The Professional Paralegal

D0144614

The McGraw-Hill Paralegal List

WHERE EDUCATIONAL SUPPORT GOES BEYOND EXPECTATIONS.

Introduction to Law & Paralegal Studies
Connie Farrell Scuderi
ISBN: 0073524638
© 2008

Introduction to Law for Paralegals
Deborah Benton
ISBN: 007351179X
© 2008

Basic Legal Research, Second Edition
Edward Nolfi
ISBN: 0073520519
© 2008

Basic Legal Writing, Second Edition
Pamela Tepper
ISBN: 0073403032
© 2008

Contract Law for Paralegals
Linda Spagnola
ISBN: 0073511765
© 2008

Civil Law and Litigation for Paralegals
Neal Bevans
ISBN: 0073524611
© 2008

Wills, Trusts, and Estates for Paralegals
George Kent
ISBN: 0073403067
© 2008

The Law Office Reference Manual
Jo Ann Lee
ISBN: 0073511838
© 2008

The Paralegal Reference Manual
Charles Nemeth
ISBN: 0073403075
© 2008

The Professional Paralegal
Allan Tow
ISBN: 0073403091
© 2009

Ethics for Paralegals
Linda Spagnola and Vivian Batts
ISBN: 0073376981
© 2009

Family Law for Paralegals
George Kent
ISBN: 0073376973
© 2009

McGraw-Hill's Torts for Paralegals
ISBN: 0073376965
© 2009

McGraw-Hill's Real Estate Law for Paralegals
ISBN: 0073376949
© 2009

Legal Research and Writing for Paralegals
Pamela Tepper
ISBN: 007352462X
© 2009

McGraw-Hill's Criminal Law for Paralegals
ISBN: 0073376930
© 2009

McGraw-Hill's Law Office Management for Paralegals
ISBN: 0073376957
© 2009

Legal Terminology
Edward Nolfi
ISBN: 0073511846
© 2009

For more information or to receive desk copies, please contact your McGraw-Hill Sales Representative.

The Professional Paralegal

DISCARD

Allan M. Tow
Suffolk University
Boston, Massachusetts

LIBRARY
FORSYTH TECHNICAL COMMUNITY COLLEGE
2100 SILAS CREEK PARKWAY
WINSTON-SALEM, NC 27103-5197

Boston Burr Ridge, IL Dubuque, IA New York San Francisco St. Louis
Bangkok Bogotá Caracas Kuala Lumpur Lisbon London Madrid Mexico City
Milan Montreal New Delhi Santiago Seoul Singapore Sydney Taipei Toronto

THE PROFESSIONAL PARALEGAL

Published by McGraw-Hill, a business unit of The McGraw-Hill Companies, Inc., 1221 Avenue of the Americas, New York, NY, 10020. Copyright © 2009 by The McGraw-Hill Companies, Inc. All rights reserved. No part of this publication may be reproduced or distributed in any form or by any means, or stored in a database or retrieval system, without the prior written consent of The McGraw-Hill Companies, Inc., including, but not limited to, in any network or other electronic storage or transmission, or broadcast for distance learning.

Some ancillaries, including electronic and print components, may not be available to customers outside the United States.

This book is printed on acid-free paper.

1 2 3 4 5 6 7 8 9 0 QPD/QPD 0 9 8

ISBN 978-0-07-340309-0
MHID 0-07-340309-1

Vice president/Editor in chief: *Elizabeth Haefele*
Vice president/Director of marketing: *John E. Biernat*
Sponsoring editor: *Natalie J. Ruffatto*
Developmental editor II: *Tammy Higham*
Marketing manager: *Keari Bedford*
Lead media producer: *Damian Moshak*
Media producer: *Marc Mattson*
Director, Editing/Design/Production: *Jess Ann Kosic*
Project manager: *Christine M. Demma*
Senior production supervisor: *Janean A. Utley*
Designer: *Marianna Kinigakis*
Media project manager: *Mark A. S. Dierker*
Outside development: *Beth Baugh*
Cover design: *Studio Montage*
Interior design: *Pam Verros, PV Design*
Typeface: *10.5/13 Times New Roman*
Compositor: *Aptara, Inc.*
Printer: *Quebecor World Dubuque Inc.*
Cover credit: *Taken by Allan Tow at The Old Royal Naval College in Greenwich, London.*

Library of Congress Cataloging-in-Publication Data

Tow, Allan M.
The professional paralegal / Allan M. Tow.
p. cm. — (The McGraw-Hill paralegal list)
Includes index.
ISBN-13: 978-0-07-340309-0 (alk. paper)
ISBN-10: 0-07-340309-1 (alk. paper)
1. Legal assistants—Vocational guidance—United States. I. Title.
KF320.L4T638 2009
340.023′73—dc22

2008001069

The Internet addresses listed in the text were accurate at the time of publication. The inclusion of a Web site does not indicate an endorsement by the authors or McGraw-Hill, and McGraw-Hill does not guarantee the accuracy of the information presented at these sites.

www.mhhe.com

Dedication

To Mary, Aimee, and Ben for their love and support.

About the Author

Allan M. Tow is an Associate Professor of Paralegal Studies at Suffolk University, Boston, Massachusetts, where he has taught since 1993. Previously he taught as a clinical instructor and directing attorney at Harvard Law School and as an instructor at Suffolk Law School. Allan was a Managing Attorney with Legal Services of the Virgin Islands and Greater Boston Legal Services. He was also a judicial clerk in Philadelphia, Pennsylvania. While a member of Suffolk's paralegal program, Allan successfully litigated several *pro bono* cases before the United States Supreme Court and the First Circuit Court of Appeals. He received a Bachelor of Arts *cum laude* from Brandeis University in Anthropology and Linguistics and a Juris Doctor *cum laude* from Boston College Law School.

Preface

Having survived a judicial clerkship, I began practicing law for the first time in the United States Virgin Islands in January 1977. With four suitcases and our cat, my wife and I started our new lives on the island of St. Thomas, she as the island librarian and I as a Staff Attorney with Legal Services of the Virgin Islands. The law office was in a charming 200-year-old Danish colonial house on Government Hill in the island's only town, Charlotte Amalie. There, I met Lillian Mitchell, who had been the office manager and secretary already for more than 10 years. To her, I was just another attorney from the States passing through like so many others she had worked with in the past. Yet, over the next four and a half years, Lillian and I would forge a friendship that lasts to this day. By working with Lillian, I truly came to understand the value of working with a paralegal.

In Chapter 1, you will read about Lillian and how the paralegal movement grew out of the establishment of legal aid offices across the country during the 1960s and 1970s. Strapped by limited budgets and the crush of indigent clients, it made sense that Lillian and others like her engage in legal work alongside legal aid attorneys pursuing the ideal of providing access to justice to those who could not afford to pay a lawyer. For me, Lillian occupies a special place, for it was she who taught me the nuts and bolts of legal practice in the island's courts. Of course, I took it upon myself to learn the law of this new jurisdiction. But it was Lillian who knew the unwritten rules of how many copies of a divorce complaint to file, where the constable's office was in order to serve the complaint, and a multitude of other details. For a new attorney just learning how to practice, I saw that the unwritten rules became equally as important as the written ones I had just started to learn.

Isolated on a Caribbean island, we were unaware that a quiet revolution was taking place on the mainland of the United States. All across the country, law firms, government offices, and agencies started to recognize that unlicensed persons could perform substantive legal work under the supervision of an attorney and thereby increase the attorney's and the legal office's productivity. Slowly but surely, the legal profession began to accept and then embrace the idea of paralegals. Soon, the American Bar Association got into the act and recognized paralegals and paralegal education as an integral part of the legal world in the United States. Now, paralegals have come into their own as legal professionals.

This book is proparalegal. That is, throughout this book, Lillian's story is just one of a dozen stories of paralegals who have succeeded in finding a place in the legal profession. Moreover, these legal professionals and thousands of others have found meaning and personal growth by working as paralegals. Ethics, an essential foundation for any profession, comes to the forefront throughout the various discussions of legal theory and legal practice. When discussing the parameters of ethical practice for paralegals, the focus for students is to find empowerment in the *authorized practice of law* for paralegals. That is, pointing out what paralegals should not do can well be accomplished by teaching students what they *can do.* In doing so, this book exhorts students to view themselves as budding professionals—*professional paralegals*.

The text is divided into three major parts. The first part provides students with a detailed overview of the paralegal profession and its growing place in the larger legal profession. Immediately thereafter, an entire chapter discusses ethics and establishes a perspective for providing the student instruction on substantive law, starting with the American legal system and then how to find and read the law. Learning the law from an ethical perspective will provide students with important early lessons about what it means to be a legal professional. The second part of the text explores basic and specialized areas of law common to traditional paralegals and some that are not so traditional. The third and final section covers the unwritten rules of the profession, including how to find suitable employment in the legal profession. This section provides instruction and counseling on the uncertainities of job searching and offers a myriad of techniques, mainstream and otherwise. This section also gives students a view of legal practice and survival techniques for the workplace.

Within each section, the chapters discuss the theory (social or economic reality), legal doctrine (sources and substance), and practice both by lawyers and specifically by paralegals. This textbook is for a course on the paralegal profession that covers the traditional topics of the paralegal profession, practical issues of the workplace, and a skills approach within an eclectic selection of substantive law topics. A skills approach discusses the substantive area of law and contains examples and exercises of how paralegals operate within those substantive areas.

Features in each chapter include:

- **A Day in the Life of a Real Paralegal** highlights the activities professional paralegals are involved in on a daily basis. It also features real paralegals who are working in the profession today.
- **Practice Tip** presents different nuances of the law and caveats to rules that alert students to the intricacies of the law.
- **Communication Tip** offers advice to help students communicate professionally and clearly in different legal environments.
- **Research This** gives students the opportunity to investigate issues more thoroughly through hands-on assignments designed to develop critical research skills.
- **Eye on Ethics** recognizes the importance of bringing ethics to the forefront of paralegal education. It raises the ethical issues facing paralegals and attorneys in today's legal environment.
- **Cyber Trip** provides Web sites and encourages students to go to the Internet to learn more about a wide array of legal issues.
- **Case in Point** offers a significant case that expands on the topics discussed in the chapter. Students consider questions based on the case to assist their understanding of the case and its relevance to the chapter materials.
- **Review and Discussion Questions** ask students to apply critical thinking skills to the concepts learned in each chapter. The Review Questions reinforce the objectives of the chapter. The Discussion Questions focus on more specific legal topics and promote dialogue among students. Both sets of questions are found at the end of each chapter.
- **Exercises** at the end of each chapter offer short scenarios to test the students' retention and understanding of the chapter materials.
- **Portfolio Assignments** ask students to use the skills mastered in each chapter to reflect on major legal issues and create documents that will become part of their paralegal portfolio of legal research. The Portfolio Assignments are useful as both reference tools and samples of work product.

The aims and purposes of this book attempt to provide students with an introduction to the skills and instruction they will be acquiring in their pursuit of a place in the legal world as a professional paralegal. The text explores and analyzes topics in a way that gets students thinking critically—not only about the law but also about the legal profession—while also encouraging them to find that legal work can actually be fun and interesting, just as Lillian Mitchell and I found working together on the island of St. Thomas.

OTHER LEARNING AND TEACHING RESOURCES

The **Online Learning Center (OLC)** is a Web site that follows the text chapter-by-chapter. The OLC content is ancillary and supplementary, as well as germane to the textbook—as students read the book, they can go online to review material or link to relevant Web sites. Students and instructors can access the Web sites for each of the McGraw-Hill paralegal texts from the main page of the Paralegal Super Site. Each OLC has a similar organization. An Information Center features an overview of the text, background on the author, and the Preface and Table of Contents from the book. Instructors can access the instructor's manual and PowerPoint presentations from the IRCD. Students may use the Key Terms list from the text as flashcards, as well as for additional quizzes and exercises.

To access the Online Learning Center for *The Professional Paralegal* visit www.mhhe.com/tow09.

Acknowledgments

Many talented and thoughtful people contributed to the completion of this book. I am particularly indebted to Dr. Glen A. Eskedal, Professor and Chair of the Education and Human Services Department at Suffolk University, whose guidance has steadied me through trials and tribulations during my 15 years at the University.

Special thanks to:

- The American Association for Paralegal Education for its support and reprint permissions.
- Martha J. Donovan, Paralegal for Offshore Offerings, Massachusetts Financial Services, and former student, who regularly visits my Securities Law class to discuss paralegal employment opportunities in the securities field.
- Stephen P. Imondi, Registered Paralegal, General Counsel's Office, Brown University, who, as Chair of the NFPA's Ethics Board, taught and impressed upon me the importance of ethics in the paralegal profession.
- Paul M. Osborne, Esq., and Catherine A. Davis, Esq., longtime close friends and former classmates, both of whom provided expertise in civil litigation and professional ethics.
- Richard L. Pennie, Adjudications Officer, U.S. Citizenship and Immigration Services, Department of Homeland Security, Colorado Springs Office, and former student.
- Brigite M. Requeijo, trilingual paralegal extraordinaire, for her constant support and friendship.
- Mark S. Rotondo, Esq., Dean's Office, Suffolk University, for his reality checks, humor, and camaraderie.
- Timothy P. Smith, Appellate Paralegal par excellence, for his encouragement, exemplary work ethic, and confidences.
- And to my colleagues at Suffolk University's Paralegal Program, Mary M. Flaherty and Graham Kelder, both remarkable teachers, and the late Lynne D. Dahlborg, close friend and mentor.

Those involved in the actual production of this book deserve high praise for their extraordinary focus, patience, and perseverance. Primary among them are Developmental Editor Beth Baugh and Project Manager Christine Demma. The reviewers—my peers and colleagues in the field—provided astute and valuable criticism on the book's content and organization. Without their prompt and ample feedback, this project would have been much more difficult.

Leigh Anne Chavez
Central New Mexico Community College

Donna Donathan
Marshall University

Karen Emerson
Southeast Community College, Nebraska

Flora F. Hessling
Wesley College

Joni Mina
Lewis-Clark State College

Adam Pincus
Kaplan University

Jeffery S. Rubel
University of Cincinnati, Clermont

Damara Watkins
Navarro College

A Guided Tour

The Professional Paralegal explores the paralegal profession and its growing place in the legal community. Emphasis is placed on ethics and how it applies to legal theory and legal practice. Students are introduced to the American legal system and how to find and read the law. Building on this foundation, the textbook walks students through specialized areas of the law, such as civil, criminal, family, and business law. It concludes with a section detailing the inner workings of a law office, tips on how to find a paralegal position, and the types of jobs paralegals might want to pursue. The many practical assignments throughout and at the end of each chapter allow students to explore the paralegal profession in more detail and test their knowledge of key concepts. The pedagogy of the book applies three main goals:

- Learning outcomes (critical thinking, vocabulary building, skill development, issues analysis, writing practice).
- Relevance of topics without sacrificing theory (ethical challenges, current law practices, technology application).
- Practical application (real-world exercises, practical advice, portfolio creation).

CHAPTER OBJECTIVES

After reading this chapter, students will have a specialized understanding of:

- Paralegals and the work they perform.
- Lawyers, with an overview of their profession.
- The history of the paralegal profession and paralegal education.
- The status of paralegals in the legal profession and the public at large.
- The licensing debate regarding how to regulate paralegals.
- Professional associations for paralegals.
- The legal workplace and the legal profession.

Chapter Objectives

Introduce the concepts that students should understand after reading each chapter and provide brief summaries of the material to be covered.

A Day in the Life of a Real Paralegal

Highlights the activities in which professional paralegals are involved on a daily basis and features real paralegals who are working in the profession today.

A DAY IN THE LIFE OF A REAL PARALEGAL

Probably the most famous paralegal in recent years is Erin Brockovich of the California law firm Masry & Vititoe. As an unemployed single mother of three children, Brockovich was offered a job as a file clerk at Masry & Vititoe, which had represented her in a car accident. While organizing a file in a pro bono case, Brockovich's interest was piqued by the sight of medical records. She was allowed to investigate the matter on her own time. Her ingenious and tireless efforts uncovered a connection between the Pacific Gas and Electric Company's pollution of the public water supply and the severely deteriorated health of hundreds of nearby residents.

A class action suit brought by Masry & Vititoe resulted in the largest settlement in a direct action lawsuit. Brockovich's heroic efforts overcame insurmountable odds and an opposition with almost unlimited resources. On behalf of 600 residents of Hinckley, California, Brockovich was instrumental in obtaining a settlement of $333 million. Her crusading efforts as a paralegal, as well as the turnaround in her life, were portrayed in the Universal Studios film *Erin Brockovich* (2000). The film was a big hit and nominated for five Academy Awards, including Best Actress for Julia Roberts' portrayal of Erin Brockovich. Brockovich worked as a consultant on the film and even acted in the role of a waitress for one scene. At the end of the film, Brockovich receives a bonus check in the amount of $2 million for her work against Pacific Gas & Electric—apparently a true fact.

While the Erin Brockovich story has inspired legions of would-be legal professionals, many have questioned the ethical conduct of Brockovich and the attorneys at Masry & Vititoe. Many of the ethical considerations covered in this chapter may alert you to those concerns.

Practice Tip

Presents different nuances of the law and caveats to the rules to alert students to the intricacies of the law.

PRACTICE TIP

When dealing with clients, avoid all possible conflicts of interest, or even the appearance of conflicts of interest, by maintaining at all times a purely professional relationship. Be sure to consult with your supervising attorney if any questionable circumstances arise that could compromise your professionalism.

Communication Tip

Offers advice to help students communicate professionally and clearly in different legal environments.

COMMUNICATION TIP

Be sure that you thoroughly understand the numerous legal terms before using them, since there are many fine line yet significant distinctions in their definition.

RESEARCH THIS

Only two states, Arizona and California, have passed laws that directly deal with paralegals. What are the requirements to become a "legal document preparer" in Arizona and California? Visit www.supreme.state.az.us/cld/ldp.htm and www.calda.org/information.asp#Legislation to research this question.

Research This

Gives students the opportunity to investigate issues more thoroughly through hands-on assignments designed to develop critical research skills.

EYE ON ETHICS

One of the most important aspects of the legal profession is its concern for ethical behavior. For almost a century, the ABA and every state have established strict rules that govern the legal profession. There are also rules that protect the public against incompetent and unscrupulous persons who may attempt to perform legal tasks. Only licensed attorneys may engage in the range of activities known as the practice of law. As you will see throughout your studies, a primary concern for paralegals is the prohibition against the unauthorized practice of law. Thus, take particular care to understand this prohibition, as well as the ethical rules governing the legal profession. Throughout this book, we will cover the all-important topic of professional ethics extensively.

Eye on Ethics

Recognizes the importance of bringing ethics to the forefront of paralegal education and practice and considers the ethical issues facing paralegals and attorneys in today's legal environment.

CYBER TRIP

Go to the ABA's Web site at www.abanet.org. What two items of federal legislation now pending before Congress does the ABA urge passage of? What reasons does the ABA give for urging the passage of these two proposed laws?

Cyber Trip

Provides Web sites and encourages students to go to the Internet to learn more about a wide array of legal issues.

Case in Point

Offers a significant case that expands on the topics discussed in the chapter, then provides questions based on the case to further assist students' understanding of the case and its relevance to the chapter materials.

CASE IN POINT

CASE SUMMARY: *TARASOFF V. REGENTS OF THE UNIVERSITY OF CALIFORNIA,* 13 CAL. 3d 177, 529 P.2d 553, 118 CAL. RPTR.129 (1974)

Prior to the California Supreme Court's decision in *Tarasoff v. Regents of the University of California*, mental health professionals were under no obligation to control the acts of their patients or to warn anyone at possible risk of harm from the patient. In the *Tarasoff* case, a psychologist who learned his patient planned to kill a former girlfriend notified the campus police orally and in writing. The patient proceeded to ingratiate himself with the parents of the ex-girlfriend and then shot her. In a suit brought by the parents, the California Supreme Court acknowledged the confidentiality duty of the psychologist and ruled that "the doctor bears a duty to use reasonable care to give persons such warnings as are essential to avert foreseeable danger arising from the patient's condition."

Two years later, in the same case, the California Supreme Court expanded its earlier ruling and explained that the therapist was under a duty "to warn the intended victim of if it is likely, to apprise the victim of a danger, to notify the police or take whatever steps are reasonably necessary under the circumstances." This ruling has been interpreted to mean that a therapist has a duty to warn and to protect because of the "special relationship" that exists between the therapist and the patient.

QUESTIONS ABOUT THE CASE

1. Do you think the *Tarasoff* case puts therapists under the same duty to report as lawyers?
2. What effect does *Tarasoff* have on a therapist's duty of confidentiality?
3. Are there any differences between therapists and legal professionals that would justify a different rule for either?

Chapter Summary

Provides a quick review of the key concepts presented in the chapter.

Summary

The paralegal profession has grown in leaps and bounds over the past 40 years. Starting in legal aid offices for the poor in the 1960s, paralegals have become recognized professionals in law offices and now work in private firms, corporations, and government offices across the United States and in foreign countries. Paralegal education comes in many different forms and has just begun to standardize. Many employers consider an associate's degree, bachelor's degree, or certificate in paralegal studies sufficient evidence of education and training. The American Bar Association has taken a major role in setting educational standards for paralegal education. Nevertheless, many feel that there should be other ways of measuring the quality of paralegal education. Moreover, other sources of input, in addition to the ABA, would ensure a more balanced and honest approach to paralegal education. The same is true of the professional status of paralegals working in the field.

Currently there is much debate about whether there should be licensing. Licensing would mean that paralegals could practice law in a limited way. Already there is a certification process, known as the CLA, which has been in existence for a long time. Established by the National Association for Legal Assistants, the certification process is a good way to measure the competency of a paralegal. Alternatively, there is also the registration process of the National Federation of Paralegal Associations, which offers PACE as a form of recognition for paralegals with education, experience, and demonstrated competence. The registration scheme of the PACE program also provides for the possibility of a limited form of licensing for registered paralegals to perform some specialized tasks involving the practice of law. Substantial controversy surrounds whether this licensing may even be possible any time in the near future. There are many questions and issues to be addressed before the establishment of a licensing process for paralegals.

Key Terms

Introduce students to basic legal terminology. Key terms are used throughout the chapters, defined in the margins, and listed at the end of each chapter. A common set of definitions is used consistently across the McGraw-Hill paralegal titles.

Key Terms

American Bar Association
ABA approval
ABA Standing Committee on Paralegals
Associate's degree
Bachelor's degree
Bar exam
Certificate
Certification
Contingency fee
Hourly fee
Law clerk
Lawyer
Legal assistant
Legal technician
License
National Association of Legal Assistants (NALA)
National Federation of Paralegal Associations (NFPA)
Paralegal
Paralegal education
Pro bono
Registration
Regulation
Training

Review Questions

1. What is the difference between certification or registration and licensure?
2. What started the growth of the paralegal profession?
3. How can legal fees be lowered by employing paralegals?
4. Why did the law degree change from an undergraduate to a graduate degree?
5. What are NALA's reasons for opposing licensing paralegals?
6. What position does NFPA take regarding the licensing of paralegals?
7. What constitutes a profession, and how is it different from an occupation?
8. Why do lawyers need a license to practice law?
9. What tasks that now constitute the practice of law might be well suited for paralegals if there were limited licensing?
10. What is the difference between education and training for legal professionals?
11. List some of the specific substantive legal tasks that paralegals may perform.

Exercises

1. Using a notepad, list as many times in one day the way in which an activity, an object, a person, or anything you come across is affected by law. Share your list with others in the class.
2. Go to the Web site for AAfPE and that the ABA's Standing Committee on Paralegals. In both cases, which schools in your state are AAfPE members or ABA approved schools? Are there any schools in your state that are listed on both sites?
3. Find the Web site for the U.S. Department of Labor Occupational Outlook Handbook at www.bls.gov/oco/ocos114.htm. Find the Job Outlook for paralegals. How much do paralegals earn?
4. Find the paralegal organization closest to your home. Find out about it, when it meets, its membership benefits and requirements, and other details.

Review Questions and Exercises

Ask students to apply critical thinking skills to the concepts learned in each chapter and tests the students' retention and understanding of the chapter materials.

Discussion Questions

1. Can you develop any additional arguments for or against licensing paralegals to perform some of lawyers' work?
2. If paralegals were to be licensed, what kinds of problems or issues can you anticipate? For instance, based on the information in the chapter, what type of education or training (or both) should be required? Should there be different types of examinations for different types of activities within the practice of law that paralegals would be permitted to do?
3. Do you think that NALA should advocate inroads into the practice of law for paralegals? What are the pros and cons of either position that NALA or any other paralegal organization might take?
4. NFPA recognizes that the licensing and regulatory issue needs further study. What areas need clarification, and what issues need to be addressed?
5. What is the practice of law?
6. How much influence or control should lawyers and the ABA have in the shape and direction of the paralegal profession and education?
7. Looking at the AAfPE definition of paralegals, could a potential ethical problem arise, because its definition omits the requirement that paralegals must work under an attorney's supervision?

Discussion Questions

Focus on specific legal topics and promotes dialogue among students.

PORTFOLIO ASSIGNMENT

Create a two- or three-page report on the type of law-related environment that interests you. The report should describe the office, the type of legal work, and the staff, as well as an explanation of why that office or type of work interests you. If possible, visit an office, take electronic pictures if permitted, and put them into your report. Otherwise, you can obtain information from the Internet about a particular law firm, government office, or other legal workplace. Prepare to present your report to your class.

Portfolio Assignment

Asks students to use the skills mastered in each chapter to reflect on major legal issues and create documents that become part of their portfolio of legal research. The Portfolio Assignments are useful as both reference tools and as samples of work products.

Brief Contents

PART ONE
About Paralegals (and the Legal Profession and the Law) 1

1 The Paralegal Profession 2

2 Ethics and Professional Conduct for the Legal Professional 26

3 Law and the American Legal System 55

PART TWO
Developing Skills for the Legal Professional 80

4 Finding and Reading the Law of Court Opinions 81

5 Legal Research and Writing 110

6 Paralegals in Action 138

7 Basic Legal Specialties for the Professional Paralegal 167

8 Legal Specialties: Family Matters 197

9 Legal Specialties: Business Matters 225

PART THREE
Entering the Profession 254

10 Using the Law in the Field 255

11 Getting the Job and Surviving in the Workplace 283

12 Examples of Legal Work by Professional Paralegals 314

GLOSSARY 337

INDEX 349

Table of Contents

PART ONE
About Paralegals (and the Legal Profession and the Law) 1

Chapter 1
The Paralegal Profession 2

What Are Paralegals and What Do They Do? 2
About Lawyers 4
History of the Paralegal Profession 5
Paralegal Education 6
Two-Year Colleges 6
Four-Year Colleges 7
Certificates 7
ABA Involvement in Paralegal Education 8
Professional Status and Licensure 9
Professional Status 9
Licensure 13
About Legal Fees and the Advantage of Paralegals 14
Professional Paralegal Organizations 15
Certification 18
The Legal Profession: The Workplace 21
Private Law Firms 21
Government Legal Offices and Agencies 21
Legal Services/Legal Aid Offices 22
Nontraditional Paralegal Positions 23

Chapter 2
Ethics and Professional Conduct for the Legal Professional 26

Ethics and Rules of Professional Conduct for the American Legal Profession 27
A Brief History of Professional Regulation: A Cultural Evolution 28
Ethics for Legal Professionals 29
Ethics for Paralegals 30
Emerging Issues in the Paralegal Movement: The Relationship between Ethics and Licensure 32
Ethics for the Professional Paralegal 37
Applied Ethics and Professional Conduct for Paralegals 38
Maintaining Client Confidentiality 38
Conflicts of Interest 43
The Unauthorized Practice of Law 47
Other Important Ethical Considerations 51

Chapter 3
Law and the American Legal System 55

Jurisprudence and Legal Theory 55
Sources of American Law and the American Legal System 57
Sources of American Law 58
Codified and Uncodified Constitutions 58
The United States Constitution 59
Article I: Legislative Power 60
Article II: The Executive Branch and Law Enforcement 61
Article III: The Judicial System 63
The State Systems and State Constitutions 71
State Courts 72
Subject Matter Jurisdiction in State Courts 74
Personal Jurisdiction 74
Alternatives to Courts 76

PART TWO
Developing Skills for the Legal Professional 80

Chapter 4
Finding and Reading the Law of Court Opinions 81

Classification of Law and Legal Materials 81
State and Federal Law 82
Civil and Criminal Law 83
The Parties 83
Crimes and Their Variations 84
The Nature of Civil Cases 86
Civil Law—Substantive Subject Areas 89
Substantive Law and Procedural Rules 92
The Hierarchy of Legal Literature 93
Court Opinions 96
Reading Court Opinions 96
Dissecting Court Opinions 97
Legal Note Taking: The Case Brief 100
Briefing a Court Opinion 101

Chapter 5
Legal Research and Writing 110

Learning to Use the Law 110
Case Reporters 111
Publication of State Court Opinions 112
Publication of Federal Court Opinions 114
Researching Court Opinions Using Digests 115
Unpublished Opinions 115
Case Law Research with Secondary Authority 116
Legal Encyclopedias 116
Treatises 116
Restatement 117
Law Reviews 117
Assorted Secondary Sources 118
Shepard's 118
Legal Research Resources Online 119
Focusing Your Research 120
Researching Statutes 120
About Statutes—Legislative Laws 122
Federal Statutes 122
A Primer on Reading Statutes 124
Federal Regulations 127
Using the Law 127
Legal Writing—The Office Legal Memorandum 128
Learning to Write in Plain English 130
Format for the Office Memoranda 133

Chapter 6
Paralegals in Action 138

Ethical Considerations 138
The Authorized Practice of Law for the Professional Paralegal 139
Civil Litigation and Procedure: Litigation Paralegals 140
Prelitigation Activities 142
Rules of Procedure 142
Beginning the Lawsuit: The Complaint 143
Filing the Complaint 145
The Defendant's Perspective 147
Other Responses to the Complaint 151
Discovery 152
Pretrial Matters 156
Trial 157
Duties of the Litigation Paralegal 158
Evidence for Paralegals 161

Chapter 7
Basic Legal Specialties for the Professional Paralegal 167

Criminal Law and Procedure 167
What Is a Crime? 169
Limitations on the Government's Power to Criminalize 169
Elements of a Crime 171
Defenses to All Crimes 173
Criminal Procedure 176
Government Investigation of a Crime 176
The Rights of the Accused 179
Constitutional Considerations During a Criminal Proceeding 180
Civil Legal Specialties 182
Torts 182
Negligence 183
Defenses to Negligence 186
Strict Liability 187
Nuisance 188
Property Law 188
Real Property and Personal Property 189
Forms of Property Ownership 189
Paralegals in Real Estate Practice 191
Personal Property 192
Transferring Personal Property 193

Chapter 8
Basic Legal Specialties: Family Matters 197

The Law of Gifts 197
The Law of Wills and Descent: A Primer 199
Wills 201
Legal Formalities for Wills 202
Types of Testamentary Gifts 204
Probate Practice for the Professional Paralegal 206
Family Law 211
Marriage 212
Support Obligations 214
Adoption 214
Miscellaneous Family Law Matters 217

Chapter 9
Legal Specialties: Business Matters 225

Contract Law for the Professional Paralegal 225
Historical Background for Contract Law 226
Traditional Contract Law 228
Elements of a Contract 228
The Offer 228
Acceptance 229
Consideration 231
Parties to a Contract 233
Genuine Assent 233
Undue Influence 234
Duress 234
Mistake 234
Fraud 234
Public Policy Considerations: Illegal Contracts 234
Consumer Issues 235
The Statute of Frauds: "Put It in Writing!" 236

The Rights of Third Parties to a Contract 237
Assignments and Delegations 237
Enforcing the Contract: Remedies 238
Rescission 238
Reformation 238
Specific Performance 238
Remedies at Law: Damages in Contract Lawsuits 240
Activities of Legal Professionals in Contract Law 242
Agency Law 244
Agents and Principals 244
Business Organizations 245
Sole Proprietorships 247
Partnerships 247
Corporations 248
Issues for the Modern Corporation 249

PART THREE
Entering the Profession 254

Chapter 10
Using the Law in the Field 255

Developing Communication Skills 256
Interviewing 256
Investigations 267
Investigatory Tools 269
In the Field 269
Bringing It Home 271
Working with Files—A Juggling Act 274
Management Systems in the Law Office 276
Tickler Systems 276
Checking for Conflicts of Interest 276
Managing Client Files 277
Time and Billing 278

Chapter 11
Getting the Job and Surviving in the Workplace 283

Self-Assessment 284
Testing for Internals 284
Evaluating the Job Market 287
College Career or Placement Office 288
Employment Agencies 288
Human Resources Departments 288
Newspaper and Internet 289
Networking 289
Paralegal Associations 289
Local and Federal Government 289
Volunteering 289
Applying for a Job 290
Résumé 290
Cover Letter 294
The Interview 295
After the Interview 298
Starting Your First Job—A Primer 299
Working Successfully in the Law Office: A Skills Approach 302
Managing Your Mind and Emotions: Stress Management 303
Communication Skills 304
Survival in the Law Office—Dealing with the Difficult Coworker 306
Dealing with the Difficult Office 309
Seeking New Horizons 310

Chapter 12
Examples of Legal Work by Professional Paralegals 314

Training at Your New Job, and Training Yourself 315
Possibilities for the Professional Paralegal 317
Criminal Law Opportunities for Paralegals 318
Paralegals in the Insurance World: Claims Adjusters and Others 320
The Health Care Professional as Paralegal 320
Paralegals in the Military: The Judge Advocate General 321
Mainstream Professional Paralegals: Specialty Opportunities 321
The Independent Paralegal: Going Out On Your Own 329
The Entrepreneurial Paralegal 329
What Paralegals Earn *331*

Glossary 337

Indexes 349

Part One

About Paralegals (and the Legal Profession and the Law)

CHAPTER 1 The Paralegal Profession

CHAPTER 2 Ethics and Professional Conduct for the Legal Professional

CHAPTER 3 Law and the American Legal System

Chapter 1

The Paralegal Profession

CHAPTER OBJECTIVES

After reading this chapter, students will have a specialized understanding of:

- Paralegals and the work they perform.
- Lawyers, with an overview of their profession.
- The history of the paralegal profession and paralegal education.
- The status of paralegals in the legal profession and the public at large.
- The licensing debate regarding how to regulate paralegals.
- Professional associations for paralegals.
- The legal workplace and the legal profession.

Law touches every aspect of our lives. The food we eat, the clothes we wear, the schools we attend, and much more have all been shaped or affected by law, in one way or another. However, few people really know what law is or how it actually operates. Those who are most familiar with law are legal professionals—individuals who are educated and trained in and work with the law. This book provides an introduction to students of law who plan to enter or merely hope to explore the world of legal professionals. As an aspiring legal professional, you are beginning a journey into a culture and tradition that has existed for centuries and that continues to develop and accommodate changes in society and technology. As you proceed in your exploration, you will see how the legal world in the United States has created a new form of legal professional: the paralegal.

WHAT ARE PARALEGALS AND WHAT DO THEY DO?

Only within the past 30 years has it been possible to obtain employment performing substantial legal tasks without having to be a lawyer. Things began to change in the 1960s. The federal government established legal aid offices for the poor across the country. At the same time, a major shift in public attitudes toward lawyers occurred, and the legal profession began to learn that much of the work performed by lawyers could be delegated to others. Free from having to perform many of the more routine legal tasks, lawyers would be able to offer services to a greater number of people and thus increase the public's access to justice. The result was that legal services could be delivered more efficiently to a greater number of people at a lower cost because a considerable amount of the work could be done by nonlawyers.

There are many other names that have been used for persons who perform important legal work without a law school degree or membership in a state bar. The labels lay advocate, **legal technician**, **law clerk**, and others have also been used to describe persons working alongside with lawyers. However, the term **paralegal** has become the most common.

Today, paralegals are well-recognized legal professionals who work in a variety of contexts as integral parts of teams that deliver legal services and perform substantive legal tasks. Law firms large and small from New York City's Wall Street to small town Main Street offices employ paralegals to perform legal research, draft court documents and contracts, prepare witnesses, gather evidence, and even represent clients at certain types of administrative hearings. In government offices, paralegals assemble and organize complex legal records, interview applicants for government benefits, and make legal decisions on those applications. With the recent globalization of the world's economy, paralegals are starting to work on international matters within accounting firms as well as law firms with overseas offices worldwide. Thus, within the past three decades, paralegals have begun to ascend in their own right as a profession within the lawyers' world.

legal technician
A nonlawyer who performs legal services, in some cases, to the public if permitted by law and which would otherwise constitute the unauthorized practice of law.

law clerk
A term formerly used to refer to a paralegal.

paralegal
A trained and educated legal professional who performs substantive work under the supervision and responsibility of an attorney.

In the actual delivery of legal services, paralegals perform substantive legal work alongside licensed attorneys. The professional tasks performed by paralegals involve critical thinking using their education obtained from **paralegal education** programs and training from internships and on-the-job experience. These tasks include case planning, development, and management; legal research; interviewing clients; fact gathering and retrieving information; drafting and analyzing legal documents; and collecting, compiling, and utilizing technical information. In fact, paralegals are often expected to perform legal research and make independent decisions and recommendations to their supervising attorney in almost any type of legal matter.

paralegal education
Formal education at a school—often a college or university—offering courses in the paralegal profession and substantive law and conferring an associate's degree, bachelor's degree, or certificate.

Many seasoned paralegals possess a tremendous amount of sophisticated knowledge in certain areas of law that makes them particularly useful to the lawyers working

A DAY IN THE LIFE OF A REAL PARALEGAL

Approaching her retirement years, Lillian Mitchell moved from her home in upstate New York to the Caribbean island of St. Thomas in the U.S. Virgin Islands, figuring that she would stay for a while just to see if the island would be a suitable retirement location. Mitchell ended up taking a job as the secretary of the newly formed legal aid office in 1966.

Funded by the federal government in its War on Poverty, the office was staffed by just one lawyer to represent economically deprived persons who could not afford a private attorney. Like public defenders, the salaries of legal aid lawyers were paid by the government to give poor people access to justice in areas such as welfare rights, divorce, landlord–tenant disputes, and other civil matters. This service is known in the legal trade as **pro bono**, meaning "for [the public] good." The idea was similar to that of charitable work and in the public interest.

pro bono
Legal representation performed voluntarily for free.

At first, Mitchell's job was entirely that of a traditional secretary: typing, filing, taking dictation, and the like. However, with the crush of poor clients seeking free legal services, she began taking instruction from her supervising attorney on how to draft sworn statements (affidavits) for clients. She also began to learn of the rules for filing and then drafting court papers and soon was interviewing clients to screen the myriad of cases that came through the office. After a while, Mitchell began to perform a host of substantial legal duties routinely, just as a lawyer would and as a modern paralegal does so today. This work was a tremendous boon to the office, which could then serve many more clients on its severely limited federal budget.

All across the country, hundreds of people like Mitchell were doing the same thing in the legal aid offices. In doing so, they established a model for the new type of legal professional, the paralegal. Lillian Mitchell finally did retire and moved back to her home in upstate New York in 1988.

alongside them. In fact, many larger private law firms and government offices rely heavily on paralegals working under the supervision of a licensed attorney. Thus, paralegals have been able to establish themselves as highly valued contributors to the flow of legal work product. Indeed, paralegals have established themselves as legal professionals, working alongside licensed attorneys. The growth of the paralegal profession has been supported and guided by licensed attorneys.

American Bar Association
A national organization of lawyers, providing support and continuing legal education to the profession.

The **American Bar Association** (ABA) is the largest nationwide professional organization for lawyers. Because of its long-standing commitment to high professional standards and its vast expertise and resources, the ABA has established standards for legal practice and legal education in every state. Since the beginning of the paralegal profession some 30 years ago, the ABA has fostered its growth and development. Still, there is a bright line distinction between two types of legal professionals: paralegals and licensed attorneys. We will begin our examination of paralegals with a brief overview of the legal profession and an in-depth history of the growth of the paralegal profession.

ABOUT LAWYERS

lawyer
Also known as an attorney, a person who is licensed by a state to engage in the practice of law.

For centuries, **lawyers** were the only individuals occupying the legal profession. At this point, they need little introduction. Lawyers represent clients, whether those clients are individuals, the government, government agencies, or various types of business entities such as corporations, partnerships, or international conglomerates. For their clients, lawyers give legal advice, prepare legal documents for courts or as contracts, negotiate business deals, enter into plea bargains, and try cases before courts and juries—the most visible and romanticized aspect of their legal duties.

Also known as attorneys, counselors, and legal advocates, lawyers must follow a long and arduous path. Becoming a lawyer requires both extensive education and formal governmental licensing, after passing a grueling two- or three-day examination, depending on the state in which they live. To begin with, an aspiring attorney needs a bachelor's degree from an accredited four-year college and graduate training for a law degree, which usually takes three years on a full-time basis. Many law schools offer evening programs that can take up to five years to complete on a part-time basis. The law degree is known as a J.D., for *juris doctor,* and is sometimes thought of as the equivalent of a Ph.D., or a real doctorate, that can take more than three years to obtain.

Until the 1960s, the J.D. was known as an LL.B., or Bachelor of Laws, an alternative to a regular undergraduate college degree for those who wished to become lawyers. Some time ago, all undergraduate degrees, both bachelors of law and bachelors of arts and sciences, took only three years to complete. However, with the ever-increasing complexity of modern American life, educators and legislators found it necessary for attorneys to have an undergraduate degree as well as a graduate law degree. Today's attorney must be able to learn complex subjects in almost each case he or she handles. The competent practice of law requires, at a minimum, the ability to write and speak clearly and effectively. Details of business and accounting practices; scientific matters such as biology, chemistry, and physics; and, of course, computers, along with an assortment of other subjects, can arise in any given case. Thus, the modern attorney must be able to study and absorb many other subjects. Now, the law degree is firmly established as a form of graduate education.

bar exam
A test administered to graduates from approved law schools that determines the applicant's knowledge of the law and ability to practice in the state.

After obtaining a J.D. from law school, an aspiring attorney must pass the **bar exam** to become licensed. As in most professions, each state regulates its own lawyers, setting the qualifications for becoming an attorney. Almost all states require that applicants pass an examination, the bar exam. Each state administers an exam spanning two days: one day of essay questions and another of entirely multiple-choice questions known as the "Multi-State." For many states, there is also an important third exam that covers professional ethics, to ensure that those wishing to become attorneys have the requisite knowledge of professional ethics. Moreover, each state has a character and moral fitness component that requires candidates to submit several references and supply details of their personal and employment history.

Once past these hurdles, the applicant is finally sworn in as an attorney-at-law and is deemed to have "passed the bar." Membership in the state's bar means that the individual is licensed to engage in the activity known as the practice of law. Like any professional license granted by the government, whether it be a license to practice medicine or to act as a certified public accountant, the license to practice law means that only those granted the license may do so. As you will see, the practice of law has been difficult to define, yet it is an activity that is regulated to protect the public from unqualified or unscrupulous persons. Like medical matters, the repercussions from faulty or unprofessional legal work can profoundly affect the lives of many people. For that reason, entry into the field of law requires much studying and training.

HISTORY OF THE PARALEGAL PROFESSION

The idea of professional tasks performed by trained and educated nonprofessionals has been well established in many areas. Most notably in the medical field, there is a wide array of para-professionals. The prefix "para" means next to or beside, as an assistant. First there were nurses, then X-ray technicians and physical therapists, and, most recently, physician's assistants. All of these "para-professionals" perform significant tasks that require training and education in the world of medicine.

Without para-professionals in the medical world, doctors would have to perform a wider range of routine tasks that could otherwise be delegated to persons with sufficient training and education to perform those tasks. Para-professional in medicine thus free doctors to perform duties that require more advanced knowledge and skills. The idea of employing para-professionals has been well known as a means for delivering professional services more efficiently to a wider range of the public.

The use of para-professionals in the legal world followed much later. The ABA formally recognized the legitimacy of nonlawyers performing legal work in 1967. In that year, the ABA issued a formal opinion that approved the use of paralegals. The ABA also formed the Special Committee on Lay Assistants for Lawyers to study the matter further. The Special Committee concerned itself with the nature of training and education for "nonlawyer assistants," the tasks they could perform, and ultimately the role of the legal profession itself with regard to paralegals.

There were also lawyers who expressed concern over the training and education of nonlawyers who would be performing legal work. At stake was the level of

CYBER TRIP

Go to the ABA's Web site at www.abanet.org. What two items of federal legislation now pending before Congress does the ABA urge passage of? What reasons does the ABA give for urging the passage of these two proposed laws?

EYE ON ETHICS

One of the most important aspects of the legal profession is its concern for ethical behavior. For almost a century, the ABA and every state have established strict rules that govern the legal profession. There are also rules that protect the public against incompetent and unscrupulous persons who may attempt to perform legal tasks. Only licensed attorneys may engage in the range of activities known as the practice of law. As you will see throughout your studies, a primary concern for paralegals is the prohibition against the unauthorized practice of law. Thus, take particular care to understand this prohibition, as well as the ethical rules governing the legal profession. Throughout this book, we will cover the all-important topic of professional ethics extensively.

professionalism that the legal profession had taken decades to establish. The fear was that the public would be harmed if legal tasks could be performed by incompetents lacking knowledge of the law or the requisite ethics, or both. These fears were well founded and resulted in the establishment of educational and supervisory guidelines for paralegals that are still in force today.

Through what is now known as the Standing Committee, the ABA continues to study the status of paralegals and develop the competency standards for their education and training. The Standing Committee also "approves" paralegal schools that meet its guidelines in a voluntary process that has generated some interesting issues. After endorsing of the concept of the paralegal, the group upgraded the Special Committee in 1975 to the status of the **ABA Standing Committee on Paralegals**, which still acts as the ABA's eyes to oversee the paralegal profession. Today, the paralegal profession continues to rise in status and stature.

ABA Standing Committee on Paralegals
A specialized committee of the ABA that oversees the paralegal profession.

PARALEGAL EDUCATION

There are now more than 1,000 paralegal schools across the country. These schools specifically offer instruction in paralegal education. Often you will come across advertisements for them on the Internet, in newspapers, and even on matchbook covers. Paralegal schools vary considerably in quality, course offerings, and facilities. They can range from correspondence or online crash courses to full-fledged bachelor's or associate's degrees from venerable public and private universities. As a result, there are three types of programs that offer education to people who aspire to become paralegals.

Two-Year Colleges

Associate's degree
A two-year college degree offered by both public and private colleges.

Formerly known as "junior colleges," these schools confer **Associate's degrees** in sciences or arts in two years on a full-time basis. There are public "community" colleges that are very reasonably priced, and there are private two-year colleges that can be quite expensive. Many students find it cost effective to attend a community college for their first two years of higher education. Then, if all goes well, the next step is to transfer into a four-year school. Two-year colleges grant associate's degrees, usually in a specific area of study such as English, math, or history. This specification is called a concentration or, more commonly, a major. At many schools, students can also major in paralegal studies, sometimes known as legal studies. Many two-year colleges offer sound paralegal education as part of an associate's degree in applied business.

Usually, an associate's degree requires taking several general education courses in English composition, history, and science. Most two-year schools require about 7 to 10 general education courses out of a total of 20 courses to obtain an associate's degree. The idea behind these general education requirements is twofold. First, the purpose of an associate's degree is to develop an educated, well-rounded person who has a minimum level of basic knowledge in certain common areas. Second, because many graduates of two-year schools go on to four-year colleges, these general education courses prepare the student for more advanced study for the bachelor's degree.

In addition to the general education courses, there are courses in a chosen subject area for a major. At two-year colleges, a major requires taking six or seven courses in a chosen subject matter. To major in paralegal studies, most two-year colleges require a combination of required paralegal courses plus one or two advanced paralegal courses. These advanced paralegal courses are called electives because the student elects or chooses them individually. The required courses usually consist of an introductory course in law and the paralegal profession, using books such as this one. Courses in civil litigation, legal research, and writing and business law constitute other required courses at many schools. Elective paralegal courses build on the basic information of the required courses and offer a greater level of sophistication in subjects such as wills and trusts, domestic relations, and even bankruptcy or administrative law.

With an associate's degree, a budding paralegal may be able to enter the workforce immediately. As time goes on, more and more people have chosen to continue their education beyond an associate's degree. Students transferring to a four-year school usually continue with the major that they selected in their two-year school. To assist graduates who wish to transfer their credits, many two-year schools have "articulation agreements" with a few four-year schools in their area. Under these articulation agreements, graduates of the two-year schools with a minimum grade point average (usually a 2.5) are automatically admitted into the four-year school with all of their course credits from the two-year school fully accepted. For many students opting to begin their postsecondary education at a two-year school, an articulation agreement offers the opportunities of a short-term educational goal with the option to continue to a four-year program.

Four-Year Colleges

The traditional **Bachelor's degree** consists of four years of full-time study at a college or university. Within the past 10 years, a growing number of four-year schools have begun to offer bachelor's degrees with a major or minor in paralegal studies or legal studies. Like their two-year counterparts, four-year colleges require students to take certain courses to satisfy general education standards, as well as the required courses for the major. The minor consists of a fewer number of courses than are required for a major. A minor indicates that the student has an appreciable level of competency in a subject, in addition to her or his major. Not all four-year schools offer minors However, in those that do, the paralegal minor may offer some flexibility in the student's course of study. For instance, a student may major in history or science as a matter of intellectual interest and simultaneously minor in paralegal studies to preserve the possibility of working as a paralegal. Sometimes a bachelor's degree that combines a science major and a paralegal minor is well suited for a position in a law firm that handles technical scientific legal matters, such as patents or copyrights.

Bachelor's degree
A college degree offered by both public and private four-year colleges and universities.

For students continuing a major in paralegal studies from their two-year school, there may be two or three more required basic courses, such as a higher level of legal research and writing, a course on contracts, and another on real estate, at the four-year school. There may also be two or three additional elective courses. Here, it can become very interesting for students. Some of the more sophisticated schools have the resources and facilities to offer advanced electives that can really pique a student's interest in the study of law. Courses such as intellectual property (i.e., the law of patents, trademarks, and copyrights), immigration law, international law, and other specialized areas can truly enhance the student's experience in paralegal education. Moreover, a graduate of a four-year program with a background in securities law and corporate law becomes more marketable to law firms interested in hiring paralegals with such highly specialized education.

The downside of a four-year bachelor's degree is the time and expense. At a private college, tuition alone can be very costly. Fortunately, the diversity in educational offerings within paralegal education has allowed for some cost-effective alternatives.

Certificates

For those who may not wish to pursue a bachelor's or even an associate's degree, many two- and four-year schools offer the paralegal **certificate**. Like the major in a bachelor's or associate's degree program, a certificate demands both required and elective paralegal courses. Most certificate programs can be completed within one year on a full-time basis and usually consist of about 10 paralegal courses. Many students

certificate
An educational credential that indicates an individual has successfully completed a prescribed course of study, usually in an occupation or profession.

FIGURE 1.1
The Paths of Legal Education and Where They Lead

Type of Legal Professional	Education	License or Credential
Attorney	B.A. or B.S. and J.D. required. Optional: LLM or SJD	License or practice issued by state
Paralegal	2-year associate's, 4-year bachelor's, or certificate	Certification or registration offered by associations

who choose certificate programs may already have a bachelor's or associate's degree and return to school as a form of retraining or to enter a second career. Other students in paralegal certificate programs have no formal education beyond secondary school but either have been working in the law field or have other relevant experience. Some paralegal certificate programs have alternative entry requirements for students without any college experience. For those students, a certificate program may require two or more nonparalegal courses, such as English composition.

Whether a student decides to pursue an associate's degree, a bachelor's degree, or a certificate in paralegal studies depends on personal circumstances, such as economics and prior education and training. The decision may also be location sensitive. In large cities, particularly on the East and West Coasts, the employment market will be more competitive for job seekers. Thus, the person with the most educational qualifications will likely be more marketable. This trend certainly does not mean that in less densely populated areas of the country, applicants for paralegal positions will be less qualified. Many persons with little or no formal education may perform just as well as someone with education. The key is the perception of the prospective employer. As will be covered subsequently in this book, students seeking the appropriate form of paralegal education and graduates of paralegal schools are well advised to keep their fingers on the pulse of the job market in their environs. A savvy graduate of a paralegal program will always try to see what is around and find out who is getting the jobs. (See Figure 1.1.)

ABA Involvement in Paralegal Education

From the outset, the ABA established itself as the guiding hand in the development of the paralegal profession. As such, the ABA's Standing Committee on Paralegals has established standards for paralegal education through its approval guidelines. Paralegal schools may apply to the ABA for voluntary "approval" of their programs. **ABA approval** is an expensive process that requires extensive documentation of the school's facilities and an onsite visit by an inspection team assembled by the ABA. Obtaining ABA approval can be very involved and costly.

ABA approval
A voluntary process for paralegal schools indicating that they meet prescribed educational standards set by the American Bar Association.

Upon meeting the specific criteria in the guidelines, the school receives ABA approval for a term of seven years. Matters such as curriculum, access to an adequate law library, the faculty's credentials, available technology, and other resources are some of the subjects of the ABA's examination. Specifically, the approval process involves an in-depth self-study regarding facilities, curriculum, faculty credentials, library facilities, community surveys for utilization of paralegals, employer surveys, graduate follow-up surveys, and many other requirements, including an initial three-day site visit. Even after obtaining approval, there is a reapproval process that requires the same level of preparation and a site visit, in addition to materials that must be submitted on an annual or biannual basis. Thus, the ABA approves only those schools that meet its guidelines and therefore have sufficient resources and depth to provide a solid legal education for paralegals.

The approval process is similar to that of any accrediting body. By attaching its seal of approval, the accrediting body has made a public statement that the accredited school meets a specified level of educational standards. Thus, the public can rely on the accrediting agency's action as a quick assurance of quality. In doing so, the accrediting agency has expended time and valuable expertise to measure the quality of a school, beyond the ability of any layperson. Accreditation also entitles a school to receive students with federal assistance.

CYBER TRIP

Go to the ABA's Web site on paralegal education at www.abanet.org/legalservices/paralegals/process.html.

What is the cost to a school that wishes to apply for ABA approval of a paralegal program?

Schools that do not have ABA approval may be just as good as those with ABA approval. Nevertheless, ABA approval stands as the unofficial standard. Otherwise, a prospective student would have to spend the time and expense to scrutinize schools in ways that the student is unable to, not knowing what exactly to look for. The guidelines, in turn, reflect what the lawyers and the legal establishment consider important for the education of paralegals. Like the Seal of Good Housekeeping or a Zagat rating for a restaurant, ABA approval is a clear signal that the school meets acceptable standards.

Only about one-third of all paralegal schools in the country have obtained ABA approval. The costs and involvement of demonstrating that a school meets ABA guidelines and the costs applying for approval may be beyond the school's budget and resources. However, many schools have sought ABA approval, primarily as a credential or marketing device to attract students over other schools. The cachet of ABA approval imparts an air of importance to the school's image and reflects positively in the larger legal community. Having the seal of approval from the ABA gives a paralegal school an appearance of legitimacy that may sway law firms and attorneys in the area to hire that school's graduates over those of other schools that do not have ABA approval. This likelihood is an important consideration, because a degree or certificate in paralegal studies is, after all, primarily an employment credential—certainly more so than an associate's degree in history or a bachelor's in anthropology.

Some schools find the ABA's approval process objectionable on philosophical grounds. As noted previously, the ABA's pervasive presence in paralegal education has stirred some controversy. Because the ABA represents the view of the country's mainstream lawyers, there may be an apparent conflict of interests. Although the ABA's Standing Committee on Paralegals allows for some input from paralegals and those who teach paralegals, the ABA's role symbolizes the dominance of lawyers over the paralegal profession. In some people's eyes, lawyers' dominance presents only one side and does not allow for other points of view. Those with this view would note that in 1986, the Standing Committee on Paralegals stated that its own ABA approval process for paralegal programs was the *best method* of assuring quality in the paralegal education. Thus, some schools choosing not to obtain ABA approval have done so under the philosophy that paralegal education, as well as the entire paralegal profession, should develop autonomously, free from the dominance of lawyers.

Realistically, however, the ABA's considerable resources and its preeminence over the nation's legal community leave few options for the growing paralegal profession. Moreover, virtually every state in the country has relied on the ABA for almost a century as a measure of legal professionalism. Its resources and the depth of its experience in all forms of legal practice are without peer. Thus, the reliance on the ABA is, on balance, quite natural. As history has shown, the ABA has fostered the growth and development of the paralegal profession.

PROFESSIONAL STATUS AND LICENSURE

Professional Status

After more than 30 years of development, the paralegal profession has started to come into its own. For the past 20 years, official reports from the United States Department of Labor have proclaimed that the paralegal profession has been one of the fastest growing professions in the country. More recently, the Department of Labor predicted that employment opportunities for paralegals would continue to grow at an above-average rate through the year 2100. During this period, we can also expect the profession to ascend to a status that is more independent of the domination of the organized bar. As the ABA will continue to foster and guide the profession as much as ever, paralegals have become firmly entrenched throughout the legal profession. Within recent years, court decisions and government agencies have commented very positively on the value of the paralegal's work. As it now stands, paralegals are well recognized by the courts as worthy of receiving professional compensation in attorney's fee awards. As you will see, courts and legislatures have increasingly regarded paralegals as an integral part of the legal profession.

Starting with the 1989 decision in *Missouri v. Jenkins,* the United States Supreme Court has said that paralegals should receive recognition under laws that grant attorney's fees if their labor contributes to the work product. Other high-level courts have been even more inspiring and stated that employing paralegals encourages the cost-effective delivery of legal services. In several other cases, courts have interpreted these laws broadly to include the paralegal's work as well. Thus, as a legal professional, the paralegal's assistance is now compensable, just as attorney's fees are under the federal Civil Rights Act, the Equal Access to Justice Act, the Bankruptcy Code, and several other laws. Moreover, extensive studies by state courts have favored the **regulation** of paralegals. For instance, in New Jersey, a study by that state's judiciary resulted in the famous Kestin Report of 1999, which favored paralegal licensure, the first official endorsement of this practice.

regulation
The government oversight and enforcement of an area to protect the public.

These laws and the court decisions interpreting them have had a significant influence on the paralegal profession in the public eye and within the legal profession. Having grown from the ranks of legal secretaries, law clerks, or file clerks, the question still remains whether paralegals have become recognized as an integral part of the legal profession. The issues regarding the paralegal as a professional become more complex. Although many regard paralegals as professionals with education from paralegal schools, the paralegal profession is still undergoing development.

In short, a person with an associate's degree, a bachelor's degree, or a certificate in paralegal studies may share a similar position with someone with a degree in history or math. To be sure, you would not call that person a historian or a mathematician. The big difference is that a person who has obtained an educational credential in paralegal studies has done so with the specific intention of preparing for employment in a law office directly after graduation. In this regard, a paralegal degree or certificate is more akin to a nursing or engineering degree, in that these degrees are specifically designed for someone who plans to work as a professional in a recognized field. Thus, a degree that prepares a person for professional work is an advanced form of vocational education, as opposed to a traditional degree in the arts or sciences.

Still, there is a difference between becoming a nurse or engineer and becoming a paralegal, even though all have the educational credentials. The difference is that nurses and engineers have to pass a state-issued qualifying exam to work within their profession. Only on passing their respective exams may they call themselves nurses or engineers. The qualifying or licensing exam is the highest form of legal recognition for a regulated profession. At this point, there is no required qualifying examination for paralegals.

So, the question is, what makes a paralegal a professional? At this point, the paralegal profession is still very young, and the answer is a bit complex and, at the same time, undergoing change. Unlike the status for other fully established professions, there are only a few laws that regulate who may enter the paralegal profession. As we

CASE IN POINT

THE KESTIN REPORT

In many states, the highest court acts as the regulatory body for the legal profession. Aided by committees staffed by lawyers, academics, and other segments of the public, the state supreme courts study issues and trends that can assist in the administration of justice. In 1999, the New Jersey Supreme Court issued a landmark report on the status of paralegals and made the following recommendations:

Recommendation 1: Paralegals in New Jersey should function under the governance and direction of the Supreme Court. The Court remains of the view that many of the tasks conducted by paralegals involve the practice of law. Those tasks, therefore, properly come within the scope of the Court's constitutional authority over the practice of law in New Jersey.

Recommendation 2: The Supreme Court, pursuant to its constitutional authority over the practice of law, should establish a regulatory scheme to govern the practice of paralegals. The Committee recommended that the Court establish a licensing system for all paralegals. Pending future evaluations of the profession, the Court has concluded that direct oversight of paralegals is best accomplished through attorney supervision rather than through a Court-directed licensing system. As noted below, the Court agrees that the obligations attorneys have as paralegal supervisors need to be set forth in greater detail.

Recommendation 3: Persons who seek to be practicing paralegals in New Jersey should be required to demonstrate compliance with minimum hour and course content requirements of paralegal programs offered by American Bar Association–approved paralegal educational programs. Although the Court would encourage those who seek to become paralegals to engage in a broad-based educational program such as that recommended by the American Bar Association, it recognizes that there are many paths available to develop the skills necessary to perform with competence as a paralegal. The paralegal community and the organized bar should work together to identify and promote educational programs that will enhance the performance of current and future paralegals.

Recommendation 4: The rules proposed by the Committee for licensing the practice of paralegals in New Jersey should be adopted by the Supreme Court. Because the Court views the supervision of paralegals as the responsibility of attorneys, it has declined to adopt this Recommendation, which proposed specific Rule amendments for a Court-directed licensing system.

Recommendation 5: The Code of Professional Conduct for paralegals should be adopted by the Supreme Court to be administered by the Committee and others in conjunction with the proposed regulatory scheme. The Court supports in principle the creation and adoption of a Code of Professional Conduct for Paralegals. The Court prefers, however, that the Code be adopted through the efforts of paralegals and attorneys and their respective associations. Such a Code would be akin to the Code of Professionalism for attorneys.

Recommendation 6: The Supreme Court should modify The Rules of Professional Conduct as recommended by the Committee to incorporate ethics and performance standards governing New Jersey lawyers in using the services of paralegals.

The Court agrees that the Rules of Professional Conduct ("RPC") should be modified to describe more comprehensively the obligations imposed on attorneys by their use of paralegals. The supervision attorneys must provide for both employee-paralegals and independent contractors must be detailed in the RPCs.

Recommendation 7: The Standing Committee on Paralegal Education and Regulation should be continued and reconstituted. The Committee should be charged with the responsibility of developing and administering standards and rules governing paralegals in conformity with this report and subject to the Supreme Court's approval.

Recommendation 8: Operating standards, guidelines and rules should be developed and administered by the Committee subject to the Supreme Court's approval.

Recommendation 9: An administrative office should be established charged with the operational responsibility for licensing individuals as paralegals pursuant to the rules governing licensure and conduct of paralegals, subject to the Committee's direction and the Supreme Court's oversight.

QUESTIONS ABOUT THE CASE

1. Other than the existing educational paths for paralegals, can you think of any additional educational or occupational requirements for paralegals?
2. Why did the Court recommend the establishment of a Code of Professional Conduct for paralegals?
3. What would be the responsibilities and duties of an administrative office that oversees paralegals?

will discuss later in this book, California became the first state to regulate paralegals directly. The state of Arizona followed with the creation of the occupation of legal document preparer.

RESEARCH THIS

Only two states, Arizona and California, have passed laws that directly deal with paralegals. What are the requirements to become a "legal document preparer" in Arizona and California?

Visit www.supreme.state.az.us/cld/ldp.htm and www.calda.org/information.asp#Legislation to research this question.

Elsewhere, the only direct regulation of paralegals comes from the unofficial forces of the marketplace. A view of the law of the marketplace clearly indicates that the demand for educational credentials is an important indication of the emergence of professional status. In the employment market, more and more employers of paralegals are looking for the educational credential of a paralegal degree or certificate. Sociologists who have studied the growth of the paralegal profession have noticed that in recent years, educational requirements for entry-level positions mark the beginnings of a transformation from an occupation to a profession. More encouragingly, there has been express recognition from the ABA, the spokes-organization for the legal profession. After years of study, the ABA decided to give paralegals their due by defining them. In doing so, the ABA in effect gave official birth to the paralegal profession. Their 1997 definition of paralegal is as follows:

legal assistant
Also known as a paralegal, a nonlawyer who performs substantive legal work under the supervision of a licensed attorney.

> *A* **legal assistant** *or paralegal is a person, qualified by education, training or work experience who is employed or retained by a lawyer, law office, corporation, governmental agency or other entity and who performs specifically delegated substantive legal work for which a lawyer is responsible.*

Although official-sounding and certainly legalistic, the definition created an initial standard for what constitutes a paralegal. Of particular note were the qualifications of education and training that distinguished paralegals and their role in a variety of legal workplaces. Concise in its rendering, the ABA definition also educated the legal community as to the utility of paralegals and their berth in the legal community. For the first time, someone other than lawyers could perform "substantive legal work." At the same time, the ABA definition indicates that the lawyers ultimately are responsible for the final work product and the work performed by the paralegal. This important gesture mollified concerns for how paralegals would fit into the legal world. These concerns came not only from attorneys but also members of the general public. Everyone had wondered who would ultimately stand responsible for legal work.

More and more attention became focused on paralegal education. Colleges, universities, and even private concerns began offering a wide range of educational offerings for those who wanted to become paralegals. To those involved with teaching prospective paralegals, **training** and education became the centerpiece of their definition of paralegals. Contrast the ABA definition of a paralegal with that by those who teach at paralegal schools. The American Association for Paralegal Education (AAfPE), the national association of paralegal educators, has come up with its own definition:

training
A form of instruction in the use of skills and the practical application of theory and principles received through education.

> *Paralegals perform substantive and procedural legal work as authorized by law, which work, in the absence of the paralegal, would be performed by an attorney. Paralegals have knowledge of the law gained through education, or education and work experience, which qualifies them to perform legal work. Paralegals adhere to recognized ethical standards and rules of professional responsibility.*

As you can see, there is a difference between the two definitions. The ABA definition is quite simple and represents the lawyer's and the public's point of view. In contrast, the AAfPE definition, which was written years later, defines paralegals in terms of the type of work they do and, more so, the education they need to do their work. Notice that the AAfPE definition is written with much more careful detail and close attention to legal and ethical concerns. This attention may reflect that paralegal educators have a more intimate understanding of the details involved with the education, training, and work of paralegals. They also realize the benefit of their position as educators of paralegals as a means to educate the public about paralegals.

Licensure

Societies all over the world grant permission to certain people to engage in well-defined activities. This permission is known as a **license**. In granting a license, society also regulates the defined activity in the interests of public safety and quality assurance. The most common example is a driver's license. Operating a motor vehicle on the public roads is a defined activity that can present a risk to the public safety if performed by unqualified or unable persons. Thus, every state requires an applicant for a driver's license to have attained a certain age and to pass some form of a written exam, as well as a road test. Without the license, an individual simply is not permitted to operate a motor vehicle on public roads. In this way, the state licensing laws regulate certain activities in the interests of public safety. State regulation of public roads is taken for granted, so much so that it would be difficult to imagine a time before driver's licenses were required. The same is true for those seeking to enter a trade or profession that requires a license.

license
Permission from a governmental unit to an individual authorizing him or her to engage in a regulated activity.

The work performed in a profession is akin to operating a motor vehicle on public roads. The law requires that the state grant permission in the form of a license before a person can engage in the activities of that profession. Successfully completing a specified educational level, passing an examination, and meeting ethical standards are the threshold requirements for obtaining a license in most professions. This standard is true for architects, doctors, engineers, and pharmacists. The same is true for electricians, hairdressers, and plumbers, if you think about it. What is important to keep in mind is that only those persons who are granted the license are allowed by law to engage in the activities permitted within the scope of that license.

COMMUNICATION TIP

As you begin your journey into the legal profession, be aware that ethical considerations require that paralegals identify themselves as such and note that they are not attorneys. Thus, when speaking with family, friends, and others about your endeavors in the law, be sure to start off with the good habit of saying that you are studying law for the purpose of entering the paralegal profession.

In theory, the purpose of professional license is to protect the public and the consumer from those who may be unqualified to engage in regulated professional activities. You can imagine the damage that could result from an unlicensed person trying to perform dentistry. To protect the public, state laws establish minimum qualifications to engage in certain activities. Someone with a license is presumed to have those minimum qualifications. In the legal world, the only licensed professionals are lawyers who are permitted to engage in the activity known as the practice of law. Like any licensed activity, practicing law without a license to do so is prohibited by law; just as driving a car without a license is illegal.

Over the years, there has been some discussion about licensing paralegals. At first, some thought that paralegals could be licensed on a limited basis to perform a certain number of routine tasks normally performed only by licensed lawyers. These tasks included processing uncontested matters in bankruptcy, housing, and domestic relations. Other assignable tasks could include conducting real estate closings and negotiating contracts and settlements. In states such as California, Minnesota, and Illinois, various consumer and lawyer's commissions have extensively studied the possibility of limited licensing for paralegals. Many idealists favored licensing, arguing that the poor and middle class would have greater access to legal services if licensed paralegals could offer their services at a more reasonable rate than lawyers. To date, however, no state has granted licenses for paralegals to engage in any form of the practice of law. Still, the issues that arose as a result of these studies provide some guidance for the future development of the paralegal profession.

The idea of a limited license for paralegals has aroused much discussion. The notion that paralegals with a limited license could work independently certainly would mean a radical shift in the definition of a paralegal. Ultimately, who would bear responsibility for the legal work? To quell such concerns, the idea of a limited license soon came to mean that a paralegal with a limited license had to work under the supervision of a lawyer. In that case, the idea of a limited licensed paralegal working under a lawyer meant that he or she could appear in court for the attorney in routine matters such as an uncontested divorce, a simple bankruptcy, or asking for a continuance of a trial. Otherwise, limited licensing could, in theory, allow paralegals to offer their services directly to the public.

Requiring paralegals to work under the supervision of an attorney keeps all of the legal work under the supervision and review of the attorney, who would be ultimately responsible. This limitation has both good and bad points. From a consumer safety point of view, keeping the paralegal's activities under the responsibility of a supervising attorney assures that the work is being watched over and accounted for by a licensed professional. However, a few observers voiced the view that paralegals could operate independently. Requiring paralegals to maintain malpractice insurance, much like compulsory car insurance, could also mollify consumer concerns. Yet the notion of an independent licensed paralegal has raised too many issues and potential problems that outweigh the potential and intangible benefits.

The arguments in favor of granting limited licenses to paralegals to work under an attorney's supervision also sound more rational. Under a limited license, paralegals would be permitted to perform some of the tasks now done legally only by lawyers, yet still under a lawyer's supervision. These permitted tasks would include matters for which paralegals would have received education and training as part of the requirements for their license. Real estate closings, court appearances in uncontested matters, representation before government agencies, and even drafting routine documents could become part of the list of activities permitted by a licensed paralegal working with a supervising lawyer. By being able to perform these tasks, a paralegals' work would free up the lawyer to perform other, more complex tasks that require greater education and training than a paralegal's.

ABOUT LEGAL FEES AND THE ADVANTAGE OF PARALEGALS

As a matter of custom and habit in England, the losing side pays the attorney's fees for the winning side, in addition to the fees for its own attorney. This tradition is known as the English rule. The reasoning for English rule is that parties will think twice about suing someone if there is a chance that they may have to pay for two attorneys instead of just their own. The English rule also encourages parties to settle the matter out of court. In the United States legal system, the parties to a lawsuit pay for their own attorneys, win or lose.

However, sometimes the English rule applies in the United States. For instance, Congress has passed some laws that reflect a strong public policy. To encourage their enforcement, many laws specifically allow for a winning party that sues under these laws to obtain attorney's fees from the losing side. As pointed out previously, the United States Supreme Court has recognized that the paralegal's contribution to the legal work product deserves compensation under attorney's fee awards to the winning party. See *Missouri v. Jenkins,* 491 U.S. 274, 285 (1989).

One of Abraham Lincoln's most famous sayings is, "A lawyer's stock in trade is his [or her] time and advice." Most lawyers charge by the hour. Depending on the location and the type of practice, **hourly fees** can range between $150 to more than $500 per hour. A lawyer's hourly rate will tend to be higher in large cities and in specialized practices such as patents or international law, or in areas such as securities (stocks and bonds), where there is a high degree of risk. The hourly rate applies to whatever the lawyer does, whether it is arguing a case, waiting for his or her turn to argue a case, writing a legal document, or engaging in simple phone conversations.

hourly fee
A form of legal fees paid to an attorney based on the attorney's hourly rate and the time spent by the attorney.

Many lawyers who advertise in the media are soliciting for personal injury cases. These advertisements tell consumers that if the lawyer is not able to obtain a monetary award for the client's injuries, there are no legal fees at all. Should the lawyer succeed in an award or settlement, the legal fee is a percentage of the amount received. Therefore, the legal fees are contingent upon receiving something from the case. The percentage of the **contingency fee** is usually structured. Commonly, the lawyer will receive 25 percent if the case is settled before going to court and a higher percentage if the case goes to trial. Contingency fees are also commonly used in collection cases in which the lawyer is asked to sue someone to collect a debt. Cases involving the purchase and sale of real estate or the settlement and distribution of a deceased person's estate (a legal procedure known as "probate") may also involve legal fees based on a percentage of the money involved.

contingency fee
The attorney's fee calculated as a percentage of the final award in a civil case.

Finally, there is the fixed or flat-fee type of arrangement. These are cases in which the lawyer knows how much time will be involved, such as simple wills, simple title searches, uncontested divorces, bankruptcies, and other routine matters. By charging a flat fee, the lawyer has made it easier for both him- or herself and the client. The client benefits from knowing that one fixed sum will take care of a simple legal matter. The flat fee also saves lawyers the administrative time and expense of keeping track of time and sending bills.

Law firms often find it economically efficient to delegate the work in fixed-fee cases to paralegals. By doing so, law firms reduce their costs of getting the case done. In hourly rate cases, delegating tasks to paralegals can save both the client and the lawyer money. The work done by a paralegal can be billed out at a lower rate, leaving tasks beyond the ability of the paralegal to the lawyer. To the lawyer, employing paralegals is a way of reducing overhead, or the costs of doing business.

As an illustration of how the use of paralegals may reduce the costs of legal fees, assume that an attorney working alone spends five hours to accomplish the task of drafting a simple will. The time to perform this legal task includes interviewing the client, preparing a draft will, reviewing the draft with the client, redrafting the will into its final form, and executing the final will with the client. Working with a paralegal, the task may be completed by delegating to that paralegal the tasks of gathering information, assembling the draft and revising it into final form, under the attorney's careful supervision. By delegating a substantial portion of those hours to a paralegal, the entire matter may be accomplished more efficiently, saving time for the legal professionals and legal fees for the client.

The result then is that more people will have greater access to legal services. However, just how to provide greater access has spawned a wide variety of opinions. A review of the various professional paralegal organizations and their positions on licensing and the regulation of paralegals provide an interesting contrast of the various points of view from working paralegals themselves.

PROFESSIONAL PARALEGAL ORGANIZATIONS

Many professionals commonly join associations or organizations that provide support to their members in the form of sharing information or lobbying for laws that benefit the profession as well as the public at large. The ABA is an example of such an organization for lawyers on a national level. At the state and local level, lawyers' associations provide the same benefits on a regional scale. Membership to these professional associations or organizations is voluntary and limited to those from the profession that pays annual dues, which are usually well worth the membership benefits. As a collective of their profession, these associations have the strength of numbers and can be highly influential in matters of the profession's expertise. An all-important concern is how the law and social practices affect the organization's profession. Probably the most important function that these associations serve for their members is the protection of the profession from overly intrusive regulation or public scrutiny.

Professions prefer to be able to operate autonomously. Instead of having the public or the legislature tell them what they can or cannot do, established professions seek to regulate themselves. One way they do so is to establish codes or rules for professions to abide by. Usually these rules embody principles of honesty and foster feelings of trust. Referring to their concerns as "ethics" creates the air of respect and high purpose for these professions. They have become more commonly known as rules of professional conduct. Another way that professions protect their membership is to remain active in the public eye and watchful of legislative or regulatory action. For new professions, these organizations are also important signs of maturation and the development of an identity as a profession.

For lawyers, the ABA first created the Canons of Professional Ethics in 1908. Then in 1969, the ABA adopted the Model Code of Professional Conduct to replace the Canons. Currently, the professional activities of all lawyers are governed by the ABA's Model Rules of Professional Conduct. These rules were the result of major revisions to the Model Code in 1983.

National Federation of Paralegal Associations (NFPA)
National paralegal professional association providing professional career information, support, and information on unauthorized practice of the law.

National Association of Legal Assistants (NALA)
A legal professional group that lends support and continuing education for legal assistants.

For paralegals, several local, state, and national paralegal associations have sprung up over the past 30 years, dedicated to the interests of paralegals. Nationally, there are two major paralegal organizations.

The **National Federation of Paralegal Associations** (NFPA) came into existence in 1974. With headquarters in Seattle, Washington, the NFPA provides a central communications network for the myriad of state and local paralegal associations—more than 60 organizations in all—divided into five regions from Alaska to Florida and everywhere in between. The NFPA is also associated with paralegal associations in eastern Canada. As such, the NFPA is essentially a federation of various paralegal organizations across the country. Still, the NFPA can count as part of its membership an additional 15,000 individual paralegals from areas that do not have local associations. As the oldest and largest paralegal organization, the NFPA may very well be the "voice of paralegals" it claims to be.

The **National Association of Legal Assistants (NALA)**, headquartered in Tulsa, Oklahoma, is a professional association for individual paralegals, now numbering 18,000 members, with local chapters all across the country. The NALA exists as an outgrowth of the Legal Assistant Section of the National Association of Legal Secretaries. NALA's evolution out of the profession's secretarial beginnings belies the occupational roots of paralegals. Like the NFPA, the purpose of NALA is to promote the growth of the paralegal profession and monitor developments in the law and public attitudes that may affect paralegals. It also provides continuing legal education to help paralegals keep up with the latest changes brought about by new legislation and court decisions. In addition, it offers assistance with professional development to inform working paralegals about how to be more effective in the workplace and thereby gain promotions and other forms of individual recognition.

CYBER TRIP

Go to the NFPA's Web site (www.paralegals.org). What are the membership criteria? Are there any provisions for paralegal students to join?

Although there are some minor differences in the structures and styles of these two professional organizations, both act and advocate in the best interests of paralegals and their profession. For instance, both the NFPA and the NALA have developed

EYE ON ETHICS

One of the most important ethical duties of a legal professional is to perform his or her professional duties competently and thoroughly. The ethical codes of NALA, NFPA, and the ABA command their members to maintain a high degree of competency through education and training. The law is constantly changing. Lawyers and paralegals must therefore continue to learn and train on the job, as well as through regular, continuing legal education courses. Thus, as you pursue your studies of law and the paralegal profession, consider what you are doing as just beginning to fulfill a professional's ethical duty.

guidelines for professional conduct. Using the traditional label of ethics, both organizations have drafted model rules of professional conduct that its members pledge to abide by as a condition of membership. As noted previously, these ethical guidelines provide society and the larger legal profession assurances that the emerging paralegal profession will govern itself in accordance with the public interest.

Both NFPA and NALA publish their own periodic journals to keep their respective memberships abreast of association activities and other developments in the law and the paralegal profession. NFPA's journal is called *The Paralegal Reporter,* and NALA publishes a quarterly journal called *Findings and Facts*. Each association holds annual national conventions and various regional meetings. At first blush, both associations appear similar. Yet, there are some major philosophical differences.

For decades, NALA has vigorously opposed licensing paralegals. The basis for its objection is four major points: (1) There is no demonstrated public need to regulate paralegals; (2) a licensing procedure would increase the cost of paralegals to employers; (3) a licensing procedure would increase the cost of legal services to the public; and (4) a licensing procedure does not allow for the growth of the paralegal profession, nor does it encourage the use of paralegals in the delivery of legal services. Initially, NALA's points appear to contradict many of the major assumptions about the paralegals' role in the legal profession. An anti-licensing position would seem an unlikely stance for a national organization that represents the interests of paralegals. However, if we examine the controversy a little more closely, we can see that NALA's position against licensing has some merit.

For more than 15 years, NALA's definition of a paralegal was actually more detailed than AAfPE's. Then, NALA decided in 2001 to adopt the more simple ABA definition. More tellingly, NALA has not taken a position on whether paralegals should be able to perform tasks that can only be done by lawyers. Quite simply, NALA's anti-licensing stance is based on the notion that licensing is unnecessary, unless the activity to be performed is regulated or restricted. At present, what paralegals do does not require a license. In 1984, NALA adopted the following definition of legal assistants:

> *Legal assistants (also known as paralegals) are a distinguishable group of persons who assist attorneys in the delivery of legal services. Through formal education, training, and experience, legal assistants have knowledge and expertise regarding the legal system and substantive and procedural law which qualify them to do work of a legal nature under the supervision of an attorney.*

For its part, NFPA defines paralegals differently. Its definition is designed in anticipation of a larger role for paralegals. Specifically, NFPA endorses a two-tiered plan to license and regulate paralegals. This plan consists of licensing and specialty licensing using a minimum level of education, continuing legal education courses, requirements for experience, and standards of ethics and character. In doing so, NFPA advocates the continued expansion of the profession, which may allow for the future practice of paralegals in areas that are now reserved only for lawyers. At the same time, the NFPA licensing proposal seeks to provide a way to assure consumer protection devices as a means of public protection. By a resolution adopted in 2002, NFPA defines a paralegal as follows:

> *A Paralegal is a person, qualified through education, training or work experience to perform substantive legal work that requires knowledge of legal concepts and is customarily, but not exclusively, performed by a lawyer. This person may be retained or employed by a lawyer, law office, governmental agency or other entity or may be authorized by administrative, statutory or court authority to perform this work.*

What we learn from all of this is that the idea of permitting paralegals to perform some of the tasks that only lawyers may do is much more complicated than it would initially seem. Thus, both NFPA and NALA have offered an alternative solution to the credential question for paralegals.

Certification

certification
The recognition of the attainment of a degree of academic and practical knowledge by a professional.

An important form of recognition in many professions is **certification**. Certification is different from licensure. Both are formal recognitions for an individual who has met predetermined qualifications. The difference is that licenses are granted by governments, whereas certifications come from private or not-for-profit organizations. The qualifications for certification may consist of achieving a certain level of education or experience at a particular occupation or passing a proficiency exam, or both. The rapid development and expansion in the high-tech field is a recent example where certification is common.

Not-for-profit organizations of computer programmers and computer system designers commonly issue a great variety of "certifications" to computer programmers. Certification for specific software expertise has become particularly prevalent in Internet applications and Web page designs. Private companies such as Microsoft, Sun, and Cisco commonly issue a multitude of certifications for their software. Like government licenses, certifications are credentials for those who qualify for them. Someone with certification in certain security software is more likely to be hired than someone without the same certification. The only difference from a license is that a person who is not certified is not legally restricted from working in that area or with a certain software program. For instance, there is nothing to prevent someone from working with computers without the available certification. It therefore follows that certifications are voluntary, yet they are assurances of some level of competency to the public.

The same type of voluntary certification for paralegals has been around for some time. For more than 30 years, NALA has offered certification to paralegals. Formerly known as a Certified Legal Assistant (CLA) designation, the certification consists of an examination that is administered regularly. To be eligible to take NALA's certification exam, an applicant must meet minimum educational or work experience requirements as a paralegal. More recently, NALA has adopted the term "paralegal" as the favored terminology. The examination is quite extensive and covers a broad range of substantive law, as well as topics on professional responsibility and communication skills for what is now known as the "certified paralegal" or "CP" designation, a registered trademark of NALA.

CYBER TRIP

Go to the Web site for NALA (www.nala.org). List the educational requirements it requires before someone can take the CLA exam.

There are also specialty examinations by which an established paralegal with a CLA certification may obtain additional distinction in an advanced specialty area of the law, such as criminal, corporate, or intellectual property law. Like their computer counterparts, paralegal certifications are employment credentials that make paralegals more marketable and more valuable. To date, there are more than 12,000 CLAs in the United States and 1,000 paralegals who have obtained a specialty or CLAS distinction. NALA claims that the CLA program has achieved national recognition as the only paralegal program to be used as a voluntary certification program by several states.

For its part, NFPA offers a similar competency examination for paralegals who may wish to become known as "registered paralegals" and therefore take the Paralegal Advanced Competency Exam, or PACE. To qualify for this examination, an individual must possess an associate's degree in paralegal studies and six years of paralegal experience or a bachelor's degree and three years' experience as a paralegal. The PACE exam is also available for those individuals who have gained four years of substantive experience as a paralegal prior to 2000. Like NALA's exam, PACE tests the individual's knowledge on fundamental topics such as ethics, legal research, and document preparation, as well as specific practice areas of law. Upon successful completion of PACE, a person gains official **registration** and may call him- or herself a "PACE-registered paralegal," or PRP.

registration
Recognition conferred upon an individual by a private organization or governmental entity.

The unique features of NFPA's PACE exam are twofold: (1) its development and administration by independent testing firms and (2) a continuing legal education requirement of 12 hours every two years. NFPA also suggests a regulatory scheme that envisions a limited form of licensing. This proposal would permit paralegals to practice law on a limited basis within specialties that are state specific. Under this scheme, those paralegals who could obtain limited licenses would be allowed to perform only those specific tasks that the limited license would permit.

To be sure, NFPA's proposed regulation presents a complex array of issues. Those specialties would have to be identified. Then the educational and competency levels necessary to perform those tasks would need development. Assuming that there are various specialty tasks that could be identified for paralegals to perform, the numerous tests and specialty licenses available to paralegals would present a complex array of questions. Who would develop and administer these tests and licenses? Who would bear the costs of overseeing the numerous and various limited licenses issued? And, most important, would the benefits of a complex limited licensing scheme justify the costs and effort required?

NALA itself admits that PACE does not address all the issues of regulation, including certification and licensing. Nevertheless, the possibility of a second level of recognition to perform specialty tasks offers a tantalizing possibility of expanding the paralegal profession. If paralegals could perform specialty tasks such as real estate closings, uncontested court matters, and even some legal advice, those tasks could very well be offered at a lower cost, and that would be in the public interest.

In the final analysis, the debate has been dictated largely by economics. Differing notions of what constitutes justice and what is in the public interest also come into play. From those who favor licensing paralegals to do some of the lawyers' work, the arguments sound highly appealing. The idea of providing greater access to justice at lower costs is highly noble and idealistic. Yet this argument ignores the economic and political reality of the industry known as the legal profession. As a matter of economics, there would be a substantial public cost involved in the regulation of licensed paralegals, as there is with regulating any occupation. Moreover, the need for licensed paralegals would differ depending on location. In many large urban areas, where there is often an overabundance of lawyers as well as law students, a paralegal licensed to do some of the lawyer's work may find it fruitless to have shelled out the costs to obtain his or her license.

These economic considerations play out on the political scene as well. Although paralegals have been able to achieve professional status after only 30 years, the organized bar has consistently and strenuously resisted allowing anyone but licensed attorneys to engage in any aspect of the practice of law. With law school applications approaching historic heights in recent years, lawyers' position on licensing is unlikely to change in the near future. More lawyers are coming out to compete with one another, and the vision of a licensed paralegal must appear as a minor irritation, or at the very least, a threat. Certainly there is nothing on the horizon that would propel the idea of licensing paralegals to perform some lawyers' tasks.

PRACTICE TIP

Once you have become a legal professional, staying connected with other legal professionals provides the great benefit of sharing information, support, and networking. Associations such as NALA, NFPA, and local paralegal associations offer a wealth of information on current trends in the law, job-hunting leads, practice tips, and other useful information. Thus, an important part of becoming a legal professional includes joining a professional association. Many paralegal schools have student-run paralegal associations. Also, check on the availability of special student memberships in national or local paralegal associations.

Thus, the reality is that the paralegal progression appears to have achieved a plateau, or stasis, at least for now. In light of these considerations, NALA's and NFPA's programs appear quite sensible, if not appropriate. Certifying or registering paralegals who have sufficient education and training with a standardized test acts as an assurance of a paralegal's competency for both employers and the public without stirring the ire of the organized bar. By maintaining this posture, the organizations have gained wide acceptance. If they had advocated to allow paralegals to engage in the limited practice of law, they would have run the certain risk of alienating the mainstream of the legal community.

There are other organizations and associations related to paralegals worthy of mention as well. The American Association for Paralegal Education (AAfPE) was founded in 1981 and acts as the national organization for paralegal educators and institutions offering paralegal educational programs. AAfPE's activities focus on developing high quality education for paralegal students. Its members represent 350 institutions that offer programs in paralegal education. Most of its members are thus two- and four-year colleges. With a membership consisting primarily of college instructors and professors, AAfPE is also the nation's primary source of scholarly authority in paralegal matters. The organization has promoted educational standards, core competencies, and statements of educational quality for paralegal education. AAfPE publishes an annual scholarly journal, a quarterly magazine, and an online news bulletin.

As the only academic voice of the paralegal profession, AAfPE holds the unique position of being able to influence the establishment of educational qualifications for paralegals. The status of a professional is largely determined by the necessary education. Thus, AAfPE has been an important voice in the growth of the paralegal profession. With regard to the licensing debate though, AAfPE has been conspicuously neutral. More specifically, AAfPE has declined to take a position on whether nonlawyers should be allowed to provide legal representation directly to clients. Nevertheless, with its academic and scholarly bent, AAfPE is probably the most likely candidate to examine the complex and myriad issues of paralegal licensing more closely.

CYBER TRIP

Go to AAfPE's Web site at www.aafpe.org/p_membership/criteria.htm. How many types of memberships are there, and what are the qualifications for each type?

The International Paralegal Management Association (IPMA) was formerly known as the Legal Assistant Management Association, or LAMA. It is headquartered in Avondale Estates, Georgia. This association represents those who manage paralegals in the legal workplace. Thus, most of its members are individuals who supervise and coordinate paralegals in larger law firms, government offices, and the legal departments of large corporations. IPMA provides an important resource for both the working professional paralegal and those who manage them. For example, IPMA provides compensation surveys to inform its members and the public about the salary scales of paralegals across the country.

Of even greater interest to the profession is IPMA's utilization survey. Available online, the survey results provide detailed information about the type of work assigned to paralegals. Interestingly, more than half of those who manage paralegals are attorneys, with the balance being office managers or human resources professionals. Of greatest interest to a working or beginning paralegal is the extensive national job bank that IPMA publishes on its Web site. These jobs include not only entry-level paralegal positions across the country but also positions for paralegal managers.

Also deserving of mention is another paralegal organization, the American Alliance of Paralegals, Inc. (AAPI). Similar to other paralegal organizations, AAPI has a certification program, as well as its own code of ethics and definition of paralegals. Unlike NALA and NFPA, AAPI fully supports regulation and licensure.

The paralegal profession has progressed through its development and adoption of rules of professional responsibility and the acceptance of various incarnations of paralegals. We next look at the paralegal profession within the context of the larger legal profession and the various forms of law-related workplaces.

CYBER TRIP

Go to IPMA's Web site at www.paralegalmanagement.org and find its most recent utilization survey. What do most of the survey respondents report regarding the type of assignments or type of work environments for paralegals?

Next, visit AAPI's Web site, www.aapipara.org, to determine its position on paralegal licensure.

THE LEGAL PROFESSION: THE WORKPLACE

Paralegals have found their way into a wide range of law-related work environments, and the list keeps growing. Wherever there is a need for legal analysis or documentation, or legal work in general, you probably will find professional paralegals working alongside lawyers and other professionals, such as accountants, bankers, and engineers. In any of these contexts, paralegals actively perform substantive legal work. Their tasks may include legal research, drafting and reviewing legal documents, interviewing and preparing witnesses, or investigating and assessing legal claims. In some circumstances, paralegals can represent claimants before administrative agencies or even preside over the hearings themselves, when provided for by law. Some of the more common situations in which paralegals work as legal professionals include the following.

Private Law Firms

By far, the most common organizational structure for lawyers is the private law firm. Traditionally formed as partnerships, law firms can consist of a single solo practitioner or thousands of attorneys. Now more commonly known as professional corporations or limited liability corporations, the modern American law firm is a private, money-making venture that evolved from the gentlemanly practice of law in England. Law firms vary greatly in the scope of their practices. Some firms are general practitioners that accept a wide range of mainstream cases, such as personal injury, domestic relations, and real estate. Other firms, usually situated in large cities, concentrate in one or two highly specialized areas, such as intellectual property, immigration, or securities. These are known as "boutique" firms, like boutique shops that sell specialty products.

The work performed by paralegals in private law firms varies greatly. In larger firms, with more than 50 lawyers, paralegals tend to specialize in particular areas. Litigation sections are most likely to use paralegals, because much of their legal work involves document drafting, analysis, and organization. Legal work in the areas of corporate and real estate are next, followed by boutique practices in bankruptcy and intellectual property. In small firms, and certainly in one- or two-attorney offices, paralegals can be expected to work on a greater variety of matters and take on a wider range of tasks in the office.

Government Legal Offices and Agencies

The government is probably one of the largest employers of paralegals. The types of jobs available to paralegals can vary even more greatly than in law firms. For instance, paralegals in the United States Department of Justice and state attorney general offices perform tasks very similar to those of their private practice counterparts.

CYBER TRIP

Go to the Web site for the Legal Services Corporation at www.lsc.gov. Where are the Legal Services Corporation (legal aid) offices near you?

However, due to the tremendous scope of governmental interaction with law, paralegals can often staff the legal advisors' offices of government agencies and engage in policy-making decisions. In the rule-making arena in which government agencies issue rules and regulations, paralegals are involved in soliciting and analyzing public input into proposed agency regulations. Some agencies, such as unemployment offices or parole boards, employ paralegals to analyze or even make decisions in cases before the agency. Less visible government paralegal positions involve legal research, drafting, and other substantive legal work.

Legal Services/Legal Aid Offices

In the eyes of many, this area is where paralegals got their official start. These offices were initiated by the federal government on a national basis beginning in the early 1960s to provide free legal representation to the poor in the government's War Against Poverty. Understaffed from the start and besieged by a crush of indigent clients, legal aid attorneys quickly learned that a greater number of cases could be served by delegating the legal work to trained nonattorneys. Soon, with some education as well as training, legal aid offices employed almost as many paralegals as they did the attorneys who supervised their work.

Many paralegals in the legal aid offices actually started to represent clients in large numbers before administrative agencies that allowed nonattorney representation. Agencies like the U.S. Social Security Administration assess the claims of many indigent persons to receive benefits such as disability, retirement, or survivors' benefits. Paralegals are expressly permitted to represent claimants for such benefits. A 1984 study showed that Social Security Administration claimants represented by nonattorneys achieved a success rate very close to that of claimants who were represented by

A DAY IN THE LIFE OF A REAL PARALEGAL

Here is the story of two paralegals and their paths to nontraditional jobs as professional paralegals:

Phyllis Crane received her bachelor's degree from Emerson College and a few years later obtained a position negotiating contracts for a *Fortune* 500 company subsidiary, Standard & Poor. To perform more efficiently and effectively on the job, Crane pursued a certificate in paralegal studies with the support of her employer. With courses such as contracts, securities law, and legal research, Crane sees a great improvement in her job performance. "Some of the material we covered, I already knew in a very general sense," she admits. However, with the actual courses and then the certificate under her belt, Crane feels confident in her work. "Now," she says, "I am more sure of what I am doing, and if I'm not sure, I have the knowledge to look it up right on my computer at work." Her supervising attorney at first was pleasantly surprised by the depth of her newly acquired legal knowledge and now has the confidence that Crane can handle the job with a greater level of certainty and expertise.

After receiving her associate's degree from a local community college, Martha Donovan transferred to a four-year school for a bachelor's degree in paralegal studies. Recently, Donovan completed her internship with the Consumer Division with the state attorney general's office. She reported that the greatest benefit she gained from school and the internship placement was seeing herself develop as a legal professional. After a few years in the legal department of some banking and investment firms, Donovan found a position in the securities field—the law of stocks and bonds—in the legal department of a major mutual fund company. Overwhelmed by the complexity and breadth of the laws and regulations involved, Donovan waded her way through drafting prospectus, analyzing detailed financial spreadsheets, and learning a whole new language. After a couple of years on the job, Donovan was assigned to handle the government compliance and annual reports for several mutual funds on her own.

attorneys. Dozens of federal agencies permit qualified paralegals to appear as representatives in their hearings for claimants or the agency itself. The same is true of many state agencies.

Nontraditional Paralegal Positions

Although not called paralegals in these fields, more and more paralegal school graduates are finding jobs performing legal work with insurance companies and financial institutions. Positions such as investigator, claims representative, office manger, title examiner, and contract coordinator are commonly staffed by graduates of paralegal programs because of the need in these positions for legal training and competent legal analysis. More recently, paralegals have begun to gain positions as legal professionals in labor unions, criminal justice systems, and even professional athletic organizations, which are increasingly the subject of legal disputes. Graduates of paralegal programs are also able to provide the ability to write clearly and effectively, research the law competently, and, above all, provide a strong sense of professionalism.

Summary

The paralegal profession has grown in leaps and bounds over the past 40 years. Starting in legal aid offices for the poor in the 1960s, paralegals have become recognized professionals in law offices and now work in private firms, corporations, and government offices across the United States and in foreign countries. Paralegal education comes in many different forms and has just begun to standardize. Many employers consider an associate's degree, bachelor's degree, or certificate in paralegal studies sufficient evidence of education and training. The American Bar Association has taken a major role in setting educational standards for paralegal education. Nevertheless, many feel that there should be other ways of measuring the quality of paralegal education. Moreover, other sources of input, in addition to the ABA, would ensure a more balanced and honest approach to paralegal education. The same is true of the professional status of paralegals working in the field.

Currently there is much debate about whether there should be licensing. Licensing would mean that paralegals could practice law in a limited way. Already there is a certification process, known as the CLA, which has been in existence for a long time. Established by the National Association for Legal Assistants, the certification process is a good way to measure the competency of a paralegal. Alternatively, there is also the registration process of the National Federation of Paralegal Associations, which offers PACE as a form of recognition for paralegals with education, experience, and demonstrated competence. The registration scheme of the PACE program also provides for the possibility of a limited form of licensing for registered paralegals to perform some specialized tasks involving the practice of law. Substantial controversy surrounds whether this licensing may even be possible any time in the near future. There are many questions and issues to be addressed before the establishment of a licensing process for paralegals.

To make matters even more interesting, there are many differing points of view within the paralegal profession. As an indication of their status as an emerging profession, paralegals have formed several different organizations and associations that provide support for members and the entire profession. Paralegals are still evolving as a profession, and working as a professional paralegal affords an exciting and meaningful way to engage in law, whether it is in a private law firm, government agency, corporate office, or any of the new emerging forums for the professional paralegal.

Key Terms

- American Bar Association
- ABA approval
- ABA Standing Committee on Paralegals
- Associate's degree
- Bachelor's degree
- Bar exam
- Certificate
- Certification
- Contingency fee
- Hourly fee
- Law clerk
- Lawyer
- Legal assistant
- Legal technician
- License
- National Association of Legal Assistants (NALA)
- National Federation of Paralegal Associations (NFPA)
- Paralegal
- Paralegal education
- Pro bono
- Registration
- Regulation
- Training

Review Questions

1. What is the difference between certification or registration and licensure?
2. What started the growth of the paralegal profession?
3. How can legal fees be lowered by employing paralegals?
4. Why did the law degree change from an undergraduate to a graduate degree?
5. What are NALA's reasons for opposing licensing paralegals?
6. What position does NFPA take regarding the licensing of paralegals?
7. What constitutes a profession, and how is it different from an occupation?
8. Why do lawyers need a license to practice law?
9. What tasks that now constitute the practice of law might be well suited for paralegals if there were limited licensing?
10. What is the difference between education and training for legal professionals?
11. List some of the specific substantive legal tasks that paralegals may perform.

Exercises

1. Using a notepad, list as many times in one day the way in which an activity, an object, a person, or anything you come across is affected by law. Share your list with others in the class.
2. Go to the Web site for AAfPE and that the ABA's Standing Committee on Paralegals. In both cases, which schools in your state are AAfPE members or ABA approved schools? Are there any schools in your state that are listed on both sites?
3. Find the Web site for the U.S. Department of Labor Occupational Outlook Handbook at www.bls.gov/oco/ocos114.htm. Find the Job Outlook for paralegals. How much do paralegals earn?
4. Find the paralegal organization closest to your home. Find out about it, when it meets, its membership benefits and requirements, and other details.
5. Take a look in the phonebook for the listings of lawyers in your local area. Identify from the listings and advertisements the various types of lawyers there are and the types of cases they handle.

Discussion Questions

1. Can you develop any additional arguments for or against licensing paralegals to perform some of lawyers' work?
2. If paralegals were to be licensed, what kinds of problems or issues can you anticipate? For instance, based on the information in the chapter, what type of education or training (or both) should be required? Should there be different types of examinations for different types of activities within the practice of law that paralegals would be permitted to do?
3. Do you think that NALA should advocate inroads into the practice of law for paralegals? What are the pros and cons of either position that NALA or any other paralegal organization might take?
4. NFPA recognizes that the licensing and regulatory issue needs further study. What areas need clarification, and what issues need to be addressed?
5. What is the practice of law?
6. How much influence or control should lawyers and the ABA have in the shape and direction of the paralegal profession and education?
7. Looking at the AAfPE definition of paralegals, could a potential ethical problem arise, because its definition omits the requirement that paralegals must work under an attorney's supervision?

PORTFOLIO ASSIGNMENT

Create a two- or three-page report on the type of law-related environment that interests you. The report should describe the office, the type of legal work, and the staff, as well as an explanation of why that office or type of work interests you. If possible, visit an office, take electronic pictures if permitted, and put them into your report. Otherwise, you can obtain information from the Internet about a particular law firm, government office, or other legal workplace. Prepare to present your report to your class.

Chapter 2

Ethics and Professional Conduct for the Legal Professional

CHAPTER OBJECTIVES

Upon completion of this chapter, students will have a basic understanding of:

- The Rules of Professional Conduct for the legal profession.
- The relationship between ethics and notions of professionalism.
- Ethics as a component of licensure in the legal profession.
- The Big Three ethical rules for paralegals: confidentiality, unauthorized practice of law, and conflicts of interest.
- Ethical duties for paralegals.
- The history and development of the American legal system and professional ethics.
- Ethical codes for paralegals.

This chapter will provide students with an overview of the all-important ethical considerations necessary for the study of law. Ethics cannot be overemphasized, and the information covered here will provide instruction in professional ethics on both a theoretical and practical level. Special attention to the ethical issues faced by paralegals in the legal workplace will assist students in applying otherwise abstract principles. This chapter continues with a discussion of professionalism as a learned occupation. Professionalism is also defined as an earnest expression of faith or belief, such as a religious or moral belief. Most people also understand the common use of the word "professional" to describe someone who performs a task requiring high expertise. Thus, something done "professionally" means doing it well as a matter of routine and with aplomb—that is, with assurance and perhaps some poise. Putting all of this together, the idea of a profession combines a vocation requiring a high degree of both education and training with high moral or ethical standards and orderly calm.

ETHICS AND RULES OF PROFESSIONAL CONDUCT FOR THE AMERICAN LEGAL PROFESSION

The main idea behind the image of professionalism is to instill confidence in the public eye. If society is going to entrust a small group of persons to perform specialized tasks that can have a profound impact on individuals as well as the public, there must be an important level of confidence and trust. This requirement is plainly true in the case of doctors, in whose hands the public entrusts its physical and emotional well-being. The same trust is given to engineers and architects who design our office buildings, bridges, and homes to stand stable and safe. By the same token, clients must be able to have the confidence that the lawyers they hire will draft documents, such as wills or contracts, that are legally effective; argue a case that has been adequately researched; and give sound advice that has insight and conforms to the current state of the law. This confidence often relies on a sense of the **ethics** of those professionals.

ethics
Standards by which conduct is measured.

Beyond the requirement to maintain a high level of professional competence, there are other equally important elements of a professional's duty, not only to his or her client but also to the public. Publicly undertaking these additional duties creates the important sense of trust. Moreover, all recognized professions are governed by ethical codes that further inculcate a positive public perception toward the profession. These

EYE ON ETHICS

The most common and prevalent ethical principle for almost every profession is the duty of confidentiality. The duty to maintain confidentiality means that the professional must ensure that information about his or her patient, client, source, or customer remains secured from others outside of the professional relationship. For most professions, the duty of confidentiality is designed to encourage the free disclosure of information to the professional involved. Thus, confidentiality builds trust and assists the professional to do his or her job. Here is a brief review of some confidentiality concerns in other professions:

Journalists often recognize three levels of confidentiality with news sources:

- *On the record* is official information provided "on the record" that may be quoted and attributed directly to the source.
- *On background* is information provided "on background" and may be attributed to a person's position, even if anonymously.
- *Off the record* is unofficial information provided "off the record" and may not be used. At any rate, journalists are frequently wary of accepting such information. "Off the record" information is sometimes used to point journalists in the direction of other sources or simply expresses a frank or personal opinion.

A ***physician'*** duty of confidentiality prohibits the disclosure of information about the patient's case and encourages the physician to take precautions to ensure only authorized access to patient information. In the course of caring for patients, physicians find themselves exchanging information about patients with other physicians. However, these exchanges are often critical for patient care and are an integral part of the learning experience in a teaching hospital.

Psychologists frequently inform their patients as follows: You have a right to expect absolute privacy and confidentiality in therapy. Without the patient's explicit consent, the therapist is prevented by law from discussing information shared during treatment sessions with anyone else. Knowing and trusting that anything you say will be safely contained in the therapeutic space is essential to meaningful therapy. In addition to maintaining absolute confidentiality, the therapist is responsible for establishing an environment that ensures privacy in every way possible.

For ***librarians***, according to the American Library Association, and in a library, the right to privacy is the right to open inquiry without having the subject of one's interest examined or scrutinized by others. This form of confidentiality is designed to promote the freedom of inquiry and to encourage the use of library materials. Confidentiality exists when a library is in possession of personally identifiable information about users and keeps that information private on their behalf. Confidentiality is the library's responsibility.

codes impose not only a duty of competence but also of honesty, fair dealing, and confidentiality. The details within the ethical codes of each profession differ, because the expertise among the various professions differs greatly, and so their ethical codes are tailored to the specifics of each profession.

Lawyers, like almost all professionals, are regulated by state laws. However, for more than a century, the ABA has been able to act on behalf of its members and offer guidance to the states in their regulation of the legal profession. As a voluntary professional association, the ABA has no direct authority over the practice of law in the United States. Instead, state court systems and state legislatures regulate lawyers on the basis of what the ABA proposes. This prime example depicts how a **profession** has successfully regulated itself by taking the initiative to promulgate its own rules of conduct, which are, in turn, adopted and incorporated into law. Thus, the ABA was able to gain credibility regarding its ability to govern its own membership of the legal profession by issuing its own specific standards that its members agreed to abide by.

profession
A learned occupation that abides by an ethical code or rules.

CYBER TRIP

On the Internet, go to the ABA's Web site to view the Model Rules of Professional Conduct at www.abanet.org/cpr/mrpc/mrpc_toc.html. (Due to limitations imposed by the legal protection of copyright laws, the ABA's Model Rules may be quoted only in their entirety, including the lengthy and extensive comments that follow each rule.)

What eight areas of concern do the rules cover? What information is protected by Model Rule 1.6, which deals with the important ethical concern for client confidentiality?

Using an Internet search engine, find the ethical rules for lawyers in your state. Is there a difference between the ABA version and the version adopted in your state?

A Brief History of Professional Regulation: A Cultural Evolution

Law and the rules regulating the legal profession have come about as the result of a long history of evolution. Originally, the existing Rules of Professional Conduct were called the "Canons of Professional Ethics," which, like many other aspects of law, had religious overtones. The inside of a courtroom can even resemble that of a church, replete with pews and alter. Some historians have likened the jury box to a variation of the choir seats at the side of a church alter. Undeniably, the courtroom judge, who enters through a separate, almost secret entrance and sits on an elevated bench, seems like a priestess of justice, complete with black robe and occasional use of Latin, dispensing justice as if they were absolutions and divine pronouncements.

The law itself has also developed from more explicit religious origins. The United States is known as a "common law" country. When the English colonists settled in the United States, they brought with them English customs and laws, known as the "common law." With those laws came a lot of English history. As you will see in subsequent chapters, American property and contract laws are direct descendants of early feudal laws, known as writs. Soon after the Norman conquest of Britain in 1066, the process started by which disputes were submitted to the monarch, who applied the common law through a system of writs that is, in large part, still in use today. Except in disputes over the ownership of land or possessions, the monarch's decisions were always in the form of monetary amounts, or judgments. Therefore, in the monarch's judgment, one person would owe another a certain sum of money. Of course, as an order of the monarch, the judgment had to be obeyed.

Other forms of disputes did not easily fit into the writ system and prompted the application of moral or religious principles, such as cases involving family relationships, charities, and matters of conscience. Deciding such matters called for the application of larger principles of right and wrong, for which the writ system could not provide adequate relief. Thus, beginning with the reign of Henry II (1154-89), these cases were delegated to ecclesiastical or religious personnel within the King's Court, who proceeded to apply principles derived from canons, or religious laws. As a result, there are many ecclesiastical symbols and customs still in use today. One of the most powerful symbols of law is the Ten Commandments.

From all of this, our society's legal culture has evolved from a combination of governmental authority, religious icons, and notions of conscience, as well as a general sense of right and wrong. These values have been reflected in works that discuss "ethics" and "morality." After centuries of development, religious labels such as "canons" have been shed for the modern language. Since 1983, the ABA has moved toward more secular labels, using for example the "**Model Rules of Professional Conduct**." Nevertheless, the idea that correct, professional behavior equates with ethical behavior is still with us, at least in name. Therefore, many people use the terms "ethical codes," "professional responsibility," and "rules of professional conduct" synonymously.

ABA Model Rules of Professional Conduct
Lawyer's ethical rules.

Ethics, one of the cornerstones of Western culture and society, originated from the study and writings of classical Greek philosophers, such as Plato and Aristotle. From this study, both classical and modern philosophers looked for a systematic set of rules that would guide a person and his or her actions. Of particular concern was the effect of a person's actions on others. Thus, an "ethical" person would perform only good deeds that would not do harm. Laws issued by governments were looked on as expressions of what constituted ethical persons and deeds.

Grafted onto classical Greek philosophy are Western Judeo-Christian ideals of ethics and the compelling Christian idea of an eternal soul, which did not exist for Aristotle or Plato. For both philosophies, the key to maintaining an "ethic" of community was based on an understanding that all life shares a common need for the basics of life, such as food, water, shelter, and factors that make the quality of life an important good in and of itself. Both Greek philosophy and Judeo-Christian ideals serve as the foundations for the rules governing the conduct of modern professions.

Ethics for Legal Professionals

A century ago, the ABA formulated the Canons of Professional Ethics, now known as the Model Rules of Professional Conduct. Virtually every state has adopted the ABA rules in one form or another. The bulk of these rules prescribe the parameters of the attorney's conduct in the actual practice of law during his or her direct dealings with clients, the courts, and the public. Consistent with the purpose of public protection, these rules command that attorneys perform for their clients competently, zealously, and diligently.

Attorneys must present their cases before a tribunal in good faith, with candor, and within the bounds of the law. Professional responsibility requires attorneys to act fairly to their opposition and discharge their professional duties with impartiality and punctuality. In the interest of the profession's integrity, attorneys must avoid misconduct or even the appearance of impropriety that would adversely reflect on his or her fitness to practice law. The aims of these rules are threefold. First, the rules establish the attorney's primary duty to his or her client: to act competently and zealously. Second, attorneys must behave honestly and forthrightly before the courts. Third, lawyers have a duty to the public to maintain an unsullied image. The **ethical rules** require legal professionals to avoid even the appearance of impropriety. This requirement means that a legal professional must stay out of trouble and away from anything that could be seen as trouble. Again, the rules helped shape the public's perception of the profession.

ethical rules
Rules or codes issued by professions to identify ethical duties.

In almost all licensed professions, members must abide by the rules of professional conduct or ethics. If they are found to have violated the rules, their license to work in the profession may be in jeopardy. Depending on the seriousness of the violation or the amount of harm caused by the violation, the sanction can range from receiving a reprimand—a slap on the wrist—to having their license revoked temporarily or permanently by the governmental authority that issues the professional license.

Because professional activity requires a license to engage in it, disciplinary action against licensed professionals effectively takes away their legal ability to work. For lawyers, this action is known as a license suspension or, in the case of revocation, disbarment. As you can see, rules of professional conduct are the primary way by which professions are regulated, which is particularly true for lawyers. The ethical rules for lawyers establish a standard of conduct that applies only to them. Lawyers

FIGURE 2.1
Sanctions for Lawyers Who Violate Ethical Rules

Sanction	Effect on Lawyer's Status
Disbarment	Terminates an individual's license to practice law. Reinstatement available after 5 years upon demonstration of rehabilitation and possibly retaking bar exam.
Suspension	Suspends an individual's license to practice law for a specified period, usually 6 months.
Interim suspension	Temporary suspension of the license to practice law pending final outcome of disciplinary proceedings.
Reprimand	Also known as a private censure, this sanction becomes a matter of public record announcing that the lawyer has engaged in improper conduct.
Admonition	Also known as a private reprimand, this sanction declares improper conduct without public disclosure and does not affect the lawyer's license.
Probation	Permits the lawyer to continue practicing law under specified conditions; can be combined with other sanctions.
Other actions or remedies	In addition to other sanctions, additional measures may include payment for costs, restitution, or attending continuing education courses.

who violate their ethical obligations are subject to disciplinary actions by their state bar association, which can impose sanctions. Depending on the severity of the violation, the sanction that may be imposed on a lawyer ranges widely. Moreover, each state has its own array of disciplinary sanctions. Figure 2.1 provides a typical list of possible sanctions that may be imposed on lawyers who violate the ethical rules.

As discussed subsequently in this chapter, a lawyer's violation of the ethical rules may be cause for civil law suits or criminal proceedings against the wayward lawyer as another form of enforcing the ethical rules. For example, a paralegal or other nonattorney working under the supervision of a lawyer could cause harm to a client's case through neglect, which would constitute a violation of the ethical rules. Under such circumstances, the supervising attorney could be sued for a form of neglect known as malpractice. Although the attorney him- or herself may not have committed the neglect, he or she is ethically and legally responsible for the acts or misdeeds of those working under him or her under the legal doctrine of *respondeat superior*—a concept discussed in detail later in this book.

Ethics for Paralegals

Paralegals themselves are not directly governed by their own rules of professional conduct or ethics. Nor do the ABA Model Rules apply to paralegals. The primary reason is that paralegals are not yet licensed. The professional conduct or ethics for the paralegal profession are indirectly governed by the same rules that govern lawyers. With the first recognition of paralegals by the ABA in 1967, it became clear that paralegals work under the supervision of attorneys, who in turn are governed by their states' rules governing attorney conduct. As noted previously, every state's rules more or less follow the ABA's Model Rules of Professional Conduct, which require attorneys to supervise paralegals working with them. The ABA rules do not specifically refer to paralegals. However, the ABA Model Rules of Professional Conduct apply indirectly.

Specifically, ABA Model Rule 5.3 provides that any attorney who employs or retains a nonattorney's services must ensure that the nonattorney's conduct is consistent with the attorney's obligations under the professional rules. The nonattorneys referred to in Rule 5.3 could include a wide range of people, such as accountants, engineers, surveyors, assessors, and even secretaries and file clerks. Paralegals are nonattorneys under that rule. As supervisors of paralegals, lawyers have an obligation to ensure that those working under their umbrella in the practice of law obey the ethical rules. Thus, if a paralegal acts unethically, the lawyer is responsible for the paralegal's conduct under the ABA Model Rules.

In 1991, the ABA decided to get into the act and published *Model Guidelines for the Utilization of Legal Assistants*, a much welcomed document that was well received by both lawyers and paralegals. The publication was most recently updated in 2004 and is now known as the ***Model Guidelines for the Utilization of Paralegal Services.*** The guidelines are directed solely at attorneys who employ paralegals and spell out the attorney's professional obligations under Rule 5.3 with regard to paralegals. Like the Ten Commandments, there are exactly ten guidelines. Primary among them are the three most important aspects of an attorney's professional conduct. The three rules requiring attorneys to maintain client confidentiality, avoid conflict of interests, and prevent the unauthorized practice of law are already well defined in the ABA Model Rules of Professional Conduct. The same three ethical rules are recast in the *Model Guidelines for Utilization of Paralegal Services* and specifically extended to situations involving paralegals.

ABA Model Guidelines for the Utilization of Paralegals
Lawyers' guidelines for delegating work to paralegals.

The guidelines offer to the paralegal profession both express limitations and some needed recognition of the paralegals' status in the legal profession. Beginning with the attorney–client relationship, the guidelines provide that attorneys are solely responsible for the legal work product, even though the paralegal may have contributed substantially to the end product. The same guideline also permits the attorney to delegate a wide range of tasks to a paralegal, short of practicing law, which only the attorney may do. At the same time, another guideline prohibits an attorney from delegating responsibility that would enable a paralegal to establish an attorney–client relationship, set fees, or give legal opinions. These limitations actually sum up the outer parameters of the work that paralegals may perform. Although the practice of law is difficult to define, establishing the attorney–client relationship involves setting fees, rendering legal opinions (advice), and appearing in court, well-understood tasks that require a license. Understandably then, the guidelines are very specific about reiterating these limitations.

CYBER TRIP

Go to www.abanet.org/legalservices/paralegals/ and find the ABA's Model Guidelines. Which guideline authorizes a lawyer to identify a paralegal on the lawyer's letterhead and business guide?

A DAY IN THE LIFE OF A REAL PARALEGAL

Probably the most famous paralegal in recent years is Erin Brockovich of the California law firm Masry & Vititoe. As an unemployed single mother of three children, Brockovich was offered a job as a file clerk at Masry & Vititoe, which had represented her in a car accident. While organizing a file in a pro bono case, Brockovich's interest was piqued by the sight of medical records. She was allowed to investigate the matter on her own time. Her ingenious and tireless efforts uncovered a connection between the Pacific Gas and Electric Company's pollution of the public water supply and the severely deteriorated health of hundreds of nearby residents.

A class action suit brought by Masry & Vititoe resulted in the largest settlement in a direct action lawsuit. Brockovich's heroic efforts overcame insurmountable odds and an opposition with almost unlimited resources. On behalf of 600 residents of Hinckley, California, Brockovich was instrumental in obtaining a settlement of $333 million. Her crusading efforts as a paralegal, as well as the turnaround in her life, were portrayed in the Universal Studios film *Erin Brockovich* (2000). The film was a big hit and nominated for five Academy Awards, including Best Actress for Julia Roberts' portrayal of Erin Brockovich. Brockovich worked as a consultant on the film and even acted in the role of a waitress for one scene. At the end of the film, Brockovich receives a bonus check in the amount of $2 million for her work against Pacific Gas & Electric—apparently a true fact.

While the Erin Brockovich story has inspired legions of would-be legal professionals, many have questioned the ethical conduct of Brockovich and the attorneys at Masry & Vititoe. Many of the ethical considerations covered in this chapter may alert you to those concerns.

For paralegals, the guidelines offer express recognition of them as professionals on the legal team. The guidelines do so by allowing attorneys to identify paralegals by name and title on the law firm's letterhead and on the paralegals' own business cards. Today, most paralegals in mid-size to large private firms and government agencies have their own business cards issued by the firm or the agency with their names printed above their paralegal title. The guidelines also permit attorneys to bill clients separately for the work performed by the paralegal. Finally, the guidelines encourage paralegals to participate in continuing education and pro bono activities. These positive measures for paralegals are clear signs from the legal establishment that recognize the paralegals' status as a legal professional.

Voluntary Ethical Codes for Paralegals

voluntary ethical codes
Ethical rules or codes issued by a professional organization as a voluntary show of professional status.

professionalism
Performing duties as a professional ethically and efficiently.

As another measure of professional status for paralegals, both NFPA and NALA have drafted their own **voluntary ethical codes**. Both NFPA and NALA are voluntary associations. The full text of those codes appear in the appendix to this book. A full-fledged paralegal need not belong to either or any professional association. However, as discussed, there are many benefits to being a member of such organizations. In addition to offering collegiality and networking opportunities, these associations provide the benefits of **professionalism** through their ethical codes. Attaining membership to either NFPA or NALA means that the professional paralegal has embraced the association's codes of ethical and professional responsibility.

confidentiality
Lawyer's duty not to disclose information concerning a client.

NFPA's *Model Code of Ethics and Professional Responsibility* was established in 1993 for its members. The Code consists of ten rules, including several "ethical considerations" modeled after the ABA's earlier Code of Professional Responsibility. Like the ABA Model Rules of Professional Conduct for lawyers, the NFPA's Model Code highlights paralegals' obligation to maintain **confidentiality**, avoid conflicts of interest, and refrain from the unauthorized practice of law. The NFPA Model Code is also tailored to paralegals and their practice. Specifically, the Code exhorts NFPA members to adhere to a high level of professional integrity and competence and to serve the public interest by contributing to the improvement of the legal system. The Code is enforced by NFPA's disciplinary mechanisms, which can include fines, reprimands, or even expulsion from membership.

For its part, NALA also has its own *Code of Ethics and Professional Responsibility,* which covers essentially the same areas and provides for sanctions for violations. Furthermore, NALA has taken the additional step of adopting the *ABA Model Guidelines for Utilizing Paralegal Services* as an additional part of the professional responsibilities of its members. Although the two associations have differed sharply on the licensing issue, they are in agreement with regard to the ethical and professional conduct of their membership and of paralegals in general. Other paralegal associations, such as the International Paralegal Management Association and the American Alliance of Paralegals, as well as local associations for paralegals, have largely adopted their own codes similar to NFPA's or NALA's.

EMERGING ISSUES IN THE PARALEGAL MOVEMENT: THE RELATIONSHIP BETWEEN ETHICS AND LICENSURE

Viewed from a variety of perspectives, the adoption of ethical and professional responsibility by codes by the various paralegal associations is an important step in achieving recognition as a profession that is entitled to the respect and confidence. As paralegals progress from an occupation to a profession, these codes of ethics and professional responsibility will begin to take on greater significance. From a public policy standpoint, the existence of enforceable ethical codes and the like are viewed

OBSERVATIONS ON MULTIDISCIPLINARY PRACTICE (AN OPPORTUNITY FOR THE PROFESSIONAL PARALEGAL)

ABA Model Rule of Professional Conduct 5.4, which has been adopted by almost every state, prohibits a practicing lawyer from sharing fees with and from becoming a partner with a nonlawyer if any part of the business entity involves the practice of law. Rule 5.4 is known as the partnership rule. Partnerships are business entities created by state laws allowing two or more persons to share expenses and profits in a common business activity. When two or more lawyers combine to form a firm, the law has traditionally required them to form a partnership or a modern variant. A partner in a partnership is like a shareholder of a corporation—a stake in the business. The difference is that a partner works actively in the business whereas a shareholder is usually a passive investor. Other than partners in a law firm, everyone else who works in the partnership does not have a stake or share. They are merely employees who can be fired or laid off at will—by the partners. Employees in a partnership cannot profit from the good fortunes of a partnership, aside from an occasional bonus made at the discretion of the partners.

Another rule that exists in every state is the requirement of a license in order to engage in the practice of law. Known more popularly as the unauthorized practice of law rules (UPL), the laws of all states thus prevent any business entity from the practice of law unless all of the principals, that is partners, of the entity are licensed attorneys.

As a result, business associations between lawyers and nonlawyers such as accountants and bankers as co-equal principles in the business entity may not offer legal services as even a part of their business activities. Hence, tax advice from an accountant and legal advice from an attorney must therefore come from two different entities for the same client even though it involves the same transaction. Estate planning and life insurance proposals for the same individual must come separately from an attorney's law office and a life insurance agency. An attorney working within a bank may not draft a will for the bank's customer. Only law firms, which consist entirely of lawyers as its partners, may engage in the practice of law. The underlying legal theory is that a business entity such as a corporation is an artificial creation which cannot practice law since it is not a natural person and possesses neither learning, good character, nor capacity to take an oath or preserve and occupy a personally confidential relation with a client. This is, of course, nonsense. It is a vestige of a bygone era. Yet, it is a concept that is still embodied the law.

Those who have defended of the combination of partnership and UPL rules prohibiting the nonattorney from law firm partnership have voiced concerns for client confidentiality, conflicts of interest as well as UPL. However, now that globalization of the world's economy is well upon us, the double-barreled impact of these two rules—the partnership rule and UPL—have unintentionally stymied the much needed growth of the legal profession in the United States. As a result, law firms in the United States are losing the battle for clients.

In the early 1990's, the large accounting firms began purchasing existing law firms and moving them to Europe in order to avoid the restraints imposed by Model Rule 5.4, and UPL on their practices. This is simply because the partnership rule and UPL laws do not apply outside of the United States. In Europe and elsewhere, accounting firms are expanding their services, offering direct legal services and actively soliciting traditional legal work as well as business management services. Thus, combining business and financial expertise with legal advice under one roof, the accounting firms operating with lawyers in Europe have established a new concept of a fully integrated model for the provision of legal services. This is known as a Multi-Disciplinary Practice firm, or an MDP.

Under this model, the benefit and the value of these firms to the client is the increased efficiency, giving business, accounting and legal advice to the client under one roof. The client benefits from the savings in the cost of professional business advice, and from the sheer convenience of obtaining a multitude of services from one office. This is precisely the point of MDP as a business model. Both the accountants and the lawyers benefit by sharing common expenses of overhead and firm management, as well as the increased marketability of their business model.

MDP's are entirely legal in Switzerland, France, Germany, and the Netherlands. Global firms such as Merrill Lynch employ top international tax lawyers. Other global MDP firms appear to be hiring the best lawyers from the United States. In recent years, up to twenty percent of the graduates of the top American law schools such as Georgetown, Harvard and NYU are taking

(continued)

jobs overseas with accounting firms, business consulting firms and MDP's. As a consequence, the American law firms are starting to lose their best lawyers as well as their clients.

Confronted with this dilemma, the ABA began studying the impact of MDP's upon the legal profession and established a Commission on Multidisciplinary Practice in 1998. The Commission's Final Report recommended that lawyers should be permitted to share fees and join with nonlawyer professionals a practice that delivers both legal and nonlegal professional services, that is, an MDP. In doing so, the Commission defined "nonlawyer professionals" as members of recognized professions or other disciplines that are governed by ethical standards, citing as examples, "accountants, psychologists, psychiatric social workers and real estate brokers", among others."

In arriving at this recommendation, the Commission tackled some of the same issues facing the paralegal movement in its quest for recognition and professional status. The Commission specifically recommended the adoption of rules that would protect three primary concerns: client confidentiality, conflicts of interest, and UPL.

Specifically, the Commission recommended that so long as the attorneys remained in control of the entity an attorney should be able to deliver legal services through an MDP. At the same time the Commission recommended that nonattorneys remain strictly prohibited from delivering legal services. The same rules of professional conduct that apply to law firms would still apply to an attorney in an MDP, even if the attorney were to act under a nonattorney supervisor.

The Commission also recommended that any nonattorney professionals who operate MDPs expressly subjects itself in writing to the oversight authority and discipline of the highest court in each state in which the MDP is operating. This requirement would thus regulate the nonattorney partner of an MDP in the same way as an attorney.

The implications of the MDP phenomenon upon paralegals are clear. Paralegals may, under the Commission's recommendation, become nonlawyer professionals because they are members of a recognized profession that is governed by ethical standards. For many years, paralegals have been governed by the same ethics and rules of professional conduct for attorneys. In fact, NFPA and NALA have voluntarily adopted codes of ethics and professional responsibility. Even the ABA has promulgated "ethics" rules specifically for paralegals in its *Model Guidelines for the Utilization of Paralegal Services*. As early as 1996, NFPA expressed the opinion that its PACE qualified as proof that the paralegals are members of a recognized profession operating under ethical standards. As such, paralegals are therefore prime candidates as equity partners in an MDP.

A very meaningful form of professional recognition for paralegals is financial. As a partner in an MDP firm, a paralegal would have a stake in the business, a say in running the business and the opportunity to work along side other legal professionals to help the business grow and prosper. Business ownership is a strong work incentive. The difference is between a mere job as an employee, and a lifetime career as a partner in an MDP.

Source: Article reprinted by permission of the American Association for Paralegal Education. Article originally printed in 19 J. Paralegal Educ. and Prac. (2003). Further reproduction of any kind is strictly prohibited.

CALIFORNIA DREAMIN'

There's an old joke that begins by asking, "When the Beach Boys song 'Good Vibrations' was number one on the top forty charts in California, what was number one on the East Coast?" The answer is, "Not sure, but six months later, it was 'Good Vibrations'." We all understood this to mean that California was in the vanguard when it came to fashion, trends and new ideas. So it came to be true that California was the first state to enact laws that purported to regulate paralegals directly. Yet these new statutes actually do little by way of regulating paralegals. Instead, they only require educational or experiential qualifications for anyone calling herself a "paralegal." As merely a title that confers nothing by way of professionally prescribed activities, the California laws do nothing more than to commandeer the word "paralegal."

Under the new California law, a person performing "substantial legal work under the direction and supervision" of a licensed attorney may not call themselves a "paralegal" unless she has a certain level of education or experience or both. Upon meeting these qualifications, any person may legally identify herself as a "paralegal" as a title "on any advertisement, letterhead, business card, sign, or elsewhere."

(continued)

The new California law then provides that a duly licensed paralegal can perform "substantial legal work," defining it as "case planning, development, and management; legal research; interviewing clients; fact gathering and retrieving information; drafting and analyzing legal documents; collecting, compiling, and utilizing technical information to make an independent decision and recommendation to the supervising attorney; and representing clients before a state or federal administrative agency if that representation is permitted by statute, court rule, or administrative rule or regulation."

However, none of those tasks require a license. The law also specifically prohibits paralegals from engaging in the un-authorized practice of law. These express prohibitions confirm that the definition of "substantial legal work," and indeed the entire statutory scheme, does not allow those qualifying as paralegals the authority to engage in the practice of law.

The nub of the matter is that within the confines of any law office, whoever performs "substantial legal work" does not necessarily have to be called a "paralegal." In fact, the law could be easily and legally circumvented by labeling the person performing substantial legal tasks anything but a "paralegal."

Other nagging issues persist. No one knows who is supposed to enforce the new law. According to officials of the California State Bar, the law will be enforced by those allegedly harmed by the putative paralegal. You could sue the paralegal for messing up your case. However, it was always the case that you could sue someone for malpractice, whether or not they called themselves a paralegal. So why have any new law? Here's what happened.

In 1989, the California State Bar created the Commission on Legal Technicians to appraise the role of independent paralegals. This was in response to the phenomenon of independent storefront operations providing paralegal services springing up all over Southern California. Unconnected with licensed attorneys, these operations charged fees for preparing legal forms and other papers which their "clients" then filed on their own. This prompted consumer advocates as well as lawyers into proposing the new law. In fact, the initial legislative proposals envisioned a limited licensure scheme to be administered by the California Department of Consumer Affairs.

However, due to heavy opposition from the organized bar and the National Association of Legal Assistants, the limited licensure aspect was deleted. What remained for the California law to regulate is merely the word "paralegal." What we are left with is the sober wisdom that effective paralegal regulation necessarily involves the notion of some kind of license. For it makes little sense to regulate solely the person without licensing that person to engage in a regulated activity such as the practice of law, if even just part of it.

Early on, observers of the paralegal movement pointed out that the regulation of professional activity requires two things. First, it identifies the general scope of activity subject to regulation. Second, it licenses the persons who are thereby permitted to engage in that defined activity in accordance with defined educational standards and governmentally sanctioned competency examinations. For example, the practice of medicine is an identified professional activity. Doctors are licensed as such to engage in the practice of medicine as a result of meeting well-defined educational standards and passing board examinations. Similarly, the practice of law is an identified (albeit vaguely) professional activity. Lawyers are licensed to practice law after successful completion of both law school and a bar exam. The same is true of electricians, plumbers, hairdressers, and licensed drivers for that matter. Thus, missing from the California law was a delineation of a scope of activity requiring a license. Paralegals are "licensed" under the California law for only their education or experience or both, but not for anything they do as such.

Perhaps it would be helpful to look at how physicians assistants ("PA's") came about. PA's do indeed practice medicine and are licensed by the state after meeting educational requirements and an exam. They have an ethics code and practice a limited range of medicine consisting of tasks that only doctors could do before. A licensed PA may make elementary diagnoses, perform diagnostic procedures, and prescribe and distribute medication directly to patient's maintenance. PA's are paid less than doctors, and PA's receive less schooling and training than doctors.

Behind the scenes, the presence of health insurance companies has had a profound effect. Insurance companies have been instrumental in the shaping the growth of licensed non-physicians in the health care world because of their independence from the profession and their overriding concern for costs.

In the legal world, there is no parallel entity or other economic incentive that could similarly propel the licensing of paralegals. For that reason, it becomes very obvious why pro bono legal

(continued)

services offices were the first to utilize paralegals as a cost effective measure for the delivery of legal services to the poor. It is simply a matter of economics.

From all of this, here is some advice: If you are a California attorney doing legal work alongside some nonattorneys, do them a favor and call them anything but a "paralegal."

Source: Article reprinted by permission of the American Association for Paralegal Education. Article originally printed in the E. Paralegal Educator, Volume 18, Number 3 (Fall 2004), and Volume 19 Number 1(Winter 2005). Further reproduction of any kind is strictly prohibited.

as necessary if not essential elements to achieving the prize of professional status and perhaps licensing. From what you have learned so far, it should be clear that the regulation of a profession by society is accomplished by the enforcement of such codes. These professional codes also serve the purpose of protecting the profession and the public from intrusion by outsiders who may be untrained or unscrupulous or both. Yet there may be some unintended results. The previous two articles present some issues now facing the paralegal profession. As you read them, notice the role that ethical codes take in a given profession.

There clearly are some unintended results from the ABA's Model Rules of Professional Conduct for lawyers. Although the rules are designed to protect the public, they may also have the effect of inhibiting the growth of a profession. Nevertheless, the legal profession and the ABA have shown some flexibility in modifying the rules to accommodate changed conditions. What is significant is the notion that ethical codes in a given profession are important aspects of the profession's recognition by society. Other than status, social recognition can eventually lead to legal recognition and the monetary rewards that can follow. However, at this point, the adoption of ethical codes by voluntary associations such as NFPA and NALA may be too simplistic an answer for the paralegal profession.

The Commission on Multidisciplinary Practice gave examples of other professionals who could be MDP partners. It named accountants, psychologists, psychiatric social workers, and real estate brokers, all of whom are professionals tested, licensed, and hence directly regulated by state law. As yet, paralegals are not licensed and are regulated only indirectly. Thus, it appears that what the Commission may have meant as possible MDP partners were those nonattorney professionals with ethical codes that would be enforceable by the same state law that licenses the nonattorney professionals. This reasoning would appear to make sense. Current enforcement provisions by NFPA and NALA do not have the force of law, so that violations of their ethical codes result only in loss of membership—not membership to a profession but to a voluntary association. Compared with a suspension or revocation of a professional license, the NFPA or NALA sanctions can hardly be called sanctions. A paralegal whose membership has been revoked could still work as a paralegal. For a professional ethical code to have any meaning, adherence to the ethical code appears to be a condition for the professional license. Licensing for paralegal is a very complex issue.

Professional ethical codes thus perform more than the function of assuring the public that the professionals in question will be performing their tasks in good faith. There is more to it than appearance and assurances. Perhaps it would be helpful to think of professional ethical codes as the terms of a binding contract between a profession and society. The members of a profession—whether it be doctors, lawyers, or accountants—promise to abide by their ethical codes in exchange for society's grant of the exclusive right to perform certain professional tasks—doctoring, lawyering, or accounting. Those individual professionals who have been found to have breached the profession's ethical code have thereby also breached their contract with society and may have their right to practice their profession suspended or revoked. This sanction is the point behind a license. A professional license is permission from the state government to engage in an activity that requires regulation because that activity can affect the public safety and at the same time promote social good. As you can see, society regulates professional activity by enforcing the profession's ethical codes.

Ethics for the Professional Paralegal

Although paralegals are not as yet licensed and the ethical codes directly pertaining to them are through voluntary associations, there are significant ways in which society regulates paralegals. The first way is through the laws that prohibit the **unauthorized practice of law (UPL)**. This direct form of regulation allows society to prohibit paralegals (and everyone else) from engaging in professional activities that are reserved exclusively for lawyers. The UPL laws are usually vigorously enforced at the state and local level. There are criminal penalties for serious violations of UPL. The story of Rosemary Furman presents an extreme example of UPL enforcement.

We will be covering the laws of torts and **negligence** in depth as an area in which many paralegals practice. For now, our focus is upon the myriad of ethical rules that govern the activities within the legal profession directly, whether you are a lawyer or a paralegal. In any law office on any given day, lawyers and paralegals make decisions based on ethical considerations, applying the ABA Model Rules of Professional Conduct, the ABA Guidelines, and the ethical codes of voluntary associations. For the most part, most lawyers and paralegals make ethical decisions as a matter of course every working day. A competent and conscientious legal professional knows the applicable rules and knows how to follow them routinely. Let's take a look at how these rules are applied in everyday professional life.

unauthorized practice of law (UPL)
Practicing law without proper authorization to do so.

negligence
The failure to use reasonable care to avoid harm to another person or to do that which a reasonable person might do in similar circumstances.

CYBER TRIP

The two largest paralegal organizations differ sharply on the issue of paralegal licensure. NALA does not feel that licensure is necessary, while the NFPA believes that paralegals should respond to legislation allowing for at least limited licensure for paralegals. Toward that end, the NFPA has promulgated a position paper and a Model Act for Paralegal Licensure. At its Web site, www.paralegals.org, find both the NFPA's position paper and Model Act.

What are the proposed educational standards for licensure? What legal tasks would a license allow paralegals to perform?

A DAY IN THE LIFE OF A REAL PARALEGAL

Rosemary Furman worked for many years as a legal secretary and court reporter in Florida. She had seen or worked on hundreds if not thousands of routine cases, such as simple bankruptcies, uncontested divorces, wills, name changes, debt collections, evictions, adoptions, and many other legal matters. Furman saw that using standardized forms distributed freely to the public would take care of these simple, routine cases, which constituted more than half of the legal work that went through the courts. She also felt that in these types of cases, most adults could handle their own cases with a little bit of advice from court clerks and, more important, without a lawyer. Because court clerks were forbidden from giving out legal advice, Furman offered an "expanded secretarial service" and charged less than one-tenth of what lawyers charged for giving the same simple advice and filling out legal forms.

Soon, Furman's business, Northside Secretarial Service, started becoming well known in Jacksonville, Florida. In 1979, the Florida Bar Association filed a civil court action against Furman and asked the court for an injunction to stop her from engaging in the unauthorized practice of law (UPL). However, Furman felt her position was moral and kept her business open, sincerely believing that her work was bringing a small measure of justice and access to the courts for many who could not afford it.

The Florida Bar Association pursued her and had her arrested. She was tried before a judge who decided her case without a jury and sentenced her 30 days in jail, also assessing court costs against her. The Florida Supreme Court heard the case, affirmed the sentence, and ordered Furman to stop practicing law without a license. The U.S. Supreme Court declined to hear the case. By this time, Furman's case had become a cause célebre and she herself something of a folk hero. The public uproar was so great that on November 27, 1984, Florida Governor Robert Graham and the Clemency Board granted Furman clemency so that she did not have to serve time in jail.

APPLIED ETHICS AND PROFESSIONAL CONDUCT FOR PARALEGALS

Most legal professionals agree that the most important ethical rules for paralegals involve the "Big Three": maintaining client confidentiality, avoiding conflicts of interest, and refraining from UPL. These particular rules apply because of the unique position that paralegals occupy in the legal profession with respect to the ethical rules. Although not directly governed by the lawyer's ethical rules, paralegals are nevertheless an integral part of the legal team that must work under the ABA Model Rules of Professional Conduct. Thus, a thorough knowledge of how these rules operate is essential.

Maintaining Client Confidentiality

Paralegals perform many of the same tasks that their supervising attorneys would perform themselves. In doing so, paralegals become privy to information about a client. In the wrong hands, some of that information could be embarrassing or even damaging to a client's case. Thus, the rule that an attorney must maintain client confidence is designed to encourage clients to make full disclosures so that the attorney can represent the client effectively. Without such a rule, clients would hesitate in making full disclosures of information that the attorney should know. Guideline 6 of the *ABA Guidelines* makes it the attorney's responsibility to make all reasonable efforts to protect client confidentiality when working with paralegals.

PRACTICE TIP

When discussing client matters, be sure that you are speaking to a person authorized to receive information about the client and that you are out of earshot of others who may not be so authorized. Thus, particular care must be taken when speaking about client matters outside the office. Outside the office, discussions concerning client matters must be done, if at all, out of earshot of those who are not within the circle of confidentiality. Refrain from discussing client matters in public places such as restaurants or even in the office's reception areas, corridors, or elevators.

The confidentiality requirement of Rule 1.6 does two things. The rule commands legal professionals to protect information about the client from disclosure. The information subject to protection is anything that the client has revealed to the legal professionals within the context of their professional relationship, including the fact that the attorney is representing the client. Information about the client that is already publicly available is not subject to the confidentiality rule, such as published information in a telephone book or the content of papers filed in court, which are generally open to public view. Thus, the rule of confidentiality does not cover information about the client that appears as a matter of public record. The rule is silent as to what a legal professional must do to maintain client confidences. Over time, a number of commonsense practices have become routinely embedded in the procedures of virtually every law office.

Quite simply, maintaining confidentiality within Rule 1.6 means that legal professionals must be sure to remain silent about their clients and their cases while in the presence of anyone outside of the office. (Remember that Rule 5.3 requires lawyers to instruct any nonlawyers working with them to act in accordance with the lawyer's ethical codes.) Of course, it is permissible to discuss client matters with others in the office as part of the activity of working on their cases. Office colleagues, such as secretaries, file clerks, and computer technicians, are covered under the same confidentiality requirements of Rule 1.6.

At home, the confidentiality requirement means that even family and loved ones are outsiders when it comes to client confidences. Telling a spouse or family member stories about client's cases may be technically permissible so long as there is no disclosure of information that would reveal the client's identity. However, the best practice is to remain silent about all client matters. Faithful observance of the ethical duty to maintain client confidentiality carries the true mark of professionalism for a paralegal. By merely remaining silent, a paralegal fulfills that professional obligation. As simple as it may sound, remaining silent requires effort and the conscious choice to maintain a client's confidence.

Other office practices specifically designed to preserve client confidences include the proper handling of files so that client names and certainly any of their documents are safely out of view of other clients. Handling files in a way that preserves client confidentiality comes about simply as a matter of sensitivity. When working on client files in or outside the office, all care should be taken to keep documents and any information pertaining to the client, including the client's name, out of the view of others. Within the office, care should be taken to ensure that files are not left about on desktops and conference tables but instead filed out of view from other clients and visitors to the office.

With the overriding duty to maintain client confidentiality, Rule 1.6 also sets out several exceptions for situations in which client confidences *may* be revealed. The rule itself contains two exceptions pertaining to the relationship between the attorney and the client. The first permits disclosures if the "client consents after consultation," which covers a variety of situations, from issuing press releases to discussing client matters with expert consultants or other attorneys. Notice that the client's consent is made *after consultation*. Under this exception, not only has the client approved of the disclosure ahead of time, but the attorney has also informed the client of the potential risks and effects of certain disclosures. This allowance is known as **informed consent**, which means that the client has agreed with knowledge of the ramifications that the disclosure may bring.

informed consent
A legal condition whereby a person can be said to have given consent based on an appreciation and understanding of the facts and implications of an action.

implied authority
The appearance of possessing the legal ability to make a legally binding contract on behalf of another.

The second exception is one of necessity. The rule states that an attorney may reveal a client confidence that is impliedly authorized. The phrase **implied authority** means that the attorney is permitted to make disclosures of client information as necessary in the course of the attorney's representation of the client. Thus, the client's authorization to make disclosures is not expressed but understood just from the circumstances. Otherwise, it would make little sense for the attorney to be bound by the duty to maintain confidentiality and therefore be unable to reveal information to a court about the client's case that is essential to an effective presentation.

COMMUNICATION TIP

Modern technology has caused legal professionals to take additional measures to maintain client confidentiality under Rule 1.6. Here is an example of a notice now common with e-mail and faxes:

> This message and any files transmitted with it are subject to attorney–client privilege and contain confidential information intended only for the person(s) to whom this e-mail message is addressed. If you have received this e-mail message in error, please notify the sender immediately by telephone or e-mail and destroy the original message without making a copy. Thank you.

The rule of confidentiality also sets out two more exceptions in which a lawyer may make disclosures of confidential client information. One of the exceptions expresses important public policy concerns that are broader than the attorney–client relationship, and the other goes directly to that relationship. During the course of representation, a client might reveal the intent to cause harm to another person. Under these circumstances, Rule 1.6 permits the lawyer to disclose information that would otherwise be protected as confidential. The reason for this exception is obvious. As stated in the wording of the rule, the lawyer's disclosure is permitted to prevent the commission of a criminal act. Here, the public interest and public protection outweigh the breach of client confidence.

At the same time, the original wording from the ABA Model Rules of Professional Conduct for this exception has generated considerable controversy. The rule states that a lawyer may reveal information in an attempt to prevent imminent death or substantial bodily harm. By using the word "may," the rule permits disclosure at the lawyer's discretion. That is, disclosure is not required. The word "imminent" also means that even if the lawyer were to make the disclosure, the threat of death or bodily harm from the client would have to be impending or immediate.

Thus, if a client informed a lawyer of plans to commit a crime that would cause death or substantial bodily harm next month or next year, the lawyer may not be permitted to disclose because the threat was not imminent. Another problem with the wording of this exception appears in the words "substantial bodily harm." What is substantial? And is there any kind of insubstantial bodily harm? Harm is exactly that. A slap on the wrist is not bodily harm, but a punch in the nose may be. Finally, the rule does not cover other types of harm that the client may intend, such as harm to financial interests, property, or a person's freedom.

CASE IN POINT

CASE SUMMARY: *TARASOFF V. REGENTS OF THE UNIVERSITY OF CALIFORNIA,* 13 CAL. 3d 177, 529 P.2d 553, 118 CAL. RPTR.129 (1974)

Prior to the California Supreme Court's decision in *Tarasoff v. Regents of the University of California,* mental health professionals were under no obligation to control the acts of their patients or to warn anyone at possible risk of harm from the patient. In the *Tarasoff* case, a psychologist who learned his patient planned to kill a former girlfriend notified the campus police orally and in writing. The patient proceeded to ingratiate himself with the parents of the ex-girlfriend and then shot her. In a suit brought by the parents, the California Supreme Court acknowledged the confidentiality duty of the psychologist and ruled that "the doctor bears a duty to use reasonable care to give persons such warnings as are essential to avert foreseeable danger arising from the patient's condition."

Two years later, in the same case, the California Supreme Court expanded its earlier ruling and explained that the therapist was under a duty "to warn the intended victim of if it is likely, to apprise the victim of a danger, to notify the police or take whatever steps are reasonably necessary under the circumstances." This ruling has been interpreted to mean that a therapist has a duty to warn and to protect because of the "special relationship" that exists between the therapist and the patient.

QUESTIONS ABOUT THE CASE

1. Do you think the *Tarasoff* case puts therapists under the same duty to report as lawyers?
2. What effect does *Tarasoff* have on a therapist's duty of confidentiality?
3. Are there any differences between therapists and legal professionals that would justify a different rule for either?

In 2001, these issues generated a heated debate within the ABA. Ultimately, the issue was left to the various states. Addressing these issues, many states have made changes to the wording of this exception. For many states, their version of Rule 1.6 does not have the qualifier "imminent" and expands the type of harm to include property and financial interests. Massachusetts has gone so far as to permit disclosure by lawyers, and particularly prosecutors, to avert fraud and the "wrongful execution or incarceration of another." Other states such as Pennsylvania and Utah have also added fraud to the list of harms that a client may have expressed the intent to commit. Still, for every state that has adopted the ABA Model Rules of Professional Conduct in some form, another has left it up to the lawyer to decide whether to make the disclosure.

Other consequences based on moral or even religious grounds were a large part of the debate when the ABA drafted the Model Rules. A brief review of the issues provides an interesting insight into the conscience of the legal world. In particular, there is a distinction between ethics and morals. They are not the same thing, though they overlap in certain respects. **Morality** consists of a collection of cultural and religious concepts regarding the difference between "good" and "bad." Ultimately, morality provides behavioral guidelines that become social traditions that vary with time and place. Anyone who has traveled abroad understands that the concepts of morality differ greatly from country to country. Morality is therefore subjective and does not necessarily follow necessity or even practicality. Moral standards speak to an individual's relationship with his or her conscience or a higher being.

morality
A value system for determining good and bad behavior.

Ethics, however, tend to be more objective. Although ethical rules also function as behavioral guidelines, ethics are actually based on practicality and fulfill narrower social functions. Notions of ethical rights and wrongs depend on the situation. Ethics also define what is "good" and "bad" but only in a narrow and sometimes artificial sense. Such is the case with professional rules, which are "ethical" as opposed to "moral" in nature. Ethics define a particular individual's relationship to a social community, such as a profession. Violation of ethical rules carries the earthly penalty of professional sanction; moral lapses are matters of conscience and faith. Exceptions to lawyer's ethical rules stand as prime examples of social utility and are created to cover unusual or unforeseen situations.

The debate over Model Rule 1.6 ultimately pitted two potentially conflicting roles of the lawyer against each other. As a legal professional, the lawyer has an undeniable duty to represent his or her client zealously. At the same time, the attorney is an officer of the court. This particular ethical rule speaks to the lawyer's relationship to his or her client, as well as to the legal community. In the American legal realm, lawyers are vested with the trust of clients, as well as a duty to seek and uphold justice. As such, lawyers must represent their clients avidly, using all legal means at hand. Yet in doing so, lawyers must remain faithful to the integrity of the legal system, actively preventing perjury and other tactics that would subvert the system. Therefore, Rule 1.6 commands that a lawyer maintain confidential client secrets. However, the main differences of opinion centered on the extent to which a lawyer should keep clients' secrets. For many, the ABA's version in the Model Rule did not go far enough, and for others it went too far. For this reason, several states such as Massachusetts, Pennsylvania, and Utah adopted their own versions of Rule 1.6.

One argument against revealing client information is that lawyers themselves create a high expectation of confidentiality and clients, therefore, have come to expect strict confidentiality. Many thought that lawyers would best be able to talk clients out of committing future harmful or criminal conduct. Thus, if clients were not able to confide in lawyers, their intentions would remain silent. As a result, the lawyers would not be able to talk their clients out of committing crimes or harm. Another point was that the discretionary, as opposed to mandatory, nature of the rule reinforces the moral duty to reveal confidences while avoiding the elevation of moral duties to ethical or legal duties. Thus you can see the difference between morality and ethics. Those who wished to maintain strict confidentiality saw the lawyer's duty to reveal as a matter of personal conscience, not an ethical duty to society.

The final exception allowing a lawyer to disclose confidential client information covers situations in which a client or others are questioning an attorney's work. Typically, these situations would include malpractice allegations against the attorney by a former client or disciplinary proceedings in which an attorney is alleged to have violated one or more provisions of the ethical codes. Under these circumstances, the rule of confidentiality does not prevent the lawyer from defending him- or herself against allegations of wrongdoing and making disclosures. Without this exception, the rule of confidentiality would prevent the lawyer from disclosing information that would be clearly relevant to the lawyer's defense, such as the client's attempt to commit fraud, other misconduct, or even illegality.

This exception is popularly known as the "self-defense exception" and expresses a public policy that clients who have committed or intended to commit wrongdoing should not benefit from the shield that is designed to protect them. Even where there is no wrongdoing by the client, the self-defense exception permits the lawyer to reveal enough client confidences to establish a defense against claims of malpractice and ineffective assistance, as a matter of fairness.

The same exception applies to actions by lawyers against their former clients. In these rare circumstances, the lawyer is permitted to make disclosures of confidential client information to collect unpaid legal fees. Recently courts have allowed lawyers to make disclosures of confidential client information to prove claims that the lawyer was wrongfully discharged from a job as in-house corporate counsel. As corporate counsel, the lawyer has one client: the corporation for which he or she works. A large part of what corporate counsel does consists of advising the corporation as to whether a certain proposed course of action or activity is legal. Because of the rule of confidentiality, all information about the corporation is entitled to the protection of confidentiality under the ethical Rule 1.6.

Yet there have been cases in which the corporate counsel has voiced strenuous objections to the corporation's management in terms of the legality of its practices, such as pollution, product safety, or even corruption and fraud. If the corporation fires the corporate counsel for making those objections, lawyers may sue the corporation for wrongful termination. Normally, information about the corporate practices to which the lawyer objected would be entitled to confidentiality. However, as one court stated, "[a] lawyer . . . does not forfeit his [or her] rights simply because to prove them he [she] must utilize confidential information. Nor does the client gain the right to cheat the lawyer by imparting confidences to him." See *Doe v. A Corp.,* 709 F.2d 1043, 1050. (5th Cir. 1983). The court meant that it would be unfair for the client to be able to hide behind the shield of confidentiality if keeping the information behind the shield would result in an injustice.

Sometimes third parties, such as the government agencies, might begin an investigation of a client for violations of administrative regulations. In defense, the client might claim that he or she had been following a lawyer's instructions. In essence then, the client would be blaming the lawyer, even if the lawyer was not a party to the proceedings between the client and the government agency. Under the ethical rule, the information that the lawyer gave to the client, as well as the lawyer's knowledge of the client's actions, would be subject to confidentiality. Nevertheless, the lawyer would be able to disclose confidential information to defend against these allegations. In this situation, the lawyer is not the object of the administrative action.

From all of this, you can see that client confidentiality is an extremely important topic in the practice of law. The rule ensuring confidentiality protects clients, the legal profession, and society. For lawyers, the ethical codes impose a duty to keep client confidences, and provide narrow exceptions for which the lawyer may disclose such information in the public interest. For paralegals, the rules operate in the same manner, although indirectly through the lawyers with whom they work. Perhaps the best way of observing this ethical duty is to maintain an air of professionalism that acknowledges your role as a paralegal. A large part of that professionalism is to guard and protect the client's interests by keeping the information about them confidential at all times.

Three Types of Client Information

Closely related to the notion of confidential client information is the rule of evidence known as the attorney–client privilege. Like the doctor–patient privilege and other types of privileges, the attorney–client privilege may be used to keep an attorney or paralegal from testifying about information they have about a client. If the client objects, the attorney or paralegal cannot testify regarding information that is subject to the attorney–client privilege. The attorney–client privilege applies to a narrower range of information than the ethical rule covering client confidences.

The attorney–client privilege to applies to (1) a client statement, made (2) to an attorney or paralegal, (3) while seeking legal advice, even if an initial consultation, and (4) in confidence outside the presence of anyone else but the attorney or paralegal. If all four conditions are met, the client may object and the **privileged information** cannot be disclosed, even if the attorney or paralegal is subpoenaed to come to court. The same type of privilege also applies to the attorney's or paralegal's notes, research, memos of conversations and impressions, conclusions, and strategies. These matters constitute information compiled by the attorney or paralegal regarding the client's case and are protected to the same extent as the attorney–client privilege by what is known as the work product doctrine.

privileged information
Information protected by law due to a special relationship, such as attorney–client.

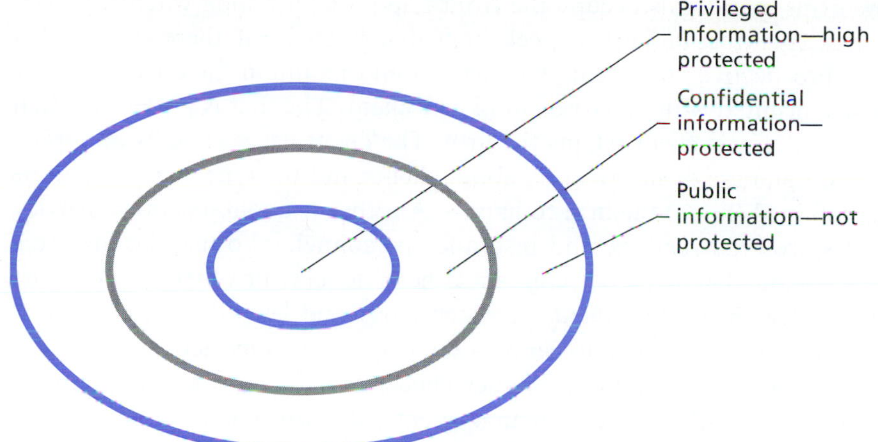

FIGURE 2.2
Three Types of Information Protected by Law

The scope of client information subject to the confidentiality requirements of Rule 1.6 is broader than the information covered by the attorney–client privilege. Rule 1.6 applies to any information in the possession of the attorney (or paralegal) from whatever source that relates to representation of the client. If this information is outside the attorney–client privilege, then the attorney or paralegal may be compelled to testify over the client's objection.

Finally, information about the client that is generally available to the public is not protected at all. This information may be obtained in a telephone book or directory that the client has usually posted or revealed voluntarily. Figure 2.2 represents the three types of client information and the protection accorded to them by law.

Conflicts of Interest

The second ethical consideration deserving of special attention by paralegals is the duty to avoid **conflicts of interest**. This duty springs from another ethical duty known as zealous representation. See Rule 1.3 of the ABA Model Rules of Professional Conduct. To represent their clients zealously, lawyers' loyalties to their clients cannot be compromised or divided. Such would be the case if a lawyer found herself representing both sides of a lawsuit or a transaction. To ensure that a lawyer has full-fledged and uncompromised loyalty to his or her client, the ethical codes require lawyers to avoid concurrent conflicts of interest if representing one client will cause a directly adverse effect on another client. The rules go on to point out that a conflict exists for the attorney if representing one or more clients will affect the attorney's responsibilities to another client or third person.

conflicts of interest
Clash between private and professional interests or competing professional interests that makes impartiality difficult and creates an unfair advantage.

Drafting these rules required considerable study and review. Innumerable scenarios can occur in the myriad of legal matters, from real estate development to wills to stock transactions to state and federal lawsuits, all of which involve attorneys and their clients as well as witnesses, experts, accountants, and others. Therefore, unlike the single rule regarding confidentiality, the ABA Model Rules of Professional Conduct contain no less than five separate rules covering conflicts of interest.

The ethical concern with conflicts of interest is obvious. If you were to hire an attorney to pursue a civil claim against another person and found out that your attorney was already representing the person you planned to sue, questions would certainly arise in your mind as to the lawyer's loyalties and whether the lawyer would act in your best interests. There would also be valid concerns about whether the lawyer would be able to maintain his or her duty of confidentiality about your case. In short, your attorney would have a conflict of interest between the two clients who have opposing interests and would be unable to represent one or both zealously.

In some law firms, paralegals occupy the front line in determining whether a conflict of interest exists. Most law firms check immediately to see if there is a conflict of interest for a prospective new client. The firm should maintain three lists, each of which should be consulted with every potential new client. The first is a client list that is updated each time a new client retains the firm. The client list is actually an alphabetically arranged database of information about clients and the type of legal matters each client has retained (hired) the firm to handle. Another list contains other parties, such as witnesses, experts, vendors, and insurance personnel, who may be involved. A third lists the various lawyers who represent others, adverse or otherwise, who are somehow connected with the new client. For each party and lawyer, a memorandum should indicate their name and relationship to the client's legal matter.

With today's computer technology, conflict checks, as they are known, may be performed quickly and easily with case management software. These software packages are integrated assemblages of many different functions that help law offices manage their clients. Conflict-checking programs are merely database applications that are custom made for law offices. With such law office software suites, conflict checking can be performed in minutes. Nevertheless, paralegals in law firms must pay careful attention to possible conflicts of interest, for ethical violations of this rule could easily and inadvertently occur.

More complex possibilities are also covered by the rules against conflicts of interest. For instance, in large firms with hundreds, or even thousands, of clients, care must be taken to ensure that the firm does not represent the parties to either side of a transaction such as the purchase and sale of a business or real estate. This type of conflict commonly comes up when a legal professional who worked for one firm now works for another law firm with adverse interests to the client of the former firm. Although there may not be any actual conflict, the situation with former employees presents the appearance of a conflict. The ethical concern is that the legal professional may have gained information about the former firm's client and use it to the advantage of the new firm's client. In this way, the ethical rules pertaining to conflicts of interest are closely related to the ethical rule of confidentiality. Yet the rule of confidentiality may not be enough. When there exists the possibility for the lawyer's or paralegal's judgment to be compromised, the rules regarding conflicts of interest step in to remove the temptation.

These rules also operate in a practical way. In today's world of high professional mobility, both lawyers and paralegals commonly switch employers, going from one firm to another. When a legal professional is disqualified from representing a certain client because of conflicts of interest, the entire firm is also disqualified. When the same legal professional starts working for another firm, the new firm may become disqualified from representing that same client. This step is known as *imputed disqualification,* because the new firm is disqualified vicariously not by its own acts or memberships but by taking on the new legal professional, which means it is disqualified by imputation.

However, this rule would work to the detriment of everyone. Disqualification may be impractical, because the new firm may already be representing that client and would have to withdraw at a point in time that would be very inopportune for the client. In addition, disqualifying the new firm would have a negative impact on the hiring and employment practices of the entire legal community. Thus, law firms would either have to turn down business or turn down new talent. Using a practical approach, both the courts and the agencies that govern lawyers have allowed a new attorney to work in a law firm, even if a client of that firm has a conflict of interest with the new attorney. The new firm may continue to represent the client as long as the new attorney is screened of and has no association with that client's case. This well-known ethical

CASE IN POINT

ETHICAL OPINION

In 1992, the District of Columbia Bar issued the following official opinion on the imputed disqualification rule as it applied specifically to paralegals.

OPINION 227—MIGRATORY PARALEGALS AND LAWYERS/IMPUTED DISQUALIFICATION/ SCREENING

If a paralegal moves from Law Firm A to Law Firm B, and that paralegal is personally disqualified from a matter pending in Law Firm B because the paralegal worked on a substantially related matter at Law Firm A, Law Firm B ordinarily may avoid imputed disqualification by "screening" the paralegal from that matter in Law Firm B. However, it is not permissible for Law Firm B purportedly to "screen" the paralegal from only that portion of the matter that is related to the paralegal's previous work at Law Firm A, and assign the paralegal to work on other, assertedly unrelated aspects of that same matter. Absent informed consent from Law Firm A's client, the paralegal must be effectively isolated at Law Firm B from the entire matter, otherwise Law Firm B risks being disqualified from that matter. In general, in the case of a migratory lawyer (as distinguished from a nonlawyer), screening plus consent of the former client is required.

QUESTIONS ABOUT THE CASE:

1. What types of disclosures must a paralegal make when switching jobs between law firms?
2. Would any disclosures made to avoid a conflict of interests violate the duty of confidentiality?
3. What is screening?

wall or barrier ensures that the confidences and any conflicts of interest are isolated from the client. In erecting this ethical wall, the firm first must have the new attorney acknowledge and accept this policy. The firm also informs its employees that the new attorney is barred from access to all files, documents, or any other matters pertaining to the client. Finally, the files are marked with warnings of the screening. The application of ethical walls and screening procedures to the imputed disqualification rule presents examples of a practical resolution of complex ethical entanglements.

A common metaphor in the legal profession to describe the protections that a law firm must take to ensure compliance with the duty to avoid conflicts is the Chinese Wall. Built over the course of thousands of years, the Great Wall of China has stood as one of the world wonders and was built to keep foreign intruders away from the Chinese civilization. By screening legal professionals with imputed conflicts of interest, a law firm is, in a way, constructing a Great Wall to avoid conflicts of interests. Specifically, Chinese Walls are used in law firms when one part of the firm, representing a party on a deal or litigation, is separated from legal professionals—both lawyers and paralegals—who may have had prior contact with certain legal matters while working for another legal office.

A legal professional who has a conflict of interest between two clients at the same time is faced with *concurrent conflicts of interest*. A conflict or the appearance of a possible conflict due to a prior relationship or previous representation is known as a *successive conflict of interest*. An example of a *successive conflict of interest* occurs when a legal professional represents a client in one type of matter and then, some time later, represents that client's spouse in an action against the former client. The difference is the time in which the lawyer in question was involved with the possible conflicting interest. *Concurrent conflicts* and *successive conflicts of interests* both share the possibility that the lawyer's judgment and ability to represent the client zealously will be negatively affected by having information from two or more adverse parties.

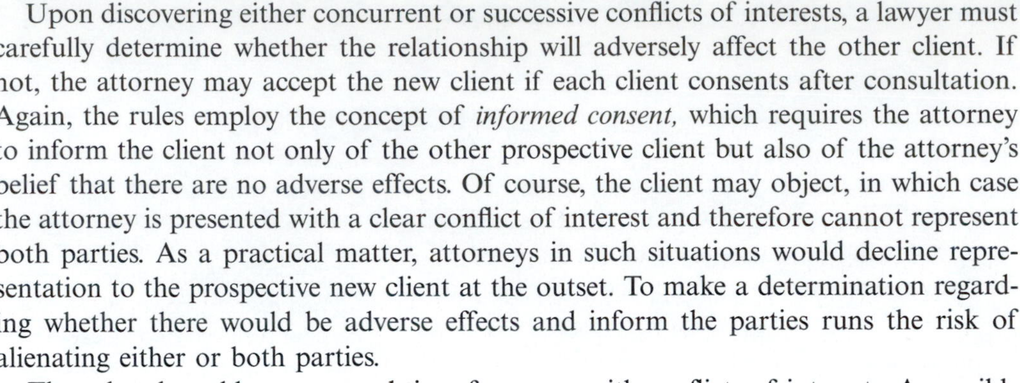

Upon discovering either concurrent or successive conflicts of interests, a lawyer must carefully determine whether the relationship will adversely affect the other client. If not, the attorney may accept the new client if each client consents after consultation. Again, the rules employ the concept of *informed consent,* which requires the attorney to inform the client not only of the other prospective client but also of the attorney's belief that there are no adverse effects. Of course, the client may object, in which case the attorney is presented with a clear conflict of interest and therefore cannot represent both parties. As a practical matter, attorneys in such situations would decline representation to the prospective new client at the outset. To make a determination regarding whether there would be adverse effects and inform the parties runs the risk of alienating either or both parties.

PRACTICE TIP

When dealing with clients, avoid all possible conflicts of interest, or even the appearance of conflicts of interest, by maintaining at all times a purely professional relationship. Be sure to consult with your supervising attorney if any questionable circumstances arise that could compromise your professionalism.

The rules also address a second tier of concern with conflicts of interests. A possible conflict of interest can arise if the client is pursuing a matter that is adverse to the interests of the lawyer or the lawyers family and friends. The conflict exists because the lawyer's representation of the client may be compromised. Because of the lawyer's close relationship with the client's opponent, the lawyer is put into a difficult position. Acting on behalf of a client's best interests as a lawyer should do, the lawyer may be acting against the interests of a friend, relative, business associate, or even him- or herself. Moreover, given the natural human tendency to favor those close to us, any lawyer would be hard pressed to comply with the ethical duty to represent the client zealously if the interests of someone close are also at stake. The problem with this aspect of the conflict of interest is that the client may be totally unaware that a conflict exists. The rules place the burden of informing the client of the possible conflict upon the lawyer. Yet under most circumstances in which the lawyer's own personal interests or those of someone close are at stake, the lawyer should discontinue or decline representation. In other situations, the lawyer *must* discontinue or decline.

As mentioned above, there are five separate rules in the ABA Model Rules of Professional Conduct when it comes to conflicts of interest. Furthermore, as you can imagine, the states have adopted them with several differing variations that would be impossible to cover comprehensively here. Consequently, applying these rules can be a very complex undertaking. Paralegals should recognize some key situations to avoid any conflict of interests. In these situations, the legal professional's conflict of interest may appear obvious, yet faithful compliance with the ethics rules of the legal profession requires sensitivity to conflicts of interests as they present themselves in practice.

- Clients as business partners. Legal professionals should exercise caution when entering into business dealings with clients. Here, the concept of *informed consent* plays a role. When entering into a business dealing with a client, the attorney must obtain the client's written consent after fully informing the client of the business terms.
- Gifts and inheritances. The attorney cannot prepare legal documents, such as a will, a trust agreement, or a deed in which the attorney receives a gift or inheritance from a client. Some states' rules also prohibit attorneys from preparing documents that leave gifts to those working under the attorney or others related to the attorney. This rule exists for the obvious reason that an attorney who is aware of both confidential information regarding client's personal and financial situation and the intricacies of the law could unduly influence the client. This danger is particularly valid in the case of elderly clients. Even though a gift from such a client may be quite valid, an attorney who prepares the technical legal documents making gifts to him- or herself appears to be self-dealing, that is, acting on his or her own behalf and not the client's best interests. Remember,

under the ethical rules, the attorney must avoid even the appearance of impropriety. An exception exists when the attorney is receiving a gift or inheritance from a relative.

- Media rights. Recently, highly popular films and television shows have vividly reenacted sensational criminal or civil matters and drawn media attention. Cases involving celebrities are particularly prone to receiving an inordinate amount of news coverage. The attorneys who represent either the prosecution or any of the parties become a point for media attention as well. Representing a client in a high-profile case is good for any lawyer's business. Yet an attorney who represents clients unable to pay for legal fees in sensational cases could very well be tempted to persuade these indigent clients to grant potentially valuable media rights. After the conclusion of the legal proceedings, the attorney would then own the rights to the client's story and could sell all or part of those rights to the media—particularly television and movies. Get the picture?

The ethical concern here is that the right to receive future compensation could affect the way the attorney handles the case. With the potential to receive payment in the future, the attorney would be acting for him- or herself and not for the client. For instance, a client might benefit from the entry of a guilty plea to lesser charges rather than going though a full trial. However, the attorney who has been given the rights to the client's story may be tempted to go through with the trial to receive greater publicity or create a highly dramatic public display. Whether the client is found innocent or guilty, the attorney will have played a "starring role" and, at the same time, increased the value of the client's story for a future film or television show.

Hence, there are ethical rules to cover this scenario. The rules do not prevent the attorney from receiving all or part of the media rights from the client. However, negotiations between the attorney and the client for the media rights cannot be entered into until after the conclusion of the proceedings that provide the subject for the media rights. End of story.

The Unauthorized Practice of Law

The third—the most important ethical rule for paralegals—rule pertains to avoiding the unauthorized practice of law (UPL). As this rule applies to lawyers, Rule 5.5 of the ABA Model Rules of Professional Conduct prohibits lawyers from assisting nonlawyers from performing duties that would constitute the unauthorized practice of law. Nonlawyers include paralegals. As highlighted previously, most states have criminal sanctions for violating UPL rules. Admittedly, few would ever suffer the fate of Rosemary Furman. Nevertheless, a paralegal cited for the unauthorized practice of law, even while working under the supervision of an attorney, may very well find him- or herself in dire straits when it comes to current or future employment prospects. Any supervising attorney would come under scrutiny and possible discipline. (See Figure 2.3.)

A wide range of opinions exists as to whether the UPL prohibitions are justified. Officially, the laws prohibiting the practice of law by anyone but lawyers are designed to protect the public interest. By permitting only those who are trained in law schools and licensed by the state after a vigorous test to practice law, the rules ensure that consumers of legal services are more likely to have a competent lawyer. If there were no laws prohibiting UPL, the public would be exposed to unlearned and untrained, or even unscrupulous, individuals for whom there is no enforceable ethical code or disciplinary bodies within the government.

Thus, the argument goes, laws prohibiting UPL are necessary, as they actually protect the public interest and consumers of legal services. For the same reason, doctors and dentists are licensed, and one would have trouble imagining seeking services

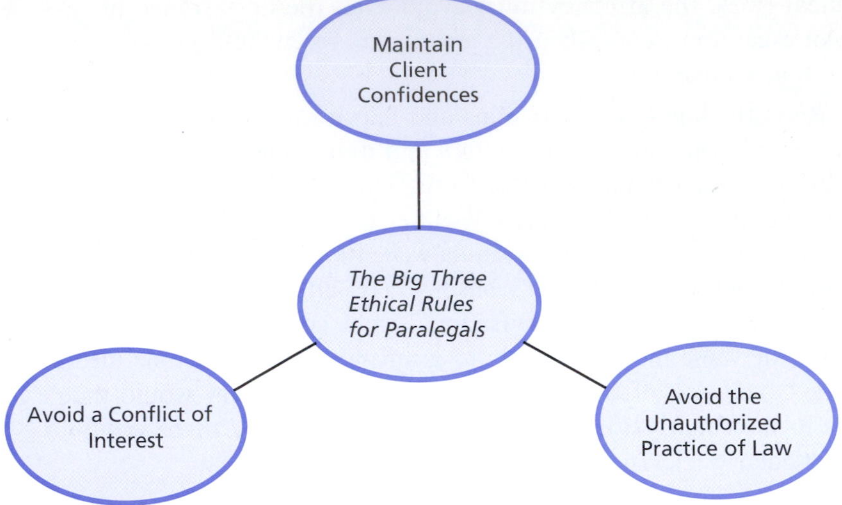

FIGURE 2.3
Big Three Ethical Rules for Paralegals

from an unlicensed individual in either of those fields. No matter how inexpensive the fee, few people would even consider having their tonsils removed by an unlicensed "doctor." By the same token, if charged with a serious crime or involved in a civil matter with a large sum of money or the custody of a child at stake, the vast majority of persons would choose to hire a licensed attorney.

However, there are many who consider the UPL prohibition as a thinly veiled mechanism to protect lawyers and their monopoly over what is known as the practice of law. They point out that the practice of law is different from medicine. Routine matters such as an uncontested divorce, a simple will, or a routine real estate transaction involve preprinted forms that even lawyers themselves use. For these and many other types of legal matters, lawyers charge too much and are actually unneeded. With medicine, the stakes are higher: Our biological health is at stake. The practice of medicine deals with physical reality. Many legal matters, in contrast, consist of only words on paper and are, in comparison, highly artificial. Medicine deals with nature, law with mere human constructs.

Thus, training in law and the license required to practice it should not apply to many aspects known as the practice of law, as Rosemary Furman pointed out to no avail. Opponents of the UPL prohibitions also point to studies that show that only a minuscule percentage of all the cases involving lay advocates actually complained about their lack of ability or competence. Nevertheless, the UPL prohibitions are with us to stay, at least for the time being. For whatever reason, UPL laws are often enforced quite rigorously, and thus, paralegals should be aware of some of the pitfalls of engaging in the practice of law even inadvertently.

A well-recognized problem persists with laws prohibiting UPL. Specifically, they fail to define specifically what constitutes the "practice of law." This gap presents something of a paradox. Normally, laws that forbid certain activities are written with enough clarity so that there is fair notice of what is lawful or unlawful behavior. This clarity would seem particularly necessary of behavior or activities for which a license is required. If the public cannot perform duties that are, by law, reserved only for lawyers, there should be some clear guidelines as to what those duties are.

Again, using a medical analogy provides some insight. Licensed doctors diagnose and treat physical medical conditions; they perform surgery and prescribe and inject medicine, among a host of other functions commonly understood to be the practice of medicine. Still, there are a host of other sub-professionals in medicine who perform similar functions for which they have a limited license. Physicians' assistants, nurses, phlebotomists, physical therapists, and many other health-care workers have the limited license to perform tasks that are also within the realm of the doctor's license. In sharp contrast, lawyers are the one and only type of licensed professionals in the entire legal world. (If you think about it, the licensing system within the medical profession presents a very strong argument for licensing paralegals.)

PRACTICE TIP

Paralegals oftentimes appear to others as lawyers, due to their appearance and demeanor. At all times, identify yourself as a paralegal to those from outside the office. In doing so, you will avoid the appearance of impropriety. Clients and others you may deal with habitually may forget, so it is important to remind them of your role as a legal professional.

Most people have a general sense of the lawyer's scope of licensed activity. However, finding the exact parameters of what constitutes the practice of law becomes crucial in determining UPL. Herein lies the problem. Clearly, representing a client in the courtroom is an activity that requires a lawyer's license. From there, drafting legal documents such as court papers and contracts might also come to mind as exclusively lawyer-like tasks that require a license. Resolving tax issues, setting up a business, advising clients about buying or selling property, and arranging personal affairs for inheritance are all activities for which people traditionally engage a licensed lawyer. Yet does every task that a lawyer undertakes require a license? Paradoxically, the only clear answer is "sometimes." Exactly what those tasks are is the subject of some debate.

Other professionals, such as accountants, bankers, insurance agents, and real estate brokers, all practice some form of law incidental to their businesses. Accountants give tax and business advice that is similar, if not exactly like, the legal advice lawyers give. After all, business and tax issues invariably involve attempts to comply with or obtain exemptions from legal requirements. Similarly, bankers set up various accounts, business arrangements, and financial packages for their customers in a way that conforms to legal requirements and uses legal documents and forms. Insurance agents sell and interpret contracts of insurance coverage for their customers in the same way that a lawyer would. Life insurance necessarily involves legal advice regarding estate planning, a well-known lawyer activity. Real estate brokers use legal forms every day for the purchase and sale of property. They routinely advise customers on the legal points of a mortgage contingency or inspector's reports. They negotiate and draft real estate purchase contracts, all in the same way a lawyer would.

However, after some wrangling many years ago, the legal tasks performed by nonlawyer professionals such as accountants and bankers have come to be considered within their respective professions and stand as exceptions to the UPL prohibitions for the sake of business expediency. There are also other exceptions. One of them comes directly from the United States Constitution.

As most Americans study in their high school civics classes, the United States Constitution guarantees several legal rights and liberties set out in the Bill of Rights—the first ten amendments. The Sixth Amendment reads as follows:

> In all criminal prosecutions, the accused shall enjoy the right to a speedy and public trial, by an impartial jury of the State and district wherein the crime shall have been committed, which district shall have been previously ascertained by law, and to be informed of the nature and cause of the accusation; to be confronted with the witnesses against him; to have compulsory process for obtaining witnesses in his favor, *and to have the Assistance of Counsel for his defence.*

The Sixth Amendment lists some of the most basic rights for those accused of a crime. The italicized portion at the end of the Amendment expresses what is known as the right to counsel, which means that those accused of a crime have a right to be represented by counsel—that is, an attorney. A hundred years after the Constitution was signed, the United States Supreme Court declared that the right to counsel in criminal matters, particularly serious ones, is a fundamental right under the United States Constitution. Fundamental rights are among the most important legal rights in the United States. Because rights declared in the Sixth Amendment are fundamental,

LIBRARY
FORSYTH TECHNICAL COMMUNITY COLLEGE
2100 SILAS CREEK PARKWAY
WINSTON-SALEM, NC 27103-5197

public defenders are paid by states and appointed to represent indigent criminal defendants unable to pay for their own attorneys.

In the case of *Faretta v. California,* 422 U.S. 806 (1975), the United States Supreme Court declared that in addition to the right to an attorney, whether paid or appointed, the Sixth Amendment also guarantees a defendant the right to represent him- or herself. Thus, people who are not licensed attorneys may perform the very same tasks that an attorney would in court for themselves. This exception to the UPL prohibition appears as an anomaly as a result of the Constitutional right to counsel. Another exception to the UPL prohibitions exists as the result of a legal anomaly. Many state and federal **administrative agencies** hold hearings that are very much like court trials. Representing both the government agency and the individual contesting the agency action may be performed by an unlicensed layperson. In fact, the person presiding over the hearing, who acts in a way very similar to a trial court judge, also may be an unlicensed layperson known as the hearings officer or administrative judge. Even though these proceedings are very court-like and the tasks performed by all those involved are the same as those that only a licensed attorney could perform, the federal and state rules governing how these agencies run permit lay, or nonattorney, representation. The primary reason for this exception is the need for efficiency in government.

administrative agencies
Governmental bodies created by state or federal laws to administer and regulate certain subjects, such as the environment, employment, or Social Security.

Almost all administrative agencies on both the state and federal level permit laypersons to navigate their way through the agency on their own. From state agencies that issue drivers' licenses or unemployment benefits to federal agencies that pay retirement benefits or collect taxes, the vast majority of people who deal with these administrative agencies do so on their own. There are also highly technically oriented agencies that require specialized attorneys or scientifically trained persons to represent an individual in his or her dealings with the agency.

For this reason, many persons who are not licensed lawyers perform legal duties with and for administrative agencies without regard to the UPL prohibitions. Many of those who are practicing a limited form of law before and within these state and federal agencies are paralegals. Outside of these few exceptions, however, paralegals should be fully aware of the UPL prohibitions. A paralegal found to have committed a UPL violation may also get the supervising attorney into trouble, because attorneys are directly prohibited under Rule 5.5 of the ABA Model Rules of Professional Conduct from being involved with anyone who commits the unauthorized practice of law.

Although the practice of law is not well defined, paralegals should take guidance from other reliable sources. The ABA Model Guidelines for the Utilization of Paralegal Services set out some parameters for the working paralegal. Remember that these guidelines are directed at attorneys, so they should provide some insight as to how attorneys should view the UPL laws with regard to working with paralegals. Guideline 3 covers what many consider the essence of the practice of law: (1) creating an attorney–client relationship, (2) setting legal fees, and (3) giving legal advice to a client. (See Figure 2.4.)

FIGURE 2.4
Three Main Forms of UPL Violations

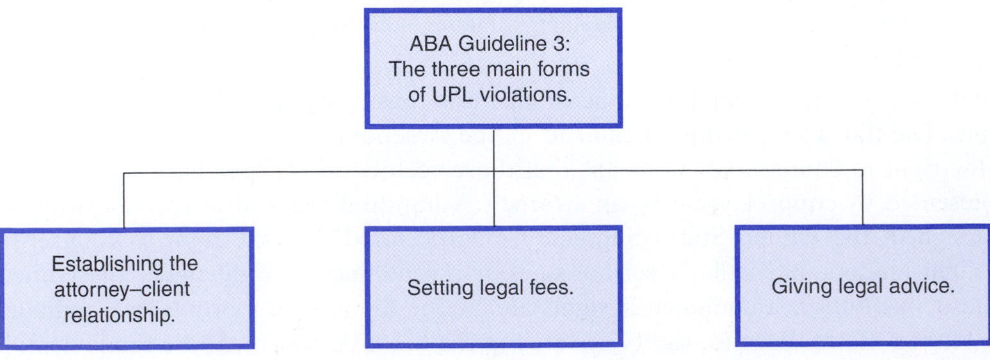

From this short list, experience has shown that working paralegals may be particularly susceptible to other prohibited activities. Paralegals work closely with attorneys and frequently end up doing the same tasks as the attorneys within the confines of the office. Thus, a paralegal may even inadvertently cross the line and unwittingly commit a violation of the UPL prohibition. At all times, a professional paralegal draws a bright line safely around any situation in which it may be possible to commit a UPL violation. In addition to Guideline 3, careful observance of the UPL for paralegals would include signing documents to be filed in court or other legal documents such as contracts or settlements, negotiating settlements directly with the parties, and giving legal advice.

PRACTICE TIP

Supervising attorneys often ask paralegals to relay specific information to a client, some of which is actual legal advice. To avoid a UPL violation, be sure to go over all of the information to be relayed with the attorney completely. Then, when speaking with the client, be sure to tell the client that you are merely conveying the information from your supervising attorney. If the client asks questions or for clarification, tell the client that you will get back to her or him immediately after consulting with the attorney.

Paralegals are on the horns of a dilemma when it comes to giving legal advice. Within the confines of the law offices, paralegals are regularly requested by their supervising attorneys or other coworkers to perform legal research on a particular client's situation and to report on their findings and analysis at a meeting or in a written memorandum. If you think about it, this activity is giving legal advice. However, reporting findings and analysis to another coworker or a supervising attorney is different from relaying the same information to a client or the public. Hence, information communicated in the office among coworkers is not a violation of the UPL prohibition against giving advice. The paralegal should develop a sense of the extent to which he or she is responsible for the flow of information.

The actual practice of law consists almost entirely of processing and parceling information in specialized legal products that vary in spoken and written format, depending on the circumstances. Lawyers, as licensed, routinely give information in the form of legal advice. Legal advice and the time it takes to render it is the lawyer's stock in trade. Thus, one can gain a sense of what really constitutes the practice of law. It is purely a communication activity, complete with its own language and customs. It is all about giving legal advice—whether to clients, to courts, or to colleagues and coworkers. Inside the law office, among colleagues and coworkers, advice flows freely without UPL constraints. Outside, a different legal environment reigns.

The possibility for paralegals to violate the UPL prohibitions arises when they deal with clients and the public, the people for whom the UPL prohibitions were designed to protect. The most helpful approach for paralegals would be to view themselves as extensions of the attorneys with whom they work. When it comes to discussing matters with clients and others, the professional paralegal conveys the information known as legal advice, at all times attributing the advice to the attorney. Thus, as a matter of prudence and caution, the paralegal acts as a conduit whenever he or she conveys information to a client or others from outside the office. This action is easily accomplished by prefacing any statement with a comment that the paralegal is relaying information from the attorney. In addition, it is advisable to limit discussions and avoid any unnecessary client contact, as a matter of professionalism.

The ABA's Model Guidelines for the Utilization of Paralegals sums up the essence of the three major ethical concerns for paralegals. According to Guideline 3, attorneys cannot give paralegals the responsibility to establish an attorney–client relationship, set the fees to be charged, or render a legal opinion for a client.

This guideline is directed toward the lawyer who has a duty to ensure that any nonlawyer working under his or her professional umbrella in the practice of law conforms to the ABA Model Rules of Professional Conduct.

Other Important Ethical Considerations

In addition to the "Big Three" ethical principles that affect paralegals in particular, there are situations in which other ethical considerations may arise.

Duty of Diligence and Competence

The ABA Model Rules of Professional Conduct and the ethical rules for paralegals impose and emphasize a duty to perform legal duties diligently and with competence. These ethical commands impose a twofold requirement on legal professionals.

- As a day-to-day matter, the duty to act diligently and competently requires legal professionals to perform their legal tasks promptly and attentively. Procrastination and disorganization, even if unintentional, could easily result in a breach of this duty. Thus, it is imperative to maintain an acute attentiveness and professionalism on a daily basis.
- The duty also requires legal professionals to keep abreast of the constant changes in the law. This updating may be accomplished by independent study or participating in continuing legal education courses and seminars. It is a simple fact of life for legal professionals that they must devote a substantial amount of their spare time to studying not only the changes in the law but also new techniques to improve the quality of their professionalism.

Duty to Report Ethical Violations of Other Legal Professionals

duty to report
An ethical obligation to report perceived unethical behavior committed by another legal professional.

A recent addition to the lawyer's ethical rules, known the "snitch" or "rat" rule, has generated considerable controversy. Rule 8.3 of the ABA Model Rules of Professional Conduct requires an attorney to report actual knowledge of serious ethical violations by another attorney to the proper disciplinary agency. Formally, this is known as the **duty to report**. Although a similar form of this rule existed in previous versions of the canons, not all states adopted it. However, after the Watergate era, the public interest called for "whistleblower" laws to combat corruption and waste, and Rule 8.3 became part of the call for the profession to regulate itself. Although broad in its wording, the rule does not require the report of every violation. Many violations of the rules of professional conduct are inadvertent, unintentional, and petty. A review of the Rule shows that the perceived violation must create serious doubt that the lawyer may not be acting forthrightly or otherwise be unfit to practice law. Commentators have observed that the rule requires (1) actual knowledge of a (2) substantial violation that does not (3) involve disclosing confidential information. These three items are known as elements. Each of these elements must exist, which requires complex issues of fact. Paralegals appear to be under the duty to report knowledge of ethics violations or misconduct by paralegals as well as by lawyers.

RESEARCH THIS

Just about every state has adopted the ABA Model Rules of Professional Conduct in one form or another. Find out if your state has adopted the ABA rules. Whether or not it has done so, do the ethical rules for lawyers or paralegals in your state impose a duty to report ("snitch")?

Summary

Ethical rules exist for almost every profession and perform several purposes. For society at large, ethical codes function as assurances that the members of the profession will adhere to high standards of conduct and the performance of their professional duties. The existence of ethical codes also may provide the basis for licensing standards for professions. Having ethical codes is one way that a profession can instill confidence in the public and thereby gain its trust. Ethical codes are also the way that society regulates a profession.

Under American law, lawyers are governed and regulated by the ABA Model Rules of Professional Conduct; earlier names for these rules used arcane language such as "ethics" and "canons." Today, the Rules of Professional Conduct are synonymous with notions of ethics, even though these rules have become highly specialized and technical. A lawyer's license to practice depends on his or her observance of these ethical rules. There are some unintended results when these rules are applied to modern business forms. Nevertheless, the ABA has shown that ethical rules are meant to apply practically for the benefit of society and the legal profession.

Although paralegals are not as yet licensed, they are indirectly governed by lawyers' ethical rules. Paralegal associations such as the NALA and NFPA have promulgated their own ethical rules for paralegals. However, unlike the lawyer's ethical rules, the paralegal association rules are conditions for association membership, not for the ability to work as paralegals. Nevertheless, ethics perform a prominent role for the paralegal profession. Paralegals must be aware of the Big Three ethical rules that can affect them almost on a daily basis. The first is the rule of confidentiality. This rule requires that all client information be kept secret.

As a practical matter, paralegals may take specific action to maintain client confidentiality. The second rule involves avoiding conflicts of interest. This rule is complex and involves the history of client representation, as well as the employment histories of the legal professionals. Finally, UPL prohibitions apply directly to paralegals because they work directly with the law and often with clients. Nevertheless, paralegals may suffer from sanctions as well as jeopardize their employers if they fail to understand or heed UPL prohibitions. Specific actions and a conscious awareness of ethical rules can avoid UPL. Other ethical concerns affecting paralegals include the duty to act diligently and competently.

Ethics are an undeniably prominent part of the legal profession. Careful study of the ethical rules for both lawyers and paralegals will go far to assist the professional paralegal.

Terms

ABA Model Guidelines for the Utilization of Paralegals
ABA Model Rules of Professional Conduct
Administrative agencies
Confidentiality
Conflicts of interest
Duty to report
Ethical rules
Ethics
Implied authority
Informed consent
Morality
Negligence
Privileged information
Profession
Professionalism
Unauthorized practice of law (UPL)
Voluntary ethical codes

Review Questions

1. What are the several functions that ethical codes provide for professions?
2. What steps must a law firm take upon finding itself with a successive conflict of interest?
3. Looking at the notion of limited licensing, what specifically could paralegals be licensed for that would have benefited Rosemary Furman?
4. Why should paralegals be particularly aware of the three main ethical rules?
5. In what way are the rules regarding zealousness and conflicts of interest interconnected with the rule to maintain confidentiality?

Exercises

1. Looking at the practice of law as a form of information processing, how would you define it to make the UPL laws clearer?
2. Write a part of an office manual for paralegals in a fictitious law office covering the practices that paralegals in the office should follow in order to observe the three main ethical rules.
3. What types of arrangements would you have to make in a law firm if the ethical rules were amended to permit taking accountants on as partners?
4. What steps would you have to take to go into business with a client?
5. After moving into a new neighborhood, you find out that your neighbor, a licensed hair stylist (and nothing more), is giving legal advice on no-fault, uncontested divorces. He is filling out legal forms and instructing his "clients" on how to proceed in certain matters themselves. Are you under a duty to report him? If so, how should you do so? If not, in what circumstances would you be under a duty to report? Prepare a class presentation of your reasons and a conclusion about the course of action you should take.
6. Many legal experts have questioned the ethical behavior of the legal professionals involved in the Erin Brockovich story. Viewing the movie with the major ethical concerns in mind, what actions by Brockovich or her supervising attorney give rise to these concerns?

Discussion Questions

1. What is the difference between ethics and morals? Are there some aspects of a profession that have both ethical and moral dimensions?
2. If you were an archaeologist, like Indiana Jones, from another culture and dug up a courthouse, what would you think you had found?
3. Why do psychiatrists have a duty to report a patient's expressed desire to do harm, whereas lawyers do not? Do you think that is fair?
4. If Rosemary Furman came to your office seeking representation to defend the UPL violations she was charged with, what arguments would you make on her behalf?
5. Do you think that the ABA should allow multidisciplinary practice? If so, what changes would have to be made?
6. How could a licensed attorney become subject to civil lawsuits or criminal proceedings for ethical lapses in the professional conduct of the attorney him- or herself or those working under him or her?

PORTFOLIO ASSIGNMENT

Assume you are a paralegal working in a criminal defense law firm. One of the firm's clients, a high-level politician, has been accused of an infamous crime. The media coverage has been intense and prolonged. The client vocally protests innocence and is willing to fight to the hilt. In exchange, the client is willing to grant the firm media rights instead of a retainer. Your supervising attorney wants to know what steps the firm would have to take for the client to grant your office media rights. Write a brief memo of one or two pages to your supervising attorney, advising about the ethical considerations involved and the actions to be taken.

Chapter 3

Law and the American Legal System

CHAPTER OBJECTIVES

Upon completion of this chapter, you will have acquired specialized knowledge on the following topics:

- Jurisprudence and prominent schools of thought in legal theory.
- Sources of American law and the common law.
- The history and development of the American legal system.
- The structure and components of the federal and state court systems.
- Jurisdiction over subject matter, persons, and things.

Chapters 1 and 2 presented the professional context of the paralegal profession and the important ethical considerations within which paralegals operate. The materials that follow are pedagogical—that is, they will teach you necessary information about the law itself and, equally as important, how to analyze a legal situation as a legal professional, without regard to a particular legal theory or philosophy. Thus begins your journey into the study of law, which will prepare you for your career as a legal professional. This chapter explains the law and the legal system in the United States and practical applications that you will encounter as a legal professional.

This chapter also will delve into an examination of the culture in which lawyers and paralegals work and thrive. Careful attention will help you gain the necessary foundation of basic information about the legal profession and the culture in which you may soon find yourself. Part of that culture consists of the philosophy with which courts and judges view the law. Thus, as part of your acculturation process, you need a basic review of the various schools of thought in law that will provide you with a backdrop of how judges sometimes approach their decision-making process. As you review these various philosophies, think about which view of the law you might favor. Looking at law in this way gives you some insights into how courts and judges approach their decision-making processes.

JURISPRUDENCE AND LEGAL THEORY

Many legal scholars believe that the functions and origins of law provide a worthwhile subject of study, known as **jurisprudence**. Since ancient times, scholars have studied law in relation to human nature, the universe, and religion. Whether dictated by a

jurisprudence
The science or philosophy of law.

single despotic emperor or developed by a popularly chosen ruling class, the law is a creature of government and reflects the values of the society it governs. Thus, in early civilizations, monarchs who claimed the legitimacy of their rule through divine right also claimed that the laws emanated from the heavens. Modern Western society has become more secular or nonreligious in its approach to law. Since the Industrial Revolution, modern societies have admitted that laws are products of social organizations and processes, which themselves are created by laws. Still, scholars debate the origins and proper functions of law in society. Here, we enter the academic and intellectual realm of legal theory.

One of the earliest legal theories is the idea of *natural law*. Like early religious laws, the theory of natural law holds that society obtains its laws from nature or the physical universe. This quaint view is actually a derivative of the notion of God-given laws, except that Nature itself or the inherent nature of human beings provides the source for law. An integral part of natural law declares that there are immutable—that is, unchangeable—principles of right and wrong that stand as eternal guideposts. Natural law acts to usher us to a preordained human destiny or purpose. Intertwined with natural law are traditional notions of morality and ethics.

Throughout history, royalty everywhere frequently claimed that they ruled by divine right. Since the days of classical Greece, the idea of government as the purveyor and protector of natural laws has heavily influenced our overall view of law. Our own Declaration of Independence even refers to the "unalienable Rights" that have been granted by the "Creator." Modern national leaders frequently claim that the forces of natural law provide the basis for their territorial expansion, national defense, or other broad-based policies that call for emotional or chauvinistic national support.

Subsequent legal theories dropped the idea that nature or religion was the source of law and took a more structural and science-based approach. For example, *legal positivism* developed soon after the American and French Revolutions. A seismic shift in legal thought, legal positivism recognized that laws are rules made by human beings and that there is no inherent or necessary connection between law and morality. The validity of laws was determined not by their content but by the process that enacted them. Thus, if laws came into being through a valid law-making process, those laws were presumed valid. In this way, notions of right and wrong or the degree to which the laws sprang from natural sources were no longer part of the analysis to test whether a law was just.

A subsidiary legal theory known as *legal formalism* also accepted the presumed validity of laws, but it also applied to the judges who interpreted those laws. Under a formalist approach, judges apply laws neutrally and thereby arrive at a "correct" result based on the rules of logic. According to formalism, the application of formal rules of logic to enact laws properly thus appears value neutral and impartial.

Legal realism came into prominence during the early 1900s with the proposition that laws are frequently contradictory or vague. Thus the realists argued that logic acted as a pretense for fair or neutral application of the law, while judges actually decided cases on the basis of their own personal beliefs and biases. Some realists urged judges to apply laws by taking other considerations into account, including extra-legal materials from disciplines such as sociology, psychology, and economics. A prevailing theory applied in many major court decisions during the 1960s and 1970s, realism has since undergone a considerable retreat. Yet the foundations of the realist movement remain with us.

Current trends in legal theory include viewing law through an economic lens. The school of thought known as *law and economics* says that law should be looked at in terms of an economic analysis. It further proposes that law is a way of conditioning behavior through rewards and punishments. More important, law and economics

School of Jurisprudence	Basic Philosophy
Natural or divine law	Law comes from nature or a Supreme Being and is valid without question.
Legal positivism	Laws that are properly enacted are presumed valid.
Legal formalism	Properly enacted laws are valid and as interpreted are applied with neutral logic.
Legal realism	Laws should reflect social policy, taking into account sociology, psychology, and economics.
Law and economics	Laws should be enacted with a view toward economic efficiency, which benefits society.
Critical legal scholarship	Laws are inherently biased in favor of those who enacted them. Judges can use anything to justify the result because law is indeterminate.

FIGURE 3.1
Various Forms of Jurisprudence

supporters say that the law uses economic incentives to influence behavior. Using economic theory, analysts predict individual responses on the basis of a broader view of both incentives and consequences. Critics of the law and economics approach instead argue that economic analysis alone should not be the sole perspective for making law, which rather should include larger social policy and humanitarian concerns.

Probably the most outspoken critics of the law and economics school come from the *critical legal studies* (CLS) field, one of the most intellectual schools of thought in legal scholarship. Drawing from such diverse fields as social theory, political philosophy, literary theory, and economics, CLS argues that the law represents the voices of the society's rich and powerful and therefore does not reflect the legitimate use of power. To prove this point, CLS adherents argue that court decisions or statutes do not actually determine the outcome of legal disputes. They note that judges can justify almost any result in a particular case with existing laws, court decisions, and other legal materials by using logical-sounding legal arguments.

All of these schools of thought, and many others, fall under the study of the science and history of law known as jurisprudence. As you can see, there is a great divergence of opinion regarding what law is, which sometimes results in a confusing disarray of ideas. You might want to think of these schools of thought as differing philosophies about why and how law exists or should exist. Like other forms of philosophy, these various legal theories represent different points of view. The study of legal theory is exactly that, theory—the stuff of college and law school professors. Nevertheless, our society places great value on learning and high academic achievement. Thus, legal theory can have an important influence on the judges and legislators who make our laws. For that reason, jurisprudence has, at times, great use in shaping a legal argument for a client to appeal to a judge who is known to subscribe to a particular legal theory. Figure 3.1 summarizes the various forms of jurisprudence.

SOURCES OF AMERICAN LAW AND THE AMERICAN LEGAL SYSTEM

Every society possesses a mechanism for creating, interpreting, and enforcing its laws through a legal system, though these systems vary greatly from country to country. Depending on several factors, such as geography, history, religion, demographics, and a host of other elements, legal systems result from traditions and practices that have developed as an integral part of each country's cultural and social history. The function of most modern legal systems is to resolve a certain limited variety of disputes among individuals, business entities, and the government and to find responsibility for crimes against the government. These disputes are legal disputes between various parties that society entrusts to its legal system to resolve.

Sources of American Law

common law
Judge-made law, the ruling in a judicial opinion.

precedent
The holding of past court decisions that are followed in future judicial cases where similar facts and legal issues are present.

As discussed in the previous chapter, the laws and legal system of the United States are derived primarily from those in England. We saw that the English legal system itself developed from Norman customs and ecclesiastical sources, incorporating local communal practices and various religious concepts. We also observed that the colonists in the United States used English **common law** to settle disputes among themselves, using the same system of writs. One unique feature of the common law is the notion of **precedent**. Under English legal traditions, judges decided the cases brought before them on the basis of the notes that lawyers and judges had taken during earlier cases. These notes, over time, were preserved and became a form of written reports regarding the application of law in case situations. Eventually, judges began to rely on these written reports as guidelines about the status of the law. From this practice developed the idea of precedent, or following the law as it had been applied in previous cases. Known in Latin as *stare decisis,* which means "to stand by the decision," the use of precedent appealed to English and then American sensibilities of equity and fairness.

The idea of applying laws equally over the entire country also benefits its legal system and social behavior. A legal system that is applied uniformly makes it easier to administrate. The use of recorded precedent promises equal treatment and promotes the perception of fairness and impartiality. Business and interpersonal dealings are also positively affected by the use of precedent, which provides both predictability and reasonable expectations for directing future conduct, which is essential for business to thrive. For instance, the idea of enforcing credit and contracts are laws that are central to business dealings. Few businesspeople would extend credit or enter into contracts that could not be enforced. In this way, precedent or the common law became a form of governance as well as a means of resolving disputes.

Each reported decision thus becomes a sort of parable, guiding social conduct. Over time, the common law legal system developed a way to organize judges' decisions and made them available so that lawyers and others could research the precedent that would apply to a particular situation. The common law doctrine of precedent, together with an accessible body of written decisions, became a major source of law that provided guidance and stability. The textural source for the common law and reported decisions also came from a well-regarded source.

Sir William Blackstone (1723–1780), a British jurist and professor of law at Oxford, published an extensive four-volume survey of the common law entitled *Commentaries on the Laws of England (1765–1769)*. Immediately, both British and American judges came to regard Blackstone's *Commentaries* as the authoritative source for the common law. To this day, American courts, including the United States Supreme Court, still quote Blackstone as the authority for a historical discussion. Almost all of the laws first used in the American colonies came from Blackstone's *Commentaries,* which also provided the basis for American law after the Revolution. Inherent to Blackstone's discussions is the theory of natural law.

Codified and Uncodified Constitutions

William Blackstone's most significant contributions to the development of British law were his descriptions of English legal history and the notion of the "Fundamental Laws of English Rights." In Volume 1 of his *Commentaries,* Blackstone traced the history of the "Absolute Rights of Individuals," declaring them as "the absolute rights of every Englishman." Blackstone reported more than a dozen significant historical events over the course of more than 500 years, starting from the Magna Carta in 1255. In doing so, Blackstone established a constitutional view of the sources of British law. That is, the sources of the power to make laws and to govern are derived from a basic document or line of documents that arose at various times.

The government of the United Kingdom is based on an uncodified constitution that consists of written and unwritten sources. As such, the **constitution** of the United Kingdom is flexible, organic, and continuingly evolving, able to respond to political and social changes, as it has since its medieval origins. The United Kingdom has a well-respected tradition of freedoms, such as free speech and other rights. However, until recently, there was no definitive written exposition of these rights. Common law precedents have been the main source of any "rights." Since its adoption in the United States, the study and use of English common law has become a part of what is known as Anglo-American jurisprudence, which acknowledges the cultural and historical sources of our laws and individual rights.

constitution
The organic and fundamental law of a nation or state, which may be written or unwritten, establishing the character and conception of its government, laying the basic principles to which its internal life is to be conformed, organizing the government, regulating functions of departments, and prescribing the extent to which a nation or state can exercise its powers.

Constitutions, written and otherwise, are the basic laws or governing documents in many countries. These documents describe the organization of the government and enumerate the powers of government and the rights of the people. You may want to think of a constitution as a kind of social contract whereby a group of people agrees to live together according to its terms in harmony and for their mutual benefit. This contract involves retaining of certain "natural" rights, accepting restrictions of certain liberties, assuming certain duties, and delegating certain powers to the government. A constitution or social contract prescribes the legal rights of individuals and the powers of government and includes certain obligations.

Those obligations include the duty to avoid infringing on the rights of others, to obey the laws, to vote, to serve on juries, and to defend the community. Under the idea of a social contract, all of the powers exercised by government have been granted from the people as a whole. Constitutions commonly are quite definite about the powers delegated to the government that it forms. Sometimes, the document is not always explicit about the duties, which can allow for some flexibility as conditions change. These social contracts also create the various governmental institutions that govern by generating a variety of laws.

As a collective of 50 individual states, each with its own limited autonomy, the United States has a dual system of government. The federal system and the state system mirror each other in their structures and allocation of governmental authority. Our examination begins with the sources of law in the United States with the federal government.

THE UNITED STATES CONSTITUTION

Another important influence on our laws has been the Roman Code of the Emperor Justinian. Known as the **Justinian Code**, the practice of putting the law in writing has greatly influenced the form of law in the United States. By having the laws in writing for public view, business and family affairs became guided by laws to which everyone could refer. Thus, both court decisions and legislative laws come to us as written laws.

Justinian Code
Written laws compiled during the reign of the Roman Emperor Justinian (483–565 AD), including a constitution and statutes that stand as models of laws for later civilizations.

The United States, in contrast to England, has a codified, or formal, written Constitution. Most countries in the world have codified or written constitutions. Codified constitutions come about as the result of a dramatic political change, such as a revolution. Such was the case with the United States. Soon after the American Revolution, each of the 13 new United States approved what is now the United States Constitution. In doing so, the newly formed states agreed to unification according to its terms, ceding some of their sovereignty for the purposes of becoming a single nation. Thus, the Constitution is the fundamental law for the nation and the basic legal document that establishes the organization of the United States government. The Constitution was adopted, or "ratified" by the states in 1787. In 1791, the first ten amendments, known famously as the Bill of Rights, were added. The document now consists of the seven original Articles, followed by twenty-seven Amendments. Amendments are changes or additions to the Constitution. Amendments must be passed by Congress and then ratified by three-fourths of the states.

As a source of law, the Constitution itself creates in the first three Articles, the three branches of government. The Constitution then enables—that is, empowers—each branch with law-making powers in various forms. They are thus a source of law. As taught in every middle-school civics class, the idea behind creating three branches of government was to create a system of checks and balances in which each branch is equal with the others. In this way, the Constitutional makeup of the United States government avoids concentrations of power by distributing governmental powers among the three branches. From this structure develops the notion of the separation of powers, which means that the three functions of government, legislative (law-making), executive (enforcement), and judicial (dispute resolution and interpretation), are defined powers confined within each branch. As a legal doctrine, the notion of the separation of powers can invalidate a governmental action as having overstepped its bounds.

The other Articles of the Constitution also are worth mentioning. Article IV deals with the states, their relationship with one another in certain enumerated respects, and the method by which new states may be added to the union. Both Hawaii and Alaska were admitted as states in 1959, following the procedures outlined in Article IV. In Article IV, the federal government is charged with the obligation of defending the states from foreign invasion and internal (domestic) strife. Article V is brief and describes the manner in which amendments may be made to the Constitution. Article VI is famous for what is known as the **Supremacy Clause**, which states that the Constitution, all laws of the United States (that is, federal laws), and treaties are the "supreme Law of the Land." This phrase means that in the event that a state's law conflicts with the Constitution, federal law, or a treaty, the state law is considered invalid and has no effect. Finally, Article VII consists of one sentence stating that a minimum of nine states are needed to approve the Constitution to form the United States.

Supremacy Clause
Sets forth the principle and unambiguously reinforces that the Constitution is the supreme law of the land.

What follows is a review of the first three Articles and the law sources they create.

Article I: Legislative Power

The first sentence of Article I of the United States Constitution begins: "All legislative Powers herein granted shall be vested in a Congress of the United States, which shall consist of a Senate and House of Representatives." This one sentence grants Congress the power to enact legislation. Of course, legislation is law that is passed by a organ of the government. These are the types of laws with which we are probably most familiar. They range from annual budget appropriations for governmental expenditures to new laws, such as consumer protection provisions. Legislative laws are specifically known as **statutes**, a particular type of law. As you will see later, statutes differ from court decisions in that they are worded very generally and are often ambiguous, because legislators cannot predict all of the future situations to which the statute may apply.

statute
Written law enacted by the legislative branches of both federal and state governments.

The United States Constitution is actually a grant of limited powers from the states to the federal government. Section 8 of Article I of the Constitution enumerates the powers of Congress, listing the subject matter areas in which Congress may enact statutes. The list is long and comprehensive and ranges from regulating commerce to declaring war to establishing post offices. At the end is the "necessary and proper clause," which has been interpreted broadly to include other matters. Several of the Amendments grant Congress the power to enact laws that affect the entire nation. The Constitution also has many restrictions on Congress's legislative power. In fact,

Section 9 of Article I contains an enumeration of several matters on which Congress may not legislate. The most famous of these restrictions is the prohibition of bills of attainder or ex post facto laws. A bill of attainder is a law from the legislature that declares a person or group of persons guilty of some crime and punishes them without the benefit of a trial. An ex post facto law is a law that makes an act a crime retroactively. These constitutional limitations come from nasty experiences with such laws that were passed in England.

The relationship between statutes and the common law can be somewhat confusing. As you can imagine, the relationship between the two has undergone volumes of historical development. However, now, this much is clear: When Congress (or a state legislature) enacts a statute that is consistent with the common law, the result is a codification of the common law; when a statute changes or limits the common law, the result is an abrogation or derogation of the common law. Sometimes, the effect of a statute on the common law is not clear. There are many rules on how to read statutes, known as canons of statutory construction. When confronted with a statue and a principle of common law on the same point, the applicable rule of statutory construction states that the two should be read together in harmony. A harmonious reading may not be possible, because there may exist an actual conflict between the two. Then, the statute prevails and applies and is said to abrogate or derogate the common law rule.

The modern residential landlord–tenant relationship is an example of an abrogation or derogation of the common law. Under the common law, the underlying assumption of a lease of property was agricultural. The tenant's main interest was to farm the land. The buildings were of secondary interest. Of course, the concept originates from feudal times. This assumption survived into modern times, so that under a residential lease, the landlord was not, under common law, responsible for the building's conditions. If the building fell into disrepair and became inhabitable, the tenant was still responsible for the rent. However, modern laws now make landlords responsible for these conditions. If the residence is not habitable according to building and health codes, then the tenant is relieved of all or part of the responsibility for the rent. In many states, the tenant may, upon proper notice to the landlord, pay for repairs and deduct the cost from the rent. Thus, modern laws that regulate the landlord–tenant relationship in residential leases abrogate the common law.

Article II: The Executive Branch and Law Enforcement

The president, the primary representative of the executive branch of government, is entrusted by the Constitution to enforce the laws of the United States. At the same time, the president and the executive branch create law in several ways.

Treaties

As the part of government responsible for foreign affairs, the executive branch negotiates and enters into treaties with foreign nations. Treaties are essentially contracts

EYE ON ETHICS

As you will see in the coverage of legal research, statutes and courts decisions are constantly changing and shaping the law. The ethical codes for all paralegal associations and the ABA Model Code of Professional Conduct require legal professionals to perform their professional duties competently. Thus, all legal professionals are under a duty to stay current with these changes. Often, a legal professional spends a few hours each month reading about new court decisions and legislation in his or her spare time. In doing so, these legal professionals are fulfilling their ethical duties.

or agreements between countries. Under international law, treaties become a form of law between the signatories—that is, the nations that agreed to them. When the president or the secretary of state signs a treaty, Article II requires that before the treaty binds the United States, it must have the "advice and consent" of two-thirds of the Senate. This rule means that the Senate must approve by two-thirds' vote a special bill that the president then signs in a process known as domestic treaty ratification. Notice that the process by which a treaty is entered into requires international contact as well as the domestic procedure of treaty ratification.

Once ratified, the treaty becomes a form of law within the United States, as well as between the United States and the foreign signatory. Under the Supremacy Clause, the treaty, like all federal law and the Constitution, is the supreme law of the land and **preempts** state law. Treaties can and do affect our everyday lives. As United States citizens, our actions while crossing international borders, carrying passports, or seeking assistance from our consular offices overseas are all affected by treaties. On a more mundane level, the price and availability of foreign-made goods, such as the cars we drive, the food we eat, and the clothes we wear, as well as the way we think of other countries, medical care, and taxes, are just some of the many ways that treaties affect our daily lives. The recent and controversial growth of gambling casinos in the United States is largely the result of treaties between the United States and Native American nations.

preempt
Right of the federal government to exclusive governance in matters concerning all citizens equally.

Administrative Agency Regulation

Just before World War I, the United States began to govern on a more sophisticated level in a more complex world by using subject matter–specific bodies known as administrative agencies. Agencies are created by laws enacted by Congress and are managed under the executive branch. Particularly as a result of the Depression, civil rights concerns, and technology, administrative agencies proliferated on both the federal and state level to regulate society with highly specialized and technical forms of laws known as **administrative agency regulations and rules**. Laws enacted by Congress were too general, and the congressional law-making process too cumbersome, to legislate matters that required high levels of expertise and technical knowledge. A single administrative agency, however, could concentrate on one specific subject matter and, using its specialized expertise and competence, formulate the necessary regulations that Congress could not. Thus, agencies such as the Federal Communications Commission, the Nuclear Regulatory Commission, and the Food and Drug Administration could assemble and employ scientists and technical experts to study an area that requires regulation. Similarly, the Social Security Administration, Federal Trade Commission, and Department of Homeland Security have specialized knowledge and training to govern in their subject matter areas. Today there are dozens of federal, state, and municipal administrative agencies that affect almost every single aspect of our lives. Some sociologists believe that we now live in what they call the "Modern Administrative State."

administrative agency regulations and rules (administrative codes)
Processes and guidelines established under the particular administrative section that describe acceptable conduct for persons and situations under the control of the respective agency.

Within just about every agency is a miniature United States government, replete with its own three branches that perform legislative, enforcement, and judicial functions. Other chapters in this book will cover administrative agencies in depth, because this area of law—administrative law—employs more than its share of paralegals. As a source of law, administrative agencies issue regulations, which they promulgate, or issue, in accordance with specialized procedures, allowing for public input. Although statutes passed by Congress are higher in status, administrative regulations have the force of law.

Agencies such as the Environmental Protection Agency have their own police force and a legal enforcement mechanism, flanked by rows of paralegals and lawyers. Their task is to enforce the law and the regulations of the agency. Most agencies have a person who occupies an executive position in the agency, called an administrator, director, or chairperson. Making policy decisions and directing the agency are some of the executive branch—like functions that, similar to the president, the administrator engages in to enforce the agency's record.

Administrative agencies also have court-like functions. For example, a deportation (now called "removal") hearing is a legal proceeding to determine whether an individual who is not a citizen of the United States is legally present or entitled to remain in this country. The hearing is very much like a trial court, including a judge, usually an administrative law judge who swears in witnesses, listens to testimony, rules on what evidence may be considered, and makes legally binding decisions by applying law and regulations. At these hearings, lawyers are commonly present to represent the government and the noncitizen. These proceedings occur within the administrative agency known as the Executive Office for Immigration Review, which falls within the Justice Department. These and the court-like administrative hearings conducted by dozens of other agencies are performing adjudication functions. Many agencies have two or more levels of adjudications. The top level makes written decisions that are published and have the weight of precedent within the agency.

Executive Orders and Prosecutorial Discretion

The president issues **executive orders** and policy directives, which indirectly have the force of law. As the enforcer of the laws, the president appoints and directs the **attorney general**, who is the chief law enforcement officer of the United States. You might want to think of the attorney general as the head lawyer for the government who takes instructions from the president on which legal issues or even social policies to pursue. One would think that the president should enforce *all* the laws of the country. However, as a realistic matter, the resources available to the attorney general make it possible to pursue only a limited range of enforcement activities. As a result, the decision to allocate legal resources to combat, say, organized crime or drunk driving constitutes a policy decision of the executive branch.

executive order
An order issued by the president of the United States or a governor of a state to another part of the executive branch of the government such as an administrative agency or law enforcement official.

attorney general
The chief law enforcement officer and head of the law office of a state or country.

Executive branch decisions to enforce environmental laws by suing large-scale polluters also constitute a policy determination to allocate resources to environmental issues. The executive branch also makes a policy decision not to take action to enforce certain areas of the law, such as corporate finance fraud. Similarly, the resource allocation decision to prosecute certain types criminals while letting others alone for the time being is a form of policymaking known as prosecutorial discretion. Whether a matter of policy or prosecutorial discretion, executive branch decisions about which laws to enforce is a form of law making.

Article III: The Judicial System

The court system of the United States performs the functions of resolving certain disputes and creating an important form of law. The court system is also an epicenter of legal activity. Largely because of the use of precedent and its theatrical nature, courtroom activity has, for better or worse, become a regular source of entertainment, providing the backdrop for mainstream films, reality television, and everything else in between. The continued and sustained popularity of television shows based on lawyers and the courts for almost half a century, since the time of Perry Mason, attest to our society's obsession. The courts themselves have also developed into their own world with a distinctive culture and language.

Some elementary terminology is in order. Lawsuit, litigation, action, matter, proceeding, and petition are just some of the names used synonymously for the same thing. The persons involved in an action in the district court have names with which

plaintiff
The party initiating legal action.

defendant
The party against whom a lawsuit or criminal proceedings is brought.

litigant
A party to a lawsuit.

almost everyone is familiar. Generally, someone involved in a lawsuit is party or litigant. The person or entity who brings a lawsuit is a **plaintiff**. The person being sued is a **defendant**. The term **litigant** refers to any party to a lawsuit. The title of the case uses the actual names of the parties, such as *Nader v. General Motors, Inc.* or *Bush v. Gore*. In a criminal matter, the party bringing criminal charges is the government or the state. The accused is the defendant. The party names in criminal cases are thus something like *United States v. Martha Stewart* or *Miranda v. Arizona*. The *v.* or *vs.* is an abbreviation for "versus."

In a few specialized types of matters, the person bringing the action is called the petitioner, and the other party is the respondent. These party titles are used in court proceedings that have traditional forms or common law origins. For instance, a petition for a writ of habeas corpus often challenges the legality of a criminal conviction. (The *writ of habeas corpus* originated in the Magna Carta.) Trial courts are presided over by a judge, or at a higher level court, the judge becomes a justice. Courts are often referred to as the bench, upon which the judge or justices sit. The term forum refers to a court in a very general sense. Some courts have personnel known as magistrates who perform quasi-judicial functions by hearing a case to make findings and recommendations to an actual judge. Magistrates also make preliminary determinations or decide simple or uncontested cases.

Article III, Section 1, of the Constitution states: "The judicial Power of the United States, shall be vested in one supreme Court, and in such inferior Courts as the Congress may from time to time ordain and establish." Congress has, by statue, created the federal judicial system, which now consists of three layers, along with some specialized courts. Congress's power to establish these courts comes from Article I, Section 8, which states that Congress shall have the power, "To constitute Tribunals inferior to the supreme Court." Exercising this power, Congress first established the federal district courts and the circuit courts of appeal.

Figure 3.2 provides a chart of the three branches of government and the types of law each branch creates.

The Federal District (Trial) Courts

trial court
Courts that hear all cases and are courts of general jurisdiction.

District courts are the backbone of the federal court system. District courts are courts of original jurisdiction, which means that they are courts with the legal authority to hear a case from its beginning. Thus, a lawsuit or criminal prosecution begins or originates in the district court. More important, the district courts are **trial courts**, which means that they hear testimony from witnesses, look at exhibits, assemble juries, and consider the lawyers' arguments. When the trial is over, the district court must determine whose evidence is more believable and make findings of fact. In doing so, the court is seeking a form of truth: what actually happened according to the evidence. Next, the court must apply the law to the facts that it found. In doing so, the court is making conclusions of law. In a civil case, an ultimate conclusion might be that the one party legally owes the other a sum of money due under a contract. For criminal cases, a conclusion of law would be that the person accused committed the acts that constitute a crime and the defendant may therefore be guilty.

FIGURE 3.2
Three Branches of Government and the Law They Create

Branch of Government	Type of Law Created
Article I—Legislature	Statutes
Article II—Executive	Treaties Administrative regulations and orders Executive orders
Article III—Judiciary (Courts)	Court decisions—precedent

Jurisdiction for Federal Court

Jurisdiction is a very broad term. For courts, **jurisdiction** means the legal authority to hear a case. Usually, a court's legal authority to hear a case comes from a statute or a constitution. Because Congress created the district courts pursuant to its constitutionally granted power to do so, it makes sense that Congress should say what types of cases those courts should hear. Early on, the thought of federal judicial power provoked philosophical discussions and even heated debate as to the role of the federal government and its relationship to the states. At stake was the remnant sovereignty still claimed by many states that wanted to run their own affairs without interference from outsiders in the newly formed federal government.

jurisdiction
The power or authority of the court to hear a particular classification of case. Also, the place or court that may hear a case, based on subject matter and/or geographic area.

The Constitution is actually vague as to what the federal judicial powers were supposed to do. After much deliberation and two centuries of development, the role of the federal courts has become known as interstitial. This term means that the federal courts fill in the gaps between the state court systems. As a result, federal district courts are known as courts of limited jurisdiction, because they can only hear a limited range of cases. To sue in federal district court, a plaintiff would first have to show the court that there is a federal statute or constitutional principle that gave the court power to hear the case. Such a law grants **subject matter jurisdiction**, authorizing the court to hear a plaintiff's case. Federal district courts are generally authorized by law to hear only two types of cases: (1) diversity of citizenship and (2) federal questions.

subject matter jurisdiction
A court's authority over the res, the subject of the case.

Diversity Jurisdiction

Federal district courts play an important role in providing an alternative forum that attempts to eliminate or reduce regional jealousies. One of the first laws passed by Congress authorized the federal district courts to hear cases in which one of the parties came from another state or even another country. This authorization is the famous **diversity jurisdiction** provision of the Judiciary Act of 1789. Much of that law is still in effect today. The assumption was that a party from another state would receive fairer treatment in the federal district court than in the local state court. This assumption was based on the fact that the federal district courts were located in large cities with sophisticated and educated populations. It was also thought that the judges sitting in the federal district court would not be as subject to local opinion and biases as a state court judge might be. Hence, the Judiciary Act of 1789 granted federal district courts the legal authority to hear cases in which one of the parties is from out of state, known as diversity jurisdiction.

diversity jurisdiction
Authority of the federal court to hear a case if the parties are citizens of different states and the amount at issue is over $75,000.

Article III
The part of the United States Constitution that creates the federal judiciary.

All federal court judges are appointed by the president with the approval of the Senate under Article III of the Constitution. The same part of the Constitution also grants the judges life tenure and a salary that cannot be diminished. Therefore, a federal judge, in good standing, could stay on the bench until retirement without regard to political sways in the White House or in Congress. Both the life-tenure and salary provisions of the Constitution are part of the system of checks and balances for the three branches of government. These provisions were meant to ensure that the federal judiciary would maintain a measure of independence from the other branches of government and freedom from local or regional biases or prejudices. Implicitly, the thought was that the federal courts should administer justice freely, unhindered by politics or parochialism. These courts are known as Article III Courts, whose hallmarks are independent, life-tenured judges. As you will see, there are other types of federal courts outside of **Article III**.

COMMUNICATION TIP

Be sure that you thoroughly understand the numerous legal terms before using them, since there are many fine line yet significant distinctions in their definition.

State court judges, in contrast, step up to the bench in a variety of ways. Many state constitutions provide for judicial appointments by the state governor with approval or nominations by a state legislative body. However, other states elect their judges for a term of years, which means the judges are subject to popularity pressures to remain in office. Because of the varying ways that a state court judge may be chosen, the fear was that the state courts would tend to favor local litigants over those from out of state. Thus, the assumption was that federal district court would be a more objective and fairer forum. This assumption was based on several factors, including the life tenure and undiminished salary provisions for federal judges and the location of federal courts, usually in medium to large-sized metropolitan areas. There is another requirement: To invoke federal diversity jurisdiction, a litigant must have a case that involves $75,000 or more in controversy, that is, in potential damages. Any matters that do not reach that monetary amount may be filed in the appropriate state court.

Federal Question Jurisdiction

federal question jurisdiction
The jurisdiction given to federal courts in cases involving the interpretation and application of the U.S. Constitution or acts of Congress.

Federal statutes grant the federal courts the authority to decide cases that raise questions arising under federal law or the United States Constitution. This authority is known as **federal question jurisdiction**, the second type of subject matter jurisdiction for federal courts. Federal question jurisdiction is different from diversity jurisdiction. Diversity jurisdiction involves a case in which one of the parties is from out of state. Federal question jurisdiction means that the case presents issues under federal law or the Constitution. In federal question cases, both parties may come from the same state, as long as the case involves federal law or the Constitution. Oftentimes, there is a federal statute that specifically authorizes a federal district court to hear a particular federal question case.

A wide range of cases can invoke federal question jurisdiction. For instance, the federal law known as the Fair Credit Reporting Act creates certain consumer rights with regard to credit reports. The act also has a provision that authorizes a federal court to hear a lawsuit claiming the violation of a right created by that act. This authorization is also true of many other rights created by federal law, such as the Americans with Disabilities Act. Most of the rights created by federal law are also enforceable by filing a lawsuit in state court. For these types of cases, the state courts have concurrent jurisdiction with the federal district courts, which means that the plaintiff may choose to sue in either state or federal court.

However, state courts may *not* hear certain types of cases arising under federal law for which Congress has given the federal courts exclusive jurisdiction. Only federal courts may hear lawsuits involving claims under admiralty (certain matters regarding boats), antitrust (monopolies and unfair competition), copyright, and patent law, among a few other types of cases. Other cases include federal lawsuits requesting the federal district court to review a decision by a federal agency. Similar to the effect of the preemption doctrine upon state legislation, the types of cases that only a federal court may hear involve matters that are entrusted exclusively to the federal government and require specialized expertise.

Federal question jurisdiction also grants subject matter jurisdiction to federal district courts for cases in which the United States or an officer is a party, the controversy is between two or more states, or the controversy is between the United States and a foreign government or foreign official. The parties involved in these situations are, by their very nature, thought to raise federal or Constitutional questions. By creating special jurisdictional statutes for the federal courts, Congress also wanted to protect certain federal interests such as foreign affairs, provide a neutral forum for interstate disputes, and maintain uniformity in the nation's tax laws.

Specialized Federal Courts

To handle complex types of cases requiring expertise, Congress has established specialized courts. Two special trial courts that have nationwide jurisdiction over other types of cases are the Court of International Trade, which hears cases involving international trade and customs issues, and the United States Court of Federal Claims, which has jurisdiction to entertain various types of claims for money damages against the United States government. All over the country, federal bankruptcy courts help debtors obtain a fresh start by eliminating or easing their debts. There are also specialized courts that Congress has established outside of Article III.

You will recall that Article III authorizes Congress to establish courts below the United States Supreme Court. In doing so, Congress created Article III courts replete with judges who are able to act independently because of their life tenure and salary provisions. In addition, Article I, Section 8, authorizes Congress, "To constitute Tribunals inferior to the supreme Court." These tribunals, or courts, are known as "legislative courts" or "Article I Courts." These courts differ from Article III courts principally in that the judges do not have life tenure and serve a term of usually ten years. Their salaries are not protected. Article I courts also do not have full judicial powers but instead only those that Congress specifically delegates. Currently, the Article I courts are U.S. Court of Veterans' Appeals, the U.S. Court of Military Appeals, the U.S. Tax Court, and the district courts for the districts of the Virgin Islands, Guam, and the Northern Mariana Islands.

Distribution of Article III Federal District Courts

There are a total of 94 Article III federal district courts. Every state hosts at least one federal district court, usually located in the state capital. The District of Columbia and Puerto Rico each have an Article III federal district court. The more populous states have up to four federal district courts (California, New York, and Texas). Each district court covers a defined geographical area known as a judicial district.

The Appellate Courts

The losing party at the trial court level may appeal the case to a higher court known as an **appellate court**. Appellate is a word that describes the type of work that these courts perform. All trial courts maintain files for each case they hear. As the lawsuit progresses, the court file grows with the addition of a wide variety of documents filed by the parties and orders entered by the court. If there is a trial, a stenographer transcribes the witness' testimony and all the evidence is marked and ruled upon, culminating in a final decision or judgment declaring the winning or prevailing party. All of these items become what is known as the court record, or everything that was before the trial court. Remember that the job of the trial courts is to make findings of fact. Once made, the trial court applies the law to the findings to arrive at conclusions of law. Both of these tasks require the trial court to have made legal rulings. It is the job of an appellate court to review the record of the trial court for any errors of law, including whether certain evidence should or should not have been considered. The party asking for the appeal is the **appellant**, and the other party is the **appellee**.

In the federal system, appeals generally go into a middle-tier or **intermediate appellate court**. Sitting just below the United States Supreme Court are the 13 circuits that constitute the federal system of the United States Courts of Appeals.

The United States Courts of Appeals

The 94 judicial districts are organized geographically into 12 regional **circuits**, each of which has a United States Court of Appeals. A court of appeals hears appeals from the district courts located within its circuit, as well as appeals of decisions of federal administrative agencies. The first eleven circuits are referred to by their assigned number. The twelfth circuit is called the District of Columbia Circuit, because it reviews matters exclusively and directly from certain agencies of the federal government centered in the District of Colombia, as well as cases from the local courts. The map in Figure 3.3 shows the geographic boundaries of the circuit courts of appeals.

appellate court
The court of appeals that reviews a trial court's record for errors.

appellant
The party filing the appeal; that is, bringing the case to the appeals court.

appellee
The prevailing party in the lower court, who will respond to the appellant's argument.

intermediate appellate court
A mid-level appellate court that reviews the decision of a lower court when a losing party files for an appeal. Further review to the highest court is often discretionary.

circuit
One of several courts in a specific jurisdiction.

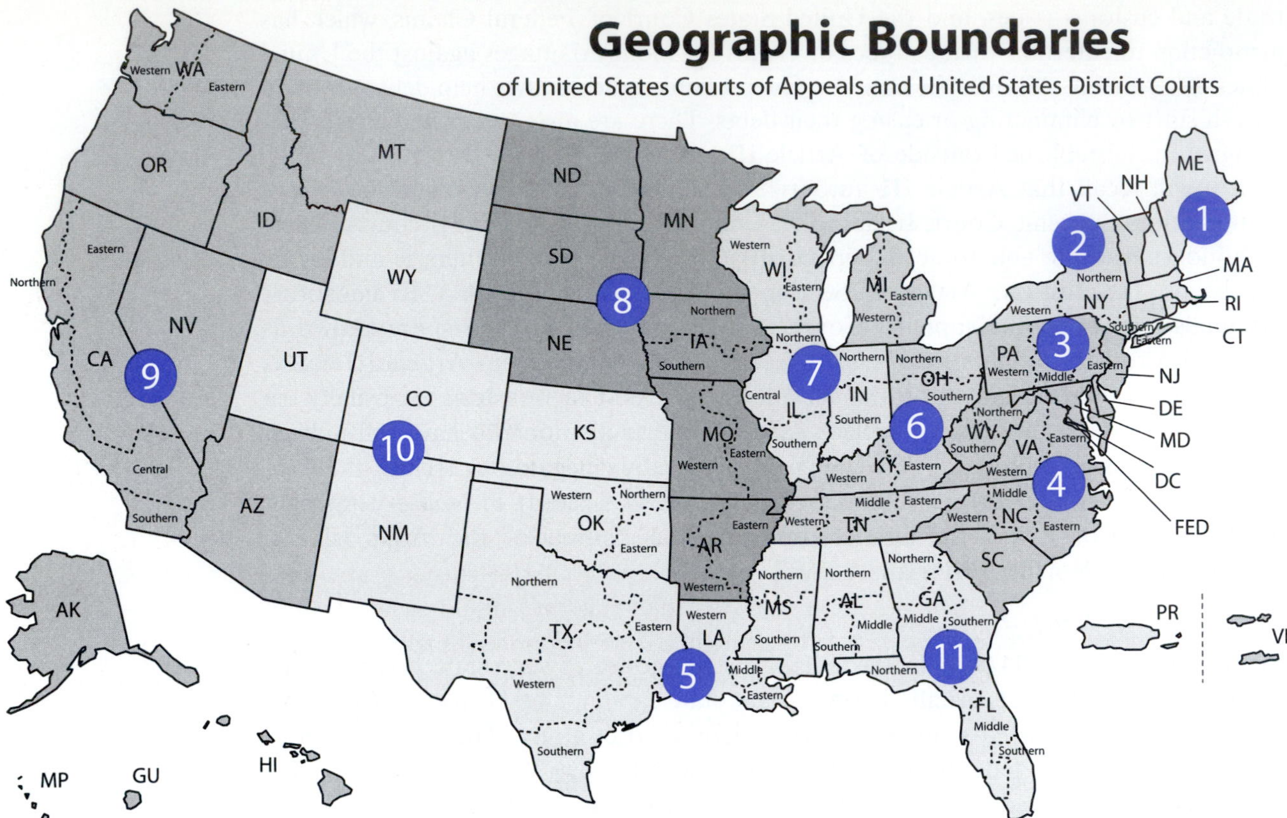

FIGURE 3.3 Geographic Boundaries of the U.S. Courts of Appeals and U.S. District Courts

Source: www.uscourts.gov/courtlinks/

Finally, there is a thirteenth circuit, known as the Federal Circuit. The Federal Circuit has nationwide jurisdiction to hear appeals in specialized cases, such as those involving patent laws and cases decided by the Court of International Trade, the Court of Veteran Appeals, and the Court of Federal Claims, among other specialized forums. The Federal Circuit is the only subject matter–specialized federal court of appeals.

At the appellate level, there are no trials. Instead, a panel of three judges reviews the record to see if the trial court has committed any prejudicial or reversible errors. That is, any error they find must be of such a nature that it could have substantially affected the outcome of the case. Appellate review involves combing through an often voluminous trial court record and performing exhaustive legal research. The lawyers for either side may file preliminary **motions** or request that the court make certain rulings, short of a final decision. The lawyer's major task in an appeal is preparing and filing the appellate brief. An appellate brief explains the party's legal position in great detail, makes legal arguments, and averages 30 to 40 pages in length.

motion
A procedural request or application presented by the attorney in court.

Either party may ask for oral argument, which the courts may grant discretionarily, taking into account the novelty or importance of the case and the number of cases to be decided. At oral argument, the lawyers present the legal points of their case before a panel of three judges. The court usually allots 10 to 15 minutes per side. During the lawyers' presentations, the three judges pepper them with questions, frequently interrupting them. A lawyer's first experience with oral argument at the circuit level is oftentimes likened to Dorothy's first appearance before the Wizard of Oz. However, with some experience, many lawyers find oral argument an enjoyable and, at times, exhilarating experience that draws on their skills of oration and persuasion. The courts of appeals hear oral argument in only a small percentage of cases.

If the court of appeals does find that the district court has committed prejudicial or reversible error, there are a number of ways that it may dispose of the case. If there is no prejudicial or reversible errors, or the court merely agrees with the outcome but for reasons different from those of the district court, the court of appeals will **affirm** the decision of the district court. The court may also **reverse** the district court's decision if there is enough error to warrant reversal. In some cases, the court of appeals will reverse and **remand**, which means that there was sufficient error, but the case is still incomplete and is being sent back, or remanded, to the district court.

affirm
Disposition in which the appellate court agrees with the trial court.

reverse
Disposition in which the appellate court disagrees with the trial court.

remand
Disposition in which the appellate court sends the case back to the lower court for further action.

The decisions made by the circuit courts of appeals are published regularly and can sometimes present momentous occasions. These decisions have the force and effect of precedent for the judicial districts within their respective circuits. Each circuit, as you will recall, consists of several judicial districts for which there is a federal district court. For instance, the First Circuit Court of Appeals, which sits in Boston, Massachusetts, hears appeals from the federal district courts within the judicial districts of Maine, Massachusetts, New Hampshire, Rhode Island and, strangely, the island of Puerto Rico. (Appeals from the courts in the U.S. Virgin Islands, which are 60 miles east of Puerto Rico, go to the Third Circuit Court of Appeals, which also covers Delaware, New Jersey, and Pennsylvania.) The decisions from the First Circuit are binding precedent upon the federal district courts within that circuit as a matter of **binding** or **mandatory authority**. In a significant way, each court of appeals acts as a supreme court within its circuit, and it would likely be a reversible error for a district court to depart from its circuit's precedent without adequate reason.

binding authority (mandatory authority)
A source of law that a court must follow in deciding a case, such as a statute or federal regulations.

The decisions of the courts of appeals from another circuit have **persuasive authority** but are not binding on a district or a circuit court from another circuit. The effect is persuasive, or helpful, but not binding. If the court of appeals for that circuit has not spoken on a particular issue, a district court within the same circuit may feel free to act on its own accord as it sees fit. You might want to think of a court of appeals as a parent of the district courts within its circuit. For the same district courts, a court of appeals in another circuit might be thought of as an aunt or uncle. In this analogy, you can see that parental orders carry an imperative, whereas those from an aunt or uncle are more attenuated. As a matter of principle at least, we must obey our parents, for their word carries the weight of mandatory authority. The kind advice from aunts and uncles may be helpful or persuasive, but it is not necessarily mandatory.

persuasive authority
A source of law or legal authority that is not binding on the court in deciding a case but may be used by the court for guidance, such as law review articles; all nonmandatory primary authority.

Appellate courts, particularly the circuit courts of appeals in the federal system, can wield considerable prestige and authority. They are often the final arbiters of federal and constitutional law for their region of the country, making interpretations and rulings that can affect millions of people living within the circuit. Moreover, the combined adjudications of a court of appeals, viewed altogether, constitute policy decisions that can often steer the behavior and conduct of businesses, governments, and individuals. Viewed statistically, the decisions of a court of appeals are fairly insulated from review by the United States Supreme Court. In the 12-month period ending on September 30, 2004, the total number of cases decided by the 12 geographical United States Courts of Appeals was 27,438 cases. Of all those cases, about 7,000 annually seek further review with the Supreme Court, which actually hears and fully decides only 80–90 cases a year. Frequently, the circuit courts will differ with one another on particular issues, known as a conflict among the circuits. Oftentimes, conflicts among the circuits are resolved by the United States Supreme Court, the highest court in the entire United States.

The United States Supreme Court

Article III of the U.S. Constitution establishes the Supreme Court. By Congressional act, the Court is staffed by eight associate justices and a chief justice. They are called "justices" as opposed to "judges" as a matter of respect. Like the rest of the federal judiciary, Supreme Court justices are appointed by the president with the Senate's "advice and consent." They are similarly accorded life tenure with a salary that cannot be diminished, and they are not subject to mandatory retirement. Currently, the Chief Justice of the Supreme Court, John Roberts, earns about $200,000 annually and is responsible for administration of the Court and for the leadership of the entire federal judiciary, which consists of more than 1,700 federal judges.

certiorari
(Cert) (Latin) "To make sure." An appellate court's authority to decide which cases it will hear on appeal.

petitioner
Name designation of a party filing an appeal or a petition.

respondent
Name designation of the party responding to an appeal.

vote of four
By tradition, a vote by four Supreme Court Justices to grant certiorari, which means that the Court will hear a case.

majority opinion
An opinion where more than half of the justices agree with the decision. This opinion is precedent.

concurring opinion
A separate opinion that agrees with the majority opinion but for different reasons.

dissenting opinion
An opinion in which a judge disagrees with the result reached by the majority; an opinion outlining the reasons for the dissent, which often critiques the majority and any concurring opinions.

plurality opinion
A rare disposition in which a greater number, but less than a majority, votes on the outcome of a case.

The Court has two types of jurisdiction, appellate and original. The Court's appellate jurisdiction brings cases from the federal courts, as prescribed by Congressional statute. The statutes allow for direct appeal and petitions for writ of **certiorari**, a request for a discretionary grant of review. In this type of proceeding, the person requesting the Court to hear the case is called the **petitioner**, and the other party is the **respondent**. State court cases may also be heard if they involve an important federal or constitutional question. For the most part, the Court hears only the cases it wants to hear, that is, by certiorari. The Court decides whether to grant a petition for certiorari and hear the case according to the importance of the legal question or if there is a conflict among the circuits. The Supreme Court begins each term on the first Monday of October and recesses in June. At regularly held conferences during each term, the justices review and vote on whether to hear a particular case. By the Court's own tradition, a **vote of four** justices will constitute a grant of certiorari, meaning that the case will be heard.

After the Court grants certiorari, the parties prepare and file briefs similar to those filed with the courts of appeals. In a few cases, the Court will hear oral argument before the entire bench of nine justices. When the Court denies certiorari, it means that the lower court ruling stands. There is no precedential effect from the Supreme Court's refusal to hear a case. Only when a case is briefed and argued, resulting in a signed opinion, has the Court made precedent. Cases are decided by a vote of the justices. A majority of the Court consists of five votes. Whether or not in the majority, the Chief Justice assigns the author of the **majority opinion**. Those justices agreeing merely sign off on the opinion by adding their names.

Others who agree with the result but for different reasons may file a **concurring opinion**. Justices who disagree dissent with the majority and may file **dissenting opinions**. At times, dissents have been vituperative or vocal. Lately, there has been the phenomenon of **plurality opinions**, in which the Court is unable to muster a majority vote of five justices. A plurality occurs when there are enough votes to decide a case a certain way, but there is a divergence of opinions on the reasons. Thus three justices may agree on the result and the reasons, then two other justices may agree on the result but for different reasons. A plurality opinion would result from the three agreeing Justices, with concurring opinions from the other two. The four who do not agree with the result would be dissenters.

The Supreme Court also has original jurisdiction over certain cases that are enumerated in the Constitution. Cases in which the states are parties or cases involving ambassadors and foreign ministers, among others, may be filed from the beginning with the Supreme Court. However, this situation is rare, and less than a handful of cases are filed in the Supreme Court's original jurisdiction each year.

RESEARCH THIS

Find a case from the federal system or any state system that was decided by a plurality decision. What was the issue presented in the case? How did the court dispose of the case? How was this case decided by a plurality?

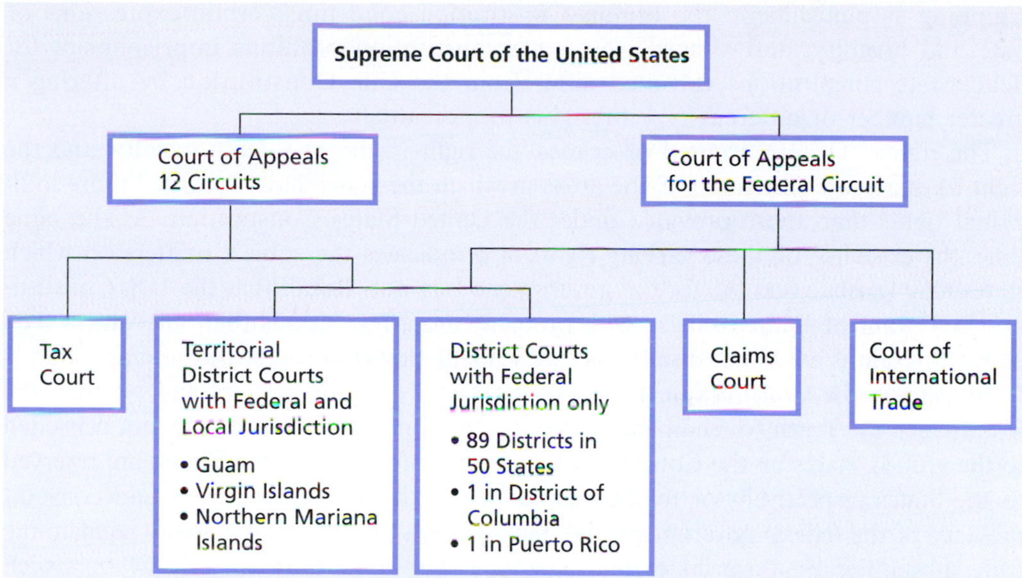

FIGURE 3.4
Flowchart of the U.S. Federal Court System
Source: Copyright © 2007 Microsoft Corporation. All rights reserved.

Almost every decision by the Supreme Court carries great significance. Every spring, the Court announces its opinions for the term. When this announcement happens, the news media, the legal community, and legal pundits all over the world cluster, rapt with attention, eager to scrutinize every word from the Court. Dozens of law review journals and scholarly books are devoted to the lengthy and detailed analyses of each term's decisions. Law professors and students of law can be seen with pens poised to note the Court's direction, the nuances of each justice's vote, and their predictions. The general public also pauses to hear the news announcing the Court's major decisions that can and often do affect their daily lives. From individual rights to governmental authority to the interpretation of federal law and the Constitution, the Supreme Court stirs the emotions and intellect of everyone within its purview. Dubbed informally as the "Supremes," every Justice has his or her place imprinted in American history. Former Justice Robert Jackson aptly described the profound effect of the Court with characteristic modesty: "We are not final because we are infallible, but we are infallible only because we are final." See *Brown v. Allen*, 344 U.S. 433, 540 (1953) (Jackson, concurring in result).

Figure 3.4 provides a flowchart of the federal court system.

THE STATE SYSTEMS AND STATE CONSTITUTIONS

The state legal systems are structurally identical to the federal system. With some minor variations, each state has a constitution, and some states have had more than one. For instance, Georgia has had ten constitutions, North Carolina three, and Massachusetts two. In some states, a succession of constitutional conventions has ratified new constitutions to replace the former. In other states, the new constitution acts as a lengthy supplement or amendment to the first, making both in force concurrently. Whether by single or multiple constitutions, each state has a founding document or law that creates three branches of government: the legislative, the executive (or gubernatorial), and the judiciary. In this way, each of these branches operates in similar fashion to their federal counterparts.

Similar to the Bill of Rights of the United States Constitution, state constitutions also declare individual rights. Typically, most state constitutions begin with a declaration of equality, freedom, and independence for all its inhabitants. Some go on to enumerate other rights. For instance, the Georgia Constitution specifically prohibits

CYBER TRIP

Trip 1: Go to www.uscourts.gov, the official Web site for the United States Federal Courts. Click on "Educational Outreach" on the upper left-hand side of the page. Explore "Contemporary Topics," in particular, "Whose Property is Intellectual Property?" Under "Witness Stand Script," you will find three examples of transcripts from trials.

Trip 2: Find the official Web site for the court system in your state. Does the state court structure differ? How well does the Web site inform you about practical aspects of bringing a case through state court?

whipping as punishment; the Illinois Constitution condemns certain expressions of hate and hostility; and almost every state constitution prohibits imprisonment for debt. State constitutions can also differ from the U.S. Constitution by offering a greater number or different type of rights to individuals.

The rights of those accused of crimes, the right to die, the death penalty, and the right to marry are just some of the areas in which the states have accorded more individual rights than those provided under the United States Constitution. At the same time, the existence of these varying rights also indicates the subject matters on which states may legislate and the federal government may not. Recall that the U.S. Constitution is a grant of limited power, with probably more restrictions than allowances. For many, this status exists because the actual seats of power are with the several states.

By signing the Constitution, the states ceded only certain powers and retained the rest. In fact, the Tenth Amendment to the Constitution states, "The powers not delegated to the United States by the Constitution, nor prohibited by it to the States, are reserved to the States respectively, or to the people." Thus, despite the pervasive and constant presence of the federal government, the state laws are the ones that actually regulate the truly substantive legal aspects of our lives. And they do so quite directly. Matters such as family relationships, property ownership, crime and punishment, public safety, businesses, and a host of other more mundane matters are almost exclusively state matters. For this reason, our drivers' licenses; license plates; birth, death, and marriage certificates; and deeds, leases, corporate documents, and contracts are all created and governed by state laws. In this way, the federal system fills in the gaps between the states and acts to unify them to form the United States. The rest is left up to the states.

The pervasiveness of the federal government is a function of the wide impact of its vast wealth, its oversight over the most basic rights, and the desire to promote the economy and other policy matters through interstate commerce. More than 50 years ago, one member of the U.S. Supreme Court viewed all the states as laboratories of reform that the federal government could later follow. One famous example is election and campaign finance reform. In the late 1800s, the California, Massachusetts, and New York legislatures realized the need for laws that would make elections more accessible and fair.

State Courts

Like state laws, the state courts are the primary centers for the legal activity that occurs across the country and the essential vehicles for dispute resolution. The state court systems are, for the most part, similar to the federal court system, consisting of three tiers: a trial court level, an intermediate appellate court, and a supreme court. Four states have different names for their supreme courts. In Maine and Massachusetts, the highest court is called the Supreme Judicial Court. Maryland and New York both name their highest court the Court of Appeals. This convention also used to be the case in Kentucky, until 1975 when it changed the name to the Kentucky Supreme Court. About ten states do not have an intermediate appellate court, so appeals go directly from the trial level to the state's highest court. Those states without an intermediate appellate level also give their highest courts discretionary appellate jurisdiction. Like the United States Supreme Court, the highest courts in many states hear only the cases they feel are important enough to hear. For many litigants in the state court, the state's intermediate appellate courts usually have the last say in a case.

Within each state, the vast amount of the nation's judicial work is funneled through the various courts. It is the state courts that handle virtually all the disputes that can be litigated. Divorce, support and child custody disputes, probate and inheritance cases, real estate, juvenile matters, most criminal cases, contracts, disputed traffic violations, personal injury cases, and a vast array of other types of cases are all heard in the state courts. Hence, the state courts are known as courts of general jurisdiction. In contrast to the federal courts, which are allowed to hear only very limited scopes of cases, the state courts have the jurisdiction to hear almost any type of case.

The state court systems differ mostly at the trial level. Some states have two or three levels of trial courts. Within the trial level, most states have several specialized courts. At the base, there are traffic courts and small claims courts. In 1996, the city of Philadelphia instituted an unusual forum, Nuisance Night Courts, to hear "quality of life crimes" and address disturbances to the city's quietude. Complete with all essential court personnel and equipment, this unique court is completely mobile and dispenses "swift and fair justice" to urban neighborhoods.

The state trial courts are commonly known as the "superior courts," which hear almost all mainstream cases involving a minimum amount of money in controversy, usually about $10,000. There is no maximum limit for these state trial courts. It is in these courts that the real action takes place. The courtroom dramas that we see on television and in movie theaters, complete with juries and parades of witnesses and dramatic orations, are the staple of the state trial courts. On almost any day of the week, with a little bit of luck, anyone can observe a trial or a formal argument just by wandering into the local courthouse. As organs of government, all courts, both state and federal, are supported by tax dollars and thus are open to the public. Figure 3.5 provides a chart of the Indiana court system, which is typical of most states' court systems.

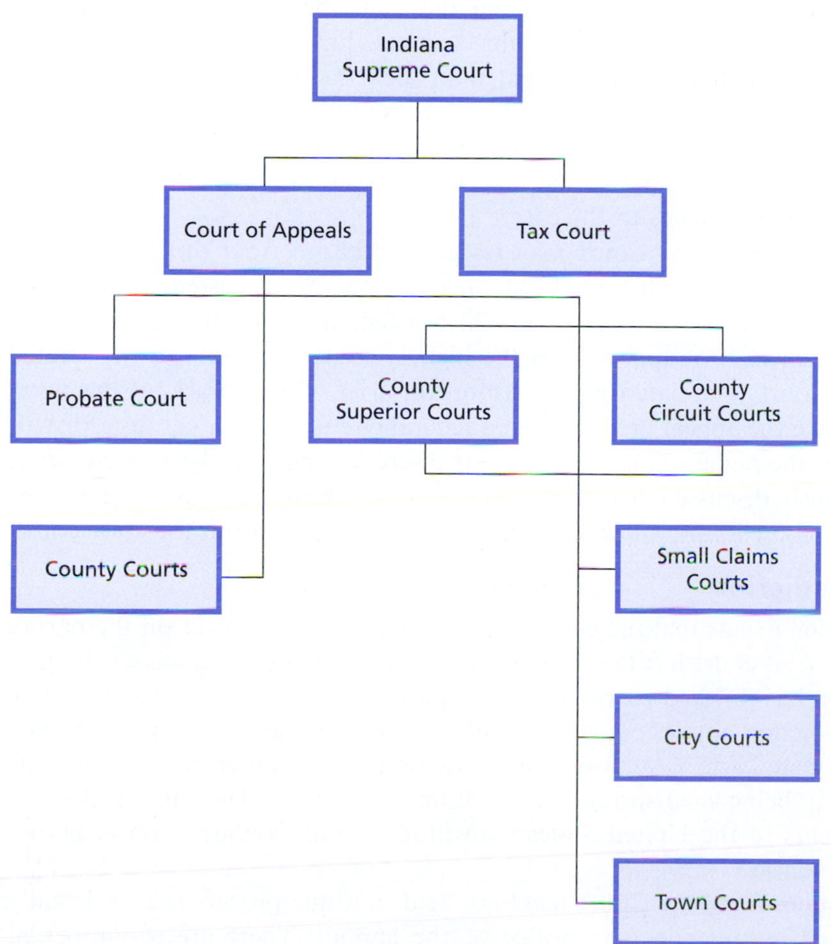

FIGURE 3.5
Flowchart of the Indiana Court System
Source: www.in.gov/judiciary/about/chart/flash.html.

Subject Matter Jurisdiction in State Courts

Previously in this chapter, we saw that federal courts are courts of limited jurisdiction. We understand this to mean that by design, the federal courts are authorized to hear only selected types of cases. For a federal court to hear a case, there must be federal subject matter jurisdiction by way of diversity or federal question. Without the specific, if not express legal authority, the federal courts do not have jurisdiction to hear a case.

In the state trial court system, subject matter jurisdiction is a different and simpler concept. As discussed previously, state trial court systems frequently have specialized courts that hear only certain types of case. Courts that hear only domestic relations cases such as divorce, adoption, and support cases are commonly known as "family court" or "divorce court." Cases involving inheritance matters, wills, and trusts are heard by a "probate court." In some large cities, evictions and other landlord–tenant disputes are heard only in a "landlord-tenant court" or "housing court." Most states have "juvenile courts" that hear only cases involving juveniles who run afoul of certain criminal laws but are too young to be treated as adults. Two states, Massachusetts and Hawaii, each have a land court that specializes in hearing only those disputes involving the ownership or boundaries of land. Thus, for state trial courts, subject matter jurisdiction simply means that if the case at hand can be heard by a specific court, the case should be filed there. For instance, a divorce case should be filed in divorce or family court, not in a housing court, which would reject a divorce case for want of subject matter jurisdiction to hear that type of case. If there is no state trial court specialized by subject matter for a particular type of case, it may be filed in the state's general trial court.

PRACTICE TIP

As you begin your study of the court system, keep a diagram or key to the court systems at hand for easy reference.

Subject matter jurisdiction is a requirement that must be met whenever a case is filed in either federal or state court. The subject matter jurisdiction requirements for federal court mean something very different than those in state court. However, for both state and federal courts, subject matter jurisdiction generally means that the court is authorized by law to hear the case at hand. Once a court has determined that it has subject matter jurisdiction over the case, the court must also be satisfied that it has jurisdiction over the parties to the case.

The United States Supreme Court may review a decision from the highest state court if the case involves a substantial federal question. As discussed, state courts may hear cases containing federal issues in which a federal law or the United States Constitution is involved. An appeal from the highest court of a state to the United States Supreme Court is initiated by a petition for writ of certiorari by the party seeking review. Like the appeal process from a federal circuit court, a petition for writ of certiorari from the highest court of a state is discretionary with the U.S, Supreme Court. As previously discussed, a vote by four justices to hear the case will grant the petition for writ of certiorari, and the Court will hear the case from the state court.

personal jurisdiction
A court's power over the individuals involved in the case; when a court has personal jurisdiction, it can compel attendance at court hearings and enter judgments against the parties.

due process
Ensures the appropriateness and adequacy of government action in circumstances infringing on fundamental individual rights; and a source of fundamental rights.

Personal Jurisdiction

Personal jurisdiction means that the court has the legal authority to act on the parties to the lawsuit. A trial court has the legal authority to act upon a person to the lawsuit if that person has received proper notice that a lawsuit has been filed against him or her. This jurisdiction applies equally to both federal and state trial courts. As you will see in more detail when we cover civil litigation, the requirement of adequate notice to the party being sued springs from notions of fairness. The Fifth and Fourteenth Amendments to the United States Constitution both contain what is known as a **due process** clause.

The United States Supreme Court has long held that due process requires that a person being sued receive adequate notice of the lawsuit. There are a number of means to notify a defendant. Without adequate notice, the court does not have

CASE IN POINT

STATE COURT SUBJECT MATTER JURISDICTION.

IN RE RICE, 68 HAW. 334; 713 P.2d 426 (1986)

Appellees Richard A. Breton and Margaret Mary Breton, as Sellers, filed a petition in the land court against Appellant Central Pacific Supply Corporation (hereinafter "CPS"), as Buyer, seeking to cancel the Agreement of Sale of a leasehold interest and for damages. The Bretons alleged that CPS had breached the Agreement by defaulting on the payment due thereon and by vacating the premises. CPS timely answered the complaint and counterclaimed against the Bretons for the breach of the Agreement and sought a rescission of the Agreement and damages. The land court, after trial, found in favor of the Bretons against CPS on both the complaint and the counterclaim. Thereafter, CPS filed a motion to set aside the findings of fact, conclusions of law and judgment, and to set the matter for a jury trial. The land court denied the motion, and CPS filed timely notices of appeal.

I. In answer to the Bretons' petition to cancel Agreement of Sale, one of CPS's defenses was that the land court lacked jurisdiction over the subject matter of the petition. The land court, after trial, concluded that it had "jurisdiction of the parties and this cause of action."

Although the issue of jurisdiction of the land court over the subject matter was not questioned at the trial level nor raised in this appeal, we hold, sua sponte, that the land court lacked jurisdiction over the subject matter of the Bretons' petition.

"The lack of jurisdiction over the subject matter cannot be waived by the parties." Meyer v. Territory, 36 Haw. 75, 78 (1942). If the parties do not raise the issue, "a court sua sponte will, for unless jurisdiction of the court over the subject matter exists, any judgment rendered is invalid." Id. at 78; see also O'Daniel v. Inter-Island Resorts, 46 Haw. 197, 377 P.2d 609 (1962). "Such a question is in order at any stage of the case, and though a lower court is found to have lacked jurisdiction, we have jurisdiction here on appeal, not of the merits, but for the purpose of correcting an error in jurisdiction." Meyer v. Territory, 36 Haw. at 78 (citation omitted).

II. The land court derives its jurisdiction from section 501-1 of the Hawaii Revised Statutes (HRS). n1 "The land court is a court of limited jurisdiction, created for a special purpose, that of carrying into effect what is known as the Torrens title scheme, derives all of its power from the statutes relating to it, and can exercise no power not found within those statutes." In Re Rosenbledt, 24 Haw. 298, 308 (1918), modified on other grounds, 25 Haw. 561 (1920).

HRS § 501-1 in relevant part reads:

> A court is established, called the land court, which shall have exclusive original jurisdiction of all applications for the registration of title to land and easements or rights in land held and possessed in fee simple within the State, with power to hear and determine all questions arising upon such applications, and also have jurisdiction over such other questions as may come before it under this chapter, subject to the rights of appeal under this chapter. The proceedings upon the applications shall be proceedings in rem against the land, and the decrees shall operate directly on the land and vest and establish title thereto.

The Bretons' petition to cancel the Agreement of Sale and for damages and CPS's counterclaim for rescission of the Agreement and for damages are both causes of action arising out of alleged breaches of the Agreement. Both are breach of contract actions over which the land court does not have jurisdiction under any of the provisions of chapter 501 of the Hawaii Revised Statutes, as amended.

The judgment of the land court is void for lack of jurisdiction. This appeal is dismissed.

QUESTIONS ABOUT THE CASE

1. What types of cases could the Hawaiian Land Court hear?
2. What does "original jurisdiction" mean?
3. Why are the parties not permitted to waive jurisdiction?
4. Where should the Bretons have filed their case?

personal jurisdiction over the defendant. Once notice has been given to the satisfaction of the trial court, the requirement of personal jurisdiction has been met, and the lawsuit may proceed. When the court does proceed, it is acting *in personnam,* which is a Latin phrase meaning that the court has personal jurisdiction and the legal authority to act on the persons named in the lawsuit. The vast majority of lawsuits involve personal jurisdiction.

In contrast to ***in personnam* jurisdiction**, a few types of lawsuits involve a dispute over the rightful ownership of property or a particular thing that is located within the trial court's geographical or territorial jurisdiction. In such cases, the court's action is focused

***in personnam* jurisdiction**
A court's authority over a party personally.

FIGURE 3.6
Types and Characteristics of Jurisdiction, and How They Are Applied

Type of Jurisdiction	Characteristics	How Applied
Personal Jurisdiction	The court's authority to act upon an individual or entity to a lawsuit as a matter of fairness.	Giving adequate notice of a lawsuit to a defendant in a manner prescribed by law.
In Rem Jurisdiction	The court's authority to act on a thing (the res) in a given controversy.	The thing in controversy must be within the court's geographical borders.
Subject Matter Jurisdiction	The court's authority to act upon a particular type of lawsuit.	The lawsuit must be filed in the proper court.
State courts	General jurisdiction.	Filing the lawsuit in the court authorized to hear it.
Federal courts	Limited jurisdiction.	1. Diversity of citizenship jurisdiction may be heard. 2. The lawsuit must present a federal question. 3. The type of lawsuit may be heard only by a certain federal court—exclusive jurisdiction.

not upon a person but upon a particular thing, known in Latin as a "res." Government seizures of property, court-supervised dispositions of inheritances, disputes about the boundary or title to property, and **admiralty** cases are examples of lawsuits in which the trial court's attention is focused on the property or thing. In such actions, whether in admiralty or other types of cases, the court's jurisdiction is called **in rem**.

admiralty
Specialized laws and courts dealing with maritime questions and offenses.

***in rem* jurisdiction**
A court's authority over claims affecting property.

Jurisdiction, in law, is a word of many meanings depending upon the circumstances. Basically, jurisdiction refers to a court's legal authority to act on a particular matter, whether it is a case, a person, or the thing in controversy. While this definition may sound simple enough, advanced students can spend an entire semester covering federal jurisdiction alone. Figure 3.6 provides a chart that summarizes the several important components of jurisdiction that are necessary for your understanding.

ALTERNATIVES TO COURTS

In recent years, both federal and state courts have experienced severe case backlogs. Litigation has also become very time consuming and expensive. To address these issues, a process of dispute resolution, alternative dispute resolution (ADR), has arisen outside of the government judicial process. The acceptance of ADR among both the general public and the legal profession has become so widespread that some courts now require some parties to resort to ADR at the outset of litigation and as a condition of continuing with the lawsuit. The ADR process offers a more efficient and cost-effective way of resolving disputes.

Specifically, ADR may proceed in several different ways. First, negotiation ADR is voluntary, and there is no third party who facilitates the resolution process or imposes a resolution. Second, ADR in the form of mediation involves a third party, known as a mediator, who facilitates the resolution process. In doing so, the mediator offers suggestions on the resolution but does not impose any final result upon the parties. Third, in collaborative law or collaborative divorce, each party has an attorney who facilitates the resolution process within specifically contracted terms. The parties reach agreement with the support of the attorneys (who are trained in the process) and mutually agreed experts.

A DAY IN THE LIFE OF A REAL PARALEGAL

As litigants have increasingly sought ADR techniques to resolve their disputes, more and more paralegals have found employment as mediators. Many paralegal schools even offer degrees or certificates in ADR for those who wish to seek specialized work as mediators or ADR specialists in law firms. Below is a list of duties performed by paralegals specializing in ADR:

- Draft motions to refer case to ADR proceeding.
- Draft demands for arbitration.
- Research and procure rules governing ADR proceedings.
- Assist with preparation of agreement containing procedures and rules the parties will use in the ADR proceeding.
- Conduct background research on the arbitrator(s), mediator(s), and/or judge(s).
- Make logistical arrangements for meeting facilities and/or hearing rooms as necessary and appropriate for the ADR proceeding.
- Assist with preparation of jury questions for summary jury trial proceeding.
- Draft documents required by settlement agreement (e.g., lien releases, property transfer documents).
- As necessary and appropriate, conduct legal research and draft ADR contract clauses.
- Store or dispose of case documents in accordance with protective orders and/or settlement agreement.

Summary

The scholarly study of law is known generally as jurisprudence, within which there are many schools of thought or legal theories. Older theories rely on the natural origins of law. Later theories applied and incorporated other disciplines, such as logic, economics, linguistics, and political theory. Jurisprudence has become a matter of academic interest that wields respect and has influenced how our laws are made and interpreted by courts and judges.

The American legal system comes to us as a result of historical development from the English laws and traditions, such as *stare decisis* or precedent. Other traditions from England include the Magna Carta and the notion of constitutions, which establish the basic organization of a government and the source for law and individual rights. In the United States, our Constitution is codified, meaning that it is a written, all-inclusive document. The United States Constitution establishes the three branches of government and the laws that each produce. A unique feature of the American legal system is its governance by numerous administrative agencies that regulate much of the technical and daily legal aspects of our lives. The Constitution also operates as a social contract to unify the states and contains several provisions setting out the relationship between the federal government and the states. As a result, the many powers of the federal government preempt the states in various areas of law, in the interest of a uniform application across the country. The United States Constitution also performs the function of declaring the most basic individual rights.

Article III of the Constitution establishes the judicial branch of government and the Supreme Court. Under the authority of Article III, Congress has created the other courts. Today, there are more than 90 federal district courts (the trial courts) and over them 13 circuit courts of appeals (appellate courts). The decisions of the circuit courts represent mandatory authority for the district courts within their geographical circuit and persuasive authority for those outside of it. The United States Supreme Court is the highest court, and its decisions are binding for the entire country. Congress has also created other courts to handle highly specialized matters. All federal courts have limited jurisdiction and can only hear diversity cases or those presenting federal questions.

Most of the judicial work in the United States is performed by the states. Similar to the federal system, state constitutions establish state court systems. Many state constitutions also create more individual rights than the federal system. State courts can vary greatly but generally are organized into a system parallel to the federal courts, with a supreme court, oftentimes an intermediate appellate court, and an array of trial courts. The main difference between the state and federal courts is in the types of cases that they hear. State courts may hear almost any kind of controversy. As a result, states commonly have a number of subject matter–specific trial courts that hear only matters, such as divorce or juvenile cases.

The state and federal court systems provide the primary forums for dispute resolution in which most lawyers and paralegals operate. Alternatives exist to resolve disputes in a process known as alternative dispute resolution (ADR). In the next chapter, we continue with our legal pedagogy by examining the law itself and how it is organized. We also delve into how legal professionals find the law and apply it in their work.

Key Terms

Administrative agency regulations and rules
Admiralty
Affirm
Appellant
Appellate court
Appellee
Article III
Attorney general
Binding authority (mandatory authority)
Certiorari (Cert.)
Circuit
Common law
Concurring opinion
Constitution
Defendant
Dissenting opinion
Diversity jurisdiction
Due process
Executive order
Federal question jurisdiction
In personnam jurisdiction
In rem jurisdiction
Intermediate appellate court
Jurisdiction
Jurisprudence
Justinian Code
Litigant
Majority opinion
Motion
Personal jurisdiction
Persuasive authority
Petitioner
Plaintiff
Plurality opinion
Precedent
Preempt
Remand
Respondent
Reverse
Statute
Subject matter jurisdiction
Supremacy Clause
Trial court
Vote of four

Review Questions

1. What is the difference between state and federal courts?
2. What is jurisprudence, and what usefulness does it have to a practicing legal professional?
3. Do we, in the United States, have a codified or uncodified constitution?
4. What is subject matter jurisdiction?
5. What is the difference between personal jurisdiction and *in rem* jurisdiction?
6. How are cases appealed to the United States Supreme Court?
7. What is the difference between ratifying a treaty and ratifying a new amendment?
8. What are the three branches of government, and what kinds of law do they produce?

9. How many circuit courts are there in the federal court system?
10. What is the difference between binding authority and persuasive authority?
11. What do appellate courts do?
12. What is the difference between federal court subject matter jurisdiction and state court subject matter jurisdiction?
13. What are the various ways that an appellate court disposes of an appeal?
14. What is the effect of the Supremacy Clause?
15. Which part of the Constitution creates the federal court system?
16. How is a concurring opinion different from a majority opinion and a dissenting opinion?

Exercises

1. Determine which federal circuit court and federal district court cover your area. What other districts are in the same circuit as your area?
2. Visit the Web site of the American Arbitration Association at www.adr.org/. What services does the association offer?
3. Using the Internet, find law firms in your area that offer ADR services to their clients.
4. Visit an administrative agency in your area. Determine what it does, and obtain a copy of any regulations it issues.
5. Find the constitution of your state. Have there been others? Is there a bill of rights? How does it compare to the federal Bill of Rights?

Discussion Questions

1. How would a critical legal studies (CLS) scholar evaluate the effect of Blackstone's work to support CLS theory?
2. Must state courts enforce a federal law? Why or why not?
3. What would prevent a state law or constitution from curtailing or limiting rights that come from the United States Constitution?
4. What concerns does the United States Constitution have that state constitutions do not?
5. Now that more than 200 years has passed since the Judiciary Act of 1789, do you think that there is still the necessity for diversity jurisdiction in the federal court system?

PORTFOLIO ASSIGNMENT

Using the Internet or any other means, research the structure of the court system for your state, and draw a diagram of the state court system, including any specialized courts. Write a three- to five-page report that answers the following questions:

- What is the name of its highest court?
- How many justices sit on the highest court?
- Is there an intermediate appellate court?
- How does the highest court hear cases?
- What types of specialized courts exist?

Part Two

The Practicing Paralegal: Developing Skills for the Legal Professional

CHAPTER 4 Finding and Reading the Law of Court Opinions

CHAPTER 5 Legal Research and Writing

CHAPTER 6 Paralegals in Action

CHAPTER 7 Basic Legal Specialties for the Professional Paralegal

CHAPTER 8 Legal Specialties: Family Matters

CHAPTER 9 Legal Specialties: Business Matters

Chapter 4

Finding and Reading the Law of Court Opinions

CHAPTER OBJECTIVES

The materials presented in this chapter will provide students with information on:

- The various classifications of law and the hierarchy of legal authorities.
- Sources of law as an introduction to legal research.
- The system of citations for court opinions.
- Analyzing court decisions and the legal principles involved.
- Distilling and defining the holding of a case.
- How to brief a case.

One of the most basic and important skills for a legal professional to develop is a thorough knowledge of the various sources of law and the ability to locate them. These are the first steps in developing the skill of performing legal research. Because research can be very time consuming and solitary, many lawyers delegate this crucial task to paralegals. In doing so, they rely upon the paralegal to be thorough and accurate. The task of having precise, up-to-date information is essential to providing competent legal representation. This chapter presents the information and techniques to develop the basic skills that a paralegal will need to perform legal research effectively and efficiently. Beginning with a review of the classifications of legal materials, this chapter will provide instruction on how to read court decisions and write a specialized form of note taking known as **case briefs**. This instruction will provide you with a necessary introduction to legal research, which, at its most basic, is a technique for finding a specialized form of information known as the law.

case brief
An objective summary of the important points of a single case; a summary of a court opinion.

CLASSIFICATION OF LAW AND LEGAL MATERIALS

Previous chapters have discussed the various sources of law. Beginning with the constitutions of the United States and the several states, we saw that official sources of law emanate from the three branches of government that these constitutions create: the legislature, the executive, and the judiciary. Each of these branches of government produces laws that vary greatly in form as well as content in the world of legal materials.

As we begin our examination of these materials, a review of the traditional organization of law into specific areas provides a helpful overview of the range of legal authority. By legal authority, we mean that the specific legal materials represent various points of law. A legal professional working in the field—paralegals as well as lawyers—perform legal research by systematically wading through legal materials to find the legal authority that might affect a client's legal position.

Within the law office, a legal professional examines each client's situation and gives it careful consideration in light of the existing legal authority. This examination must consider the client's facts as well. Whether the client is seeking to contest a government agency's decision, planning his or her estate for a family, developing a parcel of land, or defending an eviction or a criminal prosecution, the legal professional's first task is to identify the legal authority that directly or even indirectly governs the client's facts and thereby determines the client's legal position. Thus, the first step in evaluating a case is to identify the area of law applicable to the client's specific facts. Once having identified this area, the legal professional must probe further by identifying which part of that applicable law applies. The world of legal materials is vast and constantly growing. The landscape of law is classified into several different categories and subcategories. Thus, a beginning student in law must be aware of these classifications to identify that area pertaining to the client's matter at hand.

State and Federal Law

The last chapter identified one of the major classifications in American law, the distinction between state and federal laws. Specifically, the United States originated and still exists as a nation composed of several different quasi-sovereign states. Although all of the states operate in a similar fashion, each has its own form of government and laws. Each state also has its own constitution, which often mirrors the federal Constitution. At the same time, we saw that the federal Constitution is a document that each of the states has ratified as a condition for their admission to the United States, and by doing so, they ceded some of their sovereignty in the interest of a forming a single nation. Thus, the federal Constitution is different from the state constitutions, in that the federal Constitution specifically provides for the supremacy of federal government law over all state laws. As a result, federal law preempts or overrides any conflicting state laws.

At the same time, the states have the major role of governing and regulating our day-to-day lives. Often, state laws can legislate the same subject matter as existing federal

A DAY IN THE LIFE OF A REAL PARALEGAL

Paralegals often occupy the front line of a law office, particularly in the offices of small law firms and solo practitioners. As such, a paralegal may be the first person that a prospective client will meet. In an interview known as an initial consultation, paralegals will take down the information about the prospective client's situation and answer questions about the office, taking care not to give any legal advice. To be able to discuss the client's matter, a paralegal must be aware of a substantial amount of law. After taking down basic information, the paralegal discusses the client's matter with an attorney in the office. Once the paralegal and the attorney have identified the legal ramifications of the client's situation, the attorney takes over and completes the initial consultation, giving the client a legal evaluation. In this way, the paralegal and the attorney work as a team. With knowledge of the law, the paralegal is able to conduct the consultation efficiently by asking for pertinent information from the client and then discuss the matter with the attorney. From this information, the attorney can assess the situation and give the client an evaluation.

law. For instance, many if not most states have consumer laws that protect consumers from unscrupulous business practices. There are also a number of federal consumer protection laws that do the same. Another example are the state and federal antidiscrimination laws that outlaw discriminatory practices based on race, color, religion, sex, or national origin. In these and many other instances, the federal government has not declared that federal laws are exclusive and there is no preemption. Therefore, a person who feels he or she has been harmed by unsavory business practices or unlawful discrimination may seek protection under either or both federal and state laws. As noted in Chapter 3, federal law often appears to play a larger role than state law. However, state laws primarily govern our lives on a daily basis, because states are free to legislate on any matter not reserved to the federal government by the Constitution.

Civil and Criminal Law

Both the federal and state governments make the distinction between **civil law** and **criminal law**. Essentially, the difference between civil law and criminal law lies in the harm involved, the parties involved, the procedures employed, and the remedies or punishment imposed. Generally, civil laws concern themselves with the harm, whether personal, property or monetary, suffered by an individual or business entity due to the action or inaction of another party. With criminal laws, the state or federal government seeks to punish an individual (or business entity) for certain types of behavior, whether or not any harm may have resulted. In criminal law, the theory justifying the government's role as prosecutor is that the public has suffered harm.

civil law
The legal rules regarding offenses committed against the person.

criminal law
The legal rules regarding wrongs committed against society.

The Parties

A simple example of how civil law operates would be a simple automobile accident in which an individual accidentally drives his or her motor vehicle into another's. If one of the parties had caused the collision, he or she would be liable to the other civilly. Here, **liability** means that the person was found at fault and has to pay monetary damages to the other party for any injuries or damage caused to his or her property. In a civil action between the parties over the automobile collision, the harmed party—the plaintiff—would invoke the civil law of negligence against the party alleged to have been at fault—the defendant.

liability
A jury's or judge's determination that one party is responsible for injuries to another party; the basis for an award of damages.

As will be discussed at length in a subsequent chapter, the civil law known as negligence permits redress for unintentional harm in cases in which the party alleged to have caused the harm acted without the proper care under the circumstances. The harmed party could elect not to file a civil lawsuit, perhaps if the parties decided to settle the matter before a lawsuit is filed in court. In either event, the government would not become involved, as this dispute is purely a civil matter between private parties.

In a criminal matter, the government, whether state or federal, becomes very much involved. In fact, the government occupies the same position as a plaintiff in a civil action. However, in criminal cases, the government acts as a prosecutor in the criminal proceeding. The person accused of having committed a crime is the defendant. The name of the prosecuting entity is used first in the title of a criminal case, followed by the defendant's name. Thus, a criminal proceeding brought against Mary Jones by the federal government would be entitled *United States v. Jones*. State criminal cases vary in name. Sometimes the prosecutor is called "People" or "State." States that regard themselves as "commonwealths" for mere historical reasons would name the case against Jones *Commonwealth v. Jones*.

The Differences in Civil and Criminal Cases

In both civil and criminal cases, the final outcome is known as a **judgment**. Strictly speaking, a judgment merely consists of a court-issued document stating the final result of a

judgment
The court's final decision regarding the rights and claims of the parties.

burden of proof
Standard for assessing the weight of the evidence.

preponderance of the evidence
The weight or level of persuasion of evidence needed to find the defendant liable as alleged by the plaintiff in a civil matter.

clear and convincing evidence
Having a high probability of truthfulness, a higher standard being preponderance of the evidence.

verdict
Decision of the jury following presentation of facts and application of relevant law as they relate to the law presented in the jury instructions.

beyond a reasonable doubt
The requirement for the level of proof in a criminal matter in order to convict or find the defendant guilty. It is a substantially higher and more-difficult-to-prove criminal matter standard.

alibi
A defense to a criminal proceeding stating the defendant was elsewhere when the alleged crime was committed.

case. Often, a judge's signature or a certification by the clerk of court appears on the document as an indication of the document's official entry in the court's file. In civil cases, the judgment consists of a finding that the defendant is liable or not liable to the plaintiff for either a certain amount of money or subject to a court order, such as an injunction. However, in a criminal case, a judgment states whether the defendant has been found guilty or not guilty of having committed the crime of which he or she was accused. Notice that the notion of innocence is absent. In criminal cases, a judgment entered against the defendant is followed by a punishment meted out by the government.

Judgments in either type of case, civil or criminal, come about as the result of the evidence submitted by the parties. The amount and quality of the evidence varies with the type of case. In civil cases, the plaintiff must prove that his or her version of what happened was more likely than not. Thus, the plaintiff must carry the **burden of proof** in civil cases to prove his or her version of the case by a **preponderance of the evidence**. In civil cases, there can be conflicting evidence, all from credible sources. However, the judge or the jury hearing the evidence needs only to determine which version was *more likely* when reaching a final conclusion regarding what they believe actually happened. Some civil cases, such as those alleging fraud, require proof according to a higher standard known as **clear and convincing evidence**. The difference between the two burdens of proof involves both the quantity and the quality of the evidence. Clear and convincing evidence convinces a judge or jury that the plaintiff's version was *substantially more likely than not*. A jury's finding, whether in a civil case or criminal case, is called a **verdict**, which becomes the basis for a judgment.

In criminal cases, the stakes for the defendant are much higher. With a guilty verdict, the judge may impose a fine, imprisonment, or worse on the defendant. For these reasons, the amount and quality of the evidence that the government must present to support a guilty verdict at a criminal trial is much greater than in civil cases. The government must carry the highest burden of proof, that is, **beyond a reasonable doubt**. Under this standard, the government must prove its case so convincingly and conclusively that there cannot be any reasonable possibility that the defendant is anything but guilty. If, for example, there is credible evidence that there is a mistaken identity or that the defendant had an **alibi**, proving that he or she was elsewhere when the crime was committed, there is the possibility for reasonable doubt. To many, the burden of proof creates a paradox in criminal trials. Ultimately, the trial is not about whether the defendant actually committed the crime but whether the government can prove the charges beyond a reasonable doubt. The distinction between civil and criminal law is easily discernible. However, the subcategories within each area of law can present a bewildering array of legal classifications.

Figure 4.1 summarizes the more salient distinctions between criminal and civil cases.

misdemeanor
A lesser crime punishable by less than a year in jail and/or a fine.

felony
A crime punishable by more than a year in prison or death.

element
The constituent parts of a crime or civil cause of action that must be proved by the prosecution or plaintiff to establish the defendant's liability.

Crimes and Their Variations

Certain laws describe crimes and what behavior constitutes punishable behavior. Crimes are almost always defined by statutes enacted by the legislature. Almost all criminal laws set up two levels of crimes: **misdemeanors** and **felonies**. Misdemeanors are crimes that involve offensive yet petty behavior, such as disorderly conduct or shoplifting, punishable by a small fine or imprisonment for less than a year. Felonies, such as robbery, drug trafficking, kidnapping, and murder, stand for a class of more serious crimes that are punishable by imprisonment for more than a year, together with a fine assessed by the court.

Court decisions often interpret criminal statutes in a fashion that may establish precedent as to how the criminal statutes should be read. However, the statutes themselves set out the elements of what constitutes a crime. An **element** is one of several items,

Type of Case	Parties	Legal Representative	Stakes	Standard of Proof	Result or Remedy
Criminal	Government vs. individual or business entity	Prosecutor vs. defense counsel	Punishment: Fine, imprisonment, or worse	Beyond a reasonable doubt	Guilty or not guilty (if trial held)
Civil	Individuals, business entities, or government	Plaintiff and defendant, each with own counsel	Money or court order, e.g., TRO	Preponderance of evidence, sometimes clear and convincing evidence	Judgment to pay plaintiff money or court order; judgment for defendant

FIGURE 4.1 **Distinctions Between Criminal and Civil Cases**

all of which the government (the **prosecution**) must prove in court to show that the defendant has committed the crime. By presenting sufficient evidence to support each and every element for a certain crime, the government has established what is known as a ***prima facie*** case. The failure to establish a *prima facie* case will result in a dismissal of the criminal case. However, if faced with a *prima facie* case, the defendant is obliged to offer his or her own evidence to counter the government's *prima facie* case. The defendant may do so in several different ways.

Initially, the defendant may present evidence that conflicts with the government's *prima facie* case. For instance, evidence as to a mistaken identity would attempt to show that the defendant had been confused with the actual perpetrator. Other evidence to counter the government's case might attack the credibility of the government's witnesses or the authenticity of a piece of evidence. When a defendant offers no new facts and primarily disputes the government's *prima facie* case, it is known as a **rebuttal**. That is, the defendant is not presenting any explanation or excuse that is recognized by the law. The defendant's case merely rebuts the government's proof, thereby attempting to establish reasonable doubt and nothing more.

More **defenses** are available to a defendant in the form of a legally recognized justification or excuse that presents evidence that can establish additional facts. For example, an alibi attempts to prove that the defendant was elsewhere by presenting additional evidence to prove that fact. The type and quantity of proof required to establish an alibi is also prescribed by criminal laws, known as defenses. Other types of defenses to crimes constitute a form of justification, such as self-defense or insanity. Both of these types of defenses do not dispute the fact that the defendant may have committed the offense. However, the law recognizes the right to take measures of self-protection and that a person of insufficient mental capacity should not be held responsible for his or her acts. Thus, the law offers what are known as **affirmative defenses** to allow criminal defendants to either negate the criminal act or show that they did not have the requisite intent to commit the crime.

Most crimes require the government to prove, as an essential element of a *prima facie* case, that the defendant possessed the intent or ***mens rea*** to commit the crime. Like the statutes that define crimes themselves, criminal statutes also define crimes in terms of required acts and required states of mind, or "intent" to commit the crime. Thus, the prosecution must convince a judge or jury that the defendant had intended to violate the criminal statute. For example, in most states, the crime of assault and battery is committed when one person (1) tries to or does physically strike another, (2) with the intent (*mens rea*) to cause fear of harm or offensive physical contact. Once the government has presented sufficient proof to support both elements, the government has established a *prima facie* case.

A defendant accused of assault and battery would then have the choice of disproving the government's case (rebuttal). Alternatively, the defendant may wish to show

prosecution
Attorney representing the people or plaintiff in criminal matters.

prima facie
(Latin) "At first sight." A case with the required proof of elements in a tort cause of action; the elements of the plaintiff's (or prosecutor's) cause of action; what the plaintiff must prove; accepted on its face, but not indisputable.

rebuttal
Refutes or contradicts evidence presented by the opposing side.

defense
Legally sufficient reasons to excuse the complained-of behavior.

affirmative defense
An "excuse" by the opposing party that does not just simply negate the allegation, but puts forth a legal reason to avoid enforcement. These defenses are waived if not pleaded.

mens rea
"A guilty mind"; criminal intent in committing the act.

mistaken identity through evidence by establishing an alibi. Using an affirmative defense, the defendant could show the physical act was done in self-defense, meaning he or she was in fear of imminent physical harm and took action to defend him- or herself. Finally, the defendant could show that he or she did not possess the requisite *mens rea* by proving that the touching was accidental, occurred while the defendant was insane, or took place with the victim's consent. Thus, criminal statutes define the crime—behavior that is offensive to the state—and allow for legally recognized excuses for such behavior. The government must address the elements of the crime, and the defendant has the opportunity to rebut or offer an excuse recognized by law.

cause of action
A personal, financial, or other injury for which the law gives a person the right to receive compensation.

damages
Money paid to compensate for loss or injury.

remedy
The means by which a court, in the exercise of civil law jurisdiction, enforces a right, imposea penalty, or makes some other court order.

COMMUNICATION TIP

Throughout your legal studies, you will be acquiring a whole new vocabulary in legal terminology. To laypersons, these terms are often meaningless legalese. However, to a coworker in the law office, legal terms have precise meanings and are, like all forms of technical terms, a shorthand way of conveying information. Nothing betrays a novice in law more than the careless use of legal terminology. By taking care in using this newly acquired vocabulary, you will be able to communicate effectively with other legal professionals.

The Nature of Civil Cases

Civil cases follow the same pattern. Instead of a criminal statute that prescribes the elements of a crime, the elements for civil cases traditionally derive from common law or court decisions. More recently, statutes have become a major source of law to prescribe the elements necessary to prove in civil actions. Instead of constituting a crime, the elements of a civil matter make up a **cause of action** or claim for relief. Whether prompted by statute or common law, lawsuits invoking civil law are private disputes. The government may also appear in the lawsuit as one of the parties, either the plaintiff or defendant. However, the government stands on an equal footing with private parties in civil matters. Like any other party to a civil lawsuit, the government seeks to redress or acts to defend against a civil lawsuit.

Civil wrongs differ from crimes, in that the nature of the injury alleged in a civil case is a private concern. Crimes are offenses to society at large, whereas civil wrongs are usually not of public or governmental concern. Both crimes and civil wrongs can arise from the same set of facts. The act of committing the crime of assault and battery may result in the filing of criminal proceedings by the government against the perpetrator, the defendant. The same act of assault and battery could also constitute a civil wrong against the victim, who could proceed as a plaintiff against the same defendant in a civil proceeding.

As in criminal cases, a civil case consists of any number of elements, depending upon the type of case. Similarly, a plaintiff who has submitted enough evidence regarding each element in a civil case has established a *prima facie* case. The defendant in the civil action may offer counterevidence to rebut the plaintiff's *prima facie* case or negate it by proving any number of affirmative defenses available, depending on the cause of action. For instance, the crime and the civil cause of action for assault and battery may be countered by the defendant in both types of cases with the affirmative defense of self-defense.

For every civil cause of action available to plaintiffs, there are various affirmative defenses possibly available to the civil defendant. As in criminal cases, affirmative defenses in civil cases are forms of legal recognition or justification for the defendant's action. In some cases, the affirmative defense acts as a shield that reflects social policy. For instance, a contract to perform an illegal act could not be enforced by a civil action because of social policy prohibiting illegal behavior. Thus, a bet or wager is a contract that is unenforceable by a civil action in states that prohibit gambling.

As mentioned previously, the biggest differences between criminal and civil proceedings are, of course, the consequences. A criminal conviction may result in a fine, a term of imprisonment, or worse. In civil actions, a judgment may take on many different forms. People sue each other usually for **damages**—a term that generally describes judgments that award money to the victor or prevailing party. In civil lawsuits, there are a variety of monetary damages as well as nonmonetary judgments. In formal legal parlance, the judgments sought by parties to a lawsuit are known as forms of relief. You can now see why a legal basis for a civil lawsuit is known as a claim for relief. A form of relief is also known as **remedy**.

In civil actions, these forms of relief or remedies break down into two classifications known as legal relief or **equitable relief**. These classifications come to us as a result of historical developments. The classification between law and equity, often characterized as the difference between monetary damages (legal remedies) and court orders (equitable remedies), is actually far more complex. In England, the interest afforded the highest legal protection was land ownership, and then personal possessions, usually family heirlooms. For that reason, large estates remained within certain families for many centuries. Thus, the King's Court could grant a writ of ejectment, which ordered someone to leave or vacate the plaintiff's land. Although the writ of ejectment does not necessarily involve a monetary award, it was considered a legal remedy in the King's Court of Law. The same is true of the writ of replevin, by which the King's Court of Law ordered the return of a possession or heirloom to its rightful owner. With these minor exceptions, the King's Court otherwise granted monetary awards to the prevailing party.

equitable relief
A remedy that is other than money damages, such as refraining from or performing a certain act; nonmonetary remedies fashioned by the court using standards of fairness and justice. Injunction and specific performance are types of equitable relief.

Today, there are three types of monetary damages that may be awarded in a lawsuit: **Compensatory damages** are awarded for the actual loss suffered by the plaintiff. The concept is that the award is intended to compensate for the loss suffered by the plaintiff as a result of the defendant's civil wrongdoing. Thus, the award of compensatory damages restores the plaintiff back to the position he or she was in before the defendant's wrongdoing. This remedy is known as making the plaintiff "whole." There are two subcategories of compensatory damages. **Special damages** consist of lost wages or earning potential, medical expenses, property damage, and out-of-pocket expenses. Then there are **general damages** that compensate for harm for which only a subjective value may be attached. General damages would include pain, physical suffering, emotional trauma or suffering, disfigurement, loss of spousal companionship, loss of reputation, loss or impairment of mental or physical capacity, and loss of enjoyment of life.

compensatory damages
A payment to make up for a wrong committed and return the nonbreaching party to a position where the effect or the breach has been neutralized.

special damages
Those damages incurred beyond and in addition to the general damages suffered and expected in similar cases.

general damages
Those that normally would be anticipated in a similar action.

Punitive damages penalize or make an example of particularly offensive behavior by a defendant. Also known as exemplary damages, such awards are meant to make an example of the defendant as a deterrent to others. Punitive or exemplary damages are awarded only in special cases in which the conduct was especially oppressive or egregiously invidious, and they are over and above the amount of compensatory damage. Finally, there are **incidental** or **nominal damages**, which award a successful plaintiff only a token amount of damages, usually $1. Even though the plaintiff has won, the award of nominal damages represents a vindication of the plaintiff's claim, as well as disapproval of the defendant's conduct. However, due to the lack of provable loss, the plaintiff awarded nominal damages has won the war but gained only a Pyrrhic victory.

punitive damages
An amount of money awarded to a nonbreaching party that is not based on the actual losses incurred by that party, but as a punishment to the breaching party for the commission of an intentional wrong.

incidental or nominal damages
Damages resulting from the breach that are related to the breach but not necessarily directly foreseeable by the breaching party.

CYBER TRIP

Punitive damages have generated controversy. On the Internet, view the debate by visiting the following sites:

1. www.atra.org/show/7343
2. www.law.upenn.edu/bll/archives/ulc/mpda/MPDAFNAL.htm
3. www.acsblog.org/economic-regulation-employment-leading-conservative-activist-seeks-punitive-damages.html

What position do you take on punitive damages?

CASE IN POINT

PUNITIVE DAMAGES AWARDED FOR OUTRAGEOUS CONDUCT

DIXON V. INT'L BROTHERHOOD OF POLICE OFFICERS, 2007 U.S. APP. LEXIS 22891 (1ST CIR. 2007)

At the age of 23 years, Vanessa Dixon joined the Lowell Police Department in 1994, when there were fewer than 10 female police officers in a force of nearly 300. Early evaluations of her work were extremely positive, and she received special awards from her unit for her work with young people.

The day Dixon joined the police department, she automatically joined the police officers' union, the International Brotherhood of Police Officers ("IBPO"). On October 26, 1998, Dixon joined seven of her fellow officers and six corrections officers on a hired bus to travel to Boston for a union event. She was the only woman on the trip, other than the bus driver. From the outset of the trip, Dixon was subjected to gender-based criticisms by the other officers regarding what she was wearing and her presence on an all-male trip. John Leary—a police officer whom Dixon had once dated and who was sitting directly across the aisle from her—started yelling at Dixon. The shouting escalated as other people at the back of the bus joined in. The comments, directed at Dixon and a male police officer, turned offensively sexual. The male officer described the barrage as "totally inappropriate conversation, verbally abusive, threatening." Throughout all of this, the president of the local union did not intervene to stop the abuse or try to reassure Dixon when she wanted to flee.

On November 20, the very next day, Leary sought and received a temporary restraining order ("TRO") against Dixon. Leary alleged that Dixon had made threatening comments to him the evening of the bus incident. He did not explain why he had waited a month to seek protection from Dixon in the form of a TRO. Leary knew the TRO would have the result, under department policy and Massachusetts law, of forcing the police department to put Dixon on administrative leave and confiscate her weapon while the TRO was in effect. Although Dixon hired a lawyer and went to court to deny the allegations, Leary never returned to court to support his TRO or seek continued protection, allowing the TRO to expire after its initial 15-day coverage. Dixon testified she was humiliated when she had to explain her month-long absence, caused by the TRO, to the teachers, students, and parents with whom she worked at Rogers Middle School. Because of the TRO, she had to get special permission to renew her firearms permit, and she also avoided participating in outreach programs that required a background check.

After a number of other incidents, Dixon brought suit in October 2001 in the District of Massachusetts alleging discrimination and retaliation under both state and federal statutes, as well as assault, intentional infliction of emotional distress, and defamation. After an 11-day jury trial in the fall of 2005, the jury found for Dixon on the discrimination and retaliation claims. In addition to compensatory damage awards totaling $1,205,000, the jury awarded punitive damages of $1,000,000. The defendants appealed.

In affirming the award of both compensatory damages as well as punitive damages, the Court of Appeals noted that punitive damages may be awarded for conduct that is outrageous, because of the defendant's evil motive or reckless indifference to the rights of others. Vanessa Dixon has since left the police force and now teaches Criminal Justice at Middlesex Community College in Lowell, Massachusetts.

QUESTIONS ABOUT THE CASE

1. Do you think that the verdict was justified in this case?
2. What social policy aims are met by the award of punitive damages?
3. Why was this lawsuit brought to federal court? What was the basis for the federal court's jurisdiction?

injunctive relief
Court order to cease or commence an action following a petition to enter such an order upon showing of irreparable harm resulting from the failure to enforce the relief requested.

temporary restraining order (TRO)
A court order barring a person from harassing or harming another.

Equitable relief, steeped in religious and canonical traditions, varies greatly in the forms of relief available. The most prevalent forms are **injunctive relief**, or court orders commanding a party to the lawsuit to cease and desist from a certain activity. Modern-day variations of these injunctions include **temporary restraining orders** that occur frequently in domestic relations matters. In most cases that request injunctive relief, a court order may come in three stages. First, the court may grant a temporary restraining order at the outset of the action. Second, usually 10 days afterward, a court may grant a preliminary injunction, which will last during the pendency of the lawsuit. Third, there is the permanent injunction, which constitutes the final judgment of the lawsuit. Originally, common law courts fashioned these forms of equitable relief to protect landowners. Use of one's land was thus within the jurisdication of equity courts that became authorized to issue orders of abatement against a landowner who was using his or her property in a way that interfered with neighbors' use of their land.

Legal Remedies	Compensatory—Monetary Damages	Losses recognized
	Special Damages	Earnings potential Medical expenses Property damage
	General Damages	Pain and suffering Reputation Trauma Physical or mental capacity
	Punitive or Exemplary Damages	To punish extreme behavior
Ejectment		Orders trespassers off land
Replevin		Orders return of personal property
Equitable Remedies	Injunctive Relief	Types
		Temporary restraining order Preliminary injunction Permanent injunction Abatement—land use
	Contract Remedies	Specific performance Rescission Reformation

FIGURE 4.2 Remedies in Civil Actions

In actions for breaches of contracts, equity can play a large part in fashioning various non-monetary remedies for the wronged party in a transaction that has gone sour. A court sitting in equity may have a party perform its obligations under the contract by issuing an order for **specific performance**, particularly if the object of the transaction involves real estate or a unique object. If there has been a mutual misunderstanding as to the contract terms, a court may issue the equitable remedy of **rescission**, which nullifies the contract. In other cases, a court may order **reformation**, altering the contract to conform to the legal principles of fairness or justice.

specific performance
A court order that requires a party to perform a certain act in order to prevent harm to the requesting party.

rescission
A decision by the court that renders the contract null and void and requires the parties to return to the wronged party any benefits received under the agreement.

reformation
An order of the court that "rewrites" the agreement to reflect the actual performances of the parties where there has been some deviation from the contractual obligation; changed or modified by agreement; that is, the contracting parties mutually agree to restructure a material element of the original agreement.

To invoke the equity court's powers, a plaintiff needs to show that the available remedies at law (monetary damages, ejectment, or replevin) are insufficient and provide inadequate relief for a particular injury. Thus, the imposition of equitable relief applies to situations for which there is a showing of uniqueness or compelling need. Nevertheless, because of its overarching nature as the conscience of the law, equity touches every aspect of civil law. Figure 4.2 summarizes the available remedies or forms of relief in civil actions.

Civil Law: Substantive Subject Areas

Today, civil law covers an enormously vast area and grows with the passage of each new legislative year. Civil law is more ample and complex than criminal law. Beginning with the common law decisions from England, civil law has continued to expand through judicial decisions as well. Three major areas of law have provided the original sources for the branching areas of civil law. They are **property law**, contract law, and torts. From these three subject areas, almost all of Anglo-American civil law has developed. In future chapters, we will discuss these areas of law, among others, in great depth.

property law
Rights a person may own or be entitled to own, including personal and real property.

Property Law

Property law consists of rules regarding the ownership of land and personal possessions, which includes modern forms of property, such as shares of stock, patents, and copyrights. Land as a primary interest was afforded high protection under English law. Thus, property rules have taken on significant meaning in American law. Property law breaks down into two types of property. Land and those items that were intended to be attached permanently to the land are called fixtures. Thus, buildings and other permanent items, or fixtures, on the land are governed by the law regarding **real property**. Anything else that is not land or affixed to it is covered by the rules for **personal property**, which is also referred to as personalty or chattels. Caution must be taken, for the rules of property law are different depending on the type of property involved. With the growth of corporations and technology, personal property also includes **intangible property** for the legal protection of property interests in songs, computer programs, shares of stock, inventions, and financial instruments, all of which are ideas—that is, things that we cannot touch and therefore are, for obvious reasons, called intangible.

real property
Land and all property permanently attached to it, such as buildings.

personal property
Movable or intangible thing not attached to real property.

intangible property
Personal property that has no physical presence but is represented by a certificate or some other instrument, such as stocks or trademarks.

Property law also covers how interests in property are transferred. For instance, property law employs the common law concept of **title**. A person who owns a certain property, in whatever form, as a matter of law, also has title. Title is transferred to another through transactions that require certain formalities for the new owner to gain title and therefore legal ownership. Transactions such as gifts, sales contracts, and inheritance are just a few of the types of ways that transfer title. **Possession** is another concept in property that overlaps title yet often imparts different meanings. Possession applies to both land and personalty. Probably the most utilized, and certainly the most important, common law writ was for **trespass**, by which the true title holder of the property was able to enforce the most important aspect of property ownership: the legal ability to exclude others from the possession or use of property.

title
The legal link between a person who owns property and the property itself; legal evidence of a person's ownership rights.

possession
Having or holding property in one's power; controlling something to the exclusion of others.

trespass
Intentional and unlawful entry onto or interference with the land of another person without consent.

A person may have or be in possession, and even have use of, the property in question but not have title. Common examples of these scenarios include legally defined situations, such a leases or a bailment. In a lease of an apartment or a car, the lessee is paying for the legal right to use the property that the lessor owns and for which it has title. The lessee has the right of possession but does not have title. Property law rules govern the rights and obligations of the lessee and lessor with respect to each other and their relationship to the property.

A bailment is a similar situation but covered by different property law rules. Like a lease, a bailment is a legal relationship created when a person gives property to someone else. However, the person receiving the property does not have the right to use the property but is responsible for the property's care or safekeeping. Checking your coat at a restaurant or a museum or parking your car in a lot or garage may create a bailment in which you are the bailor, and the person or entity receiving the item is the bailee. The property law governing bailments imposes the obligation of taking care of the property upon the bailee. Thus, many coat checkrooms and parking garages will take steps to disclaim a bailment situation by notifying you that they are not responsible for any damage on the receipt or a sign or a written contract. Whether the law will still impose the obligation of care if the property is damaged will depend upon the circumstances. Nevertheless, you can see that the awareness of impact of property laws affects how people view the relationships created by the law. Ultimately, property laws classify property and provide for rules that describe our relationships to various forms of property.

Contract Law

Common law provided for a means to enforce a **contract**. Originally, contracts consisted merely of the undertaking of a promise. In early common law, promises were considered, at times, solemn undertakings that required enforcement as a matter of moral or ethical compulsion. However, with the rise of mercantilism and trade among the European nations, the idea of enforcing a mere promise without a mutual undertaking

contract
A legally binding agreement between two or more parties.

from the other side became obsolete. The legal elements necessary for the creation of enforceable contracts included the notion of a bargained exchange in which there was both give and take on both sides. Soon, the idea that contracts should be supported by notions of benefit and detriment from both of the parties engaged resulted in the requirement of **consideration**, or the exchange of value from both sides, as an essential element to the formation of all enforceable contracts.

consideration
An essential element of a contract consisting of a benefit or right for each of the contracting parties.

Contract law also required that the parties understood that they had indeed entered into a form of enforceable agreement, the terms to which they had agreed. The existence of an offer and acceptance also became necessary elements to the formation of a contract. Social policy concerns then came into play, so that persons of tender age or impaired mental capacity could not legally enter into contracts. Larger social policy issues also propelled the development of contract law from its common law origins. If you think about it, enforceable and cohesive contract laws are essential for trade and economic growth. If contracts were not defined by the law and could not be enforced, few would enter into business agreements. Business depends on the law's backing to be able to engage in trading and exchanges, which are the entire basis for businesses. Enforceable transactions such as extending credit, installment sales, and secured interests have given birth to commonplace devices we now take for granted, such as credit cards, mortgages, and layaway plans. Contract law is an outgrowth of a law and economics point of view. Allowing for the enforceability of contract agreements, contract law has contributed much to society's economic development.

Torts

Torts is the third of the big three areas of civil law that evolved from property law concepts. The writ of trespass was a common law remedy for the civil law violation of a person's property rights. Later, the common law courts needed to invent another writ to cover cases in which the issue was not possession or ownership of property but damage done to a person's property, including his or her physical being and reputation. The writ of trespass was developed to cover almost any wrongful damage done to a person's body, land, or personal property and, later, feelings. Now, this writ is known as a **tort**, a civil law cause of action to remedy an injury. Torts include a wide variety of civil law situations known as actionable wrongs. Unless the situation directly involves property or a contract, chances are that it is covered by tort law. Today, tort law has grown so extensively that some ideas from torts have spilled over into property and contract law.

tort
A civil wrongful act, committed against a person or property, either intentional or negligent.

Torts are divided into intentional torts, unintentional torts, and strict liability torts. Intentional torts involve actionable wrongs such as assault and battery, discussed previously. Defamation, fraud, and invasion of privacy are other forms of intentional torts in which the person committing the wrong, known as the **tortfeasor**, intended to do the harm. Such cases are actually rare in comparison to the unintentional torts, or negligence.

tortfeasor
Actor committing the wrong, whether intentional, negligent, or strict liability.

Unintentional torts, or negligence cases, make up the largest number of tort cases filed each year in the United States. As a subdivision of tort law, negligence consists of cases involving injury caused by accidents. Accidents result from the unreasonable behavior of the tortfeasor. By unreasonable, we mean that the tortfeasor did not exercise due care under the circumstances, whether it was the failure to stop at a red light or to use the proper materials in the construction of a building. The failure to use reasonable care constitutes a breach of that duty that was the cause of the injury suffered by the plaintiff. That connection is known as proximate cause. Thus, negligence has been defined as the lack of due care, which causes an injury.

Strict liability cases are torts of relatively recent creation. Strict liability cases are civil causes of action against the tortfeasor, who is engaged in an unreasonably or inherently dangerous activity. The concept of strict liability may also apply to manufacturers of products that cause injury. For either situation, the plaintiff does not have to show that the defendant was negligent. The doctrine of strict liability reflects social policy concerns over product safety and public protection from unreasonable harm. Thus, the use of explosives or radioactive materials or keeping of wild animals are examples of inherently dangerous activities for which an injured plaintiff need not show that the defendant was negligent. Similarly, for cases in which an injury results from a defective product, the plaintiff need not show that the defendant manufacturer was negligent.

The legal doctrine of strict liability furthers the social policy concerns of protecting the public from harm and encourages manufacturers to test their products rigorously. From a law and economics point of view, the strict liability doctrine balances the harm suffered by the plaintiff against any hardship to the defendant or manufacturer. By placing the economic burden on the manufacturer to compensate the injured plaintiff, the law places the responsibility on the party economically more able to absorb the costs. Placing the economic costs on the manufacturer actually passes the costs onto other consumers in the form of higher prices. As such, the manufacturer becomes the insurer of consumers who are injured by its defective products, with premiums paid by consumers.

SUBSTANTIVE LAW AND PROCEDURAL RULES

Beyond the major classifications of property, contract, and tort, other civil matters include constitutional law, domestic relations, bankruptcy, corporations, tax, and numerous other legal topics. In fact, the several types of civil law greatly outnumber criminal law. Civil laws are more pervasive because the scope of legal regulation covers almost every aspect of American life. Criminal law, in contrast, deals with a smaller but nonetheless significant aspect of human activity. Yet one constant classification shared by both criminal and civil law consists of the division between the laws that directly affect our lives and activities and the rules designed to enforce or pursue those laws.

substantive law
Legal rules that are the content or substance of the law, defining rights and duties of citizens.

procedural law
The set of rules that are used to enforce the substantive law.

Substantive laws are those laws that declare our rights, duties, and obligations. Our review of criminal law and of the several classifications of civil law present some examples of substantive laws. **Procedural laws**, however, cover the manner in which the legal system operates. Procedural rules also may be considered the rules of the game. That is, for a criminal or civil action to proceed, parties to either type of proceeding must follow procedural rules to enforce their rights under the substantive law.

Procedural rules may greatly affect substantive rights. The statute of limitations governs the time during which an action may be filed in court, whether civil or criminal. In civil cases, the time limitations to file a lawsuit for certain types of cases vary greatly from state to state. Tort actions must be filed in court within one year or up to three years depending on the type of tort. Lawsuits concerning contract matters are generally for longer periods, from four to six years. Lawsuits over property ownership have the longest statute of limitations period, some extending for more than ten years.

Although all civil causes of action are held to the statute of limitations, some crimes do not have a statute of limitations. Misdemeanors and many felonies have a three- to seven-year statute of limitations, which begins to run when the crime is either committed or discovered. Some other felonies do not have any statutes of limitations at all. Crimes such as arson, murder, and war crimes are too heinous for society to forget. However, the basic philosophy underlying statutes of limitations is known as one of repose, meaning that statutes of limitations provide closure or finality. After all, time is the great healer, and society will eventually forgive and forget. As a practical matter, statutes of limitations make sense, because over time, memories fade, evidence is lost or never found, and people prefer to get past these events and get on with their lives.

Other types of procedural rules include the rules of court procedure. In 1938, Congress enacted the Federal Rules of Civil Procedure (FRCP), a comprehensive modernization of the rules used in all the federal courts in the country. After years of in-depth study and debate by a national commission of legal experts, the adoption of FRCP for the federal court system represented a milestone in court reform. Prior to their adoption, the federal courts had been mired in hypertechnical rules that had much to do with common law forms of writs and the division between law and equity. However, these ancient procedural rules had little regard for fairness or the efficient administration of justice. With the advent of the new FRCP, law and equity were merged, and clear, succinct rules streamlined the progression of cases through the federal courts. Since 1938, almost all of the states' court systems have, with some variations, adopted the FRCP as a model for procedural rules in civil cases.

In criminal law, procedural rules play an entirely different role. Because of the severe consequences that may result and society's keen interest in maintaining public safety, criminal procedure stands sharply apart from its civil counterpart. You will recall that the burden of proof is much more strenuous in criminal cases than in civil cases. Moreover, the prominent role of the United States Constitution in criminal cases gives rise to complex issues such as the Fifth Amendment privilege against self-incrimination and other rights, as you will see later. There are also other important principles, such as the Fourth Amendment right against unreasonable search and seizure, and a host of other Constitutional issues. In fact, criminal procedure is a subject that is taught in law schools as a separate, upper-level course because of the highly specialized nature of the procedural rules involved in criminal cases.

THE HIERARCHY OF LEGAL LITERATURE

With the publication of court opinions and the enactment of new statutes every year, all 50 states and the federal government produce vast amounts of legal information. This information accumulates and builds on itself because of the tradition of precedent. In the last chapter, we described the various sources of law and described their nature and effect. We also noted that assembled together, these materials fall into a hierarchy of what is known as legal authority. By authority, we mean that these sources of law have binding effect and are the basis for decisions by courts and, more generally, behavior in our society. That hierarchy consists of an order in which these sources of legal authority should be followed. We already understand that federal law preempts or supersedes state law. Thus, sources of federal law, or federal legal authority, is almost always above state law. At the same time, both realms mirror the other in their types of legal authority. Moreover, the federal and state systems have identical regard for sources of law, in the following order of importance:

Constitution
  Statutes & Treaties
    Administrative Regulations
      Court Opinions

Court opinions actually occupy a unique position in the constellation of legal authority. Under our system of checks and balances, the courts interpret the statutes enacted by the legislature and signed into law by the executive (president or state governor). Because of the practice of using precedent, court opinions become an important source of law, particularly because of the common law traditions that were imported to the United States

CASE IN POINT

CASE SUMMARY

MARBURY V. MADISON, 5 U.S. 137 (1803)

The idea that a court's interpretation of a constitution or statute is binding on the other branches of government is known as judicial review. The power to act as the last word also includes the power to declare federal (and state) laws unconstitutional and therefore unenforceable. Events taking place early in the country's history shaped the way our legal system functions today. In the case of *Marbury v. Madison*, 5 U.S. 137 (1803), one of the most important decisions in American legal history, the United States Supreme Court established the idea of judicial review.

In 1800, the Jeffersonian Republicans defeated the Federalists and gained control of the Congress and the presidency. Outgoing Federalist President John Adams granted William Marbury a "midnight" appointment as Justice of the Peace in the last days of the presidential term. Upon gaining control, the Jeffersonians attempted to block Adams's judgeship appointments to spread their influence over the judiciary as well. Even though the outgoing Federalist-controlled Senate had approved Marbury's appointment, the commission for his judgeship remained undelivered.

Marbury sued the new Jeffersonian Secretary of State, James Madison, claiming that Madison was unlawfully withholding the commission, bringing his case directly to the U.S. Supreme Court, as allowed by a section of the Judiciary Act of 1789. John Marshall, a Federalist whom Adams had been appointed Chief Justice of the Court, foresaw that the Jeffersonians would ignore a court order in Marbury's favor. In doing so, the newly established Supreme Court's authority would be severely weakened as a coequal branch of government. Yet, at the same time, ruling against Marbury would make it appear that the Court was fearful of the new Congress and president. Either way, Marshall felt that the rule of law would be subverted.

In *Marbury v. Madison*, Marshall ruled that Marbury was entitled to the commission as a matter of law. However, Marshall also ruled that the section of the Judiciary Act that Marbury was proceeding under was an unconstitutional grant of power by Congress, because it allowed the Court to act beyond the powers granted to it under Article III of the Constitution. In doing so, Marshall censured the Jeffersonians as having acted illegally and maintained the dignity of the Court and the rule of law.

Historians and legal scholars have praised the decision as a brilliant maneuver out from a sticky spot. By saying that the Court did not have power to decide, Marshall's decision actually invested the Court with greater power. Marshall firmly established the power of the Supreme Court as the final arbiter of the meaning of the Constitution—a role that has since been respected by everyone.

The Court did not declare another act of Congress unconstitutional until 1857 and has rarely exercised its power to do so. Nevertheless, Marshall's decision established the Supreme Court as a true coequal branch of government. Later, the Court's power to act as the last word on Constitutional issues became the basis for declaring our fundamental rights.

QUESTIONS ABOUT THE CASE

1. What role does judicial review play in our governmental system of checks and balances?
2. Do you think that the Supreme Court should have the last word on how the Constitution should be interpreted?
3. Do you think that the Supreme Court should have the power to declare fundamental rights?

from England. Under common law tradition, the courts wielded considerable power in pronouncing the law as they saw fit. Even in their interpretations of statutes passed by Parliament, Congress, or a state legislature, common law courts have ended up having the final say when they apply the laws. As a result, many believe that much of our law comes to us as the result of court opinions. This belief is why judicial appointments to the U.S. Supreme Court and even state supreme courts can generate great public controversy.

What made court opinions unique in the grand scheme of things was, again, the historical development of the judicial branch. Although the court opinions appear at the bottom of all the sources of law, a court's power to make binding interpretations of constitutions and statutes commands the attention of the legal universe. The power of precedent that comes from the common law traditions we inherited from England has kept court opinions at the forefront regarding the status of a law. The meaning of any part of a constitution or a statute first comes from its own language. However, even though the meaning may be clear, a court may have something to say about that constitution or statute.

When a court has published an opinion in a case involving a constitutional provision or statute, the precedential value of the opinion affects how the statute should be interpreted in future cases. This value also applies to the way that courts interpret treaties and administrative regulations. Thus, a professionally competent technique of researching the law means reading the constitutional, statutory, or regulatory provision involved, and then seeing if any court has published an opinion that interpreted the provision. All of these sources of law—constitutions, statutes, treaties, regulations, and court opinions—declare the law and indeed are the law incarnate, so to speak. As such, they are all are referred to as **primary authority**. Primary authority is the law itself.

primary authority
The original text of the sources of law, such as constitutions, court opinions, statutes, and administrative rules and regulations.

Another form of legal materials may pertain to a source of primary authority or even to legal philosophy. Known as **secondary authority**, materials such as legal encyclopedias, legal dictionaries, scholarly works including treatises and law review articles, and even legal trade magazines, just to name a few types, have some weight as a form of legal authority. The biggest difference between primary and secondary authority is that secondary authority is not binding. Usually, the authors of secondary authority are respected practitioners, judges, scholars, and even law teachers, such as the one teaching you this course. Oftentimes, secondary authority is regarded as a source of information about what the law ought to be, as in a discussion of jurisprudence.

secondary authority
Authority that analyzes the law such as a treatise, encyclopedia, or law review article.

Secondary authority can also help a researcher learn about an unfamiliar area of law. Legal encyclopedias and treatises are materials that teach the reader, whether the reader is a student, practitioner, or judge. Legal encyclopedias explain the law in a general manner and may provide highly specific details, depending on the depth of a certain publication. Most encyclopedias consist of several volumes. Treatises usually cover one specific topic in the law. There are treatises for every area of the law, from admiralty (law of the sea) to zoning, usually written by a law professor or prominent practitioner in the field of their specialty. There are also law review articles that are published by law schools. A dozen or more varieties of secondary authority exist. Some are scholarly in their approach, whereas others are practical and expository. Again, because of the respect accorded to experts and academics, treatises, like other sources of secondary authority, may be highly influential or even forceful but certainly are not binding upon a court, which may feel free to adopt or ignore their ideas.

For the practitioner, secondary authority has some highly practical uses. When confronted with primary authority that runs against your client's situation, you might be able to find some secondary authority that criticizes the primary authority and suggests a change. Citing such secondary authority may make a good showing on behalf of your client in the face of adversity from existing primary authority. Thus, scholarly or expert opinions provided in treatises may persuade a court to find exceptions or even a new path. By the same token, the persuasiveness of secondary authority may serve the purpose of bolstering a legal position that already has the backing of primary authority, lending greater credibility and demonstrating a rock-solid position.

EYE ON ETHICS

Look up the ABA Model Rules of Professional Conduct, Rule 3.1, at www.abanet.org/cpr/mrpc/mrpc_toc.html. Is it a violation of the ethical rules to argue a legal position that is contrary to existing law? You will see that Rule 3.1 permits a legal professional to make a good faith argument to modify, extend, or even abandon existing law. In this way, the ethical rules permit legal professionals to advocate changes in the law. However, the same rule guards against taking a position that is frivolous or groundless.

FIGURE 4.3
Classification of Primary and Secondary Authority

Source	Primary Authority	Secondary Authority
	Constitutions	Legal encyclopedias
	Statutes	Treatises
	Regulations	Law review articles
	Court opinions	Legal periodicals

Certainly in the absence of primary authority on a certain point of law—and it happens frequently—using secondary authority may convince a judge to rule in your favor. Finally, secondary authority is highly useful as an educational tool. If unfamiliar with an area of law, a legal encyclopedia or a treatise can instruct a newbie within a relatively short amount of time. Moreover, the wide range of available encyclopedias and treatises provide the practitioner with various ways to self-educate, either in great detail or as a general overview. Figure 4.3 summarizes the classifications of primary and secondary authority.

COURT OPINIONS

Reading Court Opinions

Since their inception in England hundreds of years ago, published court opinions have been the bedrock of the common law system, as an essential if not central element of the tradition of precedent. As judges made law, court opinions have established themselves as not only the major source for law but also the essential explicator of the law. You will recall that the primary purpose of issuing a court opinion is to resolve the dispute before the court. Thus, court opinions are issued only on a case-by-case basis. They differ from legislative acts (statutes), in that the opinions give an explanation for the decision to the parties and their lawyers. The opinion uses a form of logic known as legal reasoning or **rationale** that is carefully examined by the parties (particularly the losing party) to see if the trial court made appropriate findings of fact and applied the correct legal principles in the correct fashion. Not all cases decided by a court result in an opinion, and not all court opinions get published. In fact, only a minuscule percentage of court cases appear in publications. Most cases are so mundane or offer so little by way of legal reasoning that an opinion or publication is not necessary or even helpful.

rationale
Stated reasoning by a court's ruling.

Court opinions that are published usually come from appellate courts, that is, the intermediate appellate courts and the highest courts. The federal system and some states also publish opinions from their trial courts. Ohio and Connecticut officially publish a few trial court opinions. New York is the only state that regularly publishes opinions of its trial courts as a matter of policy and practice. However, by and large, the opinions from the intermediate appellate courts and highest courts of the states and the federal system command the most attention and are regarded as one of the most important forms of law making. Thus, the decision to publish the opinion in a given case depends on the issues presented and the precedential value of the case. Whether an opinion should be published depends on several factors, such as the overall importance of the case or whether the case offers a new direction or modification to existing law, among other factors.

We understand that the precedent created by published court opinions constitutes a form of law and therefore primary authority. The law created by court opinions contrasts sharply with the sources of law created by other branches of government. As discussed, court opinions function to resolve a dispute between the parties before it, as well as explain how the law applies to that particular dispute. Thus, when a court issues an opinion designated for publication, law has been made. At that moment, the legal world, or at least part of it, pauses to examine the explanation or the court's rationale, because the decision will become precedent-setting law, to be followed in future cases with similar facts. Keep in mind that the precedent created by court-made law is confined to the facts of the case. Often, the facts of a particular case shape the law that is ultimately created by the court's opinion.

The biggest difference between law declared by legislative statutes and the law made by courts is the specific context of court decisions. As we noted, the rule of law made by court opinions is restricted to the facts presented in the controversy, whereas the law made by legislatures in a statute covers a wide range of general situations. Thus, when a court is deciding a case that involves a statute, or even a common law principle, the resulting decision is an interpretation of the statute or common law only with regard to the facts of the case. A close examination of a court opinion will help you understand how courts make law and, more important, how to read the form of primary authority known as court opinions, or **case law**. Case law is also known as common law, a term that is also understood to mean the law America inherited from England.

case (common) law
Published court opinions of federal and state appellate courts; judge-created law in deciding cases, set forth in court opinions.

Dissecting Court Opinions

Although there may be some variations, most court opinions fall into general patterns and share a similar structure. Cases have names identifying the parties involved. In a case name, the party that initiated the lawsuit or appeal is listed first, and the opposing party is listed second. At the trial level, the plaintiff's name comes first, and the defendant's is second. In criminal cases, the governmental entity is listed first, because it is the party bringing the case to court. At the appellate level, the party appealing ("appellant" or "petitioner") comes first, and the other party ("appellee" or "respondent") comes next. Between the two names is the abbreviation "v." or "vs." for versus. If there are more than two or more parties involved on either side, the case name indicates their presence with the Latin abbreviation, "et al.," which stands for "and others."

Usually an opinion will start by stating the facts of the case. Sometimes, preceding the facts, there may be an introductory paragraph or two in which the court summarizes the legal context of the case. Sometimes, courts may begin with an introduction that is even poetic or philosophical. Because most published opinions come from appellate courts, the next part of the opinion describes the manner in which the case had been appealed to the court, a description known as the procedural history of the case. The procedural history of a case describes how the case came to the appellate court. As you will see subsequently, the procedural history of a case may affect the questions that the appellate court will address.

Court opinions next delve into an analysis of the law and how the law applies to the facts of the case in a part known as the discussion or analysis section. The analysis is usually the longest part of the opinion and explains in detail the applicable law as part of its discussion, using a form of inductive reasoning. This part of the opinion is referred to as the rationale. Eventually, the court comes to a conclusion based on its apparent analysis of the law. The conclusion is known as a **holding** and is shaped as a legal proposition that applies to the facts of the case and sets a precedent for future cases with similar facts. The appellate court's holding is the precedent-setting law.

holding
That aspect of a court opinion that directly affects the outcome of the case; it is composed of the reasoning necessary and sufficient to reach the disposition.

More often than not, an appellate court will assemble a panel of three or more appellate judges or justices to hear a case. Each judge on the panel has one vote. Thus, opinions that are precedent setting represent the opinion of a majority of the judges hearing the case. A judge who agrees with the result and not the reasoning may write a concurring opinion, and those who disagree write dissenting opinions explaining their own views of the law. Because case law teaches and informs the reader about the latest way that a statue should be read or how the common law may affect a client's case, reading court opinions is frequently the first step in performing legal research.

In the following pages, you will read two cases—excerpts from published court opinions—that discuss the common law principle of family immunity. From these cases, you should be able to learn about this common law principle and its history in the state of California and elsewhere. These opinions use both primary and secondary authority to support their position. The Court cites Blackstone and Prosser, two secondary authorities. You may recall that Blackstone wrote the *Commentaries,* which became the primary vehicle for importing English common law into the United States. The late William L. Prosser was a law professor and author of a famous treatise, *Prosser on Torts,* universally recognized as perhaps the most respected secondary authority on tort law. His treatise is still widely used today.

As you read the *Self v. Self* opinion, see if you can identify those parts that would be considered the (1) facts, (2) procedure, (3) rationale, and (4) holding.

CATHERINE SELF, PLAINTIFF AND APPELLANT, V. ADRIAN SELF, DEFENDANT AND RESPONDENT, 376 P.2d 65 (CAL.1962)

. . .

The sole problem involved in this case is whether California should continue to follow the rule of interspousal immunity for intentional torts first announced in this state in 1909 in *Peters v. Peters.* Because the reasons upon which the *Peters* case was predicated no longer exist, and because of certain legislative changes made in recent years, we are of the opinion that the rule of the *Peters* case should be abandoned. In other words, it is our belief that the rule should be that one spouse may sue the other in tort, at least where that tort is an intentional one.

In the instant case, the problem arises under the following circumstances: The complaint for assault and battery was filed on May 5, 1961. It charges that the defendant husband on July 14, 1960, "unlawfully assaulted plaintiff and beat upon, scratched and abused the person of plaintiff," and that as a result plaintiff "sustained physical injury to her person and emotional distress, and among other injuries did receive a broken arm." As an affirmative defense, it is alleged that at the time the injuries occurred the parties were married. Thereafter, defendant filed a notice of motion for a summary judgment on the ground that a wife cannot sue a husband for tort in California. The motion for summary judgment was granted, and judgment for defendant entered [without a trial].

The common-law rule of interspousal immunity for either intentional or negligent torts is of ancient origin. It was fundamentally predicated on the doctrine of the legal identity of husband and wife (1 Blackstone, *Commentaries;* 2 Blackstone, *Commentaries* 433). This rule precluded actions between the two as to either property or personal torts. As long as this doctrine existed, the rule prohibiting a tort action between the spouses was logically sound. As Prosser points out (*Prosser on Torts* (2d ed. 1955): "If the man were the tort-feasor, the woman's right would be a chose in action which the husband would have the right to reduce to possession, and he must be joined as a plaintiff against himself and the proceeds recovered must be paid to him; and if the tort involved property, the wife had no right of possession to support the action. If the wife committed the tort, the husband would be liable to himself for it, and must be joined as a defendant in his own action." But the social order upon which this concept was predicated no longer exists.

Early in the 19th century married women's emancipation acts were passed in all American jurisdictions. These were designed to confer upon women a separate legal personality, and to give them a separate legal estate in their own property. They conferred upon a wife the capacity to sue or be sued without joining the husband, and generally, as far as third persons were concerned, made the wife separately responsible for her own torts.

From an early date it was recognized that a primary purpose of these statutes was to free the wife's property from the control of her husband. As a result, most American jurisdictions agreed that inasmuch as these statutes destroyed the legal identity of husband and wife, one spouse could recover against the other for a tort, intentional or negligent, committed against his or her property.

But this emancipation was not generally extended to the field of personal torts, most of the courts rationalizing that personal tort actions between husband and wife, if permitted, would destroy the peace and harmony of the home,

(continued)

and thus would be contrary to the policy of the law. As Prosser aptly points out: "This is on the bald theory that after a husband has beaten his wife, there is a state of peace and harmony left to be disturbed; and that if she is sufficiently injured or angry to sue him for it, she will be soothed and deterred from reprisals by denying her the legal remedy—and this even though she has left him or divorced him for that very ground, and though the same courts refuse to find any disruption of domestic tranquility if she sues him for a tort to her property, or brings a criminal prosecution against him."

In 1910 Justice Harlan in the case of *Thompson v. Thompson, 218 U.S. 611* in a dissent, in which Justices Hughes and Holmes concurred, pointed out that the old doctrine was outmoded, that the arguments in support of it were specious, and that the married women's act of the District of Columbia had so emancipated women that, properly interpreted, they should permit a tort action by one spouse against the other. Since then, the number of "majority" states adhering to the old rule has steadily dwindled, until today at least 18 jurisdictions have followed the reasoning of this dissent. Practically every legal writer in this field agrees that the old rule is archaic and outmoded, and that the minority rule is the better rule.

California has several cases adhering to the old rule. The first case to discuss the problem in California was *Peters v. Peters,* (1909), in which the action was by the husband against the wife for assault and battery. The wife, without justification, seriously wounded her husband by willfully shooting him in the leg. The court held that ". . . we are satisfied that, under the law in this state as it is, an action cannot be maintained by one spouse against the other for a battery committed during the continuance of the marriage relation. . . . The question is entirely new in this state and such cases are rare in other jurisdictions, but there is no case in favor of the right to maintain such an action."

The court squarely based its conclusion upon the reasoning that California had adopted the common law, and that at common law no such action existed. The court recognized that under the married women's emancipation acts "it is now generally held that an action at law concerning property may be maintained between them." It cited several out-of-state cases adopting the common-law rule of spousal disability as to personal torts, and particularly cited the early New York case of *Longendyke v. Longendyke,* and quoted with approval the statement in that case that "to allow such actions is 'contrary to the policy of the law and destructive of that conjugal tranquility which it has always been the policy of the law to guard and protect.'" The court went on to hold that the various code sections as they then read did not change the common-law rule in California.

None of the reasons which have been suggested in support of the common law view apply to this action. As this litigation demonstrates, any conjugal harmony of this quasi-marriage has long since been disrupted. Certainly there can be no thought of collusion between these parties.

From this analysis of the California cases it appears that the basic reasons given by the Peters case for adopting the rule no longer exist, that subsequent cases have simply cited the earlier case without analysis, and that several cases have limited the rule. The rule of the Peters case is definitely out of line with the general policy of the law of this state.

Of course, the general rule is and should be that, in the absence of statute or some compelling reason of public policy, where there is negligence proximately causing an injury, there should be liability. Immunity exists only by statute or by reason of compelling dictates of public policy. Neither exists here. That being so, these are sufficient reasons alone to justify this court in overruling the Peters case and in adopting the more modern, intelligent, and proper rule.

As already pointed out, the contention that the rule is necessary to maintain conjugal harmony—one of the reasons given in the Peters case—is illogical and unsound. It would not appear that such assumed conjugal harmony is any more endangered by tort actions than by property actions—yet the latter are permitted. For these reasons alone the old common law rule should be abandoned.

The judgment appealed from is reversed.

As you can see from the opinion in *Self v. Self,* the California Supreme Court made a somewhat momentous decision and discarded a long-held common law principle in favor of a more modern rule. In doing so, the Court's opinion offers a glimpse into legal reasoning and how the law can transform from its medieval common law origins to conform to modern-day social norms. Keep in mind that common law principles, such as interspousal immunity, had been made by English judges as they saw fit during their times. The same is true of the California Supreme Court's decision here.

Interspousal immunity was a rule adopted by the judges of the California Supreme Court in a case decided almost 100 years ago.

Since then, statutes enacted by the legislature modernized the status of married women, giving them the legal right to own property in their own name, among many other rights, to the point of becoming equals with their husbands in the eyes of the law. Although the legislation did not directly change the rule of interspousal immunity, the reasons underlying the rule were seriously eroded by these modern statutes. You may recall that statutes altering the common law have the effect of derogating or abrogating the common law, which is to say that the common law was changed or rendered obsolete by modern statutes.

The legal analysis employed in this decision is very typical of modern era court decisions involving the common law. Notice that the court first identified the common law rule, defining it and then describing the social norms or assumptions underlying the rule. These norms and assumptions provided the basis for the rule's existence. Once the Court reflected upon the modern status of women and marriage relationships, the reason for the rule's existence evaporated. Without a reason to exist, there was no necessity to apply the rule, particularly in light of modern California statutes. The Court was particularly honest in its approach, admitting that it had adopted the common law rule in the 1909 case of *Peters v. Peters,* which was the precedent case for interspousal immunity in California. Notice that subsequent reference to that precedent case was made by the use of only one of the first names of the case. This common shorthand reference applies to the same case after its first mention in the opinion. For cases in which the first party is the government, such as the state or the United States government, the other party's name is used as a short reference.

The holding or the court-made law from this case can be distilled into a single legal proposition. Stated as a rather long-winded sentence, the case law principle (that is, the holding) announced in *Self v. Self* might appear as follows: In light of the change in the status of married women, as altered by modern statutes, which emancipated their property ownership rights from their husbands' control, among other legal rights, and where no conjugal harmony remains to be preserved, the doctrine of interspousal immunity should be abandoned in cases of intentional torts, because the common law doctrine is now incompatible with modern concepts of marriage and contemporary social norms. This precedent was created by *Self v. Self.*

PRACTICE TIP

Because the law is always changing and adapting to modern conditions, it is essential for every legal professional to perform legal research thoroughly. This requirement means that the legal professional must find the latest word on the point of law involved, whether it be a recently enacted statute or a recent court opinion hot off the press.

Reasonable people will disagree as to how the holding should be worded, and that disagreement will be the fodder of future interpretations of the case and its precedential effect. In law, almost anything is debatable. In any event, it is important to note that the holding, or the case law, must be stated as a limited proposition framed by the specific facts of the case. For instance, the California Supreme Court did mention negligence in *Self v. Self.* However, the facts in that case involved an incident of domestic violence committed by the husband—an intentional tort of assault. On the same day, the California Supreme Court decided the case of *Klein v. Klein,* 376 P.2d 70 (Cal.1962). In that case, the Court was faced with the principle of interspousal immunity in a lawsuit for negligence filed by a wife against her husband for injuries she suffered on her husband's pleasure boat. Predictably, the Court similarly discarded the doctrine of interspousal immunity applied to negligence actions between spouses for similar reasons. Although the cases are certainly related, they should be read as standing for two separate and distinct legal propositions or holdings.

Legal Note Taking: The Case Brief

Reading court decisions to find relevant case law in practical life requires the specialized skill of understanding the effect of precedent and legal reasoning. Dissecting and analyzing court opinions can be a tedious and confusing task. Moreover, note taking for the purpose of studying can present a daunting assignment, particularly for working professionals who must research and carefully review several court opinions to assess a client's situation.

Both students of law and practitioners in the profession use a note-taking format known as a case brief. A case brief is to be distinguished from a trial brief or an appellate brief, which are formal and oftentimes lengthy written documents submitted to a trial or appellate court to persuade the court of the correctness of a client's legal positions. Case briefs instead serve the purpose of providing an easy-to-read formatting of the most essential elements of the court opinion. Typically, a case brief consists of one or two pages that act as a quick reference guide. As a internally prepared document in the research folder of a client's file, the case brief is an important part of a legal professionals' work for the client that can be easily read and understood by other coworkers in the office who are also working on the case. Preparing a solid and readable brief is an example of the teamwork that makes for effective and efficient legal representation.

Briefing a Court Opinion

Like any note-taking technique, the style and format of a case brief can vary depending upon personal preferences. However, most people agree on the following formulation:

1. *Title and Caption.* At the top of the brief appears the title or name of the case, consisting of the names of the parties. In documents prepared for formal submission, the name of the case is usually underlined or italicized. Following the parties' names is the case's **citation**. As you will learn in the next chapter, a citation is generally an address indicating where certain legal material may be located. There are citations for every type of legal material, both primary and secondary. You have seen these citations in this and the preceding chapters, and they may appear as mysterious numbers and letters. These are, quite simply, indications of the volume number, books, and pages on which the legal authority may be found. The citation noted for the *Self* case is 376 P.2d 65 (Cal.1962). The number 376 is the volume number of the book within the set of volumes known as the Pacific Reporter, as indicated by the "P." The "2d" is the series, indicating the second series. There is a set of volumes known as the first series that were numbered up to a certain point, after which a second series started. The number 65 is the page number where the *Self* case begins. The information in the parentheses (Cal. 1962) indicates the state and year of the decision. The Pacific Reporter covers several states within a region of the country, which is why the reference to California is necessary. The year is needed to put the case into a temporal context, because precedent is important. As we all know, precedent changes. Citing a case that is old or recent may indicate its precedential value. More recent cases may indicate current thinking that changed earlier cases; older cases that have not been overturned may show a long-held and sound legal principle.

citation
Information about a legal source directing you to the volume and page in which the legal source appears.

Self v. Self,	376	P.2d	65	(Cal.1962)
Case name	volume	Reporter	page	state & year

2. *The Facts.* Case law precedent is shaped by the facts of each case. The facts of a case are those that affect the court's ultimate decision. Courts often start off reciting the facts of the case and, unfortunately, may state many more facts than those shaped by the opinion. Thus, the task of briefing the case requires extracting the essential facts of the case—those facts that were operative in the court's decision. Fortunately, in the *Self* case, the Court stated the facts with merciful brevity. Elements of a case citation:
3. *The Procedure.* Because published court opinions come from appellate courts, the way in which the case is appealed can shape the resulting opinion, as is also true of opinions from the trial courts. Either court will state the procedural context of the case. In the *Self* case, Mr. Self was the defendant at the trial level and then the appellee before the California Supreme Court. He had filed a motion for

summary judgment with an attached affidavit stating that the couple was married when the alleged assault occurred. "Summary" in law means fast. A motion for summary judgment means that the lawsuit cannot go any further because of the existence of certain undisputed facts. Here, the undisputed fact presented was that the couple was married during the alleged events, which suggested no trial was possible because the doctrine of interspousal immunity said that husbands and wives could not sue each other for torts.

The trial court agreed with Mr. Self and entered judgment in his favor. Mrs. Self appealed directly to the California Supreme Court, bypassing the intermediate appellate court, as is possible in some situations due to the importance or novelty of the case. She was thus the appellant, and Mr. Self became the appellee. On appeal, Mrs. Self challenged the doctrine of interspousal immunity as outmoded and argued that a trial should go forward, because the doctrine was the only thing that blocked the lawsuit. This sequence of events is how the case presented the issue of interspousal immunity to the California Supreme Court.

4. *The Issue*. Every published court opinion can be distilled into a single legal proposition. Putting the legal proposition into the form of a question can be easily accomplished just by starting the issue with the word "whether." Again, people will differ as to how an issue should be stated. Generally, the issue should be stated as neutrally and narrowly as possible. For instance, as pointed out in the *Self* case, the Court's opinion did not totally discard the doctrine of interspousal immunity. It did so only with reference to the facts of the case—an intentional tort—even though the Court discussed, at some length, the issue of negligence. Many people find framing the issue the most challenging part of preparing the brief.
5. *Holding*. A "holding" is a legal term used to describe the rule of law or legal proposition established by the court's decision. Because court-made law is shaped by the facts of the case before the court, the holding is a distillation of the rule of law according to those particular facts. Courts also use the verb "to hold" synonymously with the verb "to rule." Thus, courts hold and rule, as well as make holdings and rulings.
6. *Rationale*. Also known as the reasoning, the court's rationale is the explanation part of the opinion. Notice that in the *Self* case, the reasoning appears in the form of steps that the Court took in arriving at the decision. At first the Court stated the rule, then the reasons for the rule, the statutory changes, recent trends in society and the law, and, finally, the incompatibility of the doctrine with current mores. A case brief records the major logical steps taken by the Court in short form, perhaps a sentence or two for each step, each in separately numbered parts.
7. *Comments or Critique*. Optionally, the case briefer may include his or her thoughts about the court opinion. This section will differ depending on the person and the reason the brief is being prepared. Students may wish to make comments of an academic, intellectual, or personal nature. Working professionals would comment in the case brief about how the case helps, hurts, or otherwise relates to their client's situation. Furthermore, because working professionals may use the case in papers to be filed in court, their case briefs may quote important passages from the opinion, along with the exact page on which these quotations appear. As you will see in the next chapter, the page reference to a quotation is an important matter because it provides the court with the precise location of the quoted passage. Passages from court opinions themselves are pronouncements of primary sources of law. Figure 4.4 provides a sample version of a student's brief of the case. The important thing to remember is whether the brief contains a sufficient amount of information while remaining concise—hence the use of the word "brief."

Case Brief
SELF v. SELF
376 P.2d 65 (Cal.1962)

Facts: Plaintiff ("P") wife sued husband for the intentional tort of assault resulting in personal injuries and emotional distress to her. Although a divorce was later filed, the wife's complaint alleged the assault took place while the couple was still married.

Procedure: Defendant ("D") husband filed an answer and alleged as an affirmative defense that the events took place while the couple was still married and that therefore he could not be sued for a tort in California. D moved for summary judgment, attaching an affidavit attesting to the fact that the couple was married at the time of the incident. Trial Ct. granted motion dismissing case in favor of D. P appeals directly to Cal. Sup. Ct.

Issue: Whether in light of the change in the status of married women, which has been altered by modern statutes, which emancipated their property ownership rights from their husbands' control, among other legal rights, and where no conjugal harmony remains to be preserved, the doctrine of interspousal immunity should be abandoned in cases of intentional torts as a common law doctrine now incompatible with modern concepts of marriage and contemporary social norms.

Holding: The assumptions underlying the common law doctrine of interspousal immunity have become obsolete, and the doctrine of interspousal immunity is no longer available as a defense in actions between spouses in tort actions.

Judgment: Reversed and remanded back to Tr. Ct.

Rationale:

1. Ct. states rule of Interspousal Immunity ("II") adopted as common law ("C.L.") in *Peters v. Peters* (1909), prevents suits between spouses. Reason for II was law putting Wife's ("W") property under Husband's ("H") control during marriage and idea of marriage being one unity. Thus suit by one against the other was the H suing himself, or unity suing itself.
2. Modern emancipation statutes freed W from H's control of her property as well as other rights. Still, II persisted because of idea that suits between H & W would destroy marital harmony.
3. Modern trend began w/1910 U.S. Sup. Ct. doubting propriety of II. Prosser also doubted fitness of II in modern society. Other states (N.Y.) began abrogating II.
4. Logically, reason for II no longer exists, where W is now emancipated by statute and the H & W are or will be divorced. Esp. true with policy of law should remedy an injury suffered by negligence. Immunities in general driven by public policy. Here no reason exists for keeping II, since now illogical and unsound given modern society norms. *Peters* case of 1909 overturned.

Comments: Should this be a legislative concern or should the courts take matters into their own hands? Legislature emancipated women by statue and should eliminate II by statute. On the other hand, the CL is court made and in Cal., court adopted in 1909, therefore it's appropriate for court to abrogate its own previous case law.

FIGURE 4.4 **Student Brief of *Self v. Self***

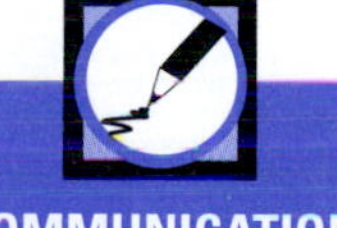

COMMUNICATION TIP

Whenever you are speaking or writing as a legal professional, particularly to colleagues, be succinct and to the point. Avoid extraneous matters or personal opinions that do not help or assist in the understanding of your communication. Similarly, avoid the use of colloquial language or slang. Every communication you make is a reflection of your professionalism. Thus, case briefs or reports on the law to coworkers should be written as professionally as possible.

As is the situation for any note-taking technique, everyone has his or her own personal style for case briefs, complete with special abbreviations and symbols. For instance, legal professionals and students frequently use the Greek letter pi (π) to indicate plaintiff and the letter delta (Δ) to indicate defendant, because these symbols are distinctive enough to stand apart, unlike using the abbreviations P and D. More important, a well-done case brief presents a clear and succinct synopsis of the court opinion. As part of the research for a client's case or as a study guide for a student, the case brief allows the reader to understand almost the entire court opinion virtually at a glance and thereby quickly grasp the pertinent case law on a particular point. Thus, your own legal research for a client, reduced to case briefs of several opinions, can provide a coworker with a quick grasp of the status of the law.

JAMES A. GIBSON, a Minor, etc., Plaintiff and Appellant, v. ROBERT GIBSON, Defendant and Respondent, Supreme Court of California

479 P.2d 648 (Cal. 1971)

OPINION: We are asked to reexamine our holding in *Trudell v. Leatherby (1931)* that an unemancipated minor child may not maintain an action against his parent for negligence. That decision, announced 40 years ago, was grounded on the policy that an action by a child against his parent would "bring discord into the family and disrupt the peace and harmony of the household." If this rationale ever had any validity, it has none today. We have concluded that parental immunity has become a legal anachronism, riddled with exceptions and seriously undermined by recent decisions of this court. Lacking the support of authority and reason, the rule must fall.

James A. Gibson, plaintiff herein, is the minor son of defendant, Robert Gibson. James' complaint alleges in substance as follows. In January 1966 he was riding at night in a car which was being driven by his father and which was towing a jeep. His father negligently stopped the car on the highway and negligently instructed James to go out on the roadway to correct the position of the jeep's wheels. While following these directions, James was injured when another vehicle struck him.

Defendant filed a general demurrer on the theory that a minor child has no right of action against his parent for simple negligence. Judgment of dismissal was entered on an order sustaining the demurrer without leave to amend. This appeal followed.

The doctrine of parental immunity for personal torts is only 80 years old, an invention of the American courts. Although the oft-compared rule of interspousal immunity reached back to the early common law, English law books record no case involving a personal tort suit between parent and child.

In 1891, however, the Mississippi Supreme Court laid the egg from which parental immunity was hatched. Citing no authorities, the Mississippi court barred a minor daughter's false imprisonment action against her mother who had wrongfully committed her to an insane asylum. The court declared that the "peace of society, and of the families composing society, and a sound public policy, designed to subserve the repose of families and the best interests of society" would be disturbed by such an action and concluded that a child's only protection against parental abuse was to be found in the criminal law. This "compelling" logic soon led the Washington Supreme Court to conclude that family peace and harmony would be irreparably destroyed if a 15-year-old girl were allowed to sue her father for rape.

Other states quickly adopted the rule, applying it to actions for negligence as well as for intentional torts, occasionally with more emotion than reason.

For example, the North Carolina Supreme Court declared of parental immunity: "If this restraining doctrine were not announced . . . it was unmistakably and indelibly carved upon the tablets of Mount Sinai."

Recently there has grown a general trend to restrict parental immunity, however, we believe that a trilogy of recent California cases in the area of intra-family tort immunity has weakened, if not eroded, the doctrinal underpinnings of the rule. For instance, in *Self v. Self,* we abrogated interspousal immunity for intentional and negligent torts. We think that the reasoning of those decisions has totally destroyed two of the three grounds traditionally advanced in support of parental immunity: (1) disruption of family harmony and (2) fraud or collusion between family "adversaries." The third ground, the threat to parental authority and discipline, although of legitimate concern, cannot sustain a total bar to parent–child negligence suits. We shall examine these arguments one by one.

The danger to family harmony was the only rationale for immunity mentioned in *Trudell*. In *Self*, however, we termed this argument "illogical and unsound." Observing that spouses commonly sue each other over property matters, we concluded that "It would not appear that such assumed conjugal harmony is any more endangered by tort actions than by property actions . . ." Indeed, as we shall discuss, infra, the risk of family discord is much less in negligence actions, where an adverse judgment will normally be satisfied by the defendant family member's insurance carrier, than in property actions, where it will generally be paid out of the defendant's pocket. Since the law has long allowed a child to sue his parent over property matters, the rationale of *Self* is equally applicable to parent–child tort suits.

We found the family harmony argument similarly unpersuasive in *Emery* when

(continued)

advanced to bar a suit between a minor sister and her minor brother. We said: "Exceptions to the general principle of liability ("For every wrong there is a remedy.") . . . are not to be lightly created, and we decline to create such an exception on the basis of the speculative assumption that to do so would preserve family harmony. An uncompensated tort is no more apt to promote or preserve peace in the family than is an action between minor brother and sister to recover damages for that tort."

Arguments based on the fear of fraudulent actions are also adequately answered. While some danger of collusion cannot be denied, the peril is no greater when a minor child sues his parent than in actions between husbands and wives, brothers and sisters, or adult children and parents, all of which are permitted in California. But we do not deny a cause of action to a party because of such a danger. . . . It would be a sad commentary on the law if we were to admit that the judicial processes are so ineffective that we must deny relief to a person otherwise entitled because in some future case a litigant may be guilty of fraud or collusion. Once that concept were accepted, then all causes of action should be abolished. Our legal system is not that ineffectual."

Moreover, we pointed out in *Emery* that concern with collusion is entirely inconsistent with the dire predictions of familial discord. The collusion argument assumes that the suit is in reality aimed not at the defendant family member but at his insurance carrier. In such case, the tort action poses no threat whatever to family tranquility; in fact, domestic harmony will not be disrupted so much by allowing the action as by denying it. The interest of the child in freedom from personal injury caused by the tortious conduct of others is sufficient to outweigh any danger of fraud or collusion.

The threat to parental authority and discipline is the only one of the traditional arguments for immunity which was not fully answered. "Preservation of the parent's right to discipline his minor children has been the basic policy behind the rule of parental immunity from tort liability."

In our view, the possibility that some cases may involve the exercise of parental authority does not justify continuation of a blanket rule of immunity. In many actions, no question of parental control will arise. Thus, the parent who negligently backs his automobile into his child or who carelessly maintains a lawnmower, which injures the child, cannot claim that his parental role will be threatened if the infant is permitted to sue for negligence. To preserve the rule of immunity in such cases, where the reason for it fails, appears indefensible.

We agree with this approach in its recognition of the undeniable fact that the parent-child relationship is unique in some aspects, and that traditional concepts of negligence cannot be blindly applied to it. Obviously, a parent may exercise certain authority over a minor child which would be tortious if directed toward someone else. For example, a parent may spank a child who has misbehaved without being liable for battery, or he may temporarily order the child to stay in his room as punishment, yet not be held responsible for false imprisonment.

Since the law imposes on the parent a duty to rear and discipline his child and confers the right to prescribe a course of reasonable conduct for its development, the parent has a wide discretion in the performance of his parental functions, but that discretion does not include the right willfully to inflict personal injuries beyond the limits of reasonable parental discipline.

We find intolerable the notion that if a parent can succeed in bringing himself within the "safety" of parental immunity, he may act negligently with impunity.

Secondly, we feel that we cannot overlook the widespread prevalence of liability insurance and its practical effect on intra-family suits. We can no longer consider child-parent actions on the outmoded assumption that parents may be required to pay damages to their children.

By our decision today we join 10 other states which have already abolished parental tort immunity. We think it is significant that since 1963, when the Wisconsin Supreme Court drove the first wedge, other jurisdictions have steadily hacked away at this legal deadwood. Of particular interest from our viewpoint is where the Alaska Supreme Court relied in part on our decisions in *Self* and *Klein*.

Applying what we have said above to the case at bench, we hold that the trial court erred in sustaining the defendant's demurrer, and hold that an unemancipated minor child may maintain an action for negligence against his parent. Consequently, plaintiff's complaint stated a cause of action and was not vulnerable to demurrer.

The judgment is reversed and the cause is remanded to the trial court with directions to overrule the demurrer and to allow the defendant a reasonable time within which to answer.

Gibson v. Gibson presents another situation in which the California Supreme Court continued to abrogate the common law doctrine of family immunity. In this civil lawsuit for negligence, the defendant filed a demurrer in response to the plaintiff's complaint. Demurrer is derived from the French and is now more commonly known as a motion to dismiss. Like the motion for summary judgment, a demurrer responds to the plaintiff's complaint by requesting that the trial court end the lawsuit before trial in the defendant's favor. Technically, a demurrer questions the legal sufficiency of the complaint at the very beginning stages of the lawsuit. Thus, courts first address preliminary questions, such as whether the lawsuit is in the correct court or, as here, whether the law allows a certain type of lawsuit. In a manner of speaking, when a defendant files a demurrer, the defendant is saying, "So what? You cannot sue me for that."

Nine years after deciding to abrogate the common law doctrine of interspousal immunity in *Self,* the California Supreme Court was faced with the related issue of parental immunity. Notice that in deciding the *Gibson* case, the California Supreme Court built upon its earlier precedent in the *Self* and *Klein* cases. At the same time, the Court acknowledged some differences. The relationship between spouses and that between parent and child stands out as an important distinction. Unlike its decision in the *Self* case, the *Gibson* Court acknowledged the role of insurance companies as available sources of compensation for injuries. At the same time, the Court actually kept a part of the doctrine of parental immunity intact.

For this case, try writing a brief on your own, keeping in mind the differences between interspousal immunity and parental immunity. As a matter of practical application, imagine that you are writing the case brief on the *Gibson* case as part of your research on behalf of a client. Imagine that your client is an insurance company that has issued an insurance policy for the parent of a child who has injured herself on the front walk of the parent's home. Would your case brief be any different if you were representing an injured child who may pursue a civil action against a parent?

RESEARCH THIS

Go onto the Internet to the site www.findlaw.com. Once there, roam around and see if you can find any cases in your jurisdiction on interspousal immunity or parental immunity. What is the current status of either form of immunity in your state?

Summary

To serve the legal needs of clients, all legal professionals possess the knowledge of the various classifications of the law. The classifications are well embedded in the training of legal professionals so that they may determine the law that affects their clients. For the beginning student in law, training in the various classifications as part of proper training provides an introduction to legal research and how to read the law. Law exists in various formats. The format that expresses legal authority is primary. Secondary authority is scholarly and may sometimes be persuasive.

An already familiar classification is the difference between state and federal laws. We understand this classification as a matter of the constitutional history of the United States. Within both the federal and state systems, there is a division between civil and criminal law. Each of those in turn contains two separate subdivisions of substantive and procedural rules, each with its own concerns and ways of declaring rights and enforcing them. Criminal law comprises a discrete area of governmental oversight of the public safety to protect the morals and welfare of the general public with laws that punish behavior regarded as harmful or dangerous. Civil law involves the rights and obligations of the entire population. Both criminal and civil law have their own variations, including standards of proof.

Much of the business of legal professionals consists of protecting or seeking to enforce client's rights. In civil law, the courts can vindicate a client's rights through the issuance of remedies, whether orders to pay monetary amounts or perform a certain act, as a result of the historic division between law and equity. To obtain a certain remedy, legal professionals resort to procedural law, which provides the means to enforce rights declared in substantive laws.

Although most laws exist ostensibly by way of constitutions and statutes, court opinions are the hidden backbone of the law. From common law traditions and historical developments in the United States, court opinions occupy an authoritative position, in which they interpret both constitutions and statutes. Thus, to determine or assess a client's legal position, court opinions provide an immediate source for legal professionals to research. Reading court opinions is a matter of training. The case brief is a professional's way to take notes on court opinions that can be easily shared with others working with the client.

Key Terms

Affirmative defense
Alibi
Beyond a reasonable doubt
Burden of proof
Case (common) law
Case brief
Cause of action
Citation
Civil law
Clear and convincing evidence
Compensatory damages
Consideration
Contract
Criminal law
Damages
Defense
Element
Equitable relief
Felony
General damages
Holding
Incidental or nominal damages
Injunctive relief
Intangible property
Judgment
Liability
Mens rea
Misdemeanor
Personal property
Possession
Preponderance of the evidence
Prima facie
Primary authority
Procedural law
Property law
Prosecution
Punitive damages
Rationale
Real property
Rebuttal
Reformation
Remedy
Rescission
Secondary authority
Special damages
Specific performance
Substantive law
Temporary restraining order (TRO)
Title
Tort
Tortfeasor
Trespass
Verdict

Review Questions

1. What is the difference between primary authority and secondary authority? Would it be possible to use secondary authority persuasively against existing primary authority?
2. Why is the government involved in criminal matters in a way that is different from the government's involvement in civil matters?
3. What is the difference between criminal and civil law?
4. How can a procedural rule affect the enforceability of a substantive right?
5. Name the component parts of a court opinion.
6. What is a *prima facie* case?
7. What is the difference between a misdemeanor and a felony?
8. What are the two forms of legal remedies that do not involve money?
9. What are the classifications of different forms of property?
10. What is the purpose of a case brief?

Exercises

1. Look up the applicable ethical rules from any of the paralegal organizations (NALA, NFPA, or others) or the ABA Model Rules of Professional Conduct to see what responsibilities are imposed upon a legal professional with respect to legal research. In what circumstances is a legal professional obligated under any of the ethical codes? Would the failure to perform research be a violation of any of those rules or codes?
2. Review the *Gibson v. Gibson* case and list the acts by parents that would still receive protection under the doctrine of parental immunity, as now defined by the California Supreme Court. Keep in mind that the parental acts receive protection because of the parent–child relationship. If the relationship did not exist, the same conduct could be the basis of a civil suit.
3. Both the *Self* and the *Gibson* cases are reported in the Pacific Reporter, Second Series. Take a trip to a law library and locate these volumes. Can you find either of these cases? List the other states that are covered in the Pacific Reporter.
4. Exchange your case briefs on the *Self* and *Gibson* cases with a fellow student. Imagine that you are both working legal professionals, working together on a case that involves the doctrine of family immunity. Do you find your fellow student's case brief understandable? Is his or her case brief an accurate and complete synopsis of the case?
5. Visit a law library and make a list of the types of secondary authorities that exist there.

Discussion Questions

1. Having laws that enforce contracts efficiently is important to societies that value commercial dealings. What would the various jurisprudence theories, such as economics and law or critical legal studies, say about this?
2. How have the courts, which are dispute resolution institutions, become a coequal law-making branch of government?
3. Viewing the types of causes of action and remedies available, what role do courts play in our government?

4. Why did the California Supreme Court think that the existence of insurance companies played an important part in the abrogation of parental immunity? Why do you think that insurance was not mentioned as a factor in the *Self* case?
5. What do you suppose happened in either the *Self* case or the *Gibson* case after the California Supreme Court's decision remanding the cases back to the trial court?
6. Our property laws are inherited from England and reflect certain social views and values. Can you think of different types of property laws from other countries or cultures that are different from ours?

PORTFOLIO ASSIGNMENT

On the basis of your research into the status of interspousal immunity in your state, prepare a report on the status of either interspousal immunity or parental immunity in your state. Address the report to a fictitious supervising attorney who has inquired into the status of the law you are addressing. Be sure to trace the common law origins and the extent to which either doctrine has been modified or abrogated by a more recent court opinion. Include as an attachment to your report briefs of any such court opinions.

Chapter 5

Legal Research and Writing

CHAPTER OBJECTIVES

After completing this chapter, students will have acquired competency in:

- Identifying primary and secondary sources of law.
- Citation form for both primary and secondary authorities.
- Using legal research aids, including digests, Shepard's, and the Internet.
- Researching statutes.
- Fundamentals of the office memorandum.
- Introductory legal writing.
- Expository writing and plain English.
- Reading statutes and cases together.

The end of Part I of this course marks your completion of basic, introductory materials necessary for your preparation as a legal professional. Part II now begins with a more advanced phase of instruction. This chapter will present specific information used in the legal world, and instruct you about the development of professional skills in that world. Advanced paralegal courses as well as practical exposure from internships, for instance, will further refine your education and training. Whether you are seeking an associate's degree, a bachelor's degree, or a certificate, the knowledge you will gain from this and succeeding chapters, and later from other paralegal courses, will constitute your professional preparation. With your basic understanding of the legal profession and a background in the structure of the American legal system, you are ready to proceed with learning the techniques and strategies for finding and applying legal materials from both primary and secondary authorities.

LEARNING TO USE THE LAW

In the last chapter, we saw how the court opinions appeared on the bottom rung of the ladder of primary legal authority. Yet the court's position as the final interpreter and arbiter of statutes and constitutions actually places it as a coequal branch of government. In fact, some say that court-made law stands at the pinnacle of primary authority. What makes the court different from the other branches of government is the way courts go about making law. Unlike legislators or the executive branch, both of which actively make law, courts make law only within the context of the disputes that appear before them. Thus, courts declare the law as part of a passive process, whereas the legislature and the executive take active roles in making new law.

Nevertheless, because of the common law tradition of precedent, court opinions themselves are often regarded as a foremost source of our laws. In both legal education and legal practice, court opinions have served to instruct and explain the law to students and legal professionals alike. This usage is largely due to the way these opinions express the law by expounding and rationalizing. Constitutions, statues, and regulations, by their very nature, are vaguely and generally worded declarations of the law and nothing more. Court opinions, in contrast, are actually stories and examples of real applications of the law. Court opinions explain how the law applies to the facts of the dispute and how they may apply differently to other types of situations. The opinions often report on the law's history and the reasons for the law's existence. They express concerns, create exceptions, and even hint as to how future cases may be decided.

In the previous chapter, we read the *Self* case, which involved an intentional tort of domestic violence. In arriving at its decision, the California Supreme Court stated that "the general rule is and should be that, in the absence of statute or some compelling reason of public policy, where there is negligence proximately causing an injury, there should be liability." In actuality, the California Supreme Court did not have to mention the negligence principle in the *Self* case at all. Indeed, negligence as a concept was not central to its decision in *Self.* Rather, the Court specifically decided that interspousal immunity is abrogated as to the intentional tort of assault and battery by one spouse against the other. Thus, negligence—which is not an intentional tort—was not at issue. We therefore may look at the quotation from the case as an observation rather than part of the court's reasoning. The Court's statement concerning negligence was not part of its holding.

The Court's statement on negligence is known as a **dictum**, which is language from a court opinion that is not necessary relevant to the decision. Because dicta (the plural for dictum) in court opinions are usually observations and not part of the holding, many people regard dicta as indications of a court's direction or inclination for future cases. Certainly this trend was true in the *Self* case, for in *Klein,* the very next case, the California Supreme Court abrogated interspousal immunity in a negligence case between spouses. At the same time, dictum is often merely that, dictum; statements in a court opinion that are off the point of the case may carry little or no portent.

dictum
(plural: dicta) A statement made by the court in a case that is beyond what is necessary to reach the final decision.

In any event, the distinction between a holding and dictum in a court opinion is an important one. Because each published court opinion expresses a rule of law that is framed by the facts of the case, cases are cited for the proposition expressed in the holding, not for any dicta. Moreover, a case's precedential value is confined to its holding. As a matter of professionalism and, at times, ethics, the ability to identify a court's holding precisely, as distinguished from dicta, distinguishes the well-trained from the less astute.

CASE REPORTERS

Because of the importance of case law as a form of instruction, as well as a source for primary authority, one of the first skills to learn is how to find cases. Almost all legal materials in law libraries are now available through the Internet or in electronic

reporters
Hardbound volumes containing judicial decisions.

case reporters
Sets of books that contain copies of appellate court opinions from every case heard and published within the relevant jurisdiction.

official reporters
Government publications of court decisions (for example, 325 Ill.3d 50).

unofficial reporters
Private publications of court decisions (for example, 525 N.E.2d 90).

regional reporters
Reporters that contain the cases of all the states in a particular geographical area.

format. However, this availability has been the case only for the past 15 years or so. For 150 years, volumes of books known as **reporters**, specifically **case reporters**, have compiled and published court opinions. Reporters have been the main source of reference for case law and exist largely because of the tradition of precedent in our system of laws.

Publication of State Court Opinions

All states began publishing their own reporters, and most continue to do so. The federal government also publishes a reporter for the United States Supreme Court. When the state or federal government publishes a reporter, it does so because a statute or court rule authorizes the publication. Reports published under legal authority, such as a statute or court rule, are known as **official reporters**. Many states have ceased their official publications and rely exclusively on private commercial companies to compile and publish the court decisions. The federal government also relies exclusively on private companies to publish reporters for opinions from the federal circuit courts of appeals and the federal district courts. State and federal reporters that are published privately are known as **unofficial reporters**. Unofficial reporters exist for all states, even those that have maintained official reporters. Thus, official and unofficial reporters often simultaneously exist for a state. Both are compilations of cases in roughly chronological order.

All state cases are unofficially reported in the National Reporting System (NRS) of the West Publishing Company. Grouped within several regions, state cases appear in families of **regional reporters** of the NRS. The regional reporters include the Atlantic Reports, North Eastern Reports, North Western Reports, South Eastern Reports, Southern Reports, and South Western Reports. Because of their large populations and amount of litigation, states such as California, Illinois, and New York have their own unofficial reporters, though these states with their own unofficial reporters also appear in the regional reporters. Figure 5.1 provides a map of the United States showing the states represented in each regional reporter.

The real-life distinction between official and unofficial reporters is slight but meaningful. The actual text of the court opinions, as it should be, remains exactly the same for both, perhaps except for the occasional misprint or typographical error. Unofficial reporters contain editorial features and research aids unavailable in the official versions. The various versions appear in different sets of books with differing appearances, names, and volume numbers. The existence of two sets of reporters for many states allows a researcher to resort to either one that may be available. The existence of two or more reporters also makes case law more accessible. However, having more than one reporter also makes life more complex, giving rise to intricate rules for citing state cases. A basic course in legal research covers these rules in depth. For now, a general overview will provide you with some useful exposure to these rules for the budding legal professional.

An In-Depth Look at Citations

Chapter 4 introduced the basic components of a case citation: volume, reporter, and page, followed by parentheses containing the court and year. Here, we take an extensive look at the world of citations—the rules of attribution for legal authority. Citations are important. The rules of citation have the eminently practical purpose of providing the reader with a means of verifying the existence of legal authority cited in any type of document. The citation may refer to a constitution, statute, regulation, or court opinion, among the host of other legal materials. Precision and accuracy in providing citations are skills that legal professionals master early in their careers. For documents submitted to courts, as well as to peers and opponents, following correct citation form

Regional Reporters (State Cases)

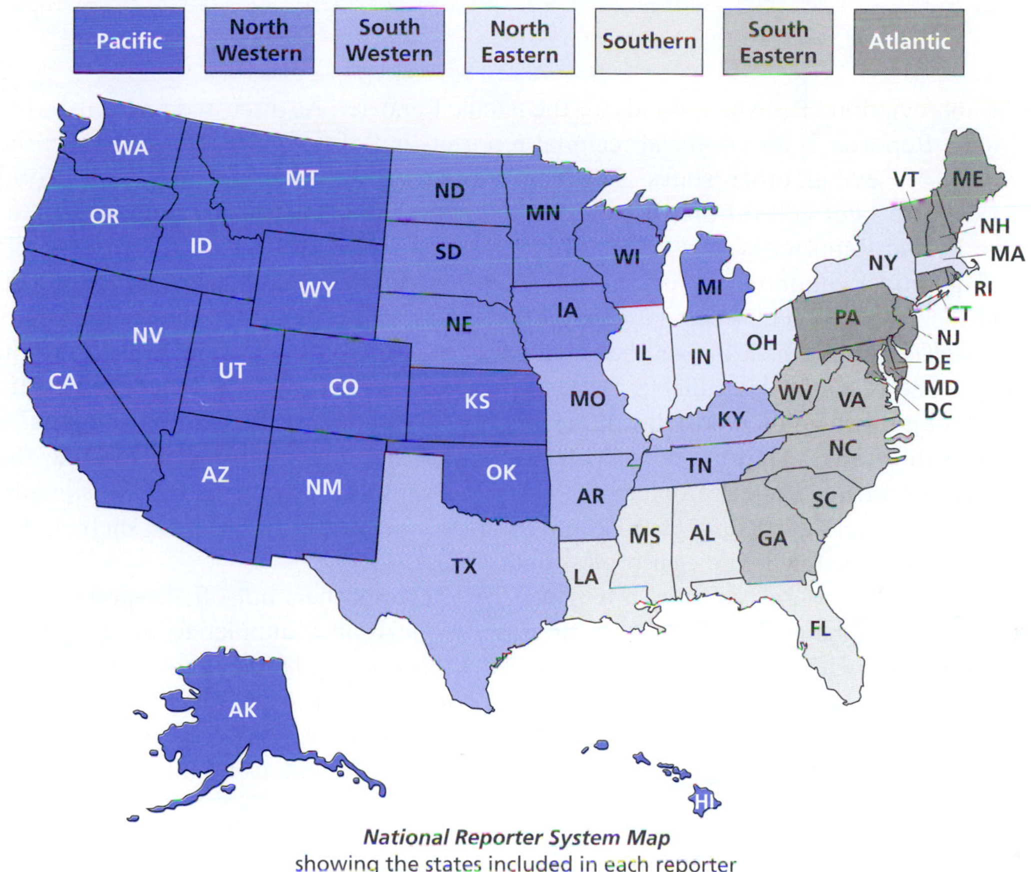

FIGURE 5.1 **Map of Regional Reporters**

Source: Obtained from http://lawschool.westlaw.com/federalcourt/NationalReporterPage.asp. Reprinted with permission of ThomsonWest.

lends credibility and professionalism to your work. In addition, citation performs the function of demonstrating or pointing to legal authority as support for a particular point. In a discussion of the doctrine of interspousal immunity, citation to the *Self* case would follow the statement that the doctrine has been abrogated. Learning citation format is the beginning of acquiring legal research skills.

Simply put, a citation is an address for the legal material cited. As we saw in the last chapter, the citation of a court opinion follows a uniform and regular format: volume number, reporter (represented by letter abbreviation), page parenthetical reference to the court (sometimes) and the year of the decision. For the cases appearing in the last chapter, we followed the rules of citation for citing California cases. The rules of citation can be so particular that they may even change depending on the context. Disagreement and vigorous debate rages as to the best citation format.

At the most basic level, two citations are necessary to cite state court cases. For instance, Figure 5.2 shows two citations for the case *State of Hawaii v. Maxwell,* 62 Haw. 556, 617 P. 2d 816 (1980). The first citation refers to the official reporter for the Hawaii Supreme Court, known as the Hawaii Reports, abbreviated as "Haw." and preceded by the volume number, then followed by the page on which the case begins. The second citation, also preceded by the volume number and followed by the page number, uses

FIGURE 5.2
Example of a Case Citation

State of Hawaii v. Maxwell, 62 Haw. 556,	617 P. 2d 816	(1980)
Case name / Official citation	Unofficial Regional citation	Year

the abbreviation "P.," which stands for the Pacific Reporter. As discussed previously, the Pacific Reporter is an unofficial regional reporter that also contains reports from the courts of several other states. The "2d" following the "P." indicates the second series, or a later edition that began after the first series reached its numerical limit. The Pacific Reporter is now in its third series, that is, "P.3d."

The proper citation form for *State of Hawaii v. Maxwell* thus consists of the official and then the unofficial (regional) cite, in that order. Citing both reporters is known as parallel citation, which allows the researcher to access either version, depending on which one is handy or available, at least in theory. You may notice that volumes are hardbound with gold-embossed volume numbers on the spines. They appear impressive and authoritative. Hardbound reporters, both official and unofficial, often line the shelves of various types of offices on televisions shows or commercials. Occasionally, media producers mistakenly place a few volumes of case reporters on the shelves of a psychiatrist's or other nonlegal professional's office.

slip opinion
The first format in which a judicial opinion appears.

advance sheets
Softcover pamphlets containing the most recent cases.

Before hardbound volumes are issued by the publisher, hot-off-the-press court opinions designated for publication appear singularly in pamphlet form, known as **slip opinions**, within days of the decision. Paperback compilations known as **advance sheets** follow as temporary case reports that come out approximately a week or two after the date of the decision. Both the slip opinions and the advance sheets are collections of the most recent decisions in unofficial reporters and eventually are replaced by hardbound volumes.

Publication of Federal Court Opinions

The United States Supreme Court

The opinions of the United States Supreme Court are the only court opinions published officially by the federal government. They appear in the official reporter called the *United States Reports,* abbreviated as "U.S." Thus, the case of *Worcester v. Georgia,* 31 U.S. 515 (1832), follows the same citation format as state cases: volume number, abbreviated name of the reporter, page number, and parenthetical reference to the year. However, the rule for citing decisions of the U.S. Supreme Court requires only the official citation and no parallel citation. Parallel citations for the United States Supreme Court exist, however, in three unofficial reporters.

Unofficially, the West Publishing Company issues the United States Supreme Court Reports, abbreviated as "S.Ct." Commonly called the *Lawyer's Edition,* the LexisNexis company publishes a set of volumes known as the United States Supreme Court Reports, Lawyer's Edition, which appear in citation form as "L.Ed." Finally, the Bureau of National Affairs, Inc., issues a weekly journal that contains recently issued Supreme Court decisions, cited as U.S.L.W, meaning United States Law Week.

Federal Circuit Courts of Appeals and the Federal District Courts

Only the West Publishing Company publishes the opinions of the intermediate appellate courts and the trial courts of the federal system. The circuit courts of appeals for all the circuits publish their opinions in the Federal Reporter, now in its third series. The opinions of the federal district courts appear in the Federal Supplement, now in its second series. Thus, the citation for the case *Saint Fort v. Ashcroft,* 223 F. Supp. 2d 343 (D. Mass. 2002), *aff'd,* 329 F.3d 191 (1st Cir. 2003), indicates that the federal district court for the District of Massachusetts issued an opinion in 2002, appearing in volume 223 of the unofficial reporter, the Federal Supplement, Second Series, beginning at page 343. The case was appealed to the Federal Circuit Court of Appeals for the First Circuit, which in 2003 affirmed the district court's decision in an opinion reported in volume 329 of the Federal Reporter, Third Series, beginning at page 191.

RESEARCHING COURT OPINIONS USING DIGESTS

Digests are an extensive set of books that are neither primary nor secondary authority. Digests serve as research aids for finding cases and are used exclusively to research court opinions on almost any given topic or area of law. The most famous and widely used digest is West Publishing's *American Digest System*. Arranged alphabetically by topic name, each of the more than 400 areas of law has an assigned key number that designates the numerous legal issues subsumed within that topic. Thus, the topic name "Child Custody" covers that area of the law, and the key numbers within that topic name indicate the various points of law dealing with child custody. After finding an appropriate topic name and key number in the digest's descriptive word index volume, a researcher can look up the topic name and number in the main volumes to find case digests, or briefs, which usually feature one-sentence summaries of cases and their citations. With these citations, the researcher may retrieve the actual case for further examination.

digest
A collection of all the headnotes from an associated series of volumes, arranged alphabetically by topic and by key number.

This ingenious system of legal research has been used for generations, ever since its invention almost 100 years ago. The digests also contain volumes known as the table of cases that provide a means to look up the citation, as well as the associated topic name and the key number of a case for which the researcher only knows the parties' names. Digests known as decennial digests cover the entire country for specific periods of time. Each regional reporter also has a corresponding regional digest. Most states have their own West digest, and some states share a digest with another state—usually a neighboring state. The federal system also has its own separate digests for all of federal courts in the nation, namely, the *Supreme Court Digest* covering the United States Supreme Court and the *Federal Practice Digest* covering the circuit courts and district courts.

Topic names and key numbers for all digests are consistent across the National Digest System. This consistency allows for the use of the same topic names and key numbers from one jurisdiction to another. Thus, the topic name "Husband and Wife" and the key number 205 pertains to the law regarding suits between spouses. Using that topic name and key number together, you will find *Self v. Self* in the California Digest as well as the Pacific Regional Digest. The same topic name and key number refer to the same issue within other regional and state digests, from Alaska to Florida and every state in between. Thus, if the doctrine of interspousal immunity has not been abrogated in a researcher's given jurisdiction, research using the same topic name and key number will supply persuasive case law from other jurisdictions.

Because of the many useful features afforded by the West key number and digest system, the unofficial versions of case reports, particularly for state cases, often are easier to use. The shelves of most law school and government law libraries contain both official and unofficial reporters for the state and federal courts. However, only unofficial West versions usually appear on the shelves of the libraries in law offices. The obvious reason for this selection is the ease with which researchers can perform legal research using the devices contained in the publications produced by West.

UNPUBLISHED OPINIONS

Not all court opinions are published officially, by West or other publishers. Courts use various factors to decide whether they will designate a certain opinion for publication. As you can imagine, a court opinion in a case that presents only mundane issues and

CYBER TRIP

On the Internet, go to the Web site for the New York State Official Reports at www.nycourts.gov/reporter/Selection.htm#Criteria.

What New York law governs the publication of its courts' opinions?

What New York State courts' opinions are published?

What factors determine whether an opinion will be published?

Why would a New York state trial court judge want her opinion published?

involves only routine application of the law has no precedential value. Publication of such a case would thus have little or no benefit. Nevertheless, an occasional unpublished opinion may have some value to a legal professional's representation of a client's cause. An unpublished opinion may become available through a network of legal professionals working in a certain area of law, for instance. However, use of an unpublished opinion may be subject to restrictions. Many court rules limit or regulate the use of unpublished opinions. Thus, it is always a good idea to check the rules of the courts in your area to see how they treat unpublished opinions.

CASE LAW RESEARCH WITH SECONDARY AUTHORITY

In Chapter 4, the discussion of secondary authority focused on its place in the hierarchy of legal materials. Specifically, secondary authority possesses, at best, persuasive weight, but secondary authority also becomes very useful as a research tool and a self-educating utility. Faced with a new area or facet of law, many legal professionals acquire immediate and thorough lessons by using secondary authority. This bountiful research tool provides elementary instruction on law, as well as citations to important primary authority.

Legal Encyclopedias

legal encyclopedia
A multivolume compilation that provides in-depth coverage of almost every area of the law.

American Jurisprudence, Corpus Juris Secundum, and *American Law Reports* are just a few of the many legal encyclopedias produced privately by commercial companies. **Legal encyclopedias** operate similarly to any other encyclopedia. Organized by topic in alphabetical order, legal encyclopedias explain each area of law in general detail as primers. Specialized legal encyclopedias also explore particular areas of the law with greater depth. Legal encyclopedias offer a crash course in discrete legal topics for even experienced legal professionals venturing into a new area for the first time. A paralegal or lawyer who has practiced for many years in litigation, for instance, may need to educate him- or herself about the rather boutique subject of international law because a treaty is at issue in a case he or she is litigating. Instead of hiring an expert or taking a course on the subject, reading a section on international law from a legal encyclopedia may be sufficient.

Some legal professionals begin their research with legal encyclopedias to obtain case citations and background information about a certain legal topic. Almost all encyclopedias provide extensive footnotes that include lists of cases, complete with citations. The arrangement usually consists of an exposition of general legal principles in the encyclopedia's text, then the cases cited in the footnotes support the legal principles discussed in the main text. Thus, much of the research is already done.

A well-organized encyclopedia makes research easier by arranging the cases cited within the footnotes by state and in alphabetical order. As you will see later in this chapter, legal encyclopedias can become extremely useful for writing a certain type of legal document to inform a colleague or supervisor about the status of the law as it applies to a case at hand. Such a legal memorandum is an objective appraisal of a client's legal situation based on a legal professional's research. Much of that research will begin in a legal encyclopedia.

Treatises

treatise
A scholarly study of one area of the law.

Treatises are written by well-known experts, such as law professors, judges, or practitioners, who provide in-depth commentary, observations, and criticisms, as well as explanations of the law. They differ from legal encyclopedias in the depth and tenor of their treatment, which is devoted to a single area of the law. Treatise authors almost always have devoted their entire scholarly careers to a single legal topic. In the *Self* and *Gibson* cases covered in Chapter 4, the California Supreme Court referred to a commonly cited treatise in cases on family immunity written by Professor William L. Prosser, a widely acknowledged expert on torts. Other authors are also as famous, such that their names are, in the legal world, synonymous with their area of expertise. Many treatises, such as *Prosser on Torts,* consist of a single volume. Others may consist of many volumes on a single topic. Probably the champion of legal treatises is the fourteen-volume treatment on the sole subject of evidence by John H. Wigmore, whose monumental work began as three volumes.

Used frequently by academics, practitioners, and law students, treatises have garnered greater respect than legal encyclopedias because of their scholarly bent. Although still within the realm of secondary authority, treatises are often granted authoritative status and respect because of the authors' preeminence and the prevalence of their use. Courts often give great persuasive weight to a point of law stated in a treatise. For practicing legal professionals, treatises are frequently found in law offices that specialize in the treatise's area of the law. Thus, a litigation specialist who regularly represents clients at trials may own the entire multivolume set of Wigmore's Evidence. Law offices that specialize in federal litigation will keep the multivolume treatise Moore's Federal Practice on-site.

Restatement

Within the past 75 years, legal observers—judges, scholars, and prominent practitioners—began to realize that the ever-growing body of case law could be stated more clearly as propositions of law, like statutes. Instead of having to wade through the clumsy language of a court opinion, sift through the facts, and distill the court's holding from amidst all the dicta, many legal scholars of the prestigious American Law Institute embarked upon the task of rewriting case law into a format similar to statutes, organized by chapter and section, into the *Restatement*. This type of assemblage is known as a **codification**, which presents law in a systematic form. In a significant way, the ***Restatement*** is a codification of case law. The Restatement also provides commentary and examples after each section that cite important cases and even dissenting views from other cases.

codification
Compiling enacted laws into an organized format.

Restatement
A recitation of the common law in a particular legal subject; a series of volumes authored by the American Law Institute that tell what the law in a general area is, how it is changing, and what direction the authors think this change is headed in.

Assembled in volumes by subject matter, such as torts, contracts, and many other topics, the *Restatement* is a well-recognized source for sophisticated research. Courts cite it more than any other secondary authority, which indicates its prestige and authority. Both the *Self* and *Gibson* cases cite the *Restatement* as an influential source for determining trends in the law.

A Word About "Pocket Parts"

Hardbound volumes are expensive and must be replaced every few years with newer editions that incorporate any changes since the earlier volumes. Before the issuance of the new hardbound volumes, updates in the law appear in paperbound **pocket parts** bound in cardboard. Every few months, and sometimes more frequently, subscribers receive pocket parts to insert in their hardbound legal encyclopedias, digests, treatises, and the *Restatement*. The cardboard backing can be inserted in a pocket on the inside of the back cover of every hardbound book to provide updated information for that hardbound volume. Law librarians at schools and law offices maintain legal materials by replacing older pocket parts with current ones. In courses on legal research and writing, and indeed in practice, competent practitioners learn to "check the pocket part first."

pocket parts
Annual supplements to digests.

Law Reviews

Among the sources of secondary authority, **law reviews** (also known as "journals") rank comparatively with the *Restatement*. However, their use remains somewhat limited to specialized situations. As we discussed in a previous chapter, law schools publish

law reviews
Periodicals edited by the top students at each law school, featuring scholarly articles by leading authorities and notes on various topics written by the law students themselves.

law reviews as scholarly sources of secondary authority that can profoundly influence the policy decisions of appellate courts. Law reviews come in a format different from that of the *Restatement*. The articles in law reviews discuss, often in minute detail, highly specialized and at times esoteric areas of the law. Written by prominent practitioners, scholars, judges, and top law students, law review articles are valuable research sources for very specific points. After completing the initial stages of research for a complex case, a legal professional would be fortunate to come across a relevant law review article that makes arguments pertinent to the case or provides a guide through a complex regulatory scheme.

Every year, law reviews across the country publish hundreds of articles on virtually every aspect of the law. Many useful articles regularly discuss recent developments in certain areas of law, such as patent and trademark or international law. Others provide a review of the past year's decisions by a state supreme court or the United States Supreme Court, keeping both practitioners and others current on important aspects of the ever-changing status of the law. Then there are law review articles that are entirely theoretical and academic. Many legal professionals find law review articles interesting reading, whether the article at hand is helpful in their practice or just provides enjoyment in their more intellectual moments.

Assorted Secondary Sources

The legal publication business does not want for lack of titles. Throughout the legal environment, magazines, periodicals, newsletters, dictionaries, guidebooks, and even legal date books designed for legal professionals proliferate. These publications are classified as practice aids rather than as a form of authority. Form books with predrafted legal documents, such as court documents, contacts, wills, and corporate documents, are even organized for the busy legal professional who just needs to fill in the blanks.

As you might imagine, many of these materials are available online or on CD-ROM. Computer programs now claim to employ a form of "artificial intelligence" that enables users to draft customized documents in a fraction of the time it would take using manual techniques. Probably no other profession produces as much published material on a regular and never-ending basis. It makes sense, if you think about it. The law is, at its most basic, about words and ideas. Moreover, these publications, whether digital or in print, are becoming increasingly available because of the constant changes in society, technology, and, indeed, the law itself. This wealth of publications is a good thing, because more and more people are becoming aware of how the law affects their lives.

Shepard's

Shepard's Citations
Reference system that reports the legal authority referring to the legal position of the case and making reference to the case opinion.

shepardizing (shepardize)
Using Shepard's verification and updating system for cases, statutes, and other legal resources.

One of the most unique and helpful practice aids for legal research is a set of volumes known as **Shepard's Citations**. Shepard's contains no explanation of law, or indeed any form of discussion at all. Shepard's is not a form of legal authority. Rather, it is purely a research tool and one of the most important ones around. Whether you are at the beginning or near the end of your research, after you have located a primary or even a secondary authority, Shepard's provides citations to those cases that have cited that authority. Arranged chronologically by volume, Shepard's consists of an exhaustive list of case citations that have cited the constitutional provision, statute, regulation, or case in which you are interested. Almost any form of legal authority may be checked through Shepard's. By using Shepard's, you are engaging in the practice of "**shepardizing**."

Every legal professional regularly shepardizes the authority he or she plans to rely on, whether that authority provides the basis of a legal assessment of a client's situation or supports a legal argument to present to a court. By shepardizing, the researcher

EYE ON ETHICS

All legal professionals have an ethical duty to represent their clients with competence. For years, the legal profession has regarded the regular use of Shepard's as fulfilling an essential part of that duty. In the case of *Taylor v. Belger Cartage Service, Inc.*, 102 F.R.D. 172 (W.D. Mo. 1984), the plaintiff's attorney filed a lawsuit on the basis of a court decision that had been restricted by a number of later decisions by the same court. However, the attorney had not shepardized the earlier case. Because of the number of rulings in later cases, there was no basis for the lawsuit. The federal district court dismissed the lawsuit and found that the plaintiff's attorney had breached his professional obligation and "willfully abused the judicial process." Thus, the court awarded the defendants more than $14,000 in legal fees. In doing so, the court stated,

> When attorneys lose sight of this duty due to laziness, greed, incompetence, or other distracting motives, the party or parties who directly suffer from the attorney's lapse must be compensated both to make them whole and to remind other lawyers that they must continuously be aware of their professional responsibility.

Id., at 180–81.

can determine the current status of a case, statute, or other legal authority; locate the most recent decisions; and find decisions involving legal or factual issues similar to those pertinent to your case. Using volumes of Shepard's in print may be a bit cumbersome at first. However, after some practice, shepardizing will become an activity as automatic as looking into your rearview mirror when driving a car. Careful and prudent practice includes using Shepard's regularly.

To illustrate, recall the *Self* and *Gibson* cases from the California Supreme Court, which had abrogated the common law doctrine of interspousal immunity in 1962. For almost 50 years in California, the doctrine of interspousal immunity had remained intact, beginning with the *Peters* decision in 1909. As the *Self* decision itself points out, the doctrine had been deeply rooted in common law for over 200 years. Thus, a seasoned practitioner during the early 1960s would rely on the doctrine in defending a civil tort action between spouses. However, you can now see that taking just a few minutes to shepardize the *Peters* decision would save the legal professional time, embarrassment, and, most important, a breach of a professional ethical duty to a client and the judicial system. This benefit is particularly the case with the state of technology now readily available. Shepard's is even easier to use in its online form, and shepardizing can be performed with a few clicks of the mouse. More often than not, practitioners, students, and scholars all use online research resources.

CYBER TRIP

Go to the Web site for the Federal District Court for the Western District of Wisconsin at www.wiwd.uscourts.gov/opinsearch/index.html.

Go to the Web site for the New Jersey State Courts at www.judiciary.state.nj.us/rules/r1-36.htm.

What are the restrictions or requirements for the use of unpublished opinions in those courts?

LEGAL RESEARCH RESOURCES ONLINE

For the past several years, two major computer-assisted legal research services, **LexisNexis** and **Westlaw**, have virtually replaced volumes of legal materials that would otherwise exist in print for a law library. With efficiency and space the premium cost concerns for most law offices, the availability of an entire law library within the confines of a single desktop computer monitor has created undiminished demand for computer-assisted legal research (CALR). Performing legal research using CALR involves techniques that are somewhat different from manually compiled research using traditional law library resources, such as digests and encyclopedias. Based on a form of mathematics known as Boolean algebra, CALR conducts searches for words and word strings, similar to using Internet search engines.

LexisNexis
Commercial electronic law database service.

Westlaw
Commercial electronic law database service.

Both LexisNexis and Westlaw employ word searches through thousands of databases, each consisting of various forms of primary authority for the dozens of state jurisdictions and the federal system. These databases consist of constitutions, statutes, regulations, and cases. Almost all secondary authority sources are available as well. In addition to using word searches, cases, statutes, or almost any material may be retrieved by entering a citation and clicking a mouse button. Once retrieved, the material is displayed on the screen for the researcher to examine. Of course, download and printing capabilities also allow users to obtain the materials and examine them more closely later. Material appearing on screen with LexisNexis also may be shepardized. In Westlaw, the researcher may use **KeyCite**, which performs a similar function. The result will be additional research information in the form of cases and secondary authority that have cited the material on the screen.

KeyCite
The Westlaw case updating and validation system, which is similar to Shepard's Citations System.

FOCUSING YOUR RESEARCH

Obtaining additional sources of authority may serve different purposes, depending on the perspective or the starting point of the research. Whether researching by computer or in a law library, securing additional legal authority may fulfill the need to amass as much support as possible for a certain point. In another situation, updating already compiled research simply validates a settled point of law, which may be all that is required under the circumstances.

Using the doctrine of interspousal immunity again as an example, a researcher looking for cases that have abrogated the doctrine in states other than California may Shepardize or KeyCite the *Self* and *Gibson* cases within the databases of any other states or the database of a secondary authority to find cases that cite both *Self* and *Gibson*. The same search performed in a database of a secondary authority would yield encyclopedia articles and recent law review articles pertaining to the doctrine. The purpose of such a research task may be to mount an attack on the doctrine of interspousal immunity in a state that maintains the common law form of the immunity. In that case, the researcher would broaden his or her search to include many different states (databases) to obtain as much authority as possible to convince the court. Legal research on this scale may take several days by a trained, experienced legal professional. Although such research may seem a tedious form of work, the excitement of being part of a team that may effect changes in the law transforms the task into one of discovery that may prove quite exciting.

At the other end of the spectrum, the research task may require only an update of what is already known, without demanding exhaustive research or compilation. In that case, the research would involve using only Shepard's or KeyCite for the purpose of ensuring that the condition of the law has not changed. For the experienced researcher, the basic task of updating is a simple job that provides positive reinforcement and confidence regarding the performance of legal work. Between the two extremes of exhaustive research and updating existing knowledge lie the day-to-day research tasks that involve an hour or so of research on a procedural issue or looking up the law cited by the opposition. Thus, depending on the purpose of the particular task, the same research tools might be used but in different ways.

RESEARCHING STATUTES

In middle-school civics class, most students learned that the legislative branch of government enacts our laws in an important form we know as statutes. Introduced as bills, these proposed laws meander through various committees and sessions until they are finally passed into law, one way or another. In both the federal Congress and the

CASE IN POINT

THE BRANDEIS BRIEF

In the 1908, Louis D. Brandeis, a prominent attorney represented the State of Oregon before the Supreme Court in the case of *Muller v. Oregon*, 208 U.S. 412 (1908). Brandeis, who later became a Supreme Court Justice himself, filed a voluminous appellate brief presenting empirical data from dozens of nonlegal sources. Now known famously as "Brandeis Brief," the filing argued that the Court should consider sociological information. This case represented the first time that the Supreme Court considered social science data as a basis for its decision. The Court ruled in Brandeis's favor and upheld the constitutionality of the Oregon law that limited the hours that laundry women could work as a health and safety measure. The Brandeis Brief is famous for its use of sociological material, and its length—113 pages. The brief also became the model for future briefs filed with the Supreme Court. Under current rules (Rule 33) of the United States Supreme Court, all briefs are now limited to 50 pages.

QUESTIONS ABOUT THE CASE

1. What problems could arise with the use of sociological materials in court?
2. How would a sociological materials be presented to a court?
3. How do courts determine the "truth" if presented with conflicting materials?
4. Today, how would a brief in excess of 50 pages be filed with the Supreme Court?

state legislatures, enacted statutes are entered in chronological order into volumes published annually for each legislative session. To make statutory research easier, these laws become codified into a set of volumes arranged by title and subject matter. Additional volumes of indexes containing alphabetically arranged descriptive words indicate the appropriate volume in which the applicable statute may be found. Annual laws, such as legislative appropriations, budgets, and the like, are not codified because of their temporary, mundane nature. Rather, codified statutes are meant to appear in compiled volumes designed for research purposes.

For instance, to research a statute that regulates the representations made by retail sales advertisements, you would first go to the index for the volumes that contain statutory compilations. Within that index, you would look up descriptive words such as advertisements, consumer protection, retail sales, and so forth. You may find an indication of the volume that contains the statue, the name or section number of the statute, or the page within the volumes that contain the statutes. Updates to codified statutes appear as pocket parts inserted into the back of each volume, even the index volumes. As is the case for any hardbound volumes of legal material, a wise researcher always checks the pocket part first.

Researching statutes is more direct than researching cases. Cases frequently discuss a wide variety of matters, ranging from facts to procedural rules to history or any number of substantive legal issues. Thus, a single case may stand for a great number of legal propositions. Moreover, the precedential law established by cases is confined to the specific facts of each case. Thus, a vast number of cases with similar facts may differ appreciably due to the nuances in their differing legal effects. Recall that the doctrine of family immunity was first abrogated by the California Supreme Court in a case between spouses involving an intentional tort and then in a later case between spouses for negligence. Subsequently, the law of family immunity was abrogated as between parents and children. However, considerations of parental supervision and childrearing kept intact part of the family immunity doctrine that did not apply to those cases between spouses.

In contrast, statutes cover more defined subject matters and are more blunt in their approach. Statutes are singular in nature and address a discrete area of activity in their broad sweep. As such, statutes are designed to cover a comprehensive range of

COMMUNICATION TIP

Once you begin performing legal research as a professional paralegal, colleagues—attorneys and paralegals alike—may inquire about your progress. Informing them that you have shepardized the major relevant court cases or read an "on-point ALR annotation" provides convenient indications of the status of your work. These and many other technical phrases and forms of shop-talk are used frequently among legal professionals. Be sure to use the jargon carefully and accurately, because it conveys specific meaning about the progress of your legal work.

activity. When legislatures act, they focus on a perceived problem and enact the legislation to correct or regulate a subject matter completely, with foresight into any number of situations. In many cases, legislative committees operate for great lengths of time, hearing testimony and gathering the information needed to anticipate laws that may be needed in a given area. Thus, looking up that area of law using descriptive words is the most common way to find the appropriate statutory law.

Reading cases is an indirect way to find statutes. As we saw in the *Self* case, the California Supreme Court discussed the effect of statutes that emancipated the status of married women as a major reason to abrogate interspousal immunity. In doing so, the Court cited those statutes and read them in light of the case, giving them a judicial interpretation. As you will see subsequently, most volumes of codified statutes contain the wording of the statutes, followed by **annotations** of cases that have discussed the statute.

annotation
An in-depth analysis of a specific and important legal issue raised in the accompanying decision, together with an extensive survey of the way the issue is treated in various jurisdictions.

As in the publication of court decisions, many states and the federal government publish their own "official" version of codified statutes, as required by law. Private publishers such as West Publishing Company and many others also publish "unofficial" versions. Some "official" versions have annotations; almost all "unofficial" versions are annotated, making them very helpful as research tools. The volumes of both official and unofficial versions are supplemented with updated pocket parts.

Similar to cases, the citation form for statutes is governed by the Bluebook and the ALWD method. However, unlike cases, statutory citations vary from state to state. Many states follow the federal citation format. Of course, statutes are eminently "shepardizable" or subject to KeyCite. When you have a citation for a statute in hand, shepardizing it will yield citations to all of the cases that have cited that statute, even in passing. Specialized symbols within Shepard's citations indicate whether the case is relevant enough to warrant reading it. Computerized shepardizing or using KeyCite will display an annotation of the case or a portion of the text that immediately surrounds the citation of that statute. This function enables the reader to determine whether the case that cited the statute is relevant to the research project at hand.

About Statutes–Legislative Laws

Statutes are a form of primary authority. They govern our everyday lives. Statutes are created by legislators who are directly elected by the voters. The legislative process, with its committees and hearings allowing for public input, clearly indicates that statutes are the result of majority decisions. Thus, statutes represent a form of governance by the rule of law in a democracy. As discussed previously, statutes occupy a higher position in the hierarchy of primary authority than do court decisions. The only exception consists of cases that interpret statutes when a court declares a statute is void because it violates a constitutional principle. Thus, for most purposes, statutes supersede court decisions, for they are a most important form of law.

Key to knowing how to research statutes is an understanding of their sources. On the federal and state levels, the publication and classification of statutes parallel each other. Our examination therefore now turns to the specifics of federal and state statutes.

slip law
The first format in which a newly signed statute appears; a copy of a particular law passed during a session of legislature.

session laws
The second format in which new statutes appear as a compilation of the slip laws; a bill or joint resolution that has become law during a particular session of the legislature.

Federal Statutes

When Congress passes a new law, that law is entered by the United States government in a paper-bound pamphlet known as a **slip law**. All of the slip laws for each Congressional session are bound together in chronological order and published in a hardbound volume called the *United States Statutes at Large*. This practice has been ongoing since 1789. Generically, the United States Statutes at Large are known as "**session laws**," meaning that they represent all legislative activity during a certain legislative session. Session laws are not research sources, for research within them

CASE IN POINT

CASE SUMMARY: CHANGING THE COMMON LAW BY STATUE

Under common law, a bank that had issued a mortgage loan on a home could foreclose and obtain possession of that home if the homeowners could not keep up with their mortgage payments. It then followed that the common law also allowed the bank to evict any tenants who were renting from the homeowner. Such was the case in New Jersey. The New Jersey Supreme Court had announced the common law in the decision, *Guttenberg Savings & Loan Ass'n v. Rivera*, 85 N.J. 617, 428 A.2d 1289 (1981).

After *Guttenberg*, in 1986, the New Jersey legislature enacted the Anti-Eviction Act (N.J. Stat. Ann. tit. 2A, §§ 18-61.1, *et seq.*) to protect tenants from evictions that were actually pretexts for obtaining higher rents or facilitating condominium conversions. In *Chase Manhattan Bank v. Josephson*, 135 N.J. 209; 638 A.2d 1301 (1994), the New Jersey Supreme Court acknowledged that the Anti-Eviction Act was a legislative act that overturned the *Guttenberg* decision, together with the common law principle that had granted banks the right to evict existing tenants. As a result of the Anti-Eviction Act, the New Jersey Supreme Court, in *Chase*, held that the foreclosing bank could not end the tenancy and evict the tenant who had been renting from the homeowner. The New Jersey Anti-Eviction Act thus provides an example of a statute that supersedes a judicial decision and the common law.

QUESTIONS ABOUT THE CASE

1. Why did the common law principle allow a tenant to be evicted?
2. Could the New Jersey court have decided the *Chase Manhattan* case the same way without the anti-eviction statute?
3. How is the effect of the anti-eviction statute on the common law similar to the effect of the statutes cited in *Self v. Self?*

would require going through year after year of legislative sessions. Session laws instead are a chronological record of what the legislature accomplished in a given year.

Official Publication of Federal Statutes

The *United States Code* (U.S.C.) is the codification of the United States Statutes at Large. Arranged in numerically ordered volumes by title number, the U.S.C. arranges all federal statutes by subject matter and assigns a title number to each topic. Citations to federal statutes appear in the following format: title number, identity of the volumes (U.S.C.), and then section number; the typographical symbol § stands for section. Thus, the citation 8 U.S.C. §1101 represents title 8 of the United States Code (U.S.C.), section 1101, which happens to be devoted to the subject of immigration and nationality.

Altogether, the United States Code consists of 50 titles, each of which encompasses a broad, logically organized area of law. Some titles are divided into subtitles and then further into parts, subparts, chapters, and subchapters. All titles have sections ("§") as their basic unit. Sections may consist of subsections, paragraphs, and clauses. For instance, there are six definitions of "child" in the United States Code for immigration purposes; they appear at 8 U.S.C. §1101(b)(1) (A)–(F). That statute's citation would read, out loud, "title eight, United States Code, section 1101, subsection (b), clauses A through F."

As required by law, the government publishes the United States Code every six months. As such, the United States Code is an "official" compilation of federal statutes. However, the statutes themselves are all that are published. For almost anyone performing research, court decisions are essential to determine how these statutes may be interpreted. For that reason, private commercial publishers also have jumped into the statute publishing business and provide annotated versions of the United States Code, mirroring the 50 titles with subjects from Armed Forces (title 10) to War and National Defense (title 50). History buffs may note that the use of the term "code," as well as the organization and arrangement of statutes according to subject matter, comes to us from Roman Law—the Justinian Code—which in turn was refined centuries later in the Napoleonic Code of 1804.

Annotated Publications of Federal Statutes

The *United States Code Annotated* (U.S.C.A.), published by West Publishing Company, contains the federal statutes in the same form as the official publication of the United States Code. Following almost every federal statute, the U.S.C.A. also provides valuable resources in the form of detailed historical information, citations to secondary sources, and, most important, case annotations. Called "Notes of Decisions," these case annotations are organized into subject groupings, because statutes can be interpreted in many different contexts. Because of the wealth of information available in the U.S.C.A., the number of volumes greatly exceeds that of the official U.S.C., which contains only the text of the statutes. As a result of its numerous research resources, extensive indexes, and ease of use, the U.S.C.A. is much more widely used.

LexisNexis publishes a similarly research-oriented set of federal statutes, called the *United States Code Service,* which also is known as the *Lawyer's Edition*. Abbreviated U.S.C.S., its organization is similar to that of the U.S.C.A., complete with volumes of indexes at the end, as well as historical information, secondary references, and case annotations after every statute. Also similar to the U.S.C.A., the LexisNexis publication provides, under the heading "Interpretive Notes and Decisions," case annotations followed by citations to the case. Annotations give the reader a synopsis of how a case that has cited the statute may have interpreted it. If the annotation reveals that the case is sufficiently related to the research project, the researcher already will have the citation so that he or she can examine the case in its entirety.

Both the U.S.C.S. and the U.S.C.A. are supplemented with pocket parts inserted in the back of each volume, including the index volumes. Thus, amendments to the statutes, changes, and recent court decisions since the publication of the hardbound volumes appear in each volume's pocket part. As with other types of hardbound legal resources, the information in pocket parts gets absorbed into any newly issued hardbound volumes.

PRACTICE TIP

Statutes can be challenging reading. It may take several readings to make sense of the entire statute. Be sure to read the entire statute before trying to get the meaning of the legislature's purpose. Unlike reported cases, statutes are worded to cover a wide range of situations and frequently provide numerous exceptions. Of course, reading reported court decisions that have interpreted the statute is essential to determine how the statue has been applied.

A Primer on Reading Statutes

For our purposes, let's assume that a new law is Civil Code §3342, which states,

> *The owner of any dog is liable for the damages suffered by any person who is bitten by the dog while in a public place or lawfully in a private place, including the property of the owner of the dog, regardless of the former viciousness of the dog or the owner's knowledge of such viciousness. A person is lawfully upon the private property of such owner within the meaning of this section when he is on such property in the performance of any duty imposed upon him by the laws of this state or by the laws or postal regulations of the United States, or when he is on such property upon the invitation, express or implied, of the owner.*

Right off the bat, we can see that the first sentence of the statute imposes strict liability on the dog owner and sweeps away the common law, "first bite free" rule. The statute, which consists of only two lengthy sentences, dismisses the common law rule in the first sentence. The last part of that sentence also says, "regardless of the owner's knowledge of such viciousness." By that phrase alone, the statute abrogates the scienter requirement in the common law. Under §3342, a dog owner is strictly liable. But liability for the dog owner is conditioned.

That is, the statute imposes liability on a dog owner depending on where the bite takes place. There are two places in which a dog owner can be liable to a bite victim. The first is a "public place." We should understand generally what this location means. The street, a sidewalk, the post office, or even a supermarket constitutes a public place because the public is allowed to enter without specific permission. Permission to be in a "public place" is implied from the circumstances.

The first sentence of the statute also mentions a second place in which a dog owner may incur liability to a victim of the dog's bite, that is, a "private place." Entering onto "private places" requires some sort of permission granted by the law or by the

CASE IN POINT

CASE SUMMARY: CHANGING THE COMMON LAW BY COURT DECISION

In 1973, the Supreme Judicial Court of Massachusetts, well-known for its adherence to the common law, joined the majority of states and abolished the status distinctions of entrants onto another's private property. *Mounsey v. Ellard,* 363 Mass. 693; 297 N.E.2d 43 (1973). After a thorough review of the common law history, the Court finally stated, "[i]t no longer makes any sense to predicate the landowner's duty solely on the status of the injured party as either a licensee or invitee." 363 Mass. at 706, 297 N.E.2d at 51.

In this decision, the Court swept away centuries of common law. The two most important concerns were land ownership and a person's social status, in that order. As a result, the common law made artificial distinctions regarding the status of persons entering upon another person's private property. At question would be the extent to which property owner owed a duty to the persons entering upon the land. If an injury occurred to the person entering, the common law allowed recovery depending upon the status of that person. The common law set up three categories.

The first and highest category were invitees, who were persons actually invited onto the property by the owner. Because the property owner had made the invitation for his/her own purposes, the common law imposed upon the property owner the duty of reasonable care. This duty meant that the invitee could sue the property owner for injuries sustained due to the owner's failure to have taken reasonable steps to make the property safe.

Licensees, the next category, consisted of those persons who entered upon another's private property for the purpose of performing a duty. Police, firefighters, letter carriers, trash collectors, and the like entered upon another's property for the purpose of discharging their own obligations. Thus, the common law regarded licensees themselves as gaining an economic benefit from their entry, because the property owner did not expressly invite them. The common law imposed a duty upon the landowner only to refrain from willfully or wantonly harming them. A licensee on the land to perform a duty had a passive acquiescence to be there. The owner's consent was implied. A licensee could sue a landowner only if the licensee's injury had been caused by a willful or reckless act of the landowner.

Finally, there were *trespassers,* who did not have any form of permission to be on another's property, whether expressed or implied. Trespassers could not sue a landowner for injuries sustained on the property.

QUESTIONS ABOUT THE CASE

1. What purpose did the common law distinctions fulfill in society?
2. What is the difference between taking reasonable care and refraining from willful or reckless acts?
3. Why do you think that social status of the person entering upon someone's land was important?

owner. A person entering onto the property with permission from the owner or with lawful authority to enter would be covered by the statute. Thus, a dog owner whose dog bit someone who is not "lawfully in a private place" at the time of the bite is not covered by the statute. So, in "private place[s]," it all boils down to whether the bite victim is, under the wording of the first sentence of the statute, "lawfully in a private place." This point is where the second sentence of the statute becomes crucial.

The second sentence defines two groups of people who may be dog bite victims "lawfully on the private property" and who therefore are protected by the statute. The first group is those persons "on such property in the performance of any duty imposed upon him by the laws of this state or by the laws or postal regulations of the United States." This wording covers dog bite victims who have permission to enter "private property," such as firefighters, law enforcement personnel, letter carriers, process servers, and a host of others who perform a "duty imposed upon him [or her] by the laws." They all have permission granted by law to be on private property and, therefore, the statute automatically covers them.

The second group of persons who are "lawfully on the property"—private property, that is—are those "on such property upon the invitation, express or implied, of the owner." Here we find a broader group of people. Friends, relatives, UPS or FedEx (or other private delivery service) couriers, dinner and party guests, and many others are actually or implicitly invited by the property owner. Implied invitations from a property owner come mainly from common experience. Even if someone has not received an actual invitation from a property owner, most people expect to be able to enter "lawfully on private property" by implication based on common experience. Thus, trick-or-treaters on Halloween, unexpected guests, solicitors, and salespersons, among others, have passive

RESEARCH THIS

Find out what your state has done to change the common law rule regarding the status of entrants onto land. Does your state still adhere to the common law, or has it taken a new direction as Massachusetts has? Have there been any developments in Massachusetts since *Mounsey v. Ellard* was decided? If you are using a digest, what is the descriptive word and key number?

or unspoken permission to ring the private property owner's doorbell. Their invitation from the private property owner is implied by the circumstances.

As you can see, statutes can say a lot more than meets the eye. Notice that statutes in general and §3342 in particular are designed to cover a broad range of situations, persons, and places. What may be a bit confusing here are the separate notions of a dog owner and a private property owner. The two may be, but do not have to be, one and the same. The statute would cover a situation in which a dog has bitten someone on private property that is not owned by that dog's owner. Then again, dog owners and private property owners may be one and the same under the statute. Many people own dogs for protection as well as for companionship. Thus, the statute also encompasses a person entering on a dog owner's land as permitted by law or by the dog owner's permission, whether expressed or implied.

It's not easy to be a statute. Starting out as a "bill" introduced in the legislature, a statute comes to us as the final product of much scrutiny, haggling, and foretelling by scores of well-trained people, on the legislative floor, in committees, and at public hearings. Statutes are meant to cover a myriad of future situations with precision and designed to address a perceived evil or promote a public good. Legislators must graft historical distinctions and make exceptions, resulting in complex and convoluted wording that stands before the people like tablets—at least until the next legislative session.

Wording is all important. With lawyers and litigants hanging on every word, the order of the words, the placement of every comma, and every other detail can shift statute's meaning, perhaps according to the point of view. One party may argue a meaning that is favorable to its cause, whereas another will argue the opposite. The judge, mindful of the precedential value of a court's interpretation, must determine what the legislature really meant to do. Caught between the need for careful, precise wording and the intent for wide and perhaps unforeseen future applications, statutes can be among the most difficult legalisms to draft. Errors and mistakes are common. Let's take a look at some.

The dog bite law, Civil Code §3342, is actually part of a California statute that is identical to another in Arizona. Take a closer look and, on the face of the statute, we can find some of the issues involved in writing statutes. In the first sentence, the statute uses "private place," whereas in the second sentence, it refers to "private property." The two most likely mean the same thing. If they do, precision drafting would have used the same phrase in both sentences. Could a clever legal professional argue successfully that "private place" and "private property" mean two different things? Could "dog" also mean "cat" or any other type of pet that bites someone? If the common law "first bite free" has been abrogated for those "lawfully" on someone's property, does that mean that trespassers have to prove scienter? Does the common law still prevail so as to disallow any remedy to a trespasser? What if the trespasser is bitten by a dog owned by someone other than the landowner? What if the dog bite victim had harassed or annoyed the dog? As you can see, §3342 leaves some room for thought—and litigation. These and other questions will remain a matter of court interpretations in future cases. As you can see, drafting statues is a difficult task, for it is impossible to foresee all of the possible situations that may arise.

CASE IN POINT

CASE SUMMARY: INTERPRETING THE DOG BITE LAW

An example of how the California dog bite statute has been interpreted can be found in the case of *Fullerton v. Conan*, 87 Cal. App. 2d 354; 197 P.2d 59 (Cal. App. 1948). In that case, a mother and her small son were visiting the home of the mother's friend. The mother had told the child to stay in the front yard and not open the gate into the backyard, where the homeowner kept a dog. The child ignored the warning and opened the gate to the backyard, where she was bitten by the homeowner's dog. The appellate court agreed with the trial court that the child was lawfully in the front yard but not lawfully in the backyard, within the meaning of the statute. Thus, the child could not recover from the homeowner, and the trial court properly dismissed the lawsuit against the dog owner.

QUESTIONS ABOUT THE CASE

1. Do you think that it was fair to hold a child to such a technically high standard?
2. Would the same result occur for a mentally challenged person?
3. Do you think the mother's admonition to stay out of the backyard was a sufficient basis to determine that the child was not legally there?

FEDERAL REGULATIONS

Much of our lives is governed by public administrative agencies whose expertise and competence in a certain subject matter make it more efficient for the agency to establish rules and regulations than for Congress or a state legislature to do so. The next time you change the battery in a home smoke detector, notice that the label advises you that the detector contains radioactive material authorized by the U.S. Nuclear Regulatory Commission.

Laws that establish government agencies, called enabling acts, usually permit agencies to promulgate regulations. Regulations issued by a government agency have the force of law and are issued through a procedure that represents a mini-democracy, even allowing for public hearings and comment. Once issued, agency regulations are published in a periodical known as the federal register and then codified into the **Code of Federal Regulations (C.F.R.)**. Both are official governmental publications. To date, there are no unofficial publications of agency regulations. The C.F.R. is arranged by title numbers that coincide with the U.S. Code. Also similar to statutes, citation to federal regulations occurs by title number, followed by "C.F.R.," and then the section number and current year of the regulation's publication in the C.F.R. Thus, student eligibility for federal Pell grants is governed by the federal regulation promulgated by the U.S. Department of Education, as illustrated in Figure 5.3.

Code of Federal Regulations (C.F.R.)
Federal agency regulation collection.

USING THE LAW

Having absorbed the broad scope of information about legal materials, you are probably ready to begin the practical application of your newly acquired knowledge. We begin this journey into the practice aspects of law by familiarizing you with how these materials may be used in everyday life of a law office.

As we discussed in previous chapters, legal practices crop up in a wide variety of contexts. From the small-town law offices of solo practitioners to the big city law firms and government offices that hire hundreds, if not thousands, of legal professionals,

34	C.F.R. §690.6	(2007)
title	section	year

FIGURE 5.3
Code of Federal Regulations (C.F.R.) Citation for Pell Grant Student Eligibility

and every place in between, the use of legal materials involves two distinct purposes: external and internal. External purposes include using legal materials to prepare documents to be filed with a court or administrative agency. This type of external use likely exists in an adjudicatory proceeding that decides a dispute between two or more parties. An adjudicatory body is a generic term for a decision-making and dispute resolution entity. These bodies may take the form of a court, agency, or even privately contracted expert in an alternative dispute resolution.

In adjudicatory proceedings, disputes pertain to facts and, at times, to how the law should apply. Therefore, documents using legal materials may explain the factual or legal position of the parties. The court or administrative agency produces a document based on the use of legal materials. During the course of the proceedings, an order may be issued. At the end of the proceedings, the court or administrative agency issues an opinion or judgment. These types of documents require preparation by legal professionals who use many of the same legal materials described in this chapter, and more. As a matter of their daily routine, these legal professionals know seemingly instinctively how to perform legal research, where to begin, and when to stop before they begin writing the document for external use.

Thus, a document for external use is prepared for use outside of the law office. Adjudicatory bodies exemplify one type of context, though there are several others. Claims made to insurance companies, correspondence to opposing parties, consumer demand letters, and opinion letters are just a few more examples of legal documents produced for external use. Because these types of documents are viewed by those outside the office, and perhaps those with opposing or adversarial interests, legal professionals must take great care with not only the accuracy of the legal research behind the document but also with the manner such documents are written. The choice of words, the tenor of the writing, and the document's overall cohesiveness are matters entrusted to seasoned and cautious legal professionals with solid training and experience. Using the fruits of their legal research as the basis for the document, legal professionals engage in the art of legal writing. For externally destined documents, the writing, generally speaking, explains and simultaneously argues.

Within the confines of a legal office, a team of legal professionals working together uses an internal mode of communication to advise one another about the benefits of any professional analysis or legal research performed by colleagues. Known as the **legal memorandum**, this internal document is a work product of legal professionals intended only for the eyes of those authorized to view its contents. The purpose of the legal memorandum is to advise, explain, and recommend. This internal document is almost always confidential in nature.

legal memorandum
Summary of the case facts, the legal question asked, the research findings, the analysis, and the legal conclusion drawn from the law applied to the case facts.

As a matter of legal status, legal memoranda (i.e., plural for memorandum, a Latin word) are entitled to a privilege known as the work product doctrine and may be kept confidential, even during litigation. As discussed in the ethics section, such documents are certainly part of the confidentiality duty owed to clients. An internal legal memorandum may even contain sensitive matters, such as legal strategies and tactics. Because of its internal purpose, the intra-office legal memorandum carries an advisory tone that honestly weighs the available facts, evaluates, and comes to a frank appraisal and final recommendation. Thus, a legal memorandum may very well come to a conclusion that is not favorable or sympathetic to the law firm's client.

LEGAL WRITING: THE OFFICE LEGAL MEMORANDUM

Whether destined for external or internal use, legal writing represents a specialized form of expository writing and may take on several different tones, depending on the context and the intent of the author. For instance, legal writing presented to a court takes on an argumentative tone to explain a certain view of the case at hand. Letters to opposing parties may explain, as well as propose or even threaten. College students frequently engage in expository writing. In term papers, student authors write in a way that provides information, explains, defines, and describes certain topics to demonstrate their acquisition of knowledge about a certain subject.

Legal memoranda go further and, at the same time, employ a more limited choice of words. The aim of legal memoranda is purely informational and evaluative. Thus, alliteration, elegant variations, the tension implied by ambiguity, and other literary considerations are of little value in the legal memorandum. In fact, legal memoranda are necessarily straightforward, focused, and quite dry in both nature and tone. However, with some experience, legal memoranda can be easy to write. The important thing to remember is that they should be easy to read, because their point is to convey information about the law and your analysis as effortlessly as possible to the reader. Keep in mind that the audience reading legal memoranda will consist of other legal professionals—peers as well as supervisors—who are reading the legal memorandum purely to assess the legal matter at hand. The legal memorandum fulfills an essential requirement of that assessment process.

For legal professionals, researching and writing legal memoranda is a regular staple of their routine tasks in the law office. At the same time, a routine task at a professional level means an undertaking that has been performed with a studied thoroughness, as well as a level of technical exactitude that indicates professionalism. As noted previously, thorough research means using any legal research tools available to find the law and updating those finds by shepardizing and examining pocket parts. The next step in preparing the legal memorandum requires careful reading and, if necessary, briefing cases for quick reference subsequently. Finally, the legal memorandum's author must be able to convey clarity through clear and concise writing that flows smoothly.

To most people, legal writing is anything but clear, concise, or smooth. The popular perception justifiably regards most forms of legal writing as verbose, repetitive, dense, endlessly technical, full of redundant phrases, and consisting of unending paragraphs. With the persistent use of Latin and archaic French, what you have is "legalese." For centuries, legal writing remained obtuse and unapproachable—which was the point. After the Norman Conquest of England in 1066, English was considered the language of commoners. By maintaining legal writing that moved beyond the understanding of most of the population, law and those involved with it could preserve their elite social status. Every now and then, various movements have attempted to reform legal writing to a form understandable by most. However, until just recently, the convoluted and incomprehensible form of legal writing remained with the legal profession.

Fortunately, modern trends favor more recent reforms to legal writing as a result of the Plain English Movement of the 1970s and 1980s. Yet old habits still die hard. Many overly cautious and busy legal professionals prefer to use language to which they are accustomed. Too preoccupied to learn a new form of written communication or too fearful of suffering unanticipated consequences, these writers allow legalese to persist, mostly as a result of poor habits or lack of skill. Nevertheless, a new generation of legal professionals understands the importance of writing in plain English. In modern legal practice, and particularly for writing legal memoranda, the author's objective should be to communicate the needed information as clearly as possible. Using plain English helps the reader understand the meaning in the least amount of time. Despite some continued resistance, the plain English movement has become firmly implanted in the American legal world.

CYBER TRIP

In 1978, President Jimmy Carter issued an executive order directing that federal agencies should write their regulations as clearly and simply as possible. Since then, numerous federal laws have required the use of plain English. Federal agencies such as the Securities and Exchange Commission have strict plain English requirements. Go to the federal government's Web site to read about the topic: www.plainlanguage.gov.

Learning to Write in Plain English

Plain English is quite easy to master. There are only a few points to remember.

Word Choice and Sentence Construction

First, plain English is clear, straightforward, and concise, using only as many words as are necessary to get your ideas across. The words chosen intentionally should be down to earth. Plain English uses interesting words but avoids ornate and flowery ones, instead preferring those in everyday use with precisely the same meaning. Sentences are short, expressing no more than two points and preferably just one. Plain English avoids vagueness, obscurity, or pretentiousness while remaining interesting to read. It is language that avoids obscurity, inflated vocabulary, and convoluted sentence constructions. It is not baby talk, nor is it a simplified version of the English language. Writing plain English focuses on the audience's ability to understand the message easily. Ostentatious words and complex sentences can only distract the reader. Using plain words and short, simple sentences, writers in plain English identify the audience's needs and attention level and tailor their work accordingly.

Clarity and Precision

Second, plain English does not oversimplify or alter meanings, which might create imprecision. Clarity and precision are complementary goals. The process of revising into plain language can uncover the ambiguities and uncertainties that dense, impersonal, convoluted writing tends to hide. A good test for the clarity of your own writing is to ask yourself whether a passage you have just written is clear. Also ask if it could have been written more clearly. Be sure to use the active voice as much as possible. Write in short sentences that flow from one idea to the next.

Using Legal Terms

Third, plain English remains possible even if your writing must include legal terms that are common in the profession as terms of art—that is, shorthand—understood by all legal professionals. Technical jargon, or legal terms of art, are but a small portion of any legal or official document. Think of them as a form of shorthand. In previous chapters, we have learned many legal terms whose meanings now are clearer to us than they would be to a layperson. For instance, the Latin term *mens rea* means the intent or state of mind to commit a crime. Proof of *mens rea* is necessary in most cases to establish that someone has committed most crimes, such as theft. Thus, we understand that mistakenly walking away with another's belonging is not a crime because of the lack of *mens rea*. To establish the crime of theft, the accused must have the intent to deprive another, unlawfully, of his or her property. Thus, the prosecution must show that the accused possessed the requisite *mens rea* to prove the crime of theft.

Incidentally, not all crimes require proof of *mens rea*. Speeding, the unauthorized possession of a controlled substance, and accidental homicide are just a few examples of crimes that may have been unintended yet still are punishable. The law dispenses with *mens rea* for various policy reasons, including that proving *mens rea* would be too difficult for the government in some cases and that there is a strong public interest in prohibiting or curtailing certain types of behavior.

Have the Mens Rea *to Write an Understandable Document*

Fourth, a plain English writer must be motivated to achieve a better document than one written in legalese. Try to read a legal document written in plain English and then another written in a more traditional fashion. As many researchers have reported, you will find that the document written in plain English is easier to read and understood in a shorter period of time. Moreover, the plain English document is more likely to be read, because readers are less likely to be intimidated or put off by it. Because

Legal Terms and Phrases	Plain English Equivalent(s)
cease and desist	stop
covenant and agree	agree
last will and testament	will
by means of, by virtue of, in accordance with	by, under
in favor of	for
prior to, subsequent to	before, after
filed a motion	moved
on even date herewith	today, date
appurtenant thereto	attached
the question as to whether	whether
notwithstanding the fact that	despite, although
in the event of	if
at this point in time	now
(s)he was aware of the fact that	(s)he knew
because of the fact that	because
adequate number of	enough, sufficient
by and through	by

FIGURE 5.4
Plain English Equivalents of Legal Terms and Phrases

readers prefer plain language and understand it better, fewer mistakes, fewer questions, and fewer complaints result. Readers will have a more satisfying reading experience and feel better about the document, and perhaps even its contents.

In short, plain English is effective expository writing, which is very important in legal practice. Most legal writing involves careful explanations of complex ideas as they apply to a myriad of factual situations. In addition, many legal documents attempt to persuade colleagues, opposing parties, and particularly judges. Thus, the purpose of the document is to convince the reader to agree with the author. Persuasive writing attempts to get readers to feel or act a certain way toward a subject. This persuasion occurs most effectively when the writing is easy, accessible, and welcoming to the reader.

Figure 5.4 provides a chart of terms and phrases often used in legal documents. The left-hand side lists traditionally used language, whereas the right-hand side provides plain English alternatives. As you progress further into law and legal language, you will be able to supply plain English—that is, easy-to-understand and down-to-earth alternatives for archaic legal phrases. This point is not to say that legal language should always be substituted with plain English. As discussed previously, terms of the art represent professional terms that can act as shortcuts. To use plain English substitutes for some terms of art may actually require more words by way of explanation. When the intended audience understands a term of art, using them may be more concise and hence preferable. In contrast, some legal terms and phrases could definitely be substituted with shorter, plain English.

Some words and phrases can and should be avoided altogether. In fact, omitting them entirely can improve readability immensely. There are innumerable examples of legalese that can be expressed equally and with greater economy in plain English, and there are various legal words and phrases that are purely redundant. As a matter of writing in plain English, avoid using *any* of the terms in Figure 5.5.

it would appear to be the case that	herewith, heretofore	in this regard it is significiant to note that
hereinafter referred to as to wit	aforementioned such, said, aforesaid	thereon, thereupon on or about
in the case now under consideration	forthwith	free and clear

FIGURE 5.5
Redundant Terms to Avoid

CASE IN POINT

COURTS USING PLAIN ENGLISH

A current hero of Plain English Movement is Judge Mark P. Painter of the Ohio First District Court of Appeals. In *Kohlbrand v. Ranieri,* 159 Ohio App.3d 140,, 823 N.E.2d 76 (2005), Judge Painter interpreted the legal phrase "free and clear title" as follows:

> Free and clear mean the same thing. Using both is an unnecessary lawyerism. Free is English; clear is from the Old French cler. After the Norman Conquest, English courts were held in French. The Normans were originally Vikings, but after they conquered the region of Normandy, they became French; then they took over England. But most people in England, surprisingly enough, still spoke English. So lawyers started using two words for one and forgot to stop for the last 900 years. . . . The Norman Conquest was in 1066. We can safely eliminate the couplets now. *Id.,* 159 Ohio App. 3d at 143–44, 823 N.E.2d at 78.

QUESTIONS ABOUT THE CASE

1. Is there a difference between an "unnecessary legalism" and a necessary one?
2. How would you react if your supervisor told you to maintain legalisms?
3. Could Judge Painter be criticized for using a whole paragraph to avoid the use of two extra words?

CYBER TRIP

One of the most beneficial ways to remember to use plain English in legal writing is to recall the title of Judge Painter's article, *How to Write for Judges, Not Like Judges.* That article appears at www.sconet.state.oh.us/rod/newpdf/1/2005/2005-ohio-295.pdf.

Examples of plain English equivalents and avoidable legalese could go on and on. These two lists are merely examples that should give you an idea of how to write in a way that is easy for the reader to understand. Being able to write clearly and concisely is a worthy skill. Having the ability to produce easily read office memoranda efficiently will distinguish you as a valuable legal professional.

Practicing Plain English

Probably the best way to learn how to write in plain English is by practicing. A good beginning exercise would be to translate legalese (legalisms) into plain English, then put the translation into a practical situation. Statutes are notorious legalisms that are fraught with complex sentences. At the same time, statutes are good faith attempts to encompass a broad range of situations, which demand that they use vague language and numerous clauses to include certain circumstances and exclude others. Clients will frequently receive advice on how a statute, particularly a new one, might affect their lives or their livelihoods. Here is a practice example for how a legal professional might use plain English at work.

Legal Analysis in Plain English

Assume that you are employed as a legal professional in a law office that represents a wealthy dog owner who is very concerned about a new state law that was recently enacted. Your colleague has pointed out that the new statute changes the common law. As we previously noted, statutes often make changes to the common law. Under common law, domesticated animals, particularly pets, were presumed tame and not dangerous by nature. Thus, owners were not responsible for any harm caused by the animal unless they knew or should have known that the animal was likely to cause harm. This common law principle came to be known as the "first bite free" rule and absolved the owner the first time that a domesticated animal bit someone. In a significant way, the common law rule acted as a shield to protect pet owners from lawsuits arising from incidents in which their pets bit someone for the first time. Usually, the rule applied to protect owners of dogs and cats.

scienter
A degree of knowledge that makes a person legally responsible for his or her act or omission.

However, after the first time, the owner was charged with the knowledge that the animal could cause harm. The legal term for the owner's knowledge is called **scienter**. The owner could be liable for any subsequent bite, because the common law presumption would no longer protect that owner. That is, once the owner had scienter that the dog could cause harm, another person who was harmed in the same way could get past the common law presumption. The victim could then sue the owner for money damages resulting from the dog bite. Thus, under the common law rule of "first bite free," pet owners could be still liable after the first incident. That is, the common law did not protect owners completely. Anyone suing an owner after the first incident would have to prove the owner's scienter as an element of their case to remove the common law barrier and proceed with the lawsuit. Once the owners had scienter—knowledge that the animal could cause harm as it had in the past—they were deemed negligent for not having taken care to protect people from an injurious animal.

This rule is known as strict liability. Stripped of their common law protection by a showing of scienter, owners were almost automatically liable for the harm caused by their animals. Strict liability in this sense means that the person suing the dog owner does not have to show scienter on the part of the dog owner, because the dog had bitten someone before. Given this history of the common law, many animal owners may be concerned about their potential exposure to liability in this new legal environment. For a long time, they felt somewhat protected by the common law presumption. Now, with the new statute on the books, insurers, breeders, and other pet fanciers who are clients of the law firm are understandably concerned what the law may mean for them. With the ink still fresh on the new law, a law firm such as yours would notify clients about the new law and give them advice about what actions to take. That advice could include whether to buy more insurance or take additional precautions regarding the maintenance of their animals, or both.

Before communicating with clients, the law office undertakes internal analysis and preparation. At some point, the firm will decide to send an advisory letter to clients whom the new law may affect. Many clients, especially business clients, expect this level of service, because they rely on their lawyers to keep them abreast of changes in the law. This situation is where the legal memorandum comes into play. To assess the legal situation, one of the legal professionals produces a legal memorandum about the effect of the new statute on the common law. Let's take a look at a typical modern statute and analyze it.

Format for the Office Memoranda

At first sight, the format for office memoranda appears formal, almost overly so. Typewritten with headings and divided into various sections, the office memorandum merely follows a format with which legal professionals are familiar and that can be read easily. The actual arrangement differs from office to office. Figure 5.6 provides an example of the various sections in an office memorandum and their function.

FIGURE 5.6
Example of an Office Memorandum

Memorandum

To: Mary M. Manager, Esq.
From: Patricia Paralegal
Re: Implications of Civil Code §3342 for Association of Dog Breeders
Date: May 22, 2007
Question Presented: You have asked me to analyze the provisions of Civil Code §3342, as it may affect our client, the Dog Breeders Association.
Tentative Answer: Civil Code §3342 abrogates the common law requirement of *scienter* for dog owners in lawsuits by dog bite victims on public places or lawfully on private places. Thus, a plaintiff does not have to prove that the dog had bitten someone before and was potentially dangerous. Thus §3342 imposes strict liability on dog owners.
Facts: Our client, the Dog Breeders Association, has requested our opinion on the probable effect that newly enacted Civil Code §3342 will have on the conduct of their member.
Analysis: Civil Code §3342, provides as follows . . .

A DAY IN THE LIFE OF A REAL PARALEGAL

Tim Smith works with the appellate section of a medium-sized law firm in San Francisco. With a degree in English and a paralegal certificate, Tim has found that he enjoys the slower pace of appeals work, which requires in-depth legal research, careful inspection of voluminous trial records, and the intellectual challenge of writing legal arguments. After a couple of years, Tim began to play a major role in the firm's appellate work. Using his education as an English major, Tim has become the go-to person for proofreading the firm's appellate briefs. Moreover, with his paralegal background, Tim helps attorneys research and draft legal arguments in the briefs to submit to the California Courts of Appeal, the California Supreme Court, and the Federal Ninth Circuit Court of Appeals. In some important cases, Tim accompanies the attorneys when they argue the case before a panel of appellate judges in both state and federal court. Tim gushes when he talks about his job in appellate work: "I love my work. It's exciting to be at the cutting edge of the law working with cases that may create precedent. I can hardly wait until I get to work on a case in the U.S. Supreme Court."

Notice that this format makes it easy for the reader to grasp the essence of the issue under discussion immediately, with the use of the Question Presented and Tentative Answer sections, without having to read the entire memorandum. For our purposes, the Facts section is brief. In other memoranda, the situation may involve complex facts, though only the relevant or operative facts are included in this section. The Analysis section starts off with a quotation of the full text of the statute so that the reader may examine it from the outset. Another style would put a quotation of the statute in the first footnote of the memorandum. Generally speaking, legal documents place footnotes at the bottom of the page.

You may be more accustomed to the practice of endnotes, which place footnotes at the end of a chapter or section. However, in legal documents, footnotes frequently present pertinent materials for the reader to refer to while reading the main text.

The Analysis section is the main component and the bulk of the memorandum. It contains the author's legal analysis and research. In more complex situations, it may be broken up further into smaller subsections. The final section, the Conclusion, should provide more description as a summary than does the Tentative Answer.

The most important thing to remember is that despite its formal appearance, the office memorandum should be easy to read. The modern legal memorandum is a common staple, if not the bulk, of the work performed by many legal professionals in almost any law office. Many legal professionals dread the prospect of legal writing. However, more and more of these legal professionals also are finding that the use of plain English and modern computerized legal research methods make it easier to produce legal memoranda. After some practice, writing office memoranda may become a fairly satisfying task.

For every legal memorandum written, the author learns new law and becomes more practiced at the art of writing in plain English. Those professionals who do obtain such practice exhibit quiet pride in their work. With the ability to store electronic versions of their memoranda, legal professionals may develop a virtual bank of memos on various topics. After a few years, their bank of legal memos, as well as other forms of legal writing, become very valuable resources. Future legal memos may incorporate those written for other cases in the past and then updated. Legal memos also may be rewritten into different forms of legal documents for submission to court.

At its most basic, essential form, law is simply words that express concepts—some highly complex, and others very elementary and simple. To be sure, the court system and its enforcement mechanisms (e.g., sheriffs, police, constables) give it force and substance. Yet for legal professionals, working in the law consists exclusively of speaking and writing in words and concepts. Court appearances and hearings before administrative agencies are the most visible task of legal professionals. Among our most prominent images of legal professionals at work are those involving courtroom dramatics, moving orations, and devastating cross-examinations.

Within the law office, images of Erin Brockovich and other legal professionals engaged in complex and formidable negotiation sessions may persist in the minds of many people and certainly in the media. Yet the truth of the matter is that legal practice, almost anywhere, is largely legal professionals producing various types of legal documents. Thus, developing research and writing skills that can assist the legal team to assemble and prepare documents efficiently constitutes an essential part of the training to become a legal professional.

Summary

With some basic knowledge about the law and the legal profession, you can begin with some basic instruction into how to find and use the law as a legal professional. Although courts are passive, law-making institutions, the opinions they generate carry great weight. Court opinions interpret and explain the law and how it applies to our day-to-day behavior. In doing so, courts provide reasons for their rulings, which in turn becomes an important source of law that applies to future situations.

Because of the importance of court opinions in our legal culture, these opinions are published and compiled in an orderly fashion by both the government and private publishers. Over the years, research aids and other publications have arisen to help legal professionals perform their legal research. Secondary legal materials, such as legal encyclopedias, treatises, and scholarly works by law reviews among others, aid the researcher by providing background information on almost every area of the law and citations to court opinions and other legal materials. These are not a form of legal authority. Secondary legal materials help with legal research and may occasionally help persuade a court or legislature.

Statutes, like court opinions, are primary sources of law that come from state and federal legislatures. Unlike court opinions, statutes are proactive sources of legal authority that are enacted as the result of a publicly perceived problem or evil. Democratic processes produce legislation that is published chronologically and then compiled topically. For both statutes and court opinions, competent legal research means obtaining the most up-to-date information about the status of the law. Devices such as pocket parts and Shepard's are research tools that allow access to the most recent changes in the law. Researching to find the most recent legal information is an integral and important part of fulfilling both professional and ethical duties. Much of the task of updating research has been made easier and quicker with the use of computer-assisted legal research.

The fruits of legal research often comes in the form of a legal memorandum. Legal professionals inform colleagues and themselves by performing research and reducing their findings to writing, which explains the law and evaluates a client's situation in light of that law. Legal memos should be efficient and easy to read. Thus, the modern trend of using plain English dispenses with archaic legalisms and long, complex writing styles, as well as with the use of legalese.

The prevailing modern trend of using plain English promotes simple, easy-to-understand writing by using straightforward language. Older forms of expressing legal concepts in wordy and archaic language are no longer useful for conveying information. Yet old habits die hard, particularly the habit of writing in a way that has persisted for centuries. However, writing in plain English can distinguish a legal professional.

Key Terms

- Advance sheets
- Annotation
- Case reporters
- Code of Federal Regulations (C.F.R.)
- Codification
- Dictum
- Digest
- KeyCite
- Law reviews
- Legal encyclopedia
- Legal memorandum
- LexisNexis
- Official reporters
- Pocket parts
- Regional reporters
- Reporters
- *Restatement*
- Scienter
- Session laws
- Shepard's Citations
- Shepardizing (shepardize)
- Slip law
- Slip opinion
- Treatise
- Unofficial reporters
- Westlaw

Review Questions

1. What are the differences between official and unofficial publications of cases or statutes?
2. What are the main differences between traditional legal research and CALR?
3. What ethical issues are implied when a legal professional performs legal research?
4. When would you go first to a primary source or a secondary source to begin your research?
5. What is codification?
6. Are digests a form of legal authority?
7. What is the difference between the United States Code and the United States Statutes at Large?
8. Which regional reporter covers your state?
9. Which court's decisions are reported in the Federal Supplement? In the Federal Reporter?
10. How do you distinguish a dictum from a holding?

Exercises

1. Visit a local law library in a government office or a nearby law school. Find the status of the dog bite law in your state.
2. Find a legal document in everyday use, such as an apartment lease, a loan agreement, or even the reverse side of your credit card bill. Try your hand at rewriting any of the provisions into plain English.
3. Find your state's equivalent of the United States Statutes at Large, which usually are called session laws. What significant laws were passed by your state's legislature in the past year?
4. Make a list of legal issues or topics of personal interest to you. Select a state or the federal realm and determine what you can find out on your own at www.findlaw.com. Write a short memorandum about the fruits of your research efforts. If you had difficulty with your research, state what problems you had.
5. Find out through Internet research or by visiting a local law library how your state's courts give effect to the *Restatement*.

Discussion Questions

1. What types of legal research tools can help a researcher perform research tasks most efficiently? Does the type of tool depend on the researcher's familiarity with particular areas of the law?
2. Should the federal or state government provide free public access to legal materials?
3. Why do some unofficial publications have names such as Deering's California Code or Wallace U.S. Supreme Court Reports (1863 to 1874)? Do you think that it is proper for private companies to publish court opinions exclusively?
4. Do you think that using plain English is an appropriate trend in law? Why or why not?
5. Drawing on the various schools of thought in jurisprudence discussed in Chapter 1, provide an explanation for the persistence of legalese. This chapter suggests that laziness and bad habits are primary reasons. What other explanations would each school of thought provide about legalisms and plain English?

PORTFOLIO ASSIGNMENT

Try your own hand at writing an office memorandum based on the dog bite statute. Assume that this morning, your supervisor has asked you to write an office memorandum that analyzes §3342 so that she can inform an association of dog breeders that the office represents. Be sure to use the format for office memoranda as shown in this chapter. The memorandum should consist of about three double-spaced pages. To gain a better perspective on the legal concerns of dog breeders, see http://animallaw.info/articles/ddusdogbite.htm.

Chapter 6

Paralegals in Action

CHAPTER OBJECTIVES

The materials presented in this chapter will provide students with information about:

- Ethical considerations for paralegals in the legal workplace.
- The *authorized* practice of law by paralegals.
- Selected topics in legal practice, specifically, civil litigation.
- A primer on evidence law for paralegals.

An essential part of the training for all legal professionals involves acquiring knowledge on a variety of legal subjects that are common to legal practice. Similar to the many courses you are taking in school, such as English, math, history, and science, law comprises various categories or subjects. These subjects are different from the classifications we learned about in Chapter 4. In that chapter, we covered the various classifications, such as federal and state laws or criminal and civil laws. In this chapter, we discuss the various subjects within each of those classifications and gain a beginning knowledge of substantive law. In studying this chapter, you will learn some of the most basic topics in law. The topics we cover thus provide the basic foundation for more advanced topics that you may cover in other courses and indeed in your continuing study of law.

ETHICAL CONSIDERATIONS

As we discussed in Chapter 2, ethics plays an extremely important role in legal practice. Ethics are an essential part of the professionalism that allows people working in the legal field to earn the public's confidence. The legal profession's ethical rules of reflect the goals of fairness and evenhandedness of the legal system. Among the many rules that apply to paralegals are those summarized in the ABA's Model Rules of Professional Conduct and the various ethical rules of the paralegal organizations such as NALA, NFPA, and IPMA. Primary among them, as you will recall, are the three most important rules for paralegals to remember: maintain client confidentiality, avoid conflicts of interest, and refrain from the unauthorized practice of law.

EYE ON ETHICS

The ethical codes of the NALA (Canon 3), NFPA (§1.8), and the ABA's Model Code of Professional Conduct (Rules 5.3 and 5.5) caution against the unauthorized practice of law. Even a lawyer's ethical codes prohibit him or her from committing the unauthorized practice of law in another state. In addition to these ethical rules, statutes in every state impose criminal sanctions for committing the unauthorized practice of law.

For the most part, paralegals may not give legal advice, and therein lies the danger. What exactly constitutes "giving legal advice" is difficult to define. At the very least, whether someone—licensed or otherwise—is giving legal advice depends on the circumstances and the information given. For instance, after finishing this and the next chapter, you will have absorbed introductory information on five separate legal subjects: civil litigation, evidence, torts, criminal law, and procedure. If a student using this textbook were to report his or her newly acquired knowledge to family members and friends, would that constitute "giving legal advice" and hence the unauthorized practice of law?

At a gut level, we are almost certain that this reporting would not be giving legal advice. Under these circumstances, merely reporting what a student has learned in the study of law is not advice, particularly because the information given is not in response to another person's specific situation. It is merely reporting. From this analysis, we gain the sense that "giving legal advice" means, at least in part, that the person provides information that is intended to counsel or advise someone. That is, the information is meant to offer guidance under the law, and the persons receiving the information are seeking legal guidance. Otherwise, telling your friends or family what you have learned is general information that is not intended to guide behavior. Thus, a large part of "giving legal advice" is defined by the context. Persons giving legal information and those receiving it understand that the information is meant to advise the legal consequences of certain situations.

THE AUTHORIZED PRACTICE OF LAW FOR THE PROFESSIONAL PARALEGAL

For many reasons, the legal workplace stands out as an exception to the unauthorized practice rules. Primarily, legal work performed in a law office does not constitute the practice of law if it is not offered to the public. Writing a memorandum of law for a colleague or supervising attorney about the specifics of a statute or court decision certainly does constitute the practice of law. However, within the context of a law office, you might think of it as the *authorized* practice of law. Remember that the person to whom you are conveying the information is a licensed attorney or another legal professional (e.g., a paralegal) working under the supervision of a licensed attorney. The research and preparation of a legal memorandum therefore constitutes a legal task delegated by an attorney who is also supervising that legal work. The legal advice in the memorandum is given to the attorney and not to the public. More important, because the attorney is ultimately responsible for the legal work performed under his or her direction, the paralegal may perform the work that the lawyer would otherwise perform.

Putting all of this together, legal advice constitutes a form of practicing law that students of law and paralegals should be careful to avoid because of the specialized

CASE IN POINT

CASE SUMMARIES: SELF-HELP BOOKS AND THE UNAUTHORIZED PRACTICE OF LAW

States differ regarding what constitutes the unauthorized practice of law. Consider two cases in which bar associations brought actions against the authors of legal self-help books.

One of the first self-help books challenged, *How to Avoid Probate,* by Norman F. Dacey, was a 300-page how-to guide that instructed laypersons about how to draft wills, inter-vivos trust agreements and other related legal documents. The book consisted of legal forms and more than 50 pages of text explaining how to fill out the forms. The New York County Lawyers Association sued, claiming that the book constituted the unauthorized practice of law. The New York Court of Appeals, the state's highest court, rejected the lawyers' claim. The Court concluded that the book was merely a statement of what the law said. The Court also noted that the unauthorized practice of law required a relationship of personal contact between two or more individuals. At any rate, the Court noted, everyone has the right to represent themselves. *New York County Lawyers Association v. Dacey,* 21 N.Y. 694, 287 N.Y.S. 2d 4322, 234 N.E.2d 459 (1967).

A similar publication that instructed individuals how to obtain their own no-fault divorce did not fare as well in Florida. In *Florida Bar Association v. Stupica,* 300 So. 2d 683 (Fla. 1974), the Florida Supreme Court found that the information in a book was detailed and specialized to a sufficient degree to constitute the unauthorized practice of law and therefore enjoined its publication. The Court concluded that the publication coincided with the advice that a lawyer would normally give to his or her client.

QUESTIONS ABOUT THE CASE

1. What does the difference in the outcomes of the two cases say about judicial decision making and the notion of justice?
2. Why are bar associations involved as parties to the lawsuits?
3. Is there a difference between giving legal advice and telling someone how to represent himself?

and technical information obtained from their studies. Understandably, learning law can often be very exciting. With just a beginning knowledge of law, you will be able to understand more deeply the stories that you hear on the news regarding pending lawsuits and even international relations.

Sharing your broadening horizons and newly acquired knowledge with friends and relatives expresses your pride in the intellectual and professional growth you are experiencing. Still, be aware that friends and relatives may be the first to ask for your knowledge of law as it pertains to them personally. Should you respond with specific legal information, you may be treading upon that nether area that approaches the unauthorized practice of law. A number of serious repercussions may follow. First, the advice may be incomplete or inadequate and thus cause harm to your friend or relative. Second, you may actually break the law. Remember Rose Furman. Third, and perhaps most profound, you may be starting a very bad habit.

Keeping these details in mind, we can now proceed into some of the more common areas of substantive law encountered in practice.

CIVIL LITIGATION AND PROCEDURE: LITIGATION PARALEGALS

As we discussed in the previous chapter, the law contains many classifications. Among the major classifications are the differences between civil and criminal law and between substantive and procedural law. To review briefly, civil laws govern the disputes

CASE IN POINT

DEFINING THE PRACTICE OF LAW

In 1967, the American Bar Association observed that the duties that would otherwise constitute the practice of law could be delegated to nonlawyers within the law office as long as the attorney was ultimately responsible for the work. In language that sounds both proverbial and practical, the ABA stated that the unauthorized practice of law does not "limit the kind of assistance the lawyer can acquire in any way to persons who are admitted to the Bar, so long as the non-lawyers do not do things that lawyers may not do or do things that lawyers only may do." See ABA Formal Ethics Opinion 316, January 18, 1967. Thus, a nonlawyer may perform duties if they fall under the ultimate supervision of an attorney and do not directly constitute the practice of law for the *public*. Therein lies the basis of the unauthorized practice rule.

QUESTIONS ABOUT THE CASE

1. What does the ABA opinion clarify about the meaning of the unauthorized practice of law?
2. What effect did the ABA opinion have on the paralegal profession?
3. What are the "things that lawyers only may do?"

A DAY IN THE LIFE OF A REAL PARALEGAL

With the ink still wet on her paralegal degree, Linda Champion set out to test the advocacy skills she loved learning as a member of her high school and college Mock Trial Teams. "Once I learned that I could major in Paralegal Studies at my school, I decided to give it a try. It looked like a way to work with law without the time and expense of law school," she reminisces.

Before the end of her first year as a litigation paralegal with a small suburban law firm, Champion was able to persuade her supervising attorney to let her help with some of the office's Social Security cases, in which clients were making disability claims. She proved herself by studying the law and the agency's procedures in detail—all on her own time. Her boss was duly impressed and supervised Champion as she began helping with cases by interviewing clients, talking with their doctors, and reviewing their medical records. Soon Champion became the office's specialized paralegal in those cases. She handled all of the paperwork, organizing, and indexing records. Champion would also help her boss during administrative hearings.

After several months, Champion received the biggest surprise: Her boss asked if she would like to try handling a disability hearing herself. The hearings require very relaxed rules of evidence, and the judges, known as administrative law judges, are less formal and imposing than those in the courts. Moreover, Champion often understood the case as well her boss did. Her boss knew that Champion was eager and highly capable. After all, Champion had been one of her boss' students at the paralegal school.

"I used to get real nervous starting the day before a hearing," Champion confesses, "but after I got used to appearing before the administrative judges, my task was focusing on what I had to do. Once I felt that focus coming on, my nervousness went away. It's fun. Everything I learned at Mock Trial came back to me." For decades, state and federal administrative agencies have permitted nonlawyers to appear as legal representatives at adjudicatory hearings. Paralegals engaged in administrative advocacy can greatly increase productivity and effectiveness in the delivery of legal services. One oft-cited study shows that Social Security Administration claimants represented by nonlawyers achieve success rates very close to those of claimants represented by attorneys.

Now, Champion appears routinely before the administrative law judges. She is always careful to point out to clients that she is a paralegal and that the Social Security Administration has special rules that allow nonattorneys to do what she does, namely, the authorized practice of law.

RESEARCH THIS

Find the statute that governs the type of evidence rules that apply in Social Security disability hearings. What Social Security regulation permits Linda Champion and other nonattorneys to represent claimants?

civil procedure
Rules used to handle a civil case from the time the initial complaint is filed, through pretrial discovery, the trial itself, and any subsequent appeal. Each state adopts its own rules of civil procedure (often set out in separate Codes of Civil Procedure), but many are influenced by or modeled on the Federal Rules of Civil Procedure.

demand letter
A letter requesting action on a legal matter.

between individuals, even if one of the parties is the government. Criminal laws are those that protect society at large, can be enforced only by the government, and involve the possible imposition of punishment. Substantive laws describe the rights we have, whereas procedural laws are those that indicate how to enforce those rights. In the subject area known as **civil procedure**, or civil litigation, we deal with procedural law regarding the litigation of civil matters.

More practicing paralegals are involved in civil litigation than in any other area of legal practice, because litigation is highly labor intensive, requiring the drafting, organizing, and analysis of court documents, as well as preparing cases for trial or settlement and even appeal. Moreover, litigation can involve almost every subject in law. A civil dispute may involve matters as disparate as a contract dispute, an automobile accident, shares of stock, a copyright infringement, or even divorces and property boundary disputes. This chapter examines civil litigation from a timeline perspective. From the steps leading to the filing of a civil action to its conclusion or appeal, paralegals are involved in almost every aspect of litigation.

CYBER TRIP

Can a paralegal perform the duties of a private investigator? The United States Department of Labor thinks so. On the Internet, go to stats.bls.gov/oco/ocos157.htm, and find the training and qualifications for a professional private detective or investigator. Presumably, a paralegal could work as a paralegal and an investigator in a law office. Almost all states (except Alabama, Alaska, Colorado, Idaho, Mississippi, Missouri, and South Dakota) have licensing requirements for people to engage in the practice known as private investigation. See www.infoguys.com/article.cfm?id=10.

Prelitigation Activities

The filing of a lawsuit generally means that attempts to resolve the matter by the parties have failed. Informal steps to settle potential disputes may involve such activities as discussions and settlement conferences. More serious prelitigation endeavors include sending a **demand letter**, in which an aggrieved party details the essence of his or her grievance and requests the other party to take certain steps to remedy the problem. In some states, particularly in consumer matters, a demand letter is required before a party may file a consumer lawsuit. If these and other prelitigation attempts to settle a dispute fail to produce a mutually agreeable resolution, litigation is often the result.

Other prelitigation activities include factual research or investigation efforts by the plaintiff in an attempt to gather evidence in preparation for the lawsuit. Quite often, law firms and the government engage private investigators to gather and preserve evidence in contemplation of a lawsuit. Far from the sleuths we envision from mystery novels, Dick Tracy comics, and the movies, professional private investigators are professionals who are licensed in most states.

Rules of Procedure

As we have discussed, court procedures under common law employed a system of writs issued by the Crown. Several types of writs authorized a plaintiff to bring a case before the Royal Court and commanded the defendant to appear. These types of writs represented the only forms of relief available in civil disputes. That is, if a certain type of dispute did not conform to any of the available writs, the court could not and would not hear the matter. Thus, the common law courts could only hear a very limited range of disputes. The problem with this approach was that the ability to create new writs amounted to the ability to create new rights. A plaintiff's rights were defined by the writs available.

In the United States, the writ system and forms of relief became known as the cause of action, meaning that the law authorized certain types of lawsuits. In the modern language of federal rules, a cause of action is synonymous with a claim for relief. After many years of development, writs and forms of action became obsolete and were replaced by a document known as a **summons** that commands parties to appear before the court regarding the dispute. Still, many common law rules of procedure followed the cumbersome and rigid writ system of pleading a case to a court.

summons
The notice to appear in court, notifying the defendant of the plaintiff's complaint.

Finally, in 1938, the United States federal court system adopted the **Federal Rules of Civil Procedure**, which authorize only one form of action, or lawsuit, known as a civil action, and merged law and equity into a single proceeding. The adoption of these new rules in all federal district courts swept away centuries of musty, old common law pleadings and combined the division between law and equity into one action: the civil action.

Federal Rules of Civil Procedure
(Fed. R. Civ. P.) The specific set of rules followed in the federal courts.

The Federal Rules also introduced modern concepts of administering justice with streamlined court procedures and authorized the use of plain English. The change was revolutionary. Under common law, a lawsuit for breach of contract required the plaintiff to use very specialized and technical language when describing the complaint. The failure to use certain words or phrases could be fatal, and the lawsuit would be dismissed *with prejudice,* which meant that the plaintiff could not bring the action again even if it were a mere technical error and the court never heard the case.

Instead, under the Federal Rules of Civil Procedure, Rule 8, all that is required is a "short plain statement of the claim." Many states have followed suit and model their own rules of court procedure after the Federal Rules. And so begins our examination of civil procedure—the rules that govern the format and content of papers filed in court, filing fees, serving papers, requests for rulings, discovery, selecting a jury, trial procedures, and appeals. Remember our previous discussion, in which we noted that these rules are a form of law known as *procedural law* and govern the procedure required to enforce the rights flowing from *substantive laws*.

Beginning the Lawsuit: The Complaint

After prelitigation activities and other negotiation techniques have failed, or even without any prior contact, a lawsuit begins with the filing of the most basic of court documents, the **complaint**. In the complaint, the plaintiff alleges the facts underlying the dispute and states the claim for relief, or the legal basis and the relief requested, whether the plaintiff is asking for money or a court order or both.

complaint
Document that states the allegations and the legal basis of the plaintiff 's claims. Also, a charge, preferred before a magistrate having jurisdiction, that a person named has committed a specified offense, with an offer to prove the fact, to the end that a prosecution may be instituted.

The complaint performs four distinct functions: (1) advising the court as to its power to hear the case, (2) telling the court the plaintiff's story, (3) setting out the legal basis or claims for relief, and (4) asking the court to award a specific form of relief or remedy. The request for relief tells the court what the plaintiff wants it to do. Under the Federal Rules, courts in civil lawsuits may award monetary damages or a court order, such as an injunction, or both. One of the major innovations brought about by the Federal Rules was the merger of law and equity, which means that a plaintiff can seek both forms of relief in one court based on a single lawsuit by making the necessary allegations within one complaint.

Drafting complaints is a common task for paralegals as well as lawyers. From beginning to end, the constituent parts of the complaint consist of the following parts: Centered at the top of the first page appears the name of the **forum** in which the lawsuit will be heard. Next appears the name of the parties and the designation of their respective roles in the lawsuit, such as plaintiff, petitioner, defendant, or respondent. The role designation of each party may differ depending on the type of proceeding or the stage of the case. For instance, at the appellate level, the party appealing is the appellant, and the other party is the appellee. In other situations, the party bringing the action or appeal is the petitioner, and the other party is the respondent.

forum
The proper legal site or location.

These party designations are commonly used in requests for writs or requests to the United States Supreme Court or a state supreme court for **judicial review**. In proceedings using these designations, the initial document is known as a **petition** instead of a complaint. Generally speaking, a proceeding instituted by a petition requests a specific type of action rather than a form of monetary or equitable relief. For instance, when a party asks the United States Supreme Court or a state supreme court to review

judicial review
Availability or power of a court to review the actions of another branch of government, such as an administrative agency.

petition
A formal written application requesting a court for a specific judicial action.

FIGURE 6.1
Typical Court System

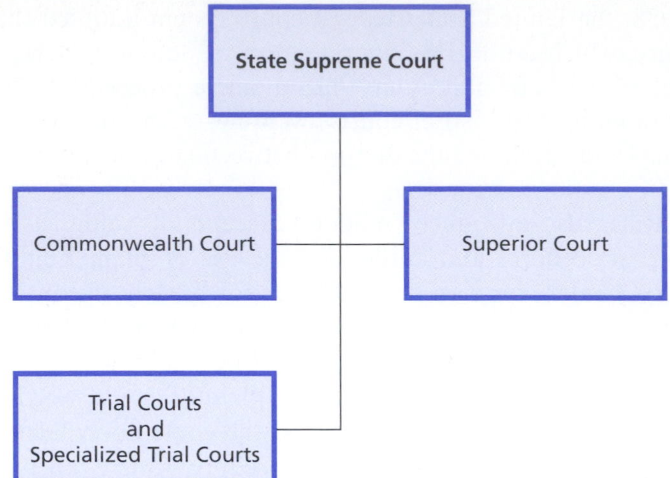

PRACTICE TIP

As part of a personal reference system, a legal professional should always maintain awareness of the structure of court systems and the routes to them from administrative agencies. Paralegals in particular can play active roles in the representation of clients for administrative agencies whose regulations permit it. If you post or file a structure chart at your work desk, you will always be sure to have a ready reference.

a decision from a lower court, it files a petition for certiorari or a petition for review. Such a petition asks the Court to review the decision by a lower forum.

Commonly, courts review the decisions of an administrative agency after a petition is filed by the party that lost before that agency. The concept of judicial review can be quite complex, involving theories of jurisprudence, political science, and government. In the federal government and in most states, administrative agencies function within the executive branch's role of enforcing laws established by the legislature. The power of courts to review the actions of an executive agency is part of the system of checks and balances.

Every state has a different mechanism for the judicial review of their agencies. The federal system acts as a model for most states. Nevertheless, there are wide differences among the states. Pennsylvania, for instance, has its own intermediate appellate level court, the Commonwealth Court, to hear appeals from that state's administrative agencies. Thus, Pennsylvania has two midlevel courts, the Commonwealth Court and the Superior Court, which hears general appeals from the trial courts. Figure 6.1 provides a chart of a typical state court system.

The part of the complaint that names the court and the parties functions as a heading known as the **caption**. After the complaint is filed, the court will assign a **docket number**, which identifies the lawsuit throughout the proceedings as a matter of administrative management. All subsequent papers filed with the court in the same lawsuit must bear the docket number in their captions.

caption
The full name of the case, together with the docket number, and court.

docket number
The number assigned by the court to the case for its own administrative purposes.

jurisdictional statement
Section of a complaint or brief that identifies the legal authority that grants the appellate court the right to hear the case.

As discussed previously, courts define their tasks very narrowly. The legislative branch establishes the courts by enacting statutes that describe the scope of the court's powers and the types of cases that the court may hear. Courts are careful not to overstep the legal authority granted to them by law. Thus, court rules, particularly in the federal courts, require that the complaint include a **jurisdictional statement**, which indicates the legal power of the court to hear a case. In state courts, the jurisdictional statement varies greatly and may simply be a statement that the parties reside within the state court's territorial boundaries. In federal courts, a jurisdictional statement includes a reference to the specific statute that authorizes the court to hear the case.

The main body of the complaint contains the factual allegations and tells the plaintiff's story. Set off in separate paragraphs, the plaintiff's factual allegations are matters that the plaintiff may eventually have to prove at trial. At a minimum, the plaintiff's complaint must *allege* a sufficient amount of facts to meet the legal requirement of establishing a *prima facie* case. As you will later discover, this legal requirement means that the plaintiff has stated a legally sufficient complaint to show that there is a possible set of facts for which the law could provide a remedy, at least on paper. In actuality, stating a *prima facie* case simply means that plaintiff has alleged enough facts to state a legal claim for which the law may provide some sort of relief.

If the complaint does not set out a *prima facie* case, the defendant should challenge the legal sufficiency of the complaint by making a request to the court that the plaintiff's complaint be dismissed for "failure to state a claim upon which relief may be granted." While this wording sounds quite technical, a motion to dismiss is one of the most common tactics defendants use to challenge the complaint. By filing a motion to dismiss for failure to state a claim, the defendant is telling the court that the complaint did not allege enough facts to invoke a legal remedy. Subsequently in this chapter, we will discuss this and various other tactics available in civil procedures from the defendant's point of view. Because of these tactics available to the defendant, the plaintiff must take care in drafting the complaint.

The most legalistic parts of the complaint are the claims for relief, also known by their old-fashioned name, causes of action. A claim for relief states an underlying legal theory that provides the legal basis for the court to grant the plaintiff relief in the form of monetary damages or a court order, such as an injunction. A complaint with more than one claim for relief must set each in separate paragraphs, known as counts. A certain set of facts may give rise to several different claims for relief stated as alternatives to one another.

The final section of the complaint is known as the prayer for relief. In this conclusionary part of the complaint, the plaintiff states what he or she would like the court to do—award damages, issue an order, or both. After this section, some formalities follow. The attorney representing the plaintiff indicates his or her name, office address, and phone number and signs the complaint. Under the Federal Rules of Civil Procedure (Rule 11), the attorney's signature constitutes a verification or certification that they are proceeding with the lawsuit in good faith and that the allegations have been made in good faith and not for an improper purpose. Some state court rules require a separate verification paragraph signed by the party or the attorney.

Once the complaint has been prepared, the next tasks include filing it with the court and then serving it on the opposing party. Filing and serving the complaint are tasks often assigned to litigation paralegals.

Filing the Complaint

Most courts require a **cover sheet** to accompany the complaint. The cover sheet is a court-issued administrative form used by the court's clerk to gather information, such as the names and addresses of the parties and their lawyers. Cover sheets also categorize the case for the court's overall administration, such as statistics and record keeping.

All courts require the payment of a **filing fee** with the complaint. Historically, filing fees have been nominal, but because the expense of maintaining courts has risen dramatically in recent years, filing fees have risen as well. In most state courts, the

cover sheet
A court-issued form that accompanies a complaint when a lawsuit is initiated in court (usually federal court) for administrative purposes.

filing fee
A fee charged by courts or other adjudicatory body required when filing a lawsuit.

EYE ON ETHICS

Whenever a legal professional submits papers to a court, an entirely new area of ethical concerns kicks in: Candor to the Tribunal. ABA Model Rule of Professional Conduct 3.3 specifically prohibits a legal professional from knowingly making false statements in papers filed with a court. The applicable paralegal association ethical codes also command integrity and forthrightness when approaching a court or other tribunal. The point is driven home by the Federal Rules of Civil Procedure, Rule 11. See www.law.cornell.edu/rules/frcp/Rule11.htm.

CASE SUMMARY: *BODDIE V. CONNECTICUT,* 401 U.S. 371 (1971)

Access to the court system is one of our most important rights. The due process clause of the Fifth Amendment has been interpreted as the source of that right. For those who cannot afford to pay a filing fee, access to the courts is effectively nonexistent, resulting in a denial of the due process right.

In 1971, the United States Supreme Court decided the case of *Boddie v. Connecticut,* 401 U.S. 371 (1971). That case involved indigent persons who could not file for divorce because they could not afford the $60 filing fee and other court costs required under Connecticut law. They brought a lawsuit challenging requirements for payment of court fees and costs for service of process. Their lawsuit claimed that the required filing fees and court costs restricted their access to the courts. The Supreme Court noted that the states have a monopoly in dissolving marriages and that marriages reflect an important aspect of society's values. The Court concluded that due process did prohibit a state from denying, solely because of inability to pay, access to its courts to individuals who sought judicial dissolution of their marriages. Thus, the Court held that a state laws requiring filing fees were unconstitutional and unenforceable for people who could not afford to pay.

After the Supreme Court's decision, state courts began a fee waiver procedure in which a person could, upon proving his or her inability to pay, still file for most forms of civil actions and even appeal cases without paying court costs. By asking the court for permission to waive filing fees and court costs, the lawsuit may proceed *in forma pauperis,* or in the form of an indigent person.

QUESTIONS ABOUT THE CASE

1. Would *Boddie v. Connecticut* apply to the California filing fee requirement for indigent defendants?
2. Does the due process right of access to the courts apply to filing fees in all cases?
3. Which standards should determine whether a litigant is indeed indigent?

filing fees for a civil case range from $100 to $200. The California Superior Court in Los Angeles County currently requires a filing fee of $320. To file a response to the plaintiff's complaint, the defendant must pay a fee in the same amount. The federal court filing fee for a civil complaint is $250. However, if you wish to have a federal agency decision reviewed by the federal circuit court of appeals, the filing fee is $450. At times, the filing fee can act as a barrier to court access.

Once the complaint has been filed, along with the cover sheet and payment of the filing fee, the court clerk assigns a docket number and, in some cases, assigns the case to a judge. At this point, the lawsuit is filed. Yet there is another important step to be taken immediately. Most courts require that the plaintiff accomplish service of process upon the opposing party within a certain time after filing the complaint. This requirement simply means that the opposing party must be officially notified that the lawsuit has been filed against them. Another court-issued form known as a summons accompanies the complaint, informs the defendant of the lawsuit, and advises the defendant to respond to the complaint to avoid the consequences of a default.

A court official or professional process server personally delivers the complaint and summons to the defendant. Delivery may be made in person or, if allowed by state court rules, by leaving the summons and complaint at the defendant's residence or place of business.

Obviously, as a matter of fairness, the court will be concerned that the plaintiff takes reasonable efforts to notify the defendant. After the court official or process server delivers the summons and complaint to the defendant, proof of service is filed with the court. Also known as a return of service, the proof of service is a document in the form of an affidavit in which the court official or process server states under oath that he or she had served the defendant. Once the court is satisfied that service was properly performed, the lawsuit may go forward. At this point, the court will have acquired personal jurisdiction over the defendant, as a matter of law. In short, acquiring personal jurisdiction over the defendant means that the court has the power and legal authority to act on the lawsuit, now that the defendant has been properly notified.

The legal requirement of giving notice to the defendant is based on notions of fairness. Technically speaking, making sure that the defendant has been properly notified satisfies the fairness requirement of the due process clause of the Fifth Amendment. After all, the defendant has, at a minimum, the right to know that he or she is being sued. Thus, the court must be satisfied that the plaintiff has taken the proper steps to notify the defendant. This requirement does not mean that the plaintiff must employ every means available to make sure that the defendant is actually notified. The due process requirement embodied in most court rules only calls for the plaintiff to take measures that are "reasonably calculated to give notice" to the defendant that the lawsuit has been filed. For this reason, service of process may be accomplished by delivering the summons and complaint to a person of suitable age and discretion at the defendant's last known address or place of business. In some situations, the defendant may be of parts unknown.

The fact that a defendant cannot be found will not necessarily prevent the lawsuit from going forward. In such situations, the plaintiff should take reasonable steps to locate the defendant. Upon notifying the court that the defendant cannot be found, the court may order substituted service. A court order authorizing substituted service permits the plaintiff to publish the summons in a local newspaper, usually once a week for three consecutive weeks. Almost every newspaper reserves a portion of its classified ads for publication of legal notices.

The publication of the summons for substituted service would appear there along with other legal notices that perform the same function. This form of service may be authorized by the court only after reasonable steps to find the defendant. It is very unrealistic to believe that any defendant would browse the newspapers on a regular basis to see if he or she is being sued, which is true of almost every legal notice published in newspapers. For this reason, service of process by publication as a form of substitute service is also known as constructive service. As with many other terms in law, "constructive" is as a legal fiction used to describe an act that approximates the actual thing. Substituted or constructive service by publication is a common example; the court may also order other forms of suitable notification efforts.

The Defendant's Perspective

When the defendant has been served with the summons and complaint, there are two realistic courses of action. The first is to prepare and file an **answer**, which the defendant must do within 20 days of receiving the complaint. An answer responds to all of the allegations in the complaint, including each of the plaintiff's counts. To each of the allegations, the defendant responds with an admission or denial. If the defendant cannot do either, the wise course of action would be to deny the allegations or state that "the defendant is without sufficient information to form a belief as to the truth of the allegations and put the plaintiff to its proof." This statement is the functional equivalent to a denial. Any allegations not denied in some form are deemed admitted. By denying the allegations, the defendant is creating issues of fact and perhaps issues of law. Answering with a denial merely forces the plaintiff to prove its case.

answer
The defendant's response to the plaintiff's complaint.

In the next part of the answer, the defendant may include its own allegations, known and labeled in the answer as affirmative defenses. In essence, affirmative defenses are legal propositions that are similar to a plaintiff's claims for relief. With affirmative defenses, the defendant alleges that the law recognizes and supports his or her version of the case. Affirmative defenses work to limit or excuse a defendant's responsibility,

CASE IN POINT

CASE SUMMARY: *MULRAIN V. MULRAIN,* 15 V.I. 149 (D.V.I. 1979)

Josephine and George Mulrain were married for four years before George up and left the island of St. Thomas, United States Virgin Islands, where the couple had been living. A decade later, Josephine decided to get divorced. Living only on Social Security retirement benefits and a small pension, Josephine was able to qualify for a legal aid attorney to represent her in the divorce action. Because George had not been seen or heard from for more than 10 years, Josephine's attorney asked the divorce court to allow for substituted service.

However, because Josephine could not afford the publication costs, her attorney asked the court if posting the summons in three different locations on the island for a month would be acceptable under the fairness notion of the due process clause. Josephine's attorney argued that the United States Supreme Court decision in *Boddie v. Connecticut* should extend to the costs of publication. Thus, the argument went, to deny the costs of publication would deny access to the due process right of access to the courts. Her attorney also pointed out that on the small island of St. Thomas (26 square miles), posting the summons in three public locations would be a cost-effective form of substitute service.

The Federal District Court for the Virgin Islands agreed and entered an order permitting substitute service. The order specifically stated that Josephine's attorney was to post the summons for a month at the courthouse, the post office, and on the old mahogany tree at the open air market in Charlotte Amalie, at the time the only town on the island. This case is reported in the Virgin Islands Reports as *Mulrain v. Mulrain*, 15 V.I. 149 (D.V.I. 1979).

QUESTIONS ABOUT THE CASE

1. If Mr. George Mulrian had not been seen or heard for so many years, what is the use of posting the summons and complaint?
2. If Mrs. Josephine Mulrain were retired and had no plans to remarry, what purpose did the divorce serve?
3. To what extent should the principle of access to the courts apply to other costs of litigation?

even if the plaintiff's claim is proven. An affirmative defense may be based on facts that might include those outside the facts claimed by the plaintiff. If a defendant makes a claim to an affirmative defense, most courts' procedural rules require that the allegations and any additional facts to support the defense must be labeled as such.

An example of an affirmative defense in a civil (or criminal) case would be the doctrine of self-defense. To illustrate how a complaint and answer would appear in a civil case, let's assume that the plaintiff has filed a complaint for assault and battery in state court (see Figure 6.2). Once the service of process has been accomplished, the defendant has filed an answer (see Figure 6.3).

notice pleading
A short and plain statement of the allegations in a lawsuit.

The complaint and answer employ the simple form of **notice pleading** and set out a brief outline of the facts surrounding the dispute. The plaintiff is alleging that the defendant struck her. The legal interest that the plaintiff is trying to assert is the right to redress for an injury intentionally inflicted by another, whether mental and physical, known as assault and battery. As you discover in the chapter on torts, this form of claim for relief is classified as an intentional tort. The defendant, in contrast, simply acknowledges that there was an encounter with the plaintiff.

Without admitting that she struck the plaintiff, the defendant claims the affirmative defense of self-defense. In doing so, the defendant is preserving her options. On the one hand, the defendant could proceed by trying to negate the plaintiff's case. That is, one tactic is to force the plaintiff to present her proof; then the defendant could deny or disprove the case. If the plaintiff merely fails to prove her case, the defendant would win. On the other hand, using the affirmative defense of self-defense gives the defendant the additional option of using a legal principle that would have the effect of excusing the defendant's behavior. Thus, if the plaintiff is able to prove her case, the defendant still could claim self-defense to excuse her behavior. The defendant would then have to step forward to prove her case for self-defense. If both parties are able to prove their claims, the winning party would be the one with the more credible case.

Mary E. Lowe, Esq.
Bar Number 67001
Shreve, Krump & Lowe
442 Glenwood Avenue, Suite 40
Mariposa City, Freedonia 10010
333-634-5789

SUPERIOR COURT OF THE STATE OF FREEDONIA—COUNTY OF MARIPOSA

Marylin Mole	)	
Plaintiff,	)	Civil Action No. 07-007
v.	)	
Patti Partee,	)	Complaint for Assault and Battery
Defendant	)	

Plaintiff complains and for causes of action alleges as follows:

1. Plaintiff is an individual and is now, and at all times mentioned in this complaint was, a resident of Mariposa County, Freedonia.
2. Defendant is an individual and is now, and at all times mentioned in this complaint was, a resident of Mariposa County, Freedonia.
3. On or about January 1, 2007, at approximately 1:30 a.m., plaintiff was in her home when she was disturbed by loud noises in the form of voices and music.
4. Seeking to determine the source of the noises, plaintiff looked out of her living room window looking into her front yard and saw defendant, who is plaintiff's neighbor, and two other persons standing on the sidewalk in front of defendant's home. Thereafter, plaintiff determined that the noise came from the defendant's home.
5. Plaintiff approached the defendant and the two other persons and requested them to lower the volume of both the music and their voices.
6. Defendant refused and belligerently told plaintiff to go back into her home. Plaintiff requested defendant again and stated that she would call the police if her request was not complied with. Defendant again refused.
7. Defendant then began exhibiting threatening gestures and shouting at Plaintiff using profane language.
8. Plaintiff again repeated her request, when defendant struck plaintiff in the face with her fist.

FIRST CAUSE OF ACTION (Battery)

9. Defendant intended to cause and did cause a harmful contact with defendant's person.
10. Plaintiff did not consent to defendant's act.
11. As a direct and proximate result of defendant's conduct, plaintiff suffered a broken nose. Plaintiff has also suffered extreme mental anguish and physical pain.
12. As a direct and proximate result of defendant's acts, plaintiff has incurred medical expenses in the amount to be determined by proof at trial, and will, in the future, be compelled to incur additional obligations for medical treatment in an amount to be determined by proof at trial.
13. As a further direct and proximate result of defendant's conduct, plaintiff's resulting medical condition caused her lost wages in an amount to be determined by proof at trial.
14. Defendant's act was done knowingly, willfully, and with malicious intent, and plaintiff is entitled to punitive damages in an amount to be determined by proof at trial.

SECOND CAUSE OF ACTION (Assault)

15. Plaintiff incorporates by reference paragraphs 1-7 inclusive, and paragraphs 11-14, inclusive, of the First Cause of Action as if fully set forth.
16. Defendant intended to cause and did cause plaintiff to suffer apprehension of an immediate harmful contact.

WHEREFORE, plaintiff demands judgment against defendant, as follows:

a. General damages in an amount to be determined by proof at trial;
b. Medical and related expenses an amount to be determined by proof at trial;
c. Past and future lost earnings in an amount to be determined by proof at trial;
d. Impairment of earning capacity an amount to be determined by proof at trial;
e. Punitive damages;
f. Costs of this action;
g. Any other and further relief that the court considers proper.

By her Attorney,

______________________________, Dated: ____________

Counsel for Plaintiff

VERIFICATION

I, Marilyn Mole, am the plaintiff in the above-entitled action. I have read the foregoing and know the contents thereof. The same is true of my own knowledge, except as to those matters which are therein alleged on information and belief, and as to those matters, I believe it to be true.

I declare under penalty of perjury that the foregoing is true and correct and that this declaration was executed at Mariposa City, Freedonia.

DATED: ____________ , ______________________________

FIGURE 6.2 **Sample Complaint**

Barry L. Love, Esq.
Bar Number 68010
Love & Moore
One Franklin Avenue, 3rd Floor
Mariposa City, Freedonia 10010
333-634-0089
Attorney for Defendant

SUPERIOR COURT OF THE STATE OF FREEDONIA—COUNTY OF MARIPOSA

Marylin Mole)	
Plaintiff,)	Civil Action No. 07-007
v.)	
Patti Partee,)	Answer to Complaint for Assault and Battery
Defendant)	

The Defendant, Patti Partee, for herself alone answers the allegations of the complaint on file with this Court and alleges as follows:

1. Answering the allegations of Paragraph 1, Defendant admits the allegations contained in that paragraph.
2. Answering the allegations of Paragraph 2, Defendant admits the allegations of that paragraph.
3. Answering the allegations of Paragraph 3, Defendant states that she is without information sufficient to form a belief as to the truth of the allegations contained in that paragraph and demand strict proof thereof.
4. Answering the allegations of Paragraph 4 of the Complaint, Defendant admits that she encountered Plaintiff in front of their homes. Defendant denies the balance of the allegations of that paragraph.
5. Answering the allegations of Paragraphs 6 through 16, Defendant denies each and every allegation contained in those paragraphs.

AFFIRMATIVE DEFENSES

FIRST AFFIRMATIVE DEFENSE—Failure to State a Claim

6. Plaintiff has failed to state a claim upon which relief may be granted and requests that this Court dismiss the complaint.

SECOND AFFIRMATIVE DEFENSE—Self-defense

7. Defendant, in defending herself, did necessarily and unavoidably exercise her right to self-defense, using no more force than reasonably necessary to prevent defendant from being injured by plaintiff.

WHEREFORE, Defendant prays that this Court enter judgment as follows:

a. Dismiss Plaintiff's complaint with prejudice;
b. Award Defendant the costs of this action; and
c. Any other and further relief that the court considers proper.

By her Attorney,

______________________________ , Dated: ______________

Counsel for Defendant

VERIFICATION

I, Patti Partee, am the defendant in the above-entitled action. I have read the foregoing and know the contents thereof. The same is true of my own knowledge, except as to those matters which are therein alleged on information and belief, and as to those matters, I believe it to be true.

I declare under penalty of perjury that the foregoing is true and correct and that this declaration was executed at Mariposa City, Freedonia.

DATED: ______________ , ______________________________

Certificate of Service

I hereby certify that I served a true and correct copy of the foregoing Defendant's Answer by depositing the same with the U.S. Postal Service, first-class mail, postage prepaid to the plaintiff's attorney, Mary Mole, Esq., Shreve, Krump & Lowe, 442 Glenwood Avenue, Suite 40, Mariposa City, Freedonia 10010, this ______ day of March, 2007.

____

Barry L. Love

FIGURE 6.3 Sample Answer

As a procedural matter, notice that the end of the answer contains a **certificate of service**, which certifies that the document was served on the plaintiff's attorney, usually on or about the same day it was sent or filed with the court.

certificate of service
Verification by attorney that pleadings or court documents were sent to the opposing counsel in a case.

The functional purpose of the complaint and the answer is to determine at the outset which facts are in dispute and on which legal theories the parties are relying.

Other Responses to the Complaint

There are a number of other avenues that the lawsuit could take after the complaint has been filed and served on the defendant.

- **Default.** The rules of most courts allow 20 days to respond to a complaint once the defendant has been served with the complaint. If there is no response to the complaint, the plaintiff may obtain a **default judgment** against the defendant. When the defendant is in default, he or she cannot participate in the lawsuit. Normally, the plaintiff receiving the default judgment still has to prove the case. In a default situation, there is no opposition, and the plaintiff's case proceeds easily. Once the plaintiff has obtained a judgment, the defendant is legally liable to the plaintiff for the amount of the judgment.

default judgment
A judgment entered by the court against the defendant for failure to respond to the plaintiff's complaint.

- **Motion to dismiss.** Instead of filing an answer, the defendant may file a **motion to dismiss**, also known as a *demurrer* (from the archaic French). A motion to dismiss challenges the legal sufficiency of the complaint or the entire lawsuit for any number of different reasons. Typically, a motion to dismiss questions whether (1) the court has jurisdiction (i.e., the legal authority to hear the case), (2) the defendant was properly served, (3) the complaint properly states a claim for relief, or (4) there should be other parties to the lawsuit, among other technicalities. A motion to dismiss thus requests the court to take a good look at the complaint to determine if, considering certain legal technicalities, the lawsuit is properly placed before the court. If not, the court will dismiss the lawsuit, leaving the plaintiff to look elsewhere or not at all. If the court denies the motion to dismiss, the defendant will have a certain amount of time to file an answer, usually 10 days from the date of the court's order denying the motion to dismiss.

motion to dismiss
A motion that dispenses with the lawsuit because of a legal defense.

- **Counterclaims and cross-claims.** Assume that in the *Mole v. Partee* lawsuit, Mole had fought back and struck Partee or that one or more of the other people present had become involved in a melee in which everyone's noses had been broken. Partee could, as part of her answer, file a **counterclaim** alleging that Mole committed an assault and battery that entitled Partee to damages. Her counterclaim would then be a form of a complaint or countersuit in the same action. Mole would then need to file an answer to the counterclaim. If Mole had named Partee and the others as additional defendants, who then made claims among themselves, the defendants would be filing **cross-claims** against one another.

counterclaim
A claim made by the defendant against the plaintiff—not a defense, but a new claim for damages, as if the defendant were the plaintiff in a separate suit; a countersuit brought by the defendant against the plaintiff.

cross-claim
A lawsuit against a party of the same side; plaintiffs or defendants suing each other (defendant versus defendant or plaintiff versus plaintiff).

- **Third-party complaint.** Finally, Partee could file a claim against someone not already a party to the lawsuit in a procedure known as filing a **third-party complaint**. In doing so, Partee would be adding a party to the lawsuit as another defendant. In what is also known as third-party procedure, Partee would file her third-party complaint and have it served in the same way that a plaintiff serves the original complaint. Once served, the third party becomes an additional defendant to the already existing action. Under common law, the procedure was known as an **impleader**, which described the process of bringing a third party into a lawsuit. When a defendant impleads another party into the lawsuit, that defendant is saying, "If I am liable to the plaintiff, then you [the third party] are liable to me." Thus, a third party complaint or impleader is a procedure specifically provided by the rules of civil procedure by which a defendant can bring another party into the lawsuit.

third-party claim
A suit filed by the defendant against a party not originally named in the plaintiff's complaint.

impleader
The involuntary addition of a new party to the litigation; a party without whom all issues raised in the case could not be resolved.

Discovery

discovery
The pretrial investigation process authorized and governed by the rules of civil procedure; the process of investigation and collection of evidence by litigants; process in which the opposing parties obtain information about the case from each other; the process of investigation and collection of evidence by litigants.

If the lawsuit proceeds, the parties next engage in what is known as **discovery**. Discovery consists of a series of mechanisms specifically provided for by the rules of civil procedure for the parties to obtain information from each other. This stage of the lawsuit can last for several months. Usually the parties interact on their own using various discovery mechanisms. When a party employs any of the discovery mechanisms, it is making a discovery request. The rules provide for either court enforcement of discovery requests that are not responded to or rejection of requests that are harassing or burdensome. For the courts to maintain a supervisory role over discovery, the rules require the parties to file their discovery requests with the court as they are served on the opposing side.

The rules usually allow five different forms of discovery, each with its own value in terms of obtaining information from the opposing party. As we take a brief look at each form, keep two things in mind: (1) What type of information can be obtained most efficiently , and (2) what role does a professional paralegal have in the law office during the discovery stage of a lawsuit? Remember that in most situations, the unauthorized practice rules permit only attorneys to sign court papers, and discovery requests are no exception. Thus, paralegals' professional role with respect to discovery, and many other matters, is entirely in house and under the supervision of the supervising attorney. The paralegals' role is therefore often invisible, because documents actually prepared by the paralegal appear under the name of the supervising attorney. With discovery, the paralegal occupies a central role in preparing and organizing the various requests and the information that is sought and received.

interrogatories
A discovery tool in the form of a series of written questions that are answered by the party in writing, to be answered under oath.

deposition
A discovery tool in a question-and-answer format in which the attorney verbally questions a party or a witness under oath.

deponent
The party or witness who is questioned in a deposition.

subpoena
A document that is served upon an individual under authority of the court, and orders the person to appear at a certain place and certain time for a deposition, or suffer the consequences; an order issued by the court clerk directing a person to appear in court.

contempt
A willful disregard for or disobedience of a public authority.

subpoena *duces tecum*
A type of subpoena that requests a witness to produce a document.

- **Interrogatories** are questions written on paper and served on all the other parties to the lawsuit. Usually, the party receiving the interrogatories has 30 days to respond in writing and under oath. Typically, interrogatories are used at the beginning of the discovery stage of a lawsuit to seek initial information from the other side about the identity of any witnesses or the location of documents, such as medical records. With the information gained from the answers received, the parties then proceed to other forms of discovery.
- **Depositions** are a common device that many legal professionals consider among the most efficient and effective ways of obtaining information. Depositions are oral examinations of a witness or potential witness taken under oath, usually in a lawyer's conference room. A stenographer or some type of device records the **deponent**—that is, the person who is being questioned. What makes depositions particularly useful is their scope. Unlike interrogatories, a party may use a deposition to question a person who is not a party to the lawsuit. Having obtained the identity of a person through the use of interrogatories or another source, a party may depose that person by sending him or her a notice of deposition.

Using a notice of deposition usually suffices to ensure that the deponent will appear at the deposition. With a recalcitrant deponent, the notice of deposition may be enforced through the use of a court-issued document called a **subpoena**. Like a summons, a subpoena is a court command. You will recall that a summons is a court-issued document, accompanied by a complaint, telling the defendant that he or she must respond to the complaint. A subpoena, in contrast, is a court command to appear and give testimony at a deposition. Subpoenas are similarly used to compel someone to appear as a witness for a trial. If the deponent fails to appear, the party requesting the deponent's appearance may make a motion to find the uncooperative deponent in **contempt** of court. A **subpoena *duces tecum*** is a command to appear and bring physical evidence, such as documents or other items specified in the subpoena.

Once the deposition is completed, the stenographer prepares a **transcript** of everything said by the person being deposed. Appearing like a play, the transcript indicates the speakers and a verbatim record of the deponent's testimony. A paralegal's assistance with depositions can play an important role in depositions. The paralegal often will be called upon to identify potential deponents and prepare an outline of the actual questions that the attorney should ask, as well as notices of deposition or subpoenas, if necessary. After the deposition, paralegals are frequently called upon to review the transcripts and prepare summaries, complete with page indexes, so that the attorney can easily locate important parts of the deponent's testimony in an easy-to-read format.

transcript
Written account of a trial court proceeding or deposition.

- Like interrogatories, **requests for production** are written requests. However, instead of asking questions, requests for production ask for documents or other evidence from the opposing parties. In the modern age of computers, the items subject to requests for production may include "electronic evidence," such as voice mail, e-mail, spreadsheets, and other items that may be stored in computers.
- Having obtained information or evidence through interrogatories, depositions, and requests for production or other means, a party may then ask the other party to admit to the genuineness of a certain item, such as a letter or agreement. A specific fact, such as ownership of a car or property, may also be subject to a request for admission. If the party receiving the **request for admission** admits to the request, there is no need to prove that fact at trial. As you might imagine, requests for admissions can help make trials more efficient. They are also self-enforcing. If a party unreasonably refuses to make an requested admission and thus forces the requesting party to prove the request at trial, the costs of proving the request may be assessed against the refusing party. Moreover, if a party fails to respond to a request for admission, the admission is deemed an established fact.
- Particularly in cases in which the plaintiff alleges physical or emotional harm, the defendant will request that the plaintiff undergo a medical or psychological exam. The party that issues the **request for examination** selects the doctor who will perform the exam. This exam is one way to determine whether a claim is valid and permits the requesting party to evaluate the extent to which it may be found liable. If, upon independent examination, a plaintiff's claim of physical or emotional harm appears well-founded, the defendants may elect to settle the matter out of court and save the time and expense of going to a trial.

request for production of documents (request to produce)
A discovery device that requests the production of certain items, such as photographs, papers, reports, and physical evidence; must specify the document sought.

request for admissions (request to admit)
A document that provides the drafter with the opportunity to conclusively establish selected facts prior to trial.

request for examination
Form of discovery that requests an examination (including medical) of an opposing party in a lawsuit.

Figure 6.4 summarizes these five discovery techniques.

Court Supervision and Enforcement of Discovery

Although the discovery process takes place outside of the courthouse, the rules require all parties to file copies of their discovery requests with the court. This requirement permits the court to supervise and enforce, if necessary, the discovery rules through

FIGURE 6.4
Discovery Techniques

Discovery Mechanism	How Performed
Interrogatories (Fed. R. Civ. Proc. 33)	Written questions answered in writing.
Depositions (Fed. R. Civ. Proc. 30)	Sworn out-of-court testimony before being transcribed.
Requests for Production (Fed. R. Civ. Proc. 34)	Written requests for documents.
Requests for Admission (Fed. R. Civ. Proc. 36)	Written requests that certain facts be admitted or denied.
Requests for Physical or Mental Examination (Fed. R. Civ. Proc. 35)	Request to have physician or mental health professional examine.

sanctions
Penalty against a party in the form of an order to compel, a monetary fine, a contempt-of-court citation, or a court order with specific description of the individualized remedy.

protective order
A court order that protects a party's information from discovery due to the existence of a privilege or other legal basis.

the use of **sanctions** and **protective orders**. Parties that have failed or refused to comply with discovery requests may be subject to orders to comply issued by the court. If the party fails to comply with the order, the court may, upon the request of the other party, assess the costs of obtaining the order to comply. In extreme cases, the court may also consider the defiant party in default and bar them from participating at trial.

Protective orders protect a party from discovery requests that are overly burdensome or excessive. You can probably imagine that a well-financed litigant could oppress its opponent by piling on innumerable interrogatories, requests for admissions and examinations, and endless depositions. Many states have rules that limit discovery for the express purpose of preventing harassment and other abusive uses of the discovery rules by limiting the number of questions in an interrogatory. Nevertheless, the rules themselves provide for protective orders at the request of the party seeking relief from oppressive discovery. By making a motion for a protective order, a party is telling the court that the discovery sought by the other side is unnecessary, was designed to harass, or both. Because all discovery is filed with the court, the judge deciding the motion for a discovery order will have ready access to the allegedly oppressive discovery request. The party seeking a protective order may also want to protect a trade secret or other sensitive information.

Protected Information Not Subject to Discovery

In a previous chapter, we briefly reviewed the notion of privilege. The law often protects certain relationships and the information that results from communication within those relationships. For instance, the law concerning the privilege accorded to doctors and their patients protects patients by allowing them to object to any requests regarding their communications with their doctors. The doctor–patient rule fosters a level of trust between doctors and their patients to encourage a free flow of information so that the physician can properly treat the patient. Thus, the information exchanged between a doctor and patient is privileged information and not, as a general matter, subject to discovery.

The same type of protection exists for the work performed on a case by an attorney or paralegal. The notes, research, and opinions that these legal professionals generate during the course of a case are deemed privileged and not subject to discovery by the other side. This form of legal protection has become known as the **work product** doctrine.

work product
An attorney's written notes, impressions, charts, diagrams, and other material used by him or her to prepare strategy and tactics for trial.

trade secret
Property that is protected from misappropriation such as formulas, patterns, and compilations of information.

Other forms of information may also be protected and available only in limited forms for discovery. Trade secrets are protected information that consist of a formula, design, pattern, customer list, or database used by a business to obtain a competitive edge. **Trade secrets** differ from patents or copyrights, in that the owner of the trade secret must take steps to protect the information. Thus, a secret formula for a soft drink that the company discloses only to its own employees would be a trade secret. Because the government does not protect this type of information by law, a trade secret could be subject to discovery, but courts have recognized that trade secrets should be accorded protection. If discovery properly requests the other side for information about its trade secret, there must be a disclosure. However, the court will, upon the responding party's request, order that the trade secret be sealed so that the information will not be available to the public.

Discovery in the Electronic Age

For decades, the discovery rules pertained to documents and physical objects. Now that communication frequently occurs electronically, matters subject to discovery

CASE IN POINT

CASE SUMMARY: THE WORK PRODUCT PRIVILEGE

In *Hickman v. Taylor,* 329 U.S. 495 (1947), the United States Supreme Court unanimously recognized the work product doctrine. The Court declared that the doctrine protects information obtained or produced by attorneys for or in anticipation of litigation from discovery under the Federal Rules of Civil Procedure.

The case involved an accident in which the defendant's tugboat sank in the Delaware River, resulting in the plaintiff's death. During discovery, the plaintiff attempted to obtain signed statements and memoranda of investigations into the accident prepared by the defendant's counsel. The defendant objected to the plaintiff's request for production of these memoranda and refused to produce them. The plaintiff then requested the trial court to order production of these signed statements and memoranda. The defendant granted the names of those who had provided statements but refused to produce the documents. The trial court ordered the defendant to produce the memoranda and issued sanctions against the defendant, which appealed to the Court of Appeals for the Third Circuit, which then reversed the trial court's order. Finally, the plaintiff sought review by the United States Supreme Court.

The Supreme Court affirmed, holding that the information sought by the plaintiff was protected by the work product doctrine. The Court reasoned that attorneys must be able to work with a certain degree of privacy, free from unnecessary intrusion by opposing parties and their counsel. The "work product" of the attorney inevitably reflects the attorney's own thoughts and mental impressions. If discovery were granted, it would create a chilling effect on the work of attorneys. As a result, much less would be written, and much more would be forgotten. The Court also observed that inefficiency and unfairness, and sharp would inevitably develop in the giving of legal advice, damaging the legal profession and the interests of justice.

QUESTIONS ABOUT THE CASE

1. Is there any overlap between the work product doctrine and the attorney–client privilege?
2. What would be unfair or damaging if a legal professional's work product were not protected?
3. Could a legal professional representing one of the parties be the subject of any discovery mechanism?

encompass electronic data as well. Known as e-discovery, the forms of information discoverable by litigants include e-mail, instant messaging chats, Microsoft Office files, accounting databases, Web sites and other electronically stored information relevant to a lawsuit.

As a result of amendments to the Federal Rules of Civil Procedure, effective December 1, 2006, data subject to e-discovery also includes metadata, that is, information about the electronic data itself, such as the original author's name, the creation date of the document, and the amount of time spent editing it. Most desktop computers will display some metadata if the user right-clicks on the file icon, then on *Properties*. Other metadata are not visible except through the analysis of a file by forensics experts.

CYBER TRIP

Melissa was the name of a computer virus first found on March 26, 1999, which spread over the Internet through e-mail. Melissa shut down Internet mail systems that got clogged with infected e-mails propagating from the virus. Although Melissa was not originally designed to cause harm, it overflowed servers and caused unplanned problems. Investigators using electronic forensics discovered metadata that uniquely identified the computer used to create the original infected document. Thus, they could demonstrate that Melissa was written by David L. Smith, of Aberdeen Township, New Jersey. Smith was sentenced to 10 years but served only 20 months in a federal prison and was fined US$5,000.

See www.usdoj.gov/criminal/cybercrime/melissaSent.htm.

Pretrial Matters

After the parties have completed the discovery stage, the complexion of the lawsuit changes dramatically. By this point, the parties know the legal position of their opponents and, more important, which facts are in dispute. Factual disputes about essential matters, such as whether an enforceable agreement exists or whether the defendant was careless in a way that caused the plaintiff's injuries, means that there should be a **trial**. We are all familiar with the drama and ritual of court trials. Television and the media remind us daily of the fact that courtroom trials perform the function of resolving legal disputes. More specifically, trial courts resolve disputes by making findings of fact and then applying the law. We discuss the fact-finding functions of trial courts in more detail later in this and other chapters. For now, the important thing to remember is that the trial court's function is to resolve disputes of fact by determining which facts gave rise to the lawsuit.

trial
The forum for the presenting of evidence and testimony and the deliberation of liability in civil cases or guilt in criminal cases.

If there are no facts in dispute, there is no need for a trial. One of the purposes of discovery is to allow the parties to determining what the opposition would be able to prove at trial. During the course of discovery, one of the parties may learn that its opposition cannot prove its side of case. To win the case without the time and expense of going to trial, the party may file a motion for **summary judgment**. Such a motion asks the court to rule in its favor as to all or part of the lawsuit, because there are no material facts at issue and the only matter to be decided is the law, which the judge is able to do without a trial. All of the facts necessary to determine the outcome of the dispute may already be part of the court record, because all of the responses to discovery are filed in court. Thus, a party moving for summary judgment would point to all of the relevant facts obtained through discovery. If an opposing party wishes to oppose a motion for summary judgment, it would point to the existence of disputed facts and therefore the need for a trial to resolve a factual dispute.

summary judgment
The disposition of a lawsuit before trial when there are no genuine issues of fact and the party requesting it is entitled to judgment as a matter of law.

If there are factual disputes that need to be resolved, trial courts often request a **pretrial conference**. Conferences can take place in a courtroom or in a judge's office, also known as the judge's **chambers**. These informal meetings between all of the lawyers involved and the judge try to determine what the trial will cover. At the conference, the parties will report which witnesses will testify, which items of evidence they plan to present, and the time needed for the trial. Remember that courts are very interested in handling cases efficiently. Thus, pretrial conferences are designed to allocate the trial court's time efficiently. As part of this procedure, the judge may

pretrial conference
The meeting between the parties and the judge to identify legal issues, stipulate to uncontested matters, and encourage settlement.

chambers
A judge's office. Trial court judges often schedule pretrial settlement conferences and other informal meetings in their chambers.

CYBER TRIP

Lawsuits and even criminal proceedings are rarely resolved by a trial. The vast majority are settled or plea bargained. According to the National Center for State Courts, the American Bar Association, and the federal government, less than 10 percent of all civil and criminal cases filed with the state and federal courts ever go to trial. The vast majority of cases are settled (or plea bargained in criminal cases) or dismissed. In some years, as few as 4 or 5 percent of all cases filed go to trial.

Nevertheless, courts and legislators at both the state and federal level have expressed alarm at the overburdened and congested condition of the trial courts across the country. In many states, a litigant may have to wait years for trial, due to the increasing number of cases pending in the nation's trial courts. As of 2003, more than 100 million cases were filed in state trial courts alone.

According to the online report at www.ncsconline.org/D_Research/csp/2004_Files/EWSC_Full_Report.pdf, which types of cases are filed the most (see page 14)? On page 39, which state has the most civil protection cases filed in its court?

ask the parties to file any additional requests that would streamline the anticipated trial. Such requests might include a **motion in limine**, asking for a court order to prevent the opposing party from presenting certain types of evidence at trial because the party asking for the court order believes that the evidence violates a privilege or other rule of law.

motion in limine
A request that certain evidence not be raised at trial, as it is arguably prejudicial, irrelevant, or legally inadmissible evidence.

Trial

When we think of the American legal system and the legal profession, nothing comes to mind more vividly than the courtroom dramas of trials. From movies to television reality shows and best-selling novels, American media culture is obsessed with the ritualized performance of legal combatants before a jury and a packed audience. At these trials, witnesses break down on cross-examination, sobbingly confessing to crimes or ulterior motives. Last-minute twists and turns rivet our attention as newly discovered evidence pops up in the courtroom, turning a sober and relentless prosecution into a gleeful revelation of innocence and redemption.

Of course, real courtroom trials usually are much less riveting. Although there are sporadic spikes of drama and occasional moments of moving oration from inspired lawyers, the daily routine of courtroom trials more frequently provoke the interest of only those involved. As discussed, the function of the trial court is to find facts. The primary reason that a case goes to trial is the existence of disputed facts. Those accused of crimes deny that they are guilty of the prosecution's accusations. Civil defendants deny that they are liable to the plaintiff for the damages alleged in the complaint. If these differences persist after the discovery has run its course, a trial supposedly resolves these disputed facts. Charged with this responsibility, trial courts perform the role of **trier of facts**.

trier of facts
Jury.

Trials occur in one of two forms. The most common is a trial before a judge sitting by him- or herself, in what is known as a **bench trial**. The judge, as the trier of fact, performs the task of finding the facts and then applies the law. Bench trials are by far the most common and efficient form of trials. After both sides have finished presenting their cases, some trial court judges announce their decisions as to the facts they find and how the law applies immediately. However, most trial court judges want to reflect on the matter, consult their notes, or perform some research before they reach a decision. When this happens, the judge has taken the matter **under advisement**. When the judge has made a decision, the court notifies the parties by mail or, in some cases, e-mail.

bench trial
A case heard and decided by a judge.

under advisement
The judge's determination of a matter to be made at a later time.

The United States Constitution and the constitutions of most states grant people the right to a **jury trial**. In the civil law traditions of most of the world, jury trials are unheard of. Yet the common law traditions we inherited from England are customs that we have grown so used to over the past two centuries that jury trials are regarded as sacred fundamental rights—that is, the right to be judged by one's peers. However, the right to a jury trial is not absolute in all situations, and the right is exercised more prevalently in criminal cases than in civil ones.

jury trial
Case is decided by a jury.

Quite frequently, however, jury trials are waived as a strategic (or even economic) decision by counsel. Attorneys handling highly technical or complex cases often advise their clients to waive their right to a jury trial, because juries may become confused by the jargon, particularly in technical or scientific cases. Only one party needs to indicate that it wishes to try the case before a jury to make it so. Once the court notes that one of the parties desires a jury trial, the case must undergo a jury selection process.

The attorney's most visible professional task for the client is court advocacy. In fact, an attorney's presence and conduct before a trial court judge have been universally recognized as well within the boundaries of the protected activity known as the practice of law. Nevertheless, paralegals frequently assist attorneys by performing

CYBER TRIP

Some courts have begun posting their decisions on official court Web sites. Often, the court posts its decision on its own Web site, then the court's clerk telephones the parties to inform them of the posting.

Trip 1: On the Internet, go to the Web site of the United States Supreme Court at www.supremecourtus.gov and click on "opinions." What is the latest opinion issued?

Trip 2: On the Internet, go to the Web site for the Maryland State Courts, at www.courts.state.md.us/. That state's highest court is the Court of Appeals. Find where that Court posts its decisions.

Pleading Stage	Discovery	Pretrial Activities	Trial	Posttrial Activities
Complaint and service of process	Interrogatories	Motion to dismiss (may occur before discovery)	Jury selection and voir dire	Posttrial motions
Answer	Deposition	Motion for summary judgment	Presentation of witnesses and evidence	Notice of appeal by losing party
Counterclaim or cross-claim	Request for production, admission, or examination	Motion in limine	Direct, cross-, redirect, and recross-examination	On appeal, preparation of transcript and briefs
Third-party claim	E-discovery	Pretrial conference		

FIGURE 6.5 Timeline in Civil Litigation

behind-the-scenes activities, even in the courtroom. During the trial, paralegals commonly assist the attorneys who are conducting the trial by collecting and finding documents and items of evidence, marshaling witnesses, and keeping track of the sometimes complex and seemingly endless array of details.

After trial, further requests are possible by either party, particularly the losing party, which may appeal the case to an appellate court. Although appellate practices are beyond the scope of this book, paralegals often play important roles in the preparation of appellate briefs, legal research and writing, and analysis of the trial transcript. Figure 6.5 provides a chart of the timeline in civil litigation and the activities occurring during each stage.

Duties of the Litigation Paralegal

Here is a overview of the duties and responsibilities that a professional paralegal may have when working in the litigation department of a law firm. Particularly in large offices, paralegals commonly are involved in every step of the litigation process, even before the complaint is filed. Using the example posed in the sample pleadings provided previously, a litigation paralegal could become involved in any of the following ways.

COMMUNICATION TIP

Many litigation paralegals involved in investigation come into contact with clients and people outside the office. As you identify yourself, be sure to say that you are a paralegal. Many consider this notification a matter of ethics. An added plus is that once it is understood that you are a paralegal, you may notice that people grow more relaxed and open.

Investigation

From the outset, paralegals are engaged in the investigation of facts; they obtain documents and medical records, interview potential witnesses and experts, and use the Internet or other sources to gather background information about a particular trade or business. The paralegal's initial investigation becomes extremely important in evaluating the case and determining how the client's goals may be achieved. These are professional decisions that can be made only on the basis of information that professional paralegals routinely gather. Working together, attorneys and paralegals develop a theory of the case, that is, the legal positions available to the client based on the evidence. In other words, if the office represents the plaintiff, the legal team may determine whether there exists enough evidence to support a complaint that alleges a claim for relief based on the legal theory of assault and battery. On the other side, the paralegal and attorney may look at the information assembled from their investigation to determine if they can prove that their client, the defendant, was acting in self-defense.

Legal Research

After performing a factual investigation, the paralegal and attorney may need to research other possible legal positions for the client. The next step may thus require additional legal research. For instance, let's assume that you represent a defendant who is being sued for assault and battery. According to an investigation of the facts, it appears that the client acted in self-defense, at least arguably. The client has informed your office that the incident occurred at a hockey arena. Your client's daughter plays for a youth hockey team that had traveled to a game held in the next town for the league championship. During the game, the client's daughter accidentally tripped a member of the other team with her hockey stick. Unharmed, the other player simply picked herself up and continued playing. The referee, whose back was turned, did not see the tripping and did not call a penalty. However, the father of the tripped player became so enraged that he scrambled onto the ice and headed toward the client's daughter. Stunned by his bold actions, the client's daughter merely stood there on the ice as the father reached out, trying to grab her by the neck. In an attempt to avoid his reach, the client's daughter swung her hockey stick to deflect his arm, causing him to slip and fall face down on the ice. The client's daughter was unharmed, slightly irritated at most by the father's impetuous act. The father suffered a fractured rib and a broken nose. As an incident during the championship game, the entire situation has been caught on videotape.

On the basis of your knowledge of the law, you are aware that self-defense is available as an affirmative defense in your state only if the defendant has retreated before applying force. Your state has also adopted, by recent judicial decision, an at-home defense, which eliminates the duty to retreat. You are aware that at least 15 states have adopted the "stand your ground" form of self-defense, which does not require a person claiming self-defense to show that he or she retreated before applying force.

To make the claim of self-defense, the legal team's job would include performing legal research of every one of the 15 states that have adopted the "stand your ground" form of self-defense. There may also be scholarly articles in law reviews and citations from legal encyclopedias that would assist the research and be worthy of citation to convince a court to adopt a novel legal idea. To represent the client zealously, the legal team also may want to convince the court that it should adopt the "stand your ground" form of self-defense, at least in this case. The defendant's legal team therefore may assign the paralegal to perform detailed legal research and design a cogent strategy regarding how to present this novel legal argument. Incidentally, as part of the thoughts, notes, and research by the legal professional, the paralegal's work in this regard would be protected from discovery by the opposition under the work product doctrine.

EYE ON ETHICS

Rule 3.1 of the ABA Model Rules of Professional Conduct requires that legal professionals exercise good faith and avoid frivolous actions in court. Stated as a prohibition, the rule is designed to prevent frivolous legal arguments that a legal professional may urge just to delay, confuse the court, or injure or harm. However, the rules of professional conduct do not affirmatively require legal professionals to make arguments that may benefit their clients if they are not yet recognized in their jurisdiction.

Both Rules 3.1 and 1.2 require zealous representation. Thus, a lawyer could, decline or neglect to make certain legal arguments that could benefit their clients. This would be consistent with the rules of professional responsibility.

Do you think that legal professionals should be under a duty of professional responsibility to make certain legal arguments? There is a first time for everything. For instance, do or should the rules have required the plaintiff's attorney to urge abrogation of the family and spousal immunity doctrines, as we saw in the *Self* and *Gibson* cases?

Drafting

Drafting the pleadings, motions, and other court documents are common tasks for paralegals in litigation departments. Whether the paralegal is part of the team for the plaintiff or for the defendant, legal documents are an important part of the work performed by the entire legal team, particularly in the discovery phase of litigation. In addition to drafting discovery requests, such as interrogatories, paralegals routinely are engaged in indexing and cataloging the vast amounts of information that are frequently exchanged. By performing these tasks, the paralegal uses his or her knowledge of law and civil procedure to arrange the information in the lawsuit so that the attorney may access it easily, especially at trial.

Assistance during Trial Preparation

At trial, the paralegal's role is regarded as supportive and, oftentimes, indispensable. Paralegals perform a wide range of tasks to support the work of the trial attorneys who supervise their work. The attorneys appear and speak on behalf of their clients before the courts. The attorneys' names and signatures appear on the pleadings and other documents filed in court, even though the paralegal may have prepared and drafted them. The paralegal also may have prepared the witnesses and marshals regarding the order in which they will take the witness stand, at the direction and under the supervision of the attorney. With full knowledge of the court documents and discovery, paralegals will have indexed and categorized the entire file for the trial attorney.

If the trial involves a jury, paralegals assist from the outset with jury selection. Juries are drawn from the local voter registration polls from within the trial court's vicinity. The court process of assembling a jury supposedly ensures an impartial group of individuals who will decide a case. The task of determining impartiality is up to both the court and the parties in a process known as **voir dire**—from the archaic French, loosely meaning "to speak the truth," by which each juror is questioned about his or her background and any connections he or she may have with the case or the parties to the case. All parties involved also have two types of challenges they may issue. The first is **peremptory challenges**, which are limited in number and may eliminate a prospective juror for no defined reason. A peremptory challenge may be based on a party's hunch or gut feeling. Each party also has an unlimited number of **challenges for cause**, with which it may disqualify a prospective juror by showing through voir dire his or her bias or personal connection with the case.

voir dire
The process of selecting a jury for trial.

peremptory challenge (peremptory jury strike)
An attorney's elimination of a prospective juror without giving a reason; limited to a specific number of strikes.

challenge for cause
A party's request that the judge dismiss a potential juror from serving on a trial jury by providing a valid legal reason why he or she shouldn't serve.

Trials notebooks are frequently three-ring binders that contain court documents and other information carefully organized for use at trial. There may be several trial notebooks, depending on the complexity of the lawsuit. As you may suspect, paralegals have a significant hand in preparing and organizing trial notebooks.

In civil matters, the plaintiff's attorney begins the trial with an **opening statement** that provides an overview of the case and tries, from the outset, to set the tone of the presentation of the evidence. The defendant follows immediately with its opening statement, which similarly explains the case from its point of view. After each side has made its statements, the plaintiff begins its case with the presentation of evidence, most commonly with sworn testimony from witnesses. Each witness is sworn in by the court clerk, and then the plaintiff's attorney questions the witness in what is known as the **direct examination**, a formal term for the questioning of a witness by the party that calls that witness. When the direct examination is complete, the other side may conduct a **cross-examination** of the witness by questioning him or her in an attempt to punch holes in the story elicited during the direct examination.

opening statement
An initial statement by a party's attorney explaining what the case is about and what that party's side expects to prove during the trial.

direct examination
Occurs when the attorney questions his or her own witness.

cross-examination
Occurs when the opposing attorney asks the witness questions.

The party that called the witness has an opportunity to rehabilitate the witness and bolster his or her original testimony by asking questions on **redirect examination**. In turn, the opposition may conduct **recross examination**. Further questioning of the witness is subject to the trial court's **discretion**. This discretion means that the trial court judge, as a sort of referee, determines whether the questioning is sufficient. The exercise of the trial court's discretion is designed to expedite the trial while giving the parties sufficient opportunity to present their evidence. Prominent in the trial court's determination is whether the jury has heard enough. Too much evidence may confuse the jury.

redirect examination
The attorney who originally called the witness asks more questions.

recross examination
A subsequent opportunity for an attorney to question by cross-examination a hostile witness.

discretion
The court's power to make decisions it deems fair and just.

At the close of the plaintiff's presentation, the defendant may move for a **directed verdict**, arguing that the plaintiff has not proven its case. Thus, the defendant is arguing that it should win. A directed verdict is very similar to the pretrial motions to dismiss and for summary judgment. All of these requests to the trial court suggest that the plaintiff, at certain points of the case, may not have the case (1) stated in its complaint, as with a motion to dismiss; (2) demonstrated by the information obtained through discovery, such as with a motion for summary judgment; or (3) shown at trial through insufficient proof, such as in the case of a motion for a directed verdict. All of these motions indicate that at some point, the plaintiff's case is either legally or factually insufficient.

directed verdict
A ruling by a judge, made after the plaintiff has presented all of her evidence but before the defendant puts on his case, that awards judgment to the defendant.

If the trial court grants a motion for directed verdict, the plaintiff has lost. If the trial court denies the defendant's motion for a directed verdict, the defendant proceeds with the presentation of its evidence. The defendant's case may consist of two aspects. The first is the presentation of evidence that rebuts the plaintiff's case or negates the plaintiff's evidence. The second consists of the defendant's presentation of evidence to prove any of the affirmative defenses it has alleged in its answer. With either aspect of the defendant's case, there will be a dispute as to exactly what happened. The defendant's attempt to negate the case contests the facts that the plaintiff's evidence has attempted to establish. Likewise, the plaintiff may attempt to negate an affirmative defense that may be available to the defendant. Either way, the judge in a bench trial or the jury in a jury trial must sift through all of the evidence to determine the facts. The fact-finding process may depend on the amount of evidence regarding a certain point, the credibility of witnesses, the cogency of their story, and many other intangibles. Whether certain facts exist and whether the trier of fact finds for one side or another is all a matter of the evidence presented.

EVIDENCE FOR PARALEGALS

Almost every law school requires second-year students to take a semester-long course in the rules of evidence. Such a course teaches students the myriad of rules that govern what may or may not be admitted into evidence in a courtroom. For those who plan to work in litigation, the rules of evidence become all important. No matter how strong a client's case may appear, the bottom line, the most important aspects of the case, depend almost entirely on whether the facts of a client's case can be proven in accordance with the evidentiary standards required by law. The amount of proof required depends on the type of case at hand.

Nevertheless, all courts in the United States have adopted rules of evidence that are essential for every legal professional to know, just to evaluate a case.

At first blush, the law of evidence appears to be an arbitrary jumble of rules that come to us from a long and meandering history of decisions from English and American courts. For instance, the long-standing and familiar rule of evidence known as the **hearsay** rule disallows as evidence any out-of-court statements offered to prove the truth of the matter asserted in the statement. A person's statement cannot be quoted by someone else in court and taken as sworn testimony. The

hearsay
An out-of-court statement offered to prove a matter in contention in the lawsuit.

hearsay rule is difficult to understand in and of itself, but then there are nearly 30 exceptions to the hearsay rule that every law student must memorize to pass a course in evidence. Every trial lawyer instinctively scrambles to his or her feet to protest "objection" whenever he or she hears an opponent's witness make a hearsay statement. Paralegals working within litigation departments are equally as knowledgeable as their lawyer counterparts when it comes to the hearsay rule and the law of evidence.

Fortunately, for our purposes, we need only introduce some of the more routine and common rules of evidence. Notice that the following rules speak to what constitutes permissible evidence. Unlike the hearsay rule, most rules of evidence state the type of evidence that is admissible or preferred. If an item of evidence does not conform to the rules, it is inadmissible, and the trier of fact may not consider it in making its decision. In contrast, hearsay, by definition, is inadmissible unless the party seeking to have a hearsay statement considered can convince the judge that an exception applies. The truth of the matter is that many hearsay statements are allowed, because there are so many exceptions.

relevant evidence
Evidence that makes the existence of any fact more probable or less probable than it would be without the evidence.

best evidence rule
To prove the contents of a document, recording, or photograph, the original writing, recording, or photograph is required.

competence
The ability and possession of expertise and skill in a field that is necessary to do the job.

direct evidence
Evidence that establishes a particular fact without resort to other testimony or evidence.

- **Relevant evidence.** All evidence introduced at the trial must have relevance to a fact that pertains to the matter being tried. That is, the evidence must have some consequence for the outcome of the lawsuit. Thus, the fact that a person was late for work or an appointment would appear to be **relevant evidence** of the allegation that the person was driving a car too fast, which resulted in an accident that is the ultimate fact to be decided. The same fact would have no bearing and thus no relevance in a lawsuit regarding a debt.
- **Best evidence rule.** The **best evidence rule** requires that the evidence come in its original form. Copies may be submitted if the party seeking to introduce the evidence does not have the original for reasons out of that party's control. Parties may agree to submit copies upon authentication of the existence of the original document during discovery.
- **Competence.** To demonstrate **competence**, a witness to information that is not technical or expert in nature must show that he or she has both legal and mental capacity, as well as firsthand experience with the facts sought to be proved. Thus, a competent witness is one without any physical or mental disability that would prevent him or her from perceiving the events and accurately relating them to the trier of fact. Competent testimony also means that the testifying witness has taken an oath or affirmation (a solemn promise) to tell the truth. On technical matters beyond the common understanding of most people, an expert witness may testify once the party offering the expert has demonstrated that the witness is competent by education, experience, or training in the field of his or her expertise.
- **Direct and indirect evidence. Direct evidence** demonstrates the existence of a fact without requiring the trier of fact to make assumptions or inferences. Thus, an eyewitness account of the events that gave rise to the controversy would constitute direct evidence, because the witness's testimony recounts the events as he or she experienced them. A document signed by the parties to an agreement would be direct evidence of the existence of that agreement.

Evidence may also prove a fact indirectly by creating an inference. Stated abstractly, an inference is a conclusion drawn from the assumed premises as a matter of probability. Evidence that directly establishes some facts may create an additional fact by inference. In a case in which the parties have no written contract, the existence of a contract may be inferred from direct evidence that shows that the action of the parties is consistent with that of parties to an agreement.

CASE IN POINT

JUDICIAL NOTICE AND ABRAHAM LINCOLN

One of the most famous cases regarding judicial notice was known popularly as the "Almanac Case." That case involved a murder prosecution in which a witness testified that he was able to see a murder committed in the dark of night. The witness stated that he was able to see the murder because the moon was directly overhead. Abraham Lincoln, who represented the defendant, William "Duff" Armstrong, then introduced into evidence the Farmer's Almanac to show that at the time, the moon was just above the horizon. Thus, Lincoln argued that the moon was at such a low angle that there could not have been enough light to see anything well enough. The jury quickly returned a not guilty verdict. Lincoln performed his legal services *pro bono* and at the same time popularized the use of judicial notice of readily determined facts.

QUESTIONS ABOUT THE CASE

1. What is the purpose of admitting evidence by judicial notice?
2. Do you think that the witness was not telling the truth as to what he saw?
3. Why would a lawyer take a case *pro bono*?

- **Judicial notice.** One of the most unique and easiest ways to establish facts is to ask the trial court judge to take **judicial notice** of a commonly known fact. In the interest of efficiency, the rules of evidence in almost every state permit judges to take judicial notice without even being asked to do so by one of the parties. By taking judicial notice, the trial court judge eliminates the time and effort required to prove the fact. The Federal Rules of Evidence define matters of which a trial court judge may take judicial notice; specifically, Rule 201 (b) states:

judicial notice
A request that a court accept evidence as fact without the necessity of further proof.

> *A judicially noticed fact must be one not subject to reasonable dispute in that it is either (1) generally known within the territorial jurisdiction of the trial court or (2) capable of accurate and ready determination by resort to sources whose accuracy cannot reasonably be questioned.*

Thus, even commonly known facts that are well-established only within the locale are subject to judicial notice. Such facts might include the existence of a traffic light at a particular intersection near the court or the wider fact that New Year's Day 2006 fell on a Sunday.

The rules of evidence regulate the type of evidence that a trial judge may admit for consideration by the trier of fact. These rules exist for several purposes. Many rules establish certain standards for evidence, designed to ensure the reliability of the evidence offered by the parties. Rules such as the hearsay or best evidence rule are prime examples of rules that ensure the trustworthiness of the evidence. At the same time, other evidentiary rules promote efficiency by foregoing the formalities of proving easily ascertainable or commonly known facts, as in the case of judicial notice. Other rules requiring relevancy and materiality eliminate unrelated or unimportant details that may confuse the jury or consume unnecessary time.

Finally, evidentiary rules may have larger roles. The rules that prohibit evidence on the basis of privilege have the broader societal functions of protecting communications in the course of special relationships. These rules have little to do with ensuring the reliability of the evidence and much more to do with protecting the relationships within which these communications are made. For instance, the priest—penitent rule—prevents the admission of statements made during a confessional. Thus the rule protects the sanctity of a confession and preserves the confidentiality of such a statement. After all, if confessions were admissible in court, very few people would feel free to go to confession. Evidentiary rules regarding privileges exist to protect certain types of relationships by making statements within them inadmissible.

Rules of evidence are of primary concern with regard to the constitutional rights of those who have been accused of committing crimes. These constitutional concerns also affect the procedure with which courts handle criminal cases, as we shall see in the next chapter.

Summary

This chapter discusses how law is used to enforce legal rights. As a step toward becoming a legal professional, a paralegal must have essential knowledge of the various subjects in law. Students new to the study of law as a professional endeavor should be particularly aware that giving legal advice represents a prohibited activity that only a licensed professional may perform. Nevertheless, legal professionals such as paralegals must understand the law and how it is applied to perform their professional tasks and communicate effectively with the legal professionals with whom they work.

Civil litigation involves several integral steps that a legal professional must take to ensure a client's legal rights. Beginning with the drafting of a complaint and the issuance of a summons, the start of a lawsuit stretches over a timeline of events. Litigants must prepare for pretrial motions that test the legal sufficiency of the complaint. Discovery and its associated enforcement mechanisms give the parties an opportunity to obtain information from opposing parties. Most rules are designed to streamline lawsuits and encourage settlements. Past the discovery stage, a matter may go to trial, in which the jury or a judge sitting without a jury will determine the facts and apply the law. Similarly, the rules regarding what evidence may be admitted, and therefore considered as part of the case, are designed to promote efficient trials and ensure the trustworthiness of evidence.

Paralegals have an important role in all aspects of civil litigation. Only lawyers may sign their names to court documents, but paralegals often draft pleadings, motions, and requests for discovery. Paralegals also work behind the scenes organizing files and managing the voluminous amounts of information in each case. At trial, paralegals can be indispensable in assisting the supervising attorney with their knowledge of law and civil procedure and evidence.

Key Terms

Answer
Bench trial
Best evidence rule
Caption
Certificate of service
Challenge for cause
Chambers
Civil procedure
Competence
Complaint
Contempt
Counterclaim
Cover sheet
Cross-claim
Cross-examination
Default judgment
Demand letter
Deponent
Deposition
Direct evidence
Direct examination
Directed verdict
Discovery
Discretion
Docket number
Federal Rules of Civil Procedure
Filing fee
Forum
Hearsay
Impleader
Interrogatories
Judicial notice
Judicial review
Jurisdictional statement

Jury trial
Motion in limine
Motion to dismiss
Notice pleading
Opening statement
Peremptory challenge (peremptory jury strike)
Petition
Pretrial conference
Protective order
Recross-examination
Redirect examination
Relevant evidence
Requests for admissions
Requests for examination
Requests for production of documents
Sanctions
Subpoena
Subpoena duces tecum
Summary judgment
Summons
Third-party claim
Trade secret
Transcript
Trial
Trier of facts
Under advisement
Voir dire
Work product

Review Questions

1. What is the difference between a cross-claim and a counterclaim?
2. How is a summons different from a subpoena?
3. What is the basis for a motion to dismiss?
4. How is a motion to dismiss different from a motion for directed verdict?
5. Why are trade secrets protected from discovery?
6. Name the various forms of discovery available under the Federal Rules of Civil Procedure.
7. What are the possible responses to a civil complaint by a defendant?
8. When is summary judgment available?
9. What is the difference between a jurisdictional statement in a federal court complaint and one in a state court complaint?
10. During the many stages of civil litigation, list the aspect(s) of litigation in which a paralegal cannot legally participate.

Exercises

1. Choose a news item from the daily paper that might give rise to a civil lawsuit. Using the facts reported, draft a civil complaint. What facts are missing that you would need to know for a complaint? Now, as the defendant, draft an answer and a motion to dismiss the complaint.
2. On the basis of the same or another news item, outline a plan of discovery that you would pursue to gather information from the opposing party. In doing so, list each discovery mechanism and what information you would ask for with each mechanism. Remember that the efficient use of discovery builds on itself. That is, the use of one type of discovery is often followed by another discovery mechanism to seek further information.
3. Visit your local courthouse and observe the activities in the clerk's office. See if you can find out how the information is received and organized. Take a look at the court-issued forms, such as a summons or a subpoena. What other forms are there, and what are they used for?
4. Visit the Web site for the United States Patent and Trademark Office (www.uspto.gov). Click on "trademark search" and find the latest trademark for Coca-Cola.

Discussion Questions

1. Why may paralegals engage in the "authorized practice of law" within a law office but not outside of a law office?
2. What do claims for relief (causes of action) and affirmative defenses have in common?
3. If the lawsuit between Mole and Partee took place in Florida, how would the "stand your ground" law affect the lawsuit differently than it would in a common law state?
4. Looking at Patti Partee's answer, why is "failure to state a claim" an affirmative defense?
5. What ethical obligations do lawyers have for the work performed by a paralegal in their employ? What ethical obligations apply to paralegals regarding their own work?
6. What is the role of a paralegal in discovery? At trial?

PORTFOLIO ASSIGNMENT

Look up and read two cases, *New York County Lawyers Association v. Dacey,* 21 N.Y. 694, 287 N.Y.S. 2d 4322, 234 N.E.2d 459 (1967) and *Florida Bar Association v. Stupica,* 300 So. 2d 683 (Fla. 1974). Write a memorandum to your supervisor, who represents the author of a self-help manual about how to plan an estate (i.e., write a will and other legal documents) without a lawyer. Your supervisor is concerned about the possible unauthorized practice of law allegations that such a book might cause the client. Analyze the two cases and determine if there are any differences or distinctions between them, considering that each case went in an opposite way.

Chapter 7

Basic Legal Specialties for the Professional Paralegal

CHAPTER OBJECTIVES

The materials presented in this chapter will provide students with basic information about the following specialty areas of law:

- Basic criminal law.
- Criminal procedure and how crimes are prosecuted.
- Selected topics in tort law.
- Basic property law.

This chapter will further your instruction in law on what are known as legal specialties. These topics in law constitute the basic legal principles on which almost all American law is based. With the knowledge you have gained in civil litigation and evidence from Chapter 6, you now will be able to proceed with more complex areas of law. This chapter covers four distinct areas of law: criminal law and procedure, torts, and property. Many people do not realize that these areas of law, which originated from medieval England, are the foundation for many of our modern laws, such as environmental protection.

We start by covering a most controversial and dynamic area of law that virtually always generates public debate and concern.

CRIMINAL LAW AND PROCEDURE

In civil cases, the parties involved proceed with their lawsuits in a private, nongovernmental capacity, using the court system to enforce their legal rights. These parties can be individuals, associations, or business entities such as partnerships and corporations. The government also engages in civil litigation quite frequently. However, in civil cases, the government acts as if it were a private litigant, enforcing or defending its legal rights in a private matter. Thus, the government can be a plaintiff or a defendant in a civil action, with the same legal rights as anyone else. An example of a civil lawsuit involving the government includes proceedings in which the government is suing or defending an action regarding a contract or tort, just as a private party would.

However, in criminal court proceedings, the government—usually the federal government or a state government—is always the plaintiff and is represented by a lawyer known as a **prosecutor**. In most states, the prosecutor is known as the **district attorney**. Federal government prosecutors are known as **United States Attorneys**. As in civil proceedings, the person or entity in a criminal proceeding is the defendant. In a criminal proceeding, the government seeks to have the courts do two things: (1) find that a person (or corporation) has committed a crime and (2) punish the defendant.

prosecutor
Attorney representing the people or plaintiff in criminal matters.

district attorney
A government lawyer who acts as the prosecutor in criminal cases.

United States Attorney
The prosecutor in charge of enforcing the federal criminal laws of the United States. A U.S. Attorney can also enforce selected federal civil statutes, such as the Civil Rights Act and antitrust laws.

Unlike civil proceedings, criminal prosecutions enforce standards of behavior imposed on all of us by criminal laws. These laws, which are always contained in statutes, are public declarations of the types of behavior deemed by society as unacceptable, to the degree that legislatures have gone through the trouble of enacting criminal laws. As such, these statues establish a duty of behavior owed by everyone to society at large. Thus, criminal laws are an important mechanism to maintain social order and public safety.

Equally important is the way in which society apprehends, tries, and punishes those who are suspected of crimes. Because of the Bill of Rights and the fundamental rights granted to us by the Constitution, the manner in which the government seeks to enforce criminal laws through the courts greatly affects the rules of court procedure in criminal cases, as well as the conduct of law enforcement officials. The resulting body of law, known as criminal procedure, goes hand in hand with the study of criminal law, which asks whether a crime has been committed. However, criminal procedure governs the entire process of enforcing criminal laws while at the same time protecting our constitutional rights.

The field of criminal justice involves the study of government's methods to maintain social order, prevent crime, enforce laws, and administer justice. A peaceful and orderly society requires the fair and efficient enforcement of criminal laws. Yet criminal law enforcement constantly raises significant public concerns. Some of the concerns involve the types of behavior that should be criminalized. Other concerns question how far police and other law enforcement officers should go to detect and apprehend suspected violators. There are also grave concerns about the manner in which guilt may be determined and who determines it. Punishment for crimes perpetually causes public outcry when that punishment is perceived as too harsh or too lenient. Because of the complex social issues involved and frequent sensational nature of the cases, criminal law receives more than its share of media and public attention.

PRACTICE TIP

As you progress in your legal studies, the points of law, practice techniques, and skills you acquire are intended for immediate use once you become a professional paralegal. Many paralegal graduates keep their class notes and books, such as legal dictionaries and other materials, for use in the law offices that employ them.

As discussed in a subsequent chapter, professional paralegals have a wide array of employment opportunities in the criminal justice area, working directly with the court system, law enforcement, prosecutors, and probation offices. These positions commonly call for students who had majored in criminal justice. However, the legal knowledge and practical skills acquired in a paralegal education have begun to sway employers in the criminal justice system to hire trained paralegals. Paralegals have begun to populate these positions in large numbers. In keeping with its concerns regarding practical professional education for paralegals, the ABA has specified that criminal justice courses do not qualify as "legal specialty" courses for paralegals. Nevertheless, many paralegal programs offer courses related to criminal law that do or could qualify as legal specialty courses, specifically designed to teach paralegal skills.

Many legal professionals engage in the practice of criminal law as a specialty. Among these criminal law practitioners, there are subspecialties. Some law firms, for instance, may specialize only in defense of those accused of "white-collar crimes." Many government prosecutors have special offices to pursue white-collar criminals. On the defense side, legal professionals who defend those accused of white-collar crimes generally work for large law firms. Smaller law offices or sole practitioners usually represent those accused of other crimes.

CASE IN POINT

WHITE-COLLAR CRIMES

White-collar crimes constitute a class of criminal prosecutions in which the accused has attained high socioeconomic status and has been charged with nonviolent crimes motivated by profit and greed. Common white-collar crimes include fraud, embezzlement, obstruction of justice, bribery, and extortion. Business executives have increasingly begun to run afoul of criminal laws in the operation of their businesses. Under the common law, corporations were considered artificial constructs without minds of their own, incapable of forming the intent necessary to be guilty of crimes. This perception has changed recently.

During the past two decades, federal and state governments have increased the number of criminal investigations of businesses and the people who run them, partly in an effort to apply criminal laws evenhandedly. Commission and prosecution of white-collar crimes are on the rise. High-profile prosecutions of large corporations have caught the attention of the press and the public with cases such as those involving Martha Stewart (obstruction of justice), Dennis Kozlowski (former CEO of Tyco, Inc., for misappropriating $400 million in company funds), Kenneth Lay (former Enron CEO, for fraud), and Jeff Skilling (former Enron official, for securities fraud and insider trading). According to the Federal Bureau of Investigation, white-collar crime is estimated to cost the United States more than $300 billion annually.

QUESTIONS ABOUT THE CASE

1. What social interests are promoted by the active prosecution of "white collar" crimes?
2. Do you think that corporations should be held responsible for the criminal acts of their employees? If so, what kinds of punishments or penalties should be levied against corporations?
3. Do you believe that "white collar" crimes should be prosecuted with as equal vigor as other crimes?

WHAT IS A CRIME?

Simply put, a **crime** is an activity or inactivity that a state or federal legislature has defined and declared as a violation of a duty owed to society that deserves punishment, such a fine or imprisonment. There are several classifications of crimes. Felonies are the category of serious crimes, such as armed robbery, arson, mayhem, murder, and rape. Although there is some variation among states, a felony generally involves a serious crime for which the punishment is at least one year of imprisonment. Moreover, imprisonment for a felony conviction is usually served in a high-security prison designated exclusively for convicted felons. Misdemeanors are lesser crimes that usually carry a punishment consisting of a fine. If the misdemeanor statute calls for imprisonment, the sentence is usually a few months in the county jail.

crime
Any act done in violation of those duties that an individual owes to the community, and for the breach of which the law has provided that the offender shall make satisfaction to the public.

Although crimes are viewed as wrongs committed against society, another way to classify crimes is based on the type of harm caused. With varying degrees of severity, crimes committed against persons are deemed the most serious. Thus, among the most serious crimes are those that cause physical injury, such as murder, mayhem, rape, assault, robbery, and kidnapping. There are also crimes against property, such as receiving stolen property, malicious destruction, theft, arson, and trespass. Finally, crimes against society at large adversely affect the public health, safety, and morals. These crimes include obscenity, prostitution, drug offenses, bribery, and espionage.

Limitations on the Government's Power to Criminalize

State and federal legislatures have considerable freedom to make certain acts or even inactions criminal. In legal parlance, when the legislature, whether state or federal, passes a statute declaring that certain specified acts constitute a crime, the legislature **criminalizes** the behavior described in the statute. Generally speaking, the government possesses broad powers to criminalize almost any behavior in the interest of public health, safety, and welfare.

criminalize
To declare a certain behavior or condition subject to criminal laws and punishment.

CASE IN POINT

COURT OPINION

CITY OF CHICAGO VS. JESUS MORALES, 527 U.S. 41 (1999)

In 1992, the Chicago City Council enacted the Gang Congregation Ordinance, which prohibits "criminal street gang members" from "loitering" with one another or with other persons in any public place. The question presented is whether the Supreme Court of Illinois correctly held that the ordinance violates the Due Process Clause of the Fourteenth Amendment to the Federal Constitution.

In the respondent's case, the trial judge held that the "ordinance fails to notify individuals what conduct is prohibited, and it encourages arbitrary and capricious enforcement by police."

The Illinois Supreme Court affirmed. It held "that the gang loitering ordinance violates due process of law in that it is impermissibly vague on its face and an arbitrary restriction on personal liberties."

We granted certiorari, and now affirm. Like the Illinois Supreme Court, we conclude that the ordinance enacted by the city of Chicago is unconstitutionally vague.

As the city argues in its brief, "the very presence of a large collection of obviously brazen, insistent, and lawless gang members and hangers-on on the public ways intimidates residents, who become afraid even to leave their homes and go about their business." We have no doubt that a law that directly prohibited such intimidating conduct would be constitutional, but this ordinance broadly covers a significant amount of additional activity. Uncertainty about the scope of that additional coverage provides the basis for respondents' claim that the ordinance is too vague.

Vagueness may invalidate a criminal law for either of two independent reasons. First, it may fail to provide the kind of notice that will enable ordinary people to understand what conduct it prohibits; second, it may authorize and even encourage arbitrary and discriminatory enforcement. Accordingly, we first consider whether the ordinance provides fair notice to the citizen and then discuss its potential for arbitrary enforcement.

First, the purpose of the fair notice requirement is to enable the ordinary citizen to conform his or her conduct to the law. "No one may be required at peril of life, liberty or property to speculate as to the meaning of penal statutes." Because an officer may issue an order only after prohibited conduct has already occurred, it cannot provide the kind of advance notice that will protect the putative loiterer from being ordered to disperse. Such an order cannot retroactively give adequate warning of the boundary between the permissible and the impermissible applications of the law.

Second, the terms of the dispersal order compound the inadequacy of the notice afforded by the ordinance. It provides that the officer "shall order all such persons to disperse and remove themselves from the area." This vague phrasing raises a host of questions.

Lack of clarity in the description of the loiterer's duty to obey a dispersal order might not render the ordinance unconstitutionally vague if the definition of the forbidden conduct were clear, but it does buttress our conclusion that the entire ordinance fails to give the ordinary citizen adequate notice of what is forbidden and what is permitted.

The broad sweep of the ordinance also violates "the requirement that a legislature establish minimal guidelines to govern law enforcement." There are no such guidelines in the ordinance. In any public place in the city of Chicago, persons who stand or sit in the company of a gang member may be ordered to disperse unless their purpose is apparent. The mandatory language in the enactment directs the police to issue an order without first making any inquiry about their possible purposes.

The ordinance does not apply to people who are moving—that is, to activity that would not constitute loitering under any possible definition of the term—[and] does not even address the question of how much discretion the police enjoy in deciding which stationary persons to disperse under the ordinance. The "no apparent purpose" standard for making that decision is inherently subjective because its application depends on whether some purpose is "apparent" to the officer on the scene.

We recognize the serious and difficult problems testified to by the citizens of Chicago that led to the enactment of this ordinance. However, in this instance the city has enacted an ordinance that affords too much discretion to the police and too little notice to citizens who wish to use the public streets.

Accordingly, the judgment of the Supreme Court of Illinois is Affirmed.

QUESTIONS ABOUT THE CASE

1. Which two aspects of the Chicago ordinance did the Court find unconstitutionally vague?
2. From considering those two aspects, what can you learn find the vagueness doctrine?
3. Why is vagueness a problem?
4. Investigate what became of the Chicago ordinance and Morales as a result of this decision.
5. To hear the case, the Court granted certiorari. Who asked the Court to hear the case?

When the government acts to protect and provide for the public, it is exercising what are known as **police powers**, or the inherent rights of a government's sovereign power. Consider, for instance, the well-justified public attention to drunk driving and domestic violence. Not too long ago, few laws and scant law enforcement attention focused on either—until the past 20 years. Police powers also include the government's authority to enforce not only criminal laws but also other laws. If you have ever read the label listing ingredients on a supermarket item, you have experienced the government's police powers, which require those labels. However, the United States Constitution imposes a number of significant limitations on what may be regarded as crimes.

police powers
The legal authority granted to governments to provide for the health, safety, welfare, and morals of society.

Criminal statutes or codes themselves are very specific. The Constitution requires specificity in criminal laws. Notions of fairness embedded in the due process clause of the Fifth Amendment to the United States Constitution have been consistently interpreted as requiring that these statutes give adequate notice of what constitutes wrongful behavior. As the previous case shows, even with the best intentions, laws may fall to Constitutional challenges. The case also describes how it was appealed through the Illinois state court system to the United States Supreme Court.

As previously discussed, the due process clauses of the Fifth and Fourteenth Amendments have been a source of fundamental rights and liberties. At the same time, the clause acts as a limitation on what statutes—whether city, state, or federal—may do. In *City of Chicago v. Morales,* the United States Supreme Court actually stated that "a law that directly prohibited such intimidating conduct would be constitutional. . . ." However, the manner in which the Chicago City Council drafted the ordinance ran into problems. Thus, the subject matter of the ordinance was a permissible exercise of the government's power to declare "intimidating conduct" criminal behavior. However, the manner in which the city of Chicago went about it was unconstitutional under the due process clause.

The other aspect to the due process clause provides a source of fundamental rights and operates differently. When laws infringe on a fundamental right, the test is whether the law being challenged is "narrowly tailored to serve a compelling government interest." This test sets an extremely high standard for the government. The following case illustrates this point.

In the next case, *Moore v. East Cleveland,* the government was attempting to regulate not families but the use of property to prevent overcrowding. However, in doing so, the law infringed on a fundamental right in a way that could not be justified under the Constitution. The due process clause thus limits the government's authority to enact criminal statutes. Other constitutional provisions also limit the scope of criminal laws.

The U.S. Constitution, Article I, Section 10, clause 3, also prohibits the enforcement of **ex post facto laws** that criminalize past acts that were not illegal when committed. This prohibition also includes retroactive increases in punishment or a retroactive application of an easier burden of proof for the government in proving a crime. The same clause prohibits **bills of attainder**—laws that impose punishment without a trial by naming a person or identifiable group of persons. Beyond these major considerations, state and federal legislatures are free to pass laws that declare criminal behavior in a wide range of human activity.

ex post facto law
Retrospective changes to the legal consequences of acts committed or the legal status of facts and relationships that existed prior to the enactment of the law. These laws are unconstitutional.

bill of attainder
A legislative act declaring a person or group of persons guilty of some crime and punishing him or her without benefit of a trial.

Elements of a Crime

For most crimes, there must be a criminal act, also called an ***actus reus***, that is described in detail by the criminal statute. Each criminal act, or *actus reus,* consists of several individual elements, which together constitute the *actus reus.*

actus reus
The guilty act.

CASE IN POINT

COURT OPINION

MOORE V. CITY OF EAST CLEVELAND, 431 U.S. 494 (1977)

East Cleveland's housing ordinance, like many throughout the country, limits occupancy of a dwelling unit to members of a single family. But [here], the ordinance contains an unusual and complicated definitional section that recognizes as a "family" only a few categories of related individuals. Because her family, living together in her home, fits none of those categories, appellant stands convicted of a criminal offense. The question in this case is whether the ordinance violates the Due Process Clause of the Fourteenth Amendment.

Appellant, Mrs. Inez Moore, lives in her East Cleveland home together with her son, Dale Moore, Sr., and her two grandsons, Dale, Jr., and John Moore, Jr. The two boys are first cousins rather than brothers.

In early 1973, the city filed a criminal charge against Mrs. Moore. She moved to dismiss, claiming that the ordinance was constitutionally invalid on its face. Her motion was overruled, and upon conviction she was sentenced to five days in jail and a $25 fine. The Ohio Court of Appeals affirmed after giving full consideration to her constitutional claims and the Ohio Supreme Court denied review. We noted probable jurisdiction of her appeal.

When a city undertakes such intrusive regulation of the family, the usual judicial deference to the legislature is inappropriate. "This Court has long recognized that freedom of personal choice in matters of marriage and family life is one of the liberties protected by the Due Process Clause of the Fourteenth Amendment."

Of course, the family is not beyond regulation. But when the government intrudes on choices concerning family living arrangements, this Court must examine carefully the importance of the governmental interests advanced and the extent to which they are served by the challenged regulation.

The full scope of the liberty guaranteed by the Due Process Clause is a rational continuum which, broadly speaking, includes a freedom from all substantial arbitrary impositions and purposeless restraints . . . and which also recognizes, what a reasonable and sensitive judgment must, that certain interests require particularly careful scrutiny of the state needs asserted to justify their abridgment.

Our decisions establish that the Constitution protects the sanctity of the family precisely because the institution of the family is deeply rooted in this Nation's history and tradition. It is through the family that we inculcate and pass down many of our most cherished values, moral and cultural.

Ours is by no means a tradition limited to respect for the bonds uniting the members of the nuclear family. The tradition of uncles, aunts, cousins, and especially grandparents sharing a household along with parents and children has roots equally venerable and equally deserving of constitutional recognition. Even if conditions of modern society have brought about a decline in extended family households, they have not erased the accumulated wisdom of civilization, gained over the centuries and honored throughout our history that supports a larger conception of the family. Out of choice, necessity, or a sense of family responsibility, it has been common for close relatives to draw together and participate in the duties and the satisfactions of a common home. Especially in times of adversity, such as the death of a spouse or economic need, the broader family has tended to come together for mutual sustenance and to maintain or rebuild a secure home life. This is apparently what happened here.

Whether or not such a household is established because of personal tragedy, the choice of relatives in this degree of kinship to live together may not lightly be denied by the State. The Constitution prevents East Cleveland from standardizing its children—and its adults—by forcing all to live in certain narrowly defined family patterns.

Reversed.

QUESTIONS ABOUT THE CASE

1. What crime had Moore committed?
2. On what fundamental right did the East Cleveland ordinance infringe?
3. The Court stated that "the family is not beyond regulation." In what ways does the law regulate families?
4. How does due process differ between this case and the Morales case?
5. How could East Cleveland prevent overcrowding without trampling on a fundamental right?

Therefore, the government must prove beyond a reasonable doubt that the accused committed each and every one of the elements of the crime as set out in the statute. The following example of a criminal statute from the Model Penal Code—a comprehensive set of criminal statutes compiled by a committee of prominent legal scholars—has been adopted in some form by almost 40 states.

Model Penal Code, §223.6. Receiving Stolen Property.

Receiving. A person is guilty of theft if he purposely receives, retains, or disposes of movable property of another knowing that it has been stolen, or believing that it has probably been

> *stolen, unless the property is received, retained, or disposed with purpose to restore it to the owner. "Receiving" means acquiring possession, control or title, or lending on the security of the property.*[1]

Reading the statute's language carefully, we can see that the elements for the crime of receiving stolen property (a form of theft) consist of a number of elements drawn from the statute's wording. To prove that a person is guilty under the statute, the prosecutor must prove (beyond a reasonable doubt) the following elements:

- Purposely receives, retains, or disposes of,
- Property that is movable,
- Of another,
- Knowing it to be stolen, and
- Without the purpose of restoring it to the owner.

Once the prosecutor has proven all elements, the government has established the *actus reus*. Without proof of all the elements, the defendant will be found *not guilty*. This result is also the case if the jury, or a judge sitting without a jury, has a reasonable doubt that the defendant may be guilty.

Notice that the quoted section of the Model Penal Code uses the words "purposely" and "knowing." These words are necessary to distinguish the crime described in the statute from innocent situations or honest mistakes. For instance, a person may unwittingly receive or even purchase an item that, unbeknownst to him or her, had been stolen. Because this person was unaware that the property was stolen, no crime has occurred. Thus, with many crimes, the prosecutor must show that the accused possesses a criminal state of mind. That is, an essential element to prove that a person is guilty of a crime requires the prosecutor to prove that the *actus reus* was committed with the intent to commit a crime. This element is commonly known as *mens rea*. Intent is always very difficult to prove, because at issue is what the person was thinking at the time. However, intent or knowledge may be inferred from the circumstances or the accused's actions.

Almost all crimes require a voluntary act. There are special situations, however, in which the law has imposed a special duty to act. Thus, the law would regard the failure to act as a crime. Here, the *mens rea* requirement becomes irrelevant. The failure to file tax returns, to pay support to a spouse or children, to register for the draft (military conscription), or to register a firearm may all constitute crimes resulting from a failure to take action. Similarly, possession of a controlled substance does not require a showing of *mens rea*. You can imagine the difficulty the government would have if criminal laws required proof of *mens rea* for drug cases and other crimes that do have such a requirement.

CYBER TRIP

On the Internet, go to www.ali.org, the Web site for the American Law Institute (ALI). Navigate to the Model Penal Code and find §233.6. What is ALI? What other publications does ALI offer? What type of legal authority does its publications offer?

Defenses to Crimes

In all criminal cases, the prosecution (i.e., the government) carries the burden of proving guilt beyond a reasonable doubt. The defendant has several options. In many instances, the defendant merely puts the government to its proof, offering no evidence of its own just to see if the government can prove its case. The law does not require any criminal defendant to prove his or her innocence or to produce any evidence at all. At most, the defendant might present witnesses in his or her own behalf to rebut (contradict) or discredit the prosecution's case. If this presentation is convincing, the finder of fact (i.e., the jury or a judge sitting without a jury) could very well find that the government has not proven its case sufficiently—either that the prosecution had

[1] Model Penal Code, copyright 1985 by The American Law Institute. Reprinted with permission. All rights reserved.

EYE ON ETHICS

Many paralegals find satisfying work with the courts and law enforcement in a variety of capacities, such as probation officers, parole officers, victims' advocates, and so forth. Be aware that as part of the court or law enforcement system, you cannot give legal advice; doing so in any of these positions would constitute the unauthorized practice of law.

not proven all the elements or that there was a reasonable doubt. Either way, the result would be a verdict of not guilty.

Similar to affirmative defenses in civil cases, there are such defenses to crimes. These defenses vary widely. Some permit the defendant to show that he or she was elsewhere when the alleged crime was committed. In doing so, the defendant would present evidence that shows it would have been impossible for him or her to have committed the crime. This defense is known as an alibi.

Similarly, the defendant may show error or ignorance for crimes that require *mens rea.* For instance, a student may leave class and accidentally take another person's backpack. Because the student had made a good faith error as to the ownership, no crime has occurred. Specifically, the crime of **theft** requires the following elements: (1) an *intentional* taking of (2) another person' property with (3) the *intent* to deprive the owner. There would have been a taking of another person's property. However, the mistaken student lacked both the intent to take another's property and the intent to deprive. Notice that what is missing is the *mens rea* requirement. The defendant's status, such as someone who is a child or is mentally incompetent, can also prevent a showing of *mens rea* as a matter of law. Those defendants would thus be unable to possess the requisite intent to commit a criminal act.

theft
The taking of property without the owner's consent.

Related to the status defense is perhaps the most controversial defense, known as the **insanity defense**. Begun as the M'Naghten Rule, the insanity defense essentially says that the defendant did not have the *mens rea* to commit a crime. More specifically, the finder of fact must be convinced that "the defendant was laboring under such a defect of reason, from disease of the mind as not to know the nature and quality of the act he was doing, or if he did know it, that he did not know what he was doing was wrong."

insanity defense
A defendant's claim that he or she was insane when the crime was committed, even if temporarily insane. Often referred to as the M'Naghten Rule.

As you can see, the available defenses focus on the defendant's state of mind. Other defenses also admit to the commission of the crime but act to avoid criminal responsibility due to the particular circumstances. All of these defenses are subject to jury deliberations, such that the jury is free to believe or disbelieve the defendant's story that constitutes the defense. Here is a partial list of defenses:

- **Entrapment.** A defendant claims he or she has been enticed or tricked by law enforcement officials into committing a crime. However, the defendant must show that he or she was not predisposed to committing the crime and that the government's enticement was the sole motivating factor.
- **Duress.** A defendant is forced to commit a crime by another who threatens the defendant, who in turn does not have the requisite state of mind to commit the crime. To avail him- or herself of a duress defense, the defendant must demonstrate a reasonable apprehension that he or she, or another innocent person, would immediately be killed or suffer serious bodily injury and that there was no reasonable opportunity to escape the threatened harm. This defense is also known as the necessity defense, in which the defendant claims that he or she committed the act to avoid a greater harm.

CASE IN POINT

CASE SUMMARY

M'NAGHTEN'S CASE, 8 TNG. REP. 718, 722 (1843)

Daniel M'Naghten, the eponym for the rule, was charged with the murder in 1843. At his trial, several psychiatrists testified that M'Naghten was delusional and suffered from the paranoid belief that the Pope and the British prime minister were conspiring against him. M'Naghten, a Scotsman, had traveled to the prime minister's office at 10 Downing Street, London, and, in a botched attempt to shoot Prime Minister Robert Peel, shot his secretary instead. M'Naghten's defense thus argued that he did not have the intent to commit murder. The jury returned a not guilty verdict.

The M'Naghten Rule has been adopted in some parts of the United States. Only those states that recognize the insanity defense have adopted the M'Naghten Rule (also known as the "right-wrong test"). Some of those states have modified the rule so that defendants need only prove that they were unable to control their actions (known as the "irresistible impulse defense"). The insanity defense is very rarely successful. Instead of a prison sentence, a defendant who succeeds with the defense usually is committed to a mental health facility. For example, Daniel M'Naghten himself was placed for 20 years in a mental asylum, where he died.

The insanity defense has become controversial because of the uncertainty in the result of the defense. Is the defendant guilty or not? Some states provide for a finding of not guilty by reason of insanity, whereas others find the defendant guilty but insane and therefore not criminally responsible. States such as Connecticut, have retained the insanity defense but have also imposed a rather harsh result in which an "insane" defendant must spend twice the average term of imprisonment in an institution. Dr. Howard Zonana, Professor of Psychiatry at Yale Medical School, has wryly commented, "So you really got to be crazy to take an insanity defense."

QUESTIONS ABOUT THE CASE

1. Should society excuse insane persons for their crimes of all sorts?
2. How should society provide treatment for insane persons who have committed crimes?
3. How should insanity be measured?

- **Self-defense.** As illustrated in the last chapter, self-defense may be used as a defense to the tort of battery, a civil action. Self-defense is similarly available in crimes alleging assault and battery. Use of force is justified when a person reasonably believes that it is necessary for the defense of him- or herself or another against the immediate use of unlawful force. Self-defense is also available for the protection of property or others who appear to be facing immediate harm. However, a person must use no more force than appears reasonably necessary in the circumstances.
- **Battered spouse syndrome.** As an expansion of self-defense, the law has come to recognize the plight of victims of domestic violence. To claim self-defense, the defendant must show that he or she was in imminent danger. A battered spouse needs to show that he or she has been the victim of numerous attacks in the past and that escape from future attacks would not be possible. Battered spouse syndrome is a relatively new legal doctrine, and not all states have adopted it. To be sure, the doctrine will undergo further changes. Now, a defendant who is accused of murder and successfully asserts battered spouse syndrome will have the charges reduced to manslaughter.

At this point, you may note the similarity between crimes and torts. The laws that cover both areas define and punish or seek compensation for bad behavior. With criminal proceedings, the government seeks punishment in the name of society and the public safety. In tort actions, the plaintiff, a private party and a victim, seeks compensation for the violation of a private interest caused by the defendant. Sometimes a civil tort action will punish the defendant by awarding punitive damages.

FIGURE 7.1
Overlapping Areas of Crimes and Torts

Crime	Tort
Murder	Wrongful death
Assault and battery	Assault: Fear of immediate harm Battery: Offensive touching
Kidnapping	False imprisonment
Criminal defamation	Defamation (libel and slander)
Criminal negligence	Negligence
Disturbing the peace	Nuisance

Oftentimes, a person who has committed a crime against a person or his or her property has also committed a tort. Figure 7.1 illustrates some overlapping areas of crimes and torts.

CRIMINAL PROCEDURE

criminal procedure
The rules and legal process for adjudicating charges that someone has committed a crime, often implicating constitutional principles pertaining to the rights of the accused.

The rules of **criminal procedure** operate in a way similar to the rules of civil procedure. However, consider the sharp differences between civil and criminal cases. In civil cases, the government occasionally appears as a party. In criminal cases, the government is always the party bringing the proceedings to court. Most important, the stakes in criminal cases can be very high. Thus, important constitutional concerns arise because of the possibility of punishment, sometimes severe, in criminal cases. The government's ample legal ability to punish through the enforcement of criminal laws is largely tempered by the Fourth, Fifth, and Sixth Amendments to the United States Constitution.

Our discussion of the Constitution's impact at this point differs from the Constitutional issues we covered earlier in this chapter. When we discussed Constitutional aspects of ex post facto laws and the Supreme Court's decisions in *City of Chicago v. Morales* and *Moore v. City of Cleveland,* we saw how the Constitution limits the types of behavior that the government can criminalize. Now we are turning to the Constitution's impact on the manner in which criminal laws are enforced.

The Constitution thus actually regulates *how* the government goes about enforcing criminal laws in three separate ways: (1) how government investigates crimes, (2) how the rights of the accused should be protected, and (3) how criminal prosecutions proceed in the courts. As we cover each of these three stages, we will take a close look at each amendments' words. You can see that these amendments specifically concern themselves with the enforcement of criminal laws.

Government Investigation of a Crime

When a crime is reported or suspected to have been committed, a police investigation ensues. That investigation's purpose is to seek and collect evidence to determine whether it is likely that a crime has occurred by interrogating witnesses and suspects and making physical and scientific inspections. In trying to determine whether a crime has occurred and who has committed it, the police and investigators have wide authority to question and obtain evidence from various sources, including private businesses and residences. The Fourth Amendment states:

> *The right of the people to be secure in their persons, houses, papers, and effects, against unreasonable searches and seizures, shall not be violated, and no warrants shall issue, but upon probable cause, supported by oath or affirmation, and particularly describing the place to be searched, and the persons or things to be seized.*

As you review the language of the Fourth Amendment, you can see that it requires police and prosecutors to follow a specific procedure in their search for evidence.

.AO 93 (Rev. 12/03) Search Warrant

UNITED STATES DISTRICT COURT for the

District of________________________

In the Matter of the Search of ________________________

(Name, address or brief description of person or property to be searched)

SEARCH WARRANT

Case Number:__________________

TO: ______________________________and any Authorized Officer of the United States

Affidavit(s) having been made before me by who has reason to believe

Affiant

that in the person of, or on the premises known as ____________________(name, description and/or location) in the District of there is now concealed a certain person or property, namely (describe the person or property) I am satisfied that the affidavit(s) and any record testimony establish probable cause to believe that the person or property so described is now concealed on the person or premises above-described and establish grounds for the issuance of this warrant.

YOU ARE HEREBY COMMANDED to search on or before

Date

(not to exceed 10 days) the person or place named above for the person or property specified, serving this warrant and making the search in the daytime—6:00 AM to 10:00 P.M. at anytime in the day or night as I find reasonable cause has been established and if the person or property be found there to seize same, leaving a copy of this warrant and receipt for the person or property taken, and prepare a written inventory of the person or property seized and promptly return this warrant to as required by law.

/S/

U.S. Magistrate Judge (Rule 41(f)(4))

at

Date and Time Issued City and State

Name and Title of Judge Signature of Judge

FIGURE 7.2 **Example of a Search Warrant for Use in a Federal Court**

Known as search and seizure, the government's power to obtain and retain evidence is directly regulated by that amendment. Notice that at the very outset, the Fourth Amendment guarantees security against "*unreasonable* search and seizure." This wording means that the Constitution allows for reasonable search and seizure. The Fourth Amendment does so by prescribing a legal method for obtaining evidence.

probable cause
The totality of circumstances that leads one to believe certain facts or circumstances exist; applies to arrests, searches, and seizures; and the commission of a crime.

The Fourth Amendment specifically authorizes the issuance of a warrant when the government shows **probable cause**. You may recall that in our discussion of evidence and civil procedure, the burden of proof varies depending on the type of case involved. In all criminal cases, the burden is "beyond a reasonable doubt." However, to obtain a warrant, the government must seek permission from a judge and present evidence that shows "a reasonable belief that a crime has been committed." That belief constitutes probable cause and stands as the legal standard necessary for the issuance of a search warrant.

search warrant
Issued after presentation of an affidavit stating clearly the probable cause on which the request is based. In particular, it is an order in writing, issued by a justice or other magistrate, in the name of the state, and directed to a sheriff, constable, or other officer authorizing him to search for and seize any property that constitutes evidence of the commission of a crime, contraband, or the fruits of the crime.

A **search warrant** is an order signed by a judge that allows the police to look in a specific place for a specific item at a specific time. (See Figure 7.2.) To obtain the warrant, the police must convince a judge that there is "probable cause" to believe that criminal activity is afoot and that a search of the location will produce the evidence to prosecute the crime. The police usually show this evidence through sworn affidavits of informants or investigators. Upon finding that there is probable cause, the judge will issue the search warrant. Without a showing of probable cause, the judge will decline to issue the warrant.

Notice that the Fourth Amendment, as specific as it is, does not specify what should happen if the police or other law enforcement officers fail to obtain a warrant. In

CASE IN POINT

CASE SUMMARY

MAPP V. OHIO, 367 U.S. 643 (1961)

Ms. Dolly Mapp and her daughter shared the upstairs part of a two-family home in a rough part of Cleveland, Ohio. In the afternoon of May 23, 1957, the local police demanded entrance to Mapp's apartment. The police had heard that a man suspected of a bombing was hiding in Mapp's house. No stranger to the law, Mapp called her attorney. Upon her attorney's advice, she refused the police entry when they failed to produce a search warrant.

Soon, more police arrived and forcibly entered her apartment. When Mapp again demanded to see their warrant, one of the policemen showed her a document, stating that it was a search warrant. Mapp snatched it out of the officer's hand, but the officer grabbed it back. At this point, things started to get worse for Mapp. Claiming that she had become "belligerent," the officer handcuffed her and dragged her upstairs. The group of police officers then proceeded to search her entire apartment and the basement to the building.

In the basement, the police found a trunk containing books, pictures, and photographs they claimed were "lewd and lascivious." Mapp disclaimed anything to do with their find, stating the trunk must have belonged to a previous tenant of the building. They nevertheless arrested Mapp for violating Ohio's criminal law prohibiting the possession of obscene materials. At trial, Mapp's attorney questioned the police officers about the search warrant, asking them to produce it. They refused, but the court found her guilty of the violation based on the evidence presented by the police. The court sentenced Mapp to 1 to 7 years imprisonment.

Mapp appealed her case to the Supreme Court of Ohio, which upheld her conviction. Undaunted, Mapp appealed to the United States Supreme Court, presenting the issue of whether evidence obtained through a search in violation of the Fourth Amendment is admissible in state criminal proceedings.

In previous rulings, the U.S. Supreme Court had declared that "any forcible and compulsory extortion of a man's own private papers to be used as evidence to convict him of a crime" violates the Fourth Amendment. *Boyd v. United States* (1886). Almost three decades later, in *Weeks v. United States* (1914), the Court ruled held that the Fourth Amendment "put the courts of the United States and federal officials . . . under limitations . . . and forever secure[d] the people, their persons, houses, papers and effects against all unreasonable searches and seizures." Thus, the Court had already ruled that the Fourth Amendment covered federal officials and that illegally seized evidence could not be used in a federal court criminal proceeding. Still, the Court had yet to decide whether the same principle applied to criminal proceedings in a state court if state officials had committed an unlawful search and seizure.

In Mapp's case, the Court ruled in a landmark decision that the exclusionary rule that protects rights guaranteed under the Fourth Amendment applied to the states as well as the federal government. Thus, the states could not use evidence obtained in violation of that amendment in state criminal court proceedings. The Court reasoned that constitutional rights would have little meaning if the state courts continued to admit illegally seized evidence. Thus, applying the exclusionary rule to the states would reduce police abuse and protect individual rights. Prohibiting court use of illegally obtained evidence would also uphold judicial integrity. The Court also considered that the exclusionary rule acted as part of the checks and balances on the executive branch. Accordingly, the Court reversed Mapp's conviction.

QUESTIONS ABOUT THE CASE

1. Mapp claimed that the seized evidence was not hers. However, what legal argument could be made that, in any event, she had a right to possess the evidence?
2. In the *Mapp* case, the United States Supreme Court balanced the protection of individual rights against the interest of public protection. Do you think that a trunk containing "lewd and lascivious books" presents a public danger?
3. What do you suppose Dolly Mapp's lawyer told her during their initial telephone conversation? Why?
4. Was Mapp justified in denying the police entry to her house? Explain your reasoning.
5. The Fourth Amendment protects "against *unreasonable* searches and seizures." What, if anything, was unreasonable in the search and seizure that occurred in Mapp's house?

Mapp v. Ohio, the Supreme Court applied the exclusionary rule to criminal proceedings in state courts as a remedy for wrongful search and seizure.

From the moment the Supreme Court handed down its decision, *Mapp v. Ohio* has continued to generate controversy. Many maintain that the decision promotes honest and legal police behavior and ensures the protection of the Fourth Amendment rights. Thus, proponents of the decision maintain that the exclusionary rule is an effective way to enforce important constitutional rights. Opponents of the exclusionary rule argue that the Supreme Court was wrong to balance public safety against individual rights. They maintain, as did the famous Supreme Court Justice Benjamin Cardozo, "The criminal is to go free because the constable has blundered."

There are several situations in which a search warrant may not be constitutionally required for law enforcement officials to make a lawful search and seizure. These situations result from several Supreme Court cases decided since *Mapp v. Ohio*. Thus, evidence seized in these situations may be admitted over the defendant's objection. As you review this list of exceptions, try to guess the justification for each one:

- Defendant has consented to the search.
- Evidence is in plain view of police.
- Where police have probable cause, automobiles and persons may be stopped and frisked.
- Protective sweeps of an area.
- Emergency situations and threats to public safety.
- Incident to lawful arrests.
- Airports and border points.

The Rights of the Accused

Constitutional considerations also greatly affect the rights of the accused once court proceedings have begun. The person accused of the crime, the defendant, is subject to **arrest** and detention to ensure his or her presence at trial. Upon a showing that the defendant does not present a danger to the community and is not likely to flee to avoid prosecution, a court will determine if the defendant is entitled to bail. The court may also consider other factors, such as the likelihood that the defendant committed the crime and the seriousness of the offense, among others. By depositing **bail** with the court in an amount determined after a hearing, a defendant may be released pending trial. In rare instances, a court may deny bail due to the seriousness of the alleged crime. At the other extreme, when there is a lesser crime and a very low flight risk, the court may release a defendant free, without any bail, on what is known as **personal recognizance**.

arrest
The formal taking of a person, usually by a police officer, to answer criminal charges.

bail
Court-mandated surety or guarantee that the defendant will appear at a future date if released from custody prior to trial.

personal recognizance
Permission to remain free of custody pending criminal proceedings.

self-incrimination
Acts or declarations either as testimony at trial or prior to trial by which one implicates himself or herself in a crime.

A few years after *Mapp v. Ohio,* the Supreme Court decided the famous case of *Miranda v. Arizona,* which held that the Fifth Amendment contains a number of rights for a person accused of a crime. Among the most important is the accused's right against **self-incrimination**. In the most basic terms, the right against self-incrimination means that an accused may not be called upon to testify at his or her criminal proceeding. Together with the presumption that an accused is innocent until proven guilty beyond a reasonable doubt, everyone has the right to remain silent, even during the investigatory phase of a criminal proceeding.

As outlined by the Supreme Court in *Miranda,* the accused has the right against self-incrimination once he or she becomes subject to custodial interrogation at the police station or when detained. Arrests can occur without questioning and without a Miranda warning. However, once the police decide to question the accused, they must first give Miranda warnings. The Fifth Amendment provides, in relevant part, for the following:

> *No person shall be held to answer for a capital, or otherwise infamous crime, unless on a presentment or indictment of a grand jury . . .; nor shall any person be subject for the same offense to be twice put in jeopardy of life or limb; nor shall be compelled in any criminal case to be a witness against himself, nor be deprived of life, liberty, or property, without due process of law.*

Notice that the Fifth Amendment's right against self-incrimination applies to statements by the accused, which may be excluded in the same way as illegally obtained evidence is. Thus, any "non-Mirandized" statements—that is, statements made without a Miranda warning—may be suppressed. Similar to consented and voluntary searches, a statement waiving those rights, after the Miranda warnings have been given, makes the voluntarily made "Mirandized" statements admissible. The right against self-incrimination has developed such that the accused's silence alone invokes the right. At trial, the prosecutor may not comment upon the defendant's refusal to take the stand on his or her own behalf. Even further, the judge at trial must instruct the jurors that they must make no negative inference from the accused's silence or refusal to take the stand.

double jeopardy
Being tried twice for the same act or acts.

acquittal
The legal and formal certification of the innocence of a person who has been charged with a crime.

The Fifth Amendment also protects an accused person against **double jeopardy**, which prohibits anyone from being prosecuted more than once for substantially the same crime after the first prosecution attempt ends in a final judgment. Based on common law origins, three essential protections are included in double jeopardy: protection from being retried for the same crime after an **acquittal**; protection from retrial after a conviction; and protection from being punished multiple times for the same offense. There are some exceptions to the rule. The primary exception to double jeopardy is known as the "separate sovereign" principle, which is unique to the United States. The principle permits the state and federal governments to try a defendant separately for the same crime, because both are regarded as two different governments or sovereigns.

Constitutional Considerations During a Criminal Proceeding

prosecutorial discretion
The legal authority granted to prosecutors to decide whether to bring criminal proceedings.

grand jury
A jury of inquiry who are summoned and returned by the sheriff to each session of the criminal courts and whose duty is to receive complaints and accusations in criminal cases, hear evidence, and decide if the defendant should stand for trial.

indictment
A written list of charges issued by a grand jury against a defendant in a criminal case. Also known as a **presentment**.

When prosecutors decide to prosecute—that is, to start a criminal case in court—they are exercising **prosecutorial discretion**. In serious cases, the prosecutors assemble grand juries to hear the evidence they present. If the **grand jury** believes the evidence shows that a crime has likely occurred, it will issue an **indictment** or **presentment**. In serious cases, prosecutors begin a formal criminal proceeding by filing an indictment with the court.

Although federal prosecutions operate with general uniformity throughout the country, the practices vary greatly from state to state. Whether the proceedings have begun in state or federal court, constitutional considerations shape what occurs within the courtroom. Whether by indictment or criminal complaint, when a proceeding has been filed in court, the criminal prosecution has begun. At that moment, the Sixth Amendment applies. That amendment states:

> *In all criminal prosecutions, the accused shall enjoy the right to a speedy and public trial, by an impartial jury of the State and district wherein the crime shall have been committed, which district shall have been previously ascertained by law, and to be informed of the nature and cause of the accusation; to be confronted with the witnesses against him; to have compulsory process for obtaining witnesses in his favor, and to have the Assistance of Counsel for his defense.*

The filing of criminal proceedings indicates the government is poised and ready to prove publicly that the accused has committed a crime. By starting criminal proceedings, the government ultimately seeks to punish the accused. That punishment may consist of a monetary fine, a term of imprisonment, or something even worse. Thus, some of the most powerful rights spring forth from the Sixth Amendment to the Constitution at the trial phase to afford legal protection for the accused. The amendment grants a number of substantive rights, described briefly next.

The right to a speedy trial ensures that the accused is not held in custody for unreasonably lengthy periods before a trial. In the federal system, the Supreme Court has held that "reasonable" depends on the circumstances. Dismissal may result from a violation of the right to a speedy trial, in which case the rule against double jeopardy would apply, and the government could not begin a second criminal proceeding for the same alleged crime. Some states such as New York and Pennsylvania have established time limits to comply with the speedy trial requirement. In New York, the prosecution must be "ready for trial within six months for all felonies (except murder)." In Pennsylvania, the rule is also six months if the accused is held in custody and one year if the accused is free. In both states, any violation of the speedy trial time limits results in dismissal of the charges.

The Sixth Amendment also requires that courts conduct criminal trials in public. This right presumes that public trials will hold the government accountable and that all parties and the court will behave properly. However, the right to a public trial may be curtailed in the defendant's interest to avoid publicity that could affect the fairness of the proceedings. The government may request a closed trial, which has become very controversial. You might understand how secret trials, out of the public's view, could create temptations for manipulation and secrecy, ultimately causing an unfair trial and injustice. Thus, the government must carry a heavy burden to show that there is "an overriding interest based on findings that closure is essential to preserve higher values and is narrowly tailored to serve that interest."

The **Confrontation Clause** of the Sixth Amendment grants the near-absolute right to have the witnesses who testify against the accused present in court and available for cross-examination. As we previously discussed, once a party has presented a witness's testimony, the other side may cross-examine that witness. Dramatic trial court scenes in the movies or on television, in which a witness tearfully recants or confesses under the pressure of cross-examination, rarely occur. Nevertheless, a skillfully and carefully conducted cross-examination can betray the witness's lack of opportunity to have observed or remembered. Cross-examination may also reveal biases or prejudices. These witness shortcomings may weaken or undermine the credibility of the testimony. The United States Supreme Court has declared the right to cross-examine one of the most important mechanisms for determining the truth at trial.

Confrontation Clause
Sixth Amendment guarantee that the accused has the absolute right to confront his or her accusers and all evidence.

The Sixth Amendment right "to have compulsory process for obtaining witnesses in his favor" allows defendants to obtain a subpoena to call forth witnesses on their own behalf. The right also includes the right to examine any documents or other physical evidence, such as weapons, particularly through scientific inspections. Thus, the accused has the constitutional right to have court clerks issue subpoenas and have them served by a court official, such as a sheriff. Prosecutors normally do not challenge a defendant's exercise of this right, but when they do, a judge must rule on the materiality of the defendant's evidence to the case.

Modern criminal procedure rules in federal and state courts include discovery, as in civil procedure. Witness lists and notices of alibi, among other requirements, thus incorporate the constitutional right to compulsory process. These rules differ from civil procedure discovery because they set out the information that both the prosecution and the defense must provide to the other in a process known as reciprocal discovery. As another benefit, criminal discovery rules prevent abuse and "ambush," that is, the use of surprise witnesses or other evidence.

The Sixth Amendment also guarantees the right of defendants to have the assistance of counsel during crucial aspects of the investigation and certainly at trial during criminal cases. Like other parts of the Constitution, the Supreme Court's interpretation of the "right to counsel" has undergone much development. Early on, the Court recognized that the right to counsel meant that a poor person should have an attorney appointed and paid by the government. However, the Court did not say how this principle would apply. Still unanswered remained the types of cases in which an impoverished person should receive appointed counsel and whether the right to counsel applied to the states.

In one of the most famous court decisions in American law, the Supreme Court held that indigents are constitutionally entitled to an attorney in all felony cases, whether in state or federal court (*Gideon v. Wainwright,* 372 U.S. 335 (1963)). As time went on, the Court expanded and clarified the right to counsel. Later cases applied the principle to any criminal proceeding that could result in a sentence of actual imprisonment, including misdemeanor (nonfelony) cases and juvenile proceedings. The Court has also extended the right to counsel to sentencing, appeals, and various other phases of criminal proceedings.

Considering the well-documented history of the paralegal profession's origins from the legal-aid movement, paralegals would appear well poised to provide indigent people with legal representation in several of the discrete and technical aspects of criminal proceedings. Employing well-trained and educated paralegals may very well help alleviate many of the concerns regarding the costs and competency of constitutionally required legal representation in criminal cases.

This coverage of criminal procedure and other legal specialties is intended to provide an overview of the types of legal work that professional paralegals commonly encounter in most law offices. As we proceed, think of the legal specialties in which a professional paralegal could become a valued part of the legal team. In particular, consider which ones appeal to you.

CIVIL LEGAL SPECIALTIES

Civil cases occupy much more of the legal profession's time than criminal cases. Less than one-fourth of all lawyers practice criminal law. Thus, with the majority of legal professionals involved in civil law, we turn to the several areas most common in law offices that engage in civil practice: tort, contract, and property law.

Torts

Closely related to criminal law, a tort is a legal term that means civil wrongs as opposed to criminal wrongs. A tort is thus a cause of action in civil practice that is recognized by law as the grounds for a lawsuit for a violation of a duty owed. Somebody behaves in a **tortious** manner when he or she violates that duty, thereby causing harm to another's body, property, or legal rights. The duties imposed under tort law depend on the relationship between the tortfeasor—that is, the person committing the tort—and the person claiming harm. Thus, in tort law, the person claiming to have been harmed will file a civil action as the plaintiff against the defendant tortfeasor.

tortious
A private civil wrong committed by one person against another that the law considers to be deserving of a remedy.

Under common law, the idea of a tort as a cause of action or claim for relief arose from the notion of trespass. Recall that under the common law writ system, civil lawsuits had to fit into a certain type of writ. As land was the most protected interest, the writ of trespass was one of the earliest ones recognized. The writ of trespass was therefore commonly used as a remedy against another person who had wrongfully entered onto another's land. By the middle ages, the law began to recognize wrongs against a person as opposed to land. Usually, such wrongs included physical harm to a person's body or property. The common law soon recognized the writ of trespass upon the case, now known as a tort.

Torts have some similarities to crimes. Recall the discussion of why assault and battery may be grounds for a civil action in tort as well as a criminal proceeding by the state. There can be civil trespass as well as criminal trespass. However, not all torts may be prosecuted as crimes. Torts are civil wrongs committed against an individual's or a private entity's legal interests. That individual or private entity then becomes a plaintiff in a civil lawsuit alleging, as a claim for relief, one or more recognized torts. In that civil lawsuit, the plaintiff would seek monetary damages, injunctive relief, or both. Ultimately, plaintiffs are enforcing private legal rights on behalf of themselves and only themselves. A crime, in contrast, may arise from the same acts (or inactions) committed by the accused and is prosecuted as an injury

FIGURE 7.3
Intentional Torts

Intentional Tort	Protected Interest
Assault	Apprehension or fear of harmful or offensive contact.
Battery	Offensive and unconsented contact with the plaintiff's person.
False imprisonment	Intentionally confining the plaintiff without legal authority.
Intentional infliction of emotional distress	Intentional and outrageous conduct that results in extreme emotional distress.
Invasion of privacy	An act that intrudes upon the plaintiff's solitude, that publicly discloses private facts, puts the plaintiff in a false light, or appropriates a plaintiff's name or likeness to obtain some benefit.
Fraud and misrepresentation	Deceiving the plaintiff for the defendant's gain.
Defamation	Oral (slander) or written (libel) defamation of the plaintiff's character.
Malicious prosecution and abuse of process	Intentional and malicious misuse of legal process to harass the plaintiff.
Trespass	The unauthorized entry onto another's land or misuse of his or her personal property (also known as chattels, or property that does not involve land).
Conversion	The interference with another's personal property.

to society at large, ultimately with the goal of punishing. Nevertheless, like crimes, torts are extensively classified.

We first examine intentional torts. An intentional tort includes actions with which the tortfeasor *intentionally* and voluntarily violates a plaintiff's legal interest. Intentional torts recognized under common law consist of the causes of action for the violation of a protected legal interest and are shown in Figure 7.3.

The list of common law torts covers a broad spectrum of situations. What they have in common is that the tortfeasor actually intended to invade the plaintiff's legal interest. Although many intentional torts come to us from England, American courts have taken a large role in recognizing whether certain behavior constitutes a tort. Over time, the list of recognized torts has continued to grow as various state courts recognize them on a case-by-case basis.

In this regard, the term "common law" takes on another meaning. We have understood the term to mean the court-made law that we in the United States inherited from England. This definition remains true. However, for torts, among other areas of the law, the term "common law" also means court-made law that a state court (usually its highest court) recognizes on a case-by-case basis. Torts are largely a matter of state law. Thus, the number and type of torts, intentional or otherwise, depends on whether the state courts or state legislature has recognized its existence.

Beyond those torts created by courts, there are also intentional torts that are authorized by statute. These occur at both the state and federal level. Statutory torts cover a wide range of behavior, ranging from "economic" torts to "human rights" torts. These statutes may authorize civil lawsuits that allege abridgments of free speech or excessive police force. These statutes also commonly allow for attorney's fees to the plaintiffs if they succeed in the lawsuit.

Negligence

Despite the great variety of situations covered by intentional torts, the tort of negligence covers a far broader range of human activity. Generally defined, negligence is a tort in which the defendant has caused an injury involving bodily harm or property damage by neglecting to conform to a duty of conduct. Proof of the defendant's intent is not necessary. Negligence law covers accidents that result from human error, from car collisions to professional malpractice to slip-and-fall mishaps in a supermarket. What is careless under the circumstances vary widely depending on the context. The elements necessary to prove negligence are, nevertheless, virtually uniform across the several states and consist of the following:

1. *The existence of a duty.* Duty is a legal obligation imposed on an individual and requires the exercise of reasonable care while performing any acts that could cause foreseeable harm to others. One of the clearest and most common examples is the laws that regulate the operation of cars. Thus, speed limits, stop signs, and other driving regulations perform the dual purpose of establishing a standard of behavior for the exercise of reasonable care and the use of motor vehicles on public roads. Similarly, building and health codes detail the minimum standards to which builders and landlords, among others, must conform. These codes also establish a minimum standard of care for the same people. The same is true of safety and health codes for electrical and plumbing, establishing a standard of care for the work performed by electricians or plumbers.

A duty of care is not always prescribed by law. Individuals considered professionals, particularly licensed professionals, are often held to a standard of care that pertains to all members of that profession. For instance, engineers and doctors are held to reasonable standards for members of their profession rather than those of the general public in cases related to their fields. Ethical codes and rules of professional conduct that apply to a professional may also set the standard of care owed.

Other ways of determining a standard of care may be through custom and habit for a particular activity or what a court thinks should be the custom and habit under the circumstances. A duty of care is thus determined from the circumstances, often in hindsight. Once established, the duty of care becomes the behavior that the defendant should have provided to the plaintiff.

2. *Breach of the duty of care owed.* The second element of negligence requires the plaintiff to prove that the defendant's behavior did not conform to the duty of care owed. If the defendant actually realized that the plaintiff was being put at risk, making the decision to continue that risk exposure breaches the duty owed. If the defendant did not actually foresee that another might be put at risk, but a reasonable person in the same situation would have foreseen the possibility, there will also be a **breach of duty**.

breach of duty
The failure to maintain a reasonable degree of care toward another person to whom a duty is owed.

3. *Causation.* Among the most complex elements in any area of the law is the third element, **causation**. Here, we have some divergence among the states. Many states use the "but for" test, which asks whether the plaintiff would have been injured *but for* the defendant's act or inaction. This standard is known as factual causation and considers whether the injury was actually caused by the defendant. Some states have a second aspect of causation that requires a showing that the plaintiff's injury was reasonably foreseeable. Some call this second aspect legal causation; in effect, it limits the range of potential plaintiffs. Thus, to satisfy the causation element, a plaintiff must show that the defendant actually caused the harm. Legal causation also requires an additional showing that the plaintiff's harm was a foreseeable result of the defendant's behavior. The *Palsgraf v. Long Island Railroad* case on the next page demonstrates the legal limits of causation.

causation
Intentional or negligent act resulting in harm or injury to the complaining plaintiff.

4. *Harm to the plaintiff.* The law of negligence exists to allow an injured plaintiff to receive compensation from the party that caused the injury. Thus, as simple as it appears, an essential element of negligence is provable **harm**. The types of harm

harm (injury)
Injury suffered as a result of a breach of a duty owed.

CASE IN POINT

COURT OPINION

PALSGRAF V. LONG ISLAND RAILROAD, 248 N.Y. 339, 162 N.E. 99 (1928)

Plaintiff was standing on a platform of defendant's railroad after buying a ticket to go to Rockaway Beach. A train stopped at the station, bound for another place. Two men ran forward to catch it. One of the men reached the platform of the car without mishap, though the train was already moving. The other man, carrying a package, jumped aboard the car, but seemed unsteady as if about to fall. A guard on the car, who had held the door open, reached forward to help him in, and another guard on the platform pushed him from behind. In this act, the package was dislodged, and fell upon the rails. It was a package of small size, about fifteen inches long, and was covered by a newspaper. In fact it contained fireworks, but there was nothing in its appearance to give notice of its contents. The fireworks when they fell exploded. The shock of the explosion threw down some scales at the other end of the platform many feet away. The scales struck the plaintiff, causing injuries for which she sued.

The conduct of the defendant's guard, if a wrong in its relation to the holder of the package, was not a wrong in its relation to the plaintiff, standing far away. Relatively to her it was not negligence at all. Nothing in the situation gave notice that the falling package had in it the potency of peril to persons thus removed. Negligence is not actionable unless it involves the invasion of a legally protected interest, the violation of a right. Negligence is the absence of care, according to the circumstances.

Here, by concession, there was nothing in the situation to suggest to the most cautious mind that the parcel wrapped in newspaper would spread wreckage through the station. If the guard had thrown it down knowingly and willfully, he would not have threatened the plaintiff's safety, so far as appearances could warn him. His conduct would not have involved, even then, an unreasonable probability of invasion of her bodily security. Liability can be no greater where the act is inadvertent.

Negligence is not a tort unless it results in the commission of a wrong, and the commission of a wrong imports the violation of a right, in this case, we are told, the right to be protected against interference with one's bodily security. But bodily security is protected, not against all forms of interference or aggression, but only against some. One who seeks redress at law does not make out a cause of action by showing without more that there has been damage to his person. If the harm was not willful, he must show that the act as to him had possibilities of danger so many and apparent as to entitle him to be protected against the doing of it though the harm was unintended. The consequences to be followed must first be rooted in a wrong.

The judgment of the Appellate Division and that of the Trial Term should be reversed, and the complaint dismissed, with costs in all courts.

QUESTIONS ABOUT THE CASE

1. Why did the court dismiss the plaintiff's lawsuit?
2. If the bag had been noticeably labeled "FIREWORKS," would the outcome have been different?
3. How is a wrongful act a negligent act?
4. What kind of negligent activity encompasses novel or extraordinary liability?

that the law will recognize varies among the states. All states allow compensation for harms that are physical (personal injury or property damage), economic (business or financial loss), or both in cases in which the loss of earnings resulted from physical injury. In defamation or invasion-of-privacy cases, the majority of states permit compensation for loss to reputation. In many states, emotional distress may be an item of damages in the case of negligence. Some states do not permit such damages.

With the beauty of simplicity in only four elements—duty, breach, causation (factual and legal), and harm—the law of negligence covers the entire gamut of unintended human error. By allowing plaintiffs to obtain compensation for injuries, negligence law acts as a specialized, self-enforcing system of economic distribution. Without an available source for recompense, an injured plaintiff, unable to work, might have to resort to governmental relief services such as welfare. Because attorney's fees are usually contingent in negligence cases, there is a strong incentive for the plaintiff's attorneys to pursue injury claims.

At the same time, negligence law establishes standards for reasonable behavior that is applicable to everyone, under threat of liability for the costs of any harm caused.

A DAY IN THE LIFE OF A REAL PARALEGAL

Behind almost every lawsuit for negligence or strict liability is an insurance company, there to defend its customer, whether that customer is a driver in a car accident or a manufacturer whose product has allegedly malfunctioned and caused injury. The legal defense team may be working within a law firm retained by the insurance company. In this recent job posting for paralegals to work on negligence defense teams, notice the skills and qualifications of the candidates they are seeking.

> Large insurance company has paralegal positions in Tampa, FL, Raynham, MA, and Wassau, WI. Paralegals assist attorneys in preparation and trial of lawsuits, including interviewing and taking statements from clients and witnesses; drafting correspondence and legal documents such as pleadings, complaints, answers, request and responses to production, motions, subpoenas, summons, discovery, services of process and notices. Review and organize documents for production. Prepare documents, exhibits and other demonstrative evidence for trail. Obtain copies of court cases, statues, law review articles and other legal references as requested by attorneys. Assist attorneys in preparation for depositions and mediation by organizing relevant documentation for specific areas of inquiry. Excellent oral and written communication skills to communicate effectively with policyholders, courts, attorneys and judges. Knowledge of court procedures. Paralegal certificate with one to three years of experience or two years nonclerical litigation experience under the direction of an attorney. College degree preferred. Knowledge of computer software products.

The law thus created the need for liability insurance. Everyone who owns an auto or home (and certainly both) must purchase insurance policies that are designed to protect the owner from any negligence, particularly the owner's own. In most lawsuits for negligence, the defendant will likely be represented by an attorney paid for by the insurance company.

Defenses to Negligence

Similar to criminal cases, a defendant in a negligence case may try to present evidence to rebut any or all of the four elements of the plaintiff's case. For instance, the defendant may present evidence that the plaintiff's injury was not caused by the defendant or was not foreseeable, thus negating the element of causation. In addition, the defendant may proffer affirmative defenses. In our coverage of civil procedure, we discussed how affirmative defenses provide a legal basis to avoid liability on the basis of recognized legal grounds. Using any affirmative defense, the defendant submits evidence in support of his or her defense. The following sections describe the most common affirmative defenses to negligence actions.

Contributory negligence

contributory negligence
The plaintiff played a large part in causing the injury; thus, fundamental fairness precludes assigning liability to the defendant.

assumption of risk
The doctrine that releases another person from liability for the person who chooses to assume a known risk of harm.

Coextensive with the duty of care that applies to all persons, the common law held that even the plaintiff owed a duty of reasonable care to him- or herself. If the plaintiff breached the duty owed to him- or herself and that breach was a cause of the injuries, the judge or jury may find that the plaintiff contributed to his or her own injuries. The legal doctrine of **contributory negligence** acted quite harshly by relieving a defendant of *any* liability to the plaintiff, even if the plaintiff had proven a *prima facie* case in negligence against the defendant.

Assumption of risk

Closely associated with contributory negligence, the **assumption of risk** is also a common law relic that can defeat a plaintiff's claim of negligence. If the defendant can show as an affirmative defense that the plaintiff voluntarily and knowingly submitted him- or herself to a situation that presented danger, there can be no recovery for any injuries suffered. Thus, if a spectator at a hockey game is injured by a puck gone astray into the stands, he or she will not be able to recover because the spectator assumed the risk.

As you can see, both defenses, contributory negligence and assumption of risk, can yield harsh results, totally defeating a fully proved case of negligence. In modern times, both doctrines have aged poorly. Out of sync with the notion of economic distribution that underlies modern tort law, the doctrines have given way in most states to more flexible standards.

Comparative negligence

As its name states, **comparative negligence** is actually a system of apportioning recovery for a tort on the basis of a comparison of the plaintiff's negligence with the defendant's. The judge or jury finds the percentage to which the plaintiff was negligent compared with the percentage to which the defendant was negligent and deducts the plaintiff's negligence from any award. Some states have a "partial" comparative negligence rule that bars any award if the plaintiff's negligence exceeds the defendant's. A "pure" comparative negligence jurisdiction merely apportions the entire award according to the negligence of the parties. For instance, in a state that has adopted the partial form of comparative negligence, the award for injuries to a plaintiff who has been found 30 percent negligent will be reduced by 30 percent. Any more than 50 percent negligence will negate any award. However in a pure comparative negligence jurisdiction, a plaintiff who has been found 75 percent negligent will still receive 25 percent of the compensation for the harm.

comparative negligence
Applies when the evidence shows that both the plaintiff and the defendant acted negligently.

RESEARCH THIS

The defenses available in a negligence action can vary greatly among the states. Some states adhere to the common law defenses of contributory negligence and assumption of risk. Most states have adopted one of the variants of comparative negligence.

What defenses to negligence are available in your state?

Find the court decision or statute that authorizes any defense to negligence in your state.

Strict Liability

At this point, you should be able to see how the law expresses (and enforces) social policy and the society's values. Negligence aims to compensate and regulate behavior. However, in some situations, the law has developed to recognize that having to prove all of the traditional elements of negligence could result in unfairness to a seriously injured plaintiff, particularly in the types of cases known as product liability.

The twentieth century's rapid technological advances brought electric appliances and gadgets into millions of American homes. When these devices do not work properly or, worse, cause injury, courts have recognized that the concept of fault, inherent in negligence cases, should not apply. Instead, the idea of strict liability imposes liability without regard to fault. As a matter of social policy, cases involving inherently dangerous activities or products that cause injury are subject to strict liability, and the plaintiff need not show negligence or fault. Because of the difficulty the plaintiff would face in proving negligence, the doctrine of strict liability imposes the burden on a defendant that is in a better financial position to absorb the costs of any injuries as part of the costs of doing business.

Nuisance

Nuisance is an anomaly in tort law. With its origins firmly planted in the thistle theory of common law, the tort of nuisance is based on the notion that a property owner is liable for the use of his or her land. A landowner has committed a nuisance by using it in a way that disturbs the quiet enjoyment of another property owner. Usual nuisance cases involve offensive noises, odors, pollution, or any other hazard that extends past the property boundary onto another's property.

Nuisances may be private or public. A public nuisance is widespread, interfering with public health, safety, peace, or convenience. A private nuisance is simply a violation of one's use of the quiet enjoyment of land. In a way, nuisances are a form of trespass but are regarded as a separate tort. Similar to strict liability cases, lawsuits for nuisances do not require the plaintiff to show fault or negligence on the part of the defendant. The primary concern is that the defendant is allegedly using his or her own property in a way that interferes with the plaintiff's use of his or her own property.

The tort of nuisance, like torts in general, is rooted in the most important and venerable concern of the common law, property. The writ of trespass, one of the original writs providing for protection against intruders on one's property, later developed into *trespass on the case.* Torts such as assault and battery still meant that the defendant had committed a trespass on the plaintiff's body, reputation, or even peace of mind. In nuisance cases, we can see the explicit underlying concerns for property rights. Under common law, property (land) was accorded the highest protection. Land meant everything to its owners—money, status, power, and legitimacy.

PROPERTY LAW

The most notable aspect of our property laws is the idea of ownership, with the accompanying power to exclude others by law. Any of us who have seen a "Private Property" or "No Trespassing" sign can appreciate the power associated with the idea of ownership. The same effect results when we write our names on our belongings. In doing so, we advertise the fact that we own that item. The law governing property thus defines the relationships that can exist between the property in question and the owner's legal rights with regard to everyone else. The idea of property ownership, though typical in almost every modern society, is not universal. In many communities around the world, past and present, the idea of ownership as we understand it is very foreign.

For instance, a school of philosophy within the Hindu religion, called Vedanta, believes that the idea of ownership separates a person from the rest of the universe—not a good thing, according to this religion. As such, ownership is an illusion that can hinder an individual's spiritual development. Vedanta ultimately holds that there is no need for ownership, as it separates the individual from the reality of the universe. In materialistically centered societies such as the United States however, the idea of ownership is quite central to the economic and social organization.

The form of government known as communism believed in the idea of collective or common ownership, such that property is controlled communally in trust for future generations. Communal ownership of property occurs when a group of people share the ownership of property among one another. In theory, any and every member of the group is free to use the property when they want, but those individuals also agree to allow all others in the group to use the property when they want.

In practice, communal ownership of property is not as widespread as individual ownership of property, but both forms of ownership exist in most societies. The United States government maintains publicly owned buildings, such as libraries and national parks, that are communally owned by all Americans. Dairy cooperatives are communal production and marketing companies collectively owned by groups of dairy farmers who have banded together to deal with their common interests and problems.

We begin our examination of property law with the legal classifications of the types of property. Keep in mind that U.S. property laws reflect the values of a society based on free enterprise and capitalism. The concept of ownership and the resultant enforceable rights and liabilities constitute an important cornerstone of U.S. society and its laws. The idea of property encompasses almost anything of value—even a right or an interest. The classifications for the types of property are therefore purely ideas designed to give legal recognition to something that society deems valuable.

Real Property and Personal Property

The law first classifies property as either real property or personal property. Real property, also known as real estate, consists of land and anything that is considered part of the land, such as wild animals and plants. The airspace above the land as well as the minerals and anything of value below the land also are considered part of the owner's interest in the land. Buildings and other items that are permanently attached to the land are considered part of the land and are known separately as fixtures.

Personal property, also known by its old-fashioned name of **chattels**, consists of any property that does not involve land. Within personal property lies the subcategory of tangible personal property, which is anything that someone can touch and move, such as your school notebook, this book, or a 16-wheel tractor trailer. Whether something is an item of personal property or a fixture can be of crucial importance, as we see in the *Far West Modular Home Sales, Inc., v. Proaps* case on the next page.

personal property
Movable or intangible thing not attached to real property.

chattel
Tangible personal property or goods.

Forms of Property Ownership

Whether the property in question is real estate, personal property, or intangible property, there are several ways in which property may be owned. A single individual who by him- or herself owns a certain property owns it in severalty—a common law term meaning property ownership by one individual. Concurrent ownership means that more than one individual owns the property in any of three possibilities:

1. *Tenant in common.* Two or more people who own the same property together may share it as **tenants in common**. As such, they each own an undivided interest that they may sell, gift, or will to whomever they wish. Their successor then becomes a cotenant with the remaining tenants. Thus, if Larry and Moe own the same property as tenants in common, and Larry sells his part to Curly, then Curly becomes a tenant in common with Moe.
2. *Joint tenants.* Two or more persons may own property as **joint tenants**. In this arrangement, each owns the property, much in the same way as tenants in common. However, upon the death of one joint tenant, the other joint tenant becomes the owner of the entire parcel, taking over as owner the part owned by the other joint tenant. This situation is known as the right of survivorship. Thus, if two sisters owned a certain property as joint tenants, the death of one sister would make the surviving sister the owner of the entire property. A joint tenancy often is created as a substitute for a will. During his or her lifetime, a joint tenant may sell or give away the interest in the property without the consent of the other joint tenant. The new tenant would then become a tenant in common with the former joint tenant, and the property would be owned by the two as tenants in common.
3. *Tenants by the entirety.* This form of ownership involves married persons who only confer upon each other the right of survivorship. A **tenancy by the entirety** is therefore a joint tenancy for married persons. The biggest difference is that a tenancy by the entirety may be dissolved by only the divorce or death of one of the spouses. Many states also permit tenancies by the entirety to become homesteads, free from attachments by most creditors.

tenant in common
A form of ownership between two or more people where each owner's interest upon death goes to his or her heirs.

joint tenant
The shared ownership of property, giving the other owner the right of survivorship if one owner dies.

tenancy by the entirety
A form of ownership for married couples, similar to joint tenancy, where the spouse has right of survivorship.

CASE IN POINT

COURT OPINION

FAR WEST MODULAR HOME SALES, INC. V. PROAPS, 43 ORE. APP. 881, 604 P.2d 452 (ORE. CT. APP. 1979)

In July 1977 the plaintiff contracted to sell a modular home to the defendants. In January 1978 the home was delivered in two sections from plaintiff's factory to the defendants' property. It was of wood construction, and was mounted and secured on a concrete foundation by bolts and nails. It was connected to sewer, water and electric outlets. When the modular home was in place it measured 60 feet by 24 feet and its accommodations included three bedrooms and two baths. The defendants and their family used it as a residence.

A dispute arose as to the purchase price and plaintiff began this action for replevin seeking return of the modular home. The trial court found that the modular home was personal property and awarded plaintiff possession. The defendants contended that the modular home was so affixed to their real property that it lost its character as personality and, therefore, was not subject to replevin.

The test for determining whether property retains its character as personal property, or loses its separate identity and becomes a fixture, is composed of three factors: annexation, adaptation and intention.

Since there is no requirement that a chattel actually be attached to the real property to satisfy the annexation test, . . . testimony illustrating the ease with which the modular home could be removed is not controlling. Rather, the fact that this chattel is a home, coupled with evidence that it was bolted and nailed to a foundation and connected to all utilities, established that it was annexed to defendants' real property. This conclusion is further supported by the fact that it would cost $4,700 to remove the modular home and restore the land.

The paramount factor in the determination of whether a chattel has become a fixture is the objective intent of the annexor to make the item a permanent accession of the freehold. The annexor's intent can be inferred from "the nature of the article, the relation (to the realty) of the party annexing, the policy of law in relation thereto, the structure and mode of annexation, and the purpose and use" for which the item was annexed. The annexor's objective, controlling intent, is determined from all the circumstances.

We begin with the presumption that a building or similar structure is a fixture and therefore a part of the real property. Also, when annexation is made by an owner of realty, an intent to affix may more readily be found. The fact that here the vendor physically placed the unit on defendants' property does not detract from defendants' status as the annexing party. Moreover, the fact that the home was to be manufactured elsewhere in two large sections before being placed on the homesite does not detract from defendants' objective intent to affix the home to their land.

A modular home has been defined as "a structure which is prefabricated in a factory and delivered to its intended site where it is installed on a foundation. . . . that once the modules were actually incorporated into completed houses, they became part of the real estate just as any other house usually does. When the houses were completed, the modules were not removable without damage to themselves or the realty. Furthermore, they were permanently fastened to their foundations, were intended to remain so, and were adapted for use as housing, as was the realty to which they were attached."

We are of the opinion that in this case the evidence is so clear that the only conclusion that can be drawn therefrom is that the modular home was a fixture of the real property and therefore not subject to an action of replevin.

QUESTIONS ABOUT THE CASE

1. What are the factors involved in determining whether something is a fixture or not?
2. What procedural error did the plaintiffs (the sellers of the mobile home) make in filing this action? If the plaintiffs' objective was to obtain payment, what type of lawsuit should they have filed?
3. Why is replevin inapplicable to this case?
4. Is this case precedent for the fact that all mobile homes are fixtures and part of the land?

deed
The written document transferring title, or an ownership interest in real property, to another person.

grantor
The person transferring the property.

grantee
The person receiving the property.

Any form of property may be transferred voluntarily by its owner, who may sell it, gift it, or pass it to another person upon his or her death. For real estate, any of these forms of transfer may be accomplished by a legal document known as a **deed**. Because the law confers the utmost importance on real estate, all transfers may be accomplished only by a written document. The deed expresses the intent of the owner to transfer the real estate. An owner who voluntarily transfers real estate is known as the **grantor**, and the person receiving it is the **grantee**. When property is transferred, the deed is all important, for it indicates the grantor's intent to transfer **title** to the grantee. Title is a common law property concept that means ownership. Legally, a person cannot own property without having title. Thus, under the law, a thief does not obtain title by mere possession. By transferring property, the lawful owner passes title to the new owner.

title
The legal link between a person who owns property and the property itself; legal evidence of a person's ownership rights.

It is also possible to lose and thereby transfer property involuntarily, such as when creditors seize property to satisfy the debts of the property owner. For instance, a bank that has loaned money to a homeowner may do so in the form of a mortgage. If the homeowner falls behind in the payments, the bank may take and sell the property to satisfy the underlying debt in a court proceeding known as a foreclosure. The state or federal government may also take an owner's land for public use through a means called eminent domain without the owner's consent. However, this seizing must be for a public purpose, and the owner must be paid just compensation for the property.

lease
A voluntary transfer of possession in property by the owner for money or other valuable consideration.

The forms of ownership are known as *freehold estates*. Other forms of legal interests in real property are recognized as less-than-freehold. They are **lease** agreements for real estate or personal property, whereby the owner does not relinquish ownership and agrees to allow another to use and occupy the property for a specified period of time at an agreed price. Students often rent apartments and houses; small business owners usually lease their shops or factories; large chain stores lease the spaces they occupy in malls; and cars and equipment are commonly leased for short periods by individuals as well as businesses.

The right to use another's property in a very limited way, known as an easement, is another common form of property interest that is less-than-freehold. An easement typically grants the right to cross over another's property or to install utility pipes or wires over- or underground.

COMMUNICATION TIP

As you learn these legal terms, be sure that you understand what they mean when you use them. Legal terms are, for the most part, precise and convey technical meanings. Careless use of legal terms can be dangerous and is a sure sign of a novice to the legal world. Try listening to how your more experienced colleagues use legal terms in conversation and in writing. In doing so, you will gain experience in the proper use of legal terminology.

Paralegals in Real Estate Practice

Professional paralegals have become indispensable as specialists in real estate law. The very nature of real estate practice lends itself well to paralegals. Real estate law is a legal specialty. Many law offices specialize exclusively in real estate law, and most large law firms and government law offices have real estate departments staffed by both practicing attorneys and paralegals.

Typically, paralegals engaged in real estate practice work closely with real estate brokers and clients to shape complex transactions in which there may be substantive legal issues, ranging from assessment to zoning. Much of the legal work in real estate requires research of public records and preparation of the necessary documents for transactions between buyers and sellers. Other parties involved in any given transaction may include banks or other financial institutions and even government agencies. Know as a **transactional practice**, real estate law rarely involves litigation but rather concentrates a professional's efforts on documentation and negotiation. Unlike litigation, for which the outcome is almost always uncertain, transactional practice focuses on the client's objective in a business deal. Transactional practice may also include the purchase and sale of businesses, stocks, and other matters that may not be related to real estate.

transactional practice
A specialized legal practice, usually in business, involving the transfer of rights and obligations.

In real estate, the primary distinction is between residential and commercial property. Residential real estate, of course, is any property that is used for a residence, whether a single family home, a condominium (or co-op), or a multi-unit dwelling. Commercial property consists of offices, retail stores, malls, and just about everything else. There is also a highly specialized segment of real estate practice known as industrial that includes factories, warehouses, and port facilities. However, the bulk of day-to-day real estate work involves residential purchase and sales transactions.

A homeowner who wishes to sell his or her home usually engages a real estate broker whose primary task is to find potential buyers. The broker does so by advertising and enlisting other brokers. Because of the repetitive nature of residential sales, brokers generally use standard forms in which the names of the buyers and sellers, the address of the property, the offered purchase price, and other details are filled into the blanks provided. Once a prospective buyer comes forward and makes an offer, the broker will forward an offer on a standard form (in some states called a binder) to the seller.

Some back-and-forth communication may occur as the seller makes counter offers. Once the seller accepts an offer as expressed in the binder, the parties enter into a formal purchase and sales agreement, which is a formal contract that sets out in detail the agreed purchase price, the rights of the parties, the date of the sale, and any other provisions. These agreements also come on a standard form, consisting of several pages. Generally, the buyer will deposit an amount equal to 5 percent of the purchase price upon signing the purchase and sales agreement. The deposit is usually kept in **escrow** with the realtor for safekeeping and eventually applied to the entire purchase price when the transaction is completed.

escrow
A legal arrangement in which an asset (often money, but sometimes other property such as art, a deed of title, Web site, or software source code) is delivered to a third party (an escrow agent) to be held in trust pending a contingency or the fulfillment of a condition or conditions in a contract, such as payment of a purchase price.

contingency
An event or provision in a contract stating that some or all of the terms of the contract will be altered or voided by the occurrence of a specific event.

Among the important parts of the agreement are the **contingencies** that enable a party to withdraw from the contract without penalty upon the occurrence of certain events. Typically, a buyer will want any of several usual contingencies. The first might be a financing contingency. Rarely is any buyer able to pay the full price for a home all at one time. Almost always, the buyer will need to obtain financing or a loan from a bank or credit union that in turn must approve the loan. Thus, a buyer will want the purchase and sale agreement to allow for the time required for a loan application and the authority to terminate the agreement if the loan application is denied. A buyer commonly needs a contingency for a building inspection as well. Undertaken at the buyer's expense, a building engineer's inspection of the home assures the buyer that there are no defects. If there is a negative building inspection report, an inspection contingency would provide the buyer with an escape hatch from the agreement.

A buyer also may wish to build an addition, make some physical changes to the property, or propose to use the property in a way that would require zoning approval by the local government, usually an official board within the city or town. At this point, the legal expertise required for such a contingency may go beyond that permitted for a realtor. A paralegal working along with the attorney for the buyer therefore would become involved to ensure that a contingency of this sort meets the client's objectives. On the basis of their experience and legal expertise, the legal team would be able to insert the proper contingency as a routine part of the negotiation process.

title search
A search of the abstract of title; the short history of a piece of property including ownership interests and liens.

After the parties agree to a purchase and sales agreement, several time-sensitive tasks are in order for both parties. The essential tasks include performing a **title search** of the property to confirm for the buyer and the financing institution that the title is clear and free of any possible claims made on the property in the past. A title insurance company often performs the title search as part of issuing an insurance policy on the property's title. For a fee known as a premium, a title insurance company will insure that the title to the property will not have a problem in the future. Banks and other financing institutions often require buyers to purchase title insurance. A paralegal working with the buyer's attorney, the bank, or the title insurance company likely will perform this search by examining all existing public records that may affect the property.

When the buyer or bank determines that property's title is acceptable and financing is "in place"—that is, approved—the parties, including the bank, will execute the purchase and sales agreement at a closing by meeting together to exchange legal documents and monies. Before this meeting occurs, the paralegals working on both sides will have prepared all of the necessary legal documents, computed the exact amount of money involved, and been the primary forces in executing the many minute details of this example of transactional practice.

Personal Property

The acquisition and transfer of personal property occur according to the same legal rules as real property. Personal property may be bought and sold, seized by creditors, made into a gift, or inherited. There are, however, some obvious differences. Land tends to stay put. Personal property does not. The finder of property may obtain title depending on whether the property is lost, misplaced, or abandoned. With lost or misplaced property, the finder is said to have a limited form of title, subject to the true owner's. Many states require any finders to turn over lost or misplaced property to an agency that looks for the owner. A finder of abandoned property, which is left by the owner with no intention of reclaiming it, acquires title by merely taking possession of it. The former owner of the abandoned property is deemed to have relinquished or abandoned title.

Another form of personal property cannot be touched: **intangible personal property**. Intangible personal property is an idea, a right, or an interest. For instance, a ticket to a sporting event such as the Super Bowl is a form of intangible property. Subject to the terms and conditions of its seller, that is, the National Football League, the ticket owner has the intangible right to attend the Super Bowl. The right to sit at a Super Bowl game may be very valuable yet at the same time intangible, because it cannot be touched. The ticket itself merely represents *the right* of the holder to enter the stadium and sit in a designated seat during the game. Similarly, cash, credit cards, bank accounts, and shares of a corporation are forms intangible personal property. We can touch plastic cards, bank passbooks, and certificates that represent those items, but they simply represent or are evidence of the intangible property recognized by the law. The property itself is an idea that is intangible.

intangible personal property
Personal property that has no physical presence but is represented by a certificate or some other instrument, such as stocks or trademarks.

An important form of intangible property, known as intellectual property, consists of patents (inventions), copyrights (artistic or literary works), and trademarks (company symbols or logos) that are forms of intellectual property that the law recognizes and protects for the person or company that owns or created it. An item of intellectual property can have tremendous value in and of itself. By securing a patent or copyright or by registering a trademark with the government, the owner obtains the right to the exclusive use of that intellectual property. Anyone who uses the property without permission may be liable to the owner in an action for **infringement**.

infringement
An act that interferes with an exclusive right.

Owners may allow other persons to use their intellectual property much in the same way that real estate is rented, by entering into a **licensing agreement**. Instead of rent, the owner receives a payment known as a royalty that, similar to rent, pays for the use of the intellectual property. The length of time that an owner of intellectual property has exclusive rights depends on a myriad of complex rules, including international agreements. For instance, the famous play *Peter Pan* was written by Sir James Matthew Barrie, who donated his copyright to the Great Ormond Street Hospital for Children in London in 1929. The amount of royalties collected by the hospital during the past 80 years is a well-guarded secret. However, by most accounts, the royalty payments have been substantial, constituting a vital source of income to the hospital.

licensing agreement
An agreement in which an owner of intangible property transfers the rights of use to another party for a fee or other valuable consideration.

Trademarks operate similarly. They are another form of intellectual property that is entitled to legal protection and may be the subject of licensing agreements to earn royalties. For instance, clothing manufacturers often pay licensing fees to use the names or logos of famous fashion designers. Licensing agreements also allow professional sports teams to earn royalties by allowing others to use team names and logos on souvenirs, baseball caps, sweatshirts, and other items. Even universities have gone to great lengths to protect their names and logos.

Transferring Personal Property

As with real property, the transfer of personal property may be accomplished by selling it, giving it away, subjecting it to inheritance rights, seizure by creditors, or, as discussed, abandonment. In some but not all circumstances, a legal document is necessary to effect a legal transfer. Certainly the transfer of intangible property requires a written document. In most states, ownership transfers of automobiles are accomplished only with a state-issued legal document such as a Certificate of Title. Otherwise,

CYBER TRIP

On the Internet, visit your school's Web site and determine if your school or another nearby school has registered its name or identity as a trademark. Most schools have a trademark program that requires special permission to use its logo or trademark. Thus, clothing such as T-shirts, sweatshirts, jackets, and sweaters, as well as key chains, mugs, glassware, stationery products, leather goods, bags, and backpacks must have special permission, or a license. Many schools use the money obtained from licensing their names and logos to fund student financial aid.

See, for example, the following sites:

www.trademark.harvard.edu/index.html#TM1 (Harvard University)

http://mark.nd.edu/ glossary-of-terms/(University of Notre Dame)

www.logos.umich.edu/guidelines/markguidelines.html (University of Michigan)

How do these schools define their protected interests?

unlike the transfer of real estate, personal property may usually be transferred by oral agreement.

Summary

Legal specialties are discrete topics in law, analogous to college courses, each with its own history and structure. An essential part of legal education and professional training requires the mastery of several legal specialties. Crimes and criminal procedure are subjects that require highly specialized expertise in legal practice. Prominent among those issues are the constitutional dimensions that restrict the types of behavior that society may criminalize.

Similar to civil procedure, criminal procedure talks about how the government may investigate and how the court system must accommodate the constitutional rights of the accused. The Constitution plays a prominent role. The Fourth, Fifth, and Sixth Amendments spell out the steps that the government and the courts must take in the treatment of the accused and the evidence that can be used to prove a crime. The United States Supreme Court has interpreted these amendments extensively, resulting in some commonly known aspects of criminal procedure, such as Miranda rights and the exclusionary rule.

Akin to crimes are civil actions known as torts. The essential difference between crimes and torts is the civil nature of torts, which are privately enforced by those claiming harm by someone else. Torts include intentional and unintentional behavior. Negligence addresses unintentional behavior or human error that causes harm. The elements of torts reflect near universal requirements that a plaintiff must prove. Nuisance, such as noise, pollution, odors, or other offensive effects, constitutes another form of tort in which the party causes harm but without regard to intent. A nuisance is a harm that may be remedied by monetary or injunctive relief.

Property is at the core of the interests that the common law was designed to protect. Unique to modern social order in capitalistic societies, property law is concerned with ownership. Property law thus defines how property may be owned, how it may be transferred, and the rights of the parties in a transaction.

Key Terms

Acquittal
Actus reus
Arrest
Assumption of risk
Bail
Bill of attainder
Breach of duty
Causation
Chattel
Comparative negligence

Confrontation Clause
Contingency
Contributory negligence
Crime
Criminal procedure
Criminalize
Deed
District attorney
Double jeopardy
Escrow
Ex post facto law
Grand jury
Grantee
Grantor
Harm (injury)
Indictment
Infringement
Insanity defense
Intangible personal property
Joint tenant
Lease
Licensing agreement
Personal property
Personal recognizance
Police powers
Probable cause
Prosecutor
Prosecutorial discretion
Search warrant
Self-incrimination
Tenancy by the entirety
Tenant in common
Theft
Title
Title search
Tortious
Transactional practice
United States Attorney

Review Questions

1. What are the differences between a misdemeanor and a felony?
2. What constitutional provisions limit the legislature in defining crimes?
3. Describe two ways that the exclusionary rule prevents the admission of a statement and an item of evidence.
4. What is the difference between a crime and a tort?
5. What is the difference between an intentional tort and negligence?
6. What are the elements of negligence?
7. What is the difference between factual causation and legal causation?
8. Name six types of intangible property.
9. How does a fixture become part of real property?
10. What is the difference between a joint tenancy and a tenancy by the entirety?

Exercises

1. Draft an ordinance that would be constitutionally valid in light of the United States Supreme Court's decision in the *City of Chicago v. Morales.*
2. Using www.findlaw.com or any other means, research the status of the insanity defense in your state. To what extent have your state's insanity defense laws changed or do they differ from the M'Naghten Rule?
3. Assume that you are a justice on the Ohio Supreme Court and write a brief dissenting opinion to the Ohio Supreme Court's majority opinion in *Mapp v. Ohio.* You can read the full story behind this case at www.crimelibrary.com/gangsters_outlaws/cops_others/dolly_mapp/index.html. Does this information affect the way you think about the case or Dolly Mapp?
4. Using www.findlaw.com or another means, find out which states still adhere to the contributory negligence rule. Which states have adopted the "pure" form of comparative negligence? (See www.mwl-law.com/PracticeAreas/Contributory-Neglegence.asp.)

5. What is the difference between the ownership form for a condominium and a cooperative?
6. A penny, a nickel, a dime, and a quarter are, in concept, tangible personal property based on the metallic value of copper (penny), nickel, and silver (dime and quarter). However, some years ago, the U.S. Mint stopped making dimes and quarters entirely from silver. Now, dimes and quarters have a middle layer of copper. Does this change the nature of their type of property?

Discussion Questions

1. Would the crime of engaging in the unauthorized practice of law be a felony or a misdemeanor? Why?
2. What factors are involved with white-collar crimes that do not exist with other types of crimes?
3. According to the Model Penal Code §233.5 regarding stolen property, what kind of situations would *not* be covered under the statue?
4. What types of crimes do not require the government to show *mens rea?*
5. What impact does the insanity defense have on the *mens rea* requirement? Would the insanity defense operate differently in a case involving a crime that does not require *mens rea?*
6. Explain illegally seized evidence, which has been popularly called the "fruits of the poisoned tree." Can you explain this metaphor?
7. What are the justifications for the exceptions to the search warrant requirement? What about cars? Search incident to an arrest?
8. Why do you suppose the Fifth Amendment requires a grand jury to determine whether a crime should be prosecuted?
9. Winston Churchill once said that the true measure of a civilized society is how it treats people accused of crimes. Do you think that the right to counsel, among the other rights accorded the accused, is a good measure of our society's civilized nature?
10. Visit the Web site for the Great Ormond Street Hospital for Children at www.gosh.org/about_us/peterpan/index.html. What legal issues would surface for a school presentation of the play *Peter Pan?*

PORTFOLIO ASSIGNMENT

At a busy department store, an undercover police officer watches and follows a small group of college students who are shopping for back-to-school items. Some of the students have made purchases, and others have apparently just tagged along. Although the students are at times boisterous, the officer sees nothing unlawful or suspicious in their behavior. After observing them for about half an hour, the officer follows the students as they exit the store. Once outside, the officer jumps in front of the students and orders them to submit to a search of their backpacks, handbags, and pockets. Before anyone can react, the officer grabs one of the student's handbags and finds a single marijuana cigarette inside. The student is arrested for simple possession of a controlled substance and taken into custody.

You are a paralegal working in the law firm that represents the student. Prepare an office memorandum for your supervising attorney, who is contemplating a motion to suppress the marijuana cigarette as evidence. Use only the materials presented in this book for the legal authority you discuss in the memorandum. The memo should be two to three pages in length. Be sure to use formal office memorandum format.

Chapter 8

Basic Legal Specialties: Family Matters

CHAPTER OBJECTIVES

Upon completion of this chapter, students will have acquired specialized knowledge in the following areas:

- The law of gifts.
- The law of wills and probate procedure.
- Family law.

With a solid grounding in some of the most basic legal specialties—civil litigation, criminal law and procedure, tort law, and property law—from previous chapters, this chapter will venture into some of the more advanced topics among the legal specialties of professional practice. The law regarding property transfers to family members constitutes a major area of legal practice. This chapter will continue with the aspect of property law that covers the voluntary transfer of property through gifts made during a person's life and upon his or her demise. The importance given to property laws in England is clearly reflected in the laws that ordain the orderly transfer of property to successive generations. Reflections of social policy appear in the flexibility of the numerous devices that permit individuals to ensure that their wealth passes according to the instructions they make during their lifetimes.

This chapter will also cover how the law governs many important aspects of our personal relationships. From birth to marriage, parentage to domestic partnership, the law creates obligations and preferences that shape the way we conduct our lives. In many ways, the law steps in when relationships no longer lend support to family members. Our exploration will reveal how the law has had to develop to define and redefine the entire notion of family. Among these topics will be in-depth coverage of the paralegal's role as part of the legal team in all of these advanced topics.

gift
Bestowing a benefit without any expectation on the part of the giver to receive something in return and the absence of any obligation on the part of the receiver to do anything in return.

THE LAW OF GIFTS

A gratuitous of property whether real, personal or intangible, is known as a **gift**. The person making the gift is called a **donor**, and the recipient is called a **donee**. Sometimes the donor is referred to as a grantor, and the donee a grantee. Gifts act as important expressions of love, affection, gratitude, or friendship. We all make

donor
The person making a gift.

donee
A party to whom a gift is given.

gifts regularly in our daily lives as a matter of routine for birthdays, holidays, graduation, and other important events. Gifts impose no legal obligation upon the donee. Under the law, the motivation for the gift is irrelevant. All that is necessary is the intent and the delivery of some sort from the donor. Yet at the same time, we understand that gifts can possess significant meaning. Even token gifts carry well-understood connotations.

Gifts of most forms of tangible personal property may be accomplished without a legal document but are nevertheless governed by law. A gift generally consists of two legal elements:

donative intent
The state of mind necessary to make a gift.

1. **Donative intent**. The donor intended to make a gift. Intent means the donor's state of mind. With gifts, the donor's intent is usually inferred through words, the relationships involved, and the circumstances. For instance, a gift may accompany a card written by the donor expressing his or her donative intent. Transfers made during holidays, anniversaries, birthdays, and other commemorative occasions carry a strong presumption of a gift, particularly if the gift is wrapped as such.

delivery (gift)
Transferring actual possession of the goods, or putting the goods at the disposal of the buyer (donee), or by a negotiable instrument giving the buyer (donee) the right to the goods.

constructive delivery
The donor's symbolic act of transferring a gift to the donee.

2. **Delivery**. The law recognizes a completed gift if the donor has made some act that indicates delivery of the gift. Donors usually accomplish delivery simply by handing the gift over into the donee's possession or to someone acting on behalf of the donee. Delivery may also be symbolic, such as when a donee hands the key to a strong box to symbolize the delivery of its contents to the donee. Delivery of a gift by the donor's execution of a legal document, such as a deed for real estate or a certificate of title for a car, is called **constructive delivery**. Therefore, the law recognizes that delivery may be impracticable due to the nature of the gift itself. Thus, the legal document acts as evidence of delivery.

Some state laws require a showing that the donee has expressed an acceptance of the gift. However, most state laws presume that the donee has accepted the gift, such as in the following statute:

> *Montana Code, 70-1-512. Constructive delivery.*
> *Though a grant be not actually delivered into the possession of the grantee, it is yet to be deemed constructively delivered in the following cases: (1) where the instrument is, by the agreement of the parties at the time of execution, understood to be delivered and under such circumstances that the grantee is entitled to immediate delivery; or (2) where it is delivered to a stranger for the benefit of the grantee, and his assent is shown or may be presumed.*

Once a gift is completed, the donor's title transfers to the donee, who becomes the new owner. The main point is that donative intent combined with delivery, whether actual or constructive, transfers title irrevocably from the donor to the donee by operation of law. The result is a completed and irretrievable gift.

Some gifts are supposed to be returned. Consider an engagement ring. Sadly, not all engagements end up in the marriage that the couple had contemplated. With luck, the deposits left with the caterer, the florist, and the dressmaker are returnable. But who gets to keep the engagement ring? Some have turned to the courts for an answer. The courts, in turn, have differing opinions.

Some courts treat the engagement ring as a completed gift if the donee can prove the elements of donative intent and delivery—usually an easy task. As a completed gift, the donee would get to keep the ring. Most courts, however, have taken the view that an engagement ring is a conditional gift. Those courts have held that the gift was made in contemplation of marriage (a condition), and until it (the marriage) occurs, the gift is not entirely completed. Thus, if the marriage does not occur, the donor has the right to get the ring back.

CASE IN POINT

COURT OPINION: *MEYER V. MITNICK*, 244 MICH.APP. 697, 625 N.W.2d 136 (2001)

When Barry Meyer, and Robyn Mitnick became engaged[,] Barry gave Robyn a custom-designed engagement ring that he purchased for $19,500. Three months later, on November 8, 1996, Barry asked Robyn to sign a prenuptial agreement and Robyn refused, and immediately thereafter, the engagement was off.

Robyn also refused to return the engagement ring and Barry filed the present action on December 2, 1996. Barry alleged that the engagement ring was a conditional gift given in contemplation of marriage and that, because the condition of marriage did not occur, the ring should be returned to him. Robyn filed a counter-complaint, alleging that the ring was an unconditional gift and that, because Barry broke the engagement, she was entitled to keep the ring.

Following a hearing on Barry's motion for summary disposition, the trial court granted summary disposition in favor of Barry. The court held that because an engagement ring is given in contemplation of marriage, the marriage itself is a condition precedent to the ultimate ownership of the ring. The court held that because the parties did not perform the condition of marriage, Barry was entitled to return of the ring. The court also determined that the issue of who ended the engagement is not determinative of ownership of the ring.

Robyn appealed arguing that since Barry was at fault in ending the engagement she should be able to keep the ring.

Most jurisdictions that have considered cases dealing with the gift of an engagement ring uniformly hold that marriage is an implied condition of the transfer of title and that the gift does not become absolute until the marriage occurs. Thus, most courts recognize that engagement rings occupy a rather unique niche in our society. Where a gift of personal property is made with the intent to take effect irrevocably, and is fully executed by unconditional delivery, it is a valid gift *inter vivos*. Such a gift is absolute and, once made, cannot be revoked. A gift, however, may be conditioned on the performance of some act by the donee, and if the condition is not fulfilled the donor may recover the gift.

We find the conditional gift theory particularly appropriate when the contested property is an engagement ring. The inherent symbolism of this gift forecloses the need to establish an express condition that marriage will ensue. Rather, the condition may be implied in fact or imposed by law in order to prevent unjust enrichment. The court determined that because an engagement ring is a symbol or pledge of a future marriage, it signifies that the one who wears it is engaged to marry the man who gave it to her. Therefore, it is given in contemplation of the marriage and is a unique type of conditional gift. We find that engagement rings should be considered, by their very nature, conditional gifts given in contemplation of marriage.

The other rule, the so-called, "modern trend," holds that because an engagement ring is an inherently conditional gift, once the engagement has been broken the ring should be returned to the donor. Thus, the question of who broke the engagement and why, or who was "at fault," is irrelevant. This is the no-fault line of cases. We find the reasoning of the no-fault cases persuasive. Because the engagement ring is a conditional gift, when the condition is not fulfilled the ring or its value should be returned to the donor no matter who broke the engagement or caused it to be broken.

In sum, we hold that an engagement ring given in contemplation of marriage is an impliedly conditional gift that is a completed gift only upon marriage. If the engagement is called off, for whatever reason, the gift is not capable of becoming a completed gift and must be returned to the donor.

Affirmed

QUESTIONS ABOUT THE CASE

1. Why did the Court hold that the issue of fault should be eliminated?
2. If fault were an issue, which party was at fault here?
3. Would Robyn have been justified in breaking off the engagement when Barry asked her to sign a prenuptial agreement after they had already been engaged?
4. Would the proposed terms of the prenuptial agreement make a difference if fault were an issue?

THE LAW OF WILLS AND DESCENT: A PRIMER

The property that is passed on to others at death has even greater meaning. Every society since ancient times has established rules for the distribution of a person's possessions upon his or her death. At stake are even larger social issues. Status, privilege, and a host of other social considerations frequently dictated how the possessions of a recently deceased person—the **decedent**—were to be handled, particularly if the decedent owned a significant amount of land or other items of high social value. Passing these items on meant the continuation of the established social order, as well

decedent
A deceased person.

as the passing of accumulated wealth to the decedent's family. To be sure, decedents wanted a voice in how their worldly possessions were to be distributed. There was also concern for the welfare of surviving family members. These issues and more remain with us today.

COMMUNICATION TIP

Planning for the future is one of the most, if not *the* most, sensitive subjects for many clients. If you think about it, coming to a legal professional to write a will and plan an estate raises issues in family relationships, as well as an awareness of the client's mortality. Thus, a professional paralegal should remember to maintain strict confidentiality and reassure the client that all matters are regarded as such. Moreover, the paralegal must approach the client and the work for the client with great sensitivity and tact.

The law of wills and probate comes to us, not surprisingly, directly from the English common law. Thus, much of the terminology survives today in much the same form. Because this area of the law concerns itself with the property rights of the decedent and those who stand in line to succeed to the decedent's property, we will build on the last chapter's coverage of property law. There, we saw that the forms of concurrent ownership—tenants in common, joint tenants, and tenants by the entirety—are the result of choices made by those who conveyed the property in that form. For instance, both joint tenancies and tenancies by the entirety allow a survivor to inherit the other half of the tenancy upon the death of the co-owner. As such, the choice to create a form of ownership acts as a substitute for a will. The law of wills and probate concerns itself with some of the choices that people may make in the distribution of their property at death.

We all accumulate property during our lifetimes, all types of property. If we were to make an inventory of everything we now own, the result would be called an **estate**, which may change over the course of a life. We may buy, sell, or give away some or all of our possessions during our lifetimes. Yet most of us leave something. Decedents leave a final estate, whether large or small. The contents of an estate become the object of scrutiny for distribution under the laws of wills and probate procedure. During their lives, everyone has the ability to make choices about how their belongings should be distributed.

The most notable method for choosing who will inherit property is accomplished by a legal document called a **will**. We are all familiar with the term. However, you may be unaware of its significance. A person who has a will is known as **testate**, or a testator. Conversely, a decedent without a will dies **intestate**. The significance of this difference is that the property of an intestate decedent passes to heirs, as provided for by statute, known as laws of **intestate succession**. The laws of intestate succession vary somewhat from state to state. However, most state intestate laws list the order in which the relatives of the intestate decedent inherit the estate property. In cases of intestacy, the property is distributed to the decedent's relatives by application of law.

Generally, the laws of intestate succession provide first for the surviving spouse, who inherits the entire estate unless there are children. If there are children, the surviving spouse inherits one-third to one-half, depending on the state. The children inherit the

estate
The total property, real and personal, owned by an individual.

will
A document representing the formal declaration of a person's wishes for the manner and distribution of his or her property upon death.

testate
The state of having died with a valid will.

intestate
The state of having died without a will.

intestate succession
State laws that direct who should inherit from a person who has died without a will.

CYBER TRIP

When a decedent leaves no heirs, his or her estate becomes property of the state. The legal principle is known as escheat. In most states, intangible estate property that escheats is regarded as unclaimed property. Escheated property includes bank deposits, insurance policies, utility deposits, stocks, and even wages. Each state varies as to how "escheat property" is turned over to a specialized government agency. State laws usually spell out the procedures it takes to find any heirs. After a specified period of time, the property may be considered abandoned. Even then, in some states, the property is held *forever.* In other states, like Virginia, the funds are loaned to a state "Literary Fund" to help finance public schools. After a period of five years, known as a dormancy period, the funds remit to the state's general fund. The Virginia Department of the Treasury reported that in 2005, $85 million in unclaimed funds were loaned to its Literary Fund. See www.trs.virginia.gov/ucp/ucpfaq.asp.

On the Internet, research what happens to escheated property in your state.

remainder of the estate, sharing it equally among them. Absent a surviving spouse and children, most intestate laws place next in line the grandchildren, then the decedent's surviving parents, siblings, and aunts and uncles. State intestate laws usually list seven or eight layers of relatives who stand in line as **heirs**. Beyond this list of the decedent's relatives in line for intestate succession, there are no relatives at law to inherit the estate. In the rare cases in which there are no heirs at law, the decedent's property goes to the state by a common law principle called **escheat**.

heirs
Persons entitled to receive property based on intestate succession.

escheat
To pass property to the state, as is done with the assets of a person who dies without a will and without heirs.

As you may have surmised, state intestate succession laws are designed to conform to what many people do anyway when they make a will. After all, the primary concern for almost any person planning for the future is the well-being of those left behind—in most cases, the decedent's spouse and any children. Thus, for many people, the intestate succession laws stand in as their will.

Wills

We all understand the underlying concept of a will: It is a legal document spelling out the author's wishes as to the distribution of the estate property. As a legal document, it is enforceable by court order but only after the death of its author, the **testator** (in common law, a woman with a will is a **testatrix**). Then and only then does a will confer gifts to those designated by the testator. Such gifts are known as **testamentary gifts**. The difference between a will and a gift is that at any time before death, the testator may change or amend the will. *Inter vivos* gifts, as we already know, are completed and final upon delivery as a matter of law.

testator/testatrix
The person who writes a will.

testamentary gift
A gift made through the will of a decedent.

Furthermore, certain events, such as marriage, divorce, or the death of a spouse, may occur that alter or nullify the will, depending on the state law involved. Other conditions also may nullify or invalidate the will, even the voluntary act of the testator. For instance, in Massachusetts and several other states, the marriage of testator—someone who already has a will—voids that will by **operation of law**, meaning that the will becomes invalid automatically without any other action by virtue of the marriage. This law makes sense as a matter of social policy, because the invalidated will could not provide for the new spouse. In this way, the law strongly favors inheritance by surviving spouses to avoid the possibility that a decedent will leave that spouse destitute, unintentionally or otherwise. Nevertheless, as we will see subsequently, the testator may, with consent, omit the surviving spouse from the will. The law of wills thus leaves the testator with the freedom to choose who may inherit through a will. As enforceable legal documents that can make substantial transfers of the testator's accumulated wealth, wills must conform to certain formalities.

operation of law
A right or liability created for a party, irrespective of the intent of that party, because it is dictated by existing legal principles.

At the outset, the law of wills requires the testator have the legal **capacity**. This requirement means that the law is concerned that people making a will do so with full awareness of the impact of their act. As our coverage of contracts will show, a person who makes a will must possess certain attributes for the law to recognize and enforce that will.

capacity
The ability to understand the nature and significance of a contract; to understand or comprehend specific acts or reasoning.

At a minimum, the testator must have *mental* capacity and reached a minimum age. In most states, mental capacity means two things:

1. The testator must understand the nature and extent of the property that he or she is giving away in the will. Knowing precisely what the testator has is not necessary; the testator simply must know within reasonable bounds what the estate property includes as a general matter.
2. The testator must recognize the identity of the persons who would be able to benefit from the will. Therefore, the testator must have an understanding of who would benefit from a will.

Similar to many other areas, the law presumes that persons under a certain age do not possess the maturity or sufficient awareness of their acts. For wills, most state laws say that a person 18 years of age or older may make a will.

RESEARCH THIS

Find the intestate succession laws for your state. Make a chart of the order in which relatives of the decedent stand in line to inherit property in the case of an intestate decedent.

Legal Formalities for Wills

A testator possessing sufficient mental capacity and age still needs to observe the formal requirements for a valid will. These requirements speak to the document itself regarding its form and content.

- *Written document.* With minor exceptions recognized in only a few states, a will must be in writing. Although the law does not require a certain size or type of print, or even that the writing be on paper, the will must exist in writing on a tangible object as a permanent and reliable record of the testator's intent and wishes. As a matter of good practice, most wills are professionally produced and typewritten on letter-size paper. However, courts have also recognized valid wills in unusual forms, such as those written on a bedpost, the bottom of a chest of drawers, and a nurse's petticoat. History is full of oddball and unusual wills that have been upheld as legally sufficient and valid.
- *Intent of the testator.* A valid will must express the testator's intent to create a will that disposes of his or her property. This requirement is formally known as an *exordium clause,* which expressly states that the testator's purpose in executing the document is to dispose of his or her property by the will.
- *Testator's signature*. The testator must sign the will. Just like a signature on a check, the testator's usual signature must appear on the will to show approval of the document. Moreover, the testator's signature must appear near what would be regarded as the logical end of the document. This requirement prevents the addition of unauthorized provisions by another person after the testator's signature. Wills usually provide for the testator's signature as part of a *testimonium clause,* which formally indicates the testator's signature as meeting the legal requirement. A careful practitioner will also have the testator sign each page of the will in the margin.
- *Witnesses' signature*. Officially speaking, the will ends with the testator's signature. Nevertheless, legal formalities include the signatures of several witnesses who must also sign the will after the testator has signed it. In doing so, the witnesses are attesting to the fact that they saw the testator sign the will voluntarily and with the appearance that he or she was aware of his or her action. Almost all states require two witnesses to a will; Vermont requires three. Even in states that only require two, a careful practitioner will sometimes have three witnesses. In a properly prepared will, the witnesses' signatures appear in an *attestation clause* that, like the testimonium clause, provides a formalized place for the witnesses' signatures.
- *Self-proving affidavit*. Attached to most modern wills is an affidavit from the testator and the witnesses stating, under oath, that the will's formalities have

been met and that they witnessed the testator's signature. A bit of history and procedure will explain why the self-proving affidavit is an essential addition to the will. When the testator has passed away, the will is submitted to a specialized state court. You will recall that there are a number of specialized state trial courts. Just about every state has a specialized trial court to receive wills in a process known as **probate**, from the Latin word, *probare,* meaning to prove. The name of these courts differs from state to state. For instance, in New York, such courts are known as Surrogate Courts; in other states as Chancery Court, because the judge's power is essentially rooted in equity. Most states call such courts the **Probate Court**. Thus, the main point of the probate process essentially involves proving the validity of the will. When proven, the court orders that the provisions of the will be carried out. An important part of proving the will's validity involves whether the witnesses saw the testator sign the will. In former times, witnesses were subpoenaed in court to testify to that fact, a cumbersome task. In many cases, the witnesses were difficult to locate, because many years may have elapsed since they signed the attestation clause. Thus, the self-proving affidavit, as a separate document accompanying the will, provides an easier means to accomplish the same result.

probate
The court process of determining will validity, settling estate debts, and distributing assets.

Probate Court
The court empowered to settle estates for those individuals who have died with or without a will.

Beyond these formal requirements, some additional items are not required, though every professionally prepared will includes them.

- *Executor*. With the testator's passing, the executor acts on the decedent's behalf and carries on as the testator's legal personality. The executor performs two distinct functions. First, the executor is the actual person representing the decedent's estate in court. Thus, even though the legal professionals represent the estate in court, they are acting on behalf of the executor. Second, the executor performs the day-to-day activities necessary to wind up the estate, such as paying outstanding bills, hiring a legal team to represent the estate, and conferring with survivors. An executor is appointed by the testator in the will. Usually, the executor is the surviving spouse, surviving child, or even a financial institution such as a bank or trust company.

A careful practitioner will usually name a second executor in the event that the first-named executor is unavailable or unwilling to act as such. A testator often executes a valid will many years, if not decades, before he or she has died. Therefore, it is a safe practice to name another person as an alternative. In the event that both persons named in the will are unavailable or unwilling, the probate court will appoint a person at the suggestion of a relative of the decedent or a **beneficiary** of the will—that is, the person who inherits from the will.

beneficiary
The person or persons named in a will or trust to receive the testator's or settlor's assets.

- ***Residuary clause***. Almost every will contains a residuary clause, which usually provides for the disposition of the bulk of the estate. Realistically, any testator is unaware of all the property he or she will own and be able to dispose of by will at the time of his or her death. Thus, a residuary clause disposes of any and all of the property owned by the decedent at the time of death. In practice, the residuary clause has become the primary part of the will's disposition. In other words, a beneficiary named in a residuary clause inherits the largest part of the estate. As you will see in the sample provided subsequently, the operative parts of the will consist of specific testamentary gifts to named beneficiaries and a residuary clause. The residuary clause makes as a testamentary gift the residue of the estate, except for those items specifically gifted.

residuary clause
A will clause that makes a testamentary gift of the remaining property of an estate after expenses and specific gifts have been satisfied.

EYE ON ETHICS

Remember that under the ethical rules for the NALA and NFPA, as well as the ABA Model Rules of Professional Responsibility, a legal professional should avoid even the appearance of impropriety. Therefore, it would be improper for a legal professional to prepare legal documents on behalf of a client who is making a gift to that legal professional.

Types of Testamentary Gifts

The law of wills has come to us after thousands of years of development and human experience. The idea behind a will has existed since Biblical times, beginning with Noah's writing and witnessed under his seal, by which he disposed of the whole world. A more authentic instance of the early use of testaments also appears (Genesis 48), in which Jacob bequeaths to his son Joseph a portion of his inheritance, double that of his brethren. With the custom of wills continuing through the Roman Empire, medieval times, and into the common law, archaic terms have remained with us today. When a will makes a testamentary gift of a specific item to a named individual, the term used depends on whether that specific gift is personal property, real property, or money. As a practical matter, these terms are sometimes used interchangeably and thus are becoming obsolete. Nevertheless, they are easy and useful to learn.

- *Bequest*. A testamentary gift of personal property. There is no specific name for the beneficiary of a bequest.
- *Devise*. A testamentary gift of real property to a devisee.
- *Legacy*. A testamentary gift of money to a legatee.

Although these terms are often used together simultaneously and repetitiously, their use displays excessive caution and has caused usages commonly known as legalese. In reality, a modern court would unlikely invalidate a will clause that *bequests* real estate instead of *devising* it. Figure 8.1 illustrates a typical simple will, that of Jennifer Craig.

Notice that Craig's will made testamentary gifts to her friends and relatives and appointed her son, Daniel Craig, as executor. This identification raises the possibility that Craig was, at least at one time, married and may have had more than one child. Of course, it is possible that Craig was single at the time she made the will. However, as discussed previously, if Craig were married at the time of her death, the will would be subject to laws that favor the surviving spouse. Here, the intestate succession laws can affect the provisions of a will.

The intestate succession laws first provide for a surviving spouse, granting the entire decedent's estate or a significant percentage of it if there are surviving children. The same provision can affect a will under the laws that allow for spousal election in the event that the decedent's will omits a provision for the surviving spouse in an amount less than the applicable intestate share for a surviving spouse. All states' laws permit a spouse to elect—that is, choose—between any share provided for in the will or the applicable intestate share accorded to surviving spouses. Thus, if Craig died as a married person, her surviving spouse could choose to take the equivalent of a surviving spouse's intestate share from her estate. The will would still be valid and the provisions still effective, to the extent of the amount of the assets remaining.

elective share
The right granted by law to a surviving spouse who may elect to take an intestate share of a decedent's spouse's estate despite any will provisions to the contrary.

In doing so, Craig's spouse's exercise of spousal election would have the possible effect of an abatement, which reduces the specific bequest, legacy, and devise in her will. By exercising a spousal election and taking an intestate share, Craig's spouse would effectively reduce the other provisions of the will. Thus, the surviving spouse would be taking an **elective share** (also known as a spousal share). The laws in most

Exordium clause →

Appointment of Executor →

Appointment of Alternate Executor →

Legacy of money →

Bequest of personal property →

Devise of real property →

Residuary clause designating the beneficiary and alternate beneficiary →

Enumeration of powers granted to Executor →

Provision for any after-born children →

Testimonium clause →

Attestation clause for witnesses →

Self-proving affidavit attached to will →

WILL OF JENNIFER CRAIG

I, Jennifer Craig, a resident of and domiciled in the City of Carlsbad, Commonwealth of Massachusetts, make, publish and declare this to be my Will, hereby revoking all Wills and Codicils at any time heretofore made by me.

FIRST: I hereby nominate, constitute and appoint as Temporary Executor and as Executor of this Will, my son, Daniel Craig, of Boston, Massachusetts, and direct that he shall serve without any sureties on his bond.

SECOND: If my son Daniel Craig, or any successor as herein defined should fail to qualify as Executor or as Trustee hereunder, the successor or substitute Executor or Trustee shall be my sister, Kristin Alley. I direct that she shall serve without any sureties on her bond.

THIRD: I hereby give, devise and bequeath the sum of $10,000.00 to my nephew, Drew Carrie, of Cleveland, Ohio.

FOURTH: I hereby give, devise and bequeath my entire collection of first edition books now located in my home in Carlsbad, Massachusetts, to my niece, Anna Sophie Robb, of Terabithia, Massachusetts.

FIFTH: I hereby give, devise and bequeath my real estate real estate with the building thereon known as 14 Bedford Road in Wolfboro, New Hampshire, containing three acres more or less, to my sister, Mia Farrel, of Los Angeles, California.

SIXTH: I give, devise and bequeath all of the rest, residue and remainder of my property of every kind and description, real or personal, wherever situated and whether acquired before or after the execution of this Will, absolutely in fee simple to my sister, Hannah Craig. If my sister Hannah Craig does not survive me, I give, devise and bequeath all of said property to my friend, Elliot Craig, of Camillus, New York.

SEVENTH: By way of illustration and not of limitation, and in addition to any inherent, implied or statutory powers granted to executors generally, my Executrix is specifically authorized and empowered with respect to any property, real or personal, at any time held under any provision of this Will; to allot, allocate between principal and income, assign, borrow, buy, care for, collect, compromise claims, contract with respect to, continue any business of mine, convey, convert, deal with, delegate, dispose of, enter into, exchange, hold, improve, incorporate any business of mine, invest, lease, manage, mortgage, grant and exercise options with respect to, take possession of, pledge, receive, release, repair, sell, sue for, to make distributions or divisions in cash or in kind or partly in each without regard to the income tax basis of such asset and in general, to exercise all of the powers in the management of my Estate which any individual could exercise in the management of similar property owned in its own right, upon such terms and conditions as my Executor may deem best, and execute and deliver any and all instruments and to do all acts which my Executrix may deem proper or necessary to carry out the purposes of this Will, without being limited in any way by the specific grants of power made, and without the necessity of a court order.

EIGHTH: Insofar as I have failed to provide in this my Will for any of my issue, whether born before or after the date of this Will or before or after my death, such failure is intentional and not occasioned by accident or mistake.

IN WITNESS THEREOF, I have hereunto set my hand and affixed my seal this _____ day of , 2007, at Carlsbad, Massachusetts.

____

Jennifer Craig

The foregoing Will consisting of four (4) typewritten pages, this and the following page containing the Proof of Will included, the two (2) preceding pages thereof bearing on the margin the signature of the Testatrix, was this _____ day of , 2007, signed, sealed, published and declared by the Testator as and for his Will, in our presence, and we, at his request and in his presence, and in the presence of each other have hereunto subscribed our names as witnesses on the above date.

__________________of________________

__________________of________________

PROOF OF WILL

Commonwealth of Massachusetts

We, ______________ and ______________, on oath state that we are the subscribing witnesses to the attached written instrument dated the _____ day of _____, 2007, which purports to be the Will of Jennifer Craig. On the execution date of the instrument, the Testator, in our presence, signed the instrument to be her Will and requested that we attest to the instrument to be his Will, and requested that we attest to the execution thereof whereupon, in the presence of the Testator each of us signed our respective names as attesting witnesses. At the time of the execution of the instrument, the Testator appeared to be over eighteen (18) years of age, of sound mind, and acting without undue influence, fraud or restraint.

Dated this _____ day of ____, 2007.

____

____

Subscribed and sworn to before me on this ____ day of July 2003.

____

Notary Public. My commission expires on:

FIGURE 8.1 **Example of a Typical Simple Will**

states empower the executor to reduce the other testamentary gifts in proportion to the entire estate. As the person carrying on the legal personality of the testator, the executor to Craig's will possesses the authority and responsibility to **marshal** the estate's assets to pay the debts of the estate, including the spousal election or taxes. The power to marshal Craig's estate, among other powers, is amply granted in paragraph seven of her will.

marshal
The act of reducing testamentary gifts provided by a will.

The right of election does not, however, apply to the testator's children. The laws of all states permit anyone to disown any and all of their children. Notice that in Craig's will there is no provision for her son, even though he was appointed executor of his mother's estate. Oftentimes, a person may have otherwise provided for his or her children during life, and, with the understanding of the children (or not), they are intentionally omitted in the will. To avoid a will contest, Craig has added the seventh paragraph of her will to make it clear that she intended to omit any children, including those born after the will had been drafted. This paragraph makes it extremely difficult, if not impossible, for any of her children to claim that they had been unintentionally omitted. Most of the time, wills are probated in a peaceful and orderly process.

After the testator has passed away, the probate professional begins the post-mortem work of probating the estate in a court proceeding. Much of this work consists of gathering the information to file in the probate court to assure the court that the testator's will was properly executed, that the creditors are notified, and that the debts are paid. When these and other assurances are fulfilled, the court issues the all-important **letter testamentary**, which is essentially a court order granting the executor the authority to carry out the will's provisions.

letter testamentary
An order issued by a probate court approving the validity of a decedent's will and authorizing the estate's distribution according to the terms of the will.

In cases in which there is no will, the estate undergoes the same probate process using different names. The process itself is called an **administration**, and the person appointed by the court to carry out the legal personality of the intestate decedent is an **administrator**. In intestate cases, the court order is a **letter of administration**, which authorizes the administrator to distribute the decedent's assets in accordance with the intestate succession laws.

administration
The court-supervised distribution of the probate estate of a person who has died without a will.

administrator
A person appointed by a probate court to handle the distribution of property of someone who has died without a will.

letter of administration
An order issued by a probate court appointing an administrator to an intestate estate and ordering the estate's distribution by the laws of intestate succession.

Whether testate or intestate, the probate proceedings occur under the court's ***in rem* jurisdiction**, in that the court is acting upon the decedent's estate. In this way, probate proceedings are unique in civil practice.

***in rem* jurisdiction**
A court's authority over claims affecting property.

Probate Practice for the Professional Paralegal

The social policy behind the probate process ensures the orderly distribution of a decedent's estates. Primary among the concerns of this process are respect for the wishes of the testator. In the administration of intestate estates, assets must be properly distributed to the rightful heirs, as provided for by the laws of intestate succession. You might think of the probate procedure as an extension of property law by which ownership is determined. The primary principle in nature is that you cannot take it with you.

Paralegals often take an active role in a probate practice. Probating an estate, whether or not a will exists, usually consists of a relatively straightforward procedure involving mostly court-printed forms. Unlike civil litigation, the probate process consists of submitting the will to the court, gathering the decedent's assets that are meant for distribution through the will, paying the decedent's debts, and distributing the net assets to those named in the will under the court's supervision. Almost everything is done by mail without any in-court appearances. Will contests, which challenge the validity of a will, are extremely rare. When they do occur, the proceedings involve typical civil litigation principles involving pleadings, discovery, trials, and the like.

For the most part, the work of legal professionals engaged in probate practice consists of pre- and post-mortem activities, that is, before and after death. Pre-mortem legal work is known generally as **estate planning**. A paralegal working under the supervision of an attorney would be able to handle much of the work in an estate planning case. From gathering information from the client to drafting wills, a paralegal is often instrumental in probate practice. For most clients, the will is the centerpiece of the estate plan. However, for more complex estates, two other devices commonly appear as essential parts of an estate plan: trusts and asset rearrangement.

estate planning
The legal practice of arranging a client's assets and affairs in contemplation of death through the use of wills, trusts, and asset rearrangement.

Trusts

The law of trusts is quite complex but deserves mention here. Essentially, a **trust** is an arrangement whereby the person creating the trust places assets (i.e., money, property, or both) in the care and management of a **trustee** for the benefit of designated beneficiaries. Frequently, with large trusts, a bank or other financial institution will act as the trustee. The trustee, like an executor or administrator, acts as a **fiduciary** to the beneficiaries, who are the "beneficial" owners of the trust property. As a fiduciary, the trustee must deal honestly and avoid any self-interest in performing his or her duties. The person creating the trust and putting the assets into it, known as the **settlor**, divests him- or herself of title to the assets and transfers title to the person assigned to take care of the property held by the trust. The trustee is the legal owner of the property but is obliged to hold and manage the property for the beneficiaries—usually children or close relatives of the settlor, or perhaps a charity—who have enforceable rights that are spelled out in the trust document.

trust
An agreement for the care and maintenance of assets by a designated person for the benefit of another or others; often used in place of a will.

trustee
A person or entity designated to care for and maintain the property placed into a trust and to follow the terms of the trust.

fiduciary
One who owes to another the duties of good faith, trust, confidence, and candor.

settlor
A person who creates a trust.

Paralegals often gather the necessary information to draft a trust document. The trust is governed by the terms of the trust document, which is essentially an agreement between the settlor and the trustee. As long as the trust conforms to state laws, the agreement is, like a will, an enforceable document. However, unlike a will, a trust becomes effective by its own terms, usually upon execution of the trust agreement and the transfer of property into it. Figure 8.2 provides a sample trust agreement.

The laws of most states allow for great flexibility in the creation of trusts. As noted previously, these laws vary and can be quite complex. This discussion of trusts is merely an introduction to a vast and intricate area of the law. Nevertheless, paralegals frequently perform important tasks in drafting trust agreements or even assisting trustees in the care and administration of trust property.

In the sample trust in Figure 8.2, notice that the settlor, Snow, directed that the property should go to the two children upon their attaining the age of 21 years. If Snow died before then, the trust would still continue in existence, providing income to the children and passing the property on to them when they reached 21 years. Although a settlor may provide any number of final dispositions for the property, including its return to the settlor, trust terms that give the property to the trust beneficiaries when they turn a certain age is most common. Trusts often operate as will substitutes for certain properties of a settlor. The same settlor may otherwise provide for the disposition of other assets through gifts or a will.

What is important to remember is that the property in a trust usually does not go through the probate process. Under the trust agreement, Snow has given the property to the trust and provided for a gift of the property to the children when they turn 21 years of age. Because of this arrangement, the property in the trust is **nonprobate property**. That is, the property does not undergo probate court supervision as a disposition of Snow's estate because the property no longer belongs to Snow.

nonprobate property
Property of the decedent that avoids the probate process due to the nature of its ownership or contractual arrangements previously made by the decedent.

FIGURE 8.2
Sample Trust Agreement

TRUST AGREEMENT

This Trust Agreement is made March 15, 2007, between Harriet B. Snow, of Brunswick, Maine, hereinafter referred to as the Settlor, and Nathaniel Hawthorne, of Bath, Maine, herein referred to as Trustee. In consideration of the mutual covenants and promises set forth herein, Settlor and Trustee agree as follows:

1. Transfer of Trust. Settlor herewith assigns, transfers, and conveys to Trustee the property described in Exhibit "A" attached hereto and made a part hereof by this reference, and receipt of such property is hereby acknowledged by Trustee. Such property, hereafter designated the Trust Estate, shall be held by Trustee in Trust for the uses and purposes and on the terms and conditions set forth herein.
2. Disposition of Principal and Income. Trustee shall administer and manage the property described in the accompanying addendum collect the income, and, after payment of all taxes and assessments and all charges to the management, apply and dispose of the net income and the principal of the Trust Estate as follows:
   a. Net income to be distributed to the Settlor's children, Edgar and Eliza Snow, of Brunswick, Maine, for the purpose of their education and maintenance.
   b. Principal to be distributed in equal shares to Edgar and Eliza Snow upon their attainment of age 21.
3. Additions to Trust. Settlor and any other person shall have the right at any time to add property acceptable to the Trustee. Such property, when received and accepted by Trustee, shall become part of the Trust Estate.
4. Irrevocability of Trust. This trust shall be irrevocable and shall not be revoked or terminated by Settlor or any other person, nor shall it be amended or altered by Settlor or any other person.
5. Compensation of Trustee: The original Trustee hereunder, and all Successor Trustees, shall be entitled to reasonable compensation for their services as Trustee.
6. Successor Trustees: If Nathaniel Hawthorne resigns or is unable to continue to act as Trustee, then Henry W. Longfellow, of Portland, Maine, is hereby appointed as Successor Trustee.
7. Governing Laws: The validity, construction, and effect of this agreement and the Trust created hereunder and its enforcement shall be determined by the laws of the State of Maine.

   In Witness Whereof, Settlor and Trustee have executed this Agreement on the date above written.

   ______________________ Settlor ______________________ Trustee
   ______________________ Successor Trustee
   ______________________ Witness ______________________ Witness

The foregoing instrument was acknowledged before me this March 15, 2008, by Harriet B. Snow, Nathaniel Hawthorne, and Henry W. Longfellow, in Brunswick, Maine.

My commission expires: ______________________ Notary Public
______________________ Date:
____

COMMUNICATION TIP

Paralegals often have substantial contact with clients. Be sure to use straightforward language and a patient tone. Moreover, when explaining the law to clients pursuant to your supervising attorney's instructions, it is crucial to use plain English. The difference between probate and nonprobate disposition of a client's property can be bewildering; be sure to explain clearly, using a minimum of legal jargon.

Asset Rearrangement

Another important aspect of making an estate plan may include asset rearrangement. The process of estate planning combines traditional notions in property law and choices about the types of ownership that the client may prefer. The last chapter discussed how property ownership devices, such as a joint tenancy and a tenancy by the entirety, operate as will substitutes, with the surviving tenant automatically assuming ownership by operation of law. Tenancies in common, in contrast, allow the property to be inherited by the heirs or devisees of each tenant in common. The difference you may notice is that the ownership forms of joint tenancy and tenancy by the entirety, as will substitutes, are not probated and as such are considered nonprobate property. By operation of law, the surviving joint tenant or the surviving spouse of a tenancy by the entirety automatically inherit the property without regard to a will.

Device	Successor	Source for Disposition to Successor
Trust	Trust beneficiaries	Trust terms
Joint tenancy	Surviving joint tenant	Operation of law
Tenancy by the entirety	Surviving spouse	Operation of law
Joint bank accounts	Surviving joint owner	Operation of law
Life insurance	Designated beneficiary	Terms of insurance contract
Annuity	Designated beneficiary	Terms of annuity contract

FIGURE 8.3
Forms of Nonprobate Property

Other devices are also available to rearrange assets into forms of ownership that act as will substitutes. Using any of these and other forms of ownership enables clients to make choices with regard to their property with a full understanding of the desired consequences. By rearranging assets in any of these forms during the life of the owner, a legal professional accomplishes important common pre-mortem estate planning for their client. Figure 8.3 lists the various forms of nonprobate property. Notice that the successor to the property or money becomes a successor as the result of trust terms, the operation of law, or the terms of a third-party contract, such as one from an insurance company.

Living Will

Also known as a health care proxy, a **living will** provides for specific directives regarding the course of treatment to be taken by caregivers or, in some cases, forbidding treatment and sometimes food and water should the person in question become unable to give informed consent ("individual health care instruction") due to his or her incapacity. Due to recent cases receiving national attention, living wills have become an integral part of carrying out a client's estate plan. Living wills fulfill the wishes of the client to avoid anguish or become a burden to family and loved ones should that client be unable to express his or her desires for health care, including when none is desired. A living will has become a common device and often provides the client with considerable peace of mind. Figure 8.4 provides a sample of a living will.

living will
A legal instrument that expresses the wishes of the person making it for health care decisions.

Legal professionals in probate practice engage in a specialty some consider a boutique practice. Their knowledge is highly specialized, because their practice involves a blend of ancient legal concepts and modern property laws. Moreover, the court procedures, though civil in nature, are unique to that area of the law. Probate practice and the laws surrounding it greatly affect the lives of clients and their family relationships and histories. At stake are hopes and wishes that have been stored up for a lifetime. Paying for college, buying homes, passing along treasured family heirlooms, and expressing family and cultural traditions are translated into the myriad of legal devices used to transfer all forms of property.

Many legal professionals with personal interests in history and family genealogies become attracted to probate practice, both pre- and post-mortem, and find great satisfaction in planning and executing a person's estate effectively and efficiently. The clients of most probate practices are persons with fascinating backgrounds and refined manners that often make it a pleasure to deal with them.

RESEARCH THIS

Consider a ruling on the right to refuse medical or life-sustaining treatment in *Cruzan v. Missouri Dept. of Health,* 497 U.S. 261 (1990).

How would a living will (health care proxy) have averted the situation?Is a living will sufficient proof of the person's wishes to discontinue life-sustaining treatment?

FIGURE 8.4
Sample of a Living Will

LIVING WILL OF
Belinda Messina

I, Belinda Messina, a resident of the City of Portland, Oregon, being of sound and disposing mind, memory and understanding, do hereby willfully and voluntarily make, publish and declare this to be my LIVING WILL, making known my desire that my life shall not be artificially prolonged under the circumstances set forth below, and do hereby declare:

1. This instrument is directed to my family, my physician(s), my attorney, my clergyman, any medical facility in whose care I happen to be, and to any individual who may become responsible for my health, welfare or affairs.
2. This statement stands as an expression of my wishes now that I am still of sound mind, for the time when I may no longer take part in decisions for my own future.
3. If at any time I should have a terminal condition and my attending physician has determined that there can be no recovery from such condition and my death is imminent, where the application of life-prolonging procedures and "heroic measures" would serve only to artificially prolong the dying process, I direct that such procedures be withheld or withdrawn, and that I be permitted to die naturally. I do not fear death itself as much as the indignities of deterioration, dependence and hopeless pain. I therefore ask that medication be mercifully administered to me and that any medical procedures be performed on me, which are deemed necessary to provide me with comfort, care or to alleviate pain.
4. In the absence of my ability to give directions regarding the use of such life-prolonging procedures, it is my intention that this declaration shall be honored by my family and physician as the final expression of my legal right to refuse medical or surgical treatment and accept the consequences for such refusal.
5. In the event that I am diagnosed as comatose, incompetent, or otherwise mentally or physically incapable of communication, I appoint my daughter, Georgiana Messina to make binding decisions concerning my medical treatment.
6. If I have been diagnosed as pregnant and that diagnosis is known to my physician, this declaration shall have no force or effect during the course of my pregnancy.
7. I understand the full import of this declaration and I am emotionally and mentally competent to make this declaration. I hope you, who care for me, will feel morally bound to follow its mandate. I recognize that this appears to place a heavy responsibility upon you, but it is with the intention of relieving you of such responsibility and of placing it upon myself, in accordance with my strong convictions, that this statement is made.

IN WITNESS WHEREOF, I have hereunto subscribed my name and affixed my seal at _____, ____________, this _____ day of ____________, 20_____, in the presence of the subscribing witnesses whom I have requested to become attesting witnesses hereto.

____

Declarant

The declarant is known to me and I believe him/her to be of sound mind.

____________________ ____________________

Witness Witness

Subscribed and acknowledged, before me on the 15th day of March 2008.

____________________ (SEAL) NOTARY PUBLIC

My Commission Expires: ____________________

PRACTICE TIP

Many legal professionals involved with family and domestic matters find it helpful to maintain a genealogy chart for their client's family file. While there are many types of genealogy charts, use a simple one showing marriages, births and other pertinent aspects of the client's family history. For examples of useful genealogy charts, visit www.misbach.org/pdfchart.

Unlike their counterparts in civil litigation, practitioners specializing in probate seldom engage in adversarial situations. Typically, the legal professionals of a probate department within large law firms engage in planning, research, and drafting activities, and any cases involving will contests are handled by the firm's litigation team. Probate work itself thus appears attractive to many who enjoy working with the law.

Many professional paralegals in this field remain for many years in the trusts and estates division of a large law firm or as a specialist in smaller firms. Their day-to-day activities consist of direct client contact, preparing filings for court submission, reviewing documents, researching and retrieving public records and

A DAY IN THE LIFE OF A REAL PARALEGAL

As the paralegal for the probate department of a medium-size law firm, Wendy Percosette has two major general areas of responsibility. First, she acts as the liaison for the firm's clients. In this role, Percosette meets with clients after they have consulted with the firm's attorney to discuss their estate plan or probate matter. Then she steps in to gather detailed information from the client and obtain their signature on necessary forms. She is also the person available for telephone calls from clients who call with questions. Careful to avoid giving legal advice, Percosette detailed notes whenever her supervising attorney gives her information that she needs to relay to clients. As Percosette clarifies, "I always tell clients that the legal advice is from the attorney; and that's backed up by my notes in the file log."

Second, Percosette keeps track of the assets that the firm helps their clients administer as executors and trustees. In this capacity, she uses the accounting and business education and the internship training she acquired at her two-year school. "The stakes can be high," Percosette reflects, "but the work is satisfying. Ultimately, what we do is to make sure to carry out the decedent's wishes, which usually means taking care of their families."

court documents, analyzing documents, assembling family genealogies, drafting wills and other legal instruments subject to a supervising attorney's review, and organizing files.

Paralegals, particularly those with a business education background, benefit particularly from accounting skills that can be useful in probate practice. In the probate process, legal professionals are often expected to assist the executor, administrator, or trustee of an estate with an accounting of both assets and debts, as well as distributions required under a will, trust, or intestate succession. Thus, a paralegal with good organizational skills, an eye for detail, and accounting training can be invaluable in setting up and maintaining an estate inventory and keeping track of the disbursements to creditors and beneficiaries alike.

FAMILY LAW

Also known as domestic relations law, **family law** covers the legal aspects of personal relationships. In many respects, family law regulates relationships by delineating the rights and liabilities of those involved in the ever-growing concept of the family. Traditionally, the "family" that the law contemplated consisted of a woman and a man married to each other and living together with their children. Issues arising from this context consisted primarily of divorce, support, and custody. However, the law's assumptions proved unsuited to the realities of modern society and even to the social reality of the past that the law declined to recognize.

family law
A body of law that applies to family relationships such as marriage, divorce, adoption, custody, and support.

The current status of the law has grown to recognize the vast array of "family" arrangements, such as single parents, extended families living together, and, in four states, civil unions or same-gender marriages. Almost entirely a matter of state statutes and state court decisions, family law also acknowledges the mobility of Americans, resulting in the nationwide adoption of uniform laws relating to prenuptial agreements, support custody, and paternity issues.

Dealing with these issues, legal professionals engaged or specializing in family law become involved with a variety of specialty legal work. As we discussed in our coverage of the court system, family law is administered by specialized state courts. In some states, these courts are called, quite plainly, "Family Court," whereas many others call these courts "Probate Court." Other names include "Supreme Court" (New York). However named, these courts become involved in family matters when things fall apart (divorce and custody), need to be artificially created (adoption), or need to be protected (guardian and conservator). Litigation procedures within these courts tend to be unique to accommodate the nature of their subject matter. Seldom do they call juries. However, these courts frequently hear requests for temporary orders at the very outset of litigation, more than their civil counterparts. These courts sit at the center of family law practice.

Marriage

marriage
A union between a man and a woman (except in Massachusetts).

A **marriage** is an interpersonal relationship that carries the state's official approval and recognition. State law enumerates the criteria for who may marry whom. As strictly a legal matter, entering into a marriage involves an exchange of duties and expectations. Absent a prenuptial agreement, the duty of reasonable support and the expectation of an equitable division of the "marital property" have become nearly standard nationwide. Family law courts never enter into the picture during a successful marriage, only unsuccessful ones.

Marriage Redefined

Within the past few years, some states have broadened the concept of marriage to include persons of the same gender. Massachusetts currently stands alone as the only state that permits two people of the same gender to marry. In *Goodridge v. Dept. of Public Health,* 440 Mass. 309, 798 N.E.2d 941 (2003), the Supreme Judicial Court, the state's highest court, held that to deny same-sex couples the right to marry violated the Massachusetts Constitution. As a result, the Massachusetts statutes regarding marriage are now read to include couples of the same gender. Even before *Goodridge,* other states had enacted legislation that has permitted same-sex couples to enter into a lawful alternative form of marriage known as a **civil union**.

civil union
In some states, a legally recognized committed relationship similar to marriage for persons of the same gender.

domestic partnership
A legally recognized relationship in some states between two individuals of the same or opposite gender who live together and share a common domestic life but are not joined in a traditional marriage or in a civil union.

Other states have created yet another form of union known as **domestic partnership**, which may include couples of opposite genders (Hawaii uses the term "Reciprocal Beneficiary Relationship"). States doing so have created civil unions and domestic partnerships by statute. The idea has stirred great controversy. On the other end of the spectrum, several states have enacted statutes or constitutional amendments prohibiting any form of union other than traditional marriages.

At the federal level, The Defense of Marriage Act, codified at 1 U.S.C. §7 and 28 U.S.C. §1738C, specifically allows states to decline recognition of a same-gender marriage lawfully entered into under another state's laws. The fear was that the full faith and credit clause of the U.S. Constitution would require states to accept a same-gender marriage from another state. The Defense of Marriage Act also prohibits the federal government from recognizing same-gender marriages for federal law purposes, such as taxes, Social Security, and other federal programs. Figure 8.5 summarizes the various ways the states have handled same-gender unions.

Both civil unions and domestic partnerships are similar to marriage. The benefits available are limited to those offered by the state, such as state taxes, inheritance, and health care decisions, to name a few. The recently created alternatives to marriage indicate our changing society and its values. Moreover, there is a greater awareness of the benefits and obligations of entering into a committed relationship and the meaning of society's growing acceptance of various lifestyles.

Termination of the Marriage

Every state has two ways to end a marriage at the insistence of at least one of the parties: annulment and divorce. The legal effects of divorce and annulment differ substantially.

annulment
Court procedure dissolving a marriage, treating it as if it never happened.

Annulment Annulment involves a court proceeding to declare a marriage void, as if it never existed. In this way, **annulment** differs from legal proceedings in an action for divorce. In a divorce, the court enters a decree ending an otherwise valid marriage, acknowledging its existence and declaring it terminated as of the date of the decree.

Status of Same-Sex Marriage Laws	State(s)
Same-sex marriage prohibited by state constitution	Alabama, Alaska, Arkansas, Colorado, Georgia, Hawaii, Idaho, Kansas, Kentucky, Louisiana, Michigan, Mississippi, Missouri, Montana, Nebraska, Nevada, North Dakota, Ohio, Oklahoma, Oregon, South Carolina, South Dakota, Tennessee, Texas, Utah, Virginia, and Wisconsin
Same-sex marriage prohibited by state statute	Arizona, Connecticut, Delaware, Florida, Illinois, Indiana, Iowa, Maryland, Minnesota, New Hampshire, New York, North Carolina, Pennsylvania, Puerto Rico, Washington, West Virginia, and Wyoming
Marriage legalized for same-sex couples	Massachusetts
Civil union for same-sex couples	Connecticut, New Hampshire, New Jersey, and Vermont
Domestic partnership for same-sex couples	California, District of Columbia, Hawaii, Maine, Oregon, and Washington

FIGURE 8.5
State-by-State Approach to Same-Gender Marriages

The grounds for an annulment differ from state to state. Generally, however, they consist of any one of the following circumstances:

1. Either spouse was already married to someone else at the time of the marriage.
2. Either spouse was too young to be married or too young and lacked required court or parental consent (unless, in some cases, the marriage continued beyond the age of consent, which validates it).
3. Either spouse was under the influence of drugs or alcohol at the time of the marriage.
4. Either spouse was mentally incompetent at the time of the marriage.
5. The marriage was based on fraud or force.
6. Either spouse was physically incapable of consummating the marriage.
7. The marriage is prohibited by law due to the relationship between the parties. This prohibition relates to the "prohibited degree of consanguity," or blood relationship between the parties. The most common legal relationship is second cousins; the legality of a marriage between first cousins varies from state to state.

Annulments distinguish between void and **voidable marriages** ones. A voidable marriage, like a voidable contract with a minor, may be declared void only at the insistence of one of the parties. Otherwise, either of the parties may elect to stay in the marriage. A void marriage is null from the outset. Nevertheless, a void marriage still requires a court decree of annulment. The effect of an annulment for either a void or a voidable marriage is the same; an annulment decree renders the marriage null from the beginning, or **void *ab initio***, Latin for "from the beginning." Nevertheless, an innocent spouse—that is, the one who is not at fault—may still obtain the financial benefits of marriage, such as the rights to community property, spousal support, child support, and equitable contributions for attorney's fees for litigation expenses.

Divorce By far the most common method of terminating a marriage is through the legal proceeding known as a **divorce**, which acknowledges that the marriage existed. Most states have a no-fault system in which the grounds for the divorce are merely "irreconcilable differences." Some states still require fault and will grant divorces on a showing of grounds, such as desertion, physical or mental cruelty, or adultery. Even in no-fault states, wrongful conduct by one party may become relevant in the court's

voidable marriage
Valid in all legal respects until the union is dissolved by order of the court.

void *ab initio*
Marriages that are void from the inception.

divorce/dissolution
The legal termination of a marriage (or civil union).

CYBER TRIP

Vermont was the first state to permit same-gender unions. On the Internet, go to www.sec.state.vt.us/otherprg/civilunions/civilunions.html.

How are civil unions recorded?

What are the legal consequences of a Vermont civil union?

How are civil unions dissolved in Vermont?

determination of spousal support, custody, or property settlement issues. These issues are usually the points of contention in divorces.

Dissolution of Civil Unions States that have adopted civil unions or domestic partnerships have also instituted procedures for dissolving civil unions and domestic partnerships.

Support Obligations

support
Periodic payments extending over time.

alimony
Court-ordered money paid to support a former spouse after termination of a marriage.

Support, also known as **alimony** or maintenance, for the lesser earning or stay-at-home spouse and any children of the marriage is usually determined by state statute, which enumerates the factors that a divorce court should consider. An award of spousal support means that one party must make payments to the other regularly, usually on a monthly basis. Generally, the numerous statutory factors can encompass not only the behavior of the parties but also the marketable skills, education, and employment histories of the couple. The law's concern is to ensure that a spouse is not left without a means of support to provide for the necessaries of food, clothing, and shelter. In California, courts are directed to consider "the standard of living established during the marriage." (Cal. Fam. Code, §4320).

custody
The legal authority to make decisions concerning a child's interests. Also, the care and control of a thing or person.

prenuptial agreement
An agreement made by parties before marriage that controls certain aspects of the relationship, such as management and ownership of property.

Complicating the issue in child support cases is the fact that any payments are made to the parent who has been awarded **custody** of the minor children. Strictly speaking, child support payments belong to the child, though they are paid to the custodial parent. A custody determination determines the parent with whom the children of the marriage will live and who will care for them on a day-to-day basis, subject to the noncustodial parent's right to visitation. State statutes list numerous factors that a court should consider, such as the wishes of the child and parents, the ease with which the child will be able to adjust with a parent, and the overriding "best interests of the child." Thus, past behavior by the parents is clearly a factor. Custody determinations can take several different forms, such as joint custody arrangements in which the parents take turns in providing the day-to-day care of the children.

The *Marriage of Riddle* case below illustrates the wide berth of factors that a court may consider in determining which parent should have custody of minor children.

Property Division

community property
All property acquired during marriage in a community property state, owned in equal shares.

separate property
One spouse is the exclusive owner.

marital estates (marital property)
The property accumulated by a couple during marriage, called community property in some states.

equitable distribution
Divides the assets acquired during the marriage between the parties.

Property belonging to a couple is subject to "equitable division" by the divorce court, absent a **prenuptial agreement**. Eight states (Arizona, California, Idaho, Louisiana, New Mexico, Nevada, Washington, Wisconsin) have **community property** laws in which each spouse owns a one-half interest in all of the property acquired during the marriage, without regard to which party's funds purchased the community property. Excepted from this pool is **separate property**, which consists of gifts and inheritances received by either of the spouses during the marriage. In a divorce, each party receives one-half of the community property. Other states that do not have community property laws have begun to follow suit by awarding one-third to one-half of the **marital property** to each party in a form of distribution known as **equitable division**.

Often, the parties or a divorce court employ experts to determine the value of the various property items subject to the court's distribution in both community and noncommunity property states. As with custody matters, state statutes guide courts to consider certain factors in ordering a distribution. The *O'Brien v. O'Brien* case below illustrates the developing concept of what constitutes "marital property."

Adoption

adoption
The taking of a child into the family, creating a parent–child relationship where the biological relationship did not exist.

Adoption was unknown to the common law. Orphans usually were institutionalized if they were not taken in by relatives. Informal adoptions existed in the form of apprentices who worked for their masters, earning their room and board. Massachusetts was the first common law jurisdiction to enact an adoption statute in 1851. Adoption is a legal

CASE IN POINT

COURT OPINION

IN RE THE MARRIAGE OF RIDDLE, 500 N.W.2d 718 (IOWA CT. OF APP. 1993)

Dorothy and Michael Riddle were married in August 1986. They have one minor child, Lauren, who was born in January 1987.

Dorothy was born in 1966. At age sixteen, she married Pat Pepples. The marriage lasted only nine months and bore one child, Ashley, in June 1983. Dorothy has sole custody of Ashley. Dorothy married Michael just prior to her sophomore year at Iowa State University. While attending college, Dorothy held a number of part-time jobs. Dorothy has now graduated from Iowa State with a Bachelor of Science degree in nutrition. She is currently employed as the chief clinical dietician at Broadlawns Medical Center in Des Moines and earns a net monthly income of $1560.

Michael was born in 1964. He attends college at Iowa State University and intends to complete his degree in elementary education in about two years. Michael currently works several part-time jobs including assistant coaching duties, handyman work for the Ames School District, and sales for the Fuller Brush Company. His net monthly income is about $1102.

In July 1990, Dorothy filed a petition for dissolution of marriage. In January 1992, the district court awarded temporary physical custody of Lauren to Dorothy.

In August 1992, following a hearing, the district court issued its dissolution decree. The court determined, among other matters, primary physical custody of Lauren should be awarded to Michael. The court ordered Dorothy to pay $351 per month in child support.

Dorothy now appeals. Dorothy contends the district court erred in awarding primary physical custody to Michael. She specifically claims the district court erred in: (1) finding Lauren's long-term best interests were best served by awarding primary physical custody to Michael; (2) separating Lauren from her half-sister, Ashley; and (3) disregarding the recommendation of the independent custodial investigator.

In child custody cases, the best interests of the child is the first and governing consideration. The factors the court considers in awarding custody bear on the "first and governing consideration," the court's determination of what will be in the long-term best interests of the child. The critical issue in determining the best interests of the child is which parent will do better in raising the child. Gender is irrelevant, and neither parent should have a greater burden than the other in attempting to gain custody in a dissolution proceeding.

We agree with the district court's finding that the issue of primary physical custody was a "close call." Both Michael and Dorothy care deeply for Lauren and her welfare. They both clearly offer Lauren a stable environment both emotionally and financially.

On our review, the record supports the finding that the long-term best interests of Lauren would be better served if Michael were the physical custodian. As Dorothy spent considerable time working and completing her degree, Michael became the primary caretaker for Lauren. Michael has done an excellent job as the primary caretaker to Lauren during the first five years of her life. As a coach, Michael takes Lauren to many of his practices and games. At trial, many witnesses testified to the close bond between Michael and Lauren.

We admire Dorothy's diligence in completing her bachelor's degree while helping to raise two children. Dorothy has found a responsible and challenging job which provides her with considerable financial stability. In comparison, we recognize Michael's future plans are not as certain and that his income is less than that of Dorothy's. However, the fact Michael is employed only by several part-time jobs and the fact he has a lower income do not constitute evidence that Michael is unable to offer Lauren stability.

Dorothy asserts she is being "punished" for having assumed the "traditional male duties" of being the family breadwinner. We do not agree. Our decision is based on an examination of which parent had been the child's primary psychological parent and with which parent the child had more closely bonded. Here, the evidence suggests Lauren has consistently demonstrated a greater emotional attachment to her father.

In our decision, we recognize the preference for not separating siblings. Admittedly, Lauren and her half sister, Ashley, are close. However, Michael is not the legal father of Ashley and he has no right to seek physical custody of Ashley in the dissolution. Michael therefore argues it would be unfair to give substantial weight to the preference for keeping siblings together because this gives Dorothy an unfair advantage in the contest for physical care of Lauren.

Here, we find the district court did have a good and compelling reason to separate Lauren and Ashley. Lauren and Michael have a close relationship, and Michael has been the primary caretaker of Lauren throughout her life. There is no evidence that Lauren and Ashley will not be able to continue their close relationship despite the separation. On our review, we find granting Michael primary physical care will better promote the long-range best interests of Lauren.

We remind Michael that liberal visitation rights are in the best interests of the children. Both parents, as joint custodians, are charged with maintaining those interests. Unless visitation with the non-custodial parent will in some way injure the child, it is not to be prohibited.

The costs of this appeal are taxed to Dorothy.

For the reasons stated, we affirm the judgment of the district court.

QUESTIONS ABOUT THE CASE

1. Do you think the outcome of the case was fair?
2. Why do you think the trial court awarded temporary custody to Dorothy, only to give permanent custody to Michael?

CASE IN POINT

COURT OPINION: *O'BRIEN V. O'BRIEN,* 66 N.Y.2d 576, 489 N.E.2d 712, 498 N.Y.S.2d 743 (1985)

Plaintiff and defendant married on April 3, 1971. Later, while plaintiff pursued his medical degree, defendant held several teaching and tutorial positions and contributed her earnings to their joint expenses. Plaintiff was licensed to practice medicine in October 1980. He commenced this action for divorce two months later. At the time of trial, he was a resident in general surgery. The trial court found that defendant had contributed 76% of the parties' income. Finding that plaintiff's medical degree and license are marital property, the court received evidence of its value and ordered a distributive award to defendant.

The court, after considering the lifestyle that plaintiff would enjoy from the enhanced earning potential his medical license would bring and defendant's contributions and efforts toward attainment of it, made a distributive award to her of $188,800, representing 40% of the value of plaintiff's medical license. The court did not award defendant maintenance. Plaintiff appeals.

The New York Equitable Distribution Law contemplates only two classes of property: marital property and separate property. The former, which is subject to equitable distribution, is defined broadly as "all property acquired by either or both spouses during the marriage and before the execution of a separation agreement or the commencement of a matrimonial action, regardless of the form in which title is held." The statute thus recognizes that spouses have an equitable claim to things of value arising out of the marital relationship and classifies them as subject to distribution by focusing on the marital status of the parties at the time of acquisition. Those things acquired during marriage and subject to distribution have been classified as "marital property."

As this case demonstrates, few undertakings during a marriage better qualify as the type of joint effort that the statute's economic partnership theory is intended to address than contributions toward one spouse's acquisition of a professional license. In this case, nearly all of the parties' nine-year marriage was devoted to the acquisition of plaintiff's medical license and defendant played a major role in that project. She worked continuously during the marriage and contributed all of her earnings to their joint effort; she sacrificed her own educational and career opportunities.

A professional license is a valuable property right, reflected in the money, effort and lost opportunity for employment expended in its acquisition, and also in the enhanced earning capacity it affords its holder.

Accordingly, in view of our holding that plaintiff's license to practice medicine is marital property.

QUESTIONS ABOUT THE CASE

1. If you were the plaintiff, what alternatives would you urge instead?
2. What is the difference between a professional license and, say, a fishing license or driver's license?
3. What role might an expert have played in the trial phase of this case?
4. Why do you think the trial court did not award Ms. O'Brien maintenance?
5. What other forms of property could qualify as "marital property" subject to distribution in a divorce?

proceeding in which a court transfers the rights and duties of the parent–child relationship from the natural parents (also known as the birth parents) to the adoptive parents.

Adoption procedures vary greatly among the states. Some require the intervention of an adoption agency, even if the birth parents agree to their child's placement with preselected adoptive parents. Other states permit adoptions without an agency, particularly if the child is related to the adoptive parents. Significant controversy still swirls around adoption involving issues of race, religion, ethnicity, and socioeconomic status. Moreover, gay and lesbian couples are permitted to adopt in a growing number of states, though a few states have enacted statutes that prohibit them from adopting.

The effect of an adoption is both a blessing and a harsh reality. A court adoption decree terminates the parental rights of the birth parents and invests the same rights in the new adoptive parents. The long-term effect of the decree is to give the adoptive parents the right to raise their new child with the values, mores, education, and religion they wish, without regard to the wishes of the birth parents. There are also constitutional dimensions that attach to becoming a parent. The United States Supreme Court has repeatedly held that parents have a fundamental due process right to decide on the educational and religious upbringing of their children. At the same time, an adoption carries with it the parental duty to care and support their new child.

The adoption process can be trying, as it involves not only the court system but also an adoption agency and the birth parents, if available. In most cases, the

CASE IN POINT

ABOUT PRENUPTIAL AGREEMENTS

Before they married, movie stars Michael Douglas and Catherine Zeta-Jones entered into a detailed prenuptial agreement. Douglas had just paid $40 million as a settlement to his ex-wife, Diandra Luker.

Although most people do not have multimillion-dollar fortunes, they do have property and other assets that could be at risk when they enter into a committed relationship. A prenuptial agreement may help secure these assets. In a prenuptial agreement, also known as an ante-nuptial agreement, a couple sets out their rights in relation to any property, income, and other assets purchased together or that they have bought into a relationship. A prenuptial agreement allows the parties to protect their separate property and other assets.

The primary purpose of a prenuptial agreement frequently is to limit the potential claims on the wealth of one of the parties to the marriage. This limit normally appears necessary when one party brings considerable wealth to the relationship or perhaps one or more of the parties has been married before and has family that might benefit from a stepparents' wealth.

Nevertheless, prenuptial agreements have been successfully challenged. Ivana Trump, a former member of the Czechoslovakian Olympic ski team, was married to Donald Trump from 1977 to 1991. During their hotly contested divorce, the divorce court set aside the prenuptial agreement between the couple. The divorce was finally settled, and the court ordered the results sealed. Rumor has it that Ivana Trump received $20 million, the family estate in Connecticut, and a $5 million housing allowance, among other items. According to sources, including A&E Television Network, Ivana Trump has since doubled her fortune through shrewd business moves.

QUESTIONS ABOUT THE CASE

1. On what grounds do you think that prenuptial agreements should not be enforced?
2. What types of safeguards should exist when couples enter into a prenuptial agreement?
3. How would you respond to a marriage proposal coupled with a request to enter into a prenuptial agreement?

adoptive parents start with the filing of a petition for adoption in family or probate court. For the court to approve the adoption, the state social services agency or a private agency completes a home study, in which a trained social worker reports in detail on the suitability of the adoptive parents' home, lifestyle, finances, and any other relevant matters. The birth parents rarely contest the adoption, and their consent, if available, must appear on the court record. With orphans, consent is not necessary.

Because of the documentation and process required for an adoption, final hearings before the court become mere formalities and generally take only a few minutes. With ritual-like demeanors, judges usually rely on the social service agency's recommendation and issue an adoption decree. For many, that decree acts as if it were a birth certificate.

Miscellaneous Family Law Matters

Guardianships

A **guardian** is a person who has the legal authority (and the corresponding duty) to care for the personal and property interests of another person, called a **ward**. A person usually gains **guardianship** because the ward is incapable of caring for his or her own interests due to infancy, incapacity, or disability. Most states laws provide that the parents of a minor child are the legal guardians of that child and that the parents can designate who shall become the child's legal guardian in the event of their death. This designation often appears in the parents' will.

Family and probate courts have the power to appoint a guardian for an individual in need of special protection. A guardian with responsibility for both the personal well-being and the financial interests of the ward is a general guardian. A person may also be appointed as a special guardian, with limited powers over the interests of the ward. A special guardian may, for example, be given the legal right to determine the disposition of the ward's property without any authority over the ward's person. In New Mexico, for instance, a form of guardianship known as a kinship-guardianship permits close relatives to assist children

guardian
A court-appointed person to care for a ward.

ward
A person, usually a minor, under the care of a court-appointed guardian.

guardianship
A legal relationship created by a court between a guardian and ward, either a minor child or an incapacitated adult. The guardian has a legal right and duty to care for the ward, which may involve making personal decisions on his or her behalf, managing property, or both.

CASE IN POINT

COURT OPINION: *ADOPTIONS OF B.L.V.B. AND E.L.V.B.*, 160 VT. 368; 628 A.2d 1271 (1993)

Appellants are two women, Jane and Deborah, who have lived together in a committed, monogamous relationship since 1986. Together, they made the decision to have and raise children, and together, they consulted various sources to determine the best method for them to achieve their goal of starting a family. On November 2, 1988, Jane gave birth to a son, B.L.V.B., after being impregnated with the sperm of an anonymous donor. On August 27, 1992, after being impregnated with sperm from the same donor, she gave birth to a second son, E.L.V.B. Deborah assisted the midwife at both births, and she has been equally responsible for raising and parenting the children since their births.

Appellants sought legal recognition of their existing status as co-parents, and asked the probate court to allow Deborah to legally adopt the children, while leaving Jane's parental rights intact. The adoption petitions were uncontested. The Department of Social and Rehabilitation Services conducted a home study, determined the adoptions were in the best interests of the children, and recommended that they be allowed. A clinical and school psychologist who had evaluated the family testified that it was essential for the children to be assured of a continuing relationship with Deborah, and recommended that the adoptions be allowed for the psychological and emotional protection of the children.

Despite the lack of opposition, the probate court denied the adoptions, declining to reach whether the adoptions were in the best interests of the children because the proposed adoptive mother "does not satisfy the statutory prerequisite to adoption."

Appellants contend that the statutory language does not prohibit the adoptions, and that such a result is inconsistent with the best interests of the children and the public policy of this state. We agree.

In interpreting Vermont's adoption statutes, we are mindful that the state's primary concern is to promote the welfare of children.

When the statute is read as a whole, we see that its general purpose is to clarify and protect the legal rights of the adopted person at the time the adoption is complete, not to proscribe adoptions by certain combinations of individuals.

When social mores change, governing statutes must be interpreted to allow for those changes in a manner that does not frustrate the purposes behind their enactment. To deny the children of same-sex partners, as a class, the security of a legally recognized relationship with their second parent serves no legitimate state interest.

Today a child who receives proper nutrition, adequate schooling and supportive sustaining shelter is among the fortunate, whatever the source. A child who also receives the love and nurture of even a single parent can be counted among the blessed. Here this Court finds a child who has all of the above benefits and two adults dedicated to his welfare, secure in their loving partnership, and determined to raise him to the very best of their considerable abilities. There is no reason in law, logic or social philosophy to obstruct such a favorable situation.

By allowing same-sex adoptions, we are furthering the purposes of the statute as was originally intended by allowing the children of such unions the benefits and security of a legal relationship with their de facto second parents.

Our paramount concern should be with the effect of our laws on the reality of children's lives. It is not the courts that have engendered the diverse composition of today's families.

We are not called upon to approve or disapprove of the relationship between the appellants. Whether we do or not, the fact remains that Deborah has acted as a parent of B.L.V.B. and E.L.V.B. from the moment they were born. To deny legal protection of their relationship, as a matter of law, is inconsistent with the children's best interests and therefore with the public policy of this state, as expressed in our statutes affecting children.

Judgment is entered granting the petitions for adoption.

QUESTIONS ABOUT THE CASE

1. Why did the Court say that the case did not involve approval or disapproval of the relationship between the two women?
2. What did the Court mean when it said that the adoption served the "paramount concern"?
3. What legal interests were served or not served if the adoption were disallowed?
4. Do you agree with the Court?

whose parents are unavailable. Thus, a kinship-guardian, such as a grandparent, may receive limited oversight authority to register children in school or make health care decisions on the children's behalf. A guardian appointed to represent the interests of a person with respect to a legal proceeding in court is a guardian *ad litem.*

Guardians *ad litem* are often appointed in divorce cases to represent the interests of minor children. The kinds of people appointed as guardian *ad litem* vary by state, ranging from volunteers to social workers to volunteer attorneys. The two divorcing parents are usually responsible for paying the fees of the guardian *ad litem,* though the guardian *ad litem* is not responsible to them at all. The guardian *ad litem*'s only job is to represent the minor children's best interests in court.

Guardians *ad litem* are also appointed in cases in which there has been an allegation of abuse, neglect, or dependency. In these situations, the guardian *ad litem* is charged to represent the best interest of the minor child, which may differ from the position of the state or government agency, as well as the interests of the parent or guardian.

Conservatorship

Related to guardians are conservators, who are also appointed by a court. Their responsibility differs in that conservators are responsible for the management of the ward's assets and finances, not day-to-day decisions or caretaking. In some jurisdictions, a **conservatorship** may be referred to as a "guardianship of the estate."

conservatorship
The court appointment of a person who manages the financial and day-to-day affairs of an incapacitated adult.

There are many circumstances in which a person is still able to live an independent life but may require assistance with his or her assets due to failing health or disability. Thus, it is not unusual for a petition to be made for the appointment of a conservator, even if the allegedly incapacitated person does not require a guardian.

The procedure for the creation of a conservatorship and the appointment of a conservator varies to some degree among the states. Typically, the person seeking the appointment of a conservator files a petition with the family or probate court in which the proposed ward resides. The petitioner is often a relative, an administrator for a nursing home or health care facility, or other interested person. A petition is ordinarily accompanied by medical affidavits or other sworn statements that evidence the person's incapacity, and it either identifies the person or persons who desire to be named conservator or requests the appointment of a conservator.

At times, the court may arrange for an independent evaluation of the proposed ward, which may involve the appointment of a guardian *ad litem,* who provides an independent report to the court on the behalf of the proposed ward. If appointed, the guardian *ad litem* will meet with the proposed ward to give advice on his or her legal rights and solicit his or her wishes, if any. The guardian *ad litem* may also examine the petitioner, health care providers, and other interested individuals, such as family, to complete the report requested by the court.

If the proposed ward contests the petition, a court hearing ensues in which counsel may be appointed to represent the proposed ward. If a conservator is appointed, the judge will issue the conservator a court order, often called a "letter of authority," which represents the legal authority of the conservator to act on behalf of the ward.

A conservator ordinarily receives compensation, subject to court oversight, for performing the duties for the estate. The compensation often is charged on an hourly basis and paid by the estate of the legally incapacitated person. If an attorney is appointed, the duties of a paralegal will entail recordkeeping and preparation of documents to be filed with the court periodically, usually annually.

Conservatorships have created some controversy. Although the conservator is supposedly under court supervision, an unscrupulous person may submit falsified records and accounts while absconding with or mismanaging the ward's assets. Moreover, a conservatorship may go on for years, as in the case of an elderly person, without clear resolution or direction. Many people fear the consequences of becoming a ward to a court-appointed conservator as a sign of vulnerability and dependency.

Many advocates maintain that a conservatorship would be unnecessary with sufficient estate planning. In addition to a will or trust, paralegals are often called upon to prepare a general durable power of attorney, which appoints a trusted individual to manage the client's personal affairs in the event of incapacity. A more limited power of attorney could also protect a client's assets in the manner proscribed by the client. To many, this option is preferable to leaving the management of assets to the discretion of a conservator or court. Figure 8.6 provides an example of a durable power of attorney.

FIGURE 8.6 Example of a Durable Power of Attorney

General Durable Power of Attorney
Effective Upon Execution

I, [NAME], a resident of [ADDRESS. COUNTY, STATE]; Social Security Number [NUMBER] designate [NAME], presently residing at [ADDRESS], as my attorney in fact (referred to as "the Agent") on the following terms and conditions:

1. Authority to Act. The Agent is authorized to act for me under this Power of Attorney and shall exercise all powers in my best interests and for my welfare.
2. Powers of Agent. The Agent shall have the full power and authority to manage and conduct all of my affairs, and to exercise my legal rights and powers, including those rights and powers that I may acquire in the future, including the following:
   a. Collect and Manage. To collect, hold, maintain, improve, invest, lease, or otherwise manage any or all of my real or personal property or any interest therein;
   b. Buy and Sell. To purchase, sell, mortgage, grant options, or otherwise deal in any way in any real property or personal property, tangible or intangible, or any interest therein, upon such terms as the Agent considers proper, including the power to buy United States Treasury Bonds that may be redeemed at par to pay federal estate tax and to sell or transfer Treasury securities;
   c. Borrow. To borrow money, to execute promissory notes therefor, and to secure any obligation by mortgage or pledge;
   d. Business and Banking. To conduct and participate in any kind of lawful business of any nature or kind, including the right to sign partnership agreements, continue, reorganize, merge, consolidate, recapitalize, close, liquidate, sell, or dissolve any business and to vote stock, including the exercise of any stock options and the carrying out of any buy sell agreement; to receive and endorse checks and other negotiable paper, deposit and withdraw funds (by check or withdrawal slips) that I now have on deposit or to which I may be entitled in the future in or from any bank, savings and loan, or other institution;
   e. Tax Returns and Reports. To prepare, sign, and file separate or joint income, gift, and other tax returns and other governmental reports and documents; to consent to any gift; to file any claim for tax refund; and to represent me in all matters before the Internal Revenue Service;
   f. Safe Deposit Boxes. To have access to any safety deposit box registered in my name alone or jointly with others, and to remove any property or papers located therein;
   g. Proxy Rights. To act as my agent or proxy for any stocks, bonds, shares, or other investments, rights, or interests I may now or hereafter hold;
   h. Legal and Administrative Proceedings. To engage in any administrative or legal proceedings or lawsuits in connection with any matter herein;
   i. Transfers in Trust. To transfer any interest I may have in property, whether real or personal, tangible or intangible, to the trustee of any trust that I have created for my benefit;
   j. Delegation of Authority. To engage and dismiss agents, counsel, and employees, in connection with any matter, upon such terms as my agent determines;
   k. Restrictions on Agent's Powers. Regardless of the above statements, my agent (1) cannot execute a will, a codicil, or any will substitute on my behalf; (2) cannot change the beneficiary on any life insurance policy that I own; (3) cannot make gifts on my behalf; and (4) may not exercise any powers that would cause assets of mine to be considered taxable to my agent or to my agent's estate for purposes of any income, estate, or inheritance tax, and (5) cannot contravene any medical power of attorney I have executed whether prior or subsequent to the execution of this Power of Attorney.
3. Durability. This durable Power of Attorney shall be irrevocable until the trust corpus is surrendered by the trustees, shall not be affected by my death or disability except as provided by law, and shall continue in effect after the surrender of the trust corpus until my death or until revoked by me in writing.
4. Reliance by Third Parties. Third parties may rely upon the representations of the Agent as to all matters regarding powers granted to the Agent. No person who acts in reliance on the representations of the Agent or the authority granted under this Power of Attorney shall incur any liability to me or to my estate for permitting the Agent to exercise any power prior to actual knowledge that the Power of Attorney has been revoked or terminated by operation of law or otherwise.
5. Indemnification of Agent. No agent named or substituted in this power shall incur any liability to me for acting or refraining from acting under this power, except for such agent's own misconduct or negligence.
6. Original Counterparts. Photocopies of this signed Power of Attorney shall be treated as original counterparts.
7. Revocation. I hereby revoke any previous Power of Attorney that I may have given to deal with my property and affairs as set forth herein.

Contd...

8. Compensation. The Agent shall be reimbursed for reasonable expenses incurred while acting as Agent and may receive reasonable compensation for acting as Agent.

   Substitute Agent. If [NAME] is, at any time, unable or unwilling to act, I then appoint [NAME], presently residing at [ADDRESS] as my Agent.

Dated: [DATE]

____

NAME
Signed in the presence of:

____

Witness

____

Witness
Subscribed and sworn to before me on [DATE]:

____

Notary Public, [COUNTY, STATE]
My commission expires on ____________.

Clients might execute a general power of attorney so that the appointed person may act for them while they are indisposed, away on business, or on vacation. However, that power of attorney is not valid if the client becomes infirm or incapacitated. A durable power of attorney is effective even after the client has become infirm or incapacitated, so that an appointed person may continue to act on his or her behalf. This person is usually a close relative or friend, who may very well become the executor of the client's estate.

The example in Figure 8.6 is by no means the only format for a durable power of attorney. Keep in mind that these devices are flexible and should be regarded as tools for achieving the client's objective. Here, the objective is to protect the client and his or her assets. Thus, the durable power of attorney accomplishes two objectives: First, it transfers the legal authority of the client to another person to act on the client's behalf. Second, and more important, it delegates the authority to make any needed decisions on the client's behalf. This significant feature gives the person receiving this authority from the client the legal authority and power to make property transfers and engage in contracts on behalf of the client. The document provisions are flexible. Well-educated and trained paralegals often draft these documents under the general instruction of their supervising attorneys.

A durable power of attorney can be worded in any fashion to achieve a specific objective with regard to all of the client's assets or just the enumerated ones. The example in Figure 8.6 could, if needed, state with specificity that the authority delegated would be confined to, say, the sale of only certain assets or agree to only a specified contract. The document could also become effective upon execution—that is, immediately upon signing, as in the case of this example—or only at the onset of the client's inability to manage his or her affairs, or other contingencies.

Summary

This chapter covers advanced topics in legal specialties and provides detailed instruction in areas that built on the more basic subjects of civil litigation, crimes and criminal procedure, torts, and property. The law of wills and contracts covers the transfer or exchange of various types of property.

In family law, the creation and termination of relationships, whether with children or spouses, involves not only these relationships but also the agreements that can affect the right to support and receive property. The legal devices of guardianship and conservatorship are designed to put someone in charge of another's life if that person is unable to manage his or her own affairs and specifically property. Overlaying all of this detail is the way in which disputes over property, contracts, and family matters are litigated in our court system. Court cases instruct us as to the various points of law and the legal consequences that flow from certain actions, such that decisions become more understandable because of the knowledge acquired from the study of civil litigation.

From here, we will be entering a new phase of study: the development of professional skills for use in virtually any legal office. In its purest form, the work engaged in by legal professionals consists ultimately of communication skills and using them effectively to communicate with clients, the courts, and others within the legal environment.

Key Terms

Administration
Administrator
Adoption
Alimony
Annulment
Beneficiary
Capacity
Civil union
Community property
Conservatorship
Constructive delivery
Custody
Decedent
Delivery (gift)
Divorce/dissolution
Domestic partnership
Donative intent
Donee
Donor
Elective share
Equitable distribution
Escheat
Estate
Estate planning
Family law
Fiduciary
Gift
Guardian
Guardianship
Heirs
In rem jurisdiction
Intestate
Intestate succession
Letter of administration
Letter testamentary
Living will
Marital estates (marital property)
Marriage
Marshal
Operation of law
Prenuptial agreement
Probate
Probate Court
Probate property
Residuary clause
Separate property
Settlor
Support
Testamentary gift
Testate
Testator/testatrix
Trust
Trustee
Void *ab initio*
Voidable marriage
Ward
Will

Review Questions

1. What is the difference between an heir and a beneficiary?
2. Why must a will be in writing?
3. What does it mean to be testate?
4. Name four forms of nonprobate property.
5. What difference is there between a holographic will and an entirely handwritten will that complies with all of the requirements for a valid will?

6. What is the difference between a will and a trust?
7. Identify the difference between an annulment and a divorce.
8. What is spousal support?
9. What is the difference between a guardian and a conservator?
10. What is a home study?

Exercises

1. Find the name of the court in your state that probates wills. Where is it located? What functions might that court have other than probating estates? Collect as many court forms and self-help brochures as are available.
2. Look up the relevant statutes in your state to determine how marital property is distributed in a divorce.
3. Using the example of a durable power of attorney, try to draft a living will or health care proxy. Check your draft against any you may find on the Internet.
4. Determine the adoption process in your state. Are there private or state-run adoption agencies? Is a home study necessary all the time?
5. Draft a will for yourself.

Discussion Questions

1. Harriet Hobbs died this morning intestate in a noncommunity property state. Identify as probate or nonprobate the following assets:
   a. Gift of $1,000 to her unrelated neighbor, made by giving the neighbor the key to her desk drawer where the money, and only the money, was kept in the presence of witnesses.
   b. Harriet's bank account jointly held with her brother.
   c. Harriet's home, which had deeded to her and her surviving husband Todd as married persons with the right of survivorship.
   d. Her personal belongings.
   e. The proceeds of her life insurance policy.
   f. Her cottage in New Hampshire, which she solely inherited last year from her father.
   g. Her Volkswagen Rabbit, owned with her sister without designation as to type of ownership.
   h. The computer she bought from Bradlee's with her own cash, right after she had had a fight with Todd, who didn't want her to buy one.
   i. An inexpensive stereo set that everyone knew she wanted her old college roommate (unrelated) to have.
   j. Her cat Kokomo.
2. Do you agree or disagree with the result in the *O'Brien v. O'Brien* case? Why?
3. Do you think that an adopted person has the right to find the identity of his or her birth parents? Do you think parents who put their children up for adoption have the right to remain anonymous?
4. What types of assurances could be built into a conservatorship to ensure honesty?
5. To what extent should the state regulate marriage? Since cohabitation is so common, what is left for the state to regulate?

PORTFOLIO ASSIGNMENT

In her will, Craig left a piece of property in New Hampshire. Because Craig is a Massachusetts resident, a Massachusetts probate court has almost exclusive jurisdiction to probate her will, particularly for the assets in Massachusetts. What about the three acres in New Hampshire she left to her sister Mia though? That property is outside the jurisdiction of a Massachusetts probate court.

The answer to this situation is clear and settled, complete with time-honored legal procedures for each state. At this point, you should be able to think through the process that a legal professional in New Hampshire and in Massachusetts must take. The following questions are clues to how Craig's New Hampshire property should be handled. Write a memorandum about Craig's estate for your supervising attorney in which you answer the following questions.

1. What type of proceeding occurs in the Massachusetts Probate Court? *In rem*, or in personnam? Explain.
2. What authorizes the executor to carry out Craig's wishes as expressed in her will?
3. What do the legal professionals ask of the Probate Court in the Massachusetts proceeding?
4. What effect does the Constitution's full faith and credit clause have in New Hampshire?
5. What court would have jurisdiction over Craig's New Hampshire property?
6. How would a probate practitioner proceed on behalf of Craig's estate in a New Hampshire probate court?

Chapter 9

Legal Specialties: Business Matters

CHAPTER OBJECTIVES

Upon completion of this chapter, students will have acquired specialized knowledge in the following areas:

- The history of contract law.
- Elements of a contract.
- The Statute of Frauds.
- Remedies and damages in contract law.
- Agency law.
- Business organizations.
- Current issues for the modern corporation.

In this chapter you will be venturing into two important business-related topics that rank high among the legal specialties of the legal profession. The laws as they affect business are essential to our economic system and occupy a central place in legal practice. Through the study of contracts, you will see how complex business transactions occur. We will explore the mechanics of how to accomplish more complex transfers of property—through contract—as both a legal and a practical matter. We will then delve into the types of business entities, such as partnerships and corporations, created by laws that allow them to own and transfer property. Our examination also will cover how the law allows these entities to come into being and the factors involved in deciding which type of entity to use. As part of this discussion, we will look at the benefits and shortcomings of most common business entities, comparing them side by side. You will see that the choice of business entity can help the business succeed and grow. For these reasons, among many others, business matters.

CONTRACT LAW FOR THE PROFESSIONAL PARALEGAL

Having progressed thus far, you have acquired a significant background in some of the important aspects of both civil litigation and property law to proceed into one of the more important of legal specialties: contract law. We all have a general familiarity

contract
A legally binding agreement between two or more parties.

with the idea of a **contract**. Contracts are agreements for an exchange of all types of property, including money, services, or other consideration. Moreover, a properly executed contract is enforceable in a court of law. Experienced businesspeople, companies, and most consumers are aware that business deals, property purchases, credit cards, and our everyday purchases are legally enforceable in civil actions. Most people take contract law for granted. Yet our lives are surrounded by contract law. In property law, purchase and sales agreements for real estate involves an enforceable contract. As you will see, principles of contract law make the commercial world go round.

HISTORICAL BACKGROUND FOR CONTRACT LAW

assumpsit
Common law writ for contracts.

The law of contracts has a long and storied history. Early on, the common law recognized a cause of action or claim for relief for contracts as it did in other areas of the law, by a writ. The writ of ***assumpsit*** (Latin for "she has undertaken") authorized an action for the recovery of damages by reason of the breach or nonperformance of a contract. Surprising to many, the writ of *assumpsit* came after the writ for trespass on the case (early tort). Because of the common law's preoccupation with property, the notion of enforcing an obligation or undertaking was still foreign to thirteenth century England. Almost 300 years later, the courts began to recognize, in certain circumstances, promises that were supported by consideration—that is, a promise made in exchange for money or other property.

CYBER TRIP

In Chapter 2, we covered various forms of jurisprudence—that is, legal theory—including the school of thought known as "law and economics." That theory urges the use of economic theory to make laws and decide cases so that the laws act as incentives or disincentives for certain behaviors. One of the most approachable explanations of law and economics is that provided by Professor David D. Friedman. Using an Internet search engine, find his Concise Encyclopedia (one-page) explanation of law and economics. How does his explanation support the historical development of contract laws?

With the arrival of the Industrial Revolution in the late eighteenth century, legislatures and courts began to understand the need for the efficient enforcement of contracts to encourage the flow of commerce. With the resulting increased economic activity occurring in England, the common law approach, which centered on property law principles, proved inadequate. Sorely lacking were any legal mechanisms in the courts to enforce obligations expressed in contracts. The first vestiges of the common law system to give way were the hyper-technical and overly formal common law pleading system that made it difficult for parties to plead their cases in court. Claims that might be acceptable to the evolving court were often out of step with any of the established ancient writ system that had persisted since feudal times.

In the United States, the movement toward a more streamlined system of court procedures resulted in code pleading and then the notice pleading system now used in modern court systems, both state and federal. Only then did contract principles develop and expand so that courts would recognize reciprocal promises as the essence of an enforceable agreement on which businesses could rely. You can imagine the difficulty that businesses and commerce in general would encounter if the agreements extending credit to a buyer for the sale and delivery of goods or services could not be enforced in court. The buyer's promise, if unenforceable, would mean nothing, and the seller of goods or provider of services would be left with nothing but an empty promise. This situation was bad for business.

A unique problem faced by the growing, industrialized America was the great variation in contract laws among the several states. Business transactions that traversed state lines or involved multistate parties became subject to a confusing mixture of state contract laws, leading to uncertainty. That uncertainty in turn acted as a barrier to the growth of commerce. Fearing that business deals with parties from another state would go unenforced in that state, many businesses preferred to stay within their own state's borders. This limit was also bad for business and stifled the nation's economic growth.

If you think about it, laws that govern business transactions create a framework of understanding and expectations, so that the parties can conduct business with the confidence that the business deals into which they enter may be enforced easily. Life in the United States for most people would be very different without at least one credit card. Little do these people realize that the use of credit cards did not become widespread until the past 30 years or so. Holding the usage back was the lack of laws that permitted banks to issue enforceable credit agreements in the form of "revolving credit accounts," which we know today as credit card accounts.

With the aid of the Internet and networked computers, modern credit cards command our lives to an extent unimagined before. Rental cars, ATMs, and even routine supermarket purchases require us to possess a credit card. This reality has resulted from developments in not only contract law but also the laws that regulate banks. The law continues to develop to protect a worldwide financial system against fraud, identity theft, and other threats to the security and stability of consumer business transactions. From this example alone, we can see that laws that protect and enforce business transactions can stimulate and encourage economic activity.

In the early 1940s, the American Law Institute and the American Bar Association began a decade-long project to establish uniform laws for the country. As we observed in previous chapters, uniform and model laws have attempted to unite the vast array of differing state laws. The Model Penal Code and the Uniform Probate Code are examples that we have covered. The need for uniform laws was especially acute for commerce; otherwise, contract enforcement would remain uncertain and confusing. Businesses transactions on a national level were too unwieldy and difficult to manage. A new system of uniform laws that permitted streamlined transactions and business deals nationally gave rise to the most successful of the uniform laws, the **Uniform Commercial Code (UCC)**.

Uniform Commercial Code (UCC)
Model laws drafted by the National Conference of Commissioners for governing commercial transactions.

The UCC has been adopted by every state and possession of the United States, with only minor variations. Keep in mind that the UCC does not rise to the level of a federal law. Nevertheless, its adoption by all of the states has greatly enhanced the growth of commerce without the encumbering need to worry about state borders. Legal professionals must still research any variations that may exist in other states' adoption of the UCC when their clients do business across state lines. However, UCC experts, usually practitioners of commercial law, are frequently aware of the several variations that exist among the states.

The UCC consists of a comprehensive scheme of ten articles, each covering the various areas of commercial and business activities. Much of its coverage spans the breadth of different types of transactions, enabling businesses to enter into many different financial arrangements that are enforceable in court. To understand its provisions requires a basic familiarity with business concerns, such as banking, credit, investments, shipping, secured transactions, and, most significantly, the sale of goods. Its provisions are detailed and numerous. Most law schools require students to take a year-long course in contracts and then another year-long course in the UCC, usually during their second year. For our purposes here, the important thing to remember is that the UCC, and the contract law that it encompasses, express the rules that make up a contract, its provisions, and the legal consequences that flow from it. The flow chart in Figure 9.1 helps to determine whether the UCC applies to certain transactions.

RESEARCH THIS

Find the codification of the UCC in your state's statutes. When was the UCC adopted in your state? What is the citation for warranties in the sale of goods?

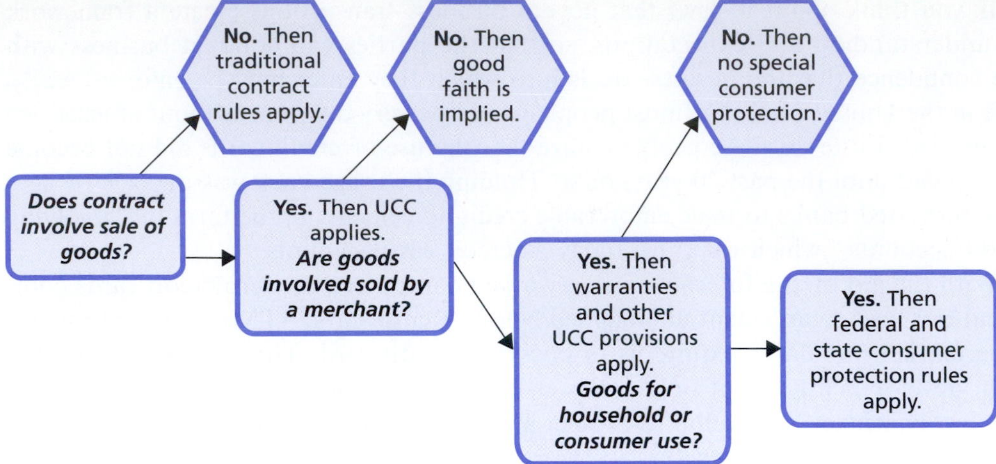

FIGURE 9.1
Determination of Whether UCC Applies

TRADITIONAL CONTRACT LAW

Similar to other areas of modern law, a contract exists upon the convergence of certain elements, namely, voluntary acts by the parties. When these elements exist, a contract, together with its terms, becomes enforceable against the parties to it and to no others. You may want to think of the terms of an enforceable contract as a form of law that lies between the parties to a contract and those parties alone. For instance, an enforceable contract for the sale and delivery of lumber to a construction site imposes a legal obligation on the buyer to pay for the goods and a coextensive legal obligation for the delivery of the specified goods by the seller.

These contract terms and the legal obligations, enforceable in court, apply only to the parties to the contract and no one else. Although this point may appear obvious, the consequence of the voluntary act of entering into a contract can have significant legal repercussions. For that reason, contract law requires certain formalities before a contract can be said to exist. Remember that contracts are made for the exchange of goods and services. In sharp contrast to *inter vivos* gifts and wills, the elements necessary for the formation of an enforceable contract are more numerous and involved. In short, a contract is formed if there exists:

- An offer,
- An acceptance, and
- Consideration.

In addition, a valid and enforceable contract takes into account important social policy considerations. Rules regarding who may enter into contracts and the types of contracts that may be legally enforced are equally important and may arise as defenses to an action for breach of contract. These rules cover:

- Competent parties,
- Legal subject matter, and
- Genuine assent to ensure against fraud, mistake, duress, or undue influence.

ELEMENTS OF A CONTRACT

The Offer

offer
A promise made by the offeror to do (or not to do) something provided that the offeree, by accepting, promises or does something in exchange.

An **offer** is a voluntary undertaking, usually in the form of a promise. That promise may be to buy or sell goods or services, to pay money, to render services, or even to forebear. An offer establishes the initial terms of a proposed contract. To constitute an offer, the person making the offer, the **offeror**, must express the initial terms with sufficient clarity and detail so that the party hearing the offer knows that a contract is contemplated. Thus, for an offer to be effective, it should communicate with sufficient reference to (1) the parties, (2) the subject matter of the proposed contract, (3) the consideration, and (4) the time in which the contract may be performed. Advertisements in newspapers, magazines, and other media outlets would not qualify under this definition. Although advertisements, particularly those for a discount or special sales event, appear to offer goods and services subject to our acceptance, they instead are deemed invitations to deal.

offeror
The person making the offer to another party.

Traditionally courts held that an offer had to conform to these requirements to be effective, which is still the case for most complex transactions and those involving the sale of real property. However, in more routine business dealings involving the sale of goods, the advent of the UCC modified the common law and made offers more flexible. Similar to statutes that abrogated common law immunities in family law, the UCC similarly modifies the common law of contracts. The UCC permits some required aspects of an offer to remain unstated, as long as there is a reasonable understanding that those aspects exist within the context of the dealings. For example, an offer to sell perishable produce that omits the time for performance is nonetheless a valid offer, because a reasonable understanding would assume performance within a short period of time before spoilage could occur.

Thus, custom and practice that usually govern a contract for such goods would be understood. However, a communication of intent without an important aspect of an offer, such as sales price, may not be considered an offer but rather the intent to receive offers, or an invitation for offers. If a friend or acquaintance expressed a desire to sell her used MP3 player and asked what price you would pay, it would not constitute an offer but rather an intention to solicit offers. The difference can be crucial. If an offer exists, a contract may be formed at the moment the offer has been accepted.

Acceptance

When a valid offer has been communicated to an **offeree**, the UCC specifies that the offeror's notification of an **acceptance** means a contract has formed. An acceptance may consist of a simple "I accept" or a sufficient communication that mirrors the offer. The test for the legal sufficiency of an acceptance is the **mirror image rule**, which states the simple requirement for legally valid acceptances. The offeree accepts the offer if the acceptance encompasses every aspect of the offer, without varying or adding to any of the offer's terms. A response to an offer that varies or adds terms does not constitute an acceptance but instead a **counteroffer**. In that case, the original offeree may respond with an acceptance that mirrors the counteroffer or make another counteroffer. If the acceptance mirrors the offer, a contract is formed when it is received by the offeree.

offeree
The person to whom the offer is made.

acceptance
The offeree's clear manifestation of agreement to the exact terms of the offer in the manner specified in the offer.

mirror image rule
A requirement that the acceptance of an offer must exactly match the terms of the original offer.

For its part, the UCC has modified the mirror image rule, simplifying and streamlining the common law. In transactions involving merchants and the sale of goods, an acceptance that does not match the terms of the offer is nonetheless effective as long as the material terms are agreed upon. Still, a legally recognized acceptance, which is essential to the formation of a contract, must accept the essential terms of the offer to be effective. As the time-honored saying goes, there must be a "meeting of the minds." More commonly, this meeting is known as **mutual assent**, which indicates both parties have agreed to the essential terms of the deal.

counteroffer
A refusal to accept the stated terms of an offer by proposing alternate terms.

mutual assent
Concurrence by both parties to all terms.

The case below illustrates how the interactions of the parties in making offers and acceptances combine to form an enforceable contract. As you read this case, consider the court's concern for the policy implications of its decision.

In the *Schreiber v. Olan Mills* case, the court referred to a "bargained-for-exchange ('consideration')" in determining whether a contract existed between the parties as a matter of law. After our discussion on offers, counteroffers, and acceptances progresses, you should be able to see that a contract can frequently involve bargaining. If

CASE IN POINT

COURT OPINION

SCHREIBER V. OLAN MILLS, 426 PA. SUPER. 537, 627 A.2d 806 (PA. SUPER. 1993)

The defendant, a Tennessee-based corporation, operates a nationwide chain of family portrait studios. In securing business, the defendant relies heavily upon "telemarketing," This practice of soliciting customers, because of the compelling quality of the telephone as a desirable medium for disseminating information, has spawned a rapidly growing billion dollar industry which includes "telemarketing," phone surveying and soliciting by phone.

Instantly, a representative of the defendant phoned the plaintiff on November 29, 1989, the result of which prompted the following letter:

> Mrs. Linda Borelli
> Olan Mills
> 547 Clairton Blvd.
> Pittsburgh, Pa. 15236
> Dear telemarketer:
>
> Today, you called us attempting to sell a product or a service. We have no interest in the product or service that you are selling. Please don't call us again. Please remove us from your telemarketing list and notify the provider of the list to also remove our name and number since we do not appreciate receiving telemarketing phone calls.
>
> We rely on the availability of our phone lines which have been installed for our convenience and not for the convenience of telemarketers. We pay for these phone lines and instruments. You do not. Please don't tie up our phone lines.
>
> Should we receive any more phone calls from you or from anyone connected with your firm of a telemarketing nature, we will consider that you have entered into a contract with us for our listening services and that you have made those calls to us and expect us to listen to your message on a "for hire" basis.
>
> If we receive any additional telemarketing phone calls from you, you will be invoiced in accordance with our rates which are $100.00 per hour or fraction thereof with a $100.00 minimum charge. Payment will be due on a net seven (7) day basis.
>
> Late payment charge of 1-1/2% per month or fraction thereof on the unpaid balance subject to a minimum late charge of $9.00 per invoice per month or fraction thereof will be billed if payment is not made as outlined above. This is an annual percentage rate of 18%. In addition, should it become necessary for us to institute collection activities, all costs in connection therewith including, but not limited to, attorney fees will also be due and collectible.

Thereafter, two phone contacts caused the plaintiff to bill the defendant for services, which, when not paid, resulted in the institution of a suit to collect $479.00 in fees. Preliminary objections were filed by the defendant arguing that the facts alleged in the complaint did not show an intent, on the part of either party or their representative, to enter into a contract.

The trial court concluded from a review of the record and law that the parties did not enter into a contract for the purchase of the plaintiff's "listening services." Not only did the court find that there was "no true and actual meeting of the minds," but, under the circumstances, there was no "'ordinary course of dealing and the common understanding of men [and women] showing a mutual intention to contract.'" This appeal followed.

The sole issue we need to concern ourselves with, in disposing of the case at bar, is whether a binding contract was effectuated between the parties so as to obligate the defendant to pay the plaintiff for his "listening-for-hire" services.

The elemental aspects necessary to give rise to an enforceable contract are "offer," "acceptance," "consideration" or "mutual meeting of the minds." Further, when seeking to enforce an agreement, one may look to the "conduct" of the parties to ascertain the acceptance of the agreement. A panel of this Court, when confronted with the question of whether "conduct" is sufficient to constitute "acceptance" of an "offer" for services provided, has held:

> It is settled that for an agreement to exist, there must be a "meeting of the minds," . . .; the very essence of an agreement is that the parties mutually assent to the same thing, . . . The principle that a contract is not binding unless there is an offer and an acceptance is to ensure that there will be mutual assent. . . .

Notwithstanding the aforesaid, it is equally well-established that "an offer may be accepted by conduct and what the parties do pursuant to the offer" is germane to show whether the offer is accepted.

Instantly, it is evident from the tenor of the plaintiff's communique to the defendant that it was in the nature of a "cease and desist" request rather than an "offer" to "listen . . . 'for hire'" to the solicitations of the defendant. As observed by the court on this point:

> The sole purpose of the November 29, 1989, letter was to encourage Olan Mills to remove plaintiff from its calling lists—and not to solicit a purchaser for "listening services." The sole purpose of any additional calls that Olan Mills made to plaintiff was to solicit orders—and not to obtain "listening services." Consequently, as a matter of law the parties did not enter into a contract.

Before a contract may be found, all of the essential elements of a contract must exist, e.g., consideration. There obviously can be no bargained-for-exchange ("consideration") if one of the parties acts without any intention of binding itself to a contract for "listening services." There was no "unconditional" manifestation on the part of Olan Mills or its representative that a contract was acknowledged by behavior of the defendant.

There was no "offer," "acceptance," "consideration" or "mutual meeting of the minds" to effectuate the elemental aspects of a contract.

Order affirmed.

QUESTIONS ABOUT THE CASE

1. What did the court decision state as a matter of precedent regarding the formation of a contract?
2. How does the mirror image rule differ from the court's test of a "meeting of the minds"?
3. What was the basis for the plaintiff's claim that Olan Mills had made an acceptance?"
4. Why, as a matter of social policy, did the court decide the way it did?

you have ever purchased a car, been to a yard sale, or visited to a foreign country where bargaining is common, you know that haggling over the price of an item is a common method of agreeing to the terms of a sale. Price haggling is just one way that parties come to a "meeting of the minds." In more sophisticated or complex transactions, other terms enter into the mix of a "bargained for exchange." Terms such as the timing for delivery of goods, the quality of goods, credit, interest rates, and a host of other contingencies enter the picture of contract negotiations. Nevertheless, the Pennsylvania court in *Schreiber v. Olan Mills* did mention the third necessary element for a contract: consideration.

Consideration

For an enforceable contract to exist, the contract must be supported by consideration. Consideration can be a difficult concept. In early contract cases, courts struggled with the concept, wondering if a contract could be enforced if the value of the exchange between the parties was, in the eyes of the court, unequal. This point of view proved unsatisfactory because courts would then become contract police, judging the value of a party's contribution from an objective point of view. Missing from this early legal equation was the notion that consideration can be highly subjective; one person's trash is another's treasure. Moreover, businesses were more interested in having their expectations fulfilled when entering into contracts. To allow a court to judge whether the consideration was equivalent for both sides was also bad for business, because courts did not take into account the customs of a particular trade, which necessarily involves a subjective evaluation.

Soon, courts began to adopt a more modern approach known as the **benefit-detriment** theory. Under this approach, the consideration flowing from both parties consisted of both a benefit and a detriment as part of the bargained for exchange. That is, each party to a contract must realize both a benefit and, at the same time, suffer a detriment. Thus, for a contract to exist, there must be an offer, an acceptance, and consideration consisting of a benefit and a detriment to both contracting parties. In a simple contract for sale, the seller would experience the benefit of receiving the sales price and the detriment of parting with the item for sale. The buyer would experience the benefit of obtaining title to the item for sale and the detriment of paying for the item.

benefit-detriment
A test for the element of consideration in a contract involving a determination of whether each party gains a benefit and suffers a detriment.

As things developed, the requirement of consideration began to take on a broader meaning. Consideration could consist of an exchange of promises, both of which could be performed in the future. Under this more flexible approach, the fulfillment of one promise can act as a condition, which then obligates the other contracting party to perform on its promise. A party to a contract could also give a promise as consideration in exchange for payment. Under this approach, often used in conjunction with benefit-detriment theory, courts need not weigh the relative values of the consideration from either side. All that matters with regard to consideration is whether there has been an exchange of promises. Thus, a promise could constitute sufficient consideration to uphold a valid contract.

CASE IN POINT

COURT OPINION

HAMMER V. SIDWAY, AS EXECUTOR, 124 N.Y. 538; 27 N.E. 256 (1891)

The question on this appeal is whether by virtue of a contract defendant's testator William E. Story became indebted to his nephew William E. Story, 2d, on his twenty-first birthday in the sum of five thousand dollars. The trial court found as a fact that "on the 20th day of March, 1869, . . . William E. Story agreed to and with William E. Story, 2d, that if he would refrain from drinking liquor, using tobacco, swearing, and playing cards or billiards for money until he should become 21 years of age then he, the said William E. Story, would at that time pay him, the said William E. Story, 2d, the sum of $5,000 for such refraining, to which the said William E. Story, 2d, agreed," and that he "in all things fully performed his part of said agreement."

In further consideration of the questions presented, then, it must be deemed established for the purposes of this appeal, that on the 31st day of January, 1875, defendant's testator was indebted to William E. Story, 2d, in the sum of $5,000, . . . on that date the nephew wrote to his uncle as follows:

> "Dear Uncle—I am now 21 years old to-day, and I am now my own boss, and I believe, according to agreement, that there is due me $5,000. I have lived up to the contract to the letter in every sense of the word."

A few days later, and on February sixth, the uncle replied, and, so far as it is material to this controversy, the reply is as follows:

> "Dear Nephew—Your letter of the 31st. came to hand all right saying that you had lived up to the promise made to me several years ago. I have no doubt but you have, for which you shall have $5,000 as I promised you. I had the money in the bank the day you was 21 years old that I intended for you, and you shall have the money certain. Now, Willie, I don't intend to interfere with this money in any way until I think you are capable of taking care of it, and the sooner that time comes the better it will please me. I would hate very much to have you start out in some adventure that you thought all right and lose this money in one year. . . . This money you have earned much easier than I did, besides acquiring good habits at the same time, and you are quite welcome to the money. Hope you will make good use of it. . . ."
>
> /s/ W. E. Story.
>
> "P. S.—You can consider this money on interest."

The trial court found as a fact that "said letter was received by said William E. Story, 2d, who thereafter consented that said money should remain with the said William E. Story in accordance with the terms and conditions of said letter."

The defendant contends that the contract was without consideration to support it, and, therefore, invalid. He asserts that the promisee by refraining from the use of liquor and tobacco was not harmed but benefited; that that which he did was best for him to do independently of his uncle's promise, and insists that it follows that unless the promisor was benefited, the contract was without consideration.

In the past, courts have defined a promise as a valuable consideration in the sense of the law may consist either in some right, interest, profit or benefit accruing to the one party, or some forbearance, detriment, loss or responsibility given, suffered or undertaken by the other. Thus, courts will not ask whether the thing which forms the consideration does in fact benefit the promisee or a third party, or is of any substantial value to anyone. It is enough that something is promised, done, forborne or suffered by the party to whom the promise is made as consideration for the promise made to him.

Thus, in general a waiver of any legal right at the request of another party is a sufficient consideration for a promise. And any damage, or suspension, or forbearance of a right will be sufficient to sustain a promise. Consideration means not so much that one party is profiting as that the other abandons some legal right in the present or limits his legal freedom of action in the future as an inducement for the promise of the first.

Now, applying this rule to the facts before us, the promisee used tobacco, occasionally drank liquor, and he had a legal right to do so. That right he abandoned for a period of years upon the strength of the promise of the testator that for such forbearance he would give him $5,000. We need not speculate on the effort which may have been required to give up the use of those stimulants. It is sufficient that he restricted his lawful freedom of action within certain prescribed limits upon the faith of his uncle's agreement, and now having fully performed the conditions imposed, it is of no moment whether such performance actually proved a benefit to the promisor, and the court will not inquire into it, but were it a proper subject of inquiry, we see nothing in this record that would permit a determination that the uncle was not benefited in a legal sense.

The order appealed from should be reversed and the judgment of the Special Term affirmed, with costs payable out of the estate.

QUESTIONS ABOUT THE CASE

1. Drawing on our coverage on wills and estates, why was the defendant named Sidway?
2. In this case, Mr. Story, 2d, the nephew, had filed his lawsuit in the trial court then known as the "Special Term," which found in his favor. An intermediate appellate court reversed, and he appealed to the New York Court of Appeals. What did the New York Court of Appeals' decision do to the two earlier decisions?
3. What was the defendant's main legal argument in this appeal?

4. What did the court mean when it decided not to inquire whether the nephews abstaining actually benefitted the uncle? What benefit did the uncle actually receive from the contract?
5. Suppose that instead of making demands on the nephew, the uncle simply promised to give the money, without conditions, as soon as the nephew turned 21 years old. This promise would be a promise of a pure gift. Is there consideration? Would such a promise be enforceable under the bargain theory? Should courts enforce such promises?

Consider in the previous case how the courts weigh the value of consideration in finding the existence of an enforceable contract.

As the development of contract law progressed, the *Hamer v. Sidway* decision marked a significant change of course that allowed parties considerable freedom in forming their expectations from an enforceable contract. Key to this change was the requirement of consideration, specifically, the nature of what constitutes sufficient consideration. By holding that mutual promises are sufficient, the idea of forbearance on the nephew's part as a detriment or peace of mind as a benefit to the uncle became of secondary importance to the court. What mattered were the parties' expectations.

PARTIES TO A CONTRACT

Previously in this chapter, we discussed the legal requirement for persons making a will. As a matter of legal capacity, we saw that minors and persons with mental deficiencies cannot make a valid will because the law does not regard them as able to understand the consequences of their actions. The requirement of legal capacity thus protects against undue influence or other forms of coercion. In contracts, the law's concerns were particularly acute, because entering an enforceable contact imposes legal obligations.

Those who are mentally infirm or incompetent are deemed incapable of entering into contracts. Any contract in which a party is found to have been incompetent at its formation is unenforceable as a **void contract**. In Chapter 8, we saw that marriages—a form of contract—may be void as a matter of public policy. Thus, a polygamous marriage would be void from the outset. There are also voidable marriages that are valid until one of the parties steps forward to declare the marriage void. The same is true with contracts.

A person to a contract who has not attained the age of majority (in most states, 18 years) has the option of opting out of the contract. If the contract is for food, shelter, or clothing, also called necessaries, the minor may disaffirm the contract but be liable for the reasonable value of any necessaries obtained. The other party to the contract with the minor runs the risk of entering the contract. The contract is a valid one, but at the minor's election, it may be declared void. As a **voidable contract**, a minor may disaffirm the contract, rendering it unenforceable.

void contract
Agreement that does not meet the required elements and therefore is unenforceable under contract law.

voidable contract
Apparently fully enforceable contract with a defect unknown by one party.

COMMUNICATION TIP

In high school English class, most of us are taught to vary our word use in a usage style known as the elegant variation. However, in law, accuracy and consistency are more important than style. Thus, when referring to a contract, avoid using any synonyms such as agreement, indenture, pact, or so forth. In different situations, those synonyms may very well mean something different than a contract.

Genuine Assent

Even if all of the parties are legally capable of entering into a contract, the contract still may be voided if there is no genuine assent. Recall that a valid contract requires a "meeting of the minds" or mutual assent, as we saw in the *Schreiber v. Olan Mills* case. There, the parties had not voluntarily assented to the formation of a contract. For that reason, the Pennsylvania court held that no contract existed. Thus, mutual assent exists when there is a voluntary agreement as to the essential and material terms of a contract.

The requirement of genuine assent is a broader concept that arises when a contracting party alleges as a defense that the contract had been entered into as a result of undue influence, duress, mutual mistake, or fraud. These defenses generally allege that there was no genuine assent and hence no meeting of the minds to form a contract. Keep in mind that the lack of genuine assent refers to the inability of one of the parties to agree to the contract because of extrinsic circumstances and relates to that party's capacity to enter into the contract freely. Undue influence, duress, mistake, and fraud are common situations that may indicate a lack of genuine consent. Used as defenses to a lawsuit based on a contract, the lack of genuine consent, if shown, will render a contract unenforceable.

Undue Influence

A party to a contract may allege the abuse of a relationship of trust, such as family members, caretakers of the elderly or infirm, or even instances in which a legal professional has induced the contract. Specifically, the allegation of **undue influence** as a defense states that the other party abused their trust, resulting in a contract that would be unfair to enforce.

undue influence
Using a close personal or fiduciary relationship to one's advantage to gain assent to terms that the party otherwise would not have agreed to.

Duress

Related to undue influence is the defense in which a party claiming **duress** alleges that he or she was threatened or literally forced and had no choice but to enter into the contract. Because of the inordinate pressure, the party is ultimately claiming that he or she could not have given genuine assent when entering into the contract. Duress cases are, as you can imagine, difficult to prove. A famous and obvious case of duress involves a treaty, which is akin to a contract between countries. In 1939, German ministers reportedly chased the president and foreign minister of Czechoslovakia around a table, forcing pens into their hands to sign a treaty that would give Germany control over their country. During these events, the Czechoslovakian president fainted and was revived from injections given by a German doctor.

duress
Unreasonable and unscrupulous manipulation of a person to force him or her to agree to terms of an agreement that he or she would otherwise not agree to. Also, any unlawful threat or coercion used by a person to induce another to act (or to refrain from acting) in a manner that he or she otherwise would not do.

Mistake

If all the parties to a contract have a misunderstanding about an important matter in the contract, a court will find that there was no meeting of the minds and therefore no contract. In what is known as a rescission, the court would render the contract void for lack of genuine assent. This decision may occur when there has been a **mistake in fact**. For rescission to be granted, the mistake must be bilateral, or a mistake on the part of both parties to the contract. One party's mistaken belief, or unilateral mistake, is not enough for a court to grant rescission. Both parties must be laboring under the mistake for rescission to be available.

mistake in fact
An error in assessing the facts, causing a defendant to act in a certain way.

Fraud

As an existing separate cause of action in tort law, **fraud** also provides a basis for a party to challenge the validity of a contract. By alleging fraud, a contracting party is saying that the other party made misrepresentations intentionally and thereby induced the other party into the contract. Fraud is a heavy assertion and can result not only in the contract's rescission but also in double or triple damages against the party found to have committed it. Thus, courts will take care to see if the party alleging it was reasonable in its belief of the other party's misrepresentation.

fraud
A knowing and intentional misstatement of the truth in order to induce a desired action from another person.

PUBLIC POLICY CONSIDERATIONS: ILLEGAL CONTRACTS

Contracts that call for an illegal act or involve an illegal matter are void and unenforceable. Courts will not enforce contracts that involve violations of the law. Contracts involving criminal conduct, illegal gambling, or contraband such as controlled

CASE IN POINT

CASE SUMMARY: "THE PREGNANT-COW CASE"

SHERWOOD V. WALKER, 66 MICH. 568, 33 N.W. 919 (1887)

Hiram Walker agreed with Theodore Sherwood, a banker, to sell him a cow of distinguished ancestry known as Rose 2d of Aberlone. The price was $80, both parties believing Rose to be sterile. When Walker discovered that she was pregnant and worth between $750 and $1,000, he refused to deliver her. Sherwood sued and prevailed in the trial court but lost on appeal. This case illustrates the contract law rules of rescission of contract by mutual mistake. Because both parties believed they were contracting for a sterile cow, there was a mutual mistake of fact and therefore grounds for rescission. Hiram Walker (4 July 1816–12 January 1899) is better known as an American grocer and distiller and the namesake for the famous distillery in Windsor, Ontario, Canada.

QUESTIONS ABOUT THE CASE

1. Would the same result have occurred if only Mr. Sherwood had known that the cow was pregnant?
2. Why does a mutual mistake result in rescission?
3. What social policy considerations are reflected in the law in this case?

substances are obvious cases. On the civil side, public policy considerations may render contracts, or parts of them, unenforceable. Usually statutes, regulations, and court decisions express concerns of public policy. For instance, in employment contracts, employers often include an anticompetition clause that attempts to prevent employees from competing with the employer after their employment has ended. Although such clauses can be valid, courts are careful to limit them to specific, reasonable times or geographic areas. Similarly, many anticompetition clauses are upheld when the former employee has acquired and plans to use specialized knowledge about customers or trade secretes obtained from the employer.

Clearer examples of contracts against public policy would be those that purport to waive certain protected rights. Contract clauses in residential leases that attempt to waive building or health code violations by the landlord are generally not enforceable. In such cases, the public policy of requiring landlords to maintain their residential apartments in accordance with health and safety codes overrides any contract that would attempt to circumvent important laws that protect public health and safety.

Consumer Issues

The rise of consumerism and the laws that protect consumers have greatly affected the state of contract law. Beginning with the UCC, the sale of goods automatically carries a **warranty** that the product will perform in the manner ordinarily expected for the purpose sold. If the goods fail or do not live up to their ordinary purpose, the purchaser or consumer has several legal options, including alleging a breach of warranty as a defense to the seller's lawsuit for nonpayment for the goods. The area of warranties can be quite complex. The UCC sets out no less than three types of warranties:

warranty
A promise or representation by the seller that the goods in question meet certain standards.

- *Implied warranty of merchantability.* Requires all contracts for the sale of goods to have a provision that the goods will meet their ordinary purpose. If the contract for sale does not include such a warranty, the law implies it into the contract.
- *Implied warranty of fitness.* Imposes on the seller a warranty that the product will be fit for a particular purpose in situations for which the buyer is relying on

PRACTICE TIP

In addition to the provisions of the UCC, many states have their own consumer laws, often called "Consumer Protection Acts." A professional paralegal should know whether his or her state has such consumer laws that increase consumer rights beyond the UCC.

the seller's expertise. Like the warranty of merchantability, the warranty of fitness is implied. An example of fitness would be the purchase of a certain type of paint, for which the buyer was relying on the seller's expertise that a particular paint would, say, prevent rust.

- *Express warranties.* Many times, goods are sold with a promise by the manufacturer or seller that guarantees the performance of the good to attract the buyer. Any limitations of an express warranty must be reasonable and not misleading.

The laws of some states grant consumers even greater rights than those in the UCC. Paralegals are often called upon to know the various provisions of the consumer protection laws in the state in which they are working.

The Statute of Frauds: "Put It in Writing!"

Since the sixteenth century, the common law has required that certain types of contracts be in writing as a precondition to their enforcement by a court. This common law principle is called the **Statute of Frauds**. As developed, the requirement of a written contract often appears as a defense to a contract action. The discussion of wills in Chapter 7 involved the same legal considerations. There, we noted that with a few minor exceptions, wills had to be in writing to be probated. The reason for this requirement was the possibility of fraudulent claims by unscrupulous persons. The same policy holds true in contracts but to a different extent. Not all contracts need be in writing to be enforced.

Statute of Frauds
Rule that specifies which contracts must be in writing to be enforceable.

The general rule is that oral contracts are enforceable. The Statue of Frauds requires that certain contracts be in writing in order to be enforcable. As a general principle of prudence, most contracts should be written with copies to all parties. In the event of a dispute or an ambiguity, the ability to resort to a written document may avert the dispute from growing into a lawsuit. Nevertheless, business and personal dealings are frequently carried on without written contracts and without problems. However, under the Statute of Frauds, which is still in effect, the following circumstances require a written contract:

1. Any agreement that involves land or fixtures, such as leases, purchase and sales, mortgages, and other transactions involving land.
2. Contracts in consideration of marriage, such as a prenuptial contract.
3. Contracts that cannot be performed within one year.
4. Contracts for the sale of goods above a certain value (usually $500.00).
5. Contracts in which one party becomes a surety (acts as guarantor) for another party's debt or other obligation.

Any contract entered into in these circumstances may not be enforced unless it is in writing. Thus, circumstances in which the Statute of Frauds applies are exceptions to the rule that oral contracts are enforceable. In practice, a formal document is not necessary to satisfy the requirement of a written agreement. Most courts have held, and the UCC provides, that only a memorandum that sufficiently sets out the general parameters of the agreement, signed by the person against whom the contract is enforced, is required.

Certainly this was the case in the *Hamer v. Sidway* case. The contract between the uncle and his nephew began as an oral agreement when the nephew was 15 years old. Six years later, the two exchanged letters that set out the details and the terms of the agreement. The letters were sufficient to satisfy the Statute of Frauds and render the contract between the uncle and nephew enforceable. As a practical matter, the requirement that a written contract is necessary to satisfy the Statute of Frauds is enforced only to prevent fraudulent claims that a contract exists. Thus, courts have permitted a canceled check or other memorandum to suffice.

THE RIGHTS OF THIRD PARTIES TO A CONTACT

Life insurance policies are probably the most common forms of contracts made between two parties for the benefit of a person who is not a party. In a classic life insurance policy, an individual enters into a contract with an insurance company. That agreement consists of an exchange of two promises, one from the individual and one from the insurance company. The individual promises to pay the insurance company an annual sum of money known as a premium for a specified period of time. The insurance company, in turn, promises to pay a lump sum amount to someone, known as the beneficiary, who has been designated by the individual upon the individual's death. The question arises: What rights does the beneficiary have to enforce the contract against the insurance company? This area of contract law is known as **third-party beneficiary** law.

third-party beneficiary
A person, not a party to the contract, who stands to receive the benefit of performance of the contract.

Third-party beneficiaries are created by a contract made by others with the intent to benefit the third-party beneficiary. When the contract indicates that intent, the third-party beneficiary has the right to sue and enforce the contract against either of the parties making the contract. Early in the development of contract law, it was thought that only the actual parties to the contract possessed the right to enforce the contract. The idea was that no one else was bound by its terms and thus did not have **privity**, a term indicating the connection between the contract and parties to it. Other types of contracts involving third-party beneficiaries abound in many different varieties. Banks often enter into agreements with parents to hold, manage, and administer funds for the benefit of their children. In such cases, the children are the intended third-party beneficiaries who have the right to enforce the agreement between the bank and their parents.

privity
A relationship between the parties to the contract who have rights and obligations to each other through the terms of the agreement.

Not all contracts that might benefit a nonparty third person give the nonparty rights to the contract. The third-party beneficiary must have been intended to receive benefits. Thus, a contract that does not intend to benefit a third party but does so incidentally does not create rights for the nonparty. For example, a contract between an apartment building owner and a contractor to replace the windows in an apartment building benefits the tenants only incidentally. The tenants cannot enforce any part of that contract. If the windows did not operate properly, any warranty, implied or expressed, in the contract between the building owner and the contractor would not be enforceable by the tenants.

Assignments and Delegations

A third party may also become involved in a contract if one of the parties to the contract delegates or assigns a part of the contract to the third party. A **delegation** occurs when a party, the delegator, transfers an obligation that was to be performed by that party to another entity, the delegatee, who then becomes obligated to perform the same obligation. An **assignment** occurs when a party, an assignor, to a contract transfers a right to receive performance (usually money) to another entity, the assignee. Various notice requirements are also part of the law of third-party assignments and delegations to ensure that the other party to the contract is aware of the assignment. In history, some limitations have developed. An assignment or delegation may not be permissible if (1) the parties to the contract agree not to permit either, (2) the assignment will change the contract's conditions, or (3) the contract was one for personal services.

delegation
The transfer of the duties/obligations to perform under the contract.

assignment
The transfer of the rights to receive the benefit of contractual performance under the contract.

Figure 9.2 provides an illustration of how an assignment operates.

FIGURE 9.2 **How an Assignment Operates**
A enters into a contract to pay B in installments for the purchase of an item. B then assigns to C, the right to A's payments so that B can satisfy a debt B owes to C. Upon notifying A of the assignment to C, B has accomplished the assignment. As a result of the assignment by B, A's payments now go directly to C. In doing so, A is still performing on the contract of purchase with B, and B is satisfying a debt obligation to C.

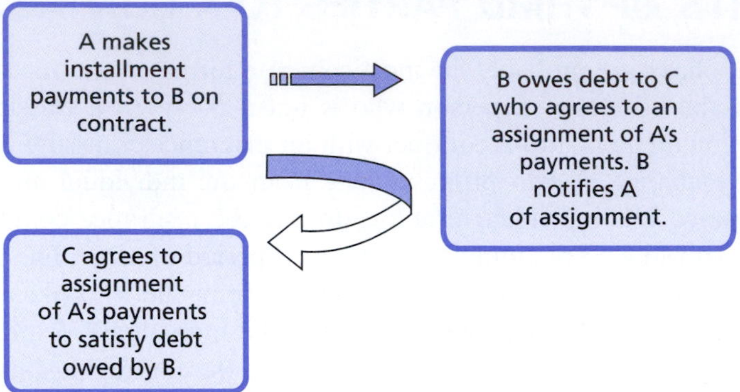

ENFORCING THE CONTRACT: REMEDIES

breach of contract
A party's performance that deviates from the required performance obligations under the contract; a violation of an obligation under a contract for which a party may seek recourse to the court.

A party that fails to perform their obligations imposed upon it by the contract has engaged in a **breach of contract**. Similar to the duty imposed by tort law, a contract establishes a duty on the parties, and the failure to carry out that duty gives rise to a cause of action or claim for relief in contract. The nonbreaching party may begin a lawsuit seeking contractual remedies. In our coverage on torts, we noted that the primary form of relief is damages—that is, monetary awards by the court. In the case of a nuisance and some other special circumstances, equitable relief in the form of an injunction may be available. Contract remedies operate a bit differently. The availability of equitable relief consists of wider forms, whereas monetary relief is more limited.

As a matter of equity, the plaintiff may obtain the following forms of relief at the discretion of the court.

Rescission

rescission and restitution
A decision by the court that renders the contract null and void and requires the parties to return to the wronged party any benefits received under the agreement.

If there has been a mutual mistake, among other circumstances, the remedy may be to rescind or set aside a contract. **Rescission** actually cancels the contract between the parties, putting the parties in the same position they were in before they entered into the contract. If needed, the court will also award **restitution** to a party that has been wronged and order the other party to return any benefits obtained under the rescinded agreement. In the pregnant cow case above, only rescission was awarded by the court since neither party had obtained any benefits. However, if one party has received a benefit in a contract involving a mutual mistake, the court may award rescission as well as restitution. In doing so, the court would be returning the parties to their respective positions before having entered into the contract.

Reformation

A court may modify or revise the terms of a contract to make it conform to what the parties understood or agreed. Reformation is most likely when the parties have entered into a binding agreement and some related writing does not conform to their agreement, due to either mistake or misunderstanding.

Specific Performance

A court may order the breaching party to perform the terms of the contract if monetary damages (known as a "remedy at law") would be insufficient to the non-breaching party. Specific performance is rare and available only in contracts for the purchase of land,

CASE IN POINT

COURT OPINION: *CAMPBELL SOUP CO. V. WENTZ,* 172 F.2d 80 (3D CIR., 1948)

These are appeals from judgments of the District Court denying equitable relief to the buyer.

June 21, 1947, Campbell Soup Company, a New Jersey corporation, entered into a written contract with George B. Wentz and Harry T. Wentz, who are Pennsylvania farmers, for delivery by the Wentzes to Campbell of all the Chantenay red cored carrots to be grown on fifteen acres of the Wentz farm during the 1947 season. The contract provides for delivery of the carrots at the Campbell plant in Camden, New Jersey. The prices specified in the contract ranged from $23 to $30 per ton according to the time of delivery. The contract price for January, 1948 was $30 a ton.

The Wentzes harvested approximately 100 tons of carrots from the fifteen acres covered by the contract. Early in January 1948, they told a Campbell representative that they would not deliver their carrots at the contract price. The market price at that time was at least $90 per ton, and Chantenay red cored carrots were virtually unobtainable

On January 9, 1948, Campbell, instituted this suit against the Wentz brothers to enjoin further sale of the contract carrots to others, and to compel specific performance of the contract. The trial court denied equitable relief. We agree with the result reached, but on a different ground from that relied upon by the District Court.

We think that on the question of adequacy of the legal remedy the case is one appropriate for specific performance. It was expressly found that at the time of the trial it was "virtually impossible to obtain Chantenay carrots in the open market." This Chantenay carrot is one which the plaintiff uses in large quantities, furnishing the seed to the growers with whom it makes contracts. It was not claimed that in nutritive value it is any better than other types of carrots. Its blunt shape makes it easier to handle in processing. And its color and texture differ from other varieties. The color is brighter than other carrots. The plaintiff uses carrots in fifteen of its twenty-one soups. It also appeared that it uses these Chantenay carrots diced in some of them and that the appearance is uniform. The preservation of uniformity in appearance in a food article marketed throughout the country and sold under the manufacturer's name is a matter of considerable commercial significance and one which is properly considered in determining whether a substitute ingredient is just as good as the original.

We see no reason why a court should be reluctant to grant specific relief when it can be given without supervision of the court or other time-consuming processes against one who has deliberately broken his agreement. Here the goods of the special type contracted for were unavailable on the open market, the plaintiff had contracted for them long ahead in anticipation of its needs, and had built up a general reputation for its products as part of which reputation uniform appearance was important. We think if this were all that was involved in the case specific performance should have been granted.

The reason that we shall affirm instead of reversing with an order for specific performance is found in the contract itself. We think it is too hard a bargain and too one-sided an agreement to entitle the plaintiff to relief in a court of conscience. For each individual grower the agreement is made by filling in names and quantity and price on a printed form furnished by the buyer. This form has quite obviously been drawn by skillful draftsmen with the buyer's interests in mind.

Paragraph 2 provides for the manner of delivery. Carrots are to have their stalks cut off and be in clean sanitary bags or other containers approved by Campbell. This paragraph concludes with a statement that Campbell's determination of conformance with specifications shall be conclusive.

The next paragraph allows Campbell to refuse carrots in excess of twelve tons to the acre. The next contains a covenant by the grower that he will not sell carrots to anyone else except the carrots rejected by Campbell nor will he permit anyone else to grow carrots on his land. Paragraph 10 provides liquidated damages to the extent of $50 per acre for any breach by the grower. There is no provision for liquidated or any other damages for breach of contract by Campbell.

The provision of the contract which we think is the hardest is paragraph 9, set out in the margin. It will be noted that Campbell is excused from accepting carrots under certain circumstances. But even under such circumstances the grower, while he cannot say Campbell is liable for failure to take the carrots, is not permitted to sell them elsewhere unless Campbell agrees. What the grower may do with his product under the circumstances set out is not clear. He has covenanted not to store it anywhere except on his own farm and also not to sell to anybody else.

We are not suggesting that the contract is illegal. Nor are we suggesting any excuse for the grower in this case who has deliberately broken an agreement entered into with Campbell. We do think, however, that a party who has offered and succeeded in getting an agreement as tough as this one is, should not come to a chancellor and ask court help in the enforcement of its terms. That equity does not enforce unconscionable bargains is too well established to require elaborate citation. All we say is that the sum total of its provisions drives too hard a bargain for a court of conscience to assist.

The judgments will be affirmed.

QUESTIONS ABOUT THE CASE

1. Campbell Soup filed the lawsuit against the Wentzes in the Federal District Court for the Eastern District of Pennsylvania. What was the basis for the federal court's jurisdiction?
2. What did the Third Circuit Court mean when it called itself a "court of conscience"?
3. Now that the Court has denied equitable relief, can Campbell Soup go back to court to try to collect damages against the Wentzes?
4. What is the difference between an illegal contract and the contract here?
5. Why did the Court refuse to enforce the contract?

CYBER TRIP

Courts acting in equity frequently engaged in the use of equitable maxims or aphorisms—concise statements expressing a general truth or wise observation. Using a search engine on the Internet, find a list of equitable maxims or aphorisms.

Which equitable aphorism did the court apply to prevent Campbell Soup from obtaining specific performance?

family heirlooms, or a truly unique subject matter. The *Campbell Soup Co. v. Wentz* case illustrates the remedy of specific performance and the role of equity in contracts.

REMEDIES AT LAW: DAMAGES IN CONTRACT LAWSUITS

Contract damages are different from tort damages because of the business context that usually surrounds contracts and historical developments. Unlike tort damages, the remedies at law available in contracts are usually limited to compensatory damages. A nonbreaching party that has suffered a monetary loss as a result of the other party's breach is entitled to an amount of damages equal to what the nonbreaching party would have received under the contract. This measure of damages is known as the **benefit of the bargain**. As with torts, an award of compensatory damages is, in theory, designed to restore the plaintiff to the position it would have been in had the breach not occurred. Yet contract damages are confined to the parameters of the contract. Damage awards focus on what the parties expected from the deal. The reason is based on social policy.

In Chapter 3, we discussed the various legal philosophies that have developed over the centuries. Prominent among them is law and economics, which urges the adoption of legal principles that encourage commerce and support business. Contracts make the world of commerce and business go round. Their efficient enforcement of contracts provides certainty and stability, which is good for business. At the same time, providing too much in the way of damages can make parties reluctant to enter into contracts and chill business activity. Thus, contract remedies do not provide for damages that would not have been foreseeable. The rule limiting contract damages was established in 1854, in the case of *Hadley v. Baxendale.* The rule of that case represents the social policy of placing the risk of loss on the party in the best position to handle it. Moreover, to go beyond the parameters of the contract would put businesses in a precarious position.

RESEARCH THIS

Research whether the status of the common law rule of *Hadley v. Baxendale* has been adopted or modified in your state. To what extent are contract damages limited?

benefit of the bargain
A measure of damages in a breach of contract action in which the damages are measured to restore the non-breaching party to the position if the breach had not occurred.

liquidated damages
An amount of money agreed upon in the original contract as a reasonable estimation of the damages to be recovered by the nonbreaching party. This amount is set forth in the contract so the parties have a clear idea of the risk of breach.

Modern courts have gone beyond the 1854 rule to allow for some incidental damages in contract cases but only for losses by the nonbreaching party for the commercially reasonable expenses incurred as a result of the other party's breach, such as the costs of inspecting and returning goods that do not conform to the contract specifications. Still, notice that these incidental damages are limited to matters within the contract and not to the loss of revenues or earnings that may have been caused by the breach.

Another form of damages in contracts cases is called **liquidated damages**. Some contracts contain clauses that are designed to avoid litigation and the computation of damages. They do so by specifying a certain amount of damages in the contract that the parties agree will provide adequate compensation in the event of a breach.

CASE IN POINT

LIQUIDATED DAMAGES

LAKEWOOD CREATIVE COSTUMERS V. SHARP, 31 OHIO APP. 3d 116; 509 N.E.2d 77 (1986)

On October 27, 1984, Angel Sharp rented a Halloween costume from Lakewood Creative Costumers. The agreement signed by Sharp provided that the costume was to be returned by November 1, 1984. The fee for the rental was $20.

The defendant failed to return the costume by November 1, 1984. Sharp testified before a referee that she had attempted to return the costume once, but that the store was closed. She then put the costume in her closet and forgot about it. Sharp eventually returned the costume on January 20, 1985.

On January 11, 1985, Lakewood Creative Costumers filed suit against Sharp in Lakewood Municipal Court, Small Claims Division. The complaint alleged that Sharp had breached her contract. The plaintiff sought to enforce a liquidated damages clause in the contract which provided that "an amount equal to one-half the rental fee will be charged for each day the costume is returned late." Under that clause, the plaintiff would have been entitled to $790 in liquidated damages from Sharp. (The costume was returned seventy-nine days late. One-half the rental fee was $10. Therefore, under the liquidated damages clause the amount due was seventy-nine times ten, or $790.) In its complaint, however, the plaintiff only sought $500 in damages.

At a hearing before a referee, a representative of Lakewood Creative Costumers testified that he definitely lost one rental of the costume, and that the costume cost $20 to make.

The referee applied the [liquidated damages] clause, and noted that based on the language of the contract, Lakewood Creative Costumers was entitled to $790. However, since the plaintiff only sought $500, the referee recommended a judgment in that amount.

The defendant filed a timely appeal, raising a single assignment of error.

Assignment of error:

"A provision in a costume-rental contract providing for payment of one-half the rental fee for each day the costume is returned late is void and unenforceable as a penalty where the rental fee is $20.00, the replacement cost of the costume is $20.00, the costume would have been rented at most for one day during the period the customer was late in returning it, and the customer would have at most been liable for the replacement cost of the costume had it been returned in a damaged condition."

A clause in a contract providing for liquidated damages in the event of a breach is valid and enforceable where the sum stipulated is in reasonable proportion to the loss actually sustained; the actual damages incurred by the breach are uncertain or difficult to ascertain; and the contract is consistent with the conclusion that it was the intention of the parties that damages in the amount stated should follow the breach thereof.

The liquidated damages clause in the instant case clearly fails under the aforementioned test. First, the sum stipulated is not reasonably proportionate to the loss sustained. The only evidence of damage by the appellee was the loss of a single rental, a twenty dollar value. Under the liquidated damages clause, however, the appellant could ultimately have been held liable for $790. A liquidated damages clause which provides for an amount nearly forty times the actual damages is not reasonably proportionate to the loss sustained, and thus is invalid.

Second, the actual damages incurred by the breach are not uncertain or difficult to ascertain. The actual damages incurred are relatively easy to ascertain. They simply consist of any lost rental sales, together with the cost of getting the costume returned. Liquidated damages are appropriate only where actual damages are uncertain or difficult to ascertain. Therefore, the clause in the case at bar is void.

Accordingly, the appellant's assignment of error is sustained.

The liquidated damages clause which provided that "an amount equal to one-half the rental fee will be charged for each day the costume is returned late" is hereby found to be void and unenforceable. The trial court's judgment is therefore reduced to the amount of actual damages proven, twenty dollars from the loss of a single rental, plus the court costs. The trial court's judgment is affirmed as modified.

Judgment affirmed as modified.

QUESTIONS ABOUT THE CASE

1. What is an "assignment of error?" What did the court mean when it "sustained" the assignment of error?
2. If Angel Sharp had agreed to the liquidated damages clause in the contract, why did the court refuse to enforce it?
3. When are liquidated damages clauses proper and enforceable in contracts?
4. What types of contracts have enforceable liquidated damages clauses?

FIGURE 9.3
Terms and Principles in Contracts

Contract Formalities	Defenses	Contract Remedies
Offer Acceptance (mutual assent) Consideration (benefit-detriment)	Lack of genuine assent • undue influence • duress • mistake • fraud Lack of legal capacity (void & voidable contracts) • under age of majority • mental incompetence Illegal subject matter (void contracts)	Monetary damages • compensatory damages • incidental damages • liquidated damages Equitable remedies • rescission and restitution • reformation • specific performance

As long as the amount specified is reasonably related to any true loss, such liquidated damages clauses are valid. Thus, a high penalty provision for the late return of a rented Halloween costume would be considered unreasonable and unenforceable, as demonstrated in the previous case.

Contract law can be the most difficult and technical area of the law to master. Certainly many students in law school will attest to this. The coverage in this chapter is intended to provide information on contracts sufficient to give students a taste of an important area of the law. Figure 9.3 summarizes the often dizzying array of terms and principles in contracts.

ACTIVITIES OF LEGAL PROFESSIONALS IN CONTRACT LAW

When parties to a contract choose to sue each other, most legal professionals agree that the onset of litigation means that the contract has failed. Once litigation has begun, the rules of contract law are both swords and shields. Questions as to whether an agreement should have been in writing, whether there is a mutual mistake, or any other issue of contract law become a matter for the litigation department of a law office.

However, legal professionals representing any party to a contract better serve their clients by carefully drafting and engaging in principled negotiation of their clients' agreements. The object of their professional efforts is to achieve their client's objective and avoid litigation. For professional paralegals, engaging in contract law involves research of the law as well as of public records, document organization, and participation in conferences and meetings in which contracts are negotiated and finalized.

From your basic knowledge of contracts and property, we can advance to another important area of practice for the professional paralegal: the law of business organizations. In this advanced legal specialty, you will see that the law creates opportunities for business-friendly environments in which to operate. In contracts, we have seen that the law promotes and facilitates commerce with several devices, such as assignments and limitations on damages. With business organizations, you will see how the law supports not only how business is done but also determines in what form business may be done. Keep in mind that in our capitalistic society, laws operate to permit business freedom and at the same time provide for the common good through legal mechanisms that protect the public. To be effective, the law must strike a balance between free enterprise and the competing interest of protecting society.

A DAY IN THE LIFE OF A REAL PARALEGAL

Paralegals with expertise in contract law are in high demand. Law firms and government agencies frequently hire contract paralegals. However, the more interesting work often comes from corporate in-house legal departments, which rely heavily on paralegals to perform important functions. The employment advertisements in Figure 9.4 seeking paralegals provide an inside view into the life of a contract paralegal.

FIGURE 9.4 Advertisements Seeking Paralegals in Contract Law

Posting Title: Contracts Paralegal

Paralegal certificate, 2- or 4-year degree from accredited institution

A global biotechnology company committed to the discovery and development of breakthrough small molecule drugs for serious diseases is seeking a full-time contracts paralegal.

Position Overview: This position will work with and support the Senior Contracts Paralegal in drafting and reviewing various types of agreements including confidentiality, consulting, commercial vendor and other services-related agreements, with a focus on information systems and software licensing.

Key Responsibilities: Direct responsibility for initial legal review and drafting of contracts to support various internal clients. Identify and refer legal issues to Senior Contracts Paralegal for review and direction. Contributes to the continued development and refinement of contract templates. Works collaboratively with and facilitates effective communication among legal department personnel, including intellectual property department to address intellectual property matters in various agreements. Works collaboratively with internal clients to set appropriate priorities and deliver results within the timelines established. Ensures appropriate entering and archiving of contracts in legal document management systems.

Position Available: Full-Time Contracts Paralegal

National leading construction management and design firm with 15,000 employees and $4.5 billion in annual revenues is looking for a dynamic person to join the firm as a Contracts Paralegal in our Englewood office. This position will provide paralegal support to the in-house legal contracts team.
Highly competitive salary and benefits.

Key Duties:

- Provide comprehensive review, analysis and negotiation of professional design and construction management service agreements and confidentiality agreements under the direction and supervision of in-house Business Group Counsel.
- Professional, precise and prompt delivery of responses and other communications with clientele is required.
- Ability to independently prioritize workload commitments in a fast-paced environment is critical.
- Demonstrated ability to recognize and assess significant risk issues (indemnity, limitation of liability, consequential damages, standard of care, termination, insurance, etc.) that typically arise in review and negotiation of professional service agreements is essential.

Qualifications:
- Experience with law firm or in-house corporate counsel, including internships.
- Two- or 4-year degree in paralegal studies from accredited school.
- Nationally accredited paralegal certification (CLA, CP or RP), a plus.
- Computer proficiency on law office software applications.

Professional Help Wanted: Contracts Paralegal
H. Co. is looking for a dynamic person to join the firm as a Contracts Paralegal in our in-house legal team. Headquartered in Denver, Colorado, employee-owned H. Co. is a global leader in engineering, construction, and operations for public and private clients. Our employees help H. Co. deliver innovative, practical, sustainable solutions helping clients develop and manage infrastructure and facilities that improve efficiency, safety, and quality of life.

Contracts Paralegal—Key Duties:

- Provide comprehensive review, analysis and negotiation of professional design and construction management service agreements and confidentiality agreements under the direction and supervision of in-house Business Group Counsel.
- Deliver professional, precise and prompt responses and other communications with clientele as required.
- Work independently and prioritize workload commitments in a fast-paced environment are critical.
- Recognize and assess significant risk issues (indemnity, limitation of liability, consequential damages, standard of care, termination, insurance, etc.) that typically arise in review and negotiation of professional service agreements is essential.

AGENCY LAW

Agents and Principals

Businesses rely almost entirely on the work performed by others. You would be hard pressed to think of a business that does not require the work of others, whether on a full-time basis or for an occasional or seasonal engagement. Restaurants engage cooks, waitstaff, maitre'ds, bartenders, and others to perform all of the functions needed. Those that perform the work on behalf of businesses are known as agents. An **agent** is a person who is authorized to act on behalf of, or in the shoes of, another person, who is known as a **principal**. The legal relationship between the two is known as an **agency**, a voluntary contractual relationship in which the principal pays for the agent's services.

agent
A person who is authorized to act for or in the shoes of another (principal).

principal
A person or entity who authorizes, by agreement or other means, another (agent) to act on behalf of the principal in a way that binds the principal in contract or tort.

agency
A legal relationship in which one party (agent) acts or represents the interests of another (principal).

independent contractor
A person who is engaged to perform a specific task that is within their specialized expertise without the supervision of the person who engaged them.

vicarious liability (*respondeat superior*)
One person, or a third party, may be found liable for the act of another or shares liability with the actor.

The most typical agency relationship is an employment situation, involving employer and employee. However, not all those who work for a business are employees. A plumber who is hired occasionally by a restaurant to fix a problem or an attorney who is retained by the restaurant to defend a debt action brought by a produce supplier is not an employee, but **independent contractor**. The legal difference between an agent and an independent contractor can be profound.

In the case of an agent or employee, the actions he or she takes on behalf of the employer are binding on the employer in both contract and tort. For instance, a bookstore employee whose job it is to order books from a publisher acts on behalf of the bookstore and creates an enforceable contract between the publisher and the bookstore. Similarly, a waiter or waitress who accidentally spills scalding hot coffee on a customer has committed the tort of negligence, causing the restaurant to incur liability. For the bookstore and the restaurant, the acts of their agents/employees have the legal effect of binding the principals/employers by operation of law. The legal principle is known as **vicarious liability**, or ***respondeat superior***, which in Latin literally means "let the master answer." The underlying public policy for this legal principle places liability on employers because they control and supervise the regular activities of those who perform their duties as an integral part of the employer's business. The legal consequences are different for situations involving independent contractors.

The law treats independent contractors differently from employees. The actions of independent contractors generally do not bind the person who has hired them, as the actions of an employee would. An independent contractor performs specialized tasks that fall within his or her expertise, which are outside the usual activities of the business that has hired them. The independent contractor chooses how and when to perform the work; that is what differentiates them from employees. Independent contractors work free from the control and supervision of those who have hired them. Usually, they are hired to deal with occasional problems or situations. Under the law, independent contractors, not the person who hired them, are responsible for their own work.

Thus, a plumber who has been engaged by a restaurant to fix an occasional plumbing problem is an independent contractor. The plumber's expertise and the plumbing work performed are clearly outside the usual activities of the restaurant. Most important, the plumber's work is performed outside the control and supervision of the person engaging him or her. Thus, the law considers it unfair to hold the person hiring the independent contractor responsible for the independent contractor's work. If a restaurant customer were harmed by the plumber's negligence, the plumber would be responsible for the harm caused by tasks undertaken as an independent contractor.

Still, as you can imagine, there are exceptions. In some situations, an independent contractor, even as such, may be regarded as an agent and thereby bind the principal.

A principal may give the independent contractor the authority to bind. Conversely, employees/agents may be held to have acted outside their authority. Thus, even though actions of an employee generally bind the principal, vicarious liability may not attach if the employee clearly acts in a way that a reasonable person would not regard as under the control of the employer. A waitress, though an employee of the restaurant, is not authorized to sell the restaurant business. Her scope of authority is limited to what people normally expect of a waitstaff person. Ultimately, the question rests on the extent to which the agent's **scope of authority** extends, as well as the amount of control and supervision of the principal.

scope of authority
Performance of duties that were expressly or implicitly assigned to the agent by the principal.

As is true of many things in law, a few guiding principles operate to promote fairness and fulfill the expectations of those who deal with agents. The following legal doctrines enumerate the types of authority that may be vested in an agent and thereby bind the principal:

- *Express or actual authority.* If the principal has led the agent to believe that he or she has the authority to bind the principal, the principal is bound. This situation arises when the principal's words or conduct reasonably cause the agent to believe that he or she has been authorized to act. In this way, an independent contractor may bind a principal, particularly in contract. An example would be an agent who makes purchases on behalf of the principal, such as a retail store or art gallery.
- *Apparent authority.* A principal's words or actions could lead a reasonable third person to believe that the agent is authorized to act on the principal's behalf. Even if the agent does not have actual authority, the third party is entitled to say that the agent's actions have bound the principal. The legal term for this right is known as "agency by estoppel." It says that the principal has acted in such a way as to lead a reasonable third party to believe that the agent has the authority to act.
- *Inherent authority, or authority by virtue of the agent's position.* To avoid fraud or other harm that an agent may cause to third parties, agents have a certain relationship to the principal. As you will read in the later chapters, a partner has the inherent authority to bind the business entity known as a partnership by virtue of his or her position as a partner. Similarly, a corporate executive has the inherent authority to bind the corporation because of his or her decision-making position within the corporation.
- *Ratification.* Even if the agent acts without authority, the principal may ratify the transaction and accept liability for the transactions entered into by the agent. Ratification may be express or implied by the principal's behavior. That is, if the agent has acted in a number of situations and the principal has knowingly acquiesced, the failure to notify all concerned of the agent's lack of authority is an implied grant of authority for future transactions of a similar nature.

From this discussion, you may sense that agency law is a complex array of legal principles that assist courts as well as businesspeople in their dealings. Agency law is a semester-long, upper-level law school course. Figure 9.5 summarizes the aspects of agency law pertinent to a budding professional paralegal.

BUSINESS ORGANIZATIONS

Legal professionals frequently advise businesspeople about the type of business entity they should operate. From the formation of a new business and through the course of a business's lifetime, legal professionals remain involved with their

FIGURE 9.5
Agency Law as It Pertains to Professional Paralegals

Type of Agent	Scope of Authority	Binding Effect on Principal
Employee	Job duties as expected or in job description	Yes
Independent contractor	Limited to specialized tasks	No
Employee or independent contractor	Express or actual	Yes, if within the express or actual scope
	Apparent	Yes, if principal led third party to believe that agent had authority to bind
	Inherent; by virtue of agent's position	Yes, if scope of authority was understood as part of the agent's position
	Ratification	Yes, when the principal expressly or tacitly approves agent's act and similar future acts

clients' form of doing business. Even after the business has achieved a high level of success, events such as the addition of new products, services, and especially new colleagues and investors cause the form of the business entity to become an ongoing concern. As you will see, the form of business entity may affect the types of property it may own, the contracts it may enter into, and other essential business activities.

At the outset, we need to understand the concept of a business entity. The idea is entirely artificial and deeply embedded in the law. As a legal reality, businesses are people and groups of people. They interact, contract, and invest as people. However, the law permits businesspeople to choose how they wish to be regarded and the legal consequences that flow from that choice. Until recently, some choices were not available. For instance, two or more professionals, such as doctors, lawyers, engineers, and accountants could, as a matter of law, adopt only one form of business entity; the partnership. However, that restriction has changed. A **business organization** is merely an idea created by law. A business entity is, for the most part, an artificial being recognized for legal and business purposes.

business organization
A form of conducting business.

As a practical matter, a business organization exists at the largesse of the state law. In many ways, becoming a certain type of business entity is akin to entering into a contract with the state. In this "contract," the consideration flowing from the state consists of the benefits that allow a business to conduct itself with ease. For its part, the business owner agrees to comply with state laws and regulations that protect the public and ensure the business's accountability. For legal professionals, specific tasks involve advising clients as to the most appropriate and favorable entity to assume, assembling documents, and filing the necessary government forms. Ongoing legal work consists of the regular maintenance required to comply with state laws and regulations. The amount of legal work depends greatly on the type of business entity that the client has assumed. Here is a review of the basic points that clients (and students) should consider.

For centuries, the law permitted three primary forms of doing business: (1) the sole proprietorship, (2) the partnership, and (3) the corporation. In the later part of the twentieth century, hybrid forms of these forms arose and have become popular types of business entities.

Sole Proprietorships

The simplest and most common form of business entity is the **sole proprietorship**. The law requires that a sole proprietor comply with a minimal number of formalities as a condition of doing business. These formalities in many cases consist only of filing a form that indicates the identity of the person doing business. To protect consumers, many jurisdictions require businesses using a **fictitious name**—a name other than the person's—to file a DBA ("doing business as") statement. This requirement is designed to reduce the possibility of confusion if two businesses were operating under the same name locally. Partnerships, corporations, and other forms of business organizations have invented some very well-known fictitious names as marketing devices. Some famous fictitious names include Acura® (Honda, Inc.), Acuvue® (Johnson & Johnson, Inc.), Slice® (PepsiCo, Inc.), and Tab® (Coca-Cola, Inc.).

sole proprietorship
A business owned by one person.

fictitious name
A name used only for business purposes different from the legal name of the person or business organization.

Other business-friendly features include complete control and the ease of management, because only one person makes all the decisions. Any of the sole proprietor's employees have a direct, often personal, relationship with the business owner. In a sole proprietorship, the sole proprietor usually handles all of the incoming money, without having to account to anyone else. Thus, expenses and business decisions belong to the sole proprietor. Taxes are easier, because the individual and the business are taxed as one and the same.

RESEARCH THIS

Find the provisions for registering a fictitious name in your state. Obtain the necessary form, usually available on the Internet. What are the requirements?

On the downside, a sole proprietor assumes all the risks of the business, including any and all of the business's liabilities. Those business liabilities may arise from a tort or a contract or both. The sole proprietor, as the business owner, is personally liable for all business debts. If the business is without sufficient assets to pay for its liabilities, the creditors may seek satisfaction of the business's debts from anything that the sole proprietor owns, including a home, jewelry, car, savings or investments, and any personal possessions that have nothing to do with the business. Thus, the risk of doing business as a sole proprietor exposes the individual's personal assets to the business's liabilities. Those liabilities may be unlimited. The legal repercussions that flow from a sole proprietorship may outweigh the benefits of control and ease of formation.

Other disadvantages include the difficulty that sole proprietors experience in raising capital for expansion and growth. Accepting investors would mean a loss of control and independence. Bank loans or other forms of debt for expansion would create additional sources of potential personal exposure to the business owner. Thus, the distinct disadvantage of a sole proprietorship is the lack of a legally recognized division between the business and the business owner. The sole proprietorship is an easy and flexible form of doing business. However, the biggest drawbacks are the possibility of unlimited personal liability and the lack of any mechanism to attract outside investment or capital to enable the business to grow.

Partnerships

Two or more individuals working together as business owners may form a partnership, which is viewed as a single business entity. A partnership is actually an agreement between the partners to pool their efforts and the assets they bring into the business. The partners also agree to share the business's liabilities. The notion of a partnership did not grow out of the perceived limitations of a sole proprietorship. Instead, partnerships developed independently from the law of agency and principal.

In a partnership, each partner is an agent for the other by virtue of his or her position as partner. Hence, each partner has the *inherent scope of authority* to bind the principal—namely, the partnership entity, along with the other partners. Each partner is an agent and can enter into legally binding contracts on behalf of the principal. The agent can also incur tort liability on behalf of the partnership. Contracts entered into by one partner for the purposes of the partnership's business are binding on the other partner. The liability incurred attaches vicariously to all partners personally in the same way as it would to a sole proprietor, exposing their nonbusiness, personal assets to the partnership's creditors. The feature of vicarious liability in partnerships has become a severe drawback and rendered traditional partnerships obsolete with the appearance of laws that permit professionals and other businesspersons to form a corporation and its variants.

Recent laws have permitted the creation of **limited liability partnerships** in which only the partnership assets may be available to creditors of the partnership, not the personal, nonbusiness assets of the individual partners. These laws have borrowed from the centuries-old concept of separating the assets and activities of a business from the business owners.

limited liability partnership
A type of partnership recognized in a majority of states that protects a partner from personal liability for negligent acts committed by other partners or by employees not under his or her direct control. Many states restrict this type partnership to professionals, such as lawyers, accountants, architects, and healthcare providers.

Corporations

The laws of all states permit individuals to create an artificial person known as a **corporation**, the most prevalent form of business entity. The business owners of corporations are **shareholders**, whose ownership is reflected by their shares in the corporation. The law recognizes the corporation as a separate and distinct entity from its owners, the shareholders. Thus, any creditors of the corporation, whether by way of contract or tort, cannot reach the shareholders' personal assets to satisfy the corporate debts. The law thus provides what is known as a shield or **corporate veil** for the shareholders, which represent the major advantage for using the corporate entity as a form for doing business. Because shares, a form of intangible property, represent business ownership, a corporation can attract investors to expand and encourage its growth without accumulating debt. Finally, corporations have perpetual existence, making for a secure and stable venue for investors.

corporation
An organization formed with state government approval to act as an artificial person to carry on business and issue stock.

shareholder
The owner of one or more shares of stock in a corporation.

corporate veil
The legal protection afforded a duly formed corporation limiting the recovery of any judgments to the assets of the corporation and not the personal assets of the shareholders, or corporate owners, in the absence of fraud, undercapitalization, or abuse of the corporate entity.

EYE ON ETHICS

Bernard Ebbert, a business client of your law firm, is meeting with you to give you the information needed to file a fictitious name registration. He tells you that your supervising attorney had advised him to do business as a corporation instead of continuing as a sole proprietor. The client tells you that becoming a corporation is too expensive and that he does not need the protection of the corporate veil because he "hides" his profits and luxury personal possessions by putting them in the name of his twin brother. He asks for your opinion. What ethical issues come to mind?

Corporate formation is simple and straightforward. In most states, all that is required is the filing of a state-issued form and the payment of a filing fee. Most states also require annual maintenance fees and reports from all corporations. In most cases, these requirements are easily complied with, but they do incur some time and expense. Corporations are also required to indicate that they are corporations by adding "Inc.," "Co.," or "Corp." after their name. In theory, the corporate designation alerts the public that they are dealing with a business entity with limited liability. In reality, most of us have little choice. Corporations with their limited liability supply virtually all the products and services we buy. In the United Kingdom, the required corporate designation notice appears as "Limited," "Ltd.," or "PLC" for a public limited company. In Spanish-speaking countries, companies are designated as such by the initials "S.A." for "Sociedad Anónima." In Germany, we often see the initials "A.G." for "Aktiengesellschaft." These abbreviations all have the same meaning and the same legal effect: to notify those who deal with them that they have the protection of limited liability or a corporate veil.

Still, there are limits to the corporate protection afforded by law. A court may "pierce" the corporate veil if the corporation does not follow proper corporate formalities, is undercapitalized, or was abused and set up as a sham to defraud. If the corporate formalities are not followed, the corporation may be deemed to be functioning not as a corporation but rather as the alter ego of its owners. To prevent the corporate veil from being pierced, it is important to keep minutes of the board meetings and not to comingle bank accounts with personal assets. These measures help ensure that the corporation will be deemed a separate entity should it be sued. Other complications and formalities may ensue. When signing documents as a corporate officer, the failure to designate a representative capacity on contracts, leases, and other instruments may result in personal liability for the person signing.

Corporate ownership is reflected by another artificial legal device known as shares or **stocks**, which represent a fraction of the corporation owned by the shareholder. Each share of stock is a unit of ownership, usually in the form of shares of **common stock**. Each share of common stock allows the shareholder one vote that can be exercised in major corporate decisions, such as buying or merging with another company. **Preferred stock** is another form of ownership and differs from common stock in that it typically does not carry voting rights but legally entitles the holder to receive a certain level of corporate profits known as dividend payments. Preferred stocks are paid dividends before any dividends can be issued to other shareholders. Depending on the size and type of corporation, there may be other types of shares or stock that have different types of benefits. Designed to attract certain types of investors and help the corporation achieve certain financial goals, hybrid forms of stock, such as cumulative preferred and different classes of stock, may be authorized by state law.

stock
A representation of ownership in a corporation.

common stock
A basic form of corporate ownership typically bearing the right to vote.

preferred stock
Corporate ownership that is paid a dividend first and does not have the right to vote on corporate decisions.

Because of the high-stakes nature of stock and corporate finance, federal and state laws regulate the way in which corporations may handle their stock. High on the list of government concerns are the way in which stock is valued and how stock may be acquired. Highly complex federal and state regulations put restrictions on and prescribe accounting methods for the valuation and issuance of stock. An example is the prohibition against *watered stock,* or an artificially inflated form of stock. The term is most commonly used to refer to a form of corporate fraud that frequently occurred under traditional corporate laws that placed a heavy emphasis on stock value. "Stock watering" was originally a method to increase the weight of cows before sale. It entailed forcing a cow to bloat itself with water before it was weighed for sale. Its introduction to the New York financial district is popularly credited to Daniel Drew, a cattle driver turned financier.

Issues for the Modern Corporation

The recent attention given to corporate scandals, such as those that affected Enron, Tyco, WorldCom, and others, has brought ethics to the forefront of the American corporate world. Congress has responded with more regulations, and many companies attempt to follow these new laws by issuing company ethical codes. At the same time, the laws recognize the vital importance of corporations and business to the nation's economy. Here are some of the more prominent issues facing corporations today.

RESEARCH THIS

In 2002, Congress passed the Sarbanes-Oxley Act in an attempt to counter corporate fraud and recent scandals. What does that act do?

Ultra Vires

ultra vires
A legal principle literally meaning "beyond the power" that holds certain transactions or acts of an agent of a corporation as unauthorized and void.

The concept of ***ultra vires*** has existed in corporate law for some time. In corporate law, *ultra vires* describes acts attempted by a corporation that are beyond the scope of its powers. Acts attempted by a corporation that are beyond the scope of its charter are void or voidable. Recall that a void matter has no legal effect whatsoever, and a voidable one is valid unless the victim takes some action to void the act or transaction. Under modern corporate law, the validity of corporate actions may not be challenged on the grounds that the corporation lacks or lacked power to act. Today, the concept of *ultra vires* may still arise in the context of the following kinds of questionable activities by corporations in some states:

- Charitable or political contributions.
- Excessive pensions, bonuses, stock option plans, job severance payments, and other fringe benefits.
- The power to enter into a partnership.
- The power to acquire shares of other corporations.
- Guaranty of indebtedness of another.
- Loans to officers or directors.

CYBER TRIP

On the Internet, go to www.rjmintz.com/double-taxation-eliminating.html. There, you will see a technique for dealing with the problem of double taxation and a possible solution from a tax attorney. Do you believe that this online advice is ethical? If the advice on this Web site had been given by an accountant, is there a violation of UPL?

Double Taxation

Many who favor the use of the corporate form complain that a distinct disadvantage is the phenomenon of double taxation. As a separate entity, corporations are taxed on their income. Any profits after taxes are, at the discretion of corporation, distributed as dividends to the shareholders, who are taxed on those dividends. The complaint is that the same money is taxed twice: once at the corporate level and once at the shareholder level. After all, the argument goes, the shareholders, as owners of the corporation, are subject twice to taxation as owners and as persons receiving dividends, that is, the profits from their own business. Recent attention to this issue has produced some interesting maneuvering.

Limited Liability Company

limited liability company
A hybrid business formed under state acts, representing both corporation and partnership characteristics.

New currents in the law have developed the **limited liability company**, or LLC, as the result of recently enacted state laws. For small businesses, the LLC offers the single taxation benefit of sole proprietorships and partnerships, as well as the corporate veil of limited liability. This new business entity first appeared in Wyoming and has spread with minor variations to every state. There are some limitations as to size, and some believe that the newness of the business form has created uncertainty that wards off ready investors.

The professional paralegal's role in working with business entities covers a myriad of duties involving public record research and the plethora of state and federal regulations. A corporation often will employ paralegals in its in-house legal departments to monitor and implement the company's compliance with the law by drafting and filing corporate documents. Other duties, whether in-house or in a law firm, include drafting corporate resolutions and preparing other corporate records, such as annual reports and shareholder agreements. Corporate work may be the most stable and profitable aspect of a law office.

Summary

This chapter covers advanced topics in legal specialties and has instructed you in detail in areas that built on the more basic subjects of civil litigation, crimes and criminal procedure, torts and property. Contract law is probably the most basic of business laws. Without contract laws, business could not operate efficiently and effectively. Contract law regulates the formation and enforcement of contracts. Businesses also rely on people working in and for them. Each and every business uses people to act for and on behalf of them, cloaking each with a certain amount of authority to act in a way that binds the business. Agency law covers those legal principles that affix contract or tort liability, depending on the expectations of the parties. In business organizations, the business entity itself is a form of property and subject to transfer or exchange. Moreover, businesses conduct their activities with their primary purpose of entering into contracts for the exchange of goods and services and accumulating property. Modern experience has raised new issues that corporations must face, as well as new forms of corporate forms. All of these matters and more are part of the legal world of business in which paralegals play important parts. Mastery of business matters in law and practice can help a new paralegal land a job in the most lucrative areas of legal practice.

From here, we will be entering into a new phase of study: the development of professional skills for use in virtually any legal office. In its purest form, the work engaged in by legal professionals consists ultimately of communication skills and using them effectively to communicate with clients, the courts, and others within the legal environment.

Key Terms

Acceptance
Agency
Agent
Assignment
Assumpsit
Benefit-detriment
Benefit of the bargain
Breach of contract
Business organization
Common stock
Contract
Corporate veil
Corporation
Counteroffer
Delegation
Duress
Fictitious name
Fraud
Independent contractor
Limited liability company
Limited liability partnership
Liquidated damages
Mirror image rule
Mistake in fact
Mutual assent
Offer
Offeree
Offeror
Preferred stock
Principal
Privity
Rescission and restitution

Scope of authority
Shareholder
Sole proprietorship
Statue of Frauds
Stock
Third-party beneficiary
Ultra vires
Undue influence
Uniform Commercial Code (UCC)
Vicarious liability (*respondeat superior*)
Void contract
Voidable contract
Warranty

Review Questions

1. What are the formalities necessary to form a contract?
2. What is a counteroffer?
3. If your client had suffered physical injury from a defective product, would you sue in tort or in contract?
4. What are the rights of a third-party beneficiary?
5. What is the UCC?
6. Why are contract laws important to business and the economy?
7. What are the primary forms of doing business?
8. What are the equitable forms of relief in lawsuits over contracts?
9. What is the difference between a LLP and an LLC?

Exercises

1. Find out how many different types of business entities are available in your state by visiting the appropriate state office or Web site. Obtain a copy of the necessary forms and brochures.
2. Find two or more sample partnership agreements that can be used in your state. Compare them; is one better than the others?
3. Research the subject of business ethics in your school's library or your school's business department.
4. Find your state's UCC office. What is it?
5. Look up the consumer protection laws in your state. Is there a state agency for consumers? In what kind of cases, if any, can the state agency or attorney general intervene on behalf of a consumer?

Discussion Questions:

1. Which Pennsylvania State Court decided the case of *Schreiber vs. Olan Mills,* and how did the case get to that Court? See www.superior.court.state.pa.us/about.htm.
2. In *Schreiber vs. Olan Mills,* the trial court granted the defendant's preliminary objections and dismissed the case without a trial, and then the plaintiff appealed. A preliminary objection is a term peculiar to Pennsylvania civil procedure. What would be the equivalent in the federal rules?
3. What types of authority do the following agents have, and who are their principals?
   - Real estate agent
   - Theatrical or talent agent

- Department store manager
- Delivery courier
- Hairdresser
- Tutor
- Private detective
- Cashier

4. Do you feel that business laws should be shaped by the law and economics school of thought or by another legal theory?
5. What are the ethical rules regarding business ventures for legal professionals?

PORTFOLIO ASSIGNMENT

Almost everyone has dreamed of owning and running their own business. From restaurants to nightclubs to bakeries to retail boutiques, people dream about getting rich and having fun while running a business that involves something they love. Write a two-page description of the kind of dream business you would love to start, either alone or with family or friends. Go to the appropriate government office in your state, or visit it online, and obtain the necessary forms for creating a corporation (usually called articles of incorporation). In this exercise, fill out the necessary form(s) as if you were doing so for real. What is the filing fee? How helpful was the office's staff or the Web site? Write down your observations from this experience.

Part Three

Entering the Profession

CHAPTER 10 Using the Law in the Field

CHAPTER 11 Getting the Job and Surviving in the Workplace

CHAPTER 12 Examples of Legal Work by Professional Paralegals

Chapter 10

Using the Law in the Field

CHAPTER OBJECTIVES

Upon completion of this chapter, students will have acquired specialized knowledge and competence in the following areas:

- Developing communication skills for interviewing clients, witnesses, and others.
- Planning an investigation and gathering physical evidence.
- Searching public records and using the Internet.
- Basic law office management.

This chapter begins a new phase of your education by introducing some of the ways in which you can learn how to apply the knowledge and skills you have gained from this course. Many professional paralegals routinely conduct interviews and perform investigations. To do so effectively and efficiently, legal professionals prepare for an interview by performing research and formulating questions beforehand. Similarly, fact investigations require preparation and the use of numerous techniques presented in this chapter.

Now that you have a fundamental knowledge of the law as a framework, it is possible to develop skills to apply this newly acquired knowledge. Lawyers and paralegals receive information that they formulate into a legal format for a variety of different eyes and ears. For the courts, legal professionals submit information from clients in the form of pleadings, motions, discovery, legal memoranda, and trials. To their adversaries, lawyers and paralegals submit information seeking settlements or accommodation of their respective clients' positions. These adversaries may include other legal professionals, insurance companies, governmental agencies, or law enforcement officials. Finally, to clients, legal professionals communicate advice, using their understanding of the law to apply legal principles and the rules of law to the client's particular situation.

The legal professional's role is thus essentially one of communication, whether the audience is the legal system, worthy adversaries, or most important, clients. This chapter will instruct and introduce you to some of the basic communication skills used to obtain information from clients, pubic records, and other sources. Although many of these activities involve the intake of information, communication skills become essential in obtaining information from any source.

DEVELOPING COMMUNICATION SKILLS

Obtaining accurate and complete information is the initial step that legal professionals take to formulate legal positions for their clients. With basic information in hand, further inquiry and investigation necessarily follow to ensure that evidence exists to prove the client's assertions. Thus, an understanding of the law of evidence, as we have covered it, becomes an essential part of preparing a client's case. Paralegals frequently act as the first point of contact for prospective clients, as well as the point person for gaining additional information from the client as the case develops. Witnesses provide other sources of information whom paralegals contact with the purposes of taking statements and preparing them for trial. To obtain information efficiently and professionally from clients, witnesses, and others, paralegals must employ a combination of legal knowledge, preparation, and, above all, communication skills.

Interviewing

Communication skills may be broken down into the basic ability to observe, listen, and respond appropriately. In almost any professional context, an interview is not about the interviewer, whether a legal, financial, or medical professional. The object of an interview is to exchange information. The legal professional seeks information that is relevant and helpful to the client's case. Therefore, the legal professional's task during the interview may be viewed as quite technical. Using the law as a blueprint, a paralegal understands, say, the elements of a certain tort, the requirements of an enforceable contract, or the various forms of property ownership. The technical aspects of law thus provide the framework or outline. Focusing on the technical information needed delineates the scope of the interview and lends professionalism to the task. What goes on during the interview should similarly be dictated by efficiency and the goal of meeting the client's expectations.

On the other side, the client may wish to obtain legal information or practical information regarding the case, such as trials or other scheduled events, and perhaps, some reassurance. Here, paralegals must exercise some caution lest they venture into the unauthorized practice of law by giving legal advice. Most agree that responding to questions about the law as it applies to their situation constitutes legal advice. Paralegals, therefore, should respond by prefacing any comments with a statement that they cannot give legal advice. Ideally, the attorney would be available soon after the client meeting with the paralegal. To be safe, responses to specific requests for legal advice should be deferred. Of course, a paralegal remains within the bounds of ethics if he or she relays legal advice directly from a supervising attorney. After a while, avoiding requests for legal advice becomes quite natural. Many paralegals find that the restriction liberates them from burden of prompting the client's expectations and emotions, frequently an unpleasant hazard in the practice of law. Largely, interviewing in this context is about understanding the role of the paralegal and conveying the parameters of this responsibility to the person being interviewed.

Beyond the formalities of communicating as a legal professional are the unwritten rules or guidelines that every professional understands. No official enforcement or sanctions exist for failing to follow any of these unwritten rules or guidelines. As we discussed in the first chapter, professionalism in behavior and appearance have a particularly important place within the legal profession. Maintaining a professional image goes a long way toward instilling confidence and trust in clients, potential clients, and the public at large.

Professional behavior comes naturally with mental focus on the task at hand, filtering out irrelevant personal feelings and maintaining proper and, if possible, pleasant decorum. This maintenance includes keeping voices at an indoor level and speaking of client matters only within earshot of those intended to hear them to guard client confidences. Conversations with colleagues and coworkers regarding client matters have no place in elevators, hallways, cafeterias, and other public or semi-public areas. Far from being overly straight-laced or uptight, professional behavior in the office often appears relaxed and casual. Comfort levels can vary from office to office and location to location.

Preparing for the Interview

Unbeknownst to many people, paralegals often occupy the first line in a law office, acting as the first point of contact with prospective clients. Although this situation does not usually happen in large law firms, medium and small firms or solo practitioners rely on paralegals to screen cases and perform **initial consultations**—the first meeting with a potential client. The types of offices in which paralegals perform initial consultations typically consist of those that engage in general practice or specialize in representing individuals as opposed to businesses or other entities. In matters such as criminal law, employment, family law, immigration, personal injury, and estate planning, paralegals in the law office are well equipped and authorized to obtain information about the potential client and the type of matter they are bringing to the office.

initial consultation
The first meeting with a prospective client in which information will be gathered, additional information requested, and the attorney–client relationship formed.

At most law offices, potential clients make inquiries about possible legal proceedings over the telephone. A receptionist may guide the caller or direct the call to an intake specialist in the office, who may be a paralegal. After determining that the caller has a matter that the office might handle, the intake specialist makes an appointment and instructs the potential client to bring in any relevant documents or papers at the appointed time. In preparation for this appointment, the paralegal at most knows only the most basic information regarding the potential client: name, address, phone number, and the type of matter for which legal assistance is sought.

Law offices use a variety of **intake forms**, each of which asks for specific information depending on the type of matter involved. A family law intake form, for instance, solicits information about the client's family composition and history, as well as the names and dates of birth of any children, spouses, and other family members. Family law intake forms may also request details of the client's financial status, such as income sources, property, and other assets. These details would be necessary if the intake form were for clients who came to the office for a will or estate plan. An intake form for a personal injury case would request a description of the incident, the nature and extent of injuries, and a medical history. These forms vary greatly and usually have been developed by one of the office's attorneys or paralegals. Depending on the type of legal matter, the forms may be very simple or quite lengthy and involved. At any rate, these forms make the initial consultation more efficient. As the interviewer, even a new paralegal can use the office's intake forms to ask the appropriate questions.

intake form
A form developed to solicit basic, case-specific information from a client during an initial consultation and at various stages afterward.

Figure 10.1 provides a sample intake form for a case in which the client wants a will. Our coverage of the subject matter of wills in Chapter 9 can now be put to practical use. As you review the following intake sheet, review the materials on wills in Chapter 8 to determine how the information collected here conforms to the law.

The interview may take place in one of several places in the law office. Generally, most law offices have a conference room for client consultations, whether for initial or follow-up meetings. These conference rooms are usually located near the reception area to control the flow of traffic within the office. For reasons of confidentiality and because of the sensitive nature of legal work, most law offices prefer to confine clients and other visitors to "public" areas of the office.

FIGURE 10.1 Sample Will Intake Form

WILL INTAKE

Date opened: ____________

Execution Date: ____________

☐Will ☐DPA Finances & Personal Care ☐DPA Healthcare

____

Personal Information:

Full name as it will appear on documents: ______________________________________

Address: ______________________________________ City: ______________ Zip: ________

Home Telephone: (________)____________________ Social Security No.: ______________

Work Telephone: (________)____________ Date of Birth: ______________

E-mail: ________________________

Marital Status:

☐Single ☐Spouse or Domestic Partner Name: ______________________

☐Married Date: ______________ Name: ______________________

☐Divorced Date: ______________ Name: ______________________

Children:

______________________ ______________________

______________________ ______________________

Living Relatives: Living Siblings:

Father: ______________________ ______________________

Mother: ______________________ ______________________

Others ____-

Will and Trust Information:

☐Prior Will Date: ______________ Prepared by: ______________________

Residual Beneficiary:

Name: ______________________ City: ______________________ State: ____________

Alternate Residual Beneficiary:

Name: ______________________ City: ______________________ State: ____________

Specific Gifts:

Name: ______________________ City: ______________________ State: ____________

Description of Item: ____

Name: ______________________ City: ______________________ State: ____________

Description of Item: ____

Name: ______________________ City: ______________________ State: ____________

Description of Item: ____

Distribution Other Than Above: ____

____

____

____

Executor: ______________________ Telephone: (________) ______________

Address: ______________________ City: ______________________ Zip: ____________

Alternate: ______________________ Telephone: (________) ______________

Address: ______________________ City: ______________________ Zip: ____________

Contd...

Miscellaneous:____

____

____

Contest Anticipated? ? No ? Yes Explain: ______________________

____

____

Post-Death Instructions:

☐Burial Where: ____________ City: ____________ State:__________

Memorial service or funeral? Describe:__________________________

____

☐Cremation Disposition of remains:_______________________________

Person who will make arrangements: ☐Executor ☐Other (see below)

Name: ____________________ Telephone: (______) ____________

Address: __________________ City: ______________ Zip:________

Any pre-arranged post-death services? ________________________

Durable Power of Attorney (Financial): ☐Immediate Springing Dependant

Agent:____________________ Telephone: (______) ____________

Address: __________________ City: ______________ Zip:________

Alternate: _________________ Telephone: (______) ____________

Address: __________________ City: ______________ Zip:________

Personal Care Provisions for dependant:__________________________

Durable Power of Attorney for Health Care:

Agent: ____________________ Telephone: (______) ____________

Address: __________________ City: ______________ Zip:________

Alternate: _________________ Telephone: (______) ____________

Address: __________________ City: ______________ Zip:________

Organ Donation: ☐No ☐Yes Specify:_____________________________

Medical Treatment Desires and Limitations Options: ☐1. ☐2. ☐3.

Special Instructions for Nutrition and Hydration: ☐A. ☐B.

Health & Safety Code §7100 Disposition of Remains: ☐Y. ☐N.

ASSETS

Real Property: ____

How held? ____

Life Insurance: ____

(beneficiaries, amounts, etc.)

Bank Accounts: ____

401(k), IRA, etc.: ____

Stocks, Bonds, etc.: ____

Other: ____

____

FIGURE 10.1 Sample Will Intake Form *(Concluded)*

PRACTICE TIP

Appearances are important if you are going to meet with a client. In the office, be sure to conform to the offices custom for dress and appearance.

For the same reason, in the event that the interviewer uses his or her own office to consult with a client, an essential part of preparation consists of clearing the desk. Client files and other papers should be kept out of view. Moreover, prospective clients are just as likely to be interviewing the law firm, assessing whether to entrust their legal matter to your firm. Shopping around for legal services has become quite common for cost-conscious individuals and business decision makers. Thus, an organized and professional appearance for the office and the legal professional will go far in making a good impression. It would be natural for a prospective client to fear that his or her legal matter will be lost or forgotten under a disarrayed pile of files and papers. Similarly, a person seeking initial advice would be put off by a legal professional's disheveled appearance.

Another important part of preparing for the interview is to review the information about the client and situation. If interviewing an existing client for the purpose of obtaining ongoing information, a professional paralegal conducts a thorough review of the client's file. In case any questions from the client arise, the paralegal's display of through knowledge about the client's situation instills confidence and trust. The two primary purposes of almost any interview with a client are to obtain accurate and complete information and to foster a professional relationship of comfort and trust that facilitates the flow of communication between the client and the legal professionals of the entire office. Clients naturally view any legal professional of an office that is handling their legal matter as a representative of the entire law firm. Thus, the conduct and appearance of the paralegal conducting an interview reflects on the firm and can make a lasting impression on the client and others—hopefully a positive one.

Professional greetings consist almost uniformly of a smile, a handshake, and an exchange of a greeting such as, "Pleasure to meet you." Eye contact is important, yet too much can be unsettling. Many cultures regard sustained eye contact as inappropriate or overly aggressive. Some otherwise knowledgeable authorities on the subject have attempted to make generalizations about these attitudes among different cultural groups. However, these generalizations serve little more than to perpetuate stereotypes. Nevertheless, knowledge of some customs can avoid discomfort or even offense.

In the United States, those seeking the assistance of legal professionals presumptively understand the rules of professional etiquette in a law office. Certainly, even a novice to the legal system and the legal profession in the United States has a basic appreciation of what constitutes professional conduct in a law office. In American culture, standard greetings and office behavior vary little and are within the bounds of most cultures of the world. During a first meeting in a professional setting, touching is limited to a cordial handshake and brief eye contact.

COMMUNICATION TIP

When communicating with persons from another culture, it is important to be aware of their customs and habits, which may differ greatly from what you are used to in American business norms.

In many parts of the Caribbean, for instance, beginning a conversation without an initial greeting such as "Good morning" is considered quite rude. In the Middle East, many cultures consider it very impolite for people to show the bottom of their feet, even inadvertently when sitting. The "okay" hand signal, using the thumb and index finger in a circle with the rest of the fingers splayed, is considered a vulgar gesture in some European countries. Professionals often receive a business card from a new acquaintance by looking at it very briefly and then putting it into their pocket. To do so when receiving a business card from someone from certain Asian countries is considered disrespectful; the card should be read and admired for a moment or two and then carefully put away.

To avoid offending a person from another culture, be sure to check with anyone in the office who has had dealings with the person or members of the same culture to see if there may be a certain etiquette or protocol to follow.

The same cultural norms are true of the behavior within the interview room, whether in a conference room or the legal professional's office. Traditionally, legal professionals conducted conferences on opposite sides of a desk, sitting opposite each other. Modern thinking regards such a traditional arrangement as hierarchical and authoritative, appropriate for some circumstances but not all. To create a comfortable setting, the following factors come into play.

- Almost all interviews take place seated at a table or desk.
- Desks tend to exude the authority of the person sitting behind them.
- Sitting at a conference table or end table conveys a more casual atmosphere.
- The relative chair height may also indicate a higher status for the person seated in a higher chair; thus, the chairs should be of equal height.
- Face-to-face seating arrangements can be too intense and even a bit confrontational.
- Side-to-side seating denotes equality, and many prefer a kitty-corner seating arrangement as more conducive to a relaxed and more productive setting.

Body language is a broad term for forms of communication using body movements, gestures, and facial expressions. Most people are generally not aware that everyone sends and receives nonverbal signals. Figure 10.2 provides some interpretations of common body language. These signals can indicate what they are truly feeling. The technique of "reading" people is used frequently. For example, the idea of mirroring body language to put people at ease is commonly used in interviews. Mirroring to a small extent puts the person being interviewed at ease, indicating that they are understood. Posture, if too attentive or stiff, may indicate unnecessary formality or discomfort. Instead, an attentive posture that is also casual and relaxed helps create a mood that is more conducive to an exchange of information.

body language
A form of communication using body movements or gestures instead of, or in addition to, sounds, verbal language, or other communication.

Taking notes in some contexts may be considered distracting. However, at an interview in the law office, an interviewer who takes notes demonstrates interest and

Body Language	Interpretation
Brisk, attentive walk	Confidence
Sitting with legs crossed, foot kicking	Boredom
Sitting, legs apart	Receptive, relaxed
Arms crossed over chest	Defensiveness
Hand to cheek	Thinking or evaluating
Touching, slightly rubbing nose	Rejection, doubt, lying
Rubbing eyes	Doubt, disbelief
Hands clasped behind back	Anger, frustration, apprehension
Locked ankles	Apprehension
Head resting in hand, looking downward	Boredom
Patting/fondling hair	Lack of self-confidence; insecurity
Rubbing hands	Anticipation
Tapping or drumming fingers	Impatience
Gesticulating with palms up	Sincerity, openness, entreating
Hands clasped behind head, legs crossed	Confidence, superiority
Pinching bridge of nose, eyes closed	Negative evaluation
Tilted head	Interested, piqued, quizzical
Stroking chin	In the process of deciding or weighing
Looking down or facing away	Disbelief
Steepling fingers	Authoritative
Biting nails	Uncertainty, insecurity, nervousness.
Pulling or tugging at ear	Indecision

FIGURE 10.2
Interpretations of Body Language

impresses upon the client that what he or she is saying is worth noting. Note taking also shows that the interviewer is listening. The use of a specific intake form, along with a notepad for added information, should accompany the interviewer. In some cases, the client's file or relevant parts of it may be handy for reference. Again, the interviewer's demonstrated familiarity with the file will impress a client regarding the paralegal's preparedness and understanding of the situation. If there is only basic information, such as name, address, and contact information, a thorough interviewer should review those items to ensure accuracy.

A professionally conducted interview results not from improvisation but from careful preparation and thoughtful questioning. The object of the interview is to bring out the personal story from the client and to put the client's knowledge center stage. It is never about the interviewer, unless the client asks; even then, responses about the interviewer's personal life should be very brief. Personal matters not germane to the client's situation may lead to unproductive tangents in the conversation and thus should be avoided. However, a complete refusal to respond may offend the client. Most agree that the best practice is to answer as briefly as possible and then move on.

Conducting the Interview

At the outset, many legal professionals consider it inadvisable to launch right into the interview unless only a few minutes have been allotted. Starting with some casual conversation will relax both of you. Innocuous discussions about the weather or current events act as ice breakers and help establish a comfort level for the client as an entry into the main topic to be discussed: the client's legal matter. Certainly after a couple of minutes of small talk, the interview's main purpose should begin. The interviewing paralegal can taking charge by broaching the discussion asking, "Well, how can this office help you?" At that point, the interview has begun in earnest, which invites the client to launch into a narrative of his or her situation.

At a certain point, the interviewer should break into the client's narrative and ask questions. The opportunity to do so may come at a pause in the client's description or when the interviewer needs to interject a question seeking clarification. Questions should be as short and simple as possible. Avoid legal terms and jargon. The object is to get the client talking in a directed fashion. Give the client time to answer. Rambling responses may be politely cut short by saying, "Fine, but let me ask you this," or even, "Good, let's move on." Begin with general questions and then focus on legally relevant details that the client may have left out. Draw out specifics by asking, "How long, how many, when?" Clients may be fuzzy about details such as specific dates. Probing further with specific follow-up questions regarding the time of year or proximity of a holiday can jog the client's memory. It may be helpful to consider the interview as a cone. At the beginning, the wide mouth of the cone is reflected in the wide berth of general questions from which the interviewer is able to elicit narrower details that fill out the picture.

The legal knowledge and skills you have acquired through education and training now come into play, as the questions you ask to follow up coincide with the legal requirements of proof or the elements of a legal principle. The rules of evidence or the Statute of Frauds may have a grave impact on a client's situation, perhaps without his or her knowledge. Thus, the paralegal's knowledge of the law should prompt questions to gather legally relevant information from the client.

paraphrasing
A technique used for interviews in which the interviewer repeats the information in his or her own words to ensure the accuracy of the information received.

After a comfort level has been achieved and the client feels at ease, several techniques can help clarify and assure the accuracy of the interview. **Paraphrasing** the client's response—that is, repeating the client's description in the interviewer's own words—can ensure the accuracy of the information. A client's description of an incident should be repeated by the interviewer so that the understanding is clear. Clients are reassured when an interviewer paraphrases their responses. Through paraphrasing, the client becomes aware that the interviewer understands. Paralegals conducting interviews may think of themselves as conducting a form of direct examination, as if in court or during an administrative hearing. Many experienced legal professionals use questions as a painter would use a brush to paint a picture of the client's version of the story. At the beginning of the interview, general questions act as broad strokes, then specific questions act as fine brushes to fill in the details and complete the picture.

Questions that ask for a one- or two-word response are known as **closed-ended questions**, which are useful for seeking clarification or minor details, such as, "What date was that?" Following a closed-ended question, encourage a continuation of the narrative with, "Go on, please," or "Then what happened?" These types of questions are **open-ended questions**, which ask for broad narrative responses. Except when paraphrasing the client, avoid using leading questions that ask a question by suggesting the answer. An example of a **leading question** would be, "Was it true that the child's father appeared angry?" At trials and administrative hearings, leading questions are, with minor exceptions, impermissible because the person asking the question is actually testifying by revealing the answer. For the same reason, during an interview, the factual information must come from the client or witness. Even the safest assumptions by the interviewer may lead a case down the wrong path.

closed-ended questions
Questions that seek a brief or one-word answer.

open-ended questions
Questions that encourage a full meaningful answer involving the person's knowledge and feelings.

leading questions
Questions that suggest the answer.

Listening and Active Listening

Perhaps the most important skill to acquire as an interviewer is the ability to listen. As simple as it may sound, listening—especially **active listening**—comes about only through experience and training. Active listening involves two behaviors on the part of the listener or interviewer. The first is difficult: The listener must suspend judgment and consciously avoid the tendency to relate the client's story to the interviewer's past associations or experiences. We all construct our reality around our own relationships and histories. When we meet someone new or find ourselves in a different situation, we gauge this new acquaintance or situation in comparison with persons or experiences from our past. In psychology, the phenomenon is known as transference and countertransference, such that listeners subjectively shape their experiences of the speaker. Although valuable as a form of understanding the dilemma of a friend or loved one, in the give-and-take of normal conversation, these psychological dynamics block the simple intake of client information in an office interview.

active listening
A structured form of listening and responding that focuses attention on the speaker and the speaker's feelings.

At this point, the professional dynamics of an interview should become apparent. A professional interview is vastly different from the conversations in our personal lives outside the office. The task of listening as a legal professional consists solely of getting the information down accurately and completely. Listening is not an act of repose. Listening requires the exercise of high concentration. Simply holding your tongue while the other person speaks isn't the same thing as listening. To really listen, you have to suspend your own agenda, forget about what you might say next, and ignore the impression you may make. Concentrate on being a receptive vehicle for the other person. But there almost inevitably comes a moment when we cease to be engrossed. We lose interest or feel the urge to interrupt. It is at this moment that listening requires the second aspect, self-control. Genuine active listening means suspending memory, desire, and judgment and, for a few moments at least, existing solely for the other person.

Having listened and understood the client, your response assures the client that you have listened and understood. This response may be verbal or otherwise. Paraphrasing is the most accurate way to provide this reassurance. Simpler methods of responding may consist of a word or two, such as "I see," "Uh-huh," and "I understand." On the nonverbal side, a simple nod may suffice. These simple responses acknowledge and assure the client that you understand and flow naturally from the task of active listening. Active listening also helps the interviewer focus on the task of receiving the information from the client. By losing a distracting sense of self-consciousness and focusing upon the client, an experienced interviewer can maintain the flexibility needed to appreciate the nuances of the client's predicament.

Just as a paralegal must develop an awareness of his or her body language, awareness of the client's body language can discern clues as to his or her feelings. Careful observation of the client's gestures, posture, and movement may provide additional information. In many cases, the legal professional is only one of a small circle of people to whom the client has entrusted his or her confidence. Picking up on nonverbal clues may provide more legally relevant information. For instance, in discussing a will or estate plan, the client's apparent anxiety regarding one of the intended beneficiaries may signal a need to make additional provisions in a will or other estate planning instrument. Further questioning may reveal that the client is concerned that this intended beneficiary, perhaps one of her children, is not known to be particularly responsible in handling his own finances. It therefore would be incumbent on the legal professional to consider other legal mechanisms.

Ending the Client Interview

When the interview has reached the tip of the cone, a final review of all the information, perhaps by paraphrasing, checks the completeness and accuracy of the information. Using an intake sheet as a checklist, review the information received once more, being sure to confirm details such as dates, names, and addresses. If you have received documents from the client, be sure to make copies and return the originals to the client before ending the interview. Finally, go over the next steps that the legal professionals in the office will take or make a list on a separate piece of paper that indicates the items that the client needs to take or provide. Frequently, clients are unaware of all the details or additional documents needed. In some cases, an interviewing paralegal will give the client a self-addressed, stamped envelope, along with the list of items, so that the client can mail the missing information or additional papers. If the firm has provided you with business cards, be sure that the client is aware of the office's phone number and e-mail address so that he or she will be able to contact you directly if any questions arise.

If the interview is an initial consultation, the end of the interview with the paralegal should be followed by a discussion with an attorney from the firm, unless previous discussions have established the attorney–client relationship. In many situations, the client will have already decided to **retain**—that is, hire—the firm to pursue the client's legal matter. Upon ending his or her part of the interview, the paralegal will say something like, "It was nice to meet you; let me get the attorney to come to speak with you." After departing the conference room, the paralegal usually discusses the matter privately with the attorney, giving a concise overview of the details covered. The attorney then consults with the client to confirm some of the more important information and provide some initial legal analysis, often in the presence of the paralegal.

retain
To hire a legal professional.

With knowledge about the type of case before the interview, the legal team can have ready the necessary forms and other documents for the client to sign. When the attorney has taken over the interview, these authorizations often have been prepared

EYE ON ETHICS

Remember that one of the three major concerns of the prohibition against the unauthorized practice of law is establishing the attorney–client relationship. Both major national paralegal associations and the ABA have specific rules in this regard. By definition, the creation of the attorney–client relationship consists of entering into an agreement for the delivery of legal services. Thus, paralegals may conduct initial interviews and collect information from the client. Once the client agrees to hire the firm, a licensed attorney must enter into the actual retainer agreement to create the attorney–client relationship.

for the client to sign once he or she has retained the firm. If the client's matter involves an administrative agency, almost all agencies require a client's signature on specific forms from the agency, authorizing the law firm to review the client's records and appear as the legal representative.

Every law office maintains a variety of internally generated **authorization letters**, or releases, that authorize the law firm to obtain a client's personal records, such as medical, employment, or criminal record information. Unlike a retainer agreement, a paralegal may obtain a client's signature on the release to obtain information or verification without an attorney present. Paralegals are frequently called upon to obtain client authorization for obtaining or viewing records.

authorization letter
A letter the client provides the attorney granting permission to contact employers, doctors, or other individuals who have records that relate to a case.

Figure 10.3 provides an example of a release of the client's medical records from a hospital or doctor's office.

As soon as practical after the interview, review handwritten notes to flesh out any abbreviations or other shorthand devices that may need deciphering. Depending on the protocol in your office, the intake sheet and any notes should a basic part of the client's file once the office accepts the case. In a growing number of offices, the person performing the interview enters the information from the intake sheets and accompanying notes into the firm's computer network through a time and reporting software system. In your haste while taking notes, you may have written abbreviations for words that won't mean anything to you a day or two later. In

FIGURE 10.3
Example of a Release of a Client's Medical Records

Shrieve, Krumpp & Loh
Attorneys and Counselors at Law
925 Sterling Street
Silver Springs, Nevada
775-577-4336

Authorization for Release of Medical Records

To: Dr. Maryann Glendon

I hereby authorize you to provide a copy of my medical records to Edward Loh, Esq., or his designee at Shrieve, Krumpp & Loh. Kindly regard any copy of this authorization as effective as an original of the same. This authorization is effective immediately and remains in effect until I revoke it in writing.

______________________ Date:_______

Horace Silver
442 Glenwood Avenue
Silver Springs, NV 89429
775-555-1212
SSA #026-356-9966
Date of Birth: January 28, 1950

short, fill in whatever gaps exist in your notes to allow anyone to understand what has transpired.

Interviewing Witnesses

The same skills for interviewing clients also apply to interviewing witnesses. Preparation, focus, and active listening skills apply to contacts with witnesses. Some differences deserve mention.

lay witness
Any witness not testifying as an expert witness and who may not testify as to conclusions or opinions.

expert witness
A witness with specialized knowledge or expertise in the subject of testimony.

Lay witnesses are those persons who have seen or experienced aspects of the client's case, such as observers of an accident or the signing of a contract. A lay witness may also be a person familiar with the parties or the general surroundings of an incident in question. **Expert witnesses** possess technical education or training for which they are retained to give an opinion regarding a technical aspect of the case. Experts are almost never personally involved with the case and can act as either consultants to help evaluate a case or as potential witnesses testifying in court. These witnesses are also made available to the other party during litigation for the purpose of discovery and can include accountants, engineers, and medical professionals. When one party reveals, as it must, that a potential witness, whether lay or expert, may testify on their behalf, the opposing party may depose them during the discovery phase of the litigation.

adverse (hostile) witness
A witness whose interests or perspective are potentially damaging to the case of an opposing party.

Interviewing either type of witness at the earliest stages of the case helps the office litigation team strategize ways to bolster or minimize the impact of their intended testimony. This benefit is particularly true for experts for the opposition. A common tactic in dealing with the experts for the opposition challenges their qualifications to act as experts. Unusual tactfulness can reduce the amount of hostility that can come from an adverse witness—that is, a witness whose position is unfavorable to the client's case. Do not expect an **adverse witness** to be willing or even available for an interview. An adverse witness often will refuse an invitation for an interview with legal professionals representing the opposing side. Other than through certain discovery mechanisms, there is no law that requires them to speak with you. However, the likelihood of an uncooperative response should not preclude an attempt to contact them.

Even the most minimal contact with a witness deserves a notation in the file. A file memo or a witness's statement written and signed by the individual stands as a record of the statement and can, in some circumstances, be used at trial as either a corroborating or impeaching aid to litigators when the witness is on the stand. The important similarities that witnesses have to clients for interview purposes are the professionalism with which they should be approached. Antagonizing an adverse witness may harden his or her opposition to your client. At the same time, a friendly and professional approach will do no harm and may yield, in some rare instances, some surprising results. You never know.

EYE ON ETHICS

When a potential witness is represented by another attorney, ethical rules prohibit legal professionals from contacting the potential witness, unless his or her attorney consents. Thus, once a potential witness is contacted, it is essential for the legal professional to ask at the outset whether he or she has an attorney. If so, ask for the name and contact information of the attorney, cease communication, and consult your supervising attorney. See, for example, ABA Model Rule of Professional Conduct 4.2; NALA Canons 3 and 10 (incorporating the ABA Model Rules); and NFPA Rule 1.2, EC-1.2(b).

INVESTIGATIONS

Paralegals frequently perform **field investigations** to locate information outside of the office. Similar to witness statements, the fruits of field investigations can stand as evidence. With the advent of the Internet and search engines, paralegal investigations turn up a wealth of information that may lead to other sources of evidence from other witnesses or public records. In the legal trade, information sought in this way is known as **informal discovery**, meaning that the format of a field investigation is neither restricted nor enforced by any court rules or laws. Subject only to the cooperation and willingness of those from whom information is requested and the laws protecting privacy, the success of informal discovery depends on the initiative and resourcefulness of the investigating paralegal. As described later, one of the best forms of obtaining information through informal discovery is through the Freedom of Information Act.

field investigation
Factual research performed outside the office, including viewing public records, interviewing witnesses, photographing crime or accident scenes, or other research.

informal discovery
Obtaining information about the opposition's case through means other than the procedural rules of discovery.

The world of information available outside the law office often appears as a bottomless pit into which an investigating paralegal casts his or her fishing net. The vast array of public records, libraries, databases, and even court records is enough for a starting point. At the outset, understand and identify the aspects of your client's case that require proof.

This identification may be accomplished in two steps. First, make a chart of the elements necessary to your client's claim. Some legal research may be necessary for an accurate list of the elements of a particular claim of defense in your state. Second, for each element, fill in the evidence that you already have for your client's case. Determine with your colleagues whether there is enough evidence. List the other items of proof that would be necessary or desirable.

Figure 10.4 lists the legal elements and items of proof necessary to prove the case. In the case of an automobile accident in which your office represents the plaintiff, assume that the defendant's suspected negligence could have been due to the failure to stop at a red light. Listing the general elements of negligence, the plaintiff's case would be proven by seeking information that would prove each of the four elements.

Figure 10.4 is a simple illustration of how the beginning of an investigation would proceed. Note that there is, necessarily, a fair amount of overlap with the number of elements that a single item of proof provides. For instance, a police report may be used to satisfy several elements, along with other forms of evidence. The chart also lists some of the possible sources of proof for each element. Brainstorming with experienced colleagues could lead to other sources of proof. Also note that the chart may indicate any necessary legal research regarding damages for pain and suffering. At any rate, once started, the proof chart sets out in an organized manner the tasks needed to start an investigation. By no means should the chart's itemization of proof be considered exhaustive. As the investigation continues, items on the proof side could change or become longer and more detailed.

Remember that no matter how much material you are able to amass on behalf of your client, the rules of evidence apply. The best claim or defense will be worthless if the materials to prove either cannot be admitted as evidence in court. Thus, the fruits of a well-planned investigation always should be viewed through the lens of the rules of evidence. In Chapter 6, you studied a primer for paralegals regarding some of the rules of evidence. These rules—laws actually—are designed to ensure the reliability of evidence and determine whether a certain item of evidence may be admissible in court. If the evidence is admissible, it will be considered proof of an element in a cause of action. At the same time, a trier of fact (judge or jury) is free to disregard or disbelieve evidence that is unquestionably admissible under the laws of evidence. Thus, as a practical matter, legal professionals routinely amass as much

Elements of Negligence	Possible Proof Available
DUTY OF CARE—Stop sign and traffic regulation establish duty to obey and to stop.	1. Photograph of stop sign. 2. Police report describing intersection. 3. Testimony of plaintiff. 4. Witness familiar with intersection. 5. Governmental documentation of the stop sign's existence from the city, state, or public safety agency.
BREACH—Defendant breached duty to stop by failing to stop at stop sign.	1. Police report indicating that defendant had failed to stop. 2. Testimony of plaintiff. 3. Diagram of position of cars made for insurance. 4. Any traffic citation issued to defendant. 5. Testimony of witnesses at scene.
CAUSATION—Defendant's breach of the duty to stop caused the plaintiff harm factually and legally.	1. Police report describing incident as reported. 2. Testimony of plaintiff. 3. Testimony of any witnesses present. 4. Damage to vehicles indicating the angle of impact and the spot of impact as the cars collided.
HARM—Plaintiff suffered property damage to car and personal injuries including medical expenses, lost wages, and pain and suffering (if permitted under state tort law). Legal research needed to see if pain and suffering are compensable items of damages in this jurisdiction.	1. Photograph of damage to car. 2. Mechanics' statement and estimate. 3. Emergency room report. 4. Testimony of plaintiff as to: a. pain and suffering. b. injuries suffered. 5. Medical records. 6. Employment records showing lost time. 7. Testimony of family members, doctor, and others.

FIGURE 10.4 List of Legal Elements and Possible Items of Proof

tangible evidence
Evidence that can be touched, picked up.

real evidence
Evidence in the form of objects involved in a case or that actually played a part in the incident or transaction in question, such as a weapon.

documentary evidence
Any evidence represented on paper that contributes to supporting the legal position and/or verbal testimony of witnesses, for example, medical billing records or cancelled checks.

digital or electronic evidence
Evidence stored or transmitted in digital form, such as metadata or computer-generated documents or images.

evidence as they can during the investigatory stage of a case. Before trial, only the most convincing evidence will be used.

With these practical considerations in mind, the rules of evidence also classify the various types of evidence. Under the rules of evidence, each type of evidence carries with it specialized rules that must be followed to be admissible. Admitting a photograph into evidence does not require the identification or testimony of the photographer. Instead, a competent witness need only testify that a photograph is a fair and accurate representation of the scene. The classification for various types of evidence, in practice, also function to guide the legal professional in organizing the evidence obtained through investigatory efforts. Consider the following list of the types of evidence. As you review them, try to fit each form proof from the proof chart into the following classifications.

- **Tangible evidence** is any evidence introduced in a trial in the form of a physical object, intended to prove a fact in issue on the basis of its demonstrable physical characteristics. Physical evidence can conceivably include all or part of any object.

  Physical evidence also includes:

- **Real evidence**. Objects involved in a case or that actually played a part in the incident or transaction in question. Examples include a written contract, a defective part, the murder weapon, or the gloves used by an alleged murderer.
- **Documentary evidence**. Any form of documents, such as memoranda, correspondence, contracts, or a will.
- **Digital or electronic evidence**. Any information stored or transmitted in digital form, such as metadata or computer-generated documents or images.

EYE ON ETHICS

Whether performing duties in or outside the office, paralegals must identify themselves as such to those they encounter. Both the NALA and NFPA ethical codes specifically provide that a paralegal's title must indicate his or her status (NFPA Rule 1.7), and that paralegals must disclose this status (NALA Canon 5). These commands are particularly important when the paralegal acts on behalf of the firm's client outside of the office. Identifying yourself merely as someone from a law firm would make most people assume that you are an attorney, particularly those outside the office who have had little or no contact with legal professionals. Thus, to comply with your ethical duties, identify yourself as a paralegal right from the outset. You may actually find that people will feel more comfortable talking to a paralegal than to an attorney.

- **Testimonial evidence**. Oral recitations and statements from a witness made at trial under oath or solemn declaration.
- **Demonstrative evidence**. Prepared representations of an object or event to be used at trial, such as photos, x-rays, videotapes, movies, sound recordings, diagrams, forensic animation, maps, drawings, graphs, animation, simulations, and models.

testimonial evidence
Oral statements made by a witness under oath.

demonstrative evidence
Any object, visual aid, model, scale drawing, or other exhibit designed to help clarify points in the trial.

Investigatory Tools

At the outset of an investigation, resort to in-office tools: the telephone, correspondence, and computer resources. Many of the items of proof listed in the chart in Figure 10.4 could be obtained easily using in-office investigatory tools. Telephone inquiries to the insurance company or the police department, followed by correspondence accompanied by appropriate releases, routinely obtain the requested reports. Similarly, correspondence to the appropriate medical personnel at the emergency room, the ambulance drivers, attending physicians, or other sources, along with the client's release, should be sufficient to obtain the requested documentation. The paralegal should also maintain the names, addresses, and telephone numbers of those persons involved in the client's situation as part of the list of witnesses who would be available to testify. From there, an investigating paralegal would be able to venture out of the office to obtain statements from those involved.

In the Field

Information obtained through the in-office investigation assists the planning of the steps needed for a field investigation. Organized into discrete tasks, a paralegal might begin with statements from the mechanics or salvage personnel involved. The police report obtained through telephone and correspondence inquiries may list any witnesses that were present at the scene of the accident. If the investigating paralegal locates any witnesses, it is advisable to refresh their memories of the scene using a diagram of the scene as an aid, such as the one shown in Figure 10.5.

Notice how the diagram also suggests possible camera angles if photographs were possible at the scene. In more complex cases, law firms often retain **forensics** experts who are expert witnesses educated and trained to reconstruct accidents using photography and other visual devices that may be used in court to show how the accident occurred, based on the available information. However, in more simple cases, a paralegal or others armed with a simple point-and-shoot digital camera can produce photographs that may be used as evidence.

The lawyer's ethical rules, the Model Rules of Professional Conduct, specifically Rule 3.7, generally prohibit a party's lawyer from testifying and could arguably apply to lawyers' paralegals. However, the admission of a photograph as an evidentiary rule

forensics
The practice of applying various scientific techniques to the examination and comparison of biological evidence, trace evidence, impression evidence (e.g., fingerprints, footprints, tire tracks), controlled substances, ballistics (firearm examination), and other evidence for court use in criminal or civil matters.

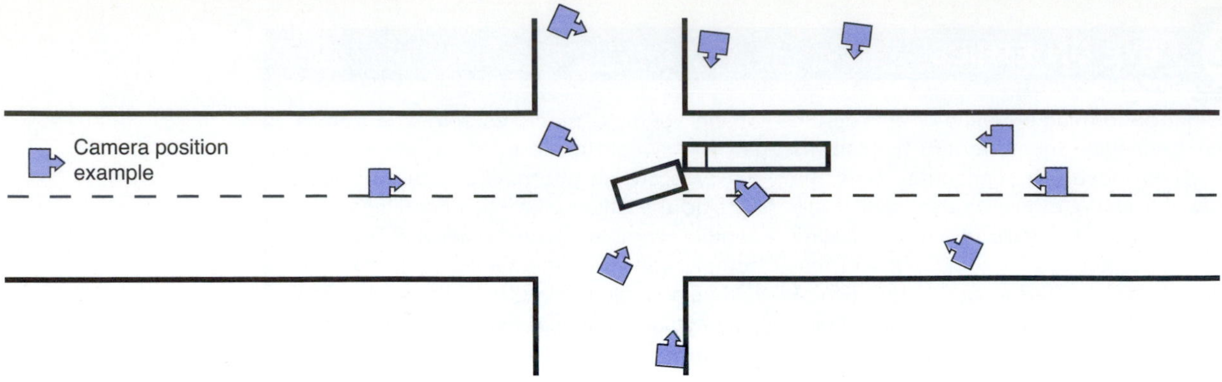

FIGURE 10.5 Diagram of a Scene of an Accident

PRACTICE TIP

Unlike many areas of law, the law of evidence does not regulate or guide behavior. The law of evidence guides legal professionals and courts in determining what items of proof are legally admissible forms of evidence. Thus, knowledge of the rules of evidence is best applied when evaluating whether a document or statement may be admitted in court. That evaluation is done only in the legal professional's mind or in discussion with others working on the same legal team.

does not require the testimony of the person who took the photograph. As indicated in the proof chart in Figure 10.4, the plaintiff's testimony alone could establish the necessary legal foundation for the admissibility of a photograph, as long as the party attempting to admit the photograph into evidence can offer testimony that the photograph is an accurate representation of the scene. This requirement usually means someone must testify that the photograph accurately portrays the scene as viewed by that witness.

Probably among the more challenging investigatory tactics is tracking down witnesses or other persons who could possess relevant information pertaining to the client's case. In our example, police reports list the names and contact information of any witnesses who were present at the scene of the accident. The possibility that any one of them could agree to produce a statement on the client's behalf makes it worthwhile to seek them out. There are many other methods for the investigatory activity known as locating people. The following are some popular sources worth looking into.

The Internet

Search engines abound with free and fee-based person location services. Some offer background checks and credit status, together with details on any court judgments filed on that person. Other resources furnish:

- Vital statistics (e.g., www.vitalrec.com).
- Links to the motor vehicle department of every state can trace registration and license information (e.g., www.usatrace.com/ssmv.html).
- Genealogy (e.g., www.genhomepage.com, www.ancestry.com).
- Business information about companies (e.g., www.yahoo.com, www.hoovers.com, www.sec.gov [publicly held companies], www.switchboard.com).

In addition to providing electronic access to the most comprehensive law library, private companies such as Lexis-Nexis and Westlaw offer the use of extensive online databases to find a person's address, telephone number, and even any professional licenses.

United States Postal Service

If an individual has requested that the U.S. Postal Service forward mail to a new address, his or her new address is available. If you send an envelope to the old address and mark it, "Change of Service Requested," the USPS will provide the new address.

Public Records

Court records are indexed and usually well organized, which facilitates searches for any civil or criminal proceedings, past or present, listed by party name. Entire court files may be available in the county of the individual's residence. At a minimum, it is worth checking.

If you have the individual's address, you can obtain information on any property owned by that individual in the land registry of all states, many of which have free online access. Within the same city or town of the individual's property, you can also obtain property taxes, assessment values, and the date of the last tax payment. The building and health departments of most cities maintain information on safety inspections, permits, construction plans, and other regularly maintained information that may pertain to a client's case. Of particular interest to many plaintiffs would be citations for any infractions of building or health codes.

Government Business Records

As we discussed in our coverage on business entities, almost all businesses must publicly file information about the nature of their businesses, the structure, and the persons behind the business entity. Of particular interest would be the business's designation of its **registered agent**. A registered agent is an individual designated to receive service of process when a business entity is a party in a legal action, such as a lawsuit or summons to testify in court or at a deposition. As a condition of doing business, the law requires that businesses indicate the name and address of a registered agent, making the business entity accountable and accessible to the public in the event of a dispute.

registered agent
A business or individual designated to receive service of process when a business entity is a party in a legal action such as a lawsuit or summons.

RESEARCH THIS

Research whether your state has its own freedom of information act. What is the citation? What state agencies does it cover? What are the formalities necessary to initiate a request?

Freedom of Information Act

The federal government and many states have statutory procedures for obtaining information from their administrative agencies. That information may be about the agency, how it operates, and any data on individuals. A treasure trove of information is available through state or federal **Freedom of Information Act (FOIA)** requests. Paralegals and other legal professionals routinely obtain information from state or federal agencies through FOIA. First-time FOIA users visit the agency's office or Web site to determine that it possesses the information sought and how to file a FOIA request, whether by filling out a special agency form or writing a letter.

Freedom of Information Act (FOIA)
A federal or state law that permits access to information held by government agencies.

CYBER TRIP

On the Internet, go to www.uscis.gov, click on *Immigration Forms*, and find the Freedom of Information Act request form (Form G-639). Where is this form filed, and what kind of information is available through this form?

Bringing It Home

In practice, a thorough investigation may take place over the course of several weeks or longer. Factors such as the time necessary to allow for responses to phone and correspondence inquiries, accommodating the schedules of potential witnesses to be interviewed, and the delays in receiving public records require flexibility and organization for an investigating paralegal. Above all, patience and the ability to juggle several balls in the air will eventually pay off, if just by teaching experience. Remember that of the several leads you may start with, some may end up as dead ends. Potential witnesses may blow off appointments, and record keepers may forget or lag behind in promised responses, resulting in some frustration. Some may actually refuse or never respond.

CASE IN POINT

EVIDENCE LAW CONSIDERATIONS

PEOPLE V. LUGASHI, 205 CAL. APP. 3d 632; 252 CAL. RPTR. 434 (1988)

Avraham Lugashi appeals a conviction by the court for grand theft of more than $25,000, and four counts of receiving payment for items falsely represented to credit card issuers as having been furnished. He contends that the trial court erred in admitting computer-generated evidence.

The evidence established that in June 1984, six computer tapes containing complete account information for up to 60,000 Bank of America Visa credit card customers were stolen. The stolen information was copied, sold, and reproduced into counterfeit credit cards. The counterfeit cards appeared similar to genuine cards, but lacked certain embossed symbols and the magnetic strip containing correct account information for the actual customers. Between September 12 and October 16, 1984, 44 fraudulent charges totaling over $67,000 were made at appellant's oriental rug stores using counterfeit credit cards without knowledge or consent of the legitimate account holders. Appellant admitted to the police making the sales or completing the paperwork on 37 of those charges.

None of the charges were made by the actual account holders. Moreover, in the expert opinion of a Los Angeles Police Department Bunco Forgery Detective, a Wells Fargo Bank Special Agent and a Wells Fargo Loss Control Specialist, many of appellant's admitted transactions involved additional indicia of fraud.

At the time of the alleged "sales," these transactions were entered at appellant's stores on a credit card verification terminal and simultaneously recorded electronically on computers maintained by the issuing banks, third party companies which conduct verification for banks, and Wells Fargo, with which appellant maintained an account into which all credit card sales were deposited.

Each night, Wells Fargo runs a program known as a "dump" which reorders the entries by customer and merchant account numbers. Shortly thereafter, a tape is made of the "dump" from which a microfiche record is prepared and maintained. Although the actual merchant and bank copies of the fraudulent charges, deposit slips, and appellant's sales invoices were entered in evidence, the merchant queries and system responses were gleaned from printed copies of the microfiche.

Appellant's objection to introduction of the computer generated records because an inadequate foundation had been laid under the business records exception to the hearsay rule was overruled.

Appellant contends the trial court abused its discretion in admitting the computer data under the business records exception to the hearsay rule. Appellant argues that respondent produced no evidence regarding Wells Fargo's hardware, software, or its maintenance and accuracy.

Appellant's contention is unpersuasive. The majority of other states and some federal courts rejected similar proposals, adopting a better reasoned and more realistic test for admissibility of computer evidence. We agree with these courts.

Appellant argues computer-generated business records are admissible under the business records exception to the hearsay rule if a proper foundation has been laid. To establish a foundation, it must be shown that the computer equipment is standard, that the entries are made in the regular course of business at or reasonably near the time of the happening of the event recorded, and that the sources of information and the method and time of preparation are such as to indicate trustworthiness and justify admission.

Moreover, the bulk of other jurisdictions addressing this issue adopted similar analyses and upheld admission of computer records with similar or less extensive foundational showings over similar objections.

Thus, there was no abuse of discretion and the challenged evidence was properly admitted.

Affirmed.

QUESTIONS ABOUT THE CASE

1. When the court stated that it was following the law from the majority of decisions, to what principle of law was it referring?
2. How does this decision guide an investigator?
3. What is the underlying rule of the case that indicates how certain records may be admissible as evidence?
4. Looking at the proposed list of proof in the proof chart in Figure 10.4, what kind of foundation is necessary for each type of proof you have listed?

A DAY IN THE LIFE OF A REAL PARALEGAL

After working for five years as a librarian, Mary Lee obtained a certificate in paralegal studies at a local community college. Her most interesting course was environmental law, and she considered herself very fortunate to find a job with a law firm with an environmental law department. There, she found that environmental law paralegals frequently fall into two types of practice: regulatory (compliance) and litigation. Both practice areas require some of the same knowledge and skills. On the regulatory side, the paralegals dealt with federal, state, and local environmental regulations, whereas the litigation practice relied heavily on knowledge of civil procedure, case law research, and general litigation skills, especially discovery. Lee chose the regulatory side and eventually worked her way into the position of the firm's FOIA specialist.

Her duties include preparing FOIA requests to agencies to obtain required documents in response to agency information requests. With her library background, she also organizes and maintains documents obtained from FOIA, not only for cases but also for the office knowledge base. As her skills and knowledge increased, Lee began to prepare client applications for regulatory permits for air emissions, water discharges, mining reclamation, hazardous waste generation, storage, and transport and disposal, all under an attorney's direction. Lee found that her job offered the perfect blend of her organizational skills as a librarian and knowledge of the law she gained in paralegal school. "I liked being a librarian," Lee recalls. "Organizing information was at the core of library science; but becoming involved with the law and using both library science and law as I do here makes for fascinating work."

The effectiveness of your efforts is largely a function of your ability to charm or cajole them into cooperation. The truth of the matter is that you have little means to coerce them into giving any information. Thus, keep in mind that if you feel that the information held by a person or an entity is important enough for the client's case, formal discovery methods may be utilized to obtain the information once litigation has commenced.

Keeping track of unproductive leads could become useful after the lawsuit has been filed. Those sources could be subject to discovery, particularly depositions. In our coverage on civil litigation, we discussed how it is possible to depose record keepers even though they and the entities they work for are not parties to the lawsuit. Depositions are backed by the enforcement mechanism of contempt by the court. Once a lawsuit has started, nonparty information sources may be subpoenaed to give sworn testimony at a deposition. A subpoena *deuces tecum* for a deposition will require a deponent to appear at the deposition with the records in question. With this in mind, an investigating paralegal will keep the supervising attorney abreast of investigation efforts. The records of your unfruitful efforts at informal discovery should be kept as possible objects once formal discovery mechanisms become available.

Once an investigation, both in and out of the office, has been completed, the investigating paralegal's next tasks involve analysis and evaluation of the information gathered. First, thoroughly review the information against your proof chart. Questions should arise. Are all or most of the elements of the client's case covered? What types of information are needed? Consistency in factual details is important; review for any discrepancies in dates, times, or other details. Are they resolvable? Do any discrepancies you perceive affect the credibility of the source? Certainly your supervising attorney should be alerted to any problems with the information you have gathered.

Second, organize and index the fruits of your investigation into an easy and pragmatic format that will permit easy access by your coworkers. Soon, you will see that the proof chart may become more complex and involved. The proof chart often develops into a notebook, with subject dividers for each element that requires proof,

file memo
A formal memorandum prepared by a legal professional to summarize investigations or legal research on a client matter.

case management
Keeping track of the progress or status of the file and proactively organizing the work of both the attorney and the paralegal.

malpractice
Negligence committed by professionals in the course of their professional duties for which they may be civilly liable.

CYBER TRIP

Law office management is good for business. The American Bar Association has assembled a wealth of resources for the solo practitioner, as well as larger offices, with everything from literature on how to set up a solo practice to advice on using office technology. Publications and products now abound to assist legal professionals in the four specialty areas of law office administration: (1) finance, (2) marketing, (3) management, and (4) technology. As discussed, paralegals frequently occupy important positions in many law firm management roles, particularly in technology. Of the four areas listed, find one that may suit you.

See www.abanet.org/lpm/resources/management.shtml.

within which are separate folders for each source. In some situations, once an investigation has been completed, a **file memo** about the investigation provides a helpful summary that memorializes your efforts for any other member of the legal team to review and continue working on the case. Writing the file memo will also help you think through any aspect of the case that requires additional attention. Your thoughts and conclusions thus become an important part of the work on the case. For instance, it is important to make note of the impressions you received from witnesses' body language and overall behavior during the interview. These small details may become relevant later.

WORKING WITH FILES—A JUGGLING ACT

Case management in a law office pertains to the important function of keeping track of the workload and covers many aspects of office activities. In our coverage of torts, we saw that the tort of negligence establishes a duty of care that everyone must follow in the everyday activities they perform. From activities such as driving a car to constructing a building, the persons performing those activities must exercise the duty of care that applies to that certain activity. Everyone who operates a motor vehicle has a duty to observe traffic regulations that impose speed limits and stop at stop signs. The failure to live up to those duties may be viewed as negligence, subjecting the violator to liability in civil lawsuits. The duty imposed by negligence varies with the activity.

Professionals are held to a standard of care that applies to their respective professional activities. The failure to carry out their professional duties can result in a form of negligence known as **malpractice** and expose the professionals to civil liability. There is also the possibility that the state agency issue the professional license could begin disciplinary proceedings against the professional for revocation or suspension of the professional's license. For lesser infractions, a state agency may issue a reprimand against the professional that does not affect his or her ability to continue practicing. However, an agency's reprimand may appear in the agency's records, which are always open to the public. The issuance of a reprimand tarnishes the marketability of the professional, making present and potential clients wary of retaining that professional.

Admittedly, the *Bowman v. Doherty* case below represents a somewhat extreme situation. Sadly, however, the occurrence of malpractice is not uncommon. Lawyers and legal professionals find themselves in a potential malpractice situation more often than they care to admit. Use an Internet search engine to look for the term, "legal malpractice," and you will find dozens of law firms and consultants that specialize in legal malpractice. Understandably, this information can be disheartening for a budding legal professional. The truth of the matter is that the vast majority of legal professionals work hard for their clients, acting diligently and promptly. Notice that Bowman's second attorney resolved his matters quickly and effectively.

Chances are that a lack of proper management systems or even the awareness of them has plagued legal professionals who have fallen prey to malpractice claims, or worse, disciplinary proceedings. One contributing factor is that law schools do not teach law office management skills or even the need to manage legal work. Rarely do law schools offer a course on law practice management. In most medium- and large-sized firms, professional managers, many of whom have masters' degrees in business administration, perform the actual office management. As professional managers, they remain law firm employees whose job it is to maintain the organizational integrity of the office. Many administrators of law firms are also well trained

CASE IN POINT

LAWYER MALPRACTICE

BOWMAN V. DOHERTY, 235 KAN. 870, 686 P.2d 112 (1984)

This is a legal malpractice case tried to a jury in the Shawnee County District Court.

Michael Bowman was arrested for giving a worthless check on December 27, 1978. Bowman arrived at the initial appearance without an attorney and was released upon posting a bond. The judge informed the plaintiff of his right to an attorney and continued the case to January 22, 1979.

On January 19, Bowman telephoned Harold Doherty, a Topeka attorney, who had helped Bowman with previous legal matters. The plaintiff claimed he retained Doherty to handle this case. Bowman advised Doherty of his upcoming court appearance. Doherty told Bowman he would take care of the matter. Doherty called the district attorney's office and made arrangements with one of the deputy district attorneys for the case to be continued for two weeks. Later, Doherty assured Bowman the matter would be taken care of.

No continuance was arranged for with the district court. Bowman and Doherty failed to appear in court on January 22, 1979. The judge declared a bond forfeiture and ordered a warrant be issued for Bowman's arrest.

Bowman called Doherty again, and the parties agreed to meet to discuss the case. A day or two later Bowman met with Doherty in his office to discuss the matter. According to Bowman, Doherty said, "I will take care of it. This is no problem, don't worry about it."

Several weeks later, in late February or early March of 1979, Bowman received a letter from the sheriff's office, stating he was in contempt of court for failure to appear on January 22. The letter advised Bowman would be arrested if he did not present himself at the Shawnee County Courthouse. After receiving the letter, Bowman called Doherty and described the letter to him. Doherty told Bowman to come in to his office and bring the letter with him. Bowman went to Doherty's office and showed him the letter. According to Bowman, Doherty said, "I know what this is, I will take care of it." Doherty took no action.

Approximately one month later, on April 13, 1979, Bowman was arrested at his residence on a charge of aggravated failure to appear. Upon his arrival at the courthouse, Bowman was allowed to make a telephone call to Mr. Doherty, but was unable to reach him. Bowman then was booked into the county jail where he was held for two or three hours. Bowman eventually called his father who came down to the courthouse to post bond for his son's release. Bowman was handcuffed for three or four minutes while he was moved from his jail cell to the room where the bond papers were signed. The handcuffs caused Bowman to suffer some physical pain.

Later that same day, after Bowman had been released from jail, Bowman's father telephoned Doherty, informed him of the situation, and asked to have an appointment with Doherty. Doherty told Bowman's father to come to his office in the morning. Early the next morning, both Bowman and his father met with Doherty in his office. Bowman's father then asked Doherty what needed to be done to take care of the cases. After reviewing the court papers, Doherty replied that they needed to appear at the next docket which was May 1, 1979. Doherty promised to appear in court for Bowman on May 1.

Doherty arranged to have both of Bowman's cases continued from the May 1 docket to the May 10 docket. Bowman and his father were notified by Doherty that the cases had been continued. Father and son appeared in court May 10. Doherty did not appear. Judge Hope recommended that Bowman and his father hire another attorney, which they did. Once the new attorney had been hired, both of Bowman's cases were resolved.

At the conclusion of the jury trial, the plaintiff was awarded $100.00 in actual damages for physical pain and suffering, and $900.00 in punitive damages. The jury refused to award the plaintiff any damages for loss of personal freedom. After apportioning the negligence, the trial court entered judgment in favor of the plaintiff in the amount of $50.00 in actual damages and the total amount of punitive damages of $900.00.

Both parties appealed.

Doherty, an attorney, should have known full well that his client's bond would be forfeited and his client placed in jail if the matter was not properly handled. The act of the attorney which led to the injury suffered by his client was the failure of the attorney to act, which caused the client to be placed in jail and deprived of his freedom. One being negligently deprived of his freedom suffers an injury which could cause mental distress.

An attorney is obligated to his client to use reasonable and ordinary care and diligence in the handling of cases he undertakes, to use his best judgment, and to exercise that reasonable degree of learning, skill and experience which is ordinarily possessed by other attorneys in his community. The duty of an attorney to exercise reasonable and ordinary care and discretion remains the same for all attorneys, but what constitutes negligence in a particular situation is judged by the professional standards of the particular area of the law in which the practitioner is involved. Here, Doherty was involved in the practice of criminal law. Doherty was hired to represent Bowman in an alleged criminal check case. Whether or not Bowman's loss of freedom, for failure to appear before the court when required, was due to Doherty's deviation from the appropriate standard for an attorney.

Lawyers, like other professionals, are required to have and exercise the learning and skill ordinarily possessed by members of their profession in the community.

The jury determined Doherty was a wrongdoer and assigned the sum of $900.00 as punishment to Doherty. The trial court properly refused to reduce the punishment assessed by the jury against Doherty's conduct by the negligent fault apportionment assigned all the parties to the occurrence.

The judgment of the trial court is reversed and the case remanded for a new trial.

QUESTIONS ABOUT THE CASE

1. What is the difference in damages between a contract action and a tort action, and how did it make a difference in this case?
2. Make out a proof chart for the plaintiff case and list the legal theories for each element and the proof that was shown at the trial, as reported in this decision.
3. Why did the court not require an expert to prove Bowman's case? Under what circumstances would an expert be necessary for a legal malpractice case?
4. The court stated that, "Lawyers, like other professionals, are required to have and exercise the learning and skill ordinarily possessed by members of their profession in the community." Do you think that a legal malpractice case should be judged by the community standard or by something more objective?

in high-technology and responsible for keeping the law office's computer and IT systems current and running smoothly and securely. Some large firms can employ several personnel whose sole task is to work the law firm's computer systems. As discussed in Chapter 1, a paralegal education and training can also qualify a person for the role of an office manager.

CYBER TRIP

On the Internet, go to the Web site for the International Paralegal Management Association (IPMA) at www.paralegalmanagement.org. Locate the IPMA's most recent Utilization Report. What are the four practice areas in which paralegals are mostly engaged? What is the most prevalent education requirement for paralegals responding to the IPMA's survey?

MANAGEMENT SYSTEMS IN THE LAW OFFICE

From the moment that a client's case has been reviewed for possible acceptance by a law office, several activities come into play as a matter of the overall management of the law office.

Tickler Systems

In the *Bowman v. Doherty* case, the attorney Doherty would have benefited from a **tickler file**, also known as a calendar and docket control system. These legal management mechanisms in manual form often consisted of a large blackboard with an overlay of a calendar of two to three months. Each court date or deadline for every case in the office would be entered on this centralized calendar. Support staff would also place a tickler card, about the size of a file card, on a legal professional's desk or office mailbox to warn him or her in advance of an upcoming deadline or event. Of course, much of this activity has been computerized so that one person in the office is responsible for entering important dates and events. Court hearings, due dates for filing court papers such as responding to discovery or filing an appeal, statutes of limitations, real estate closings, and other important events are brought to legal professionals' attention on their computer screens, with an alert window that pops up ahead of time. These computer programs for calendar and docket control often require the legal professional to respond to the alert.

tickler file
System of tracking dates and reminding what is due on any given day or in any given week, month, or year.

Checking for Conflict of Interest

As we discussed in Chapter 2, one of the most important ethical concerns is the potential for conflict of interest. Serious repercussions can result from taking on a client whose interests conflict with those of a present or previous client. The ethical rule of avoiding conflict of interest actually implicates another ethical rule: the duty to maintain client confidences and the fiduciary duty that lawyers have toward their clients.

As a fiduciary, the legal professional owes the client the highest standard of care, loyalty, and trust. Thus, the legal professional cannot put his or her personal interests before his or her duty. Other than the fee arrangement voluntarily entered into by the client, the legal professional must not profit from the position as a fiduciary. For law offices run by solo practitioners, the check for conflicts often rests on the memory of the practitioner and others in the office. However, with the real possibility that a faulty memory could create an ethical nightmare, a more reliable system for conflict checks would be the better choice. Prior to the availability of the high-tech office equipment, the legal professional's memories often prevailed over cumbersome manual methods as the method of choice. Of course, computers now can perform a conflict check task in seconds. Software programs now prevalent in almost all law offices perform the task of **conflict checks** as a small part of the larger task of administrating and organizing the law office.

conflict check
A procedure to verify potential adverse interests before accepting a new client.

Managing Client Files

A manila file folder filled with papers randomly thrown in, unsecured, runs the risk of jeopardizing the legal professional as well as the client in a number of ways. Important client documents and court papers may go unnoticed and become lost. Worse, lost documents might fall into the wrong hands, such as, say, an opposing party. Even in the hands of an innocuous finder, the legal professional has possibly breached his or her duty to maintain client confidences. At crucial moments, such as a trial, a negotiation session, or even a client conference, bumbling through a disorganized file wastes time and leaves a poor, unprofessional impression. For the legal professional, an efficiently organized file saves time and is well worth the small amount of effort to maintain.

A visit to the file organizer aisles of any number of office supply stores will reveal the dizzying array of products and methods for organizing a client file. From simple to complex and voluminous files, how they can be organized becomes a matter of personal preference and even taste. There are only a few guidelines to managing an organized client file.

1. To maintain client confidentiality, many legal professionals use assigned numbers on the tabs of client file folders, encoding the client's identity with a number. In doing so, the client's name remains unrevealed to roving eyes, whether the file is inside or outside the office.
2. The information in the file for most clients consists of the following groups, which should be maintained consistently in separate, assigned parts of the file:
   a. Client contact information, such as name, telephone numbers (home, work, and cell numbers clearly marked).
   b. Court documents, such as pleadings, orders, and the like, possibly arranged in chronological order from bottom up, attached with a two-hole fastener at the header. On top of all court papers lies a **docket entry sheet** that lists each document by number, in chronological order with the corresponding number tabs on each document. With more involved court cases, pretrial documents and motions are kept separate from discovery papers. Trial preparation papers generally occupy a separate notebook or a series of notebooks.
   c. Copies of noncourt-related papers, usually client-generated documents such as reports, ledgers, photographs, contracts, leases, birth certificates, and the

docket entry sheet
A court management document that details the papers filed in a court case in chronological order.

like. As with court documents, a top sheet list and tabs on the documents provide easy reference.

d. Correspondence between the office and the client or any others.

e. Notes, research, and file memos performed by any of the legal professionals working on the client file.

f. The retainer agreement and billing information, which is highly sensitive. Most law offices maintain this information in an entirely separate file and keep it together with the same files for other clients in a part of the office separate from the substantive files.

3. Depending on how the office encodes its clients for file purposes, all client files should be kept in a central location and taken only by the legal professional working on them at that moment. Many law offices have file rooms staffed with full-time employees whose responsibility consists of keeping track of client files. Systematically, a ledger keeps track of every time a legal professional signs out a file from the file room and then returns it, much like a library.

Time and Billing

time slip
An office form used to keep track of billable hours performed by legal professionals.

In the days before the extensive use of computers, legal professionals manually kept track of their billable time. Using a ledger system, every time a legal professional worked on a client's matter on an hourly basis, he or she would fill out a **time slip**, part of which was carbonized on the back. The time slip consisted of a bank check–sized paper on which the legal professional would enter the client's name and the actual times work had begun and ended. Parts of the information on the time slip made a carbon impression on an underlying ledger. At the end of the day, the legal professional would turn in his or her time slips for the day. Each time slip represented a billable event for each client, with the amount of time spent and the actions taken by the legal professional noted on it. Sophisticated coding systems developed almost universally.

CYBER TRIP

Using an Internet search engine, search for the term "time and billing." Browse through the numerous Web sites offering computer programs for law firms. Notice the features available and make note of them. What features from any of these programs would assist a legal professional in complying with the ethical rules? What features assist in the management of a law office?

Every month, the client would be billed on the basis of the number of hours accumulated from all of the time slips handed in by the legal professionals during the course of the month. The hourly rate for any legal professional varies depending on his or her status in the law firm. Senior partners bill their time at the highest rate. The amount lessens for junior partners, associates, senior paralegals, and then support staff. The underlying ledger sheet kept track of each legal professional's productivity for the day. The more hours that a legal professional could enter on time slips, the greater that individual's productivity. Thus, the ledger system of time slips kept track of both the billable amount owed by each client and the amount of hours the legal professional was able to bill.

Computers have greatly automated the manner of recording and tracking billable time and the legal professional's productivity. These programs make it easier to enter time slips, compute the billing, and keep track of a legal professional's productivity almost automatically.

The status of a paralegal has risen considerably since the inception of the paralegal profession in the late 1960s. The United States Supreme Court contributed to the profession's growth by acknowledging that paralegals could bill hourly under federal statutes that allowed a winning party to obtain legal fees from the other side. Now that you have become proficient at reading cases, the Supreme Court decision as presented here should have more meaning. As you read it, keep in mind that the fees discussion of this case constitutes only a small part of a very complex and extensive lawsuit.

CASE IN POINT

ATTORNEY'S FEES AWARDS AND PARALEGALS

MISSOURI V. JENKINS, 491 U.S. 274 (1989)

This is the attorney's fee aftermath of major school desegregation litigation in Kansas City, Missouri. We granted certiorari, 488 U.S. 888 (1988), to resolve a question relating to fees litigation under 42 U. S. C. § 1988.... Should the fee award compensate the work of paralegals and law clerks by applying the market rate for their work?

Both Benson and the LDF employed numerous paralegals, law clerks (generally law students working part time), and recent law graduates in this litigation. The court awarded fees for their work based on Kansas City market rates for those categories. It therefore awarded fees based on hourly rates of $35 for law clerks, $40 for paralegals, and $50 for recent law graduates.

Missouri's second contention is that the District Court erred in compensating the work of law clerks and paralegals (hereinafter collectively "paralegals") at the market rates for their services, rather than at their cost to the attorney. While Missouri agrees that compensation for the cost of these personnel should be included in the fee award, it suggests that an hourly rate of $15—which it argued below corresponded to their salaries, benefits, and overhead—would be appropriate, rather than the market rates of $35 to $50. According to Missouri, § 1988 does not authorize billing paralegals' hours at market rates, and doing so produces a "windfall" for the attorney.

The parties have suggested no reason why the work of paralegals should not be similarly compensated, nor can we think of any. We thus take as our starting point the self-evident proposition that the "reasonable attorney's fee" provided for by statute should compensate the work of paralegals, as well as that of attorneys. The more difficult question is how the work of paralegals is to be valuated in calculating the overall attorney's fee.

If an attorney's fee awarded under § 1988 is to yield the same level of compensation that would be available from the market, the increasingly widespread custom of separately billing for the services of paralegals must be taken into account. All else being equal, the hourly fee charged by an attorney whose rates include paralegal work in her hourly fee, or who bills separately for the work of paralegals at cost, will be higher than the hourly fee charged by an attorney competing in the same market who bills separately for the work of paralegals at "market rates." In other words, the prevailing "market rate" for attorney time is not independent of the manner in which paralegal time is accounted for. Thus, if the prevailing practice in a given community were to bill paralegal time separately at market rates, fees awarded the attorney at market rates for attorney time would not be fully compensatory if the court refused to compensate hours billed by paralegals or did so only at "cost." Similarly, the fee awarded would be too high if the court accepted separate billing for paralegal hours in a market where that was not the custom.

Nothing in § 1988 requires that the work of paralegals invariably be billed separately. If it is the practice in the relevant market not to do so, or to bill the work of paralegals only at cost, that is all that § 1988 requires. Where, however, the prevailing practice is to bill paralegal work at market rates, treating civil rights lawyers' fee requests in the same way is not only permitted by § 1988, but also makes economic sense. By encouraging the use of lower cost paralegals rather than attorneys wherever possible, permitting market-rate billing of paralegal hours "encourages cost-effective delivery of legal services and, by reducing the spiraling cost of civil rights litigation, furthers the policies underlying civil rights statutes." It has frequently been recognized in the lower courts that paralegals are capable of carrying out many tasks, under the supervision of an attorney, that might otherwise be performed by a lawyer and billed at a higher rate. Such work might include, for example, factual investigation, including locating and interviewing witnesses; assistance with depositions, interrogatories, and document production; compilation of statistical and financial data; checking legal citations; and drafting correspondence. Much such work lies in a gray area of tasks that might appropriately be performed either by an attorney or a paralegal. To the extent that fee applicants under § 1988 are not permitted to bill for the work of paralegals at market rates, it would not be surprising to see a greater amount of such work performed by attorneys themselves, thus increasing the overall cost of litigation.

Such separate billing appears to be the practice in most communities today. In the present case, Missouri concedes that "the local market typically bills separately for paralegal services," and the District Court found that the requested hourly rates of $35 for law clerks, $40 for paralegals, and $50 for recent law graduates were the prevailing rates for such services in the Kansas City area. Under these circumstances, the court's decision to award separate compensation at these rates was fully in accord with § 1988.

Amicus National Association of Legal Assistants reports that 77 percent of 1,800 legal assistants responding to a survey of the association's membership stated that their law firms charged clients for paralegal work on an hourly billing basis. Brief for National Association of Legal Assistants as Amicus Curiae 11.

The courts below correctly granted a fee enhancement to compensate for delay in payment and approved compensation of paralegals and law clerks at market rates.

Affirmed.

QUESTIONS ABOUT THE CASE

1. The National Association of Legal Assistants appeared in the Supreme Court case as amicus. What do you think was its legal position?
2. What type of activities did the Supreme Court note that paralegals could perform?
3. Do you think that employing paralegals can actually reduce the costs of litigation, as the Supreme Court surmised?
4. What do you think about the idea of billing separately for paralegals at above cost?

Summary

Well-trained paralegals can perform the invaluable tasks of interviewing and investigating on behalf of a client's case. Paralegals can also specialize in the administration of a law office and assist in its management. All of these professional activities require the development of skills that are backed by specialized training in the law. With legal training, the ability to putting the "nuts and bolts" of a client's case together in a well-run and -organized office constitute the hallmarks of a professional paralegal.

From the moment a potential client steps into the office, a well-trained paralegal is fully capable of performing the basics for an initial consultation. With properly developed communication skills and the ability to read the client's behavior, the paralegal's role is to obtain the necessary information efficiently and promote trust and credibility. In criminal and civil proceedings, the underlying facts represent the heart of the case. Techniques such as a proof chart apply legal knowledge together with the practical ability to obtain and find ways to prove facts. This approach requires knowledge of substantive law as well as the law of evidence. Resourcefulness and persistence in going after facts through interviews, the Internet, and public records help build a client's case.

No matter how good the facts may be for a client, the case may not survive without the proper foundation of provable facts. In the office or in the field, an effective investigating paralegal can become an invaluable member of a litigation department of any law office.

A paralegal can further or broaden his or her professional worth by assisting with the organization and management of a law office. As a legal professional, paralegals must work with the law office's management systems, such as file organization, tickler systems, and time and billing programs. With the computer dominating almost all law office work, a paralegal with the ability to work well with programs can become an invaluable part of any legal team.

Key Terms

Active listening
Adverse (hostile) witness
Authorization letter
Body language
Case management
Closed-ended questions
Conflict check
Demonstrative evidence
Digital or electronic evidence
Docket entry sheet
Documentary evidence
Expert witness
Field investigation
File memo
Forensics
Freedom of Information Act (FOIA)
Informal discovery
Initial consultation
Intake form
Lay witness
Leading questions
Malpractice

Open-ended questions
Paraphrasing
Real evidence
Registered agent
Retain
Tangible evidence
Testimonial evidence
Tickler file
Time slip

Review Questions

1. What are the primary ethical concerns for paralegals when they conduct interviews in the office? What other concerns arise when a paralegal conducts interviews and investigations outside the office?
2. What are the communication skills that help facilitate an initial interview?
3. What is an intake form, and how is it helpful to a legal professional?
4. What kind of body language would be best suited for conducting an interview in or outside of the office?
5. What is a registered agent, and how is that person's identity important?
6. What is a proof chart, and how does it assist the legal professional?
7. What is the difference between informal discovery and formal discovery?
8. What types of computer software can help fulfill a legal professional's ethical duties?
9. What are some ethical concerns regarding time and billing?
10. What is a docket entry sheet?

Exercises

1. Many furniture companies specialize in office equipment and furniture. Visit the showroom of one to see the assortment and variety of office accoutrements available. What would you pick out for yourself? What types of images do these items project?
2. Using their most embarrassing moment (real or conjured), practice an interview with a classmate and reduce the interview to a file memorandum. You may also use a news clipping or past event as the incident.
3. Visit a major office supply store and familiarize yourself with the file organizing systems and products available for use in a law office. If you were a law firm paralegal whose job it was to establish a uniform filing system for the office, what would you need to know before picking out a particular system or product? Would you choose more than one type?
4. Official governmental forms for most federal and state agencies appear on the Internet for easy access. Visit the following Web sites or similar others to familiarize yourself with their forms. Can you find the form that a client would need to sign for you to represent him or her before these agencies?

   Social Security at www.ssa.gov/online/#Other

   Veterans Administration at www.va.gov/vaforms/

   Next find the Internet site for obtaining criminal records in your state. For example,

   PA at www.usdoj.gov/eoir/formslist.htm

   NY at www.courts.state.ny.us/apps/chrs/

   WA at www.wa.gov/wsp/crime/crimhist.htm

5. Review various office management and technology periodicals and Web sites, such as Law Office Computing, Law Office Management, PC World, CNET.com, or Zdnet.com. List the various law office management technology tools you would want to work with in a law office that would fulfill the big three ethical duties: (a) avoiding the unauthorized practice of law, (b) avoiding conflicts of interest, and (c) maintaining client confidentiality.

Discussion Questions

1. If a client or a prospective client asks for legal advice or for your opinion as to the prospects of his or her case, how should you respond?
2. Why are releases and authorizations necessary to obtain the client's own personal information? What types of information require formal written client authorizations?
3. You may recall that a legal professional's thoughts, impressions, and theories are protected from discovery by the opposing party under the work product doctrine. Is it ethical if your supervising attorney directs you to write a memo of a witness's interview that includes your thoughts and impressions in order to protect the memo from discovery?
4. In one scene from the famous film *Erin Brockovich* (Universal Pictures, 2000), Julia Roberts, playing the character of the film's eponym, embarks on an investigation in which she searches records in a public utility office. There, she entices the male governmental employee into cooperating by wearing a revealing, low-cut blouse. Do you think this action constituted ethical behavior? Visit:
   http://paralegals.org/displaycommon.cfm?an=1&subarticlenbr=796
   www.nala.org/code.htm.
5. How is the Supreme Court's decision in *Missouri v. Jenkins* important to the paralegal profession?

PORTFOLIO ASSIGNMENT

On the basis of what you have learned from the substantive areas of law presented in previous chapters, draft three separate intake forms that you might use in an office for (1) a criminal defense case, (2) an car accident case, and (3) a property transfer case.

Be sure that the form asks for all of the information necessary for that type of case.

Chapter 11

Getting the Job and Surviving in the Workplace

CHAPTER OBJECTIVES

Upon completion of this chapter, you will have acquired knowledge on:

- Assessing yourself and your professional goals.
- Techniques for entering the legal profession.
- Succeeding in the legal workplace.
- Approaching a legal assignment.
- Surviving, dealing with, and understanding difficult coworkers.

This chapter provides an overview of perhaps the most practical and personal part of a professional paralegal's initial training. This and Chapter 12 cover the techniques for entering the legal profession, for succeeding in the workplace, and for assessing your personal goals. Unlike many of your fellow students, who have focused their studies by majoring in subjects such as history or literature, your course of study has led you down a distinctly professional path. So far, you have been exposed in detail to a whole different world of professionals working in law, what they do, and the work environments they inhabit.

The final part of this course centers on entering and navigating through the process of obtaining employment in the legal profession. This chapter will cover the customs and habits for, and even some backdoor routes to, searching for and flourishing in a legal job. Thus, in a very different way, you will be applying your knowledge about the law and the legal profession for your own direct benefit.

Newcomers in any professional field often feel overwhelmed by the myriad of options, strategies, and uncertainties. The prospect of entering the professional job market for the first time can create great anxiety. Undoubtedly, the primary source of this anxiety is the apprehension that accompanies being judged by prospective employers. Rest assured that you are not alone. Everyone, even the most experienced and seasoned professional, feels the disquieting tug of distress that accompanies the pursuit of any job application. Although the legal field often appears unshakably stable, the truth of the matter is that even among the top law firms and government offices, attrition among lawyers has steadily risen during the past few years. Despite some appearances, today's legal profession in the United States has become known for the mobility of its members—lawyers as well as paralegals.

Given this constant movement within the legal profession, you can expect many paralegals to have followed the same path that you will soon take in seeking employment. In the past 40 years, since the birth of the paralegal profession, a few paths have become well worn. Once lawyers learned of the economy and efficiency that legal aid societies gained by employing paralegals, government and then large law firms jumped onto the bandwagon creating permanent slots for paralegals among their ranks. Since then, a number of other inroads have developed offering paralegals significant opportunities in less traditional professional venues. Simply knowing the strategies and techniques for securing any of these and other employment opportunities can go a long way toward reducing the apprehension about applying for your first job.

Although there is no single method or guide for success to finding employment as a paralegal, most agree that there are certain steps that almost everyone should take *before* embarking upon the job search. For most, taking these steps instills self-knowledge and an understanding of the world they are about to enter. With this knowledge—about yourself and the employment market—you will have acquired a significant amount of power and control over your expectations, as well as those of the people you will encounter. For many, this knowledge helps reduce the anxiety about searching for a job and instills self-confidence, whether among first-time career job seekers or those who have left the ranks of the employed for a few years to raise a family and returned to school to "re-tool."

SELF-ASSESSMENT

self-assessment
An initial step of the career planning process that involves gathering information about yourself to make an informed career decision.

The first step (always the hardest) is to learn about yourself by undergoing a **self-assessment**. As painful as it may feel in the beginning, a self-assessment has the direct benefit of instilling confidence about your own likes and dislikes, as well as what you have to offer a prospective employer. Making a self-assessment for the purposes of beginning a job hunt helps by providing focus and direction. The task of making a self-assessment involves learning two important aspects about yourself: (1) the priorities and values that can guide you to a job that fits your personality and (2) the skills and education you can bring to a law office. Viewed this way, the exercises presented here will help you become aware of your own personal internal and external dynamics. "Knowing yourself" is probably the most potent advantage you can have.

Testing for Internals

The field of psychology creates categories of personality "types." We all should be aware that each person is an individual, and that labels are often inappropriate and can lead to "profiling." Nevertheless, instead of thinking in terms of "types," consider the following exercises as personality traits. This exercise is also a fun way to create an initial self-assessment. Ask yourself the following questions, being careful to write down your answers honestly and completely. A self-assessment draws on an individual's past experiences. As you do so, keep in mind that there are no correct answers; These questions are designed to create self-awareness.

Self-Assessment Exercise 1: Communicating and Working with Others

For the most part, working in the legal profession is a highly social activity that requires individuals to work together and communicate effectively. After all, at its most basic level, the legal practice is about communication. Throughout any workday, legal professionals regularly meet to discuss a number of work-related items, such as the facts of a client's situation, the applicable law, or the strategy that the legal team should pursue. To see where your own personality traits will steer you, ask yourself the following questions:

1. To what degree do you find it easy or difficult to discuss personal feelings or opinions?
2. Do you prefer socializing or building relationships with others before or after starting work tasks with them?
3. When a coworker expresses an opinion with which you disagree, do you voice your opinion or remain silent?
4. Do you prefer to work with others or alone?
5. Is the pace with which you work slower or faster than that of others with whom you have worked?
6. Do you become impatient or frustrated when things move too slowly or too rapidly?
7. To what degree does working with others on a regular basis cause stress or motivation?
8. When faced with aggressive or assertive people, do you become assertive or do you retreat?
9. When faced with having to make a difficult decision, do you immediately formulate a course of action or ponder the situation?
10. When in new social situations, do you tend to be approachable or more formal and business-like?

Again, there are no correct answers to these questions. Nevertheless, depending on your responses, these questions may help you develop a greater awareness of your own work habits as a function of your personality traits. There is nothing positive or negative about having any one or a combination of these personality traits. For instance, knowing that you feel more comfortable keeping to yourself or that you tend to feel more productive in a more socialized atmosphere may guide you in seeking the type of employment situation that best suits you. What is important is to understand how you relate to situations and to the people in the workplace. Even more important is understanding what talents and skills you can offer. In doing so, you will be developing **self-esteem**—confidence in yourself and your abilities.

self-esteem
A realistic respect for or favorable impression of oneself; self-respect.

The legal workplace can vary greatly depending on location, size, and the nature of the work performed. As we discussed at the beginning of this book, larger law offices in large cities tend to be formal and hierarchical. The greater the number of employees, the more structure and governance become apparent. Office organization and internal systems, such as accounting mechanisms for time and billing, file maintenance, and personnel supervision, take on greater sophistication and presence in larger urban offices. Moreover, in larger offices, legal professionals and others tend to perform more specialized tasks. In contrast, solo practitioners and small law offices are well known for their more informal and, at times, relaxed atmosphere. At the same time, paralegals working in smaller environments can be expected to take on a wider range of duties for a wider range of case types.

Within these various settings, the type of legal work performed in a law office can greatly shape the office's personality. Even in large firms, each department within the firm takes on its own distinctive culture. For instance, an office that performs primarily litigation tends to be fast paced, punctuated with rushed activity regularly to meet court deadlines. Legal professionals engaged in litigation have been characterized as intense, argumentative, and cunning. They love the drama of the courtroom, their stage. Accomplished trial attorneys make good actors. Preparation for the various aspects of trials, depositions, and settlement conferences take litigation professionals to a variety of courts and other law offices. Litigation files are voluminous, filled with pleadings, discovery materials, notes, and legal research. Telephone calls and e-mails are of vital importance, because litigation offices often have to juggle their time among experts, witnesses, the various courts, and their clients and adversaries. Emotions can run the gamut as the litigation professionals experience the thrill of victory or the sobering crush of defeat.

In contrast, offices specializing in trusts and estates or corporate matters engage in an area of law that requires careful planning and meticulous wording. The atmosphere is usually quiet and subdued. Legal professionals focus on the completion of a final document or group of documents, such as an estate plan or a corporate financing structure. Client contact is minimal and occurs during hushed, ceremonial, in-office conferences for signing formal documents, such as deeds, wills and trusts, corporate resolutions, and copious contractual agreements. Trust and estate professionals are known for their pensive and meticulous nature and take special interest in family histories. They know arcane and esoteric rules of property law and estate planning backward and forward. Rarely are trust and estate professionals engaged in adversarial proceedings. Their primary aim, indeed their *raison d'être,* is to plan for the future. For them, death is a realization event.

Corporate law departments and law firms, in contrast, are more aggressive and formal. Their domain exudes prestige, power, and money. Some excitement may occur with public offerings in which a corporation offers its shares to the public for the first time. Their offices are festooned with trophies that proudly memorialize successful initial public offerings they have handled. Corporate legal professionals are businesspeople who possess the art of making the deal. They are at their best when schmoozing.

boutique law firm
A law firm that specializes in a technical area of the law offering clients customized service.

Recently, many paralegals have obtained employment in **boutique law firms**, which specialize in discrete areas of law, such as intellectual property, immigration, tax, or bankruptcy. These firms are particularly apt to hire paralegals because much of the legal work involves gathering information to complete forms used in specialized courts, administrative agencies, and government offices. The client's objective is the result of a process as opposed to a contested trial verdict or a final document. With the exception of removal proceedings (formerly known as deportation), matters handled by boutique firms are usually initiated once the legal professionals have fully examined a client's situation and decided to participate in the process of obtaining, say, a visa to enter the United States, a patent, or a discharge of debts in bankruptcy.

form practice
A type of law practice that involves the use of forms generated by courts and administrative agencies, usually a specialty area of law such as probate or social insurance program.

Often known as a **form practice**, much of the work of a boutique legal professional consists of completing and filing government forms—often extensive ones—along with documentation that substantiates the information requested in the forms. Discussions between legal professionals often use specialized language, sprinkled with shorthand references to form numbers and alphanumeric abbreviations. Customarily, boutique law firms possess specialized law libraries and computer software that can generate the required forms. As a result, working with boutique law firms tends to involve substantial client contact and carries a certain rarified air that comes with highly specialized knowledge expertise.

As you begin your job search, first determine the type of work that would best suit your personality and preference. Location and the availability of employment for paralegals may limit your choices. Nevertheless, as discussed further into this chapter, an evaluation of the job market could reveal some pleasant surprises.

Self-Assessment Exercise 2: Personal Preferences

A meaningful self-assessment should also include inquires into some of the more pragmatic areas of life. Thus, personal preferences, which are the result of your values and living circumstances, deserve careful attention. Several factors can come into play that can have more bearing on your choices and decisions during the process of seeking employment. Beyond the personality traits you may become aware of, this next level of self-assessment inquires into the real-life aspects of working for a living.

Highly practical factors include the importance you may place on commuting time, salary, prestige, community service, and work hours. These factors, with perhaps some other considerations, can act as filters for your job search by helping eliminate those positions that do not fit your particular circumstances or preferences. Because of family or other commitments, a lengthy commute may not be desirable. School loans understandably play a part in deciding to take a higher paying position, even if you have to put up with a long commute. For others, a strong desire for pride in the workplace can make a prestigious law firm or high-level government office more attractive. Working in law also may be a way to commit to help a discrete clientele or further a heartfelt cause. Early in the paralegal movement, paralegals that enlisted in the "War on Poverty" during the 1960s began working for the poor in legal aid offices across the country. Now, such ethical considerations can mean performing legal work from within an environmental group, a children's charity, or the in-house legal department of a faith-based organization.

A sound self-assessment, as outlined here, may be accomplished easily during a brief, reflective afternoon or evening alone or while chatting with family, friends, or others who know you well. Try writing down your thoughts in an organized fashion, setting apart your perceived personality traits from practical factors. The urge to keep your written thoughts private would be understandable, perhaps for sharing only with confidants or teachers. Afterward, try another exercise that allows you to assess yourself more critically and could help you achieve self-improvement.

Actors frequently engage in similar exercises. One notable exercise consists of devising two columns on a sheet of paper, listing in one column five or six of your strengths, such as a pleasant personality or punctuality. In the other column, list a few of your weak points or aspects of yourself that could use improvement, such as procrastination or poor posture. By doing so, you will have identified some of your less desirable personality traits that could actually change through your own conscious decision. If you perceive yourself as shy and withdrawn, for instance, engaging in this exercise could be just the beginning of a new professional persona.

The basic point of these exercises is to help you identify yourself as a budding professional in a most positive light. Some facets of everyone are out of our practical control—innate physical makeup, bodily limitations, and other parts of yourself that are not susceptible to change. Because these facets are beyond anyone's practical control, we accept these limitations and, at the same time, free ourselves from worrying about them. As simple as it may seem, this technique is tried and true; for many, it can be an invaluable tool for self-evaluation as you position yourself for entry into the job market. Don't sweat the stuff that is beyond your control.

CYBER TRIP

With high-technology in full swing, most law offices, particularly boutique firms, regularly use specialized software to generate forms for submission to government agencies and specialized courts, saving many hours of time and paperwork. Using basic databases, most of these programs initially prompt the legal professional for specific client information that is saved to a database. Once the information has been entered, the legal professional can call up a needed form that has been "populated" with the client information in the appropriate spaces, or fields, ready for printing and submission to the government agency or court.

Using an Internet search engine, enter "practice systems" or "document assembly." What types of computer expertise would be required to become a law office's point person? Would such a position be consistent with the definition of a paralegal?

EVALUATING THE JOB MARKET

Finding places to apply for jobs takes a bit of ingenuity and persistence. Seeking out sources of information about jobs is actually a matter of common sense and sensibility. Trends in the law and fluctuations in the local and national economy alter the availability of the type of positions available in law. Real estate practice, for instance, can rise and fall appreciably in direct proportion to the price of land and houses.

Economic downturns can boost debt collection practices for creditors and their legal professionals in the same way when more debtors seek out bankruptcy and consumer law practitioners. A strong economy, in contrast, may cause a rise in corporate maneuverings such as mergers and acquisitions. Changes in the law and even current events can spike activity in a particular area of legal practice.

Awareness of factors such as the economy can come about by paying particular attention to some of the more specialized topics in the news. Information about the current economy comes to us daily through broadcast outlets and print media. By making an occasional and inexpensive investment, you can gain a wealth of detailed information on the economy from readily available newsstands in publications such as *The Wall Street Journal, Baron's, Money,* and *Fortune*. These and other publications are also freely available in the reading rooms at most public libraries. Local libraries are also great sources for information on local developments that could affect the type of employment available for paralegals. With these sources in mind, information on actual job openings is probably close at hand. The following sections describe some sources available to job seekers, right on the well-beaten path.

College Career or Placement Office

career or placement office
A support office of a school that assists students in finding suitable employment through counseling and maintaining job listings.

This source of job postings and other services should be your first stop. Almost every school, college, or university has a **career** or **placement office** that exists to help its students find employment, and more. Some schools, due to budgetary limitations, have offices that can only post job openings as they occur locally. Other schools offer more extensive services, such as workshops for creating a résumé and developing interviewing techniques. These offices are also sources of information about the types of jobs that have been available in the past and the pay scale for new graduates.

Employment Agencies

Private firms, also known as headhunters or recruiters, are paid by prospective employers to find legal talent—lawyers, paralegals, and mangers. Unlike the career counselors at your school, these firms actually represent the employers who pay the firm to perform the service of finding a pool of job applicants. Thus, support in the form of résumé review or interview tips is generally unavailable at employment agencies. However, these firms are sources of specialized information, such as salary and the qualifications that employers are generally seeking. Their task is to obtain and screen, according to the employers' specifications, qualified applicants, who are then interviewed by the firm and the prospective employer. Care should be taken to ensure that the firm is reputable. Very rarely should the job applicant pay these firms.

Human Resources Departments

human resources (personnel) department
The department in an organization dealing with matters involving employees, such as hiring, training, labor relations, and benefits.

Most corporations, whether scientific, manufacturing, high-tech, or other, have their own in-house legal departments staffed by attorneys and paralegals. Recently, these in-house legal offices have taken advantage of the skills and knowledge of paralegals by hiring them in large numbers, under the supervision of one or two in-house attorneys. For these in-house corporate law offices, the corporation is their one and only client, which generates enough legal work to keep a small law office busy. The employment opportunities in these environments are discussed in greater detail in Chapter 12 but deserve mention here. If you have an interest in the legal environment of a particular industry, its **human resources department** would be an excellent source of information about any job opportunities in in-house legal departments.

Newspaper and Internet

The classified section of every newspaper commonly lists advertisements for jobs, known as the help-wanted ads. The number of advertisements for jobs increases as the week progresses, usually culminating with the most ads in the Sunday paper. The ads are often grouped together or categorized according to job type. Thus, paralegal positions may appear under the category of "Legal" or even "Paralegal." In larger cities, weekly and some daily newspapers devoted exclusively to the community's legal profession are the most direct way of finding job openings for those with some experience. First-time job seekers need not be deterred by ads for experienced paralegals. Internships from a paralegal program can frequently qualify as experience. Reading legal newspapers such as the *Philadelphia Intelligencer,* the nation's oldest law journal, can also keep you abreast of recent events in the local legal community that affect the job market.

CYBER TRIP

Many legal newspapers and law journals that post job opportunities now appear online. Although the news content is available only to paid subscribers, the notices for available openings are usually accessible free without a subscription. Other online resources service the legal community exclusively. See, for instance, www.lawcrossing.com or www.lawjobs.com. Some operate in the fashion of a database, through which a job seeker can hunt specifically paralegal positions and even refine the search by area of law and location. Similar to other general online employment services, such as www.careerbuilder.com or www.monster.com, the Web sites accept résumés to post for review by prospective employers. Many law firms, large and small, also have Web sites listing open positions, in addition to the biographies and specialty areas of their personnel.

Networking

According to many studies, using personal contacts and making new contacts has proven to be one of the most successful methods of finding employment. Becoming known through a local paralegal association is one form of networking. Informing friends and family that you are on a job search with your newly acquired legal expertise may be equally effective in landing a job. As surprising or unorthodox as it may seem, **networking** succeeds because many employers prefer to hire someone based on a direct personal reference. By using networking, an employer will save the time and expense of advertising or retaining an employment agency to fill an available position.

Paralegal Associations

As part of your networking efforts, it is wise to maintain contact with your local paralegal association. Attending social events or training seminars can be an effective way of getting your name out there, as well as getting inside information about law firms' culture and employment conditions. A Web search for "paralegal association" in your area should turn up a site for a nearby association. The association's Web site should have information about how frequently members meet and how to contact them.

Local and Federal Government

One of the largest employers of paralegals is government: municipal, county, state, and federal. These positions are, like others, available online on their Web sites. The federal government's Web site, usajobs.gov.opm, is easy to navigate and operates similarly to legal and general online employment Web sites by providing for database searches and résumé posting.

Volunteering

A bit off the beaten path to employment is the idea of volunteering your legal expertise as a paralegal. Most law firms, particularly mid- and large-sized firms probably shun this idea, but solo practitioners and some small firms may, in certain limited circumstances, allow you to spend a month or so as a volunteer, even on a part-time basis. Not-for-profit organizations, such as legal aid offices, actually welcome the idea of volunteer paralegals. Similar to the volunteer movement among lawyers, the idea of donating time in exchange for some training and expertise is now well-embedded in the legal community. Government offices such as the attorney general and district attorney frequently run programs for volunteers with legal expertise to handle consumer matters, victims' assistance, and other areas suitable for paralegals. Volunteering can benefit a job seeker by providing a venue for networking and an opportunity to gain credible experience. It also can happen that a volunteer whose work is highly appreciated is eventually hired.

networking
The process of actively seeking associations and friendships for the purpose of establishing a supportive system of sharing information, particularly in job seeking.

A DAY IN THE LIFE OF A REAL PARALEGAL

Upon graduation, Audrey Masterson had her paralegal certificate in hand, but no jobs were anywhere to be seen. The fact that Masterson lived in a semi-rural area did not help her job prospects. Feeling down on her luck, she tried networking, talking to friends and former classmates about her job search. She even joined a support group for women looking to get back into the workforce. At one meeting, Masterson heard that the local prosecutor's office was looking for part-time volunteers to assist with a victim's assistance project funded by a government grant.

Located at the local courthouse, the prosecutor's office was only a few miles from Masterson's home. She sent in her résumé and cover letter, and after a short interview, she found herself interviewing crime victims and their families. Masterson found the work fascinating, particularly because she conducted the interviews amidst all the goings-on in the courthouse. Between interviews, she would wander into the courtrooms and listen to the hearings and trials taking place, and then to the clerk's office to learn how cases progressed through the system. She also began to know most of the courthouse employees, including a few judges, and many of the attorneys who came to the courthouse to represent their clients.

After a few months, one of those attorneys asked Masterson to visit her office to see if she would be interested in working as a domestic relations paralegal. With her paralegal certificate and experience in the courthouse and the victim's assistance project, Masterson was well suited to begin working in a real paralegal's job. Within a couple of years, she has become well known in the local legal community. Her job takes her out of the office frequently, searching through public records, interviewing witnesses, and filing papers in the courthouse where she started as a volunteer.

APPLYING FOR A JOB

Résumé

résumé
A brief, written account of personal, educational, and professional qualifications and experience, prepared by a job applicant.

With knowledge about the job market, employment opportunities, and, more important, yourself, the next steps consist of learning how to present yourself and your qualifications to prospective employers. By far, the most common format to display your qualifications is the **résumé**. The importance of the résumé cannot be understated. Interviews with prospective employers are granted solely on the basis of a résumé and often nothing more. At the same time, there are only a few guidelines for an effective résumé; even then there is considerable disagreement over what should and should not appear. Yet most people acknowledge that one résumé that sparks the interest of one prospective employer may appear mundane to another. Time and chance happen to all.

Sophisticated job applicants may frequently have two or more different résumés, each appealing to a particular market segment of potential employers. One résumé may highlight matters of the applicant's background that might appeal to a private law firm, whereas another version may emphasize matters that would interest a government office, and a third would be appropriate for submission to a nonprofit organization emphasizing experience and interest in its work. The difference lies in the aspects of your life and experiences that you choose to include or amplify. When applying for a position that appears particularly attractive and well suited to you, a résumé customized for that position takes only a few minutes to draft. Keep in mind that a prospective employer will sort through a stack of résumés, giving each one only a couple of minutes at most before deciding whom to interview. Thus, the résumé should try to attract attention from the outset.

Looking at the process from the perspective of the employer, a résumé acts as a form of marketing brochure, much like the ones vendors of office equipment or stationery send. An impressive résumé may not automatically get your foot in the door, but a poor résumé can eliminate you from the process from the very outset. The résumé is a vehicle with the specific purpose of winning an interview. An effective résumé does not merely recount your personal history. An effective résumé presents you in the best light possible by selling you to the prospective employer. An effective résumé should convince the employer that you possess the education, experience, and skills to succeed at this new position.

Creating a résumé is actually just a matter of arranging information into an acceptable format or template. Thus, résumés generate information as they are created. That is, once you have decided on a particular format, the information about you should flow into each segment in which it belongs. Commercially available résumé-building software follows the same idea by merely establishing a format for inputting data. Unfortunately, résumé-building software can also be inflexible by offering only one or two different formats, which are not easily imported into a standard word processor. Prevailing wisdom favors simply keeping a résumé as a word processing document for updating and rearranging as your career progresses. Although the process of drafting your first résumé may appear daunting, you will find that everyone continually revises their résumés throughout their careers. Even seasoned professionals with many years of professional experience regularly maintain a current résumé or even several versions.

EYE ON ETHICS

When drafting your résumé, be sure not to amplify or inflate any aspect of your personal qualifications. Although we all wish to be viewed in the best possible light, the most honest light is preferable. False information on a résumé would betray serious ethical flaws on the part of the job applicant.

For many, a résumé performs as more than part of a job application. Over the course of your career, you may be called on to provide a current résumé for purposes other than applying for a job. Consider the following reasons for keeping an updated résumé on hand:

- Résumés are frequently kept on file by an employer to maintain contact information about all employees' current addresses and telephone numbers.
- Once you have joined the ranks of legal professionals, your employer may wish to display your résumé as a part of the credentials of the firm or office, together with your coworkers', to support the firm's ongoing marketing or on its Web page.
- Having a current résumé on your computer makes it easy to send in an e-mail or by postal delivery to a casual acquaintance for the purpose of building a network connection or alliance with colleagues from other law firms.
- References will sometimes request a résumé so that they may have something to mention when asked to provide a recommendation.
- Résumés are often attached to applications for grants, graduate school, or promotions with your current employer.
- Reviewing and redrafting your résumé can help clarify your professional direction, qualifications, and strengths; boost your confidence; or start the process of a career change. In this way, redrafting a résumé acts as an ongoing exercise in self-assessment.

At the entry level, a résumé may lack direction or a focus because of the absence of actual work experience. Employers are used to seeing résumés in which the applicant is seeking to build on previous legal experience. Thus, a person with years of experience from a number of professional positions will usually appear to be on a specific career path or trajectory. For a new entrant to the legal profession, a specific professional objective is difficult for a prospective employer to glean unless the résumé states the applicant's **career objective** clearly and succinctly. Without an objective, an entry-level job applicant's résumé could appear muddled and mediocre. A well-stated objective at the head of a résumé helps distinguish it from the many others an employer receives. For this reason, many experienced professionals frequently customize their résumés by redrafting at least their objective.

career objective
A statement at the beginning of a résumé stating the job applicant's goals and providing focus for the prospective employer.

Stating an objective requires some thought. Avoid highly generalized or vague statements such as, "To obtain a position with a forward-looking organization with which I may fully utilize my education and skills." The more specific and positive, the better your résumé will appear to others. At the same time, it is important not to be so specific as to limit yourself. Instead, tailor your objective to the job requirements, as you understand them, while leaving some room for flexibility. Think of the objective as the thesis statement in a college paper. As one of the last sentences of your introductory paragraph to a paper, the thesis statement provides the reader with a "guide" to your essay. It states succinctly what you are going to say in more detail throughout your paper. Similarly, a specific and well-written statement of your objective at the head of your résumé makes the rest of the information flow to fit your objective and thereby impresses the reader.

COMMUNICATION TIP

One thing that all prospective employers agree on is that mistakes, typos, and poor grammar in a résumé or cover letter can be the death knell for otherwise promising job applicants. Errors may very well indicate carelessness or a lack of attention to detail, particularly in a situation in which you should be trying to make a most favorable impression. Proofreading carefully and sharing your drafts with friends and colleagues for them to proofread can eliminate mistakes.

Instead of using flowery (and meaningless) language, state your objective by focusing on the type of position for which you are applying. Specifically mention the objective of becoming a paralegal, interested in the area of law required by the position and perhaps the location of the office. For example, a simple and effective objective may state, "Career objective: Litigation paralegal with an intellectual property firm in south Florida." Notice that a clear and detailed objective section often distinguishes one résumé from others without objectives or with objectives that are weak or too general. Most employers review résumés quickly at first, with an eye toward eliminating applicants. As the selection process progresses, further attention focuses on the relative merits of those résumés that have made the first cut.

Another technique to make a résumé stand out includes a **synopsis** or **highlights** section right after the objective. Provided briefly at the beginning of a résumé, this section supports the objective statement by amplifying particular skills, achievements, or any experience highly relevant to the employer's work. Here, it may be advantageous to choose words carefully to remain brief and succinct. You can feel free to use some legal jargon or buzzwords, which are shorthand terms that save space and draw greater attention to your résumé. Think of the summary section as a movie trailer, in which the more impressive parts of your qualifications are stated to entice the reader to keep reading. Thus, a summary might include specific involvement with an area of the law, special skills, or academic awards.

synopsis or highlights
A part of a résumé following the career objective that summarizes the applicant's qualifications.

Speaking of academics, a frequent question is whether to include your grade point average (GPA). The current custom and fashion holds that a résumé should include a GPA of 3.0 or higher, as well as a GPA in your major of 3.0 or greater, though be sure to designate it as a "Major GPA." Of course, omitting a GPA may betray that your GPA is less than 3.0. In that case, take the initiative of explaining any causes for your academic situation in a cover letter or during the interview. Having to hold down a full-time job, childcare responsibilities, language difficulties, and the like are respectable if not laudable reasons for less-than-stellar academic performance. Mentioning these or any other life difficulties are perfectly acceptable topics of discussion and help portray you as hardworking, diligent, and responsible.

Even after following this discussion or any other formula for writing a résumé, expect that chance and happenstance will play a large part in whether your résumé gets noticed. You may come across a position that is exactly the one you are looking for or one for which you feel perfectly qualified. Remember that résumés are meant to introduce you to a prospective employer. As unfair as it may be, the résumé is the entry point for an interview. However, whether you are selected for an interview is a function of many factors other than your résumé, even if it is perfect. Above all, recognize that the hiring process is often replete with fickleness and oversight. Thus, keep your résumé in its proper perspective. Like all résumés, it is an initial marketing brochure.

Figure 11.1 provides a sample résumé that follows a widely accepted format. Notice the use of the objective and synopsis.

In addition to the objective and synopsis, other components of the résumé consist of education, experience, and activities. Together, these categories make up the template of items whose details are continually updated. As time goes on, experienced professionals often add other components, such as affiliations, which lists memberships in

FIGURE 11.1
Sample Résumé

Daisy M. Jacobs

Campus Address:	Permanent Address:
315 Leaverton Hall	442 N. Sheridan St.
St. Joseph, MO 64507	Wheeling, MO 64688
816-532-1132	660-888-8680

D.Jacobs@gmail.com
Cell: 718-345-1212

Objective: Litigation paralegal in probate and domestic relations law with a law firm in south Florida.

Summary:
- Bachelor's degree in Legal Studies, ABA approved.
- Proficient with LexisNexis and Westlaw, MS Office, and research on the Internet.
- Fluent in Spanish, working knowledge of Italian.

Education: Bachelor of Science, Criminal Justice, Legal Studies emphasis, Class of 2009
Western Missouri State University, Saint Joseph, MO 64507
Representative courses taken include:
Legal Research, Litigation, Real Property, Legal Computer Applications, Tort Law, Legal Drafting, Domestic Relations, Probate Law, Advanced Legal Research.

Experience: Legal Assistant (part-time), May 2007 to present
Thompson, Rowe & Stuttgard, LLC, St. Joseph, MO
- Assisted in preparation of divorce and adoption cases.
- Developed intake forms and case management systems.
- Established Excel spreadsheet macros for computation of support requests.
- Extensive use of LexisNexis and Internet research.

Administrative Clerk, January 2005 to September 2006
Mayberry Health Services, Chillicoth, MO 64601
- Maintained automated monthly payroll and benefits system.
- Organized patient files and appointment schedule
- Ordered office supplies and maintained inventory

Activities:
- Member, Legal Studies Association, Western Missouri State University
- Student Legal Assistant, Legal Aid of Western Missouri, St. Joseph, MO
- Residence Assistant, Leaverton Hall, 2008-09

References and writing sample available on request.

professional organizations. Political or religious involvement should be kept to a minimum and mentioned only if you have achieved a high level of activity or an important position in the organization to show leadership capabilities. Readers may consider these items irrelevant, and readers' reaction can be uncertain. Likewise, personal information such as marital status and whether you have children should be kept to a minimum. Current wisdom holds that if there is some question as to the propriety of information to include, leave it out, unless it relates somehow to the position being sought.

Cover Letter

Every position you apply for must be accompanied by a job application cover letter, even if you are applying online. In that case, the actual e-mail message could represent the cover letter, with a word processing file with your résumé attached to it. The function of the cover letter is to introduce you to the prospective employer. Begin by indicating your interest in the specific position sought, if responding to a job advertisement, or your interest in the position in which you would be generally interested. Next, explain how your qualifications fit the position, referring to the experience listed in your résumé or any other pertinent aspect of your training (e.g., a course relevant to the employer's work) or activities. The letter should be very brief, no longer than three short paragraphs. Here, you may mention any personal matters, such as particular challenges or skills that you feel are particularly relevant. The important thing to remember is that the letter should act as a brief introduction that highlights your background. As painful as it may seem to write, the cover letter should be very simple. Figure 11.2 provides a sample cover letter.

FIGURE 11.2
Sample Cover Letter

Daisy M. Jacobs
315 Leaverton Hall
St. Joseph, MO 64507
816-532-1132

May 31, 2008

Martha Ferrari, Esq.
Ferrari & Rolls
4000 Ponce de Leon Boulevard
Suite 800
Coral Gables, FL 33134

Dear Ms. Ferrari:

I am very interested in the position of family law paralegal listed with the Career Services Office at Western Missouri State University. Enclosed is my résumé. As indicated in my résumé, I will be graduating with a Bachelor's of Science in Legal Studies from an ABA-approved program. I have taken courses in Domestic Relations Law and Probate Law, both of which were my favorite courses. Please note that I also have two years experience as a paralegal with a local law firm and as a volunteer with the family law unit of Legal Aid of Western Missouri. I am fluent in Spanish.

Ferrari & Rolls is of great interest to me because of the extensive domestic relations work of your office. While working in my current position and as a volunteer, I have been able to apply my classroom knowledge to practice. I have also found working with clients in family law matters particularly gratifying. Please note that I have substantial computer and administrative skills to contribute. I am very interested in relocating to south Florida, where several members of my family reside.

I believe that the combination of my experience and strong organizational skills are well suited to the position you described. Thank you for your consideration. I look forward to receiving your reply.

Sincerely,
Doris M. Jacobs

Enc.

In the sample cover letter, Jacobs amplifies some aspects already listed in her résumé that would be of particular importance to the position sought and has added other items that help introduce her to the law firm.

As with the résumé, the cover letter should be free of any typographical or grammatical errors. Such errors are often fatal from the outset. Employers are aware that job applicants must put their best foot forward. Thus, an error indicates carelessness and a lack of attention to detail. As a mechanical matter, both the résumé and the cover letter should appear on the same color (white, buff, gray, or ivory) and type of paper, of at least 20-pound weight. Both should be typed in the same font and typeface (usually 12-point, Times New Roman). Typically, résumés and cover letters are mailed in a legal size envelope (number 10). Some employment experts advocate sending by Priority Mail, which gives the job application greater distinctiveness.

As a matter of efficiency, apply for several jobs simultaneously. With the ease that computers offer, the first step of the admittedly painful process of looking for work can be attacked in one sitting. Sending unsolicited applications to firms and other law offices as part of a mass mailing usually produces few if any responses. However, success with an unsolicited application is not unknown. After finding some available positions from various sources, such as advertisements and a school career or placement office, try mailing a few unsolicited applications at the same time that you apply for known openings. Many job applicants, both paralegals and lawyers, use a famous publication known as *Martindale-Hubbell.*

The *Martindale-Hubbell Law Directory* was first published in 1868 to provide bankers, merchants, lawyers, and other professionals with information about reliable lawyers in every major city. It is one of the oldest and best known catalogues of lawyers in the United States. The directory and the digest are updated annually. In the directory, firms are rated for their legal expertise and ethical conduct, the highest rating being "AV." The AV rating has become the gold standard for lawyers. Now owned and operated by LexisNexis, the directory is available on the Internet and has become a major source of information for clients searching for attorneys, as well as for job applicants, both lawyers and paralegals.

The Interview

Interview Preparation

Whether or not you are aware of it, the processes of self-assessment, job market evaluation, and other activities provide good preparation for an interview. The knowledge you have acquired should have familiarized you with specifics, such as entry-level salaries, benefits, and general knowledge about the legal profession for the area to which you are applying. Once you have been contacted for an interview, there may be cause for celebration, because your résumé and cover letter made the first cut. However, this point is when earnest interview preparation should begin.

Start by assembling a folder in which you keep a few extra copies of your résumé and cover letter. It should also include writing samples from prepared research and writing projects or assignments from any legal work. Samples from schoolwork should be free of any marks or comments from your instructor; those from any actual legal work should obscure any information that would identify a client on any samples you submit to maintain confidentiality. This folder should also contain notes on research you will do about the prospective employer. Collect as much information as you can find about the firm through sources like its Web site or *Martindale-Hubbell*. Valuable information that published sources cannot provide, such as reputation or office culture, can be obtained from friends or acquaintances who may have had contact with the firm. Networking would yield some contacts for this type of information.

Nervousness in anticipation of the interview is common, if not expected to some degree, even among experienced job seekers. Thinking about the interview process rationally helps reduce anxiety. Keep in mind that an interview is a face-to-face exchange of information. Dress, body language, choice of words, and eye contact are all part of the communication process. Again, try looking at the process from the employer's viewpoint. From this perspective, you will be able to imagine the likely questions and concerns, such as whether the applicant's skills match the position and whether the applicant will fit well into the office. At its base, an interview should be a friendly, albeit somewhat formal, discussion about you and the workplace.

Temper your eagerness by concentrating on what you would like to know about the concrete aspects of the job and the office. At the same time, expect questions about your background and details of items in your résumé. You may wish to anticipate opportunities to explain "holes" or weak points in your background, including your academic record or time gaps in your past employment. The circumstances surrounding these points might have been connected with unpleasant or unfortunate life events. In that case, find a way to explain how you overcame or "moved beyond" a troubling period of your life. Then, after no more than a beat, be prepared to take a bit of control of the interview by asking a question about the office or the firm. In doing so, you will have tactfully responded to a difficult point and shifted to a more upbeat topic. Much of the background work that will enable you to make such a response may very well come from your earlier self-assessment.

The Interview

Plan your trip to the interview site, leaving plenty of time to get there and arriving 10 to 15 minutes before the appointed time. If unfamiliar with the surroundings, it would be a good idea to visit the site ahead of time as a "dry run" so that you can accurately estimate travel time. Of course, maintain a professional appearance, with a folder and a date book in hand or in a briefcase. Proper business attire includes a conservative suit with shirt (white or light blue) and a tie for men, and comparable business attire for women.

The formalities of the interview itself begin with your arrival at the employer's office. The most important item to bring with you is an appropriate attitude. Leaving plenty of time for traveling will avert feeling rushed or hassled from fighting traffic, finding a parking space, or bumping through crowded public transportation routes. Before entering the building, take a moment to compose yourself, stopping at a nearby restroom if necessary. Avoid making unreasonable requests or speaking down to the receptionist; he or she, like others you encounter in the office, could very well report negatively to your interviewer afterward. When the interviewer arrives in the reception area, remember to stand. In the United States, the custom is to shake hands while maintaining eye contact.

Depending on the size and formality of the employer firm, the interview may take place with one person or several from the firm. From the start, the type of questioning will vary greatly. You can expect to explain your strong points and any weak points. Although discussing these topics may seem difficult, there is an easy and appropriate approach to your response. Begin by responding with generalities about your good points, such as self-taught computer knowledge to show your initiative or organizational skills that you acquired from past experiences. Referring to items in your résumé provides credible and concrete examples in your responses to questions.

Discussing weak points is a bit trickier. Never deny that you have weaknesses, at the risk of appearing insolent or egotistical. At all times, show pride in yourself while maintaining a discernable amount of modesty by mentioning weaknesses, such as being a workaholic, overly demanding with yourself, or a worrier. Alternatively, explain that your computer skills need updating or that you tend to become too immersed in your work, making it difficult to keep track of your time. Follow by stating that the available position is an opportunity to improve on your weaknesses.

Inappropriate or illegal questions present a more delicate situation. Questions about your age, affiliations, ethnicity, race, marital or family status, disability, or health conditions are generally impermissible and may be discriminatory. They could also have been asked innocently. Exercising tact is a far easier task than filing a lawsuit, and even then, you are confronted with some choices, each with attendant risks. Reminding (if not informing for the first time) the interviewer of the question's illegality will severely reduce your chances of obtaining an offer. Skirting the question, if possible, and changing the conversation to your commitment to your career may be the best tact. The final choice would be, under extreme circumstances, to end the interview, thank the questioner for his or her time, and leave. You will be surprised at how relieved you will be upon leaving the office of an employer for which you would not want to work.

Even if you know everything you need to know about the firm, your own questions say something about you to the interviewer. Asking questions from the list below tends to reflect positively on you:

- Does the firm provide training or support continuing legal education for paralegals?
- What technical or computer resources exist?
- How many billable hours are expected of a paralegal?
- Are there other areas of legal practice planned?
- What is the evaluation and review process?
- What project or case has been of particular importance to the firm?
- What growth possibilities exist for paralegals in the firm?

Remember that an interview is a two-way exchange. The first interview acts only as an introduction. In subsequent interviews, salary, benefits, and the like become topics of discussion. Thus, take care not to raise issues of compensation and working conditions during the first interview. At the end of the interview, maintain an upbeat posture by expressing continuing interest and, of course, gratitude for the opportunity.

Be sure to keep track of the names of those who interviewed you and certainly the primary contact person. Customarily, they will have given you a business card. If they have not, certainly ask for one before you leave. Enter the contact information in your folder and make a note of your impressions and what was discussed for future reference. You will also need the contact information for the postinterview letter. In that letter, preferably a typewritten one, make the following points: (1) Thank the contact person for the meeting, (2) confirm your interest in working with the firm, and perhaps (3) mention a specific item discussed that piqued your interest. As meaningless and servile as a postinterview letter may seem, it performs the important purpose of keeping your application in the interviewer's consciousness. As a widely accepted convention, the postinterview letter also gives the impression of thoroughness and decorum. It never hurts to kiss up a little bit.

A week or two later, feel free to call your contact to inquire as to the status of your application. If no action has been taken, pleasantly express the same gratitude and interest and hang up gently. Rejections are always difficult. If and when they come, decide to move on and feel relief at not having to make a decision. An offer, in contrast, requires studied evaluation.

CYBER TRIP

Find the prevailing salary for an entry-level paralegal in your area. See www.nala.org/Survey_Table.htm, www.paralegals.org/displaycommon.cfm?an=1&subarticlenbr=33, and www.collegegrad.com/entryleveljob/entrylevelparalegaljobs.shtml.

After the Interview

Fielding an Offer

The excitement and flattery that can come with a job offer can often cloud a rational evaluation. Most of the time, an employer will make an offer over the telephone, followed by a confirming letter. Having interviewed and learned about the job, you are aware of the duties and responsibilities. Subsequent interviews and discussions may have already covered salary and benefits. Nevertheless, a formal offer of employment, even telephonically, should state the job title, salary, and a brief but complete description of the fringe benefits, such as health insurance, vacation, and the like. If the offer is incomplete, you owe it to yourself to ask. The employer will fully expect questions. After all, an offer basically means that the employer wants you to take the job and be happy about it. Once the offer has been made, the ball is in your court.

At this point, the information gathered from your evaluation of the job market provides a basis for appraising an offer. Primary among your findings would be the prevailing salaries for entry-level paralegals, including the pay differential between the private sector and the public sector. Specific salary and benefits information is available from the national paralegal associations and through word of mouth from local associations. Thus, comparing the offer against this information provides a sound and rational approach. A salary higher than the prevailing rate could be justified for an entry-level paralegal on the basis of special abilities. For example, advanced skills in computers or in a foreign language that is useful to the firm could command a salary higher than the prevailing rate. However, absent these or other factors, greater expectations could price you out of the market.

Most employers will not expect an immediate response to an offer. Give yourself a few days to mull it over, which should be enough time to do some further research. Other considerations could also come into play. Your job market evaluation should have revealed the degree of competition for paralegal jobs. The economy, the number of paralegal schools in the local area, and the breadth of the local legal community can affect the job market for paralegals. If you applied for the position through a professional employment agency, consider it an ally from which you could seek some guidance. Employment agencies, as part of their services, often will facilitate the negotiation process. For most job seekers, salary is the prime consideration in evaluating a job offer. Nevertheless, working conditions deserve ample consideration before you respond to an offer. A higher than prevailing salary can prove to be of little solace in a job for which there is no support or training or that requires too far of a commute. Ultimately, you may need more information about the employer to make a rational decision.

While the offer is still pending, ask to spend a couple of hours—a morning or an afternoon—in the office. Ask to "shadow" one of the current employees, preferably a paralegal. Many employers would be impressed by the request, as you will appear cautious and thoughtful. If you do so, take care not to engage in the work or express opinions, lest your application be reconsidered. Treat the visit as a way of testing the commute from your home. Once in the office, politely and quietly observe as much as you can about the physical layout and your intended office or cubicle to sense whether you feel the job would be a good fit. Tactfully inquire about fringe benefits, if needed. Express gratitude upon leaving, and if asked, give an indication of your response period. If, after experiencing the commute, benefits, office environment, and other aspects of the offer, you believe they appear to fall within acceptable ranges, you will have acquired pretty much all you need to know to begin your negotiations in earnest.

Parameters for negotiating the salary may have been established by the advertisement or posting. It would be natural to seek the high end. However, a delicate approach would be to ask for a salary within a given range that approaches the high end. For instance, if the range advertised indicates between $35,000 and $40,000 a year, and that range comports with your research, try asking for a salary figure between $38,000 and $40,000. Yet also prepare yourself to accept an offer at the lower end of this range. Unless the candidate possesses special abilities, an employer will seldom cave in to the high end, particularly for first-time job seekers. An applicant who is coming from another job has a distinct advantage. It is usually understood that a working applicant is seeking, among other things, a higher salary when moving to a new position.

Once you have accepted the position, after salary and other conditions have been agreed upon, confirm the starting date, and take the time to withdraw other pending applications as a matter of courtesy. Also take the time to inform your school. Like any professional school, paralegal programs have a vested interest in placing their students. Moreover, by taking the job, you have established a beachhead for future graduates from your school looking for work.

Dealing with Rejection

As improbable as it may seem, Michael Jordan—widely regarded as the best basketball player ever—was rejected when he first tried out for his varsity high school basketball team. Rejection happens to everyone. Dealing with rejection can be very difficult. Probably the most important advice is not to take a job rejection personally, but learn and move on. This process may be difficult if you really wanted the job. If that is the case, you should have already learned that wanting something badly only sets you up for a bad case of rejection. The hiring process, as noted, is arbitrary and well out of an applicant's control. Recall that an important part of the self-assessment process discussed at the beginning of this chapter calls for you to list matters that are out of your control. Thus, do not fret over matters out of your control.

Still, the sting of a rejection can smart. Here are some tips for dealing with and getting past a job rejection:

- Get out of the house—frequently. Many people instinctively react to rejection by withdrawing, hiding themselves, and staying at home for extended periods. However, the longer you stay burrowed away, the more difficult it will be to get over the feelings brought about by rejection. Avoid this vicious cycle by forcing yourself to get out and get out often. Movies can be very helpful, especially if they involve high action or drama or even horror. Experiencing deep emotions vicariously has the positive psychological effect known as a catharsis, a healthy release.
- Treat yourself. Whether it is an item of clothing or that espresso maker you have always wanted to buy, but held off on purchasing, now may be the time to give your morale a needed lift. Go ahead and buy something nice for yourself, using another psychological technique, retail therapy.
- Find comfort in the company of a loved one. Friends and family who care would love to hear from you and lend a sympathetic ear. That's what they're there for: to be called on during your times of need. Combining the previous two tips, perhaps you could go out with a friend or family member and treat yourself to a nice meal as you chat and laugh your rejection away.

None of these tips will get you that job you wanted. But they may, after a while, convince you that perhaps you did not want that job so badly after all.

STARTING YOUR FIRST LEGAL JOB—A PRIMER

Once the elation of having received and accepted a new job, especially a first job, has settled, the sober yet exciting task of starting a career in the legal profession begins.

Rumor has it that Queen Elizabeth II of England advised her son, Prince Charles, that "Dress gives one the outward sign from which people can judge the inward state of mind. One they can see, the other they cannot." The wisdom to be gleaned from the Queen's statement is that first impressions are based on appearance. Although you have made a sufficiently positive impression to get the job, your coworkers will continue to judge you as they continue to formulate an impression of you as you begin working with them. First impressions are unfair because they are based, at best, upon incomplete and therefore inaccurate information: outward appearance. Worse, first impressions tend to last. It is easier to make a positive first impression than to overcome one that may be less than favorable. There are some tried-and-true ways of maintaining the positive first impression you made to get the job.

- Anticipate and plan to meet your employer's expectations of you. Review the hiring process and your visits to the office. Recall any work product that you may have seen, the behavior and dress of the legal professionals there, and, most important, the office policy or personnel handbooks. These and more are items that you should adopt for yourself when at work. Rather than feeling burdened or overwhelmed when taking assignments, try to accept work gladly while feeling free to ask questions or seek guidance.
- Be on time. Punctuality for office meetings or conferences with higher-ups is particularly noticeable. Resist the inclination to follow the habits of others whom you may observe arriving to work or meetings late. Establish and adhere to your own standards. In doing so, you will earn respect and a noticeable reliability that your employer will appreciate.
- Demonstrate diligence and strive for excellence. The workday in just about every office technically ends at 5:00 p.m. When that hour strikes, you will notice that the legal professionals in the firm usually keep working, while others, such as the receptionists or file clerks, leave for the day. As a legal professional, your success depends on getting your job done to the best of your abilities, which often means staying until you feel that *you* have finished for the day. This commitment may mean staying later, but not always. Modern professionals recognize quality-of-life issues. Inordinate hours and unreasonable demands can lead to unhappiness and burnout, which may in turn adversely affect productivity in the long run. Thus, it is entirely possible to demonstrate a sincere effort to produce high-quality legal work for every assignment without having to work a slavish amount of hours. A large part of being a professional means establishing your own standards. Most firms are attentive to a reasonable "quitting time" and allow legal professionals to establish their own.
- Be sure to review and proofread all documents you prepare. They should be free of any typographical and grammatical errors before leaving your hands or your computer. Simply using the word processor's spelling and grammar checker may prove insufficient. Recall that once you have completed an initial draft, you should give yourself a few hours or a day before reviewing it for any errors.
- Communicate professionally at all times. In any law office, the modes of communication take on several different forms. Traditionally, communication occurred by voice, on the telephone, or on paper, in memos and notes. In today's electronic age, forms of communication can take place via e-mail, instant messaging, or text messages to name just a few. These new modes of communication increase your visibility with the office personnel, and, consequently, the chances of communicating in a way that may be considered inappropriate. Whatever form in which you communicate within the office, be sure to avoid appearing or sounding unprofessional. Speak in a firm but soft-spoken voice, use proper grammar and diction, and certainly stay away from slang or improper

language. Far from appearing overly formal and stiff, these tactics allow you to develop a relaxed, approachable, and, at the same time, professional demeanor in the law office.

With these considerations in mind, you will be well on your way to developing a professional persona once you have decided to do so. Learn to behave as a professional. Contrary to popular belief, acting consists of showing true feelings as opposed to feigned or pretended ones. Whether or not people realize it, they apply acting theory to real life. We all behave differently depending on the situation in which we find ourselves. We shape our tone of voice, facial expressions, and physical movements to fit the various circumstances of our lives. For example, we behave differently in front of our parents than we do with friends. Yet in any situation we find ourselves, the feelings and emotions we exhibit are genuine. We cease to act truthfully if our behavior is designed to manipulate or deceive. Such intended behavior can often be detected as untruthful and cause difficulty in the future. David Mamet, the famous American playwright and acting coach, thus cautions, "Always tell the truth—it's the easiest thing to remember." One of the greatest method actors in America, Marlon Brando, once said,

> *It is a simple fact that all of us use the techniques of acting to achieve whatever ends we seek, whether it is a child pouting for ice cream or a bawling politician bent on stirring the hearts and pocketbooks of potential constituents. Statesmen the world over would have amusingly short careers without the aid and judicious application of this craft of acting. Why the perception persists that there is a distinction between the professional actor and those of us who act naturally out of out daily needs is a puzzle. It is hard to imagine that we could survive in this world without being actors. Acting serves as the quintessential social lubricant and a device for protecting our interests and gaining advantage in every aspect of life.*[1]

In addition to your time, appearance, and commitment, engaging in other activities will help advance your professional development and your career. If your employer is willing to pay for them, take advantage of lectures and seminars offered by the local professional associations, particularly those from paralegal organizations. If you must pay for them yourself, do so to the extent you are able. Large firms often conduct seminars that are important to attend so that you appear attentive and can absorb new information that will help you in your work. They are also opportunities for networking and establishing positive work relationships.

Keep up with changes and trends in the law, particularly in your practice field, by reading various publications available in your office. Regularly visit your local law library or Web sites that provide reports about the latest news and developments in the law in your spare time. Setting aside two or three hours a month should be sufficient. Keeping up with the law often is a matter of browsing. Legal newspapers and journals you combed through to evaluate the legal job market and look for job openings will suddenly take on new meaning. Now that you have succeeded in obtaining legal employment, those same publications furnish the latest news in and about the legal community. Frequently, they report on the latest court decisions, regulatory and legislative changes, and practice tips. Keeping up with the law and the legal culture, you will be surprised at the positive effect it has on maintaining your professional identity.

Of course, the help wanted announcements in local legal journals should be of continuing interest to you. Browsing them will keep you abreast of the constantly changing job market, a reflection of the economy and its effect on the legal community. It is always a good idea to see what may be available for you in the future.

---

[1] Marlon Brando, Forward to Stella Adler, The Technique of Acting, 1–2 (1988).

WORKING SUCCESSFULLY IN THE LAW OFFICE: A SKILLS APPROACH

time management
The practice of systematic, priority-based structuring of time allocation and distribution among competing demands.

One of the most important skills to develop in the legal workplace is **time management**, the skill or technique used to plan and schedule work tasks. Remember that as a legal professional, your time translates into money. As they do for their lawyers, most firms keep track of the time paralegals spend on a client's case, using computerized time and billing programs and billing the client an hourly rate for the paralegal's work. The programs also track the legal professional's efficiency and productivity. You can be sure that your supervisor, if not the client, will raise an eyebrow if a certain task has taken an inordinate amount of time to complete. Time management is extremely important and an easily learned skill.

Determine immediately any deadlines looming for the work assigned to you. These deadlines may consist of extremely important ones imposed by statute or regulation. Failing to file a complaint before the expiration of the statute of limitations may constitute malpractice. The same is true with court-imposed deadlines. Other deadlines may come from your supervisor, whose job it is to regulate the flow of work. Within these restrictions, you may wish to impose deadlines on yourself to complete certain tasks as a measure of self-regulation.

to-do list
A form of time management involving listing tasks in order of importance as reminders of goals for the workday.

As an initial strategy, set goals and write them down to formulate an action plan. We all have done this, managing our daily lives similarly by making a simple **to-do list**. An everyday example would be a grocery list. Setting up a daily or weekly to-do list will guide you through your workload while ensuring tasks that could be forgotten without the list get completed. As a simple measure, double-space the list so that you can insert other tasks as they may arise or as you delve into your work in more detail. Think of the to-do list as an inventory or checklist; once a task is completed, check or cross it off. Software applications also can be used. Several popular e-mail formats bundle task list applications, as do most PDAs. Several free Web-based task list applications are available with the click of a mouse.

prioritization
The act of listing or dealing with matters in their order of importance.

With deadlines set, determine which tasks (i.e., items from the to-do list) deserve greater or lesser priority, engaging in a practice known as **prioritization**. Rewriting the list, rearrange from top to bottom the priority with which you should approach the daily or weekly list of tasks. Often, especially with legal work, a complex case or a phase of a case may present a seemingly overwhelming amount of work, too much to think of as a single task. Simplify by carefully dissecting and breaking down the work into discrete tasks, prioritizing each one. In this way, you will make the work more manageable. Notice that the to-do list will then take on an even more orderly and structured form, setting out sub-to-do lists for each task. Of course, any list will be of little value unless you actually use it. Using these lists as your guide for your daily and weekly work schedule, among other practices, will help you achieve greater efficiency and professionalism.

As you plod though more difficult or complex work, roadblocks or obstacles will inevitably appear, making you feel mired in an inescapable morass. Several techniques may help. First, do not feel alone, helpless, or inadequate. Observe the other legal professionals around you and notice that they occasionally take breaks to visit the water cooler or restroom, start another task, or discuss their blockage with a colleague. All of these are valued techniques for dealing with being stuck. Realize that you're stuck. The technique of taking a break or beginning another task has the beneficial effect of reenergizing your thought processes, giving your brain a rest, and allowing it to come up with other ideas for tackling the task. A short walk around the block or coffee break helps the brain to start afresh.

Second, the problem could stem from the fact that you are a novice whose inexperience has caused the blockage. In that case, conferring with an experienced or trusted colleague may show you new ways of going about approaching the work. Do not expect yourself to be able to tackle any assignment without asking for help. Experienced legal professionals have collected tricks and techniques of the trade known as legal practice. They have learned them through experience and from asking questions themselves. You will find that breaking through blockage and completing a task or project that has plagued you is an important learning experience. The feeling can also be a bit exhilarating. When obstacles occur in the future, you now have gained confidence in your ability to overcome such obstacles.

PRACTICE TIP

Using an Internet search engine, enter "task list" to obtain a number of Web sites that offer free downloadable software. Many of these programs are generic time management accessories not designed with a legal professional in mind. In reviewing the ones available, consider what features a legal professional might want in such a program. Make a list of the features you would find important for a task list program that would suit you, and make it a practice to use the program regularly. Even if you have not yet begun working, you will find that using a program as a matter of time management will give you more time and help get more things done, whether it is schoolwork, errands, household chores, or even your social life.

Third, avoid interruptions by taking some control over your working environment. After assembling your to-do list, estimate the time required to accomplish a given task. Performing legal research, writing memos, and reviewing complex files, among other similar tasks, require studied concentration over several hours at a sitting. Telephone calls, social visits from colleagues, and other distractions can break your train of thought, resulting in wasted time as you attempt to regain your concentration after the interruption. Arrange the order in which you begin such tasks in accordance with your daily schedule. If necessary, block out the specific hours of the day needed to accomplish burdensome tasks in your datebook. Before beginning, close the door to your office and inform the receptionist to hold all calls as you slough through the work.

Fourth, another technique for controlling your environment is to schedule difficult or complex tasks during periods of peak efficiency. As a form of self-awareness, determine the times during the course of a workday when you are most efficient. Put quite simply, are you a "morning person" or an "evening person"? Depending on the answer, schedule the difficult tasks—those that require more focused attention than others—accordingly. Almost uniformly, everyone's lowest point of efficiency occurs right after lunch through the early afternoon. For this reason, some cultures, particularly in warm climates, set aside a siesta period. For the same reason, afternoon tea, the traditional serving of tea (caffeine) and snacks, begins at 4:00 p.m. During those periods, be sure to give yourself a break or a strong cup of coffee as the circumstances and the flow of work require. Time management is a small part of **stress management**.

Managing Your Mind and Emotions: Stress Management

Understand what stress is. Basically, stress is the "wear and tear" our bodies experience as a result of our day-to-day lives. Stress affects us both physically and emotionally. Unduly stressful situations can cause distrust, rejection, anger, and depression, which in turn can lead to other problems. In fact, most illnesses are related to unrelieved stress. Deadlines, competitive work environments, confrontations, and the occasional and inevitable frustrations of working in law create stress. Only the unrealistic person (or an eternal optimist) believes that stress can be eliminated. The realist or pragmatist approaches the problem by engaging in stress management.

stress management
The practice of identifying the causes of stress, reducing its effects, and relieving existing stress brought on by the workplace.

Stress management is all about raising your own awareness. Become aware that you are in control of most aspects of your life. At the same time, recognize that you can manage the sources and change your response to stress in the workplace. Consider the following techniques of stress management:

1. Become aware of the stressors, the causes of your stress, and your emotional and physical reactions. In office situations, we tend to ignore or gloss over our own feelings. As a first step toward stress management, become aware of when you feel distressed and the events or sources that cause you stress.
2. Recognize what you can change. Itemize the steps you can take for each source of your stress; for each item, determine what you can change to avoid or reduce the stress it produces. Avoiding or reducing exposure to sources of your stress, like toxic coworkers, can go a long way toward managing stress.

3. Take control of yourself (self-control). Emotions often feel like involuntary responses, but we have more control over our emotions than we think. Thus, try to reduce the intensity of your responses to stress. Meet and confront your enemy, as the saying goes. Chances are that things are not as bad as they seem. Decide to adopt a more moderate view of the sources for your stress. Tell yourself not to overreact.
4. Adopt exercises and techniques that moderate your physical reactions to stress. Taking a walk or breathing deeply and slowly can dissipate stress. Other relaxation techniques can reduce the rapid heart rate, muscle tension, and heightened blood pressure that are telltale signs of the onset of stress.
5. Take care of yourself. Build your physical reserves. Exercise regularly. Eat healthy. Maintain an appropriate weight. Avoid stimulants such as caffeine and certainly nicotine. Sleep well and at a consistent schedule. At work, take breaks. Use any exercise or health facilities at or near the workplace.
6. Create sources of positive energy. Make sure your to-do list is realistic. Do not be too demanding of yourself, but also expect some frustrations and even failures. Develop supportive friendships and workplace relationships. Most important, be a friend to yourself.

Communication Skills

Legal work is all about communication. At its most basic, legal professionals' calling constitutes, in its entirety, oral and written communication. More specifically, a legal professional receives communications from a client and translates, in whole or in part, the client's information into a specialized language and particular format to courts, administrative bodies, and opposing counsel, among others. Think of the legal professionals in your office as a computer and the law as several forms of computer programs. Inputting client information begins the processing cycles and routines generated by the computer programs, the law. Legal professionals, at the core of the central processing unit, make decisions about how to process the input of client data by which laws or computer programs, guiding (and guarding) the journey. On the output end come pleadings, memos, correspondence, and spoken words in the form of argumentation, rhetoric, and legal advice. Thus, with communication as its core function, a large part of a legal professional's duty is to safeguard the client's data to maintain confidentiality. Within the law office, the professional's duty also includes ensuring the accuracy, completeness, and propriety of the various forms of communication produced.

Paralegals and other legal professionals communicate with their coworkers in a variety of formats: typewritten, both hardcopy (paper) and electronic (e-mail, instant messages), and by spoken word. When they do so in whatever format, the communication is a reflection of its author.

Written Communications

In the office, a paralegal's correspondence, including memos, e-mail, instant messages, and other written communications, continue to act as a reflection of his or her skill and capabilities long after they have been produced. Sitting in a file drawer or on the office's file server for an indeterminate period and within eyeshot of anyone with access, typographical and grammatical errors can stick out like sore thumbs. Thus, paralegals must take the utmost care in producing flawless written work. Resorting regularly to dictionaries and style manuals, in either hardcopy or electronic form, can drastically reduce the chance for error.

Even after using a computerized spellchecker, carefully proofread the final product for errors in word choice that a spellchecker would not flag. For instance, a spellchecker will not notice that you have mistakenly typed *than* instead of *then,* because both are spelled correctly. This fault is often the problem with spellcheckers, as well as grammar and style checkers. Early grammar and writing style programs scanned a document for wordiness and usage that was trite, clichéd, or misused. Using simple pattern matching, these programs consisted of lists of several thousand phrases traditionally considered poor writing. The list of suspect phrases included alternate wordings for each phrase. Thus, a checking program would simply break a text into sentences, check for any matches in the phrase dictionary, flag suspect phrases, and show an alternative.

True grammar checking poses more difficult and complex issues. Computer programming languages have highly specific and structured rules of syntax and grammar, which is not the case for natural languages. There are innumerable exceptions in real usage that a grammar-checking computer program can miss. As with the words priority, prioritize, and prioritization, many words represent different parts of speech, greatly increasing the complexity of a true grammar checker. Already, a grammar checker's task is difficult and involved enough. With each use, a grammar-checking program finds and defines each sentence, check each word in the dictionary, and then applies thousands of grammatical rules to detect errors. No small feat.

Beyond grammatical errors, checking for style opens up an entirely new set of issues. For instance, most consider using the passive voice poor style but not an error. Elegant variation with the choice of a repetitive concept may be preferable, except in a technical context such as law. For instance, if referring to the existence of a contract, most legal professionals would not later use the word agreement or compact for the sake of accuracy and consistency.

Oral Communication

During meetings and even informal one-on-one conferences, particularly with supervisors and higher-ups, the skill of oral communication also includes the ability to listen and observe. As we discussed previously, visual clues such as body movement, tone of voice, eye contact, and gesticulation constitute important parts of spoken communication. In the give-and-take of normal conversation, psychological dynamics can block the simple intake of information. Feeling intimidated, wanting to make a positive impression or be accepted, among a host of other psychological dynamics, can interfere with listening. Listening is a skill that requires the exercise of high concentration.

COMMUNICATION TIP

Communication is not just about how to express your thoughts. A very important part of communication is listening. Active listening means focusing on the speaker and suspending your own thoughts or judgments.

Active listening is different from reading comprehension or merely listening to the words being spoken. Written words remain on the page for us to review over again if we missed the meaning the first time. Spoken words, however, exist only in the moment they are uttered. Simply holding your tongue while the other person speaks is not the same thing as listening. To really listen, you have to suspend your own agenda, forget about what you might say next, and concentrate on being receptive to the speaker and engrossed in what he or she is saying. Without noticing, we can lose interest or feel the urge to interrupt. It is at this moment that listening takes self-control. Active listening requires suspending memory, desire, and judgment and existing for the other person. A good listener thus focuses on being able to understand what the speaker is trying to convey and indicating that he or she understands what the speaker is saying.

Except when listening to a speech, persons engaged in a conversation customarily take turns—though not necessarily equal turns—speaking and listening. A few rules of thumb help us decide when to speak and when to listen. Never assume that you should say more than the other person. The human brain is hardwired for oral communication. However, thinking strategically about listening and choosing to meet conversational goals are an acquired skill. A skilled listener anticipates the purpose of the conversation and makes choices accordingly.

For the most part, valid business or professional purposes for a conversation include exchanging information. Particularly in an employment situation, the information needs consist of the needs of the speaker, another coworker, or the client. Part of the exchange of information entails whether you accurately understood what the speaker said. Thus, as you take assignments, discuss cases, or receive instruction, you are receiving information.

Indicate that you understand by repeating the information to the speaker in summary or paraphrased form. Taking notes is a way of indicating that you are absorbing the information. Certainly if you do not understand, ask questions fearlessly. A simple question asking for a clarification indicates that you understand. Of course, having to ask questions, particularly on points of law, betrays your lack of knowledge. Understandably, you may fear displaying a lack of knowledge by asking questions. However, no one can realistically expect a recent graduate or an entry-level paralegal, let alone an experienced professional, to possess vast amounts of legal knowledge. Nevertheless, it may be difficult to ask questions of some people. In that case, make a note of your question so that you can discuss it later with an ally or trusted coworker.

A conversation could have the purpose of building working relationships. Collegial respect and coworkers who have good experiences working together tend to work more effectively. Personal style can make an enormous difference. Developing and maintaining positive personal relationships can be one of the most important components of workplace conversations. Having an enjoyable or productive conversation can help coworkers feel valued, respected, and even liked. As such, conversations can become a key component of having a good day or even a good job, as well as boosting motivation and productivity.

For every conversation, and for every choice you make in that conversation, remind yourself of the purpose of the conversation and the choices you can make. Be aware of your choices. Choose to focus on the speaker. Take a moment to structure what you are going to say. Decide how much detail to go into or what to ask. If you aren't certain what structure works best, try clarifying before you start. Clarifying gives you an opportunity to observe the other person, who may have no interest in what you have to say, as communicated by appearing disinterested or agitated while as you seek clarification. At this point, you may wish to seek clarification from another, more receptive colleague.

Survival in the Law Office—Dealing with the Difficult Coworker

In almost every workplace, there is at least one difficult person. Unfortunately, this is also true in the legal workplace. People enter the legal profession for several different reasons. Some become legal professionals because they have strong verbal skills and enjoy the structured and nuanced use of rhetoric. Others are attracted to the philosophy-like logic and deductive reasoning found in legal thought. Precedent and the social context of past legal events fascinate history buffs. Still others study law to pursue justice on behalf of the poor, the environment, or a cause. Money is a common reason for becoming a legal professional. These are thought of as healthy reasons for entering the legal profession, but there are some who go into law for less noble reasons.

Psychological studies note that the legal profession can attract individuals who work in law for negative reasons. The unique nature of the legal profession may lend itself well to those whose personalities wish to persecute or control others. The opportunity to engage in courtroom combat or theatrics and the power-driven, hierarchical nature of many aspects of legal practice have special appeal for those with difficult personalities. In one study, psychologists have identified three basic personality disorders that are frequently drawn to law. The first is the narcissist, who is self-centered and has a need to be admired. The second is the obsessive compulsive, characterized as inflexible, rigid, and stingy. Finally, there is the antisocial, the con-man whose shallow manipulative nature is masked by charm and charisma. In every profession and every walk of life, throughout civilization, there have been difficult people. Over time, civilized people have developed techniques for dealing with them.

First, we need to define our terms. An obnoxious coworker is merely that, obnoxious, and, in most circumstances, harmless. Difficult persons come in all colors, sizes, and shapes. Their offensive or destructive behavior is what makes them difficult. Whether it is persistent offensive language or unprofessional work habits, a difficult person becomes problematic when he or she targets you personally to undermine your work and hence your professional standing. At that point, the person becomes "toxic," and some action is in order. In a more perfect world, difficult people would not exist, and if they did, management would take remedial action to protect productive and positive employees. Until we all get there though, there are several suggestions for the productive and positive. Although it may be unsettling to learn that none of these suggestions is a panacea, it should be reassuring to hear that you are not alone and help could be on the way.

Second, unprofessional behavior that is personally directed can have a shocking effect. A reality check will help confirm whether the person in question is indeed a problem in your work life. For a short period of time, say, a month, make notations in your datebook of the person's offensive behavior on the day it occurs. After a while, you will have assembled documentation, a record, that may or may not quantify your feelings. The regular and repeated occurrence of negative or destructive behavior, whether words or deeds or both, should satisfy you and others that there is a problem. Your documentation also has the power of convincing those around you of the extent of the problem, if necessary. Therein lies the real rub: choosing the person with whom to discuss the problem.

Many believe that you should take action as soon as possible. Allowing the situation to continue unattended may raise more problems. The negative effect of your emotions could fester and increase your anger. Decide to take concrete action once you are fully aware of what is happening. A solution or some type of resolution will not occur unless you do something. Left unaddressed, the situation could regress from bad to worse. Speaking with the coworker in question should be the first option. Privately and calmly, identify for the coworker the behavior that is bothering you. Be principled in your approach by informing this person that his or her behavior is destructive to the clients or the firm. Offer the possibility that the behavior may have been unintended.

Having made contact, some kind of pact may be possible. One form of agreement could agree to disagree. Here, personal dislikes move to the sidelines, which permits both employees to appreciate different approaches to the work. Under the aegis of a truce, focusing on the work is easier. It may be possible to exchange limited forms of alliances. Peace comes once both share the main goal to get along despite their differences.

Another approach advocates confronting the coworker. The argument in favor of this approach is based on principles of self-esteem. Establishing reasonable standards for your own life and requesting coworkers to respect them tests the coworker's own

"Toxic Office," *Legal Management* (January/February 2004), p. 53.

standards. In effect, enforcing reasonable standards of behavior continues a principled approach and at the same time makes a demand. The coworker's refusal to accede to reasonable standards of behavior will only make him or her look bad. A refusal is also a signal, a highly negative one.

appeasement
The act of granting concessions to potential adversaries to maintain peace and avoid future hostile behavior.

If needed, give ground in a technique known as **appeasement**. For the sake of avoiding conflict, this method offers the line of least resistance. Many consider this approach a concession to the coworker's demands. Principle has been set aside, at least for now. However, the lack of principle can prove to be bothersome. Appeasement tolerate oppressive or offensive behavior implicitly. Appeasement is a short-term or occasional tact to avert an uncomfortable scene or angry confrontations. However, the emotional cost to the appeaser can take its toll by forcing him or her to submit to a hostile work environment. Psychologists point to spiraling self-esteem and victimization as likely results of a prolonged situation of appeasement.

There is the option of speaking with management, but it also carries some risk. Before doing so, consider whether your relationship with the appropriate individual in management is amenable to bad news. An unreceptive manager could very well expect that coworkers resolve their own interpersonal issues. Too many discussions about the "problem" could tarnish your reputation and brand you as a complainer or one-issue person. Unfortunately, management is often much too concerned with bottom line and other logistic issues to concern itself with something that affects only two people in the office. If the coworker's behavior affects productivity, clients, or a number of other coworkers in the office, management should heed your call. At this point, the documentation may suffice as proof of the dilemma. Issues and documentation that affect the firm's productivity, and hence profitability, present a "business case" worthy of attention.

As a matter of collegiality and respect, do not drag in any allied coworkers without their express consent. Difficult people can pose a problem that management may wish to ignore or pay scant attention to due to stretched resources or a lack of wherewithal. Moreover, a management solution may be less than satisfactory to you, or even risky.

avoidance
The act of keeping away from certain people or situations to avert confrontations or unpleasant situations.

Staying away from a stressful coworker could be a possible long-term solution if the work situation allows you to separate yourself. A self-imposed policy of **avoidance** may still cause residual stress, because it is not possible to avoid someone altogether, especially in a small office. Having to watch your back constantly can also have a negative effect on your feelings about going to work. A management-structured program of separating or isolating the difficult coworker, if it can be accomplished, would be preferable and make the avoidance a sanctioned resolution.

Ultimately, the problem of difficult coworkers is an age-old problem that is only beginning to draw the attention of human resources professionals. Unfortunately, the legal industry has been slow to attend to interpersonal issues in the workplace. Recent studies have shown that almost half of American workers polled indicated that they have worked with an abusive coworker or supervisor. A slowly growing movement advocates legal redress against employers who knowingly permit abusive behavior and hostile work environments to persist. Several states, including Connecticut, Kansas, Massachusetts, New York, and Oklahoma, have recently introduced anti-workplace bullying legislation. However, there are no existing laws, and courts have consistently held that absent such laws, there is no legal remedy. Studies show sharp regional differences in the occurrence of those reporting abusive or hostile work environments. Southern workers (34 percent) are less likely to have experience with an abusive boss than are their Northeastern (56 percent) and Midwestern (48 percent) counterparts.

CASE IN POINT

SEXUAL HARASSMENT

LITTELL V. ALLSTATE INS. CO.

In 1996, Patricia Littell started her job as a paralegal in the legal office of Allstate Insurance Co. in Albuquerque, New Mexico. Two years later, Allstate hired Todd Aakhus to work as an attorney in the same office. Aakhus began sexually harassing Littell and failed to stop even after she told him to do so. Littell reported that she had been punished when she protested about the constant barrage of Aakhus's sexual jokes and innuendoes. Littell testified that Aakhus always talked about sex and demeaned women.

She followed the company's stated procedures concerning sexual harassment to no avail. In fact, once Littell began objecting to Aakhus's behavior, he began criticizing her work performance and denied her leave to tend to a family emergency. By 2002, Littell had had enough and requested a leave. Allstate refused, and Aakhus escalated his harassment. Aakhus at times would follow Littell around the office threatening and yelling at her until his face was purple. Littell eventually left her job.

Littell's attorneys filed a lawsuit for sexual harassment in the First Judicial District Court in Santa Fe, New Mexico. In 2005, a jury awarded Littell $1 million in punitive damages and another $360,000 in compensatory damages for the loss of her job and the emotional distress she suffered. Littell stated that she hoped the verdict sent a message to Allstate and the rest of the country. Her victory was upheld on appeal. Two other women from the same office, a secretary and an attorney, also pursued claims against Allstate.

QUESTIONS ABOUT THE CASE

1. In Littell's civil action against Allstate, what causes of action did she allege?
2. What steps would or should be taken when encountering a workplace environment such as the one Littell experienced?
3. Do you think that Allstate was to fault for Aakhus's behavior in light of the fact that there were office procedures for handling sexual harassment?

Dealing with the Difficult Office

Most modern legal professionals consider themselves enlightened, respectful, and law abiding, but the law office can be less than a perfect world. Although no laws require coworkers or supervisors to be nice people, there are laws that protect many important aspects of your personal integrity. The problem is how to identify and protect your legal rights to personal integrity. At stake is not only your job but also your self-esteem. Studies show that workplaces that promote self-esteem are more productive. By the same token, hostile work environments can adversely affect productivity and, worse, overall quality of life outside the workplace. The difference between the difficult coworker and the difficult workplace is that in certain respects, the law affords some protections. Federal law and many state laws protect workers from hostile and discriminatory work environments.

RESEARCH THIS

Federal laws provide protection from workplace discrimination on the basis of several grounds. On the Internet, go to www.eeoc.gov. What types of discrimination are of special concern to the United States Equal Employment Opportunity Commission? What is sexual harassment? How would a victim of discriminatory treatment seek redress?

What laws exist in your state that offer protection from discriminatory treatment or hostile work environments?

Seeking New Horizons

The last straw in dealing with a difficult work situation is to leave for another job. Throwing in the towel may appear that you have given up. Nevertheless, having gone through the job hunting and hiring process, you are now well equipped to seek a more positive work environment, older and wiser. Chances are that you have learned from a nasty experience and will be better able to assess a potential work situation. A primary concern would be the appearance of an early departure from your last job. Tactics such as avoidance and appeasement may help prolong an uncomfortable workplace as you allow for the passage of time. Adopting those tactics—sucking it up and sticking it out for a while—could go a long way to providing you with the solace of quitting in the near future for greener pastures. During this period, try mending your relationships with trusted higher-ups who could provide references.

As you begin to look for a new employment situation, anticipate the problem of having to explain your departure to a prospective employer. Negative remarks concerning past employment at an interview will almost certainly doom your chances of obtaining more desirable employment. Thus, concentrate on the work experience you have gained and the professional growth that could be gained from specific aspects of your prospective employer. Expressing the desire to work in a more sophisticated firm that can offer better resources and a wider range of practice areas always sounds good.

Experience is the best teacher. So as you seek another job, discrete inquiries during future job interviews may provide clues about the healthfulness of another employment situation. Avoid appearing to be prying or alerting prospective employers that you want to leave a bad situation. However, tactfully phrased questions could go unnoticed. For instance, asking why the previous person left the position could be masked as interest in your own professional development. If possible, contact that former employee for more candid information.

An inquiry about turnover rates could appear to seek information as to the stability of the firm. High turnover rates are a clue to an unpleasant environment.

An innocuous inquiry about office policies such as attire and office resources may smokescreen further inquiries into how the firm ensures workplace respect. Examine the firm's written personnel policy manual, if available, to see if there are provisions for handling harassment complaints and protection from retaliation. Other signs observable in the prospective workplace may provide additional clues. Evidence of workaholism may reveal potential exploitation by firms that ignore reasonable working hours and other conditions like workplace safety or employee wellness. The lack of **diversity** in a geographic area in which the general population is more diverse provides a telltale indication of the workplace atmosphere. Inquiry as to the firm's diversity efforts may bring evasiveness or defensiveness—a probable confirmation of less than generous attitudes toward diversity. An honest answer admitting the lack of diversity and the implementation of earnest efforts to diversify speaks volumes.

diversity
The quality of multicultural, ethnic, and racial presence in the workplace.

Other telltale responses deserve particular attention as you explore a potential new workplace. A prospective employer's defensiveness or discomfort with seemingly harmless questions are signs that management may be inattentive or inept with interpersonal issues in the office. Respond to interviewer questions about your reasons for asking questions about the workplace environment by saying that you enjoy serious and productive work environments where you spend much of your waking hours. A good employer would normally take interest in an applicant who appears careful and thorough. Pride in the workplace is usually evident. Defensiveness or difficulty in speaking about the workplace environment may indicate a lack of pride, among other problems.

Recent studies confirm that difficult coworkers behave poorly toward others largely because of their insecurity. Well-trained and productive workers threaten insecure people, who respond by trying to undermine a colleague who inadvertently outshines them or just appears to be able to do so. Bad behavior and bullying designed to oppress or undermine makes the difficult coworker feel powerful and effective. Meeting potential coworkers can now take on greater meaning. If you did not visit the office of your last employer before accepting that offer, the bad experience there may motivate you to visit before accepting an offer from a new one. As you do so, be tactful as you ask about supervisors, the flow of work, the office atmosphere, and the like. With experience from your previous position—work experience as well as life experience—you will be able to see things anew and in greater depth. You will be able not only to anticipate a problem office but also eliminate options that are not a good fit for you. This ability takes knowing yourself and the legal world you have chosen to enter.

The information presented herein is but a microcosm of the vast possibilities that exist in the legal world, which is filled with challenges and opportunities. Possibilities are endless. Consider a paralegal position in a foreign country working with American laws as well as foreign laws. Another fertile area for paralegals is international law with its worldwide application and global outlook. As discussed in the next chapter, truly adventurous paralegals are beginning to go out on their own as independent contractors working under the supervision of a number of attorneys.

Summary

Seeking employment as a legal professional requires self-knowledge, perseverance, and skill. Luck is also a large element, as in other areas of life. A very important first step is to make a self-assessment consisting of two exercises to make yourself aware of your personality traits and professional goals. A sound self-assessment is an invaluable aid in selecting the type of legal jobs to pursue. For any profession, cultural norms and practices present a format and method for entering the profession. Before actually looking for the appropriate job, evaluate the job market for legal trends, local conditions, and economic circumstances that affect the availability of desirable positions.

Before targeting possible positions, carefully prepare a professional résumé and cover letter. Two or three different versions of your résumé that amplify certain parts of your background and experience provide flexibility in applying for targeted positions. Remember that the résumé and cover letter market your skills to prospective employers, enticing them to invite you for an interview. Interviewing for a job is an exercise in tact and observation. Various techniques may help put your best foot forward. While obtaining an offer is somewhat a matter happenstance, sound research and appropriate behavior are essential for succeeding at the interview. Knowledge about the prospective employer and an agreeable, professional demeanor may turn chance in your favor.

Success in the legal workplace starts with viewing yourself as a model employee. It is often helpful to put yourself in the position of your employer and ask what you would expect from a model employee. Demonstrate initiative, industriousness, and punctuality, among a host of other qualities to make that all-important first impression. Taking work assignments as a novice legal professional, you will invariably have many questions or concerns. Success depends on acquiring the skill of time management and taking control of your working environment. Develop another facet of self-awareness by determining the optimum times for accomplishing certain tasks.

Almost every workplace can have difficult people. Workplace survival depends on your ability to cope or confront the difficult coworker. Management's ability or inclination to assist may not exist. Thus, various techniques can help make the situation tolerable, at least while buying you time to resort to the job market again. Most legal professionals implicitly acknowledge problematic work environments. For most, working in the legal profession is a satisfying and rewarding experience. The meteoric rise of paralegal programs and the competitiveness in the profession are testaments to a stable and sound vocation. Legal professionals tend to be highly educated, astute, and sociable. The opportunity for success as a legal professional is in your own hands.

Welcome to the legal profession.

Key Terms

Appeasement
Avoidance
Boutique law firm
Career objective
Career or placement office
Diversity
Form practice
Human resources (personnel) department
Networking
Prioritization
Résumé
Self-assessment
Self-esteem
Stress management
Synopsis or highlights
Time management
To do list

Review Questions

1. What is the purpose of a self-assessment?
2. What are the two aspects of a self-assessment?
3. Name the various sources for finding employment opportunities as a paralegal.
4. What are the most important parts of a résumé?
5. What is the purpose of a cover letter?
6. How should you dress for an interview?
7. What are the factors to consider when assessing a job offer?
8. What is professional behavior?
9. What is the relationship between time management and stress management?
10. Why are objectives and highlights important aspects of a résumé?

Exercises

1. Perform both parts of a self assessment, and put it in writing.
2. To see the myriad of forms used by boutique firms, see www.uscourts.gov/bkforms/bankruptcy_forms.html#official or www.uscis.gov/portal/site/uscis.
   Click on Immigration Forms and review the various forms available.
3. Go to your local courthouse and visit the clerk's office. Obtain as many forms issued by the court for public use as you can. Organize them in a folder for use as an in-office reference.
4. Find an advertised paralegal position and research as much information as you can obtain about the position and the employer. With a friend or relative acting as the employer, stage a mock interview.
5. Find the qualifications for a law office administrator at www.alanet.org/home.html. Is this a position for which a paralegal could qualify?

Discussion Questions

1. Would it be possible to institute a courthouse volunteer paralegal for the day program? What issues and problems does this idea present? How would a paralegal operate differently than a volunteer lawyer of the day?
2. Applying acting theory to behavior in a law office, what decisions can we make to help ourselves appear diligent and professional? What qualities do we want to project?

3. Would it be appropriate for a law firm to "test" your response by asking questions that are considered legally inappropriate? How would you respond?
4. What techniques are available to counter procrastination?

PORTFOLIO ASSIGNMENT

After doing a self-assessment, determine at least two kinds of employment you would be suited for, taking into account your own preferences. For each of these types of jobs, draft a résumé and a cover letter. Make a list of questions you might want to ask at an interview for each type of job.

Chapter 12

Examples of Legal Work by Professional Paralegals

CHAPTER OBJECTIVES

After completing this chapter, you will have achieved an understanding of the following:

- Obtaining sources for professional training and continuing legal education.
- The types of work environments that frequently employ paralegals, including more recent, cutting-edge workplaces.
- Starting your own paralegal practice and the unauthorized practice of law concerns for the independent paralegal.

With your basic introduction to the paralegal profession complete, this chapter will continue with aspects of the paralegal profession. Specifically, in this chapter, you will experience what it is like to perform actual legal work as a professional paralegal. First, we will look at some techniques that paralegals use to obtain training and continuing legal education. Second, we will cover some examples of the actual work that can be performed by paralegals in specialized areas of the law and specialized workplaces. Third, this chapter will introduce the idea of going out on your own as an independent paralegal, exploring the outer boundaries of paralegal activity. We thus will cover the phenomenon of the independent professional paralegal. Some paralegals are going out on their own, establishing a paralegal practice. Therefore, we will discuss some specific ethical issues that independent paralegals encounter in the workaday world.

Thus far, you have learned many things about the law and the legal profession. Moreover, you have acquired specialized knowledge and basic skills that paralegals use in legal practice. Applying that knowledge, however, requires yet another skill. In the legal workplace, putting your knowledge and skills into practice requires hands-on experience. Knowledge of the law and the basic skills of researching and writing alone are insufficient to accomplish basic legal tasks often completed by paralegals. Thus, as you begin to work in the profession, become aware of the need for training throughout your entire career.

TRAINING AT YOUR NEW JOB, AND TRAINING YOURSELF

The skills acquired from a hands-on training go beyond applying theory from the classroom. What you learn in the classroom is **education**, which involves acquiring knowledge and developing the powers of reasoning and judgment. Training, in contrast, involves the application of that acquired knowledge and the powers of reasoning and judgment. In addition to seeing how law actually applies in a particular case, hands-on training teaches you how to handle a file, how (and when) to speak or correspond with clients, what forms to fill out, where to file papers, and a host of other skills that would be impossible to learn in school without an **internship**. For this reason, many paralegal programs offer internships for students in their last year. These internships place students with various law offices or workplaces that deal with law. Students receive great benefits from internships by obtaining hands-on experience before they graduate. Moreover, students usually receive course credit from their internships.

education
The act or process of imparting or acquiring general knowledge; developing the powers of reasoning and judgment.

internship
Any official or formal program to provide practical experience for beginners in an occupation or profession.

A DAY IN THE LIFE OF A REAL PARALEGAL

After receiving her associate's degree from a local community college, Mary Petrino transferred to a four-year school to obtain a bachelor's degree in Paralegal Studies. In her senior year, Petrino completed an internship with the Consumer Complaint and Mediation Program of the Attorney General's office. She reported that the greatest benefit she gained from the placement was seeing herself develop as a legal professional. Beginning with a daylong briefing session, she and her fellow interns started their internship placements by becoming familiar with the office and its operations. After meeting with their assigned supervisor, the interns received instruction in the substantive law for their department's specialty. With this briefing, she started her semester's internship as a consumer mediator.

As a student-mediator, Petrino's task was to investigate and help settle consumer complaints that had been filed with the Attorney General. Under the supervision of an experienced mediator, Petrino would contact both the consumer and the merchant to find some common ground between the two. "The most difficult part," she recalled, "was keeping my opinion and feelings to myself. This was hard at the beginning, but after a few times, I soon realized that my task was just to listen and get a feeling for the nature of the dispute." From this facet of the job, Petrino was able to get a clearer understanding of her role as a mediator and as a paralegal. "I started to realize that my personal thoughts about the situation were irrelevant to the process. *And that was okay.* Once I really started to listen to the parties and get a sense for a way that they could settle their differences, I knew I had crossed the line into becoming a professional. It's about getting the job done," she mused.

Many times, Petrino found that the root of the numerous complaints she handled was a lack of communication. In these situations, Petrino saw that her position as a mediator was to facilitate a settlement by building a bridge between the parties. As a mediator, Petrino's knowledge of the law became a tool for striking an acceptable agreement between the parties. Instead of giving the parties legal information, Petrino effectively put her knowledge of the law from the classroom and internship training to use in shaping and finalizing a settlement between the parties. The internship training cautioned against voicing a legal opinion. Offering legal advice would not only be counterproductive but also violate the legal prohibition against the unauthorized practice of law. "Only lawyers are allowed to give direct legal advice, and anyways, giving that kind of advice wasn't my job," Petrino remarked.

These and many other aspects of her internship placement with the Attorney General's office have provided Petrino, as well as many other students, the professional and interpersonal skills required in the working world of law. She summed up by noting, "Sure, it was a wonderful experience. It tied together the things I had learned in my paralegal courses like Alternative Dispute Resolution and Consumer Law. Now, I have the internship on my résumé. And that gives me confidence and credibility when I apply for a job after I graduate. That's very cool."

Depending on the location, a school's paralegal program could have arrangements for a wide range of internship offerings, particularly in large cities with well-developed legal communities. During internships, paralegal students receive hands-on training. They also receive experience, helping them become both skilled and marketable. Internships also serve to give the paralegal a taste of what it is like to work in a particular office or **practice area**—that is, the area of law in which a legal professional specializes or concentrates.

practice area
That part of the law in which a legal professional practices as a specialty or concentration.

When you begin working, the availability of training opportunities varies depending on the resources in the office. Ideally, a law firm invests in its new employees by training entry-level paralegals and attorneys to help ease their transition from the theory learned in school to the legal practice of the office. Often, firms train their new employees using **mentoring programs** that match a new employee with one of the firm's experienced legal professionals. For small firms, mentoring acts as the most efficient method of training. Also known as "at the elbow" training, mentoring allows the newly hired legal professional to learn from example. Watching the mentor perform specific tasks in a real case, the new paralegal employee is trained by closely observing the legal professionals around him or her. Soon, the mentor delegates discrete tasks, such as drafting a memorandum of law or an affidavit. Later, having observed most of a particular type of case or parts that are permissible for a paralegal to perform, the paralegal will be able to work on similar cases in the future, self-directed.

mentoring program
A workplace support relationship in which a senior professional mentors a newly hired professional.

continuing legal education (CLE)
Continued legal competence and skills training required of practicing professionals.

practice manuals
Published or in-house guides to practice in certain areas, often part of a continuing legal education topic.

PRACTICE TIP

Many firms use in-house practice manuals and checklists routinely, often to the extent that the law itself becomes just a backdrop. When using these practice aids, be sure to familiarize yourself with the underlying law, regulations, and procedural rules. You will find that your knowledge of the practice will become much deeper and more satisfying.

Outside of the office, local bar associations and paralegal organizations often offer training for experienced legal professionals, usually at a reasonable cost. Employers may willingly pay to have their staff attend these seminars. Lasting one day, a half-day, or an evening, these seminars are commonly known as **continuing legal education** or CLE and consist of lectures by a group of panelists, complete with visual presentations. The written materials distributed at these seminars are specific and practical guides to legal practice. Written by local or regional experts, the materials become valuable reference resources for use in the office. Most legal professionals agree that CLE materials are the best way to keep up with the law. The CLE subjects can cover: annual surveys of significant court decisions or legislation; highly specialized boutique areas of law; administrative law; and trends in municipal zoning. Local or state bar associations sponsor most CLE seminars designed for attorneys and are usually open to paralegals.

Also designed for working professionals are regularly published **practice manuals**. Similar to CLE publications, these manuals actually function as "how-to" books, which contain sample pleadings, forms, and practice tips. Practice manuals come in both beginner and advanced versions and are updated regularly with pocket parts or loose-leaf inserts. Many law offices regularly maintain their libraries with practice manuals, which not only cover specialty "boutique" areas but also state specific basics for court procedures and evidence. With statutes and cases readily available on the Internet, smaller offices often purchase and rely on practice manuals in their law libraries as an efficient and cost-effective method of maintaining primary reference materials.

In this chapter, we will explore practice areas that commonly engage the work of paralegals. An experienced paralegal assigned to any of these practice areas would be able to handle such cases from start to finish. After some time, specialty cases become "routine" cases, that is, cases that are commonplace and require no more than a basic knowledge and understanding of the practice area. These are the types of cases that a newly hired paralegal could receive as a first assignment. Routine cases are those that a law firm in that area of practice is poised to handle efficiently and effectively.

When a client has retained the law firm, a legal professional, often a paralegal, sits down with the client to complete the intake form, as we described in Chapter 11. An office often will fashion intake forms from spreadsheet programs so that information or data input may be performed on a computer as well as on paper. More sophisticated electronic intake forms come in database programs so that the information can be sorted and arranged to suit the particular use. Practice area computer programs or automated document assembly programs perform the same function and reduce paper use. After the user inputs the information, the program can print out the documents or completed forms needed for submission to a court or government agency. Using well-designed intake forms and computer programs saves time and effort. The legal professional knows exactly what to ask and is able to obtain all the necessary basic information from the client in one sitting.

Checklists are another form of internally developed practice guides that operate in the same way as intake forms. In certain types of legal proceedings, a court or government agency will require the submission of several documents, such as birth or marriage certificates. Sometimes the documentation required by law can be extensive. Thus, a checklist functions as a handy reminder for the file to be checked off as the documents arrive from the client or other sources. The legal professional usually gives a copy of the checklist to the client. Other forms of checklists are never seen by clients and are intended only for internal use. These checklists remind the legal professional of the sequence of tasks involved in a particular type of proceeding, sometimes known as practice checklists. In the file, a practice checklist prompts the legal professional to complete his or her next task.

After a fashion, internally developed intake forms and checklists act as practice guides or an informal type of training that assists the legal professional in routine cases. Their use is particularly welcome to the novice legal professional who, by using them, learns exactly what to ask of the client, what documents to obtain, and what to do next. They are similar in function to the proof chart we saw in Chapter 10. The use of a proof chart assisted the practitioner in sorting out the evidence and reminded the practitioner of the necessary elements to prove a negligence case. When precedent-making court decisions or newly enacted statutes or regulations appear, a committee consisting of the legal professionals within the practice area in the office usually work together to revise and ensure that their intake forms and checklists conform to the changes in the law.

Mentoring programs, practice manuals, CLE, and in-office practice aids are just a few mechanisms common to almost all legal workplaces that help legal professionals work ethically and more efficiently.

In Chapter 1, we pointed out the various workplaces that employ paralegals. Throughout this book, we have discussed how paralegals have used their knowledge of the law in various situations. Traditionally, private law firms and legal aid organizations have been the primary employers of paralegals. Recently however, paralegals have begun to occupy positions formerly held by licensed attorneys. Insurance companies, government agencies, and even the military employ paralegals to perform legal work. Paralegals now work with the law in many other settings and areas of the law never before imagined. As an important part of your understanding of the possibilities for paralegals, we will continue with coverage of a few of these new legal environments and specialty areas that employ the modern professional paralegal.

CYBER TRIP

Using an Internet search engine, enter the phrase "litigation software." After viewing the numerous vendor Web sites, compare three of the various software programs in terms of (1) the features they have, (2) the prices, and (3) whether these programs actually make litigation easier.

Technologically savvy paralegals are frequently called upon to act as the point person for their office's technology needs. For an office of five lawyers and five paralegals all engaged in civil litigation, which program would you be able to recommend?

checklist
Internally developed instruction and guide for legal professionals in a specific area of practice, listing steps, documents, or both for the legal professional to follow and gather.

POSSIBILITIES FOR THE PROFESSIONAL PARALEGAL

Let's begin with a review of the classic definition of a paralegal. Recall that the most recent ABA pronouncement defines a paralegal as follows:

> *A legal assistant or paralegal is a person qualified by education, training or work experience who is employed or retained by a lawyer, law office, corporation, governmental agency or*

other entity who performs specifically delegated substantive legal work for which a lawyer is responsible.

Focusing on the work performed by paralegals, notice that the ABA defines the work as "delegated substantive legal work for which the lawyer is responsible." This part of the definition makes two points: (1) the tasks performed by paralegals consist of work that could otherwise be performed by lawyers who have delegated certain tasks, and (2) the work is ultimately under the supervision of a lawyer. Of course, belying the definition are concerns for the unauthorized practice of law. Thus, the definition necessarily includes the requirement of lawyer supervision and responsibility.

Yet at the same time, notice that the workplaces include "law office, corporation, governmental agency or *other entity*...." With these considerations in mind, we can see that the available workplaces for paralegals are limited only by the unauthorized practice rules. Thus, any entity—not just law offices, corporations, and governmental agencies—are potential workplaces. As long as a licensed attorney is available to act as a supervisor and stand responsible, the substantive legal work may be performed by a paralegal. Giving legal advice, going to court, and establishing the attorney–client relationship are still off-limits for paralegals, as they are for all nonlawyers. Those off-limit activities are never within the scope of a paralegal's duties. Here is a brief description of some situations in which the paralegal may perform substantive work.

Criminal Law Opportunities for Paralegals

Chapter 7 provided extensive coverage on criminal law and criminal procedure as a basic legal specialty for paralegals. For the most part, that coverage focused on the paralegal's role as part of the defense or prosecution team. As such, our coverage was from the perspective of a legal professional working directly with criminal proceedings for either the prosecution or the defense. From that perspective, you learned about various crimes, their elements, and the constitutional limits on laws criminalizing behavior. Also included in your instruction were the several aspects of criminal procedure, such as the Miranda rule and the law of search and seizure. Thus, your instruction included the information that prosecutors and criminal defense use in their respective practices. Still, the area of criminal law encompasses a wider range of possibilities for paralegals.

Parole and Probation Officers

After a successful prosecution, the wheels of our criminal justice system still turn, and employment opportunities abound for those with legal training and a penchant for assisting an individual's return to society. After a conviction, the individual may be sentenced to confinement or allowed to remain free under supervision. In either situation, a legal professional who is part of the criminal justice system (usually the courts) works with the individual toward his or her rehabilitation. For those who have been sentenced to a period of confinement, the sentence may also provide for a period of **parole** after the individual's release.

parole
Release under court supervision from jail, prison, or other confinement after having served part of a criminal sentence.

parole officer
An official of the criminal justice system who supervises parolees who are released from confinement.

During the period of parole, the individual reports to a **parole officer**, who monitors the parolee to ensure that his or her behavior complies with the conditions of parole, such as abstinence from drugs or alcohol. Other conditions may require the individual to participate in rehabilitation or community service. The probation officer's duties include monitoring the individual and filing reports with the court. These reports, like memoranda of law, analyze the individual's case in a purely legal context. Occasionally, an individual on parole may appear to have failed to abide by the conditions of parole. When that happens, the parole officer must decide whether the individual has violated his or her parole and must return to confinement. Thus, parole

RESEARCH THIS

Sentencing has been a subject of great interest and controversy. More than 20 years ago, the Federal Sentencing Commission issued the United States Sentencing Guidelines (USSG) to establish an equitable and uniform standard for sentencing. Find the following with regard to the USSG.

1. The citation to the USSG.
2. The latest United States Supreme Court decision involving the USSG. What did the Court hold in that decision?

officers must possess a thorough knowledge of court procedures, criminal law, and the specialized area of corrections law, which covers sentencing, prisoners' rights, and the administration of the criminal justice system.

Probation is another method of sentencing an individual who has been convicted of a crime. However, probation consists only of a period of court supervision instead of incarceration. In less populated areas of the country, parole officers also perform the duties of a **probation officer**, whose function is similar to that of a parole officer. In addition, a probation officer's duties include investigating the individual's background, family, and personal history for inclusion in a **presentencing report** that assists the court in determining a sentence in a particular case. In the federal courts and some state courts, a probation officer's presentencing report includes an extensive investigation of the individual and, applying laws known as **sentencing guidelines**, recommends a sentence or range of sentences. To perform these duties, a probation officer must be trained and educated in the same areas of law as parole officers.

Both parole and probation officers are an integral part of both the state and federal criminal justice system, which consists of law enforcement professionals, prosecutors, and the courts. Parole and probation officers also occupy the unique position of acting as a bridge between the courts and the individual under the system's supervision. Their investigations, reports, and knowledge of the law assist the courts and prosecutors in determining sentences or other dispositions of criminal proceedings. Even before a criminal trial or plea occurs, probation officers provide input when an individual—usually a first time offender of a minor crime—seeks **pretrial probation** as an alternative to entering a plea. Under such a disposition, the individual remains under the officer's supervision for a short period before any trial to ensure his or her good behavior. After successful completion of the pretrial probationary period, the proceedings are dismissed. Whether the supervision occurs before or after a trial or plea, both parole and probation officers exercise not only legal judgment but also compassion and understanding for the lives of those individuals who have wandered astray from the law. Indeed, they often play an instrumental role in the individual's rehabilitation.

Traditionally, the educational qualifications for parole and probation officers require a four-year degree in criminal justice, social work, or a related field. Employment opportunities are also available in the criminal justice system for those with paralegal training. Compared with their counterparts who have studied criminal justice, those with paralegal training are arguably better suited because of their more rounded and practice-oriented education. This qualification is particularly true of paralegals educated at schools that have ABA approval or meet similar standards of practical orientation in their coursework. An internship with a parole or probation officer also would give a student not only a taste of what criminal justice system professionals do but also the hands-on experience that may qualify him or her for a position in that field. An added plus is that a paralegal degree provides more employment options in law than just criminal justice.

probation
A court-imposed criminal sentence that, subject to stated conditions, releases a convicted person into the community instead of sending the criminal to prison.

probation officer
An officer of the criminal justice system who supervises a person on probation.

presentencing report
An official postconviction report of a convict's background and resources and the details of the criminal offense committed, written by the probation department for court use in determining a sentence.

sentencing guidelines
A group of laws that establish guidelines for judges to use in determining the appropriate sentence in a criminal matter.

pretrial probation
A pretrial disposition of a criminal matter, agreed to by both parties, that provides for a brief period of probation.

CYBER TRIP

On the Internet, find the U.S. Department of Labor's occupational outlook for parole and probation officers at www.bls.gov/oco/ocos265.htm#earnings. On the site, find the following information: What are the qualifications? How much do parole and probation officers earn? What is the government's projection regarding growth in the occupation?

claims adjuster
A law-trained insurance company employee who assesses and settles claims between the insured and the insurance company.

insurance law
A specialty legal practice surrounding insurance, including insurance policies and claims.

legal nurse consultant
A licensed, registered nurse with specialized training as a paralegal.

CYBER TRIP

Insurance claims provide fertile ground for paralegals seeking to work for either attorneys or insurance companies. On the Internet, check out the following sites:

- http://iwin.iwd.state.ia.us/iowa/OIC?occ=131031&occtype=SOC&area=01000019&action=full.
- www.dcba.org/brief/sepissue/2004/art30904.htm.

What is the pay scale for paralegal claims adjusters in Iowa? On the basis of the information provided by the DuPage County (Illinois) Bar Association, determine what steps a claimant should take to ensure that his or her claim will receive full consideration.

Paralegals in the Insurance World: Claims Adjusters and Others

When people buy insurance for cars, homes, businesses, or health care, they are entering into a contract with an insurance company. In that contract, the company promises to compensate for losses due to an accident, calamity, or medical care in exchange for the consumer's payment of premiums to the insurance company. The terms of that contract list the types of losses that the company promises to cover, both with regard to the types of damage or health conditions and the monetary limits of coverage. Thus, an insurance company assesses a consumer's claim for coverage within the confines of the insurance policy, a legally binding document.

When a claim is made to an insurance company in, say, a car accident, the consumer provides documentation of the loss in the form of police reports, photographs, and an appraisal of the vehicle's damage by a trained auto mechanic. Once this documentation has been submitted to the insurance company, a **claims adjuster** reviews it to determine whether the claim is covered and the amount of the claim the company should pay to the consumer. The consumer may, in many instances, offer additional evidence about the accident's cause and the cost of repair or replacement. However, a claims adjuster makes the ultimate determination for the insurance company. In doing so, the claims adjuster is making a decision based on both contract and negligence law, as well as **insurance law**, another specialty area that covers the rights and obligations of the insurance industry. Using specialized training as a paralegal with knowledge of law, the claims adjuster can judge whether the claim is covered and, if so, the amount of monetary damage to be paid.

In health insurance companies, paralegals perform the same duties as their claim adjuster counterparts. Requests for coverage for various types of medical procedures or conditions are reviewed by health insurance paralegals to determine whether the procedure or condition is covered under the health insurance policy and applicable laws. In many situations, the patient may appeal a denial of coverage. These appeals are decided by a paralegal who works under the supervision of an attorney who also works for the health insurance company. In a way, the paralegals and the supervising attorneys have only one client: the insurance company. The concept of an in-house legal team is commonplace in the corporate insurance world.

The Health Care Professional as Paralegal

As we discussed in Chapter 1, many working professionals from other fields seek a paralegal degree or certificate to prepare themselves for a career change. The study of law may lead to an entirely new career, separate and distinct from their previous endeavors. For others, a paralegal degree or certificate combines their previous education, training, and work experience with a new career in law. Currently, a popular option comes from the medical field in the position of **legal nurse consultant**.

The legal nurse consultant (LNC) is a licensed, registered nurse with specialized training as a paralegal. With training and experience from both the medical and the legal worlds, an LNC is able to advise both medical and legal professionals about the standards and guidelines of healthcare practices. A LNC often reviews and analyzes medical records to determine the merits of a particular case. In doing so, the LNC evaluates whether there was a possible breach of duty on the part of a healthcare practitioner or facility. If litigation commences, LNCs assist legal professionals by educating them about medical terminology. In addition, legal professionals may employ an LNC to interview witnesses or exhibits during discovery or at trial. Finally, LNCs practice in a wide variety of legal and medical environments, including government, law firms, insurance companies, hospitals, and consulting firms, to name just a few.

An LNC receives legal education and specialized training from various types of schools. Many paralegal schools offer LNC certificates, as do nursing schools, health science programs or institutions of continuing education. The LNC certificate conferred by an educational institution acts as an employment credential. Like mainstream paralegals, LNCs are not yet licensed. However, professional associations for LNCs offer certifications similar to NALA's Certified Legal Assistant program or NFPA's Registered Paralegal certification. In short, an LNC acts as a liaison between the legal and the healthcare professions and institutions.

COMMUNICATION TIP

Almost all legal professionals perform legal writing in one form or another, whether a sentencing or probation report or a file memo. Be sure to use the *plain English* concepts covered in Chapter 5. It's not only what you say, but also how you say it.

Paralegals in the Military: The Judge Advocate General

The United States military—the Air Force, Army, Marines, Navy, and Coast Guard—possesses its own court system. The legal professionals working in that system are known as the Judge Advocate General's Corps, or **JAG**. Consisting of judges, lawyers, and paralegals within the military, these legal professionals have undergone highly specialized training in U.S. military law, known as the Uniform Code of Military Justice. Their duties involve the defense and prosecution of military (and some civilian) personnel in specialized military proceedings called courts-martial in courts of inquiry. The JAG also provides service members with a wide range of legal services without charge and assists military combat operations by advising commanders on the law surrounding armed conflict.

The Uniform Code of Military Justice covers all internal military justice affairs of the United States. Created by an act of Congress in 1951, the code establishes identical systems of courts-martial in all branches of the nation's armed forces. Paralegals working in this system are known as **legal specialists**. They provide legal and administrative support in such diverse areas as international law, contract law, and military court procedures. Their knowledge is highly specialized. Legal specialists perform research into military court decisions and the laws and regulations covering military personnel for JAG defenders, judges, and prosecutors.

In doing so, JAG legal specialists process legal claims and appeals, and prepare records of hearings, investigations, courts-martial, and courts of inquiry.

JAG (Judge Advocate General's Corps)
Legal professionals trained in U.S. military law who work in the military justice system.

legal specialist
A paralegal working within the military legal system assisting judges, Army lawyers, and unit commanders with legal matters and judicial work.

Mainstream Professional Paralegals: Specialty Opportunities

For paralegals wishing to engage in specialized areas of the law outside of traditional law firms, opportunities abound in corporations, educational institutions, nonprofit organizations, and specialized government agencies. The following sections describe some fascinating legal environments for paralegals.

In-House Corporate Counsel

In the past, legal professionals working in corporate in-house legal departments were regarded as having settled for less pay and more reasonable hours than in a private law firm. Moreover, the suburban setting of most corporate headquarters was attractive to many compared with the hustle and bustle of big city law offices. Their legal tasks consisted mostly of giving legal advice to the various corporate departments

RESEARCH THIS

Military law is a highly specialized area with its own legal professionals, court system, and court procedures.

1. Find the citation to the Uniform Code of Military Justice in the United States Code.
2. What international treaties are involved in the application of U.S. military law?

CYBER TRIP

A variety of resources exists for the new LNC profession and those seeking to enter it. On the Internet, find:

1. The Web site for the American Association of Legal Nurse Consultants. Once there, find out how long LNCs have existed.
2. Find three schools that offer an LNC certificate. Are there any LNC schools in your state?

and outsourcing litigation and other more complex legal work. More recently, however, many corporations have come to rely more heavily on their in-house counsel to take on broader, more substantial work, including litigation.

Still, with only one client, the corporation, life can be a bit less hectic for an in-house corporate paralegal while still offering a wide variety of legal issues to keep the paralegal's interest. Many attorneys and paralegals working within a corporate in-house counsel's office prefer the wider range of work in contrast to the ultra-specialization that occurs in many private law firms. These legal professionals analyze their corporation's policies and their effects on the company's employees, the environment, contract negotiations, corporate structure, international law, taxes, and a host of other issues. Reporting to the top levels of management, in-house legal paralegals have the luxury of amassing a wealth of experience and knowledge with access to the company's top executives.

Other benefits accrue because there is only one client to serve. Having one client means not having to juggle cases. In-house corporate legal professionals engage in some litigation on behalf of their company. However, most do so on a limited basis, and many do not at all. As a result, paralegals can occupy an important role with diminished concern for the unauthorized practice of law. Along with their coworker attorneys, corporate in-house legal professionals serve as the personal advisors to their company. Moreover, the emphasis is on teamwork and not time sheets. As legal professionals with only one client, time sheets, if used at all, simply ensure the legal professional's efficiency and not billable time.

The type of business conducted by the corporation often defines the prevailing type of legal work handled by the in-house counsel. A software or computer company will, by nature, dictate the type of legal work encountered by the in-house legal team. The intellectual property laws of copyright, patent, trademark, and licensing take their place as a high priority to protect the company's software and hardware products. Similarly, the in-house legal teams of companies that handle chemicals and petroleum are experts in environmental law and compliance with government regulations for handling toxic waste and hazardous materials. Nonprofit corporations with in-house legal staff require uncommon expertise in the causes and concerns of the nonprofit corporation's general goals and purposes. For instance, advocacy groups for the elderly, animal rights groups, and faith-based causes often rely on their in-house legal teams for advice about the laws that affect the subject matter of their concerns. Of unique interest are nonprofit organizations such as the one in which you may be a student.

Colleges and Universities

Most colleges and universities have their own legal staff similar to corporate in-house offices. From within their institutions, these legal professionals are Jacks- and Jills-of-all-trades, performing a wide variety of legal duties as they arise. Like their corporate counterparts, they represent only one client: the institution. The legal issues commonly addressed by these specialized in-house legal professionals cover the law of contracts, education law, employment law, and compliance with government regulations for matters such as federal grants, student policies, and accreditation issues.

In-house legal professionals usually work from within their educational institution. In many cases, that setting is more pleasant and preferable to traditional urban law offices. Many educational institutions are located in pleasant, manicured surroundings with access to athletic facilities and cultural events. A paralegal's duties could include responsibility for the computer operations of the general counsel's office, preparing draft documents for review, handling public records requests, performing contract prereviews, preparing cases and investigations, and, of course, legal research.

A DAY IN THE LIFE OF A REAL PARALEGAL

Stephen P. Imondi, RP, has been employed as a legal assistant with Brown University's General Counsel's office in Providence, Rhode Island. Prior to working at Brown, he was an aide in Rhode Island's Lieutenant Governor's Office, working in various capacities along the way. Imondi is a general paralegal but does much of his work in the areas of litigation, nonprofit corporate law, employment law, education law, and legal research.

Imondi has an impressive list of credentials. He obtained an associate's degree in business administration from the Community College of Rhode Island and then bachelor's and master's degrees in public administration from Roger Williams University. Next he obtained a certificate in paralegal studies from the American Institute for Paralegal Studies. Imondi was the first paralegal in Rhode Island to complete the National Federation of Paralegal Associations (NFPA) Paralegal Advanced Competency Exam (PACE) and earned the designation "Registered Paralegal" (RP). He reflects, "I never thought I would go through so much school. After a while, I just got into it."

As a part of the legal team at Brown, Imondi assists the general counsel and other attorneys with the legal work that supports the university's policies by performing advanced legal research and drafting policy statements. His supervisor, Beverly E. Ledbetter, Vice President & General Counsel, speaks at many legal issues seminars in higher education. Imondi compiles most of the materials she uses for her outlines and PowerPoint presentations, which also keeps him up to date on the latest issues in higher education law. Imondi admits that the work is challenging and, at times, hectic. The legal issues can be unique and not what paralegals usually see if they work in a more traditional law firm. He also adds that it's fun being in a university setting: "All around us there are great places to eat, concerts, and fascinating lectures from famous people. Plus the athletic and cultural facilities like the gym and the museums always make it an interesting and fun place to work as a legal professional."

Title Examiners and Abstractors

In Chapter 7, we covered one of the basic paralegal specialties, real estate law, and learned that the concept of title meant ownership. At the same time, other interests taken on voluntarily or otherwise may affect real estate ownership interest. A property owner may wish to borrow money and use the real estate as security for the loan. You may recall that we discussed how most homebuyers pay for most of the purchase price of the home by taking on a mortgage from a bank. In doing so, the homebuyer agrees that the bank can take over or foreclose on the home if the buyer cannot make the monthly loan payments. Banks protect their interest in the home by recording their interest with a Registry of Deeds—a state or county government office that keeps public records of land ownership and other interests in land, such as mortgages.

There are also other interests that could be recorded on a parcel of real estate involuntarily. Real estate taxes levied by the city or county government that go unpaid for an extended period may result in a **tax lien**, recorded to secure the amount of tax owed on that property. When the property is sold, the city is entitled, by virtue of the recorded lien, to receive payment of the back real estate taxes. Both mortgages and tax liens, as well as other items, are recorded for two reasons. First, recording preserves the interest of the party making the recording. Second, the recording is notice to the world that the recording party has an interest in the property. Recorded interests thus affect the property's title by indicating that a party other than the owner has an interest in the real estate.

tax lien
A legal claim placed on real estate by a governmental authority that is owed money for unpaid property taxes.

Paralegals known as **title examiners** search public records and examine property titles to determine a property title's legal condition. In these positions, title examiners have contact with realtors, banks, homebuyers, sellers, and contractors as part of their research. They copy or summarize recorded documents affecting title to property, such as mortgages, trust deeds, and contracts. They may also prepare and issue insurance

title examiner
A law-trained person who researches the title to property for any encumbrances and imperfections.

policies that guarantee the condition of the property's title. Paralegals perform title examinations work for specialized title insurance companies, real estate companies, or even independently. As such, title examiners must have a thorough knowledge of real estate law as well as the law of wills and trusts. Some paralegals in this field also prepare real estate **abstracts**.

abstract
A short history of a piece of land that lists any transfers in ownership, as well as any liabilities attached to it, such as mortgages.

abstractor (title examiner)
A law-trained person who searches public records and examines titles to determine a property title's legal condition.

Paralegals known as **abstractors** write summaries of pertinent legal or insurance details, sections of statutes, or case law from reference books for examination, proof, or ready reference to a certain parcel of real estate. Like title examiners, abstractors search titles to determine if the title deed is correct. Abstractors perform these duties for a variety of purposes. They may also compile lists of mortgages, contracts, and other title-related documents by searching public and private records on behalf of law firms, real estate agencies, banks, and others who handle real estate issues.

The skills required to perform the work of title examiners and abstractors include research and investigation skills and an understanding of legal terms. Like all legal professionals, they must be aware of any new legal developments in the real estate laws of their state and other states. Because title examiners and abstractors come into contact with a variety of different people, good communication and organizational skills will assist them in their research and in preparing reports for the benefit of others. The nature of the work is highly detailed, exacting, and thorough. Title examiners and abstractors become used to spending many hours searching public records, as well as recognized experts in the intricacies of real estate law.

Government Agencies—Federal and State

For those interested in public service, many federal and state agencies employ paralegals to perform substantive and important legal work on behalf of the government. Each agency has its own laws and regulations, and paralegals working within them can act as advocates, researchers, and even hearing officers who make decisions in cases involving individuals appearing at the agency hearings.

At the federal level, dozens of agencies need the legal expertise of paralegals. The United States Citizenship and Immigration Services, the Federal Communications Commission, the Social Security Administration, and the Veterans Administration, among many others, regulate within their respective subject matters. On the state level, departments of motor vehicles regulates drivers' licenses and auto registrations. Other state agencies may regulate insurance companies and businesses in accordance with state law. Whether state or federal, governmental agencies employ a bevy of legal professionals to administer the laws in a variety of ways. Over the past 30 years, paralegals have come to replace the lawyers that once performed the same legal tasks they currently do.

For decades, state and federal administrative agencies have permitted nonattorneys to appear as legal representatives at **adjudicatory hearings**, held for the purpose of determining the rights and obligations of an agency. Paralegals engaged in administrative advocacy can greatly increase productivity and effectiveness in the delivery of legal services. Studies have shown that Social Security Administration claimants represented by nonattorneys achieve a success rate very close to that of claimants represented by attorneys.

adjudicatory hearings
Trial-like proceedings held by administrative agencies to determine legal rights under the agency's jurisdiction.

Many governmental agencies hold hearings or interviews with individuals and companies regarding the grant or revocation of operating licenses, monetary grants, and other benefits. In many instances, paralegals decide these and other cases on behalf of state and federal agencies. Using their legal education and on-the-job training in the agency's regulatory substantive laws and procedures, paralegals increasingly are becoming an important part of the agency's decision-making functions. At administrative hearings, paralegals rule on the admissibility of evidence and write decisions in unemployment, disability, and even immigration cases.

A DAY IN THE LIFE OF A REAL PARALEGAL

After receiving his bachelor's degree in paralegal studies, Richard Pennie applied for the position of District Adjudications Officer with the Department of Homeland Security's Citizenship and Immigration Services. One of his favorite courses in paralegal school was Immigration Law. Pennie enjoyed the intricacies and international flavor of that area of the law. With surprising speed, the government responded to his employment application. After a series of interviews and a security clearance, Pennie spent three months in the government's training facility, where he learned from top to bottom the administrative processes used to determine applications for permanent residence and citizenship in the United States. Soon, he found himself actually deciding the cases he had studied in school.

From an office in the local federal office building, Pennie reviews the evidence submitted by applicants and verifies their authenticity and accuracy. Each day, applicants appear at the Citizenship and Immigration Services office for scheduled interviews about their applications. Following detailed procedures, Pennie determines whether the applicant deserves to become a permanent resident or U.S. citizen. Cases in which the applicant seeks permanent residence based on a marriage to a U.S. citizen are the most challenging. In these cases, Pennie must determine whether a bona fide marriage exists between the parties or whether there is an attempt to commit fraud upon the system. Coincidentally, he ended up deciding a couple of cases in which the instructor of his Immigration Law course represented the applicant.

"Sure it was awkward," Pennie recalls. "Fortunately, my instructor is a straight-shooter and the evidence was clear and well organized. Whether the applicant is represented by a friend or foe, you just have to call it by the numbers. That's the professional way to get things done."

THE INDEPENDENT PARALEGAL: GOING OUT ON YOUR OWN

In this chapter and elsewhere, we have broached the notion that a person with a paralegal education can work for lawyers as an independent contractor. That is, a paralegal could hang a shingle, like a solo practicing attorney, and work as a freelance legal professional hired on a case-by-case basis by lawyers in firms or other entities. These days, paralegals are going out on their own to become independent paralegals.

Let's revisit the ABA's most recent definition of a paralegal:

> *A legal assistant or paralegal is a person qualified by education, training or work experience who is employed or* ***retained*** *by a lawyer, law office, corporation, governmental agency or other entity who performs specifically delegated substantive legal work for which a lawyer is responsible.*

Notice that the ABA definition uses the word "retained." This terminology means that a paralegal may work for "a lawyer, law office, corporation, governmental agency, or other entity" on an independent basis. Not too long ago, the unauthorized practice rules appeared to prevent this type of arrangement. However, after four decades of legal development in courts and legislatures, the idea of an independent paralegal has gained acceptance. Hand-in-hand with this change, courts and legislatures have begun to refine the idea of the unauthorized practice of law. Consider the following chronology of events:

New York, 1967—The highest state court in New York held that a nonattorney could not be convicted of violating the unauthorized practice laws by authoring a book entitled *How to Avoid Probate*, which contained advice on taking advantage of legal procedures. *N.Y. County Lawyer's Assn. v. Dacey,* 21 N.Y.2d 694, 287 N.Y.S.2d 422, 234 N.E. 2d 459 (1967).

Oregon, 1975—The Oregon Supreme Court decided that the sale of legal forms and instructions on how to use them did not violate the state's unauthorized practice laws because there was no attorney–client relationship between the buyer and seller. *Oregon State Bar v. Gilchrist,* 272 Or. 532, 538 P.2d 913 (1975).

Colorado, 1976—An independent paralegal acting as a scrivener, filling out divorce forms, could not be prosecuted for violating the unauthorized practice laws because the paralegal was merely filling out the forms by using the exact words of the person seeking the divorce. *Colorado Bar Ass'n v. Miles,*192 Colo. 294, 557 P.2d 1202 (1976).

Florida, 1978—The Florida Supreme Court reversed an earlier decision and held that legal forms with instructions *and* direct contact between the seller and the buyer to fill out the forms did not violate the state's unauthorized practice laws, as long as the seller fills out the forms using the exact words of the buyer. *Florida Bar v. Brumbaugh,* 355 So. 2d 1186 (Fla. 1978).

California, 1984—California dissolved the state's unauthorized practice enforcement office and assigned enforcement to criminal prosecutors who enforce the unauthorized practice laws only in cases of fraud or misrepresentation.

Washington, 1985—Real estate brokers who draft purchase and sales agreements for real estate transactions did not violate the state's unauthorized practice laws, according to the Washington Supreme Court. *Cultum v. Heritage House Realtors, Inc.,*103 Wash.2d 623, 694 P.2d 630 (1985). The Court recognized that realtors would be performing legal tasks normally done by lawyers but found that the public interest would be better served by offering a choice of legal services.

California, 1987—The California Legislature permitted immigration specialists to give advice in immigration matters for a fee if they disclosed that they were not attorneys. *Cal. Bus. & Prof. Code, §22441.*

Florida, 1991—In *Florida Bar re Advisory Opinion—Non-lawyer Preparation of Pension Plans,* 571 So. 2d 430 (Fla. 1990), the Florida Supreme Court refused to adopt the Florida Unauthorized Practice Laws Committee's recommendation that nonlawyers designing and preparing pension plans constituted the unauthorized practice of law. The Court was not convinced that there was a public need for the protection sought by the committee.

South Carolina, 1993—The South Carolina Supreme Court concluded that certified public accountants who were not lawyers could legally represent clients before administrative agencies and probate court. *In re Unauthorized Practice of Law Rules Proposed by the South Carolina Bar,* 309 S.C. 304, 422 S.E. 2d 123 (S.C. 1992).

Washington, 1999—In *Perkins v. CTX Mortgage Co.,* 137 Wash. 2d 93, 969 P.2d 93 (Wash. 1999), the Washington Supreme Court declined to find that the activities of a mortgage company that assisted mortgage applicants with filling out financing documents constituted an unauthorized practice of law.

These and other developments in the law indicate a clear trend toward refining social policy and public attitudes about what lawyers do and what nonlawyers may not do. Specifically, legislatures and courts have begun to refine the outer boundaries of the prohibition against the unauthorized practice of law.

For centuries, the lawyer's realm was defined by the tasks that lawyers performed in the course of representing their clients. As a result, the lawyers themselves defined what constituted the *authorized* practice of law. In doing so, they also defined what nonlawyers should not do—that is, the *un*authorized practice of law. Society adopted the lawyers' definition and established the justifications for the unauthorized practice laws. Primary among the justifications were social concerns for protecting the consumers of legal services against the incompetent lay practitioners and fraud by the unscrupulous. For decades, if not longer, these social concerns were sufficient to uphold the prosecution of the unlicensed who dared to encroach into the lawyers' realm.

During the mid-1960s, wider social concerns regarding the provision of legal services began to arise. First, courts and legislatures saw an unmet public need for legal services. Second, there was public concern for the high cost of quality legal services. For these reasons among others, the traditional view of the unauthorized practice laws gave way to a more utilitarian view. Thus, nonlawyer professionals such as bankers, certified public accountants, real estate brokers, and financial analysts were and are able to give legal advice and prepare legal documents with impunity.

The case summaries contain a common thread that saves nonlawyer professionals from prosecution, namely, a lack of need for public protection. In those cases, courts had begun to assume that the nonlawyer professionals would be acting competently and professionally as they engaged in tasks clearly related to their professions. What caught the ire of the bar associations in those cases was that the same tasks overlapped with lawyers' tasks. Therefore, the nonlawyer professionals' encroachment on the lawyers' turf was merely technical and did not threaten the basic public concern for incompetence or fraud. In such circumstances, the courts felt uncomfortable convicting a nonlawyer professional who had performed his or her lawyer-like duties in good faith.

For paralegals, a parallel perspective becomes apparent. From humble beginnings as file clerks, office clerics, and legal secretaries, paralegals have now come into their own as legal professionals. The fact that the ABA has gone so far as to "approve" paralegal schools by establishing detailed guidelines for educating paralegals is strong evidence that mainstream lawyers consider educated paralegals worthy of consideration as legal professionals. On a more official level, the same may be said of the Supreme Court's holding in *Missouri v. Jenkins* that a paralegal's billable time can be counted as attorneys' fees. What differentiates paralegals from other nonattorney professionals, such as accountants and real estate brokers, is that the professional tasks that paralegals perform are often the same ones attorneys perform.

As unlicensed legal professionals, paralegals are nevertheless subject to the unauthorized practice rules, as is everyone else except for licensed attorneys. For paralegals, the lynchpin of the unauthorized practice rules is the prohibition against giving legal advice. However, as we examined in Chapter 10, paralegals working in a law office discuss their legal evaluation of a client's matters with coworkers who are attorneys or other paralegals. Paralegals also perform legal research about a specific client situation and reduce their thoughts and conclusions to a memorandum of law read by other legal professionals. Whether by spoken or written words, the paralegal indeed gives legal advice. However, because the advice goes to coworkers and not the public, the unauthorized practice of law prohibition does not apply. Simply put, by giving legal advice to attorneys, paralegals are not practicing law as long as the attorney supervises the paralegal and remains responsible for the final work product. That is what freelance or independent paralegals do.

CASE IN POINT

FREELANCING AS AN INDEPENDENT PARALEGAL

IN RE: OPINION NO. 24 OF THE COMMITTEE ON THE UNAUTHORIZED PRACTICE OF LAW, 128 N.J. 114, 607 A.2d 962 (1992)

The New Jersey Supreme Court Committee on the Unauthorized Practice of Law (the "Committee") concluded in Advisory Opinion No. 24, 126 N.J.L.J. 1306, 1338 (1990), that "paralegals functioning outside of the supervision of an attorney-employer are engaged in the unauthorized practice of law." Petitioners are several independent paralegals whom attorneys do not employ but retain on a temporary basis. They ask the Court to disapprove the Advisory Opinion.

Like paralegals employed by attorneys, independent paralegals retained by attorneys do not offer their services directly to the public. Nonetheless, the Committee determined that independent paralegals are engaged in the unauthorized practice of law because they are performing legal services without adequate attorney supervision. We agree with the Committee that the resolution of the issue turns on whether independent paralegals are adequately supervised by attorneys. We disagree with the Committee, however, that the evidence supports a categorical ban on all independent paralegals in New Jersey.

The State Bar Association's Subcommittee on Legal Assistants ("Legal Assistant Subcommittee"), the National Association of Legal Assistants ("NALA"), and the National Federation of Paralegal Associates ("NFPA") provided the Committee with information on regulation, education, certification, and the ethical responsibilities of paralegals.

After receiving those submissions, the Committee held a hearing at which four independent paralegals, three employed paralegals, and three attorneys testified. All the independent paralegals testifying before the Committee were well qualified. One independent paralegal noted that as an NALA member she is bound by both the ABA Model Code of Professional Responsibility and the ABA Model Rules of Professional Conduct. The independent paralegals stated that although they had worked with many attorneys during their careers, they had worked solely for those attorneys and only under their direct supervision.

Client contact varied for each independent paralegal. Some see the attorney's client in the attorney's office, while others meet outside of the office. One paralegal testified that she carefully ensures that clients understand that she is not an attorney and that she cannot, as a paralegal, answer legal questions.

Three paralegals who were full-time employees of law firms also testified before the Committee. Each paralegal represented a paralegal organization, such as NFPA or NALA. They explained that many independent paralegals are members of those organizations and that both organizations have developed guidelines and standards for their paralegal members.

All three employed paralegals expressed support for independent paralegals who work under the direct supervision of an attorney and who do not provide services directly to the public.

Two attorneys appeared before the Committee. One testified that as long as attorneys supervise independent paralegals, that those paralegals do not work full-time for one attorney or firm does not matter. The second attorney, a sole practitioner, testified that independent paralegals provide many benefits to both small firms and the general public alike.

The Committee concluded that attorneys are currently unable to supervise adequately the performance of independent paralegals, and that by performing legal services without such adequate supervision those paralegals are engaging in the unauthorized practice of law.

We granted petitioners' request for review, and the Chairperson of the Committee granted their motion to stay the enforcement of its finding.

No satisfactory, all-inclusive definition of what constitutes the practice of law has ever been devised. None will be attempted here. That has been left, and wisely so, to the courts when parties present them with concrete factual situations. Essentially, the Court decides what constitutes the practice of law on a case-by-case basis.

The practice of law is not subject to precise definition. It is not confined to litigation but often encompasses "legal activities in many non-litigious fields which entail specialized knowledge and ability." Therefore, the line between permissible business and professional activities and the unauthorized practice of law is often blurred.

The Court disagreed that a non-lawyer's preparation of an inheritance-tax return for another person constituted the unauthorized practice of law. The Court emphasized that "in cases involving an overlap of professional discipline we must try to avoid arbitrary classifications and instead focus on the public's realistic need for protection and regulation." Applying that standard, the Court permitted CPAs to prepare inheritance-tax returns subject to the condition that the accountant notify the client that an attorney's review of the return would be helpful because of the legal issues surrounding its preparation.

There is no question that paralegals' work constitutes the practice of law and constitutes the unauthorized practice of law. However, an exception exists if their supervising attorney assumes direct responsibility for the work that the paralegals perform. Consequently, paralegals who are supervised by attorneys do not engage in the unauthorized practice of law.

Availability of legal services to the public at an affordable cost is a goal to which the Court is committed. The use of paralegals represents a means of achieving that goal while maintaining the quality of legal services. Paralegals enable attorneys to render legal services more economically and efficiently. During the last twenty years the employment of paralegals has greatly expanded, and within the last ten years the number of independent paralegals has increased.

(contd.)

Independent paralegals work either at a "paralegal firm" or freelance. Most are employed by sole practitioners or smaller firms who cannot afford the services of a full-time paralegal. Like large law firms, small firms find that using paralegals helps them provide effective and economical services to their clients. Requiring paralegals to be full-time employees of law firms would thus deny attorneys not associated with large law firms the very valuable services of paralegals.

The utilization of paralegals has become, over the last 10 years, accepted, acceptable, important and indeed, necessary to the efficient practice of law. Lawyers, law firms and, more importantly, clients benefit greatly by their work. Those people who perform para-professionally are educated to do so. They are trained and truly professional. They are diligent and carry on their functions in a dignified, proper, professional manner.

A lawyer often delegates tasks to clerks, secretaries, and other laypersons. Such delegation is proper if the lawyer maintains a direct relationship with his/her client, supervises the delegated work, and has complete professional responsibility for the work product. This delegation enables a lawyer to render legal services more economically and efficiently.

The ABA definition expands the role of a legal assistant to include independent paralegals, recognizing that attorneys can and do retain the services of legal assistants who work outside the law office.

Under both federal law and New Jersey law, and under both the ABA and New Jersey ethics rules, attorneys may delegate legal tasks to paralegals if they maintain direct relationships with their clients, supervise the paralegal's work and remain responsible for the work product.

Neither case law nor statutes distinguish paralegals employed by an attorney or law firm from independent paralegals retained by an attorney or a law firm. Nor do we. Rather, the important inquiry is whether the paralegal, whether employed or retained, is working directly for the attorney, under that attorney's supervision. Safeguards against the unauthorized practice of law exist through that supervision. Realistically, a paralegal can engage in the unauthorized practice of law whether he or she is an independent paralegal or employed in a law firm.

Although the ABA requires that paralegals be qualified through work, education, or training, the State currently requires neither certification nor licensure for paralegals. No regulatory body exists to prevent unqualified persons from working as paralegals. However, the same is true with regard to employed paralegals. No rule requires that either employed paralegals or independent paralegals belong to any paraprofessional organization. Thus, only those paralegals who are members of such organizations are subject to regulation. Again, the problem is not with independent paralegals but with the absence of any binding regulations or guidelines.

Regulation may also solve another ethical problem—conflicts of interest.

The appearance of and potential for conflict will increase dramatically when independent paralegals offer their services to multiple law firms to assist them in litigated matters. The paralegal may be sensitive to avoid functioning for two adversary attorneys in the same case. Nevertheless, the potential for conflict with the number of different law firms represented by the one paralegal. The problem is exacerbated and uncontrollable when the relationships multiply by virtue of a single, independent paralegal representing multiple law firms.

We again conclude that regulations and guidelines can be drafted to address adequately the conflict-of-interest problem. For example, as urged by paralegal associations, there could be a requirement that paralegals must keep records of each case, listing the names of the parties and all counsel. Before undertaking new employment, paralegals would check the list. Likewise, attorneys should require the paralegals to furnish them with such a list. The attorney could thus examine whether such matters would conflict with the attorney's representation of a client before retaining that paralegal. Regulation can also remedy any problems resulting from the attendant problem of paralegals sending correspondence directly to clients without the attorney's review and approval.

Regulation and guidelines represent the proper course of action to address the problems that the work practices of all paralegals may create. Although the paralegal is directly accountable for engaging in the unauthorized practice of law and has an obligation to avoid conduct that otherwise violates the Rules of Professional Conduct, the attorney is ultimately accountable. Therefore, with great care, the attorney should ensure that the legal assistant is informed of and abides by the provisions of the Rules of Professional Conduct.

We conclude that given the appropriate instructions and supervision, paralegals, whether as employees or independent contractors, are valuable and necessary members of an attorney's team in the effective and efficient practice of law.

We modify Opinion No. 24 in accordance with this opinion.

QUESTIONS ABOUT THE CASE

1. Why did the Committee say that independent paralegals violate the unauthorized practice of law rules?
2. Under what conditions is it legally and ethically permissible to delegate legal work to a nonattorney?
3. Why is the central problem the lack of binding regulation?
4. What should the regulation of independent paralegals take into account, according to the Court?
5. What suggestions did the Court make to avoid conflict of interest by independent paralegals?

The Entrepreneurial Paralegal

Deciding to become an independent paralegal requires an entrepreneurial spirit. An independent paralegal is in business for him- or herself, very much like a lawyer who is a solo practitioner. The big difference, of course, is that instead of having clients in the traditional sense, an independent paralegal has lawyers. That is, lawyers and law firms are the "clients" or customers of the independent paralegal. Lawyers and

EYE ON ETHICS

The New Jersey Supreme Court's opinion appears to give a ringing endorsement of the idea of independent paralegals. However, keep in mind that the opinion applies only to paralegals working in New Jersey.

Every state has its own ethical rules. Although the ABA Model Rules of Professional Conduct have been adopted in most states, many states have modified some of those rules. In some cases, entire sections of the Model Rules have been changed or eliminated. Thus, paralegals outside of New Jersey who are interested in working independently should carefully research their own state's laws, ethical rules, and court decisions to ensure that an independent paralegal can legally and ethically perform legal work for the attorneys in that state.

law firms choose to retain independent paralegals on a case-by-case basis for reasons of economy and efficiency to get their work done. Independent paralegals are preferable to full-time employees in many instances, because once the delegated task or assignment has been completed, the costs required to do the work have also ended. Thus, the lawyer or law firm becomes free of the constant overhead of paying a full-time employee. Hiring an independent paralegal on a case-by-case basis is also more economical because paralegals charge less than an independent lawyer would.

Consider a situation in which a lawyer, law firm, or in-house legal department suddenly finds that they need to determine whether a certain parcel of real estate has any title problems. If title examination were not within their usual realm of legal activities, it would make perfect sense to hire an independent paralegal for the sole purpose of performing a title search. An independent paralegal with knowledge and experience as a title examiner or abstractor would certainly fit the bill to perform that single task efficiently. Once complete, the hourly fee to perform the title examination becomes a one-time cost.

The same would be true in situations in which a lawyer, law firm, or in-house legal department is experiencing a temporary work overload. Siphoning some of the work to an independent paralegal would be a convenient and economical delegation that ends once normality returns. Thus, an independent paralegal could step in and assist with the flow of legal work to perform the task of indexing discovery, organizing litigation documents, or any other legal tasks on a temporary basis. Once the work overload has eased, both the independent paralegal and the law firm are free from each other and return to their normal routines.

The advantages to becoming an independent paralegal can be numerous. In Chapter 11, we discussed situations in which a full-time paralegal may confront challenging personalities in the legal workplace. An independent paralegal is able to pick and choose not only the type of work but also the legal professionals with whom to work. Free from the dictates of a law office hierarchy, an independent paralegal may decline to take on work without having to worry about the consequences. At the same time, an independent paralegal can choose to work on a temporary basis for "regular" customers time and time again. Having built a trusting and cooperative business relationship, an experienced independent paralegal will have developed a fair measure of goodwill. This process is often how business operates, even in the legal world.

As a businessperson, the independent paralegal will find him- or herself in the same situation as anyone else trying to establish him- or herself in business. Essential to this process is marketing, developing a professional appearance, and providing a personal touch. After all, an independent paralegal is providing and selling an important professional service.

A DAY IN THE LIFE OF A REAL PARALEGAL

Seeking a career change, Donald Czarnecki obtained a certificate in paralegal studies at Suffolk University in Boston, Massachusetts. With the ink still wet on his certificate, Czarnecki decided to go into business for himself. The usual path for paralegals—working as a lawyer's assistant in an established office—was too confining. With the spirit of a true entrepreneur, he rented his own office space near his home and put out his own shingle: *Essex County Paralegals, Inc.*

"Pounding the pavement," Czarnecki worked hard to establish himself as a freelance independent paralegal. "I knew that I had to be aggressive to be able to get the work. I had the skills. The rest was up to me," Czarnecki recalls. With countless phone calls and direct mailings of professionally printed brochures that he wrote himself, Czarnecki marketed his business to solo practitioners, law firms, and corporate legal departments. Within a few months, the work started flowing in at a steady rate. Initially, Czarnecki started doing legal research for lawyers, spending much of his time in law libraries and online using computerized legal research aids. Now, the bulk of his work involves obtaining public documents for law firms and national corporations.

"Every day is different," says Czarnecki. "One day I'm at the Secretary of State's office looking up corporate documents or filing articles of incorporation; then it's to the Registry of Deeds to search a title. Tomorrow I may be at the courthouse, researching court orders and judgments. I love my work and I'm my own boss."

Yet Czarnecki scoffs at the suggestion that he is a success. "I'm just happy to bring home a decent pay check," he reports. Czarnecki then quietly adds that he just bought a new car that he uses in his business. When asked to pinpoint any part of his paralegal education that has helped him the most, Czarnecki replied, "It's beyond the great training and education I received at my school. I guess if you ask me for any one aspect, it's the confidence from having that certificate."

The future looks very bright for Czarnecki and his venture. Last month he hired his first full-time employee—another graduate from his school. Already, he's planning to hire another full-time paralegal. With evident pride, Czarnecki assures his listener that "It was scary at first, but once things started to get going, I was in business."

WHAT PARALEGALS EARN

The United States Department of Labor's Bureau of Labor Statistics performs regular periodic studies of the occupational outlook of tens of thousands of jobs and professions in the country. For paralegals, the occupational outlook is very bright. In its most recent study, the government reports that:

> *Employment for paralegals and legal assistants is projected to grow* much faster than average *for all occupations through 2014. Employers are trying to reduce costs and increase the availability and efficiency of legal services by hiring paralegals to perform tasks formerly carried out by lawyers. Besides new jobs created by employment growth, additional job openings will arise as people leave the occupation. Despite projections of rapid employment growth, competition for jobs should continue as many people seek to go into this profession; however, experienced, formally trained paralegals should have the best employment opportunities.*[1]

This projection reflects the highest job growth rate that the government provides.

In real terms, "much faster than average" means an increase of 27 percent or more. In contrast, the job growth rate for lawyers falls two notches lower, at "as fast as average," or 9–17 percent. Moreover, notice that the study reported that those who wish to become paralegals through formal training will be best suited to find work in an increasingly competitive job environment. Of course, this recommendation

[1] Source: www.bls.gov/oco/ocos114.htm#outlook (2007).

FIGURE 12.1
Average Paralegal Salaries by Year
Source: Data obtained from NALA: www.nala.org/04_Survay_SEC4.pdf.

Year	Total Compensation	Salary	Bonus
2005	$46,862	$44,373	$3,393
2004	$46,074	$43,002	$2,909
2000	$40,474	$37,946	$2,449
1997	$36,435	$33,494	$2,026

FIGURE 12.2
Regional Differences in Paralegal Salaries
Source: Data obtained from NALA: www.nala.org/04_Survay_SEC4.pdf.

Region	Salary	Total Compensation
Region 1–New England/East	$49,305	$51,479
Region 2–Great Lakes	$42,266	$44,415
Region 3–Plains states	$40,565	$42,694
Region 4–Southeast	$43,168	$45,460
Region 5–Southwest	$45,194	$47,709
Region 6–Rocky Mountains	$40,558	$43,609
Region 7–Far West	$51,993	$55,760

means that those with credentials in the form of a certificate or degree from a two- or four-year paralegal program will be in a better position to obtain employment as paralegals.

The earnings for paralegals vary greatly depending on several factors, such as training, geographic location, and type of employer. As we discussed in Chapter 1, large law firms and employers in urban areas tend to pay the highest paralegal salaries. In smaller firms or rural areas, the pay is less. Of course, this contrast is true for almost any occupation or profession. The Bureau of Labor Statistics reports that:

> *In May 2004, full-time wage and salary paralegals and legal assistants had median annual earnings, including bonuses, of $39,130. The middle 50 percent earned between $31,040 and $49,950. The top 10 percent earned more than $61,390, while the bottom 10 percent earned less than $25,360. Median annual earnings in the industries employing the largest numbers of paralegals in May 2004 were as follows:*
>
> - *Federal Government, $59,370*
> - *Local government, $38,260*
> - *Legal services, $37,870*
> - *State government, $34,910*[2]

Keep in mind that these figures represent the median, or mid-range. The information from the NALA is even more optimistic. The NALA also conducts periodic surveys of paralegal salaries from its members. Figure 12.1 displays its survey results from the past 10 years.

The NALA survey also revealed regional differences, as shown in Figure 12.2

For its part, the NFPA's survey also provides information about hiring requirements. Its survey shows that almost half of its members' employers require a bachelor's degree. Many employers prefer to hire graduates from an ABA-approved paralegal program, and others—more than one-third—require experience as a paralegal. From this summary, you can see that salaries are largely a function of location and experience. For those entering the profession for the first time, the availability of information is crucial to a job applicant's ability to negotiate an appropriate salary. Luckily, paralegal associations and the U.S. Labor Department regularly publish and update salary information. The placement office at your school may also have salary information. Knowledge is power.

[2] Source: www.bls.gov/oco/ocos114.htm#earnings.

With knowledge about the prevailing salaries for paralegals in the area, a job applicant with an offer can approach an interview with greater confidence. Salary negotiations are always delicate. Advertisements for paralegal positions often state a salary range, but many others will not mention the salary. Nevertheless, salary information is a common topic during the interview. If asked by a prospective employer what salary would be expected, a tactful answer provides a range consistent with the location and the applicant's experience. By the same token, asking for salary information at the interview in the form of a range safely sets the stage for future negotiations that ensue after the offer is made.

A wise person, however, understands that salary is not everything. It may very well appear that a salary that is lower than expected will become acceptable in light of other factors. Consider the following when deciding whether to accept a position.

- *Flexible work hours.* Legal professionals are almost never paid for overtime. Yet flexible attitudes toward work hours could include "comp time" for extra hours previously worked and applied to times when the workload slackens.
- *Benefits.* The monetary value of health insurance that covers medical, dental, and prescription medicine can add up to thousands of dollars more that you would otherwise have to pay for healthcare services. If coverage extends to spouses/partners and children, the value of health insurance increases astronomically. Daycare and relocation costs are benefits that may be offered. Vacation days, pensions, parking or public transportation subsidies, and life/disability insurance are additional factors.
- *Professional growth.* Many employers pay a variety of expenses that can help with professional growth. Employers commonly pay for professional association dues, tuition, and books for continuing legal education. Some large firms will pay for some or all of the tuition for another degree, such as a master's degree in business administration or a law degree.
- *Advancement.* Based on your own research about the employment conditions in your area and your knowledge of the employer's staffing, the potential ability and opportunity to achieve a senior or supervisory capacity can outweigh salary considerations alone. Does the employer provide representation in various practice areas that might expand your horizons? Is the employer expanding or growing? Is high performance recognized through bonus incentives?
- *Location and travel.* Workplace location means commute time, which influences quality of life. Assess the office location and how the commute will affect other commitments in your life. Location considerations also include the surrounding area's safety and available resources, such as shopping and other conveniences near the workplace. If the position requires travel, the frequency and reimbursement methods should be weighed depending on your personal circumstances. Some professionals enjoy traveling as a break from the routine and an opportunity to explore. Others consider traveling drudgery and a distraction. Understandably, those with family and other personal responsibilities may prefer to avoid traveling altogether.
- *Office resources.* Being a professional means, in large part, performing high-quality work efficiently and with a minimum of fuss. Yet getting the job done professionally requires the right tools. When assessing a potential legal workplace, the accessibility of the right resources that can assist you as a legal professional can greatly affect your productivity. A modern law office should, at a minimum, have up-to-date computers for everyone, Internet and online legal research, practice-specific software, and adequate support personnel.

Summary

As in any profession, staying current with changes in the law and the overall legal profession is essential to a paralegal's continuing success in the legal workplace. Before graduation, participation in an internship program provides the benefit of gaining hands-on training and real work experience. Once employed in the law office, paralegals can stay current by enrolling in continuing legal education courses and reading practice manuals designed for legal professionals. The law office itself may have mentoring programs and other internal mechanisms to keep its legal professionals up to date on the law and its latest developments.

Traditionally, paralegals have worked for law firms and legal aid offices. However, with growing recognition of the paralegal profession, other professional avenues have opened for persons learned and trained in the law who are not lawyers. Outside law firms, opportunities for the professional paralegal abound in almost every area of the law, such as law enforcement agencies, insurance companies, and corporations, including not-for-profit organizations, colleges, and even the military. Some government agencies hire paralegals in important decision-making roles, such as hearing officers and adjudicators.

Building a business as an independent paralegal is a way to become self-employed in the legal profession. With lawyers, law firms, and others as "clients" or customers of the independent paralegal, concerns for the unauthorized practice of law take on new and more profound meanings.

The future is extremely bright for the paralegal profession and those who chose to enter it. All indications indicate that the professional paralegal will experience the highest rate of growth, with salaries and other forms of compensation rising rapidly. Through formal education, training, and experience, a paralegal can expect to receive a warm welcome from potential employers for many years into the future.

These are great times to be a professional paralegal.

Key Terms

Abstract
Abstractor (title examiner)
Adjudicatory hearings
Checklist
Claims adjuster
Continuing legal education (CLE)
Education
Insurance law
Internship
JAG (Judge Advocate General's Corps)
Legal nurse consultant
Legal specialist
Mentoring program
Parole
Parole officer
Practice area
Practice manuals
Probation
Probation officer
Presentencing report
Pretrial probation
Sentencing guidelines
Tax lien
Title examiner

Review Questions

1. What are the benefits of participating in an internship?
2. What is the difference between a mentoring program and an internship?
3. What is the difference between a parole officer and a probation officer?
4. What is the difference between an LNC certificate and LNC certification?
5. Based on what you learned in Chapter 8, how would you arrange your assets to avoid the probate process?

6. How do parole and probation officers serve both individuals and the criminal justice system?
7. How do claim adjusters determine whether their insurance companies should pay for a claim?
8. What types of determinations can government adjudicators make?
9. What are the primary ethical concerns for independent paralegals?
10. What can you expect to earn as a starting paralegal?

Exercises

1. Using the Internet, find schools that offer study in criminal justice. What additional courses or areas of study should a paralegal student take to qualify as a parole or probation officer?
2. Find out whether there are any independent paralegals in your area. Are there any individuals who offer services to fill out legal forms or other "legal" work?
3. Visit a courthouse and find the parole or probation department. Observe the activities and try to speak to any of the officers.
4. Find out where information about deeds and property ownership is kept in your area. If possible, make a visit to observe and identify those who are title examiners and abstractors.
5. Browse the want ads, particularly those in legal newspapers, to see what the salaries are for paralegals.
6. Find out if your school has an in-house legal department. Where is it on campus? If possible, visit that office and try to speak with the legal professionals there.

Discussion Questions

1. Identify the ethical duties for which mentoring programs, practice manuals, continuing legal education, and in-office activities assist the legal professional's work.
2. How can paralegals occupy positions formerly held by licensed attorneys consistent with the prohibition against the unauthorized practice of law?
3. Are legal professionals who work at places other than law firms bound by the rules of confidentiality?
4. How should an independent paralegal guard against conflict of interest?
5. What steps should an independent paralegal take to set up his or her business?

PORTFOLIO ASSIGNMENT

Research the current status of the law in your state to see if an independent paralegal can set up shop. Write a memorandum of law that analyzes in detail whether your state's laws permit a paralegal to hang out a shingle and go into business. If you are in New Jersey, choose another state.

[illegible]

[illegible]

[illegible]

[illegible]

Glossary

A

ABA approval A voluntary process for paralegal schools indicating that they meet prescribed educational standards set by the American Bar Association.

ABA Model Guidelines for the Utilization of Paralegals Lawyers' guidelines for delegating work to paralegals.

ABA Model Rules of Professional Conduct Lawyer's ethical rules.

ABA Standing Committee on Paralegals A specialized committee of the ABA that oversees the paralegal profession.

abstract A short history of a piece of land that lists any transfers in ownership, as well as any liabilities attached to it, such as mortgages.

abstractor (title examiner) A law-trained person who searches public records and examine titles to determine a property title's legal condition.

acceptance The offeree's clear manifestation of agreement to the exact terms of the offer in the manner specified in the offer.

acquittal The legal and formal certification of the innocence of a person who has been charged with a crime.

active listening A structured form of listening and responding that focuses attention on the speaker and the speaker's feelings.

actus reus The guilty act.

adjudicatory hearings Trial-like proceedings held by administrative agencies to determine legal rights under the agency's jurisdiction.

administration The court-supervised distribution of the probate estate of a person who has died without a will.

administrative agencies Governmental bodies created by state or federal laws to administer and regulate certain subjects, such as the environment, employment, or Social Security.

administrative agency regulations and rules (administrative codes) Processes and guidelines established under the particular administrative section that describe acceptable conduct for persons and situations under the control of the respective agency.

administrator A person appointed by a probate court to handle the distribution of property of someone who has died without a will.

admiralty Specialized laws and courts dealing with maritime questions and offenses.

adoption The taking of a child into the family, creating a parent–child relationship where the biological relationship did not exist.

advance sheets Softcover pamphlets containing the most recent cases.

adverse (hostile) witness A witness whose interests or perspective are potentially damaging to the case of an opposing party.

affirm Disposition in which the appellate court agrees with the trial court.

affirmative defenses An "excuse" by the opposing party that does not simply negate the allegation but puts forth a legal reason to avoid enforcement. These defenses are waived if not pleaded.

agency A legal relationship in which one party (agent) acts or represents the interests of another (principal).

agent A person who is authorized to act for or in the shoes of another (principal).

alibi A defense to a criminal proceeding stating the defendant was elsewhere when the alleged crime was committed.

alimony Court-ordered money paid to support a former spouse after termination of a marriage.

American Bar Association A national organization of lawyers, providing support and continuing legal education to the profession.

annotation An in-depth analysis of a specific and important legal issue raised in the accompanying decision, together with an extensive survey of the way the issue is treated in various jurisdictions.

annulment Court procedure dissolving a marriage, treating it as if it never happened.

answer The defendant's response to the plaintiff's complaint.

appeasement The act of granting concessions to potential adversaries to maintain peace and avoid future hostile behavior.

appellant The party filing the appeal; that is, bringing the case to the appeals court.

appellate court The court of appeals that reviews a trial court's record for errors.

appellee The prevailing party in the lower court, who will respond to the appellant's argument.

arrest The formal taking of a person, usually by a police officer, to answer criminal charges.

Article III The part of the United States Constitution that creates the federal judiciary.

assignment The transfer of the rights to receive the benefit of contractual performance under the contract.

Associate's Degree A two-year college degree offered by both public and private colleges.

assumpsit Common law writ for contracts.

assumption of risk The doctrine that releases another person from liability for the person who chooses to assume a known risk of harm.

Attorney General The chief law enforcement officer and head of the law office of a state or country.

authorization letter A letter the client provides the attorney granting permission to contact employers, doctors, or other individuals who have records that relate to a case.

avoidance The act of keeping away from certain people or situations to avert confrontations or unpleasant situations.

B

Bachelor's Degree A college degree offered by both public and private four-year colleges and universities.

bail Court-mandated surety or guarantee that the defendant will appear at a future date if released from custody prior to trial.

bar exam A test administered to graduates from approved law schools that determines the applicant's knowledge of the law and ability to practice in the state.

bench trial A case heard and decided by a judge.

beneficiary The person or persons named in a will or trust to receive the testator's or settlor's assets.

benefit of the bargain A measure of damages in a breach of contract action in which the damages are measured to restore the nonbreaching party to the position if the breach had not occurred.

benefit-detriment A test for the element of consideration in a contract involving a determination of whether each party gains a benefit and suffers a detriment.

best evidence rule To prove the contents of a document, recording, or photograph, the original writing, recording, or photograph is required.

beyond a reasonable doubt The requirement for the level of proof in a criminal matter in order to convict or find the defendant guilty. It is a substantially higher and more-difficult-to-prove criminal matter standard.

bill of attainder A legislative act declaring a person or group of persons guilty of some crime and punishing him or her without benefit of a trial.

binding authority (mandatory authority) A source of law that a court must follow in deciding a case, such as a statute or federal regulations.

body language A form of communication using body movements or gestures instead of, or in addition to, sounds, verbal language, or other communication.

boutique law firms A law firm that specializes in a technical area of the law offering clients customized service.

breach of contract A party's performance that deviates from the required performance obligations under the contract; a violation of an obligation under a contract for which a party may seek recourse to the court.

breach of duty The failure to maintain a reasonable degree of care toward another person to whom a duty is owed.

burden of proof Standard for assessing the weight of the evidence.

business organization A form of conducting business.

C

capacity The ability to understand the nature and significance of a contract; to understand or comprehend specific acts or reasoning.

caption The full name of the case, together with the docket number, and court.

career objective A statement at the beginning of a résumé stating the job applicant's goals and providing focus for the prospective employer.

career or placement office A support office of a school that assists students in finding suitable employment through counseling and maintaining job listings.

case brief An objective summary of the important points of a single case; a summary of a court opinion.

case (common) law Published court opinions of federal and state appellate courts; judge-created law in deciding cases, set forth in court opinions.

case management Keeping track of the progress or status of the file and proactively organizing the work of both the attorney and the paralegal.

case reporters Sets of books that contain copies of appellate court opinions from every case heard and published within the relevant jurisdiction.

causation Intentional or negligent act resulting in harm or injury to the complaining plaintiff.

cause of action A personal, financial, or other injury for which the law gives a person the right to receive compensation.

certificate An educational credential that indicates an individual has successfully completed a prescribed course of study, usually in an occupation or profession.

certificate of service Verification by attorney that pleadings or court documents were sent to the opposing counsel in a case.

certification The recognition of the attainment of a degree of academic and practical knowledge by a professional.

certiorari (Cert) (Latin) "To make sure." An appellate court's authority to decide which cases it will hear on appeal.

challenge for cause A party's request that the judge dismiss a potential juror from serving on a trial jury by providing a valid legal reason why he or she shouldn't serve.

chambers A judge's office. Trial court judges often schedule pretrial settlement conferences and other informal meetings in their chambers.

chattel Tangible personal property or goods.

checklist Internally developed instruction and guide for legal professionals in a specific area of practice, listing steps, documents, or both for the legal professional to follow and gather.

circuit One of several courts in a specific jurisdiction.

citation Information about a legal source directing you to the volume and page in which the legal source appears.

civil law The legal rules regarding offenses committed against the person.

civil procedure Rules used to handle a civil case from the time the initial complaint is filed, through pretrial discovery, the trial itself, and any subsequent appeal. Each state adopts its own rules of civil procedure (often set out in separate Codes of Civil Procedure), but many are influenced by or modeled on the Federal Rules of Civil Procedure.

civil union In some states, a legally recognized committed relationship similar to marriage for persons of the same gender.

claims adjuster A law-trained insurance company employee who assesses and settles claims between the insured and the insurance company.

clear and convincing evidence Having a high probability of truthfulness, a higher standard being preponderance of the evidence.

closed-ended questions Questions that seek a brief or one-word answer.

Code of Federal Regulations (C.F.R.) Federal agency regulation collection.

codification Compiling enacted laws into an organized format.

common law Judge-made law, the ruling in a judicial opinion.

common stock A basic form of corporate ownership typically bearing the right to vote.

community property All property acquired during marriage in a community property state, owned in equal shares.

comparative negligence Applies when the evidence shows that both the plaintiff and the defendant acted negligently.

compensatory damages A payment to make up for a wrong committed and return the nonbreaching party to a position where the effect or the breach has been neutralized.

competence The ability and possession of expertise and skill in a field that is necessary to do the job.

complaint Document that states the allegations and the legal basis of the plaintiff's claims. Also, a charge, preferred before a magistrate having jurisdiction, that a person named has committed a specified offense, with an offer to prove the fact, to the end that a prosecution may be instituted.

Confrontation Clause Sixth Amendment guarantee that the accused has the absolute right to confront his or her accusers and all evidence.

concurring opinion A separate opinion that agrees with the majority opinion but for different reasons.

confidentiality Lawyer's duty not to disclose information concerning a client.

conflict check A procedure to verify potential adverse interests before accepting a new client.

conflict of interest Clash between private and professional interests or competing professional interests that makes impartiality difficult and creates an unfair advantage.

conservatorship The court appointment of a person who manages the financial and day-to-day affairs of an incapacitated adult.

consideration An essential element of a contract consisting of a benefit or right for each of the contracting parties.

constitution The organic and fundamental law of a nation or state, which may be written or unwritten, establishing the character and conception of its government, laying the basic principles to which its internal life is to be conformed, organizing the government, regulating functions of departments, and prescribing the extent to which a nation or state can exercise its powers.

constructive delivery The donor's symbolic act of transferring a gift to the donee.

contempt A willful disregard for or disobedience of a public authority.

contingency An event or provision in a contract stating that some or all of the terms of the contract will be altered or voided by the occurrence of a specific event.

contingency fee The attorney's fee calculated as a percentage of the final award in a civil case.

continuing legal education (CLE) Continued legal competence and skills training required of practicing professionals.

contract A legally binding agreement between two or more parties.

contributory negligence The plaintiff played a large part in causing the injury; thus, fundamental fairness precludes assigning liability to the defendant.

corporate veil The legal protection afforded a duly formed corporation limiting the recovery of any judgments to the assets of the corporation and not the personal assets of the shareholders, or corporate owners, in the absence of fraud, undercapitalization, or abuse of the corporate entity.

corporation An organization formed with state government approval to act as an artificial person to carry on business and issue stock.

counterclaim A claim made by the defendant against the plaintiff—not a defense, but a new claim for damages, as if the defendant were the plaintiff in a separate suit; a countersuit brought by the defendant against the plaintiff.

counteroffer A refusal to accept the stated terms of an offer by proposing alternate terms.

cover sheet A court-issued form that accompanies a complaint when a lawsuit is initiated in court (usually federal court) for administrative purposes.

crime Any act done in violation of those duties that an individual owes to the community, and for the breach of which the law has provided that the offender shall make satisfaction to the public.

criminal law The legal rules regarding wrongs committed against society.

criminalize To declare a certain behavior or condition subject to criminal laws and punishment.

criminal procedure The rules and legal process for adjudicating charges that someone has committed a crime, often implicating constitutional principles pertaining to the rights of the accused.

cross-claim A lawsuit against a party of the same side; plaintiffs or defendants suing each other (defendant versus defendant or plaintiff versus plaintiff).

cross-examination Occurs when the opposing attorney asks the witness questions.

custody The legal authority to make decisions concerning a child's interests. Also, the care and control of a thing or person.

D

damages Money paid to compensate for loss or injury.

decedent A deceased person.

deed The written document transferring title, or an ownership interest in real property, to another person.

default judgment A judgment entered by the court against the defendant for failure to respond to the plaintiff's complaint.

defendant The party against whom a lawsuit or criminal proceeding is brought.

defense Legally sufficient reasons to excuse the complained-of behavior.

delegation The transfer of the duties/obligations to perform under the contract.

delivery (gift) Transferring actual possession of the goods, or putting the goods at the disposal of the buyer (donee), or by a negotiable instrument giving the buyer (donee) the right to the goods.

demand letter A letter requesting action on a legal matter.

demonstrative evidence Any object, visual aid, model, scale drawing, or other exhibit designed to help clarify points in the trial.

deponent The party or witness who is questioned in a deposition.

deposition A discovery tool in a question-and-answer format in which the attorney verbally questions a party or a witness under oath.

dictum (plural: dicta) A statement made by the court in a case that is beyond what is necessary to reach the final decision.

digest A collection of all the headnotes from an associated series of volumes, arranged alphabetically by topic and by key number.

digital or electronic evidence Evidence stored or transmitted in digital form, such as metadata or computer-generated documents or images.

direct evidence Evidence that establishes a particular fact without resort to other testimony or evidence.

direct examination Occurs when the attorney questions his or her own witness.

directed verdict A ruling by a judge, made after the plaintiff has presented all of evidence but before the defendant puts on a case, that awards judgment to the defendant.

discovery The pretrial investigation process authorized and governed by the rules of civil procedure; the process of investigation and collection of evidence by litigants; process in which the opposing parties obtain information about the case from each other; the process of investigation and collection of evidence by litigants.

discretion The court's power to make decisions it deems fair and just.

dissenting opinion An opinion in which a judge disagrees with the result reached by the majority; an opinion outlining the reasons for the dissent, which often critiques the majority and any concurring opinions.

district attorney A government lawyer who acts as a prosecutor in criminal cases.

diversity The quality of multicultural, ethnic, and racial presence in the workplace.

diversity jurisdiction Authority of the federal court to hear a case if the parties are citizens of different states and the amount at issue is over $75,000.

divorce/dissolution The legal termination of a marriage (or civil union).

docket entry sheet A court management document that details the papers filed in a court case in chronological order.

docket number The number assigned by the court to the case for its own administrative purposes.

documentary evidence Any evidence represented on paper that contributes to supporting the legal position and/or verbal testimony of witnesses, for example, medical billing records or cancelled checks.

domestic partnership A legally recognized relationship in some states between two individuals of the same or opposite gender who live together and share a common domestic life but are not joined in traditional marriage or in a civil union.

donative intent The state of mind necessary to make a gift.

donee A party to whom a gift is given.

donor The person making a gift.

double jeopardy Being tried twice for the same act or acts.

due process Ensures the appropriateness and adequacy of government action in circumstances infringing on fundamental individual rights; and a source of fundamental rights.

duress Unreasonable and unscrupulous manipulation of a person to force him or her to agree to terms of an agreement that he or she would otherwise not agree to. Also, any unlawful threat or coercion used by a person to induce another to act (or to refrain from acting) in a manner that he or she otherwise would not do.

duty to report An ethical obligation to report perceived unethical behavior committed by another legal professional.

E

education The act or process of imparting or acquiring general knowledge; developing the powers of reasoning and judgment.

elective share The right granted by law to a surviving spouse who may elect to take an intestate share of a decedent's spouse's estate despite any will provisions to the contrary.

element The constituent parts of a crime or civil cause of action that must be proved by the prosecution or plaintiff to establish the defendant's liability.

equitable distribution Divides the assets acquired during the marriage between the parties.

equitable relief A remedy that is other than money damages, such as refraining from or performing a certain act; nonmonetary remedies fashioned by the court using standards of fairness and justice. Injunction and specific performance are types of equitable relief.

escheat To pass property to the state, as is done with the assets of a person who dies without a will and without heirs.

escrow A legal arrangement in which an asset (often money, but sometimes other property such as art, a deed of title, Web site, or software source code) is delivered to a third party (an escrow agent) to be held in trust pending a contingency or the fulfillment of a condition or conditions in a contract, such as payment of a purchase price.

estate The total property, real and personal, owned by an individual.

estate planning The legal practice of arranging a client's assets and affairs in contemplation of death through the use of wills, trusts, and asset rearrangement.

ethical rules Rules or codes issued by professions to identify ethical duties.

ethics Standards by which conduct is measured.

executive order An order issued by the president of the United States or a governor of a state to another part of the executive branch of the government, such as an administrative agency or law enforcement official.

expert witness A witness with specialized knowledge or expertise in the subject of testimony.

ex post facto law Retrospective changes to the legal consequences of acts committed or the legal status of facts and relationships that existed prior to the enactment of the law. These laws are unconstitutional.

F

family law A body of law that applies to family relationships such as marriage, divorce, adoption, custody, and support.

federal question jurisdiction The jurisdiction given to federal courts in cases involving the interpretation and application of the U.S. Constitution or acts of Congress.

Federal Rules of Civil Procedure (Fed. R. Civ. P.) The specific set of rules followed in the federal courts.

felony A crime punishable by more than a year in prison or death.

fictitious name A name used only for business purposes different from the legal name of the person or business organization.

fiduciary One who owes to another the duties of good faith, trust, confidence, and candor.

field investigation Factual research performed outside the office, includnig viewing public records, interviewing witnesses, photographing crime or accident scenes, or other research.

file memo A formal memorandum prepared by a legal professional to summarize investigations or legal research on a client matter.

filing fee A fee charged by courts or other adjudicatory body required when filing a lawsuit.

forensics The practice of applying various scientific techniques to the examination and comparison of biological evidence, trace evidence, impression evidence (e.g., fingerprints, footprints, tire tracks), controlled substances, ballistics (firearm examination), and other evidence for court use in criminal or civil matters.

form practice A type of law practice that involves the use of forms generated by courts and administrative agencies, usually a specialty area of law such as probate or social insurance program.

forum The proper legal site or location.

fraud A knowing and intentional misstatement of the truth in order to induce a desired action from another person.

Freedom of Information Act (FOIA) A federal or state law that permits access to information held by government agencies.

G

general damages Those that normally would be anticipated in a similar action.

gift Bestowing a benefit without any expectation on the part of the giver to receive something in return and the absence of any obligation on the part of the receiver to do anything in return.

grand jury A jury of inquiry who are summoned and returned by the sheriff to each session of the criminal courts and whose duty is to receive complaints and accusations in criminal cases, hear evidence, and decide if the defendant should stand for trial.

grantee The person receiving the property.

grantor The person transferring the property.

guardian A court-appointed person to care for a ward.

guardianship A legal relationship created by a court between a guardian and ward, either a minor child or an incapacitated adult. The guardian has a legal right and duty to care for the ward, which may involve making personal decisions on his or her behalf, managing property, or both.

H

harm (injury) Injury suffered as a result of a breach of a duty owed.

hearsay An out-of-court statement offered to prove a matter in contention in the lawsuit.

heirs Persons entitled to receive property based on intestate succession.

holding That aspect of a court opinion that directly affects the outcome of the case; it is composed of the reasoning necessary and sufficient to reach the disposition.

hourly fee A form of legal fees paid to an attorney based on the attorney's hourly rate and the time spent by the attorney.

human resources (personnel) department The department in an organization dealing with matters involving employees, such as hiring, training, labor relations, and benefits.

I

impleader The involuntary addition of a new party to the litigation; a party without whom all issues raised in the case could not be resolved.

implied authority The appearance of possessing the legal ability to make a legally binding contract on behalf of another.

***in personam* jurisdiction** A court's authority over a party personally.

***in rem* jurisdiction** A court's authority over claims affecting property.

incidental or nominal damages Damages resulting from the breach that are related to the breach but not necessarily directly foreseeable by the breaching party.

independent contractor A person who is engaged to perform a specific task that is within their specialized expertise without the supervision of the person who engaged them.

indictment A written list of charges issued by a grand jury against a defendant in a criminal case. Also known as a **presentment.**

informal discovery Obtaining information about the opposition's case through means other than the procedural rules of discovery.

informed consent A legal condition whereby a person can be said to have given consent based on an appreciation and understanding of the facts and implications of an action.

infringement An act that interferes with an exclusive right.

initial consultation The first meeting with a prospective client in which information will be gathered, additional information requested, and the attorney–client relationship formed.

injunctive relief Court order to cease or commence an action following a petition to enter such an order upon showing of irreparable harm resulting from the failure to enforce the relief requested.

insanity defense A defendant's claim that he or she was insane when the crime was committed, even if temporarily insane. Often referred to as the M'Naghten Rule.

insurance law A specialty legal practice surrounding insurance, including insurance policies and claims.

intake form A form developed to solicit basic, case-specific information from a client during an initial consultation and at various stages afterward.

intangible personal property Personal property that has no physical presence but is represented by a certificate or some other instrument, such as stocks or trademarks.

intermediate appellate court A mid-level appellate court that reviews the decision of a lower court when a losing party files for an appeal. Further review to the highest court is often discretionary.

internship Any official or formal program to provide practical experience for beginners in an occupation or profession.

interrogatories A discovery tool in the form of a series of written questions that are answered by the party in writing, to be answered under oath.

intestate The state of having died without a will.

intestate succession State laws that direct who should inherit from a person who has died without a will.

J

JAG (Judge Advocate General's Corps) Legal professionals trained in U.S. military law who work in the military justice system.

joint tenant The shared ownership of property, giving the other owner the right of survivorship if one owner dies.

judgment The court's final decision regarding the rights and claims of the parties.

judicial notice A request that a court accept evidence as fact without the necessity of further proof.

judicial review Availability or power of a court to review the actions of another branch of government, such as an administrative agency.

jurisdiction The power or authority of the court to hear a particular classification of case. Also, the place or court that may hear a case, based on subject matter and/or geographic area.

jurisdictional statement Section of the brief or a complaint that identifies the legal authority that grants the appellate court the right to hear the case.

jurisprudence The science or philosophy of law.

jury trial Case is decided by a jury.

Justinian Code Written laws compiled during the reign of the Roman Emperor Justinian (483–565 ad), including a constitution and statutes that stand as models of laws for later civilizations.

K

KeyCite The Westlaw case updating and validation system, which is similar to Shepard's Citations System.

L

law clerk A term formerly used to refer to a paralegal.

law reviews Periodicals edited by the top students at each law school, featuring scholarly articles by leading authorities and notes on various topics written by the law students themselves.

lawyer Also known as an attorney, a person who is licensed by a state to engage in the practice of law.

lay witness Any witness not testifying as an expert witness and who may not testify as to conclusions or opinions.

leading questions Questions that suggest the answer.

lease A voluntary transfer of possession in property by the owner for a money or other valuable consideration.

legal assistant Also known as a paralegal, a nonlawyer who performs substantive legal work under the supervision of a licensed attorney.

legal encyclopedia A multivolume compilation that provides in-depth coverage of almost every area of the law.

legal memorandum Summary of the case facts, the legal question asked, the research findings, the analysis, and the legal conclusion drawn from the law applied to the case facts.

legal nurse consultant A licensed, registered nurse with specialized training as a paralegal.

legal specialists A paralegal working within the military legal system assisting judges, Army lawyers and unit commanders with legal matters and judicial work.

legal technician A nonlawyer who performs legal services, in some cases, to the public if permitted by law and which would otherwise constitute the unauthorized practice of law.

letter of administration An order issued by a probate court appointing an administrator to an intestate estate and ordering the estate's distribution by the laws of intestate succession.

letter testamentary An order issued by a probate court approving the validity of a decedent's will and authorizing the estate's distribution according to the terms of the will.

LexisNexis Commercial electronic law database service.

liability A jury's or judge's determination that one party is responsible for injuries to another party; the basis for an award of damages.

license Permission from a governmental unit to an individual authorizing her to engage in a regulated activity.

licensing agreement An agreement in which an owner of intangible property transfers the rights of use to another party for a fee or other valuable consideration.

limited liability company A hybrid business formed under state acts, representing both corporation and partnership characteristics.

limited liability partnership A type of partnership recognized in a majority of states that protects a partner from personal liability for negligent acts committed by other partners or by employees not under his or her direct control. Many states restrict this type partnership to professionals, such as lawyers, accountants, architects, and healthcare providers.

liquidated damages An amount of money agreed upon in the original contract as a reasonable estimation of the damages to be recovered by the nonbreaching party. This amount is set forth in the contract so the parties have a clear idea of the risk of breach.

litigant A party to a lawsuit.

living will A legal instrument that expresses the wishes of the person making it for health care decisions.

M

majority opinion An opinion where more than half of the justices agree with the decision. This opinion is precedent.

malpractice Negligence committed by professionals in the course of their professional duties for which they may be civilly liable.

marital estates (marital property) The property accumulated by a couple during marriage, called community property in some states.

marriage A union between a man and a woman (except in Massachusetts).

marshal The act of reducing testamentary gifts provided by a will.

mens rea "A guilty mind"; criminal intent in committing the act.

mentoring program A workplace support relationship in which a senior professional mentors a newly hired professional.

mirror image rule A requirement that the acceptance of an offer must exactly match the terms of the original offer.

misdemeanor A lesser crime punishable by less than a year in jail and/or a fine.

mistake in fact An error in assessing the facts, causing a defendant to act in a certain way.

morality A value system for determining good and bad behavior.

motion A procedural request or application presented by the attorney in court.

motion in limine A request that certain evidence not be raised at trial, as it is arguably prejudicial, irrelevant, or legally inadmissible evidence.

motion to dismiss A motion that dispenses with the lawsuit because of a legal defense.

mutual assent Concurrence by both parties to all terms.

N

National Association of Legal Assistants (NALA) A legal professional group that lends support and continuing education for legal assistants.

National Federation of Paralegal Association (NFPA) National paralegal professional association providing professional career information, support, and information on unauthorized practice of the law.

negligence The failure to use reasonable care to avoid harm to another person or to do that which a reasonable person might do in similar circumstances.

networking The process of actively seeking associations and friendships for the purpose of establishing a supportive system of sharing information, particularly in job seeking.

nonprobate property Property of the decedent that avoids the probate process due to the nature of its ownership or contractual arrangements previously made by the decedent.

notice pleading A short and plain statement of the allegations in a lawsuit.

O

offer A promise made by the offeror to do (or not to do) something provided that the offeree, by accepting, promises or does something in exchange.

offeree The person to whom the offer is made.

offeror The person making the offer to another party.

official reporters Government publications of court decisions (for example, 325 Ill.3d 50).

open-ended questions Questions that encourage a full meaningful answer involving the person's knowledge and feelings.

opening statement An initial statement by a party's attorney explaining what the case is about and what that party's side expects to prove during the trial.

operation of law A right or liability created for a party, irrespective of the intent of that party, because it is dictated by existing legal principles.

P

paralegal A trained and educated legal professional who performs substantive work under the supervision and responsibility of an attorney.

paralegal education Formal education at a school—often a college or university—offering courses in the paralegal profession and substantive law and conferring an associates degree, bachelor's degree, or a certificate.

paraphrasing A technique used for interviews in which the interviewer repeats the information in his or her own words to ensure the accuracy of the information received.

parole Release under court supervision from jail, prison, or other confinement after having served part of a criminal sentence.

parole officer An official of the criminal justice system who supervises parolees who are released from confinement.

peremptory challenge (peremptory jury strike) An attorney's elimination of a prospective juror without giving a reason; limited to a specific number of strikes.

personal jurisdiction A court's power over the individuals involved in the case; when a court has personal jurisdiction, it can compel attendance at court hearings and enter judgments against the parties.

personal property Movable or intangible thing not attached to real property.

personal recognizance Permission to remain free of custody pending criminal proceedings.

persuasive authority A source of law or legal authority that is not binding on the court in deciding a case but may be used by the court for guidance, such as law review articles; all nonmandatory primary authority.

petition A formal written application requesting a court for a specific judicial action.

petitioner Name designation of a party filing an appeal or a petition.

plaintiff The party initiating legal action.

plurality opinion A rare disposition in which a greater number but less than a majority votes on the outcome of a case.

pocket parts Annual supplements to digests.

police powers The legal authority granted to governments to provide for the health, safety, welfare, and morals of society.

possession Having or holding property in one's power; controlling something to the exclusion of others.

practice area That part of the law in which a legal professional practices as a specialty or concentration.

practice manuals Published or in-house guides to practice in certain areas, often part of a continuing legal education topic.

precedent The holding of past court decisions that are followed in future judicial cases where similar facts and legal issues are present.

preempt Right of the federal government to exclusive governance in matters concerning all citizens equally.

preferred stock Corporate ownership that is paid a dividend first and does not have the right to vote on corporate decisions.

prenuptial agreement An agreement made by parties before marriage that controls certain aspects of the relationship, such as management and ownership of property.

preponderance of the evidence The weight or level of persuasion of evidence needed to find the defendant liable as alleged by the plaintiff in a civil matter.

presentencing report An official postconviction report of a convict's background and resources and the details of the criminal offense committed, written by the probation department for court use in determining a sentence.

pretrial conference The meeting between the parties and the judge to identify legal issues, stipulate to uncontested matters, and encourage settlement.

pretrial probation A pretrial disposition of a criminal matter, agreed to by both parties, that provides for a brief period of probation.

prima facie (Latin) "At first sight." A case with the required proof of elements in a tort cause of action; the elements of the plaintiff's (or prosecutor's) cause of action; what the plaintiff must prove; accepted on its face, but not indisputable.

primary authority The original text of the sources of law, such as constitutions, court opinions, statutes, and administrative rules and regulations.

principal A person or entity who authorizes, by agreement or other means, another (agent) to act on behalf of the principal in a way that binds the principal in contract or tort.

prioritization The act of listing or dealing with matters in their order of importance.

privileged information Information protected by law due to a special relationship, such as attorney–client.

privity A relationship between the parties to the contract who have rights and obligations to each other through the terms of the agreement.

pro bono Legal representation performed voluntarily for free.

probable cause The totality of circumstances that leads one to believe certain facts or circumstances exist; applies to arrests, searches, and seizures; and the commission of a crime.

probate The court process of determining will validity, settling estate debts, and distributing assets.

Probate Court The court empowered to settle estates for those individuals who have died with or without a will.

probation A court-imposed criminal sentence that, subject to stated conditions, releases a convicted person into the community instead of sending the criminal to prison.

probation officer An officer of the criminal justice system who supervises a person on probation.

procedural law The set of rules that are used to enforce the substantive law.

profession A learned occupation that abides by an ethical code or rules.

professionalism Performing duties as a professional ethically and efficiently.

property law Rights a person may own or be entitled to own, including personal and real property.

prosecution Attorney representing the people or plaintiff in criminal matters.

prosecutor Attorney representing the people or plaintiff in criminal matters.

prosecutorial discretion The legal authority granted to prosecutors to decide whether to bring criminal proceedings.

protective order A court order that protects a party's information from discovery due to the existence of a privilege or other legal basis.

punitive damages An amount of money awarded to a nonbreaching party that is not based on the actual losses incurred by that party, but as a punishment to the breaching party for the commission of an intentional wrong.

R

rationale Stated reasoning by a court's ruling.

real evidence Evidence in the form of objects involved in a case or that actually played a part in the incident or transaction in question, such as a weapon.

real property Land and all property permanently attached to it, such as buildings.

rebuttal Refutes or contradicts evidence presented by the opposing side.

recross examination A subsequent opportunity for an attorney to question by cross-examination a hostile witness.

redirect examination The attorney who originally called the witness asks more questions.

reformation An order of the court that "rewrites" the agreement to reflect the actual performances of the parties where there has been some deviation from the contractual obligation; changed or modified by agreement; that is, the contracting parties mutually agree to restructure a material element of the original agreement.

regional reporters Reporters that contain the cases of all the states in a particular geographical area.

registered agent A business or individual designated to receive service of process when a business entity is a party in a legal action such as a lawsuit or summons.

registration Recognition conferred upon an individual by a private organization or governmental entity.

regulation The government oversight and enforcement of an area to protect the public.

relevant evidence Evidence that makes the existence of any fact more probable or less probable than it would be without the evidence.

relief An interim or final court order in favor of the party requesting it.

remand Disposition in which the appellate court sends the case back to the lower court for further action.

remedy The means by which a court, in the exercise of civil law jurisdiction, enforces a right, imposes a penalty, or makes some other court order.

reporters Hardbound volumes containing judicial decisions.

request for admissions (request to admit) A document that provides the drafter with the opportunity to conclusively establish selected facts prior to trial.

request for examination Form of discovery that requests an examination (including medical) of an opposing party in a lawsuit.

request for production of documents (request to produce) A discovery device that requests the production of certain items, such as photographs, papers, reports, and physical evidence; must specify the document sought.

rescission A decision by the court that renders the contract null and void and requires the parties to return to the wronged party any benefits received under the agreement.

rescission and restitution A decision by the court that renders the contract null and void and requires the parties to return to the wronged party any benefits received under the agreement.

residuary clause A will clause that makes a testamentary gift of the remaining property of an estate after expenses and specific gifts have been satisfied.

respondent Name designation of the party responding to an appeal.

Restatement A recitation of the common law in a particular legal subject; a series of volumes authored by the American Law Institute that tell what the law in a general area is, how it is changing, and what direction the authors think this change is headed in.

résumé A brief, written account of personal, educational, and professional qualifications and experience, prepared by a job applicant.

retain To hire a legal professional.

reverse Disposition in which the appellate court disagrees with the trial court.

S

sanctions Penalty against a party in the form of an order to compel, a monetary fine, a contempt-of-court citation, or a court order with specific description of the individualized remedy.

scienter A degree of knowledge that makes a person legally responsible for his or her act or omission.

scope of authority Performance of duties that were expressly or implicitly assigned to the agent by the principal.

search warrant Issued after presentation of an affidavit stating clearly the probable cause on which the request is based. In particular, it is an order in writing, issued by a justice or other magistrate, in the name of the state, and directed to a sheriff, constable, or other officer authorizing him to search for and seize any property that constitutes evidence of the commission of a crime, contraband, or the fruits of the crime.

secondary authority Authority that analyzes the law such as a treatise, encyclopedia, or law review article.

self-assessment An initial step of the career planning process that involves gathering information about yourself to make an informed career decision.

self-esteem A realistic respect for or favorable impression of oneself; self-respect.

self-incrimination Acts or declarations either as testimony at trial or prior to trial by which one implicates himself or herself in a crime.

sentencing guidelines A group of laws that establish guidelines for judges to use in determining the appropriate sentence in a criminal matter.

separate property One spouse is the exclusive owner.

session laws The second format in which new statutes appear as a compilation of the slip laws; a bill or joint resolution that has become law during a particular session of the legislature.

settlor A person who creates a trust.

shareholder The owner of one or more shares of stock in a corporation.

Shepard's Citations Reference system that reports the legal authority referring to the legal position of the case and making reference to the case opinion.

shepardizing (shepardize) Using Shepard's verification and updating system for cases, statutes, and other legal resources.

slip law The first format in which a newly signed statute appears; a copy of a particular law passed during a session of legislature.

slip opinon The first format in which a judicial opinion appears.

sole proprietorship A business owned by one person.

special damages Those damages incurred beyond and in addition to the general damages suffered and expected in similar cases.

specific performance A court order that requires a party to perform a certain act in order to prevent harm to the requesting party.

statute Written law enacted by the legislative branches of both federal and state governments.

Statute of Frauds Rule that specifies which contracts must be in writing to be enforceable.

stock A representation of ownership in a corporation.

stress management The practice of identifying the causes of stress, reducing its effects, and relieving existing stress brought on by the workplace.

subject matter jurisdiction A court's authority over the res, the subject of the case.

subpoena A document that is served upon an individual under authority of the court, and orders the person to appear at a certain place and certain time for a deposition, or suffer the consequences; an order issued by the court clerk directing a person to appear in court.

subpoena duces tecum A type of subpoena that requests a witness to produce a document.

substantive law Legal rules that are the content or substance of the law, defining rights and duties of citizens.

summary judgment The disposition of a lawsuit before trial when there are no genuine issues of fact and the party requesting it is entitled to judgment as a matter of law.

summons The notice to appear in court, notifying the defendant of the plaintiff's complaint.

support Periodic payments extending over time.

Supremacy Clause Sets forth the principle and unambiguously reinforces that the Constitution is the supreme law of the land.

synopsis or highlights A part of a résumé following the career objective that summarizes the applicant's qualifications.

T

tangible evidence Evidence that can be touched, picked up.

tax lien A legal claim placed on real estate by a governmental authority that is owed money for unpaid property taxes.

temporary restraining order (TRO) A court order barring a person from harassing or harming another.

tenancy by the entirety A form of ownership for married couples, similar to joint tenancy, where the spouse has right of survivorship.

tenant in common A form of ownership between two or more people where each owner's interest upon death goes to his or her heirs.

testamentary gift A gift made through the will of a decedent.

testate The state of having died with a valid will.

testator/testatrix The person who writes a will.

testimonial evidence Oral statements made by a witness under oath.

theft The taking of property without the owner's consent.

third-party beneficiary A person, not a party to the contract, who stands to receive the benefit of performance of the contract.

third-party claim A suit filed by the defendant against a party not originally named in the plaintiff's complaint.

tickler file System of tracking dates and reminding what is due on any given day or in any given week, month, or year.

time management The practice of systematic, priority-based structuring of time allocation and distribution among competing demands.

time slip An office form used to keep track of billable hours performed by legal professionals.

title The legal link between a person who owns property and the property itself; legal evidence of a person's ownership rights.

title examiner A law-trained person who researches the title to property for any encumbrances and imperfections.

title search A search of the abstract of title; the short history of a piece of property including ownership interests and liens.

to-do list A form of time management involving listing tasks in order of importance as reminders of goals for the workday.

tort A civil wrongful act, committed against a person or property, either intentional or negligent.

tortfeasor Act of committing the wrong, whether intentional, negligent, or strict liability.

tortious A private civil wrong committed by one person against another that the law considers to be deserving of a remedy.

trade secret Property that is protected from misappropriation such as formulas, patterns, and compilations of information.

training A form of instruction in the use of skills and the practical application of theory and principles received through education.

transactional practice A specialized legal practice, usually in business, involving the transfer of rights and obligations.

transcript Written account of a trial court proceeding or deposition.

treatise A scholarly study of one area of the law.

trespass Intentional and unlawful entry onto or interference with the land of another person without consent.

trial The forum for the presenting of evidence and testimony and the deliberation of liability in civil cases or guilt in criminal cases.

trial court Courts that hear all cases and are courts of general jurisdiction.

trier of facts Jury.

trust An agreement for the care and maintenance of assets by a designated person for the benefit of another or others; often used in place of a will.

trustee A person or entity designated to care for and maintain the property placed into a trust and to follow the terms of the trust.

U

ultra vires A legal principle literally meaning "beyond the power" that holds certain transactions or acts of an agent of a corporation as unauthorized and void.

unauthorized practice of law (UPL) Practicing law without proper authorization to do so.

under advisement The judge's determination of a matter to be made at a later time.

undue influence Using a close personal or fiduciary relationship to one's advantage to gain assent to terms that the party otherwise would not have agreed to.

Uniform Commercial Code (UCC) Model laws drafted by the National Conference of Commissioners for governing commercial transactions.

United States Attorney The prosecutor in charge of enforcing the federal criminal laws of the United States. A U.S. Attorney can also enforce selected federal civil statutes, such as the Civil Rights Act and antitrust laws.

unofficial reporters Private publications of court decisions (for example, 525 N.E.2d 90).

V

verdict Decision of the jury following presentation of facts and application of relevant law as they relate to the law presented in the jury instructions.

vicarious liability (*respondeat superior*) One person, or a third party, may be found liable for the act of another or shares liability with the actor.

void *ab initio* Marriages that are void from the inception.

void contract Agreement that does not meet the required elements and therefore is unenforceable under contract law.

voidable contract Apparently fully enforceable contract with a defect unknown by one party.

voidable marriage Valid in all legal respects until the union is dissolved by order of the court.

voir dire The process of selecting a jury for trial.

voluntary ethical codes Ethical rules or codes issued by a professional organization as a voluntary show of professional status.

vote of four By tradition, a vote by four Supreme Court Justices to grant certiorari, which means that the Court will hear a case.

W

ward A person, usually a minor, under the care of a court-appointed guardian.

warranty A promise or representation by the seller that the goods in question meet certain standards.

Westlaw Commercial electronic law database service.

will A document representing the formal declaration of a person's wishes for the manner and distribution of his or her property upon death.

work product An attorney's written notes, impressions, charts, diagrams, and other material used by him or her to prepare strategy and tactics for trial.

Index

A

AAfPE; *see* American Association for Paralegal Education (AAfPE)
Aakhus, Todd, 309
AAPI; *see* American Alliance of Paralegals, Inc. (AAPI)
ABA; *see* American Bar Association (ABA)
ABA approval, 8–9
Abandoned property, 193
Abatement, 88, 89
Abrogation of the common law, 61
"Absolute Rights of Individuals" (Blackstone), 58
Abstractors, paralegal opportunities with, 323–324
Abstracts, 324
Acceptance
 as contract element, 91, 229–231
 of a gift, 198
 in real estate sales, 192
Access to the courts, 146
Accused, rights of, 179–180
Acquittal, 180
Action, 63
Active listening, 263–264, 305–306
Actual (express) authority, 245
Actus reus, 171–173
Adams, John, 94
A Day in the Life of a Real Paralegal
 adjudicatory hearings, 141
 advertisements for contract law jobs, 243
 alternative dispute resolution (ADR), 76
 areas of responsibility, 211
 beginning of profession, 3
 colleges as employer, 323
 estate tracking, 211
 ethical conduct, 31
 Freedom of Information Act (FOIA) specialist, 273
 freelancing, 331
 immigration law, 325
 initial consultation, 82
 internships, 315
 legal writing, 134
 negligence teams of insurance companies, 186
 nontraditional positions, 22
 unauthorized practice of law (UPL), 37
 volunteering, leading to employment, 290
Adjudicatory body, 128
Adjudicatory hearings, 141, 324
Adjudicatory proceedings, 128
Administration (will), 206
Administrative agencies, 50, 127, 128
Administrative agency regulations and rules (administrative codes), 62–63
Administrator (will), 206
Admiralty, 66, 76
Admonition, 30
Adoption, 214, 216–217, 218
Adoptions for B.L.V.B. and E.L.V.B. (1993), 218
ADR; *see* Alternative dispute resolution (ADR)
Advance sheets, 114
Adverse (hostile) witness, 266
Advertisements
 for employment opportunities, 289
 not a contract, 229
 seeking paralegals for contract law jobs, 243
Advice and consent, 62
Affidavit, self-proving, 202–203
Affirm, 69
Affirmative defense, 85, 86, 147–148
Age
 contracts and, 91, 233
 of testator, 201–202
Agency, 244
Agency by estoppel, 245
Agency law
 authority, scope of (types), 245, 246
 independent contractors and, 244–245
 parties in, 244
 vicarious liability and, 244
Agent, 244, 271
Age of majority, 233
Airspace above land, 189
Alabama, 142, 213
Alaska, 60, 142, 213
Alibi, 84, 174
Alimony, 214
Alternative dispute resolution (ADR), 76, 77
ALWD (Association of Legal Writing Directors) method, of statute citation, 122
Amendments, to United States Constitution, 60; *see also individual Amendments*
American Alliance of Paralegals, Inc. (AAPI), 21, 32
American Association for Paralegal Education (AAfPE), 12–13, 20, 21
American Bar Association (ABA), 4, 156
 Canons of Professional Ethics (1908), 16, 28, 29
 Commission on Multidisciplinary Practice (1998), 34, 36
 credibility of, 28
 defined, 31
 diligence and competence, duty of, 52
 dominance of lawyers over paralegal profession, 9
 ethical concerns summary, 51
 guidance to states in regulation of legal profession, 28
 Guideline 3: parameters for working paralegal, 50–51
 Guideline 6: client confidentiality, 38
 independent paralegals, 330
 Model Code of Professional Conduct (1969), 16
 Model Guidelines for the Utilization of Paralegal Services, 34
 Model Rules of Professional Conduct, 16, 28, 29
 1.3: conflicts of interest, 43–47
 1.6: client confidentiality, 38–43
 3.7: attorney and paralegal prohibited from testifying, 269
 5.3: attorney obligations to nonattorney employees, 30–31
 5.4: sharing fees with nonlawyer, 33–34
 5.5: unauthorized practice of law, 47–51
 8.3: duty to report, 52
 modern language usage, 28–29
 not applicable to paralegals, 30
 paralegal definition, 12, 317–318, 325
 practice of law, defining, 141
 recognition of paralegals, 5
 Special Committee on Lay Assistants for Lawyers, 5
 Standing Committee on Paralegals, 6, 8–9
 Uniform Commercial Code (UCC) and, 227
 unintended results, 36
American Digest System, 115
American Jurisprudence, 116
American law, sources of, 58–59
American Law Institute, 117, 173, 227
American Law Reports, 116
American Library Association, 27
Americans with Disabilities Act (ADA), 66
Amicus National Association of Legal Assistants, 279
Anglo-American jurisprudence, 59
Annotations, 122, 124
Annual laws, 121
Annulment, 212–213
Answer, 147–148, 150–151
Ante-nuptial agreement, 216
Anti-Eviction Act (New Jersey), 123
Antitrust, 66
Anti-workplace bullying legislation, 308
Aphorisms, 240
Apparent authority, 245
Appeasement, of difficult coworker, 308
Appellant, 67
Appellate brief, 68, 101
Appellate court, 67
Appellate jurisdiction, 70
Appellate review, 68
Appellee, 67
Application, job; *see* Job, applying for
Applied ethics
 client confidentiality, 38–43
 conflicts of interest, 43–47
 unauthorized practice of law (UPL), 47–51
Aristotle, 29
Arizona, 12, 213, 214
Arkansas, 213
Armed robbery, 169
Arrest, 179–180

Arson, 92, 169
Article I (legislative) courts, 67
Article III courts, 65, 67
Articles, of the U.S. Constitution; *see* United States Constitution
Artistic works, 193
Assault, 169
Assault and battery, 85–86
Assent, in contracts, 233–234
Asset rearrangement, 208–209
Assignment, 237–238
Associate's degree, 6–7, 8, 10
Assumpsit, 226
Assumption of risk, 186–187
"At the elbow" training, 316
Attorney, 4; *see also* Lawyer
Attorney–client privilege
  confidentiality and, 42–43
  defined, 265
  discovery and, 154
Attorney fees, 14–15, 278–280, 327
Attorney general, 63
Authority
  of agents, 245, 246
  binding (mandatory), 69
  legal, 82, 93–96
  persuasive, 69
  primary, 95, 96
  secondary, 95, 96
Authority by virtue of the agent's position, 245
Authorization letter, 265
Avoidance, of unpleasant coworker, 308

B

Bachelor of Laws (L.L.B.) degree, 4
Bachelor's degree, 7, 8, 10
Bail, 179
Bailment, 90
Bankruptcy Code, 10
Bar exam, 4–5
Bargained for exchange, 231
Bargaining, 231
Barrie, James Matthew, 193
Battered spouse syndrome, 175
Bench, 64
Bench trial, 157
Beneficiary, 203
Benefit-detriment theory, 231
Benefit of the bargain, 240
Bequest, 204
Best evidence rule, 162
Beyond a reasonable doubt, 84, 172, 177
Bilateral mistake, 234–235
Bill (legislative), 126
Billable time, 278, 302
Bill of Rights, 60, 168
Bills of attainder, 61, 171
Binder, 192
Binding (mandatory) authority, 69
Blackstone, William, 58–59, 98
Bluebook, 122
Boddie v. Connecticut (1971), 146
Body language, 261
Borelli, Linda, 230
Boutique law firms, 21, 209, 286
Bowman, Michael, 275–276
Bowman v. Doherty (1984), 274, 275–276
Boyd v. United States (1886), 178
Branches of government, as source of law, 60, 64; *see also individual branches*
Brandeis Brief, 121
Brandeis, Louis D., 121
Brando, Marlon, 301
Breach of contract, 89, 238–241
Breach of duty of care owed, 184
Breton, Margaret Mary, 75
Breton, Richard A., 75
Bribery, 169
Briefs, 68, 100–106, 121
Brockovich, Erin, 31
Brown v. Allen (1953), 71
Bullying, 308, 311
Burden of proof, 84, 93, 177
Bureau of National Affairs, Inc., Supreme Court decisions (U.S.L.W.), 114
Business organizations
  corporations, 248–251
  defined, 246
  generally, 245–246
  partnerships, 247–248
  sole proprietorships, 246–247
"But for" test, 184

C

Calendar and docket control system, 276
California
  community property laws, 214
  election and campaign finance reform, 72
  "legal document preparer" in, 12
  limited licensing for paralegals, 13
  regulation of paralegals in, 34–36
  same-sex marriage law, 213
  unauthorized practice of law (UPL) rulings, 326
California Department of Consumer Affairs, 35
California State Bar, 35
California Superior Court, 146
California Supreme Court, 40, 121–122
  Gibson v. Gibson (1971), 104–106, 117, 119
  Klein v. Klein (1962), 100, 105, 106
  Peters v. Peters (1909), 98, 99, 100, 119
  Self v. Self (1962), 98–100, 102, 105, 106, 111, 116–117, 119
Campbell Soup Co. v. Wentz (1948), 239
Canons of Professional Ethics (1908; ABA), 16
Capacity, 201
Caption, in complaint, 144
Cardozo, Benjamin, 179
Career objective, 292
Carter, Jimmy, 129
Case brief, 81, 100–106, 121
Case in Point
  attorney's fees awards and paralegals, 279–280
  Brandeis Brief, 121
  Case Summary
  Boddie v. Connecticut (1971), 146
  Florida Bar Association v. Stupica (1974), 140
  Hickman v. Taylor (1947), 155
  Mapp v. Ohio (1961), 178
  Marbury v. Madison (1803), 94
  M'Naghten's Case (1843), 175
  Mulrain v. Mulrain (1979), 148
  New York County Lawyers Association v. Dacey (1967), 140
  Sherwood v. Walker (1887; "pregnant-cow case"), 234
  Tarasoff v. Regents of the University of California (1974), 40
  Court Opinion
  Adoptions for B.L.V.B. and E.L.V.B. (1993), 218
  Campbell Soup Co. v. Wentz (1948), 239
  City of Chicago v. Jesus Morales (1999), 170
  Far West Modular Home Sales, Inc. v. Proaps (1979), 190
  Hammer v. Sidway, as Executor (1891), 232–233
  Lakewood Creative Costumers v. Sharp (1986), 241
  Meyer v. Mitnick (2001), 199
  Moore v. City of East Cleveland (1977), 172
  O'Brien v. O'Brien (1985), 217
  Palsgraf v. Long Island Railroad (1928), 185
  In re the Marriage Riddle (1993), 215
  Schreiber v. Olan Mills (1993), 230–231
  duty of confidentiality, 40
  evidence law considerations, 272
  freelancing as an independent paralegal, 328–329
  imputed disqualification, 45
  judicial notice, 163
  judicial review, 94
  Kestin Report (1999; New Jersey Supreme Court), 11
  lawyer malpractice, 275–276
  legalisms and Plain English, 132
  negligence, 185
  practice of law, defining, 141
  prenuptial agreement, 216
  punitive damages for outrageous conduct, 88
  sexual harassment, 309
  state court subject matter jurisdiction, 75
  status of persons entering private property, 125
  statute interpretation, 127
  statutes superseding judicial decision and common law, 123
  white-collar crimes, 169
Case law, 97
Case management, 274
Case management software, 44
Case reporters, 112–115
Catherine Self, Plaintiff and Appellant, v. Adrian Self, Defendant and Respondent (1962), 98–100; see also *Self v. Self* (1962)
Causation, 184
Cause of action, 86, 142, 145
Censure, 30
Central Pacific Supply Corporation, 75
Certificate, 7–8, 10
Certificate of service, 151
Certificate of Title, 193–194
Certification, 18–21
Certified Legal Assistant (CLA) designation (NALA), 18–19
Certified paralegal (CP) designation, 18
Certiorari, 70
Challenges for cause, 160
Chambers (judges'), 156
Champion, Linda, 141
Chancery Court, 203
Chase Manhattan Bank v. Josephson (1994), 123
Chattels, 90, 189, 190
Checklists, 317
Checks and balances, 60, 93
Children
  guardianships for, 217–219
  same-sex adoptions, 218
Child support, 214, 215
Chinese Wall, 45
Circuits, 67
Citation, of case, 101, 112–114

City of Chicago v. Jesus Morales (1999), 170, 171, 176
Civil action, 83, 86–89
Civil cases
consequences of, 86
criminal cases distinguished from, 83–84, 85
government as party to, 176
nature of, 86–89
parties in, 167
Civil law, 140, 142
contract law, 90–91
criminal law distinguished from, 83, 92
property law, 89–90
substantive subject areas, 89–92
torts, 91–92
Civil legal specialties; *see* Legal specialties
Civil litigation and procedure, 140
answer, 147–148, 150–151
complaint, 143–147, 149, 151
discovery, 152–155
duties of the paralegal, 158–161
evidence for paralegals, 161–164
prelitigation activities, 142
pretrial matters, 156–157
rules of procedure, 142–143
time line, 158
trial, 157–158
Civil procedure, 142
Civil Rights Act, 10
Civil union, 212, 213, 214
Claim for relief, 142, 145
Claims adjuster, 320
Clarity, in writing, 130
Clear and convincing evidence, 84
Client interview
authorization letters, 265
body language, 261
caution about, 256
conducting, 262–263
ending, 264–266
initial consultation, 257
intake forms, 257–259
legal professional's task during, 256
listening and active listening, 263–264
note organization following, 265–266
note-taking, 261–262
object of, 256, 262
paraphrasing, 262–263, 264
preparing for, 257–262
professional image/conduct, 257, 260
question types, 263
reviewing information, 260
traditional arrangement, 261
unwritten rules/guidelines, 256–257
Closed-ended questions, 263
Code of Ethics and Professional Responsibility (NALA), 32
Code of Federal Regulations (C.F.R.), 127
Codification, 117
Codified constitutions, 58–59
Codified statutes, 121
Collaborative law, 76
Collection cases, 15
Colleges, 6–7; *see also* Education
paralegal opportunities with, 322
as source of job leads, 288
Colorado, 142, 213, 326
Colorado Bar Ass'n v. Miles (1976), 326
Commentaries on the Laws of England (1765–1769; Blackstone), 58, 98
Comments/critique, in court opinion, 102
Commercial real estate, 191
Commission on Multidisciplinary Practice (1998; ABA), 34, 36
Common law, 28
changing, 126
contracts, 226
corporate crime, 169
court power under, 94
defined, 58
status of persons entering private property, 125
statutes and, 61
statutes superseding, 123
torts under, 182
wills, 200
written contracts, 236–237
Common stock, 249
Communication skills; *see also* Client interview; Witness interview
listening and active listening, 263–264, 305–306
oral, 305–306
written, 304–305
Communication Tip
avoiding synonyms in contracts, 233
careless use of legal terms, 191
client confidentiality, 39
correct use of shop-talk and jargon, 121
cultural differences, understanding protocol, 260–261
identifying oneself as paralegal, 13, 158
legal terms, understanding of, 65
listening and active listening, 305
mastering legal terminology, 86
plain English and clarity, 208, 321
professionalism in communication, 102
proofreading, 292
wills and confidentiality, 200
Communism, 188
Community property laws, 214
Company symbols/logos, 193
Comparative negligence, 187
Compensation, for harms, in negligence, 185
Compensatory damages, 87, 89
Competence
duty of, 52
of witness, 162
Complaint, in civil action, 143–147, 149, 151
Computer-assisted legal research (CALR), 119–120
Computers; *see* Technology
Concentration/major, in college study, 6–7
Concurrent conflicts of interest, 45–46
Concurrent ownership, 189
Concurring opinion, 70
Conditional gift, 198, 199
Confessions, to a priest, 163
Confidentiality
attorney-client privilege and, 42–43
of client interview, 260
Commission on Multidisciplinary Practice (1998; ABA) and, 34
defined, 32
duty of, among different professionals, 27
exceptions to, 39–42
maintaining, 38–43
NFPA rule, 32
Confidentiality notice, for e-mail and faxes, 39
Conflict checks, 44, 277
Conflicts of interest
Commission on Multidisciplinary Practice (1998; ABA) and, 34
ethics, professional conduct, and, 43–47
office management system and, 276–277
Confrontation Clause (Sixth Amendment), 181
Connecticut, 96, 213, 308
Consent, 39, 46
Conservatorship, 219, 221
Consideration (contract law), 91, 231–233
Constitution(s)
codified and uncodified, 58–59
defined, 59
as source of law, 95
state vs. federal, 82–83
Constitution, U.S.; *see* United States Constitution
Constructive delivery, 198
Constructive service, 147
Consultation, initial, 82
Consumer issues, contracts and, 235–236
Consumer rights, 66
Contempt of court, 152
Contingencies (property law), 192
Contingency fees, 15
Continuing legal education (CLE), 316
Contract law, 90–91
activities of legal professionals in, 242–243
historical background, 226–228
for the professional paralegal, 225–226
statutes of limitations and, 92
traditional, 228
Contract remedies, 89
Contract(s)
acceptance, 229–231
assignments and delegations, 237–138
benefit of the bargain, 240
breach of, 89
breach of contract, 238
consideration, 231–233
consumer issues, 235–236
defenses to lawsuit based on duress, 234
defined, 226
elements of, 228–233
fraud, 235
genuine assent in, 233–234
illegal, 235–237
incidental damages, 240
liquidated damages, 240–242
mistake, 234–235
offer, 228–229
oral, 236
parties to, 233–235
reformation, 238
remedies (enforcing), 242
remedies at law (damages)
rescission, 234, 238
specific performance, 238–241
Statute of Frauds, 236–237
terms and principles in, 242
third-party rights, 237–238
undue influence, 234
void and voidable, 233
written requirement, 236–237
Contributory negligence, 186
Cooperatives, 188
Copyrights, 193
Corporate veil, 248, 249
Corporations, 169, 248–251
Corpus Juris Secundum, 116
Counsel, right to, 181–182
Counselor, 4
Counterclaim, 151
Counteroffer, 229
Court advocacy, 157–158
Court of International Trade, 66–67, 68
Court opinions; *see also* Legal research
dicta in, 111
digests of, 115
dissecting, 97–100
function of, 96–97
impact of, 94–95
importance of, 111

Court opinions—*Cont.*
law of, finding and reading, 81–106
legal note taking (case brief; briefing), 100–106
legal reasoning/rationale in, 96
posted on Web sites, 157
reading, 96–97
as source of law, 93–94, 111
statutes distinguished from, 60
of Supreme Court, types, 70
unique position of, 93
unpublished, 115–116
vagueness of criminal laws, 170
Court procedure, 93
Court records, 67, 271
Courts; *see also* Article III courts; Federal court; State courts; United States; Constitution; United States Supreme Court
alternatives to, 76, 77
appellate, 67
family matters, 211–212
intermediate appellate, 67
Nuisance Night Courts, 73
superior, 73
trial, 64
United States courts of appeals, 67–69
Courts of limited jurisdiction, 65, 74
Courts of original jurisdiction, 64
Court system, 144
Cover letter, with job application, 294–295
Cover sheet, for complaint, 145
Coworkers, difficult, 306–309
Crane, Phyllis, 22
Credentials, education for, 8
Credit cards, 227
Creditors, seizure of property by, 191
Crime(s)
civil wrongs distinguished from, 86
classifications of, 169
defenses to, 173–176
defined, 86, 169
government investigation of, 176–179
quality of life, 73
torts and, 175–176, 182–183
types, 84–86
voluntary element, 173
white-collar, 169
Criminal cases
civil cases distinguished from, 83–84, 85
consequences of, 86
government as party to, 176
parties in, 168
Criminal discovery, 181
Criminalize, 169
Criminal justice, 168
Criminal law, 142, 168, 170
civil law distinguished from, 83, 92
paralegal opportunities in, 318–319
procedural rules in, 93
Criminal procedure, 168
constitutional considerations during a criminal proceeding, 180–182
defined, 176
Fourth Amendment and, 176–177
government investigation of a crime, 176–179
rights of the accused, 179–180
U.S. Constitution and, 176
Criminal proceedings
constitutional considerations during, 180–182
punishments in, 175
Criminal statutes, 171–173
Critical legal studies (CLS), 57
Cross-claims, 151
Cross-examination, 160, 181
Cruzan v. Missouri Dept. of Health (1990), 209
Cultum v. Heritage House Realtors (1985), 326
Cultural differences, understanding protocol, 260–261
Cumulative preferred stock, 249
Custodial interrogation, 179–180
Custody, 214, 215
Czarnecki, Donald, 331

D

Dacey, Norman F., 140, 325–326
Damages; *see also* Relief; Remedy
in contract lawsuits, 240–242
defined, 86
incidental, 240
liquidated, 240–242
types, 87, 89
DBA (doing business as), 247
Deadlines, 302
Decedent, 199
Decennial digests, 115
Decision-making entity, 128
Declaration of Independence, 56
Deed, 190
Defamation cases, 185
Default judgment, 151
Defendant, 64, 83, 147–148, 150–151; *see also* Defense
Defense
affirmative, 85, 86, 147–148
to contract lawsuit, 234–235, 242
to crimes, 173–176
defined, 85
insanity as, 85, 174, 175
to negligence, 186–187
self-defense, 41, 85, 148, 175
Defense of Marriage Act, 212
Delaware, 69, 213
Delegation, third parties to a contract and, 237–238
Delegation of tasks, 15
Delivery
of complaint and summons, 146
of a gift, 198
Demand letter, 142
Demonstrative evidence, 269
Demurrer, 106, 151
Department of Homeland Security, 62
Deponent, 152
Deportation (removal) hearing, 63
Deposit, 192
Depositions, 152, 273
Derogation of the common law, 61
Descent; *see* Wills
Devise, 204
Dictum, 111
Digest, 115
Digital (electronic) evidence, 268
Diligence, duty of, 52
Directed verdict, 161
Direct evidence, 162
Direct examination, 160
Disbarment, 29, 30
Disciplinary action, against licensed professionals, 29–30
Disclosure, of confidential information, 39–42
Discovery, 181, 273
court supervision and enforcement of, 153–154
defined, 152
in the electronic age, 154–155
informal, 267
protected information not subject to, 154
subpoena and, 152
types, 152–153
Discretion
prosecutorial, 63, 180
of trial court, 161
Discrimination, workplace, 309
Dismissed with prejudice (lawsuit), 143
Dispute resolution entity, 128
Dissenting opinion, 70
Dissolution of civil union, 214
District attorney, 168
District of Columbia, 213
District of Columbia Bar, 45
District of Columbia Circuit, 67–68
Diversity, as indicator of workplace atmosphere, 310
Diversity jurisdiction, 65–66
Dividends, 249
Divine right, 56, 57
Divorce, 213
Divorce court, 74
Dixon, Vanessa, 88
Docket entry sheet, 277
Docket number, 144
Documentary evidence, 268
Doe v. A Corp. (1983), 42
Doherty, Harold, 275–276
Domestic partnership, 212, 214
Domestic relations; *see* Family law
Donative intent, 198
Donee, 197
Donor, 197
Donovan, Martha, 22
Dormancy period (escheated property), 200
Double jeopardy, 180
Double taxation, of corporations, 250
Douglas, Michael, 216
Drafting of legal documents, as litigation paralegal duty, 160
Drew, Daniel, 249
Drug offenses, 169
Due care, 91
Due process
defined, 74
family living patterns and, 172
as limitation on statutes, 171
notice of lawsuit required by, 74–75
notification of lawsuit, 147
Durable power of attorney, 219–221
Duress, 174, 234
Duty, 184
Duty of care, 184
Duty to report, 39, 52

E

Earnings, of paralegals, 298, 331–333
Easement, 191
Economic partnership theory, 217
Economic torts, 183
e-discovery, 155
Education
AAfPE and, 12–13
ABA involvement in, 8–9
associate's degree, 6–7, 10
Bachelor of Laws (L.L.B.) degree, 4
bachelor's degree, 4, 7, 10
certificates, 7–8, 10
four-year colleges, 7
juris doctor (J.D.) degree, 4

for lawyers, 4
maintaining competency through, 17
paths of, and where they lead (figure), 8
training distinguished from, 315
two-year colleges, 6–7
Ejectment, 87, 89
Elective share, 204, 206
Electronic (digital) evidence, 268
Element(s)
of civil cases, 86
of contract, 91, 228–233
of a crime, 171–173
of criminal cases, 84–85
defined, 84–85
of negligence, 184–185
Embezzlement, 169
Eminent domain, 191
Employees
in agency law, 244–245, 246
of sole proprietorship, 247
Employer/employee, as agency situation, 244
Employment agencies, 288
Employment opportunities; *see also* Education; Job, applying for; Workplace types
colleges and universities, 322
in criminal justice area, 168
criminal law, 318–319
estate planning, 210–211
future of, 9–10
government agencies, federal and state, 324
health care, 320–321
in-house corporate counsel, 321–322
insurance, 320
location and, 8
military, 321
parole and probation officers, 318–319
sources of job leads, 287–289
title examiners and abstractors, 323–324
Enabling acts, 127
Engagement ring, as conditional gift, 198, 199
English rule, 14
Enron, 169, 249
Entrapment, 174
Entrepreneurial paralegals, 329–330
Environmental Protection Agency (EPA), 62–63
Equal Access to Justice Act, 10
Equitable division of property, 214, 217
Equitable maxims, 240
Equitable relief, 87, 88
Error, prejudicial and reversible, 69
Escheats, 200, 201
Escrow, 192
Espionage, 169
Essex County Paralegals, Inc., 331
Estate, 200
Estate planning
asset rearrangement, 208–209
as career, 210–211
defined, 207
living will, 209–210
trusts, 207–208
Ethical codes, 29
Ethical rules, 29
Ethics, 138–139; *see also* Professional conduct
defined, 27
history of, 28–29
for legal professionals, 29
licensure and, 32–37
morality distinguished from, 40–41
Multi-Disciplinary Practice and, 33–34
for paralegals, 30–32, 37
rules of professional conduct and, 27–32
voluntary ethical codes, 32
Evidence
in civil and criminal cases, 84
in civil litigation, 161–164
investigations and, 272
types, 268–269
Evidentiary rules, 163
Examination, in trial, 160–161
Exclusionary rule, 178–179
Executive branch, U.S. Constitution and, 61–63
Executive Office for Immigration Review, 63
Executive orders, 63
Executor, 203
Exemplary damages, 87, 89
Expert witnesses, 266
Ex post facto laws, 61, 171
Express (actual) authority, 245
Express warranties, 236
External purposes, of legal materials, 128
Extortion, 169
Eye contact, 260
Eye on Ethics
attorney-client relationship, 265
avoiding frivolous actions in court, 159
confidentiality, duty of, 27
duty to stay current with changes, 61
good faith argument to modify, extend, or abandon existing law, 95
hiding of profits and possessions, 248
identifying oneself as paralegal, 269
impropriety of gifts to legal professional, 204
independent paralegals, 330
knowingly making false statements in papers filed with a court, 145
maintaining competency through education and training, 17
résumé, honesty in, 291
shepardizing, 119
unauthorized practice of law (UPL), 5, 139, 174
witnesses, 266

F

Facts, of a case, 101
Fair Credit Reporting Act, 66
Fair notice requirement, 170
Family court, 74, 211–212
Family immunity, 106
Family law; *see also* Legal specialties, family matters
adoption, 214, 216–217, 218
conservatorship, 219, 221
courts, 211–212
defined, 211
"family" arrangements, 211
guardianships, 217–219
intake form for, 257
living patterns and due process, 172
marriage, 212–214
support obligations, 214, 215
Faretta v. California (1975), 50
Far West Modular Home Sales, Inc. v. Proaps (1979), 190
Federal Circuit, 68
Federal circuit courts of appeals, 114–115
Federal Communications Commission (FCC), 62, 324
Federal court, 143; *see also* Federal Rules of Civil Procedure (FRCP); United States Constitution
flowchart of system, 71
jurisdiction for, 65
life-tenured judges, 65
opinions, publication of, 114–115
search warrant (example), 177
specialized, 66–67
subject matter jurisdiction, 74
Federal district (trial) courts, 64, 65, 114–115; *see also* Article III courts
Federal judicial system, 64
Federal law, 60, 82–83, 129
Federal Practice Digest, 115
Federal question jurisdiction, 66
Federal regulations, 127
Federal Reporter, 114
Federal Rules of Civil Procedure (FRCP)
attorney signature on complaint, 145
defined, 143
e-discovery and, 155
importance of, 93
judicial notice and, 163
Federal Sentencing Commission, 319
Federal statutes, publications of, 122–124
Federal Supplement, 114–115
Federal system, 59; *see also* United States Constitution
Federal Trade commission (FTC), 62
Fees
attorney's, 14–15, 278–280, 327
contingency, 15
fixed/flat, 15
hourly, 15
lawyer prohibited from sharing with nonlawyer, 33–34
paralegals' impact on, 14–15
Felony, 84, 92, 169
Feudal laws, 28
Fictitious name, 247
Fiduciary, 207–208, 276–277
Field investigation, 267
Fifth Amendment
double jeopardy prohibited, 180
due process clause, 74–75, 147, 171
privilege against self-incrimination, 93, 179–180
File management, 277–278
File memo, 274
Files, confidentiality of, 38–39
Filing, of a complaint, 145–147
Filing fee, 145–146
Findings and Facts (NALA), 17
"First bite free" rule, 132–133
Fixed fees, 15
Fixtures, 90, 189, 190
Flat fees, 15
Florida, 213, 326
Florida Bar Association, 37
Florida Bar Association v. Stupica (1974), 140
Florida Bar re Advisory Opinion—Non-lawyer Preparation of Pension Plans (1990), 326
Florida Bar v. Brumbaugh (1978), 326
Florida Supreme Court, 37
Food and Drug Administration (FDA), 62
Foreclosure, 191
Forensics, 269
Formbooks, 118
Form practice, 286
Forum, 64, 143
Fourteenth Amendment, due process clause, 74–75, 171, 172
Fourth Amendment, search and seizure/warrants, 93, 176–177
Fraud, 169, 235
FRCP; *see* Federal Rules of Civil Procedure (FRCP)
Free and clear, 132

Freedom of Information Act (FOIA), 267, 271
Freehold estates, 191
Freelance paralegals, 325–330
Friedman, David D., 226
Frivolous actions, 159
Fullerton v. Conan (1948), 127
Full faith and credit clause, 212
"Fundamental Laws of English Rights" (Blackstone), 58
Furman, Rosemary, 37, 48

G

General damages, 87, 89
General jurisdiction, 73
General power of attorney, 221
Genuine assent, in contracts, 233–234
Geographical jurisdiction, 75–76
Geographic boundaries, of United States courts of appeals and district courts, 68
Georgia, 71–72, 213
Gibson v. Gibson (1971), 104–106
Gideon v. Wainwright (1963), 181–182
Gifts
  conflict of interest and, 46–47
  inter vivos, 201, 228
  law of, 197–199
  testamentary, 201, 204, 206
"Giving legal advice," 139
Global firms, Multi-Disciplinary Practices and, 33–34
Goodridge v. Dept. of Public Health (2003), 212
Government, limitations on power to criminalize, 169, 171
Government agencies
  confidentiality disclosure and, 42
  paralegal opportunities in, 324
  as source of job leads, 289
Government business records, for locating witnesses/people, 271
Government legal offices/agencies, as workplace, 21–22
Graham, Robert, 37
Grammar checking, 305
Grand jury, 180
Grantee, 190
Grantor, 190
Guam, 67
Guardian, 217
Guardian *ad litem*, 218–219
Guardianship of the estate, 219
Guardianships, 217–219
Guilty verdicts, punishment following, 84
Guttenberg Savings & Loan Ass'n v. Rivera (1981), 123

H

Habeas corpus, 64
Hadley v. Baxendale (1854), 240
Hammer v. Sidway, as Executor (1891), 232–233, 236
Harlan, John Marshall, 99
Harm
  in negligence, 184–185
  types, 169
Hawaii, 60
  land court, 74, 75
  Reciprocal Beneficiary Relationship, 212
  same-sex marriage law, 213
Hawaii Reports, 113–114
Headhunters, 288
Health care, paralegal opportunities in, 320–321
Hearsay rule, 161–162
Heirs, 201
Henry II (1154–89), 28
Hickman v. Taylor (1947), 155
Highlights section, on résumé, 292
Holding
  in court opinions, 102
  defined, 97
  dictum distinguished from, 111
Hostile (adverse) witness, 266
Hostile work environment, 309
Hourly fees, 15
Housing court, 74
How to Avoid Probate (Dacey), 140, 325–326
How to Write for Judges, Not Like Judges (Painter), 132
Human resources (personnel) departments, as source of job leads, 288
Human rights torts, 183

I

Idaho, 142, 213, 214
Illegal contracts; *see* Contracts
Illinois, 13, 213
Illinois constitution, 72
Immigration law, 325
Immunity
  family, 106
  interspousal, 98–100, 106
Immutable principles of right and wrong, 56
Imondi, Stephen P., 323
Impaired mental capacity, 91
Impleader, 151
Implied warranty of fitness, 235–236
Implied warranty of merchantability, 235
Imprisonment, for felony conviction, 169
Imputed disqualification, 44–45
Inalienable rights, 56
Incidental damages, 87, 240
Independent contractors
  in agency law, 244–246
  paralegal as, 325–330
Indiana, 73, 213
Indictment, 180
Indigents, right to counsel, 181–182
Individual health care instruction, 209
Industrial Revolution, 226
Inference, 162
Informal discovery, 267
Information; *see* Confidentiality
Informed consent, 39, 46
Infringement, 193
Inherent authority, 245
Inheritances, conflict of interest and, 46–47
In-house corporate counsel, paralegal opportunities with, 321–322
Initial consultation, 82, 257
Injunctive relief, 88, 89
In personnam jurisdiction, 75–76
In rem jurisdiction, 76, 206
In re: Opinion No. 24 of the Committee on the Unauthorized Practice of Law (1992), 328–329
In re Rice (1986), 75
In re the Marriage Riddle (1993), 215
In re Unauthorized Practice of Law Rules Proposed by the South Carolina Bar (1992), 326
Insanity defense, 85, 174, 175
Insurance
  liability, 186
  paralegal opportunities in, 320
  title companies (real estate), 192
Insurance law, 320
Intake forms, for client interview, 257–259, 316–317
Intangible property, 90, 193, 248
Intellectual property, 193
Intent
  to commit a crime (*mens rea*), 85
  contracts and, 229
  donative, 198
  proving, 173
  of testator, 202
Intentional torts, 91, 148, 183
Interim suspension, of license to practice law, 30
Intermediate appellate court, 67
Internal purposes, of legal materials, 128
International law, 62
International Paralegal Management Association (IPMA), 20–21, 32, 276
International trade, 66–67
Internet
  credit cards use and, 227
  job advertisements on, 289
  for locating witnesses/people, 270
  research resources on, 119–120
Internships, 315
"Interpretive Notes and Decisions," 124
Interrogatories, 152
Interspousal immunity, 98–100, 106, 111
Interview; *see* Client interview; Job interview; Witness interview
Inter vivos gift, 201, 227
Intestate, 200
Intestate succession, 200–201, 204
Invasion-of-privacy cases, 185
Inventions, 193
Investigations
  as duty of litigation paralegal, 158
  evidence, types of, 268–269
  field investigations, 267
  file memo, 274
  final steps in, 271, 273–274
  informal discovery, 267
  in-office tools for, 269
  in-the-field tools for, 269–271
  legal theories and possible items of proof, 268
Invitees, 125
Involuntary transfer of property, 191
Iowa, 213
IPMA; *see* International Paralegal Management Association (IPMA)
Irreconcilable differences, 213
Irresistible impulse defense, 175
Issue, in court opinion, 102

J

Jackson, Robert, 71
James A. Gibson, a Minor, etc., Plaintiff and Appellant v. Robert Gibson, Defendant and Respondent (1971), 104–106
Job, applying for; *see also* Job interview
  after the interview, 298–299
  cover letter, 294–295
  interview, 295–297
  résumé, 290–294
Job interview
  during, 296–297
  fielding an offer, 298–299

inappropriate/illegal questions, 297
negative remarks about prior employer, 310
preparing for, 295–296
rejection, 299
seek information about office atmosphere and politics, 310–311
Joint tenancies, 200, 208, 209
Joint tenants, 189
Journalists, duty of confidentiality and, 27
Journals (legal), 117–118
Judeo-Christian ideals, 29
Judge, 64
bench trial and, 157
life-tenured, 65, 67
state court, 65–66
Judge Advocate General's Corps (JAG), 321
Judgment, 28, 83–84
Judicial notice of commonly known fact, 163
Judicial review, 94, 143–144
Judicial system, 63–71; *see also* United States Constitution
Judiciary Act of 1789, 65
Jurisdiction
appellate, 70
for claims for money damages against the United States, 67
defined, 65, 76
diversity, 65–66
for federal court, 65
federal question jurisdiction, 66
general, 73
limited, 65, 74
original, 64, 70
personal, 74–76, 147
in personnam, 75–76
in rem, 76, 206
subject matter, 65, 74, 76
types, characteristics, and way applied, 76
Jurisdictional statement, 144
Juris doctor (J.D.) degree, 4
Jurisprudence
Anglo-American, 59
schools of thought on, 55–56
Jury selection, 160
Jury trial, 157
Justice (judge), 64, 69–70
Justinian Code, 59, 123
Juvenile court, 74

K

Kansas, 213, 308
Kentucky, 72, 213
Kestin Report (1999; New Jersey Supreme Court), 10, 11
KeyCite
defined, 120
focusing of research and, 120
of statutes, 122
Kidnapping, 169
King's Court, 28, 87
Kinship-guardianship, 217–218
Klein v. Klein (1962), 100, 105, 106
"Knowing," 173
Kohlbrand v. Ranieri (2005), 132
Kozlowski, Dennis, 169

L

Lack of due care, 91
Lakewood Creative Costumers v. Sharp (1986), 241
LAMA; *see* Legal Assistant Management Association (LAMA)
Land (real property), 90
Land court, 74, 75
Landlord-tenant court, 74
Landlord-tenant relationship, 61
Law
American, sources of, 58–59
classification of, 81–92
development of, 28–29
Law and economics, theory of, 56–57, 226, 240
Law clerk, 3
Law degree (J.D.; *juris doctor*), 4
Law enforcement, powers from U.S. Constitution, 61–63
Law reviews, 95, 117–118
Laws, 127
Lawsuit, 63, 143
Lawyer
bar exam and, 4–5
defined, 4
disclosure of confidential information, 39–42
education for, 4, 8
sanctions, for violation of ethical rules, 29–30
Lay, Kenneth, 169
Lay witnesses, 266
Leading questions, 263
Leary, John, 88
Lease, 90, 191
Lee, Mary, 273
Legacy, 204
Legal advocate, 4
Legal assistant, 12, 17
Legal Assistant Management Association (LAMA), 20
Legal authority, 82, 93–96
Legal capacity, 201
Legal dictionaries, 95
Legal documents, drafting, 160
Legal encyclopedias, 95, 116
Legal ethics; *see* Ethics
Legal formalism, 56, 57
Legal literature, 93–96
Legal malpractice, 274–276
Legal memorandum
aim of, 129
audience for, 129
defined, 128
format, 133–135
Plain English Movement and, 129–133
work product doctrine and, 128
Legal note taking, 100–106
Legal nurse consultant (LNC), 320–321, 322
Legal positivism, 56, 57
Legal realism, 56, 57
Legal reasoning, 96
Legal research, 110–111; *see also* Court opinions
as duty of litigation paralegal, 158–159
case reporters
citations, 112–114
civil and criminal law, 83, 85
civil cases, nature of, 86–89
civil law: substantive subject areas, 89–92
classification of law and legal materials, 81
computer-assisted legal research (CALR), 119–120
crimes and their variations, 84–86
defined, 81
defined, 95
digests, 115
federal, 122–124
federal court opinions, 114–115
federal regulations, 127
focusing, 120
formbooks, 118
generally, 120–122
law reviews, 117–118
legal encyclopedias, 116
legal literature, 93–96
legislative laws and, 122
online and Internet resources, 119–120
pocket parts, 117
practice aids, 118–119
primary authority, types of, 95, 96
reading, 124–126
Restatement, 117
secondary authority and computer programs, 118
Shepard's Citations (shepardizing), 118–119
state and federal law, 82–83
state court opinions, 112–114
substantive law and procedural rules, 92–93
the parties, 83–84
treatises, 116–117
unpublished opinions, 115–116
using the law, 127–128
Legal services/legal aid offices, 22–23
Legal specialists, in military law, 321
Legal specialties
agency law, 244–245, 246
business matters, 225
business organizations, 245–251
civil legal specialties, 182–188
contracts, 228–242
contract law, 225–228, 242–243
crime and, 169–176
criminal law and procedure, 167–168
criminal procedure, 176–182
family law, 211–221
family matters, 197
for the professional paralegal, 167–194
gifts, 197–199
property law, 188–194
wills and descent, 199–211
Legal technician, 3
Legal terms, use of, 130, 131
Legal theory, 55–57
Legal trade magazines, 95
Legislative (Article I) courts, 67
Legislative power, from U.S. Constitution, 60–61
Less-than-freehold property interest, 191
Letter of administration, 206
Letter of authority, 219
Letter testamentary, 206
LexisNexis, 114, 119–120, 124
Liability
of party to lawsuit, 83
strict, 91, 187
torts and, 91
vicarious, 244, 248
Liability insurance, 186
Librarians, duty of confidentiality and, 27
Libraries, as source of job leads, 288
License agreement, 193
Licensees, 125
License/licensure; *see also* Unauthorized practice of law (UPL)
certification distinguished from, 18
defined, 13
education for, 8
ethics and, 32–37
limited, 13–14

License/licensure—*Cont.*
- NALA opposition to, 17, 37
- requirement for practicing law, 33
- state bar membership and, 5
- state government and, 37

License suspension, 29
Licensing fees, 193, 194
Life insurance policies, third parties to a contract and, 237
Life-tenured judges, 65, 67
Limited jurisdiction, 65, 74
Limited liability company (LLC), 250–251
Limited liability corporations (LLCs), 21
Limited liability partnership, 248
Limited licensing, 13–14, 35
Lincoln, Abraham, 14, 163
Liquidated damages, 240–242
Listening, 263–264, 305–306
Literary works, 193
Litigant, 64
Litigation, 63
Littell, Patricia, 309
Littell v. Allstate Ins. Co. (2005), 309
Living will, 209–210
L.L.B. (Bachelor of Laws) degree, 4
Logos, 193
Louisiana, 213, 214
Lugashi, Avraham, 272
Luker, Diandra, 216

M

Madison, James, 94
Magistrates, 64
Magna Carta, 59, 64
Maine, 69, 72, 213, 214
Maintenance (alimony), 214
Major/concentration, in college study, 6–7
Majority opinion, 70
Malicious destruction, 169
Malpractice, 274–276
Mamet, David, 301
Management systems
- conflicts check, 276–277
- file management, 277–278
- tickler file, 276
- time and billing, 278–280

Mandatory (binding) authority, 69
Manufacturers, strict liability of, 92
Mapp, Dolly, 178
Mapp v. Ohio (1961), 178–179
Marbury, William, 94
Marbury v. Madison (1803), 94
Marital property, 214, 217
Marriage
- domestic partnership, 212
- as form of contract, 233
- redefined, 212
- same-gender, 212, 213
- termination of, 212–214

Marshal, 206
Marshall, John, 94
Martindale-Hubbell Law Directory, 295
Maryland, 72, 213
Masry & Vititoe, 31
Massachusetts
- anti-workplace bullying legislation, 308
- constitutions of, 71
- disclosure of confidential information by lawyer, 40, 41
- election and campaign finance reform, 72
- federal district court and, 69
- first adoption statute (1851), 214
- land court, 74
- same-sex marriage law, 212, 213
- Supreme Judicial Court, 72, 125
- voiding of wills in, 201

Masterson, Audrey, 290
Matter, 63
Mayhem, 169
Media rights, attorney-client conflict of interest and, 47
Meeting of the minds, 230–231, 233–234
Melissa computer virus, 155
Mens rea (a guilty mind), 85–86, 130, 173
Mental capacity (contracts), 91, 233
Mentoring programs, 316
Metadata, 155
Meyer, Barry, 199
Meyer v. Mitnick (2001), 199
Michigan, 213
Military, paralegal opportunities in, 321
Minnesota, 13, 213
Minors, 233
Miranda v. Arizona, 179–180
Mirandized statements, 180
Mirror image rule, 229
Misdemeanor, 84, 92, 169
Mississippi, 142, 213
Missouri, 142, 213
Missouri v. Jenkins (1989), 10, 14, 279–280, 327
Mistake in fact, 234–235
Mitchell, Lillian, 3
Mitnick, Robyn, 199
M'Naghten, Daniel, 175
M'Naghten Rule, 174
M'Naghten's Case (1843), 175
Model Code of Ethics and Professional Responsibility (NFPA), 32
Model Code of Professional Conduct (1969; ABA), 16
Model Guidelines for the Utilization of Legal Assistants (ABA), 31
Model Guidelines for the Utilization of Paralegal Services; *see* American Bar Association (ABA)
Model Penal Code, 172–173, 227
Model Rules of Professional Conduct (ABA), 16; *see* American Bar Association (ABA)
Modern Administrative State, 62
Monetary damages, 87, 89
Montana, 198, 213
Moore, Dale, Jr./Sr./Inez/John, Jr., 172
Moore's Federal Practice, 117
Moore v. City of East Cleveland (1977), 171, 172, 176
Morality, 28, 40–41
Mortgage, 191
Motion for directed verdict, 161
Motion for summary judgment, 102, 106, 156
Motion in limine, 157
Motions, preliminary, 68
Motion to dismiss, 145, 151
Mounsey v. Ellard (1973), 125
Muller v. Oregon (1908), 121
Mulrain v. Mulrain (1979), 148
Multi-Disciplinary Practice, ethics and, 33–34
Multi-State bar exam, 4–5
Murder, 92, 169
Mutual assent, 229

N

NALA; *see* National Association of Legal Assistants (NALA)
Napoleonic Code, 123
National Association of Legal Assistants (NALA), 35
- Certified Legal Assistant (CLA) designation, 18–19
- *Code of Ethics and Professional Responsibility*, 32
- description and purpose, 16
- *Findings and Facts*, 17
- guidelines for professional conduct, 17
- opposition to paralegal licensing, 17, 37
- paralegal, defined, 17
- paralegal salaries, 332
- voluntary ethical codes, 32

National Association of Legal Secretaries, Legal Assistant Section, 16
National Center for State Courts, 156
National Digest System, 115
National Federation of Paralegal Association (NFPA)
- description and purpose, 16
- guidelines for professional conduct, 17
- licensure and, 37
- *Model Code of Ethics and Professional Responsibility*, 32
- paralegal, defined, 17–18
- Paralegal Advanced Competency Exam (PACE), 19
- *Paralegal Reporter*, 17
- paralegal salaries, 332
- voluntary ethical codes, 32

National Reporting System (NRS), 112
Native Americans, 62
Natural law, 56, 57
Nebraska, 213
Necessary and proper clause, 60
Negligence
- aims of, 187
- assumption of risk, 186–187
- comparative, 187
- contributory, 186
- defenses to, 186–187
- defined, 37, 183–184
- elements of, 184–185
- parties in claim of, 83
- standards for reasonable behavior, 185–186
- strict liability and, 187
- unintentional torts and, 91

Nevada, 213, 214
New Hampshire, 69, 213
New Jersey
- federal district court and, 69
- Kestin Report of 1999, 10, 11
- same-sex marriage law, 213
- state courts, 119

New Jersey Supreme Court, 123, 330
New Mexico, 214, 217–218
Newspapers, job advertisements in, 289
New York
- anti-workplace bullying legislation, 308
- Court of Appeals, 72
- election and campaign finance reform, 72
- published court opinions, 96
- same-sex marriage law, 213
- speedy trial, 180–181
- Surrogate Courts, 203
- unauthorized practice of law (UPL) rulings, 325–326

New York County Lawyers Association v. Dacey (1967), 140, 325–326
New York Equitable Distribution Law, 217
New York State Officer Reports, 116
NFPA; *see* National Federation of Paralegal Association (NFPA)
Nominal damages, 87
Non-Mirandized statements, 180

Nonmonetary remedy, 89
Nonprobate property, 207, 209
Nontraditional paralegal positions, 22, 23
Norman conquest, 28, 58
North Carolina, 71, 213
North Dakota, 213
Northern Mariana Islands, 67
Northside Secretarial Service, 37
"Notes of Decisions," 124
Note-taking
  in client interview, 261–262
  in oral communication, 306
Notice, of lawsuit, 146–147
Notice pleading, 148
Nuclear Regulatory Commission (NRC), 62
Nuisance, 188
Nuisance Night Courts, 73
Nullification, of wills, 201

O

O'Brien v. O'Brien (1985), 217
Obscenity, 169
Obstruction of justice, 169
Offer
  as contract element, 91, 228–229, 230
  of a job, 298–299
  in real estate sales, 192
Offeree, 229
Offeror, 229
Office management, 274
Official reporters, 112; *see also* Legal research
Off-the-record information, 27
Ohio, 96, 213
Oklahoma, 213, 308
On-background information, 27
Online research resources, 119–120
On-the-record information, 27
Open-ended questions, 263
Opening statement, 160
Operation of law, 201
Oral argument, 68
Oral communication, 305–306
Oral contracts, 236
Oregon, 213, 326
Oregon State Bar v. Gilchrist (1975), 326
Original jurisdiction, 64, 70
Outrageous conduct, 88
Ownership, of property, forms of, 189–191

P

PACE (Paralegal Advanced Competency Exam; NFPA), 19
Pacific Gas and Electric Company, 31
Pacific Reporter, 114
Painter, Mark P., 132
Palsgraf v. Long Island Railroad (1928), 185
Paralegal(s)
  advantage of, 14–15
  authorized practice of law for, 139–140
  beginnings of profession, 2, 3
  under California law, 34–36
  contract law for, 225–226
  defined, 3
  definitions, 12–13, 17–18, 317–318, 325
  earnings of, 331–333
  education for, 6–9
  entrepreneurship of, 329–330
  ethical guidelines for, 30–32
  ethics and, 138–139
  first days on the job, 299–301
  generally, 3
  history of, 5–6
  identifying oneself as, 13
  imputed disqualification and, 44–45
  Kestin Report (1999; New Jersey Supreme Court), 10, 11
  legal fees and, 14–15
  majority of in civil litigation, 142
  probate practice for, 206–211
  in real estate practice, 191–192
  under supervision of attorney, 14
  tasks, 3
  training, 315–317
  voluntary ethical codes for, 32
Paralegal Advanced Competency Exam (PACE; NFPA), 19
Paralegal associations, as source of job leads, 289
Paralegal education, 3, 12; *see also* Education
Paralegal Reporter, The (NFPA), 17
Paraphrasing, in client interview, 262–263, 264, 306
Paraprofessionals, 5
Parole, 318–319
Parole officer, 318–319
Partial comparative negligence, 187
Parties
  to a contract, 233–235
  to a lawsuit, 64
  in negligence claim, 83
Partner, 33
Partnership rule, 33–34
Partnerships, 247–248
Patents, 193
Pennie, Richard, 325
Pennsylvania
  disclosure of confidential information in, 40, 41
  federal district court and, 69
  intermediate appellate court, 144
  same-sex marriage law, 213
  speedy trial, 180–181
People v. Lugashi (1988), 272
Pepples, Pat, 215
Peremptory challenges, 160
Perkins v. CTX Mortgage Co. (1999), 326
Permanent injunction, 88, 89
Perpetual existence, of corporations, 248
Personal injury cases, 15, 257
Personality types, 284–287
Personal jurisdiction, 74–76, 147
Personal property, 90, 190; *see also* Property law
Personal recognizance, 179
Personality, 90
Person location services, 270
Personnel (human resources) departments, as source of job leads, 288
Persuasive authority, 69
Persuasive writing, 131
Peters v. Peters (1909), 98, 99, 100
Petition, 63, 143–144
Petitioner, 64, 70
Petrino, Mary, 315
Philadelphia, Pennsylvania, Nuisance Night Courts, 73
Philadelphia Intelligencer, 289
Photography, as investigative tool, 269–270
Physical evidence, 268–269
Physicians, duty of confidentiality and, 27
Physicians' assistants (PAs), 35
Piercing the corporate veil, 249
Placement offices (college), as source of job leads, 288
Plain English Movement, 129–133
Plaintiff, 64, 83
Plato, 29
Plurality opinion, 70
Pocket parts, 117, 124
Police powers, 171
Possession (property law), 90
Power of attorney
  durable, 219–221
  general, 221
Practice aids, 118–119
Practice area, 316, 317
Practice manuals, 316
Practice of law; *see also* Unauthorized practice of law (UPL)
  defining, 48, 141
  in determining UPL, 49
  elements of, 51
Practice Tip
  client confidentiality, 38, 260
  confidentiality and sincerity, 210
  conflicts of interest, 46
  consumer laws, of states, 236
  diagram/key to court systems, 74, 144
  identifying oneself as paralegal, 49
  keeping study materials for job use, 168
  legal research, thoroughness of, 100
  practice manuals and checklists, 316
  professional association membership, 20
  reading statutes, 124
  rules of evidence, knowledge of, 270
  task list computer program, 303
  unauthorized practice of law (UPL), 51
Prayer for relief, 145
Precedent
  court opinions and, 93, 97, 111
  defined, 58
  power of, 94–95
  theatrical nature of, 63
Precision, in writing, 130
Preempt, 62
Preemption doctrine, 66
Preferred stock, 249
Prejudicial error, 69
Preliminary injunction, 88, 89
Preliminary motions, 68
Prelitigation activities, 142
Premium, 192
Premortem work; *see* Estate planning
Prenuptial agreement, 214, 216
Preponderance of the evidence, 84
Presentencing report, 319
Presentment, 180
Pretrial conference, 156
Pretrial matters, 156–157
Pretrial probation, 319
Price haggling, 231
Priest-penitent rule, 163
Prima facie case
  in civil cases, 86
  defined, 85
  established in complaint, 144–145
Primary authority, 95, 96
Principal, 244
Prioritization, 302
Privacy, 27; *see also* Confidentiality
Private censure, 30
Private investigator, paralegal as, 142
Private nuisance, 188
Private reprimand, 30
Privileged information, 42–43
Privity, 237
Probable cause, 177
Probate, 15, 203
Probate court, 74, 203, 211

Probation
 as attorney sanction, 30
 for person sentenced of a crime, 319
Probation officer, 319
Pro bono, 3
Procedural laws, 92–93, 142, 143
Procedural rules, 92–93
Procedure, in case briefing, 101–102
Proceeding, 63
Process server, 146–147
Products, strict liability and, 92
Profession, 28
Professional, 26
Professional conduct, 27–32; *see also* Ethics
 client confidentiality, 38–43
 in client interview, 257, 260
 conflicts of interest, 43–47
 unauthorized practice of law (UPL), 47–51
Professional corporations, 21
Professionalism, 26
Professional organizations, 15–21
Professional regulation, 28–29
Professional responsibility, 29
Professional status, 9–13
Prohibited degree of consanguity, 213
Promise, 232
Proof, items providing, 268
Proof of service, 146
Proofreading, 292, 304–305
Property, crimes against, 169
Property division, after end of marriage, 214
Property law, 89–90
 ownership, forms of, 189–191
 personal property, 189, 192–194
 persons entering another's property, 124–126
 real estate practice, paralegals in, 191–192
 real property, 189
 transfer and, voluntary and involuntary, 190–191
 in world communities, 188
Prosecution, 85
Prosecutor, 168
Prosecutorial discretion, 63, 180
Prosser, William L., 98, 117
Prosser on Torts, 98, 117
Prostitution, 169
Protected information, not subject to discovery, 154
Protected interests, in torts, 183
Protective orders, 154
Proximate cause, 91
Psychologists, duty of confidentiality and, 27
Publication, service of notice by, 147, 148
Publications, 17
 case reporters, 112–115
 legal literature, 93–96
Public limited company, 249
Public nuisance, 188
Public policy considerations, contracts and, 235–237
Public record(s)
 confidentiality and, 38–43
 for locating witnesses/people, 271
Puerto Rico, 69, 213
Punishment
 for crimes, 168
 for felony conviction, 169
 for misdemeanor conviction, 169
Punitive damages, 87, 88, 89
Pure comparative negligence, 187
"Purposely," 173

Q

Quality of life crimes, 73

R

Rape, 169
Ratification
 in agency law, 245
 of United States Constitution, 60
Rationale, 96, 102
"Rat" rule, 52
Real estate cases, 15
Real estate law, 191–192
Real estate practices, 287–288
Real evidence, 268
Real property, 90, 189
Rebuttal, 85
Receiving stolen property, 169
Receptionist, 257
Reciprocal Beneficiary Relationship (Hawaii), 212
Recross examination, 161
Recruiters, 288
Redirect examination, 161
Reformation, 89, 238
Regional digests, 115
Regional reporters, 112, 113; *see also* Legal research
Registered agent, 271
Registration, 19
Regulation, of paralegals, 10
Regulations
 corporate, 249–251
 as primary authority, 95
Reinstatement, of attorney license, 30
Relevant evidence, 162
Relief
 claim for, 142, 145
 equitable, 87, 88
 prayer for, 145
Remand, 69
Remedy; *see also* Damages
 for breach of contract, 238–241
 defined, 86
 exclusionary rule as, for wrongful search and seizure, 178–179
 summarized, 89
Remedy at law, 238
Removal (deportation) hearing, 63
Rent, 191
Replevin, 87, 89
Reporters, 112–115; *see also* Legal research
Repose, 92
Reprimand, 30
Request for admission, 153
Request for examination, 153
Request for production, 153
Rescission, 89, 238
Rescission of contract by mutual mistake, 234–235
Research; *see* Legal research
Residential real estate, 191
Residuary clause, 203
Respondeat superior, 30, 244
Respondent, 64, 70
Restatement, 117, 118
Restitution, 238
Restraining order, 88
Résumé, 290–294
Retain, 264, 325
Return of service, 146
Reverse, 69
Reversible error, 69
Revocation, of license, 29
Revolving credit accounts, 227
Rhode Island, 69
Riddle, Dorothy/Michael, 215
Right of election, 204, 206
Right of survivorship, 189
Right to counsel, 49–50
Right-wrong test, 175
Risk
 assumption of, 186–187
 of sole proprietorship, 247
Robbery, 169
Roberts, John, 70
Roman Law, 123
Royal Court, 142
Royalties, 193
Rules of procedure, 142–143
Rules of professional conduct, 29

S

Salary, for paralegals, 298, 331–333
Same-gender marriage, 212, 213
Same-sex adoptions, 218
Sanctions
 against lawyers who violate ethical rules, 29–30
 for refusal to comply with discovery requests, 154
Sarbanes-Oxley Act, 250
Schreiber v. Olan Mills (1993), 229–231, 233
Scienter, 132–133
Scope of authority
 for agents, 245, 246
 of partners, 248
Screening, of legal professionals with imputed conflict of interest, 45
Search and seizure, 93, 177
Search warrant, 177–178
Secondary authority, 95, 96; *see also* Legal research
Securities and Exchange Commission, 129
Self-assessment, 284–287
Self-defense, 85, 148, 175
Self-defense exception, to client confidentiality, 41
Self-esteem, 285
Self-incrimination, privilege against, 93, 179–180
Self-proving affidavit, 202–203
Self v. Self (1962), 102, 105, 106, 111
Sentence construction, 130
Sentencing guidelines, 319
Separate property, 214, 217
Separate sovereign rule, 180
Separation of powers, 60
Service of process, 146–147, 148, 151
Session laws, 122–123
Settlor, 207–208
Severalty, 189
Sexual harassment, 309
Shareholders, 248
Shares, 248, 249
Sharp, Angel, 241
Shepardizing
 focusing of research and, 120
 of statutes, 122
Shepard's Citations (shepardizing), 118–119
Sherwood, Theodore, 234
Sherwood v. Walker (1887; "pregnant-cow case"), 234

Sixth Amendment
  Confrontation Clause, 181
  right to counsel, 49–50, 181–182
  right to obtaining witnesses, 181
  speedy and public trial, 180–181
  substantive rights, 180
Skilling, Jeff, 169
Skills approach, to successful work
  communication skills, 304–306
  difficult coworkers, 306–309
  difficult office, 309
  job change, 310–311
  prioritization, 302
  stress management, 303–304
  time management, 302
  to-do list, 302
Slip law, 122
Slip opinions, 114
Smith, David L., 155
Smith, Tim, 134
"Snitch" rule, 52
Social contract, 59
Social Security Administration (SSA), 62, 324
Software; *see* Technology
Sole proprietorships, 246–247
South Carolina, 213, 326
South Dakota, 142, 213
Special Committee on Lay Assistants for Lawyers (ABA), 5
Special damages, 87, 89
Special guardian, 217
Specialized federal courts, 66–67
Specific performance, 89, 238–241
Speedy trial, 180–181
Spellchecker, 304–305
Spousal election, 204
Spousal support, 214
Standard of care, 184
Standing Committee on Paralegals; *see* American Bar Association (ABA)
Stare decisis (to stand by the decision), 58
State bar associations, 5
State constitutions, 71–72, 82–83
State courts, 72–74; *see also* Federal Rules of Civil Procedure (FRCP)
  cases forbidden to hear, 66
  general jurisdiction, 73
  judges in, 65–66
  opinions, publication of, 112–114
  personal jurisdiction, 74–76
  subject matter jurisdiction, 74, 75
State law, 60, 82–83
State legal systems, state constitutions and, 71–72
State of mind, 174; *see also Mens rea*
States, powers provided by Tenth Amendment, 72
Statute of Frauds, 236–237
Statute of limitations, 92–93
Statute(s)
  citation form for, 122
  codified (written), 121
  common law and, 61
  court decisions distinguished from, 60
  defined, 60, 122
  federal, publications of, 122–124
  interpretation of, 127
  process of creating, 126
  reading, 124–126
  researching, 120–126
  as source of law, 95
Statutory torts, 183
Stenographer, 67, 152, 153
Stewart, Martha, 169
Stocks, 249
Stock watering, 249
Stolen property, 169
Story, William E./William E., 2d, 232–233
Stress management, 303–304
Strict liability, 91, 92, 133, 187
Subject matter jurisdiction, 65, 74, 76
Subpoena, 152
Subpoena *duces tecum*, 152, 273
"Substantial legal work," 35
Substantive law, 92–93, 142, 143
Substantive rights, 180
Substituted service, 147
Successive conflict of interest, 45–46
Summary, 102
Summary judgment, motion for, 102, 106, 156
Summons, 142, 146–147, 148
Superior courts (state), 73
Support obligations, after end of marriage, 214, 215
Supremacy Clause, 60, 62
Supreme Court; *see* United States Supreme Court
Supreme Court Digest, 115
Supreme Law of the Land, 60
Surrogate Courts, 203
Survivorship, right of, 189
Suspension, of license, 29, 30
Symbolic delivery, 198
Synopsis, on résumé, 292
System of checks and balances, 60, 93

T

Tangible evidence, 268
Tarasoff v. Regents of the University of California (1974), 40
Taxes
  double taxation, of corporations, 250
  for sole proprietorship, 247
Tax lien, 323
Taylor v. Belger Cartage Service, Inc. (1984), 119
Technology; *see also* Internet
  case management software, 44
  computerized shepardizing, 122
  computer programs for secondary sources, 118
  computers for billable time, 278, 302
  confidentiality notice, for e-mail and faxes, 39
  conflict-checking software, 44, 277
  court decisions posted on Web sites, 157
  e-discovery, 155
  form-generating software, 287
  free downloadable software, 303
  litigation software, 317
  Melissa virus, 155
  online and Internet research resources, 119–120
  online job advertisements, 289
  practice area computer programs, 317
  task list computer program, 303
Temporary restraining order (TRO), 88, 89
Temporary suspension, of attorney license, 30
Tenancy by the entirety, 189, 200, 208, 209
Tenancy in common, 208, 209
Tenants in common, 189
Ten Commandments, 28, 31
Tennessee, 213
Tenth Amendment, 72
Territorial jurisdiction, 75–76
Testamentary gifts, 201, 204, 206
Testate, 200
Testator, 201
Testatrix, 201
Testimonial evidence, 269
Texas, 213
Theft, 169, 174
Third parties, confidential disclosure and, 42; *see also* Contracts
Third-party beneficiary law, 237
Third-party complaint, 151
Thompson v. Thompson (1910), 99
Tickler file, 276
Timekeeping, for billable hours, 278–280, 302
Time management, 302
Time slip, 278
Title
  of case, 101
  limited form (property), 193
  to real estate, 190–191
  transference of, 90
Title examiners, paralegal opportunities with, 323–324
Title insurance company, 192
Title search, 192
To-do list, 302
Tortfeasor, 91, 182
Tortious, 182
Torts, 91
  under common law, 182
  crimes compared to, 175–176, 182–183
  defined, 182
  economic, 183
  human rights, 183
  intentional, 148, 183
  punishments in, 175
  statutes of limitations and, 92
  statutory, 183
Trademarks, 193, 194
Trade secrets, 154
Training, 17
  checklists, 317
  continuing legal education (CLE), 316
  defined, 12, 315
  education distinguished from, 315
  internships, 315
  mentoring programs, 316
  practice area and, 316
  practice manuals, 316–317
Transactional practice, 191
Transcript, 153
Transference of property, 90
Treaties, 61–62, 95, 234
Treatises, 95, 116–117
Trespass (property law)
  common law and, 182
  as crime against property, 169
  defined, 90
  persons on private property, 124–126
  torts and, 91
Trespass on the case, 188
Trial, 156–158
Trial brief, 101
Trial courts, 64
Trial notebooks, 160
Trial preparation, 160–161
Trier of facts, 157, 163
Trudell v. Leatherby (1931), 104
Trump, Ivana/Donald, 216
Trust (confidence), 27
Trust (estate planning), 207–209
Trustee, 207–208
Tyco, Inc., 169, 249

U

Ultra vires, 250
Unauthorized practice of law (UPL), 47–51
  California law and, 35
  Commission on Multidisciplinary Practice (1998; ABA) and, 34
  defined, 37
  partnerships and, 33–34
  prohibition against, 5, 139, 174, 325–329
  real-life example, 37
Unclaimed funds, 200
Uncodified constitutions, 58–59
Under advisement, 157
Undue influence, 234
Uniform Code of Military Justice, 321
Uniform Commercial Code (UCC), 227–228
  defined, 227
  warranties and, 235–236
  written contracts, 236–237
Uniform Probate Code, 227
Unilateral mistake, 235
Unintentional torts, 91
United Kingdom, 59
United States Attorney, 168
United States Citizenship and Immigration Services, 324
United States Code (U.S.C.), 123
United States Code Annotated (U.S.C.A.), 124
United States Code Service (*Lawyer's Edition*), 124
United States Constitution, 59–60
  administrative agency regulation, 62–63
  appellate courts, 67
  Article I: legislative power, 60–61
  Article II: executive branch and law enforcement
  Article III: judicial system
  Articles IV, V, VI, VII, 60
  bills of attainder and, 171
  codified (written), 59
  distribution of Article III federal district courts, 67
  diversity jurisdiction, 65–66
  executive orders, 63
  ex post facto laws and, 171
  federal district (trial) courts, 64
  federal question jurisdiction, 66
  full faith and credit clause, 212
  government investigation of a crime, 176–179
  jurisdiction for federal courts, 65
  prosecutorial discretion, 63
  regulation of government enforcement of criminal laws, 176
  Sixth Amendment, 49–50
  specialized federal courts, 66–67
  specificity of criminal laws requirement, 171
  Supremacy Clause, 60, 62
  terminology, 63–64
  treaties, 61–62
  United States courts of appeals, 67–69
  United States Supreme Court, 69–71
United States Court of Federal Claims, 67, 68
U.S. Court of Military Appeals, 67
U.S. Court of Veterans' Appeals, 67, 68
United States courts of appeals, 67–69
United States Department of Justice, 21–22
United States Department of Labor, 9–10
United States Postal Service, for locating witnesses/people, 270
United States Sentencing Guidelines (USSG), 319
U.S. Social Security Administration, 22–23
United States Statutes at Large, 122, 123
United States Supreme Court, 37
  access to the courts, 146
  adoption and parents' rights, 216
  appellate jurisdiction of, 70
  attorney fees, 278
  Blackstone's *Commentaries* and, 58
  due process and notice of lawsuit, 74–75
  establishment of, 69
  exclusionary rule as remedy for wrongful search and seizure, 178–179
  justices, 69–70
  Mapp v. Ohio (1961), 178–179
  Miranda v. Arizona, 179–180
  original jurisdiction of, 70
  publication of opinions, 114
  recognition of paralegals, 10, 14
  right against self-incrimination, 179–180
  right of defendant to represent him- or herself, 50
  right to counsel, 49–50, 181–182
  right to cross-examine, 181
  significance of decisions, 71
  speedy trial, 180–181
  vagueness of criminal laws, 170, 171
  workings of, 70
  work product doctrine, 155
United States Supreme Court Reports (L.Ed.), Lawyer's Edition, 114
United States Supreme Court Reports (S.Ct.), 114
U.S. Tax Court, 67
Universities, paralegal opportunities with, 322
Unofficial reporters, 112; *see also* Legal research
Unprofessional behavior, 307
Unpublished opinions, 115–116
Unreasonable search and seizure, 93
Use of force, 175
Utah, 40, 41, 213

V

Vedanta, 188
Verdict, 84, 161
Vermont, 213
Veterans Administration, 324
Vicarious liability, 244, 248
Virginia, 200, 213
Virgin Islands, 67, 69
Void *ab initio*, 213
Void/Voidable contract, 233
Void/Voidable marriage, 213, 233
Voir dire, 160
Voluntary ethical codes, 32
Voluntary transfer of property, 190
Volunteering, leading to employment, 289, 290
Vote of four, 70
V./vs. (versus), 64, 97

W

Wages, of paralegals, 298, 331–333
Walker, Hiram, 234
War Against Poverty, 22
War crimes, statutes of limitations and, 92
Ward, 217
Warranty, 235–236
Washington (state), 213, 214, 326
Watered stock, 249
Weeks v. United States (1914), 178
Western Judeo-Christian ideals, 29
Westlaw, 119–120
West Publishing Company, 112, 114, 115, 122, 124
West Virginia, 213
Whistleblower laws, 52
White-collar crime, 169
Wigmore, John H., 117
Wigmore's Evidence, 117
Wills
  defined, 200, 201
  example, 205
  generally, 199–201
  intake form for, 258–259
  legal capacity of testator, 201
  legal formalities for, 202–204
  mental capacity of testator, 201
  nullification of, 201
  probate practice for professional paralegals, 206–211
  testamentary gifts, 201, 204, 206
Wisconsin, 119, 213, 214
Witnesses
  locating, 270–271
  types of, 266
Witness interview, 265
Word choice, 130
Workplace discrimination, 309
Workplace types; *see also* Employment opportunities
  government legal offices and agencies, 21–22
  legal services/legal aid offices, 22–23
  nontraditional positions, 22, 23
  private law firms, 21
Work product doctrine, 128, 154, 155
WorldCom, 249
Writ of certiorari, 70
Writ of habeas corpus, 64
Writs, 28, 142
Written communication, 304–305
Wyoming, 213

Z

Zealous representation, 159
Zeta-Jones, Catherine, 216
Zonana, Howard, 175